TWO HOUSES, TWO KINGDOMS

Catherine Hanley is a writer and researcher specialising in the Middle Ages. She is the author of *Matilda*, *Louis* and *War and Combat 1150–1270*, and is a contributor to the *Oxford Encyclopedia of Medieval Warfare and Military Technology*.

Further praise for *Two Houses, Two Kingdoms*:

'Hanley's eye for narrative detail vividly brings events to life . . . The attention paid to women and children as crucial participants in dynastic rule is refreshing.'
Emily Joan Ward, *History Today*

'Epic in scope but intimate in focus . . . An authoritative overview of a pivotal period in the development of both nations.'
BBC History Revealed

'Hanley brings to life the royal families of England and France in this exciting period, through their interactions as close bedfellows (literally), brothers (and sisters) in arms, petulant rivals and bitter enemies.'
Anne Curry, author of *Henry V: From Playboy Prince to Warrior King*

'This book creates a picture of kingdoms like siblings, connected but destined to be at war. A must-read for anyone interested in the entwined stories of medieval kingdoms and dynasties.'
Matt Lewis, author of *Richard III: Loyalty Binds Me*

T0279360

TWO HOUSES, TWO KINGDOMS

A HISTORY OF FRANCE AND ENGLAND
1100–1300

CATHERINE HANLEY

YALE UNIVERSITY PRESS
NEW HAVEN AND LONDON

For information about this and other Yale University Press publications, please contact:
U.S. Office: sales.press@yale.edu   yalebooks.com
Europe Office: sales@yaleup.co.uk   yalebooks.co.uk

Set in Adobe Caslon Pro by IDSUK (DataConnection) Ltd
Printed in Great Britain by Clays Ltd, Elcograf S.p.A

Library of Congress Control Number: 2023935504

ISBN 978-0-300-25358-0 (hbk)
ISBN 978-0-300-27297-0 (pbk)

A catalogue record for this book is available from the British Library.

10 9 8 7 6 5 4 3 2 1

For Susan

CONTENTS

CONTENTS

ILLUSTRATIONS

Plates

14. Louis, the son and heir of Philip Augustus, arrives in England after being invited to take the throne. Parker Library, MS CCCC 16 II, fol. 50v. Reproduced by kind permission of the Parker Library, Corpus Christi College, Cambridge.
15. Lincoln Castle.
16. Lincoln Cathedral.
17. The Battle of Sandwich, 1217. Parker Library, MS CCCC 16 II, fol. 56r. Reproduced by kind permission of the Parker Library, Corpus Christi College, Cambridge.
18. Louis IX and his mother, Blanche of Castile.
19. The Sainte-Chapelle, Paris.
20. Henry III marries Eleanor of Provence. Album / Alamy Stock Photo.
21. Detail of the tomb of Louis of France, the son and heir of Louis IX.
22. Edward I pays homage to Philip III.
23. Edward I and his wife, Eleanor of Castile. History and Art Collection / Alamy Stock Photo.
24. Philip IV and his family. Art Collection 3 / Alamy Stock Photo.

Tables

Maps

ACKNOWLEDGEMENTS

A S EVER, I'D LIKE TO start by thanking Heather McCallum at Yale University Press and my agent, Kate Hordern, who between them made this book possible. The team at Yale's London office, including Marika Lysandrou, Felicity Maunder, Lucy Buchan and Katie Urquhart, have been wonderful; and as the production process entered the final straight the eagle eyes and expertise of copy-editor Clive Liddiard, proofreader Chris Shaw and indexer Ian Craine have been invaluable. Many thanks to them all.

I'd like to express my appreciation to the University of Exeter for the honorary research fellowship that enabled me to consult a great deal of material that would otherwise have been inaccessible; I have also benefited enormously from the friendliness and collegiality of fellow medievalists there during my visits to the campus. Access to physical research resources is sometimes difficult when one lives rurally, and I am very fortunate that Karen Collings, at the small but perfectly formed public library in Wiveliscombe, Somerset, did not blanch at some of my more outlandish inter-library loan requests and happily tracked down all sorts of obscure volumes.

A number of academic colleagues were kind enough to discuss or read through drafts of various chapters for me and to offer extremely valuable feedback. Sophie Thérèse Ambler's unrivalled knowledge of Simon de Montfort was very much appreciated, as she kindly advised on all the sections dealing with him, while also helping me to sort out my Savoyards from my Lusignans and my bishops from my barons. Matthew Bennett's comments on Anglo-Norman warfare and my interpretation of it were invaluable, as were his notes on some of the specific terminology involved (including the fact that I had somehow managed to confuse the radius of a circle with its diameter). Peggy (E.A.R.) Brown generously shared her expertise on Philip the Fair, entering into correspondence and sending me a number of her own research publications, all of which greatly informed my thinking on a king who was initially among those less familiar to me. Andrew Buck and John D. Hosler between them went through every part of the book that mentions the crusades, and particularly the chapter dealing with the siege of Acre; their detailed comments and advice saved me from many an error of interpretation and the occasional outright howler, as well as pointing me towards sources I had been unaware of. Sean McGlynn read the sections on the construction and siege of Château Gaillard, as well as providing continuous support, encouragement and (when legally permitted!) tea throughout a planning and writing process that has lasted several years. Kathleen Neal advised me on Edward I and his politics, and kindly sent me an advance copy of one of her own publications on the subject, enabling me to rewrite a section I'd been finding particularly tricky. Paul Webster read through all those parts of my text dealing with Thomas Becket, as well as entering into correspondence on the subject of the Anonymous of Béthune, whose chronicle, oft-cited in the present volume, he was editing for publication at the time. Ellie Woodacre's expertise on medieval queens was invaluable as she advised on and provided references for the chapters featuring Isabella of Angoulême, Blanche of Castile and Eleanor of Provence. I am extremely grateful to all of these people for their time, expertise, generosity and goodwill. Needless to say, any remaining errors or infelicities in any of these sections of the book are my own; I'll be happy to defend them, probably with a well-organised infantry formation rather than a mass of aristocratic cavalry.

On a personal level, my family have, as ever, been incredibly supportive. Much of the first draft of this book was written during the lengthy UK-wide lockdown periods of 2020 and 2021 (which historians of the future will no doubt analyse in detail), so we were all at home together for many weeks. I owe a great debt of gratitude to all the schoolteachers who set work for our children and continued teaching them in the difficult circumstances that prevailed – I certainly couldn't have done such a fantastic job, and this book would never have been written if I'd tried.

Inspirational teaching is never forgotten, and I'd like to take this opportunity to step back a little into the past and thank Penny Eley and Penny Simons, who jointly supervised my PhD thesis some two decades ago now. I would never have got to this point if they hadn't guided my first attempts at proper writing – and yes, I *still* remind myself constantly of those three words you used to write in the margins of pretty much every draft chapter I ever sent you.

Finally, I would like to express my gratitude to my dear friend and former colleague Susan Brock, who indefatigably reads everything I write these days and always improves it with comments of pinpoint accuracy. This book is dedicated to her.

KINGS AND QUEENS OF FRANCE
IN THE TWELFTH AND THIRTEENTH CENTURIES

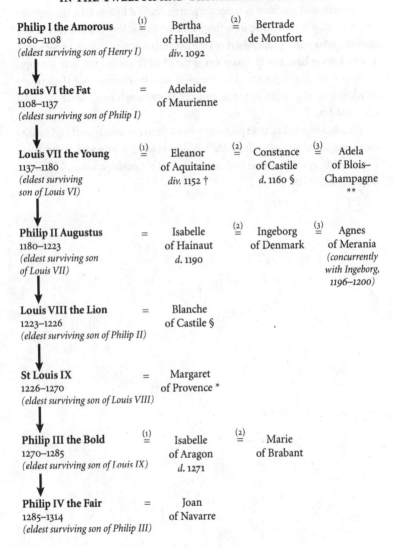

Philip I the Amorous ⁽¹⁾= Bertha ⁽²⁾= Bertrade
1060–1108   of Holland   de Montfort
(eldest surviving son of Henry I)   div. 1092

↓

Louis VI the Fat = Adelaide
1108–1137   of Maurienne
(eldest surviving son of Philip I)

↓

Louis VII the Young ⁽¹⁾= Eleanor ⁽²⁾= Constance ⁽³⁾= Adela
1137–1180   of Aquitaine   of Castile   of Blois–
(eldest surviving   div. 1152 †   d. 1160 §   Champagne
son of Louis VI)   **

↓

Philip II Augustus = Isabelle ⁽²⁾= Ingeborg ⁽³⁾= Agnes
1180–1223   of Hainaut   of Denmark   of Merania
(eldest surviving son   d. 1190   *(concurrently*
of Louis VII)   *with Ingeborg,*
                                              1196–1200)

↓

Louis VIII the Lion = Blanche
1223–1226   of Castile §
(eldest surviving son of Philip II)

↓

St Louis IX = Margaret
1226–1270   of Provence *
(eldest surviving son of Louis VIII)

↓

Philip III the Bold ⁽¹⁾= Isabelle ⁽²⁾= Marie
1270–1285   of Aragon   of Brabant
(eldest surviving son of Louis IX)   d. 1271

↓

Philip IV the Fair = Joan
1285–1314   of Navarre
(eldest surviving son of Philip III)

† Eleanor of Aquitaine was queen of France 1137–52 and queen of England 1154–89.
* Eleanor of Provence and Margaret of Provence were sisters.
§ Constance of Castile was the great-aunt of Blanche of Castile, who was the great-aunt of Eleanor of Castile.
** Adela of Blois–Champagne, queen of Louis VII of France, was the niece of King Stephen of England.

KINGS AND QUEENS OF ENGLAND
IN THE TWELFTH AND THIRTEENTH CENTURIES

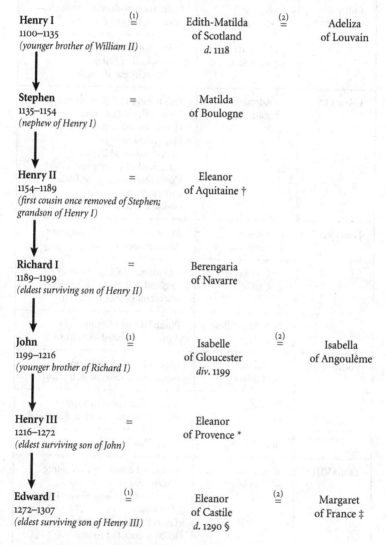

Henry I ⁽¹⁾ ≗   Edith-Matilda   ⁽²⁾ ≗   Adeliza
1100–1135   of Scotland   of Louvain
(younger brother of William II)   *d.* 1118

Stephen   =   Matilda
1135–1154   of Boulogne
(nephew of Henry I)

Henry II   =   Eleanor
1154–1189   of Aquitaine †
(first cousin once removed of Stephen;
grandson of Henry I)

Richard I   =   Berengaria
1189–1199   of Navarre
(eldest surviving son of Henry II)

John ⁽¹⁾ ≗   Isabelle   ⁽²⁾ ≗   Isabella
1199–1216   of Gloucester   of Angoulême
(younger brother of Richard I)   *div.* 1199

Henry III   =   Eleanor
1216–1272   of Provence *
(eldest surviving son of John)

Edward I ⁽¹⁾ ≗   Eleanor   ⁽²⁾ ≗   Margaret
1272–1307   of Castile   of France ‡
(eldest surviving son of Henry III)   *d.* 1290 §

†   Eleanor of Aquitaine was queen of France 1137–52 and queen of England 1154–89.
*   Eleanor of Provence and Margaret of Provence were sisters.
‡   Margaret of France, queen of Edward I of England, was the daughter of Philip III of France.
§   Constance of Castile was the great-aunt of Blanche of Castile, who was the great-aunt of Eleanor of Castile.

FRENCH ROYAL CHILDREN

Philip I	by Bertha of Holland	Constance, princess of Antioch Louis VI, king of France
	by Bertrade de Montfort	Philip, count of Mantes Florus, lord of Nangis Cecile, princess of Galilee
Louis VI	by Adelaide of Maurienne	Philip, king-designate of France Louis VII, king of France Henry, archbishop of Reims Hugh, *died young* Robert, count of Dreux Peter, lord of Courtenay Constance, countess of Blois and Toulouse Philip, archdeacon of Paris
Louis VII	by Eleanor of Aquitaine	Marie, countess of Champagne Alix, countess of Blois
	by Constance of Castile	Margaret, junior queen of England and queen of Hungary Alice, countess of Ponthieu
	by Adela of Blois	Philip II, king of France Agnes, empress of Byzantium
Philip II	by Isabelle of Hainaut	Louis VIII, king of France unnamed twin boys, *died young*
	by Agnes of Merania	Marie, duchess of Brabant Philip Hurepel, count of Boulogne
	illegitimate	Peter Charlot, bishop of Noyon
Louis VIII	by Blanche of Castile	unnamed daughter, *died young* Philip, *died young* Twin boys (Alphonse? and John?), *died young* Louis IX, king of France Robert, count of Artois John, *died young* Alphonse, count of Poitou and Toulouse

Louis VIII *cont.*	by Blanche of Castile	Philip-Dagobert, *died young* Isabelle of France Stephen, *died young* Charles, count of Anjou and king of Sicily
Louis IX	by Margaret of Provence	Blanche, *died young* Isabelle, queen of Navarre Louis, heir to the French throne Philip III, king of France John, *died young* John-Tristan, count of Valois Peter, count of Alençon Blanche, infanta of Castile Margaret, duchess of Brabant Robert, count of Clermont Agnes, duchess of Burgundy
Philip III	by Isabella of Aragon	Louis, *died young* Philip IV, king of France Robert, *died young* Charles, count of Valois
	by Marie of Brabant	Louis, count of Évreux Margaret, queen of England Blanche, duchess of Austria
Philip IV	by Joan of Navarre	Margaret, *died young* Louis X, king of France Isabelle, queen of England Blanche, *died young* Philip V, king of France Charles IV, king of France Robert, *died young*

ENGLISH ROYAL CHILDREN

Henry I	by Edith-Matilda of Scotland	Matilda, empress William Adelin, heir to the English throne
	illegitimate	Robert, earl of Gloucester Richard fitzRoy Matilda, duchess of Brittany Matilda, countess of Perche Matilda, abbess of Montvilliers Reginald, earl of Cornwall
Stephen	by Matilda of Boulogne	Eustace, count of Boulogne Mary, countess of Boulogne William, count of Boulogne
Henry II	by Eleanor of Aquitaine	William, *died young* Henry the Young King Matilda, duchess of Saxony Richard I, king of England Geoffrey, duke of Brittany Eleanor, queen of Castile Joanna, queen of Sicily John, king of England
	illegitimate	Geoffrey, archbishop of York William, earl of Salisbury
Richard I	illegitimate	Philip of Cognac
John	by Isabella of Angoulême	Henry III, king of England Richard, earl of Cornwall Joan, queen of Scots Isabelle, empress Eleanor, countess of Pembroke
	illegitimate	Richard of Dover Joan, lady of Wales
Henry III	by Eleanor of Provence	Edward I, king of England Margaret, queen of Scots Beatrice, duchess of Brittany Edmund, earl of Lancaster Katherine, *died young*

Edward I	by Eleanor of Castile	Katherine, *died young*
		Joan, *died young*
		John, *died young*
		Henry, *died young*
		Eleanor, countess of Bar
		Unnamed daughter, *died young*
		Joan of Acre, countess of Gloucester
		Alfonso, *died young*
		Isabelle (?), *died young*
		Margaret, duchess of Brabant
		Berengaria, *died young*
		Mary, a nun at Amesbury
		Elizabeth, countess of Holland
		Edward II, king of England
	by Margaret of France	Thomas, earl of Norfolk
		Edmund, earl of Kent
		Eleanor, *died young*

OTHER NOBLE AND ROYAL HOUSES

France	
Anjou	**Count Fulk IV** and his wife, **Bertrade de Montfort** (*see also de Montfort in France*)
	Fulk V, their son, and his wives **Ermengarde of Maine** and **Melisende of Jerusalem** (*see also Jerusalem*)
	Geoffrey, **Matilda** and **Sybil**, Fulk V's children by Ermengarde
	Geoffrey's wife, **Matilda of England**, formerly empress, Matilda's husband, **William Adelin of England**, and Sybil's husbands **William Clito** and **Thierry of Alsace** (*see also the Empire, Flanders*)
	Henry II of England, **Geoffrey fitzEmpress** and **William fitzEmpress**, Geoffrey's sons by Matilda
	Hamelin of Anjou, Geoffrey's illegitimate son, and his wife **Isabel de Warenne**, countess of Surrey (*see also Surrey*)
	Baldwin III and **Amalric I**, Fulk V's sons by Melisende, kings of Jerusalem (*see also Jerusalem*)
Artois	**Count Robert I**, a younger son of Louis VIII, and his wife **Matilda of Brabant**
	Robert II and **Blanche**, later queen of Navarre and countess of Lancaster, their children (*see also Navarre, Lancaster*)
	Philip, Robert II's son
Blois and Champagne	**Count Theobald IV of Blois**, also **Theobald II of Champagne**
	Henry I of Champagne, Theobald V of Blois, Stephen I of Sancerre, William Whitehands, archbishop of Reims, and **Adela**, queen of France, his children (*see also Blois, Champagne*)
Blois	**Count Theobald V of Blois** and his wife, **Alix of France**
	Louis I and **Alix**, abbess of Fontevraud, their children
	Theobald VI, Louis's son
Boulogne	**Countess Matilda I** and her husband **Stephen of Blois**, Theobald IV's younger brother, later king of England
	Eustace, William and **Mary**, their children
	Eustace's wife, **Constance of France**, later countess of Toulouse, William's wife, **Isabel de Warenne**, countess of Surrey, and Mary's husband, **Matthew of Alsace and Flanders** (*see also Toulouse, Surrey, Flanders*)
	Ida, Mary and Matthew's daughter, and her husband **Renaud de Dammartin**

Boulogne *cont.*	**Matilda II**, Ida and Renaud's daughter, and her husband **Philip Hurepel** of France
	Joan, Matilda and Philip's daughter
Brittany	**Duke Alan IV**
	Conan III, his son, and his wife **Matilda**, illegitimate daughter of Henry I of England
	Conan IV, Conan III's grandson
	Constance I, Conan IV's daughter, and her husbands, **Geoffrey of England, Ranulf de Blundeville**, earl of Chester and **Guy de Thouars** (*see also Chester*)
	Arthur I and **Eleanor**, her children by Geoffrey
	Alix, her daughter by Guy, and Alix's husband **Peter of Dreux** (*see also Dreux*)
	John I and **Yolande**, Alix and Peter's children
	John II, John I's son, and his wife **Beatrice of England**
	Arthur II, John and Beatrice's son
Champagne	**Count Henry I of Champagne** and his wife, **Marie of France**
	Henry II, their elder son, later king of Jerusalem (*see also Jerusalem*)
	Theobald III of Champagne, their younger son, and his wife, **Blanche of Navarre** (*see also Navarre*)
	Theobald IV, Theobald and Blanche's son, later **King Theobald I of Navarre** (*see also Navarre*)
Dreux	**Count Robert I,** a younger son of Louis VI
	Robert II and **Philip**, bishop of Beauvais, his sons
	Robert III and **Peter**, later duke of Brittany, Robert II's sons (*see also Brittany*)
Flanders	**Count Baldwin VII**
	Adela of Flanders, Baldwin's aunt, queen of Denmark (*see also Denmark*)
	Charles I the Good, Adela's son
	William I Clito, a distant relative, and his wife **Sybil of Anjou** (*see also Anjou*)
	Thierry I of Alsace, a distant relative, and his wife **Sybil of Anjou**, formerly married to William Clito

Flanders *cont.*	**Philip I, Matthew, Peter** and **Margaret**, Thierry and Sybil's children
	Philip's wife, **Elisabeth of Vermandois**, Matthew's wife, **Mary, countess of Boulogne**, and Margaret's husband **Baldwin VIII of Flanders**, also **Baldwin V, count of Hainaut** (*see also Boulogne*)
	Baldwin IX, Margaret and Baldwin's son
	Joan, Baldwin IX's daughter, and her husbands **Ferrand of Portugal** and **Thomas of Savoy** (*see also Provence and Savoy*)
	Guy of Dampierre, Joan's nephew
Lusignan and La Marche	**Hugh IX de Lusignan**
	Hugh X, his son, and his wife, **Isabella of Angoulême**
	Hugh XI, Guy, Geoffrey, William, Aymer and **Alice**, Hugh X and Isabella's children
	Hugh XII, Hugh XI's son
de Montfort	**Amaury III de Montfort, count of Évreux,** and his sister, **Bertrade de Montfort**, countess of Anjou and queen of France, children of Simon I (*see also Anjou*)
	Simon (known as either Simon IV or Simon V) **de Montfort**, Amaury III's great-grandson, Albigensian crusade leader
	Amaury VI and **Simon** (known as V or VI), his sons (*see also de Montfort in England*)
Toulouse	**Count Raymond V** and his wife, **Constance of France**, formerly countess of Boulogne (*see also Boulogne*)
	Raymond VI, their son, and his wife **Joanna of England**
	Raymond VII, Raymond and Joanna's son
	Joan, Raymond VII's daughter, and her husband **Alphonse of Poitiers**, a younger son of Louis VIII

England

Chester	**Richard d'Avranches**, 2nd earl
	Hugh de Kevelioc, 5th earl, grandson of Richard's cousin and successor
	Ranulf de Blundeville, 6th earl, Hugh's son, and his wife **Constance of Brittany** (*see also Brittany*)
Cornwall	**Earl Richard**, a younger son of King John, later king of Germany, and his wives **Isabel Marshal** and **Sanchia of Provence** (*see also the Empire,*

Cornwall *cont.*	*Striguil and Pembroke, Provence*)
	Henry of Almain, his son by Isabel
	Edmund of Cornwall, his son by Sanchia
Gloucester	**Robert I**, 1st earl, an illegitimate son of Henry I
	William, 2nd earl, his son
	Isabelle, countess of Gloucester, William's daughter, and her husbands **King John, Geoffrey de Mandeville** and **Hubert de Burgh**
Lancaster	**Edmund**, 1st earl, a younger son of Henry III, also a claimant to Sicily, and his wife **Blanche of Artois** (*see also Sicily, Artois*)
	Thomas, 2nd earl, **Henry**, 3rd earl, and John, their sons
de Montfort	**Simon** (known as Simon V or Simon VI) **de Montfort**, and his wife **Eleanor of England** (*see also de Montfort in France*)
	Henry, Simon, Amaury, Guy, Richard and **Eleanor**, their children
Striguil and Pembroke	**Countess Isabel de Clare**, and her husband, **William I Marshal**
	William II, Richard, Matilda, later countess of Surrey, and **Isabel**, later countess of Cornwall, their children (*see also Surrey, Cornwall*)
	John Marshal, William I's nephew
Surrey	**Countess Isabel de Warenne** and her husbands **William of Blois**, also count of Boulogne, and **Hamelin of Anjou**, both designated 4th earl (*see also Boulogne, Anjou*)
	William de Warenne, 5th earl, Isabel's son by Hamelin, and his wife **Matilda Marshal** (*see also Striguil and Pembroke*)
	John de Warenne, 6th earl, William and Matilda's son

Scotland

Kings of Scots	**William I the Lion**
	Alexander II, his son, and his first wife **Joan of England**
	Alexander III, Alexander II's son by his second wife, and his first wife **Margaret of England**
	Margaret, Alexander III's daughter by Margaret, later queen of Norway
	Margaret, 'the Maid of Norway', Margaret's daughter by King Eric II

The Empire	
Emperors and kings of Germany	**Henry V** and his wife **Matilda of England** (*see also Anjou*)
	Lothar III, a distant relative
	Frederick I Barbarossa, Henry V's great-nephew
	Henry VI, Frederick I's son, and his wife **Constance of Sicily** (*see also Sicily*)
	Philip of Swabia, Henry VI's brother
	Otto IV, great-grandson of Lothar III
	Frederick II, Henry VI's son
	Richard of Cornwall, elected although unrelated, and his wife **Sanchia of Provence** (*see also Cornwall, Provence*)
	Adolf of Nassau, elected although unrelated
Provence and Savoy	**Count Raymond-Berengar IV of Provence** and his wife, **Beatrice of Savoy**
	Margaret, later queen of France, **Eleanor**, later queen of England, **Sanchia**, later queen of Germany, and **Beatrice**, later countess of Provence and queen of Sicily, their daughters (*see also the Empire, Sicily*)
	Amadeus, Thomas, later count of Flanders, **William, Peter, Philip** and **Boniface**, later archbishop of Canterbury, Beatrice of Savoy's brothers (*see also Flanders*)
Denmark	
Royal house	**Cnut IV** and his wife, **Adela of Flanders** (*see also Flanders*)
	Charles the Good, their son, later count of Flanders
	Ingeborg of Denmark, queen of France, and her brothers **Cnut VI** and **Valdemar II**, all children of Valdemar I
Aragon	
Royal house	**James I**
	Peter III and **Isabella**, later queen of France, his children
	Alfonso III, Peter III's son

Castile	
Royal house	**Constance of Castile**, daughter of Alfonso VII, later queen of France
	Alfonso VIII, Constance's nephew, and his wife **Eleanor of England**
	Henry I, Berengaria I and **Blanche**, later queen of France, Alfonso and Eleanor's children
	Ferdinand III, Berengaria's son
	Alfonso X and **Eleanor**, later queen of England, Ferdinand's children
	Berengaria, Ferdinand and **Sancho IV**, Alfonso X's children

Navarre	
Royal house	**Sancho VI the Wise**
	Sancho VII the Strong, Berengaria, later queen of England, and **Blanche**, later countess of Champagne, his children (*see also Champagne*)
	Theobald I, Blanche's son, also **Theobald IV of Champagne**
	Theobald II and **Henry I**, Theobald's sons, and Henry's wife **Blanche of Artois** (*see also Artois*)
	Joan I, Henry and Blanche's daughter, later queen of France

Sicily	
Royal house	**William II** and his wife **Joanna of England**
	Tancred of Lecce, William's illegitimate cousin
	Constance of Sicily, William's aunt, and her husband **Emperor Henry VI** (*see also the Empire*)
	Frederick II, Constance and Henry's son
	Conrad IV, Frederick's son
	Conradin, Conrad's son
	Manfred, an illegitimate son of Frederick II
	Edmund of England (claimant) (*see also Lancaster*)
	Charles I, a younger son of Louis VIII of France, and his wife **Beatrice of Provence** (*see also Provence*)
	Peter III of Aragon and his wife **Constance**, Manfred's daughter

Jerusalem	
Royal house	**Baldwin II**
	Melisende, his daughter, and her husband **Fulk of Anjou** (*see also Anjou*)
	Baldwin III and **Amalric I**, their sons
	Baldwin IV, Amalric I's son
	Baldwin V, Baldwin IV's nephew
	Sybil, Amalric I's daughter and Baldwin V's mother, and her husbands **William of Montferrat** and **Guy de Lusignan**
	Isabella, Amalric I's daughter and Sybil's half-sister, and her husbands **Conrad of Montferrat** and **Henry II of Champagne** (*see also Champagne*)
	Maria of Montferrat, Isabella's daughter by Conrad, and her husband **John of Brienne**

Selected popes

Urban II 1088–99	**Innocent III** 1198–1216
Callixtus II 1119–24	**Honorius III** 1216–27
Innocent II 1130–43	**Gregory IX** 1227–41
Celestine II 1143–44	**Innocent IV** 1243–54
Eugenius III 1145–53	**Urban IV** 1261–64
Alexander III 1159–81	**Clement IV** 1265–68
Lucius III 1181–85	**Martin IV** 1281–85
Celestine III 1191–98	**Boniface VIII** 1294–1303

Note: table contains only those popes mentioned by name in the text.

Map 1 England

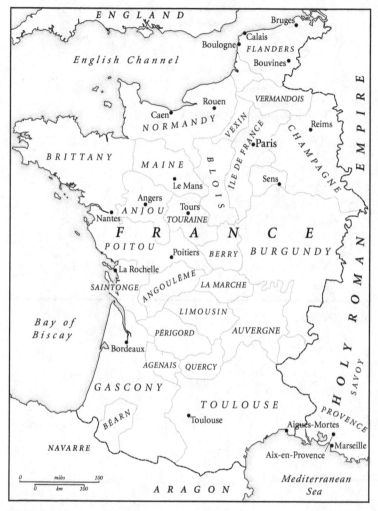

Map 2 France

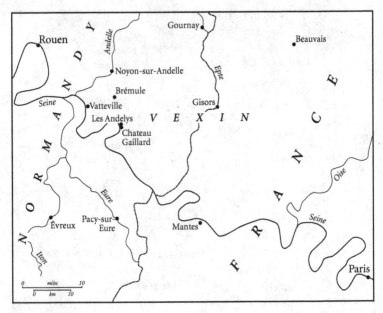

Map 3 The Vexin

Map 4 The Empire and the kingdom of Sicily

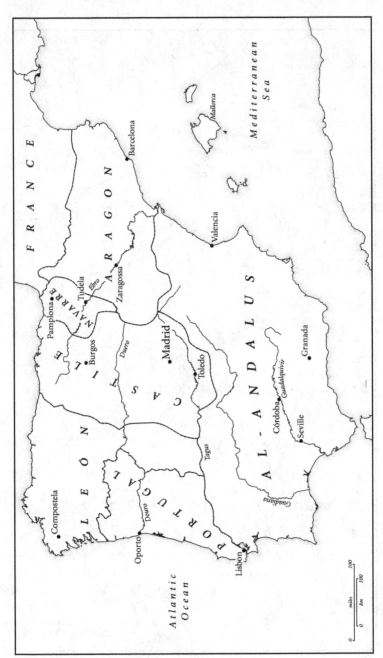

Map 5 The Spanish kingdoms

INTRODUCTION

THIS IS A BOOK about *people*.

In the twelfth and thirteenth centuries, the personal could influence the political to a great extent, and nowhere is this better exemplified than in the relationship between the ruling houses of France and England, whose members waged war, made peace and intermarried – sometimes almost simultaneously – in a complex web of relationships. These people, these kings and queens, siblings, children and cousins, held positions determined by birth; positions that often involved playing a role on the national and international stage from a very young age. Their life stories, their formative experiences and their interpersonal relationships shaped the context of decisions and actions that had the potential to affect the lives and livelihoods of millions.

The dynasties had not always been so close. Prior to 1066 England's primary relationships had been with the Scandinavian countries, but the accession of William the Conqueror – the duke of Normandy and therefore a vassal of the French king – inevitably meant that the nature of interactions would change.[1] Until the early twelfth century, meanwhile, France was a rather loose collection of counties and duchies that owed nominal overlordship to a king who exercised direct control over only a small royal domain centred on Paris.[2] All of this would change dramatically, and, as we will see, a great deal of that development was driven by the personalities of individuals on both sides of the Channel.

The two centuries from 1100 to 1300 featured a compelling cast of characters in both realms. The monarchs we will meet include Richard the Lionheart, King John, Eleanor of Aquitaine, Blanche of Castile, Saint Louis, Philip Augustus and one of France's greatest but lesser-known kings, Louis the Fat. Each was, in turn, supported or hindered not only by family, but also by a group of self-interested nobles and by some equally pivotal figures who came from the lower echelons of society and rose to be great clerics or warriors. And the story is certainly not all about men: some of the most fascinating and influential personalities of the two dynasties – as well as the majority of those who were ill-treated for no reason other than their birth – were women.

There were myriad ways in which the personal experiences of individuals could influence wider concerns at this time, and we will encounter many of them as the story progresses. The vagaries of infertility, child mortality, illness or accident could upset even the best-laid plans of kings and queens, and the way in which people reacted to unexpected events could turn fate in a completely different direction from the one they had envisaged. How a king dealt with the tragedy of his son and heir drowning in a ship wreck or being killed by a pig in the streets of Paris could have an enormous effect on the future of his realm. The death of a king caused his administration to cease immediately, and a sudden death – or one that left no clear successor – could throw a realm into disarray. Such an event could bring opportunities for those cunning and proactive enough to seize them, as could the accession of a child to the throne, something that happened several times during the period covered by this book and which inevitably caused sharks to circle. That the very idea of a child king could be contemplated, in a society where a monarch was also expected to be a war leader, demonstrates the importance to contemporaries of the concept of dynastic power[3] – and dynasties, however great or small, are formed by people.

* * *

This book is not a biography of any single individual, nor a narration of any single event; it is, rather, the tale of two intertwined dynasties that shaped the present and the future of England and France, told through the stories of the people involved. A symbol used frequently in the Middle Ages was that of Fortune's wheel, turning to raise some up and make others fall, and this is an image that perfectly illustrates the shifting balance of power between the two dynasties.[4] The lands under the control of the English king once reached to within a few miles of Paris, and those ruled by the French house, at their apogee, crossed the Channel and encompassed London itself.

In order to tell this tale, I will concentrate on the relationship *between* the houses, not on activities that either of them carried out individually – so, for example, the struggle for the English throne between Stephen and Matilda will not be a main focus, and nor will Edward I's campaigns in Wales or Scotland; neither will Louis VII's crusade to the Holy Land or the French Albigensian wars. This emphasis on the inter-relationship is also why the book opens in 1100, rather than, say, 1066: 1100 marked the first moment of real, dramatic interaction between the dynasties. *Two Houses, Two Kingdoms* covers some ground that will no doubt be familiar, but it will also include plenty of other material that is much less well known, particularly to English-speaking readers. There is a tendency, in Anglophone writing about this period, to concentrate on the trials and tribulations of the English ruling house; it becomes the major protagonist while the French only make sporadic appearances when they need to serve as antagonists. This will not be the case in this book, where I will genuinely seek to tell the story of the relationship from both sides.

Another feature of some earlier historical writing, when it focuses on the big picture of kingdoms and politics, is a lack of attention to women. Thankfully this has been addressed in recent years with a notable flowering of studies on queenship and the publication of biographies of female individuals and works that bring to light the reality of women's lives in the Middle Ages.[5] I will capitalise on this movement by featuring the stories of a number of pivotal female characters alongside their male contemporaries. Some of these women are well known, such as Eleanor of Aquitaine, the only woman ever to be queen of both France and England, and Blanche of Castile, France's regent for many years and arguably more of a 'female king' than a queen.[6] Others are not, even though they had remarkable life stories and influenced the events of their time in different ways. These women may have started off as pawns, but later they carved out vital roles for themselves, or personified peace via their marriages; some disrupted the reigns of kings, even though they spent their lives locked away; and many would fight by any means necessary to secure the future of their children and their dynasty.

Sources

There is a wide variety of primary sources available for the study of our period. Some are official records, such as charters, grants, financial and exchequer documents, and I will refer to these where appropriate, along with letters both private and public ('letters patent') where they remain extant. In order to put flesh on the bones of the story about *people*, however, we need to know more about what contemporaries thought of them, what was said of them and how they were depicted in the popular media of their own day. To this end, the book relies to a great extent on the more narrative sources available, the accounts of chroniclers and other observers. Of course, these writers all had their own biases about their subjects (as do modern historians, of course, as we admit more freely these days), and I will discuss these as they arise.

Another bias of chroniclers leads us back to the problem mentioned above: the omission of women or the minimising of their contributions to the politics of their time. This is, in some respects, a double problem: not only did the overwhelmingly male chroniclers of the twelfth and thirteenth centuries not see women's lives, personalities and actions as important, but the equally overwhelmingly male first editors and translators of these texts in the nineteenth century made no move to address this. One way in which this is illustrated is the tendency for women not to be named in the sources, or for their names to be confused or contradictory. Sometimes this merely takes the form of variant spellings (for example, Joan/Joanna), but the logic behind other, more obvious, discrepancies is difficult to discern: Isabelle of Hainaut, the queen of Philip II of France, is referred to in some texts as Elisabeth, while the daughter of Matilda of England and Henry the Lion of Saxony is called Richenza in German chronicles and Matilda in English ones. Sometimes there is a political dimension, such as the case of the queen of Henry I of England, who was known as Edith before her marriage and Matilda after it. And at other times women's names are not given at all: there are numerous instances in chronicles of women being referred to only as 'the daughter of' a male magnate, without being afforded the dignity of a name of their own. The daughter of Isaac Komnenos of Cyprus, for example, was captured as a young girl by Richard the Lionheart, held for ransom, taken with his entourage to the Holy Land and brought back to Europe; twice married, she returned to Cyprus after her father's death to stake an unsuccessful claim to it, and then fled to Armenia – and all without a single contemporary bothering to record her name. While we cannot now discover the names or the preferred names of these long-dead women, we can at least make sure that we include their actions in the tale of the two dynasties. The information in the sources is there; it just needs to be searched for more carefully in order to redress the balance.

Our primary sources are also sometimes vague on the details of royal or noble childhoods: there is a tendency for members of dynasties simply to appear fully formed at the point when they take their place on the national or international stage. However, by that time such individuals had already led lives that were often rich in incident. A girl might have been sent away for marriage at an early age; a boy might have been destined for a lower-key career before being thrust unexpectedly into the limelight following the death of an older brother; either might have suffered the loss of one or both parents or of any number of siblings whom they loved and for whom they grieved. The heir to a throne might have taken on the duties of governance (even if only in name) from a very young age as part of his training for kingship; and, indeed, the crown itself might have been placed on his head rather earlier than anticipated. Several of the kings we will meet acceded to their thrones while still in their teens, and two were even younger than that, taking on the responsibility for their realms and their younger siblings while still pre-pubescent themselves. A number of the queens were also crowned while still pre-teen, with some pressured into sexual relationships and pregnancy almost straight away. Much of the history of the two dynasties is the story of children, and through careful analysis of sources I hope to be able to bring their early lives more into the spotlight than has generally been the case.[7]

Names and titles

With so many individuals to write about over the two centuries covered in this book – some of them much better known than others – it was inevitable that I would end up with a slightly idiosyncratic naming system. As far as possible French, German and Spanish personal names have been anglicised, so I write of, among others, Philip, William and Margaret (rather than Philippe, Guillaume and Marguerite); Henry and Frederick (rather than Heinrich and Friedrich); and Ferdinand and Peter (rather than Fernando and Pedro). However, I make a few exceptions for the sake of clarity: for example, Louis VII of France had two daughters of the same name, and so I have retained the French spelling of Alix for the elder of the two, but for the younger I have amended to the English Alice. The queen of Louis VIII was called Blanca in her homeland of Castile, but is more generally known today by the French Blanche, and so I have retained this usage. Some other names, such as Rotrou and Berengaria, have no exact English equivalent, and so I have used the most commonly recognised form, as I have for Saladin and various popes.

A perennial issue with writing about the Middle Ages is the restricted range of first names in use, and the consequent repetition and potential confusion. I have attempted to address this in several ways. The ambiguity in contemporary texts over the form and spelling of women's names can be used to positive effect in order to differentiate them: thus, various individuals will be referred to consistently as Adela/Adelaide/Adeliza or Isabel/Isabelle/Isabella. This was not an option for all names, and so I have sometimes used titles or toponyms such as Empress Matilda or Matilda of Boulogne.

Male names tend not to have so many variants, and so I have, where necessary, used repetition of titles (such as King Philip and Count Philip) to avoid any confusion. Some noble families, and French comital houses in particular, tended to pass the same name on through the generations – was there ever a lord of Lusignan who was not called Hugh? – so where even a construction such as 'Count Robert of Dreux' would be ambiguous, I have used numbers: Robert I of Dreux, Robert II of Dreux, and so on.[8] I have made a distinction between 'of', which relates to a place of origin, or to a title in either full or abbreviated form (Blanche of Castile; William, earl of Salisbury; Raymond of Toulouse), and 'de', which is used for what might recognisably be described as a family name (Saer de Quincy, earl of Winchester; Renaud de Dammartin, count of Boulogne).

It is unfortunate, for the purposes of clarity and possibly even sanity, that every single French king we will meet is called either Philip or Louis – a tradition that ran unbroken from 1060 to 1316 – but various strategies have been employed as necessary, and they should be readily distinguishable. Different kingdoms have different traditions of referring to their monarchs, for example the use of numbers, nicknames or a combination of both, and so

I have tried to use whatever is the most common and recognisable form for each individual, even when this system is not entirely consistent with itself.

In terms of titles, most (king, queen, abbot, bishop) are self-explanatory and were the same in different jurisdictions; the exception is that I have used 'earl' for the holder of English counties and 'count' for the holders of French or Norman ones, even though they were equivalent ranks, to highlight the fact that the same individuals could hold multiple titles on both sides of the Channel.

Place names have been anglicised where a suitable form exists (Normandy, Castile, Rome), and left in the original (Mantes, La-Roche-aux-Moines) where not.

Terminology and potential pitfalls

Although for the sake of simplicity I will refer throughout the book to the kings of England and France, the official titles of the monarchs of the two realms in the twelfth century were *rex Anglorum* 'king of the English' and *rex Francorum* 'king of the Franks', as they were kings of people, not places; the first to use the titles *rex Angliae* 'king of England' and *rex Franciae* 'king of France' were John (r. 1199–1216) and Philip II Augustus (r. 1180–1223), respectively. The difference is subtle, but the earlier form implies rulership by consent of the people and accession to the throne via acclamation, rather than solely by heredity (although heredity was, of course, also an important factor). The 'of the people' construction survived in the title 'king of Scots' until 1605, and is still used by the king of the Belgians.[9]

The two houses of the book's title are, of course, the ruling dynasties of France and of England. While the former can simply be referred to throughout as 'Capetian' (that is, descended from Hugh Capet), the latter is more complicated. To start with, at least, the English monarchy was very much a cross-Channel institution, and so in the earlier stages of the book I will refer to its kings as 'Anglo-Norman'. Geoffrey of Anjou – who married into the royal house, rather than being a member of it by birth – is generally known by the soubriquet 'Plantagenet'; he did not pass this on to his children as a hereditary surname (the first of his descendants to use the name in this way was Richard, duke of York and unsuccessful claimant to the throne in the fifteenth century), but it has become such accepted shorthand for the

English ruling house that I will use it from his son Henry II onwards, regardless of anachronism. I prefer this to 'Angevin', the other potential candidate for the family appellation, to avoid any confusion with matters relating specifically to the region of Anjou.

There is a discussion to be had about what exactly constitutes 'English' and 'French' during the twelfth and thirteenth centuries. William the Conqueror was the king of England, but he was by birth a Norman and therefore also 'French'.[10] In what sense did his descendants and their subjects consider themselves 'English' forty years after his conquest, when our period begins, and then later again? And what of those nobles who held lands in both England and Normandy? Much work has been done in recent years on the subject of the development of national identity in the Middle Ages, and it is a theme I will touch upon at various points in the text; but for the sake of simplicity I will sometimes use 'English' or 'the English barons' to mean 'those who held lands in England', regardless of their place of birth or their other estates. In order not to go too far down the road of anachronistic nationhood, however, I will refer to 'dynasties', 'realms' and 'kingdoms', rather than 'countries' or 'nations'.[11]

Money

Sums of money are mentioned at various points in the book, and have the potential to be confusing. In both England and France there were twelve pennies (*deniers*) in a shilling (*sou*) and twenty shillings or 240 pennies in one pound (*livre*). However, a French or 'Parisian' pound (*livre parisis*) was worth less than an English pound sterling, and so the amounts were not quite equivalent. An Angevin pound (*livre tournois*), as used in Anjou or Normandy, was worth still less – between a quarter and a third of a pound sterling during the two centuries we cover. To avoid confusion, where I mention pounds I will generally mean sterling, and will note instances of other currency as such.

An accounting denomination used frequently in the twelfth and thirteenth centuries was the mark, which in both kingdoms was 13s 4d (160 pennies) or two thirds of a pound. For most of our period, however, the only actual coins in circulation were the silver penny in England – which could be cut into halves or quarters if necessary – and the silver *denier* (1d) and *obol* (½*d*) in France. Transporting money therefore involved the inconvenience of carrying around large and heavy sacks or barrels of pennies, to be counted or weighed out; for substantial sums, kings might carry with them 'treasure' in the form of valuable plate or other precious items. In the last third of the thirteenth century the first gold *écus d'or* (a gold coin equivalent in value to a *livre tournois*) and silver *gros d'argent* (1 *sou tournois*) were minted in France, the latter becoming the exemplar for the silver groat (worth 4*d* sterling) in England.

I have made no attempt to give modern equivalents for sums of money; instead, I have made comparisons with twelfth- or thirteenth-century incomes, prices or purchasing power, which should help to give an idea of how much a sum was worth in contemporary terms.[12]

Reading this book

In order to appeal to as wide a range of people as possible, *Two Houses, Two Kingdoms* offers a number of different types of reading experience. Anyone who wishes to read the main text from start to finish without consulting the notes may do so without loss of meaning; the story is all there. The notes serve two purposes: firstly, to give references for the quotes from primary source material; and, secondly, to provide further information about characters or events that are only touched on briefly in the main text – something that was inevitable when there was so much material to cover. In these discussion notes, I have chosen deliberately to point the reader to secondary sources that are in general widely available, predominantly full-length books from trade publishers rather than articles in journals that require academic or institutional library access. Those readers who wish to explore the various topics raised in the book in greater depth will find at the end of the volume a full scholarly bibliography that lists all works consulted, whether cited in the notes or not.

PART I

TWO HOUSES COLLIDE

> CHAPTER ONE <

THE NEW KINGS

I T WAS CHRISTMAS IN THE year 1100, and the king of England was
holding his seasonal court at Westminster. Bright fires roared in the
hearths to stave off the freezing winter chill, the aroma of roasting meat
filled the air and the nobles of the kingdom were gathered together to eat,
drink and jostle for position in the new regime.

The undisputed centre of attention was the stocky, dark-haired King
Henry I, a restless and energetic man of around thirty-two years of age. He
had been very busy during the past few months. On 2 August he had been
in the New Forest when his elder brother, King William II Rufus, had been
killed by a stray arrow during a hunting party; making the most of the unexpected opportunity, Henry rushed to nearby Winchester in order to secure
the royal treasury and then rode in haste for London, where he was crowned
king at Westminster Abbey on 5 August. His somewhat tenuous claim was
bolstered by his being the only one of William the Conqueror's sons who
could claim porphyrogeniture – that is, that he had been 'born in the purple'
to a reigning king – whereas his brothers had entered the world as merely
the sons of the duke of Normandy.[1] To add to this, Henry bolstered his
position by taking an eminent wife, marrying on 11 November Edith,
daughter of the late Malcolm III Canmore, king of Scots, and his wife
Margaret (later St Margaret), who was herself descended from the old
Anglo-Saxon royal line. By Christmas 1100, therefore, Henry found himself
in a very favourable position as he summoned his nobles to court, able to
demonstrate his power and his patronage. He and his queen, whose name

had been changed to Matilda, the better to appeal to Anglo-Norman sensibilities, engaged in a crown-wearing ceremony in order to emphasise their divinely approved royal status, and he hosted a great banquet for the assembled nobles and churchmen.[2]

Among the guests at the banquet, seated in the place of honour between the king and the archbishop of Canterbury, was one who owed no allegiance to Henry but rather represented the rarefied circles in which Henry would now move: Louis, the eldest son of King Philip I of France and already recognised as 'king-designate' of that realm. It was the custom of the Capetians, the ruling house of France, for each king to crown his eldest son and designated successor within his own lifetime. This practice brought two major advantages: France had not only a king, but also a 'junior king', who could learn his trade from his father, and the realm would not dissolve into chaos upon the monarch's death, as his successor was already in place.[3] Louis was around eighteen or nineteen years old, and was trusted by his father, who was not in good health, to act as his royal and diplomatic representative. He was known to enjoy a good meal, and so doubtless appreciated the fine fare that was on offer as Henry 'received him honourably as the son of a king, and showed him great favour in every way'.[4] The two men were second cousins, Louis's paternal grandfather and Henry's maternal grandmother having been siblings.

All seemed well. But hot on the heels of the prince came an unexpected communication from France: a letter under the seal of King Philip asking Henry to detain Louis in England and imprison him for the rest of his life.

This was both unprecedented and astonishing. But there was another surprise to come: after some confusion (Henry discussed with his advisors how 'absurd and unseemly' such a request was) it became clear that the missive came not from Louis's father but rather from his stepmother, who was trying to unseat him as heir to the throne. Louis was in a dangerous position, despite his recognition as junior king. He was the eldest son of Philip I, by his first marriage to Bertha of Holland; but when Louis was only around ten years old, his mother had been repudiated by the king, who then eloped with a French noblewoman, Bertrade de Montfort. Despite the fact that both Philip and Bertrade had living spouses (she was the wife of Fulk IV, count of Anjou, and the mother of his son, the future Fulk V), they were 'married' in 1092, and the relationship persisted despite King Philip's excommunication by the pope. Bertrade bore the king two sons, Philip and Florus, and she was apparently determined that one of them should succeed him on the French throne. Such ambitions might seem far-fetched, given the boys' unorthodox lineage, but it was still within living memory that a bastard had gained the crown of England; Bertrade had all to gain, and Louis everything to lose.[5]

Henry's first contact, as a king, with the house of Capet was probably meant to be low key and informal; it had turned out to be a head-on collision. But the unexpected situation presented him with an interesting diplomatic dilemma: should he begin his reign in England by interfering in the internal politics of France? And, if so, should he side with the king's wife, who evidently had much influence now, or with the king's son, who would have it later? Potential gains might be made either way by a canny tactician. Henry himself was new to his crown – and he had come to it via unconventional means, as we will discuss further below – so he had to be careful not to do anything that might lessen the majesty and the status of kingship, lest others interpret it as meaning that his own position was negotiable. He 'firmly declined any part for himself or his men in a scheme so evil and altogether repugnant for a king' and 'immediately sent a message to Louis, advising him out of kindness to withdraw peacefully, and sent him and his companions back to France loaded with many gifts'.[6] Henry and Louis remained – for now – on good terms.

Louis returned to France, where he spent the next few years acting on behalf of his father to subdue various rebellious barons while simultaneously trying to stay a step ahead of his stepmother's machinations.[7] Henry, meanwhile, had concerns of his own, and in the early years of the twelfth century it seemed as though the king of England and the future king of France, kinsmen as they were, might have little to do with each other.

* * *

The feudal relationship between the men holding the titles of *rex Francorum* and *rex Anglorum* had altered several times during the preceding half-century. Until 1066 there was little to link them, but the accession of William I meant that the king of England was also the duke of Normandy, who, by virtue of that position, was a vassal of the king of France. This situation had prevailed until William's death in 1087, at which point he left the duchy of Normandy to his eldest son, Robert Curthose, and the crown of England to his second, William Rufus. The expectation was, no doubt, that each would go on to produce sons of his own, and thus as the generations passed the relationship between the king and the duke would become more distant; Normandy would remain part of France, and the duke would recognise the French king as his overlord, while England under its king would go its own separate way.

This arrangement faltered, however, in several respects. William Rufus and Robert Curthose each coveted the inheritance of the other, and each was supported by various barons who controlled estates on both sides of the Channel and found it easier to owe allegiance to a single overlord. The brothers made abortive attempts to invade each other's lands, but the conflicts ended in stalemate with an agreement that each would keep his own territory for now, but that he would name the other as his heir. As they were both unmarried and childless at the time, everybody was reasonably happy with the outcome.[8]

In November 1095 Pope Urban II preached his great call for crusade, and Curthose was one of the first and the highest-ranking men to respond. He mortgaged Normandy to Rufus for the sum of 10,000 marks (£6,667) in cash, in order to raise and equip a force, and set off for the East. During the war that would later become known as the First Crusade, he won great renown.[9] With an enhanced reputation and a new wife – who would hopefully, in due course, provide him with an heir – he set off on the road back to Normandy in the summer of 1100.

Unluckily for Curthose, he was not yet home when William Rufus died unexpectedly, and so rapid was Henry's move that he was already the crowned and anointed king of England by the time Curthose arrived in Normandy. For Robert to lose the throne to one brother, who had always been his particular rival and their father's favourite, was one thing; to be leapfrogged a second time by the baby of the family, fifteen years his junior, was another. And the situation was further complicated when both brothers celebrated the birth of heirs at around the same time. Henry and Edith-Matilda's first child, Matilda, was born in February 1102; Robert Curthose trumped the arrival of a daughter when his wife Sybil of Conversano gave birth to a son, William Clito, in October of the same year; but Henry countered with a son of his own, William Adelin, who was born in August 1103.[10] Each brother was now fighting for his heir and his lineage, as well as his own rights – although only Henry had the potential for more children, as Duchess Sybil died from childbirth complications, leaving all Curthose's hopes invested in William Clito.

Open warfare ensued in Normandy, with the now-ailing Philip I of France doing little to intervene, and his son Louis either content to look on and await the outcome of events, or lacking the resources or the parental permission to intercede. The culmination of the fraternal conflict came in September 1106, when Henry was besieging the castle of Tinchebrai (in south-west Normandy, about 30 miles south-west of Falaise), which was held for Curthose. Curthose brought his own army up behind Henry's encircling forces in an attempt to relieve the castle, and there was an effort at mediation; but Henry's offers seemed designed to goad rather than to conciliate. He called Curthose 'a duke in name only, openly mocked by your own servants', and suggested that he should hand over control of the duchy to Henry so that he could live 'without toil or responsibility': 'You can then enjoy feasts and games and all kinds of amusements in comfort. I for my part will undertake all the labours necessary to preserve peace, and will faithfully keep my promises while you rest.'[11] Curthose declined this rather patronising offer and decided to settle the issue in battle.

The armies faced each other on open ground outside the castle; both sides dismounted to fight (not an uncommon tactic at the time, as having knights in the line encouraged the common footsoldiers to hold their ground), and Curthose's knights charged. He was first among them; he might have proved himself less adept at politics than his little brother, but he was a distinguished warrior and crusader, and nobody doubted his courage. The momentum of the charge pushed Henry's line back but could not break it, and the press grew thicker as nobody could move any further, the combatants having to hack away at anyone they could reach. But Henry had a back-up plan: he had kept a cavalry wing in reserve, and they charged into Curthose's stationary troops with devastating effect. The commander of Curthose's rearguard fled, leaving him with no additional defence from that direction, and still unable to move either forward or back. Many of his men were killed and others were captured, including the duke himself.[12]

Robert Curthose was taken to Rouen, and from there to England and then Wales, where he would remain captive for the rest of his life. Henry moved on to the ducal castle at Falaise, where he encountered William Clito, who was just short of his fourth birthday. The little boy was – understandably, given his age and the circumstances – 'trembling with fear', but in a rare act of compassion, Henry let him go.[13] Clito was confided to the care of one Helias de St Saëns, who was married to Clito's adult half-sister (an illegitimate daughter of Robert Curthose's youth whose own name has not come down to us). The reasons for Henry's seemingly uncharacteristic generosity are not spelled out by any contemporary, but they may be inferred: he was acting punctiliously while safeguarding his own reputation. Imprisoning the brother who had been in armed conflict against him was an acceptable course of action, but revenging himself on that brother's dependants was not – the murder or ill-treatment of a blameless infant would be indefensible, even in twelfth-century Normandy.

Clito was safe for now. He would not always be four years old; his survival and release provided the potential for trouble in the future, if he could outlive the perils of childhood. Louis, meanwhile, had been watching events carefully, working out how he could use the situation to best advantage in his own plans for the strengthening and aggrandising of the French monarchy's sphere of influence, once the crown was his. The opportunity came soon: Philip I died on 29 July 1108, and (Bertrade de Montfort's erstwhile plans notwithstanding) there was no question that he would be succeeded on the throne by Louis.[14] Louis, now around twenty-six years old and a veteran of years of campaigning against rebellious barons, was crowned on 3 August. After many years of the indolent rule of Philip I, France now had a king who was young, energetic and ambitious.

It takes more than two men to start a war; but in an age of personal monarchy, the personalities and decisions of kings carried much greater weight in the equation than they might have done centuries later, and the conflict between the kingdoms would be characterised during the next two decades by the way in which Henry and Louis comported themselves. Henry could be cruel and was certainly not averse to fighting when he needed to (as he had done at Tinchebrai), but he was a clever man who preferred strategy to violence as a way to achieve his goals: he 'swept away the designs of his enemies ... as if they had been spiders' webs, and had the pleasure of crushing them without shedding the blood of his own men', as one contemporary put it. Louis, meanwhile, at least during this early period of his life, was full of energy and devoted to military campaigns.[15] Each king's character and influence was to become evident as France and England took their first steps towards war.

* * *

Louis went on the offensive almost immediately after his accession, seeking to impose his royal authority in two ways. Firstly, he required Henry to pay homage to him for Normandy. Homage was a ritual act of great significance, and one that will appear frequently in our narrative, so a short explanation might be of use at this point. As we noted above, the king of France was (in theory at least) the overlord of the duchy of Normandy, and could therefore expect to receive homage from the dukes in the same way he received it from his other counts and vassals. However, this was more complicated than it appeared. The man offering the homage was expected to kneel before his overlord – a clear and public indication of his inferior status. This was generally considered to be acceptable for those who really were the overlord's acknowledged subordinates, but the problem in this particular case was that since 1066, other than a brief intermission, the duke of Normandy was also the king of England. Although the two territories were separate, and it would be the duke paying homage, onlookers would still be treated to the sight of the king of England kneeling before the king of France.[16] The intermission in question was the short reign in Normandy of Robert Curthose, in between his father's death and his own overthrow, and there is some circumstantial evidence that he had paid homage to Philip I for Normandy. However, as he was not also a king, this presented no problem; and in any case, his homage was personal and not binding upon his successor as duke.[17] Henry was not willing to compromise his royal dignity and he refused to perform the act.

The second way in which Louis attempted to impose his new royal will was by instructing that two of the castles on the Norman–French border be either handed over to neutral castellans or destroyed. This border area was known as the Vexin, divided into regions known as the 'French Vexin' and the 'Norman Vexin'; the exact boundaries fluctuated over the years, but they lay nominally on either side of the River Epte. One of these castles was the fortress of Gisors, which lay on the Norman side of the Epte, near the river and commanding the road between Rouen and Paris, and which was thus of great strategic importance. Henry, far from complying with Louis's wishes, moved immediately to take personal control of Gisors from the man who had been holding it since the time of Robert Curthose. He did not need to resort to violence: the castle was taken not by storm, but by agreement (Henry was said to have 'used flattery and threats' against the castellan), which meant that it was not damaged in a siege and remained defensible.[18] Louis was not yet in a position to launch a military campaign on the scale that would be needed to attack Gisors, but he retaliated by pillaging and burning the lands of one of Henry's barons, Robert, count of Meulan.

The kings met in force in March 1109 at the borders of their territories, at the bridge of Neaufles on the Epte – as rivers often formed a natural border between two territories, it was not uncommon for meetings to take place on the 'neutral ground' of bridges over them. In this particular case the bridge appears to have been in a state of disrepair, which precluded the possibility of any accidental combat breaking out on it; but the whole event was otherwise filled with bluster and bravado, with Louis going so far as to challenge Henry to single combat – an offer that was, predictably, declined.[19] There was not much in the way of a definitive outcome, or at least not as far as Louis was concerned: Henry retained the castle in question, and rendered no homage for Normandy. The kings, having each by now some idea of what they were up against in the other, agreed a two-year truce and departed.

The years of 'peace' that followed were marked not by any open warfare between England and France, but rather by a series of lower-level incidents involving rival barons – either with or without the tacit approval of their overlords – that resulted in pillage, murders and mutilations.[20] A major gain for Henry (and loss for Louis) occurred when Theobald IV, count of Blois, defected; he was a vassal of the French king, but Henry I was his uncle (Theobald's mother Adela was Henry's sister), so he evidently felt that his prospects would be better served by switching allegiance. Theobald brought together a coalition of barons with grievances against Louis, and Henry encouraged them to rebel against the French king.[21] Louis defeated them but did not then have sufficient resources to fight Henry as well, or to reopen the question of the control of Gisors.

Meanwhile, there had been developments in other parts of France, with Henry's political tentacles spreading further. Brittany was Normandy's immediate neighbour to the south-west, and the two duchies had experienced a thorny relationship in the past; now Henry took advantage of the recent abdication of the duke, Alan IV, by marrying his own illegitimate daughter Matilda to Alan's teenage son and successor, Conan III.[22]

The two counties to the immediate south of Normandy, Maine and Anjou, were under the control of the same man. This was Fulk V, count of Anjou (whose mother, as we saw earlier, had eloped with King Philip); he had inherited Anjou from his father in 1109 and gained control of Maine in right of his wife, Ermengarde, who was the only child and heiress of Elias, count of Maine, who had died in 1110. Fulk and Ermengarde had at this stage no son, but two infant daughters. Henry arranged for the elder, Matilda, to be betrothed to his son William Adelin, and Fulk agreed to bestow the county of Maine on his daughter as her dowry. A *dowry*, sometimes also known as a marriage portion, was the land or goods a woman brought with her to a marriage, to be controlled by her husband. The term should not be confused with a very similar one, *dower*, which was lands or other incomes provided by a husband for his wife's financial support, which would remain hers for her lifetime if he should predecease her. We will encounter both dowries and dowers frequently as we go on, for now noting only that as young William Adelin and Matilda of Anjou were respectively aged ten and two at the time of their betrothal, actual control of any lands belonging to either of them would rest with Henry.

Louis VI was put very much on the back foot by both these marriage arrangements, and in March 1113 he reluctantly agreed to a treaty that recognised Henry as overlord of both Brittany and Maine. Peace held, although one contemporary's conclusion that the two kings were 'bound in an alliance of friendship amid general rejoicing' is probably overstating the enthusiasm felt by at least one party.[23]

* * *

Among the many duties of kingship in the twelfth century was the provision of male heirs. Henry's legitimate son was recognised by all as his eventual successor and was already being introduced to the world of politics. Louis, meanwhile, was now in his early thirties and unmarried. From 1104 to 1107 he had been betrothed to Lucienne of Rochefort, who was a child at the time. It does not appear that the betrothal ever led to a formal marriage, and it was either annulled or repudiated while she was still underage.[24] His accession to the throne meant that he would need to choose a bride carefully, and in 1115 his choice fell upon Adelaide of Maurienne, who was the daughter of Count Humbert II of Savoy and Gisela of Burgundy, but also (and perhaps more significantly) the niece of the man who would shortly be elected Pope Callixtus II. Adelaide fulfilled her primary duty by producing an heir, Philip, within a year of the wedding. She would go on to bear Louis a total of eight children (one daughter and seven sons, six of whom survived infancy), and she was also politically active in support of her husband. Her name appears on forty-five royal charters, and they were dated with her regnal year as well as his.[25]

A peace of sorts lasted until April 1116, when hostilities were renewed in the French and Norman Vexins. Henry's earlier gesture of clemency towards little William Clito was returning to haunt him: Clito was now fourteen and becoming a viable candidate to rival Henry in Normandy (although not in England, or at least not yet). All those who were not favourably disposed towards Henry were naturally inclined to support the claims of Clito, and Henry found himself fighting against a coalition of Louis, Fulk V of Anjou – his daughter's betrothal to Henry's son notwithstanding – and Baldwin VII, count of Flanders. Baldwin was a kinsman of both Henry and Clito; his grandfather had been the brother of Matilda of Flanders, the queen of William the Conqueror who was Henry's mother and Clito's grandmother.[26]

Other barons who had reason to be dissatisfied with Henry's rather authoritarian rule in Normandy joined the Clito faction, thereby allying themselves with the king of France, and by the spring of 1118 the fighting had become intense.[27] Henry was not helped by the devastating blow of the loss of his wife, Queen Edith-Matilda, in May of that year; not only had he been personally fond of her, but she had served effectively as his regent in England while he was on his frequent sojourns in Normandy. England would now have to be left in other hands whenever he was on the other side of the Channel.

Shortly before Christmas 1118, Count Fulk defeated Henry's Anglo-Norman forces in what appears to have been a decisive, though unfortunately ill-recorded, engagement at Alençon in southern Normandy.[28] Henry's life was then endangered by an assassination attempt at the hands of a treasurer of his own household, causing him paranoia ever afterwards: 'Frightened thoroughly . . . he changed beds often and, dreading night's terrors, regularly increased his armed guards. He also ordered that a shield and sword be placed before him every night while he slept.'[29]

But Fortune's wheel, as ever, turned again, and Louis's coalition fell apart. Henry wooed Count Fulk of Anjou away by celebrating the wedding of William Adelin and Matilda; the bride was still only eight years old, well below the accepted canonical age, but the marriage meant that Fulk would, in due course, be the father of the queen of England, a much better position than anything Louis could offer him. Count Baldwin of Flanders had been injured fighting against Henry's forces in the autumn of 1118, and after lingering for months he eventually succumbed to his wounds in July 1119. Baldwin had no children, and so he had named as his heir his cousin Charles, later known as Charles the Good, who was the son of Baldwin's aunt Adela and her first husband, King Cnut IV of Denmark.[30] On acceding in Flanders, Charles naturally had immediate concerns of his own, including fighting off a number of other contenders for the comital title, and he had no time to spare for Clito, Henry or Louis. If Louis wanted to continue his conflict with the English king, he would have to do so on his own.

* * *

It is tempting to see warfare in the twelfth century – and in the Middle Ages as a whole – as being characterised by pitched battles; they do, after all, live long in the memory. But in fact they were rare occurrences and conflict was more likely to take the form of attempting to deprive an enemy of his resources, in the form of castles, personnel, money or food. Two examples from the next phase of Louis and Henry's war illustrate this.

The first was Louis's attack on the castle of Les Andelys in the spring of 1119. Castles were of pivotal importance in any conflict, serving a tripartite function. Firstly, they demonstrated the prestige and authority of the owner: in a world of mostly single-storey, wattle-and-daub buildings, they dominated any landscape in which they were situated. Secondly, they served a defensive purpose. Defensive architecture was at this time ahead in the ongoing race against offensive weaponry, and capturing castles was difficult:

it could be done, but it was arduous, expensive and time-consuming. In basic terms, this meant that anyone who owned or held a castle, particularly a stone one, was in a very favourable position indeed. They had an obvious advantage over anyone lower down in the hierarchy – who could be attacked at any time because they had no solid walls behind which they could retreat – and they were in far less danger either from their peers or from their social superiors. The holder of a castle, even if besieged and outnumbered, could normally manage to negotiate a settlement, as the besieging party would rather come to terms than have to spend months camping outside the walls, with all the attendant dangers such as hunger, disease and loss of campaign momentum.

Thirdly, and this is perhaps less well known, castles served an important offensive purpose. The range of influence of a castle, and the area it controlled, was not limited to the length of a bowshot from the walls; rather, it amounted to half a day's ride (allowing time to go out and then return before nightfall), or some 10–15 miles in every direction. Castellans could roam around the local countryside by day and then sleep behind closed gates at night; stores could be kept and stockpiled in safety, both for the benefit of the garrison and to stop them falling into the hands of marauding enemies. No attack on an enemy's lands, therefore, could be complete until his castles were captured, as the stronghold would offer the opportunity to regroup and counter-attack; and a series of castles built close enough to have overlapping circles of influence would be a formidable obstacle.[31]

Capturing a castle based in someone else's land was therefore very advantageous, if it could be done without great expenditure in terms of time, money or loss of life. In effect, this meant taking it through tricks and treachery, rather than siege, and Louis achieved just such a coup at Les Andelys, a fortress situated on the River Seine, well inside the Norman part of the Vexin. In the spring of 1119 he made contact with the castellan in advance of his planned attack; the exact details of their agreement are unknown, but the result was that the castellan took some of Louis's men back with him and hid them under straw in a storehouse. When Louis approached the castle himself in plain sight the next day, the men leaped out from their hiding place, pretended at first to be defending troops, and then switched their war-cry to the French 'Montjoie' and attacked. The garrison were caught completely off guard and fled.[32]

Les Andelys was thereafter for many months a major French outpost within eastern Normandy, from where Louis's forces could make frequent sorties to pillage and devastate crops and villages. Those who tilled the land could not possibly stand against trained and armed warriors, so they had no defence except to run and hide, returning later to find if anything was left of their homes and livelihoods. The net result was that they would be starving and thus unable to pay tithes or taxes, which in turn deprived their overlords of precious resources.

Ravaging and burning was not limited just to the countryside, and this leads us on to our second illustrative example. When King Henry moved against Évreux (about 25 miles south-west of Les Andelys), he burned the entire town to the ground. The unfortunate citizens 'scattered in all directions and, having lost all their possessions, were forced to wander wretchedly from one strange cottage to another'.[33] They had no recourse to justice, no claim for compensation; their misfortune was that they were considered, in the grand scheme of things, to be not important individuals in their own right but rather a general economic resource to be exploited. The destruction of the town also had significant additional consequences in terms of fear, mistrust (why would anyone wish to owe allegiance to a lord who could not protect them?), disruption to trade and a decrease in revenue.

Louis and Henry were engaged in a war of attrition, a situation that might continue for some time until something decisive happened. As we noted briefly above, pitched battles were rare in comparison to sieges, skirmishes and ravaging; but sometimes they did occur, and one such – although small in scale – was about to have profound consequences for the two kingdoms.

It came about almost by accident. On 20 August 1119, King Henry and a force of some 500 knights, including three of his sons (William Adelin, then sixteen, plus his older half-brothers, the illegitimate Robert and Richard fitzRoy) were engaged in ravaging the area around Noyon-sur-Andelle (now Charleval), a castle held by the English king that was about 10 miles north of the French-controlled Les Andelys. King Louis and William Clito – on whose behalf the French king was still ostensibly acting – were, meanwhile, riding north from their own base with an army in order to make an attempt on the castle of Noyon. Neither king seems to have realised that the other was in the vicinity until they actually came into sight of each other.

When Henry became aware that Louis was approaching, he split his men into three groups: 400 dismounted and formed up into two separate divisions, while the remaining 100 remained mounted. He then awaited the French attack. The bellicose Louis was not about to turn down the opportunity for a fight, but – either through recklessness or simply because he saw no need – he made little effort to form his force of around 400 knights into any kind of order. Instead, he allowed them, all remaining mounted, to make an impetuous and undisciplined charge.

The result was disastrous. Some of the charging French knights were beaten back by those Anglo-Normans who had remained mounted; those who did succeed in breaking through the cavalry were immediately surrounded by Henry's dismounted and well-organised divisions of knights, who killed the horses and captured their riders. All was over within an hour, with negligible fatalities on either side but some 140 French knights taken prisoner. King Louis and William Clito both escaped, but were forced to flee on foot in an ignominious manner after losing their horses in the melee.

Although the Battle of Brémule, as it became known, was of short duration and did not result in great loss of life, it is an event of great significance in the history of Anglo-French conflict, not least because it was one of the very few occasions on which a king of England and a king of France took the field against each other. Louis, although not injured or captured, suffered a huge loss of face, and both he and Clito had to endure the shame of having Henry and William Adelin pointedly return their horses to them as 'gifts'.

Contemporary chroniclers put different interpretations on the battle, depending on their own allegiances and points of view. The French abbot Suger, for example, a supporter of the French king, attempted a positive spin by claiming that Louis 'deemed it unworthy to plan carefully for battle' but was taken aback by the 'surprisingly well-aligned and positioned ranks of the enemy'; he then 'returned to Andelys as decently as possible'. The *Anglo-Saxon Chronicle*, on the other hand, notes rather more bluntly that 'there the king of France was put to flight and all his best men seized'.[34]

After his defeat at Brémule Louis appealed to Pope Callixtus (his wife's uncle), who met Henry at Gisors in early November 1120 in order to broker a treaty; Henry had the upper hand in these negotiations, and the results were favourable to him.[35] Under the terms of the peace, his heir William Adelin would perform homage to Louis for Normandy. This was something of a double win for the English king: firstly, he avoided having to kneel in public himself; and, secondly, in accepting William Adelin's homage, Louis had to promise to be a good lord to him – which meant also that he was accepting his legitimacy as heir, and therefore repudiating all support for Clito's claims to Normandy. A further stipulation of the treaty was that all territories captured by both kings during the course of the war were to be returned – except the sticking point of long duration, Gisors, which Louis was forced to concede to Henry.

Henry was thus the great winner from the negotiations, and he was understandably pleased with himself: 'The king, then, having either subdued or made terms with all who had rebelled against him, having prosperously completed everything according to his wish, in unusual gladness returned to England.'[36] He made his way back through Normandy to Barfleur, from where he embarked on 25 November 1120 in triumph and with great hopes for the future.

⇒ CHAPTER TWO ⇐

TRAGEDY, CRISIS AND MURDER

ENRY'S ROYAL ENTOURAGE WAS TOO large to be transported on a single ship, comprising as it did not only his family and other nobles, but also their many servants, grooms and attendants, and all the clerks and administrators necessary for the household and itinerant government to function. A whole fleet therefore awaited him at Barfleur, and all the necessary preparations for the crossing of the Channel began.

As he waited to embark, Henry was approached by the captain of a new vessel called the *White Ship* who said that he would be honoured to convey the king personally. Henry declined, having already made other arrangements; but his seventeen-year-old son William Adelin – perhaps wishing to be away from the eye of parental authority for the duration of the passage, or perhaps struck by the fine, sleek ship – persuaded the king to allow him and his friends to take up the offer. William therefore boarded the *White Ship*, along with his illegitimate half-siblings Richard fitzRoy and Matilda, countess of Perche; his cousins, the brother and sister Stephen and Matilda of Blois; Matilda's husband Richard, the earl of Chester; and the youthful heirs to a number of other English titles and estates. Stephen of Blois disembarked shortly before the ship sailed, thus unwittingly changing the course of English royal history; his avowed reason was that he was suffering from a stomach upset, but it is also possible that he left because he felt (rightly, as it turned out) that 'there was too great a crowd of wild and headstrong young men on board'.[1]

Henry took his place in another ship, in the rather more sober and digni-fied company of his eldest illegitimate son Robert, earl of Gloucester, his eldest nephew, Theobald IV of Blois, and various other members of his close household. He sailed on the evening tide and enjoyed an uneventful passage across the Channel; after disembarking in England he made his way to Clarendon in Wiltshire, where he waited for William Adelin and the rest of the court to catch up.

And he waited.

As time went by and young William still did not arrive, perhaps Henry started to worry. He would have been right to do so because – although nobody had yet summoned up the courage to tell him – the awful tidings had already been received: the *White Ship* had struck a rock and sunk shortly after leaving Barfleur. William and all his noble companions were dead, drowned in the cold, dark waters of the Channel. Eventually the terrified nobles could hide the news no longer, and Theobald of Blois came up with the idea of finding a young boy, an innocent, to break it to the king. The tearful child performed his duty, and Henry, in a state of collapse, 'was led into a private room, [and] gave way to bitter laments'.[2]

'O God, what a catastrophe and what sorrow there was!', lamented one twelfth-century commentator.[3] But the sorrow was not only for Henry, extreme as his personal losses had been; it was also for England. The succession to the crown had been blown wide open, for William Adelin had been Henry's only legitimate son, and the realm was now ruled by a man in his fifties with no obvious heir.

Over in France, King Louis could compare his own family and succession situation favourably with that of his rival, as he was by now the father of two sons – the elder already recognised as king-designate – with a third on the way and every hope of more.[4] He could not, of course, make any kind of case for the English throne for himself or his children, but the situation did provide him with the opportunity to take advantage of the uncertainty and to discompose Henry further. The obvious way to do this, and the one which Louis pursued with alacrity, was to resurrect his support for William Clito. Others saw things the same way. Fulk V of Anjou had lost his alliance with England: his nine-year-old daughter Matilda had fortunately not been on board the *White Ship*, being not yet old enough to cohabit with her husband; but she was now a widow who would in due course be returned to Fulk.[5] If Fulk wished to realise his ambitions of being the father of the queen of England, and in time the grandfather of a king, he would have to make alternative arrangements. With Louis's agreement, and at the urging of his uncle Amaury III de Montfort, count of Évreux (of whom we shall hear more below), Fulk betrothed his second daughter, Sybil, to William Clito. The wedding took place in 1123, and Fulk bestowed the county of Maine – which had been under Henry's control since William Adelin's marriage – as Sybil's dowry.[6]

By this time Henry's dynastic plans were falling apart. His heir was dead. His only other legitimate child, Matilda, was married to Emperor Henry V and settled in Germany, with as yet no children of her own who might fill the succession void. The king himself had married again shortly after the *White Ship* disaster, but – despite the fact that she travelled everywhere with him – his new young queen Adeliza of Louvain had not become pregnant in three years of marriage.

The claims of William Clito to be named as heir were strong. He was, after all, the only son of William the Conqueror's eldest son, so there were many barons both in England and in Normandy who saw the kingdom and the duchy as his by right. Moreover, Clito had shown himself to be an active and capable young man, and he was viewed with some personal sympathy on both sides of the Channel. But Clito's illustrious lineage was exactly the reason why Henry could *not* name him as heir, in the light of his own rather unorthodox rise to power: in short, if he were to name Clito as his successor on the basis that he was Robert Curthose's son and William I's grandson, questions would arise as to why the young man was not king and duke already.

Rebellion on Clito's behalf broke out in Normandy in 1123, backed inevitably by King Louis and also now by Count Fulk, Clito's new father-in-law, and a (surprisingly large, to Henry at least) number of others.[7] This put many barons in a difficult position because the war was one of close kinsmen. And even if their loyalty to the king was steadfast, they must have had at the back of their minds the fact that he could not last forever, and that their own futures would be best protected by ensuring that they supported the winning candidate to succeed him. This state of affairs made it very difficult for King Henry to know whom to trust:

In the general confusion that always occurs in conflicts between kinsmen he [Henry] was unable to trust his own men. Men who ate with him favoured the cause of his nephew and his other enemies and, by prying into his secrets, greatly helped these men. This was indeed more than civil war, and ties of blood bound together brothers and friends and kinsmen who were fighting on both sides.[8]

One of the leaders of the rebellion was Amaury III de Montfort, who was Count Fulk's uncle (and the brother of Bertrade de Montfort, former queen of France) and who seems to have been an extraordinarily persuasive man. Among those whom he induced to join the rebellion was the teenaged Waleran de Beaumont, count of Meulan (son of Robert, the previous count, whose lands had been ravaged by King Louis in 1109), who had formerly been a protégé of Henry's. Amaury and Waleran agitated in Normandy while William Clito and Fulk attacked some of Henry's strongholds in Maine.

The conflict in Normandy took, for a while, the usual form of ravaging, sieges and counter-sieges, much to the detriment of the local population.[9] But then an armed engagement occurred that was to change the course of the rebellion.

The rebels had been active in the Vexin, and they held the fortification of Vatteville, approximately 8 miles west of Les Andelys. King Henry did not advance on it in person, having too many other calls on his time, but his troops established a siege there and built a siege tower (a tall counter-construction, sometimes also called a belfry, from which arrows and missiles could be aimed downwards over the defending fortification's walls). In one of the chess-like manoeuvres so common in warfare of this period, Amaury de Montfort and Waleran de Beaumont had approached Henry's encircling forces from behind on the evening of 25 March 1124 and captured the siege tower, thus relieving the pressure on Vatteville.

Satisfied with their gain, Amaury, Waleran and their men set out the next day to ride back to Waleran's own lands at Beaumont-le-Roger, about 35 miles to the south-west. But unknown to them one Odo of Borleng, a commander of a different division of Henry's forces, had learned of the attack and was waiting at Bourgthéroulde, about halfway on their return journey. The precise location is not known, but the sources agree that he and his men had set their ambush at a point where the road emerged from a forest. Some of them remained on horseback, but the rest dismounted, forming a dense mass of infantry, and Odo also placed archers on the flanks of his front line. Then they waited.

The Norman rebels became aware of their enemy as they emerged from the forest, and a discussion ensued; Amaury argued against an engagement, but the younger and evidently more hot-headed Waleran ignored him, charging directly at the infantry with a group of knights. Not one of them reached Odo's line, as his archers did their work. As was customary at the time, they aimed their arrows not at the knights themselves, but rather at their horses – this stopped the charge very effectively, but also avoided killing too many knights: they were more valuable alive, as they could be ransomed. Following the failure of Waleran's initial charge the two main forces moved to engage each other, but the momentum was with Odo, whose disciplined and well-formed infantry were victorious. Amaury managed to escape, fleeing over the border to France, but Waleran and some eighty other knights were captured.

King Henry was glad to hear news of Odo's victory, and he was determined to be ruthless in order to crush the rebellion while he had the opportunity. Amaury de Montfort had eluded him, Waleran was imprisoned and some of the lesser knights who had fought against him were ransomed, according to normal practice; but Henry sentenced three of the other ringleaders to be blinded, a cruel fate for a fighting man in the twelfth century and one that was generally carried out with agonising brutality. The sentence was executed on two of the condemned men, but the third chose to commit suicide by beating his head repeatedly against a wall in his prison cell, rather than suffer the punishment.

Even though none of the principal protagonists – King Henry, King Louis, William Clito – were present at the Battle of Bourgthéroulde, the engagement was a pivotal moment in the conflict. Although most of the rebels were captured, rather than killed, this put them *hors de combat* while negotiations for their ransom and release took place; the consequent loss of so many fighting men from the cause meant that the rebellion was effectively over. The battle also illustrates that a well-disciplined formation of infantry was easily a match for a cavalry charge by knights. The monk and chronicler Orderic Vitalis, in his account of the engagement, puts these words in the mouth of Amaury de Montfort: 'See, Odo Borleng and his men have dismounted; you can be sure that he intends to fight resolutely until he has won the day. A mounted soldier who has dismounted with his men will not fly from the field; he will either die or conquer.'[10]

William Clito, abandoned by his erstwhile allies, was left without the means to continue his campaign: 'He wandered from house to house in foreign lands, living in great fear and poverty. His uncle's arm was long and powerful and formidable to him, for Henry's might and reputation for wealth and power were known far and wide.'[11] Henry now used that long arm to consolidate his gains, deploying his military and political resources to move not only against Clito, but also against Louis and France itself.

One of the great trump cards in King Henry's possession was his strategic alliance with Emperor Henry V, thanks to the marriage between him and the king's (legitimate) daughter, Matilda. This alliance had been formed as long ago as 1110 – Matilda had been shipped overseas for her betrothal to the twenty-something emperor when she was just eight – and although the two men had not met in person since that time, they kept up a frequent correspondence.[12] In the summer of 1124, following the victory at Bourgthéroulde, the king persuaded his son-in-law to plan an invasion of France from the north and east, the idea being that Louis would be caught between the two Henrys and crushed.

But King Henry had greatly underestimated the influence that Louis, after more than a decade of energetic rule, now wielded in France. Previously, although Louis was in name king of the whole realm, just as his forefathers had been, in reality France was a relatively loose collection of great duchies and counties whose lords all owed allegiance to the king, while he maintained direct control only over the royal holdings around Paris and the Île-de-France.[13] But now, faced with the threat of the massed forces of the Empire on one side and King Henry of England on the other, he used all the power and influence that he had been accumulating via non-stop action since the days of his youth. Abbot Suger of Saint-Denis, a contemporary of Louis and an eyewitness to all that transpired, has the fullest account of this episode.[14] He begins by detailing the scale of the threat:

> The emperor assembled the greatest possible host of Lotharingians, Germans, Bavarians, Sueves [Swabians] and Saxons. Feigning a movement elsewhere, he was plotting a surprise attack against the city of Reims, on the advice of the English king Henry. The emperor intended

to destroy the city suddenly or besiege it, and thereby subject it to ... suffering and shame.

But Louis, says Suger, learned of the plot and immediately took decisive action. He 'bravely and boldly called up a levy' and then, without waiting for it to arrive, hurried to attend to important spiritual matters, riding to the abbey of Saint-Denis, just north of Paris, to ask France's patron saint for help:

> Offering prayers and gifts, he [Louis] begged him [St Denis] from the bottom of his heart to defend the kingdom ... for the French have a special privilege from him: if another kingdom should dare invade theirs, the relics of that blessed and wonderful defender himself ... are placed on the altar in order to defend the kingdom; and the king had this done with solemnity and devotion in his presence.

Louis placed the abbey's holy relics on the altar, and then took up a standard that would henceforward be used as a rallying point for all French kings in times of war: the *oriflamme*.[15] He then 'sent forth a mighty call for all of France to follow him', and the French responded as enthusiastically as he could have wished:

> The customary fighting spirit of France became angry at this unaccustomed brazenness of its enemies. Stirring itself on all sides, it sent forward select forces of knights, the very strongest men ... from all directions we gathered together in great strength at Reims. Numerous hosts of knights and foot soldiers came into view, and they seemed to devour the surface of the earth like locusts, not only along the courses of the rivers but also over the mountains and the plain.

Suger goes on to note that members of this host came from many different parts of France, including such luminaries as Count Theobald IV of Blois (currently back in Louis's fold, rather than that of his uncle Henry), the counts of Champagne, Vermandois, Nevers and Flanders, and the duke of Burgundy. Those from even further afield, such as the duke of far-flung Aquitaine, also supported the king, 'but the length of the journey and the short notice did not allow them time to gather their forces in order to punish severely this insult to the French'. It was, in short, not simply Louis and a group of vassals who were ready to repel the invasion; it was the kingdom of France.[16]

Abbot Suger, of course, was concerned to present King Louis in the best light, and some of his descriptions (not to mention his estimates of the actual size of the army) verge on the fanciful. However, what is beyond doubt is that Louis had gathered together in common cause nobles and troops from a much wider area than any king of France had managed before; and also that the unexpected and unprecedented show of strength and unity persuaded the emperor to cancel his planned invasion. 'The French went home,' concludes Suger, 'having won a grand and prestigious victory, which was just the same as or even superior to an actual triumph in the field.' King Louis ceremonially replaced the holy relics and the *oriflamme* at the abbey of Saint-Denis, until such time as they should be needed again.

King Henry's plans were thwarted; in the absence of an invasion from the emperor, it would have been foolish to launch an unsupported one of his own, so he was reduced to attempting to damage his nephew's prospects by having Clito's marriage annulled. Much of the younger man's current influence and resource stemmed from the fact that he was married to Fulk of Anjou's daughter Sybil, but Henry made a persuasive case to the Church (accompanied by a donation of 'an enormous quantity of gold and silver and other valuables') that the young couple were related within a prohibited degree. That this was entirely politically motivated, rather than a spiritual concern, is illustrated by the fact that the degree of relationship between William Clito and Sybil of Anjou was exactly the same as that between William Adelin (Clito's cousin) and his wife Matilda of Anjou (Sybil's sister), a match Henry had arranged himself.[17]

King Henry's success in this endeavour was to backfire, as we shall see later in this chapter, and in the meantime he suffered another blow to his ambitions: his alliance with the Empire dissolved following the death of Emperor Henry in the spring of 1125.[18] As his marriage to Matilda had been childless, his death prompted an election in Germany, which was won by Lothar, duke of Saxony, who subsequently became Lothar III.[19] The new monarch had no particular interest in an alliance with England, and so that relationship was lost.

Emperor Henry's death also affected the still-unresolved and increasingly urgent question of the English succession. Henry I's second marriage had not produced a child, after five years, and as he neared the age of sixty he was having to face up to the fact that he would father no more legitimate sons, so an alternative solution would need to be found. The situation in Germany resulted in Empress Matilda (a childless widow of twenty-three and Henry's only remaining legitimate issue) leaving the Empire to return to Normandy and then England, so her name could be included in the mix as Henry was pressured to designate an heir.

Matilda and William Clito were considered the two principal candidates, but there were two other possibilities. The first was Robert fitzRoy, earl of Gloucester and the eldest of Henry I's many illegitimate offspring. He had been his father's loyal man for all his life and had risen to prominence and riches thanks to this; he was by now in his mid-thirties and a reliable, if sometimes uninspiring, lieutenant. However, both his illegitimacy and his less-than-stellar maternal lineage counted against him: his mother was probably a non-noble woman of Caen, in Normandy, while King Henry's legitimate children were descended via Edith-Matilda from the royal Anglo-Saxon house as well as the kings of Scotland.[20] The other alternative candidate was Theobald IV of Blois, the son of Henry's sister Adela. Theobald's claim was also problematic, as he was not only a vassal of Louis but also a man who, as we have seen, had his own interests very much to the fore and did not hesitate to waver in his allegiance accordingly. Meanwhile, naming Clito was, for the reasons discussed earlier in this chapter and the ongoing conflict, out of the question.

None of the claims of the three male contenders, therefore, were straightforward. Neither was Matilda's, of course, for the simple reason that she was female. However, she was the only one who was a legitimate child of Henry I and Edith-Matilda, descended from all three royal houses, and she was also the only one who could claim porphyrogeniture. Given that Henry I had made use of this theory in asserting that his own right to the throne was superior to that of Robert Curthose, it may have added weight to Matilda's claims. After some deliberation, the king took the unprecedented step of naming a female heir to the English crown: he announced at his Christmas court of 1126 that Matilda was to succeed him on the throne, and on 1 January 1127 the assembled barons swore to uphold her rights.[21]

None of this pleased King Louis, who now threw his considerable and increasing political weight behind his own protégé, William Clito. Clito had lost his alliance with Anjou following the forced annulment of his marriage, but Louis turned Henry's success against him when he managed to arrange an even better match: Clito would marry Jeanne de Montferrat, who was the half-sister of Queen Adelaide. The wedding took place within a month of Henry's announcement that Matilda would be his heir and, tellingly, Louis endowed Clito with the French Vexin as part of the marriage settlement, giving him resources and a sphere of influence right on the Norman border. Clito, now, in his early twenties, in his prime and a veteran of years of conflict and campaigning, immediately led an armed force to Gisors, where he issued a formal claim to Normandy, and 'the Normans respected him as their natural lord'.[22]

And then, as if to underline that Fortune had turned her wheel and that Clito was currently her favourite, he and Louis were the beneficiaries of an unexpected and scandalous event that sent shockwaves reverberating throughout Europe.

* * *

The county of Flanders was located in a crucial position in western Europe, both geographically and politically. It owed allegiance – nominally at least – to the king of France, but it was also situated on the border of the Empire, and it controlled the shortest Channel crossings to England. Most sea trade between the Scandinavian nations and the Mediterranean passed along its coast, and it was a thriving hub of international commerce. Being count of Flanders, then, was both prestigious and challenging, and since his accession in 1119 Charles I, known as 'the Good', had walked the diplomatic tightrope between the neighbouring kings and the emperor with great skill. He had also governed Flanders justly and well, ensuring peace and prosperity, and instituting reforms that helped the poor. He was, as his epithet implies, both devout and popular.[23]

On 2 March 1127 Charles entered the church of St Donatian in Bruges to attend Mass. But, unbeknown to him, a gang of 'traitors . . . all with drawn swords beneath their cloaks' entered, and what happened next outraged all Christendom:

Those wretched traitors, already murderers at heart, slew the count, who was struck down with swords and run through again and again, while he was praying devoutly and giving alms, humbly kneeling before the Divine Majesty. And so God gave the palm of the martyrs to the count, the course of whose good life was washed clean in the rivulets of his blood and brought to an end ... He surrendered his spirit to the Lord of all and offered himself as a morning sacrifice to God ... The bloody body of such a great man and prince lay there alone.[24]

For details of this heinous crime, and of the violent events in Flanders that followed, we are indebted to an extraordinary narrative written by a man named Galbert, a notary of Bruges, who was not only an eyewitness but one who was writing day by day under some fairly extreme circumstances. 'I had no suitable place for writing,' he tells us:

I did this in the midst of such a great tumult and the burning of so many houses, set on fire by lighted arrows shot on to the roofs of the town ... and in the midst of so much danger by night and conflict by day. I had to wait for moments of peace during the night or day to set in order the present account of events as they happened, and in this way, though in great straits, I transcribed for the faithful what you see and read.[25]

Sometimes we are forcibly reminded that the political was also the personal, and that real people lived, worked, hoped, suffered and died during the historical events that we examine. Galbert's text will be the main source for the rest of this chapter, as we picture him scribbling fearfully by candlelight in order to bring it to us.

Any cold-blooded murder was shocking enough, but in this specific case the aggravating factors piled up one after the other. Charles was the count, and beloved by most of his people. He was a kinsman of the king of France (Charles's mother, Adela of Flanders, was the half-sister of Louis's mother). The murder occurred while he was praying in church. And, perhaps most damningly of all to contemporaries, the perpetrators were men of low birth. This was a crime against Flanders, against the king and against God; it was an outrage to the natural order. Chaos ensued in the power vacuum that followed, a civil war beginning among rival candidates to succeed Charles, and the innocent citizens being subjected to much opportunistic violence and looting.

The situation offered both trouble and potential to King Louis. Up until this point Flanders, although technically owing allegiance to him, had been a quasi-independent state, but now he took his chance to impose royal authority, assuming the privileges of overlordship while ostensibly helping to bring peace and control. Within a fortnight of the murder he had arrived in Flanders in person and announced that justice must be done. He had the perpetrators of the crime – members of an ambitious but relatively low-ranking group who 'were trying to remove their branch of the family from under [Charles's] lordship' – hunted down. No punishment was too harsh for those who had transgressed in so outrageous a fashion, and they were put to death in a range of excruciating, humiliating and inventive ways.[26]

Once Charles's murder had been avenged, the question of who was to succeed him needed to be addressed. The answer was not clear-cut, as he had no children and no brothers, so a motley collection of cousins and second cousins were able to put themselves forward for consideration. A competition ensued, involving several candidates who could all trace descent from Count Baldwin V, who had ruled Flanders from 1037 to 1067. The early front-runner, mainly because he was the only one of the contenders who was in Flanders at the time, was one William of Ypres; but he was illegitimate, and thus his claims were soon set aside as bigger hitters entered the fray.[27]

Flanders, as we noted above, was a rich county of strategic importance to both England and France, so naturally both kings tried to influence the succession – and, just as naturally, they favoured different candidates. Henry initially seemed to offer support to any of the claimants who would stand against Louis's choice, but he eventually settled on Thierry of Alsace – whose maternal grandfather had been Baldwin V's younger son – promising him both political and financial support.

Henry was on this occasion to be outwitted by Louis, who demonstrated not only astute diplomatic skills but also the increasing power and influence of the French crown. His nomination for the title of count was none other than William Clito, Henry's nephew. Clito's paternal grandmother Matilda (the queen of William the Conqueror) had been Baldwin V's daughter, so he did have a hereditary claim, but it was inferior to that of Thierry and indeed to those of several other candidates. This was of no matter, as it tran-spired: Louis used his position as overlord to summon the Flemish barons to a week-long assembly at Arras, during which time he dismissed the claims of others and put forward Clito's. It worked, and Clito was proclaimed count on 28 March 1127, less than a month after Charles's assassination.

Although this was technically an election, there seems to be little doubt that Louis's influence was the deciding factor. Galbert, in his up-to-the-minute journalistic account, tells us that the barons returned from Arras 'after designation of the count *by King Louis*' and that 'the leading men of the land of Flanders, *on the order and advice of the king*', had elected William Clito. Suger, writing later, agrees, noting that Louis '*installed* as count of Flanders William the Norman, the son of Count Robert'.[28]

William Clito was a boy no longer, a wanderer and exile no more. He was a fit and active man of twenty-four who now had a prestigious title, along with the accompanying land and resources, a high-ranking wife and the backing of the French crown. Louis – in what was no doubt a combina-tion of support for his protégé and a desire to discomfit King Henry – also made it clear that he favoured Clito as the heir to the duchy of Normandy, by right of his imprisoned father's claim and in preference to Henry's daughter, Empress Matilda. The French king remained in Flanders for some weeks, touring the main cities with the new count as Clito received the homage of his subjects.[29]

This was all very worrying for Henry. Not only was Clito's rise dangerous for his succession plans in Normandy, but it also potentially impacted on his position as king of England – for who knew what Clito might be capable of, with the right combination of heredity, riches and baronial support?

Immediate action was necessary, and Henry took it. First, he brought economic pressure to bear by imposing sanctions on trade with Flanders. Flemish wealth was founded on trade, and so merchants of non-noble birth had more influence in the county than might have been the case elsewhere in France or England; and once the reality of the sanctions began to bite they looked on Clito with a much less favourable eye. Henry's efforts to discredit his nephew were, in fact, assisted by Clito himself: he saw Flanders only as a mine of resources, a means to an end in his greater struggle for Normandy, and he also had very little experience of government; thus, he ended up alienating both the barons and the merchants.[30]

Henry now moved to surround Clito's lands with allies of his own. His father-in-law Godfrey was count of Louvain and duke of Lower Lorraine, and was able to harm Flemish trade interests in that part of the Empire; his nephew Stephen of Blois was count of Boulogne and therefore able to harass Flanders from that direction. And Henry now moved to secure his position on the southern borders of Normandy via yet another alliance with the house of Anjou: he arranged for his daughter, Empress Matilda, to marry Count Fulk's son and heir Geoffrey. Geoffrey was at this point not old enough to be formally married (he was thirteen to the rather unimpressed Matilda's twenty-five), so the betrothal was agreed, with the wedding to come the following year. We will hear more of Matilda and Geoffrey in the next chapter.

In the meantime, King Henry continued to promise money and support to anti-Clito factions within Flanders, and to reiterate his support for the candidature of Thierry of Alsace. He also ordered his nephew Stephen to begin a military campaign on the Flemish border from his base in Boulogne. To this last, Clito was able to respond effectively. He may have been – like his father before him – an inexperienced and possibly even inept administrator, but he also resembled Robert Curthose in that he was a talented and courageous warrior. And, having spent nearly all of his life involved in various conflicts, he was by now also an experienced campaigner. He took up arms, and by the summer of 1127 had forced Stephen to agree to a three-year truce. So serious was the situation that Henry crossed the Channel in person in August.

Despite his military prowess, Clito continued to lose the support of rich trading towns, and he found his grasp on Flanders slipping. By the early spring of 1128 he was obliged to ask Louis for help, writing a letter to the French king that included the following passage:

Behold my powerful and inveterate enemy, namely the king of the English, who has long grieved at my success. Now he has brought together innumerable knights and vast amounts of money; and out of pure spite he labours to take away from you and from ourselves a section of the most faithful and powerful men of your realm, confident in the number of his men and still more in the quantity of his cash.[31]

Louis, having gone to such trouble to have Clito installed in Flanders, and having so much riding on the outcome there, now needed to take action if his advantage were not to slip. He arrived in the county in April 1128, but was almost immediately wrong-footed by a shrewd manoeuvre by Henry. The English king was by now in Normandy, and he marched his troops as far as Épernon, between Paris and Chartres, remaining there for eight days, 'as safely as if he were in his own kingdom'.[32] That he was prepared to risk all-out war by advancing so deep into French territory shows how serious he felt his nephew's threat to be; and his gambit worked. Louis was far from happy at having Henry so close to his own capital, and – Clito or no Clito – he had to look after his own concerns first. He withdrew from Flanders and returned to his own domains, whereupon Henry, his point made, left Épernon and rode back to Normandy.

Louis did not set out for Flanders again. He was, by this time, starting to suffer from poor health due to his weight ('his body was heavy, weighed down as it was by burdensome folds of flesh; no one else ... would have been able to ride a horse when hampered by such a dangerously large body')[33] and a further active military campaign did not, perhaps, appeal. Clito was on his own.

The young man could not hope to match the amount of money that Henry was prepared to pour into his campaign, and he lost more political ground when Thierry of Alsace was elected count of Flanders by the citizens of Bruges on 30 March 1128, almost exactly a year after they had acclaimed Clito.[34] Clito's only option was to try to win by military might, and now he did something that made him even more unpopular with his Flemish subjects: he put out a call to his supporters in Normandy, and soon Norman barons and knights began flooding over the Flemish border to help him. He was now, in effect, at the head of a hostile invasion force in his own county. Flanders was 'so torn by dangers, by ravaging, arson, treachery, and deceit that no honest man could live in security'.[35]

By the summer of 1128 William Clito was in a favourable position, even without support from France, and his cause looked ever more hopeful when he won a great victory over Thierry at Axspoele in June. Thierry and his men were besieging a castle that was loyal to Clito; he, approaching from behind, divided his host into three parts, sending two forward and keeping the other hidden. The stakes were high: 'Both the counts were fighting as if they offered themselves to death, rushing into the midst of hostile arms; they had decided beforehand to die in battle rather than be expelled from the countship.'[36] When the fighting was at its height, Clito's third division made a sudden attack, turning the tide all his way, as fresh men entered the fray in which he, 'bold in spirit and strong in body', was laying about him furiously. Thierry was forced to flee the field, retreating with his defeated troops to Bruges, where there was much 'weeping and sighing' as the relatives of the slain heard of their losses.[37]

Clito moved to press his advantage, and within a couple of weeks of the battle he rode with his army to besiege Thierry's castle of Aalst. But his cause was destined to die there in north-eastern Flanders, in the most anticlimactic fashion imaginable. During a direct attack on the castle on 27 July Clito was knocked off his horse and, before he could defend himself properly, was wounded in the hand by the spear of a footsoldier.[38] He made what he thought would be a temporary withdrawal from the fray in order to have it treated, but the wound festered. He 'began to complain of pain striking his heart', and 'the whole arm up to the elbow turned as black as coal'. He saw that his end was inevitable and took vows as a monk shortly before he succumbed to blood poisoning some four or five days after sustaining the injury.[39] 'William, the young count of Flanders, died, and with him all the power and daring of those who had supported him against his uncle crumbled away', wrote a contemporary. 'They had no one to lead them in their rash pride after they lost the young leader for whose sake they had ravaged the fields of Normandy with fire and sword.'[40]

Thierry of Alsace now found himself 'acceptable to the kings of both realms, France and England, and they freely granted him investiture'; he was to bring peace and stability to Flanders after the successive violent, childless deaths of the last four counts in a row.[41] He later married Sybil of Anjou, who had briefly been Clito's wife and who was by now the sister-in-law of Henry I's daughter and heir, Empress Matilda.

Clito's death had an immediate effect on the relationships between France and England and between the two ruling houses: Louis and Henry concluded a peace that would be more long-lasting than their previous efforts, mainly because there was, at this point, nothing left to fight about. Louis was certainly not about to take up arms on behalf of Robert Curthose, who was still alive (although no doubt devastated by the news of his son's death) – he was in his seventies and had been in captivity for over twenty years.

Henry was now unchallenged, but he, too, was growing older. At the time of Clito's death in the summer of 1128 Henry was around sixty, a good age for a man of such responsibility who was rarely out of the saddle, but one at which he would surely soon have to think about slowing down. Louis was only in his late forties but he was, as we noted earlier, not in good health, and thus it was that both kings began to turn their minds to the new generation.

≥ CHAPTER THREE ≤

TWO HEIRS AND TWO HEIRESSES

THE HEIR TO HENRY'S THRONE was, in fact, an heiress: his daughter, Empress Matilda. She had lived the first eight years of her life in England, and then the next fifteen in the Empire as consort to Henry V. During part of that time she had been appointed as his regent in Italy, a position of great responsibility and one that showed his trust in her abilities.[1] Widowed in 1125, she had returned to Normandy and England, being designated heir to the throne in January 1127. If she were to continue in that position, she would need to remarry in order to have children of her own; and Henry's choice, as we have seen, fell upon Geoffrey of Anjou, an alliance that would help in the ongoing conflict with the dangerous William Clito and his backer King Louis. The delayed wedding took place on 17 June 1128, the now fourteen-year-old Geoffrey being immediately invested as count of Anjou, as his widowed father Fulk was about to leave western Europe permanently – he had been chosen by Baldwin II, king of Jerusalem, as the husband for his daughter and heiress Melisende.[2]

Matilda and Geoffrey's wedding festivities were hardly over when news arrived of William Clito's unexpected and (from their point of view) fortuitous death at Aalst. This altered Matilda's situation materially, but whether or not Henry might have chosen a different husband for his daughter had Clito died earlier is immaterial: the Angevin marriage had taken place and everyone would have to live with the consequences.

Henry's hope that the union would soon produce a male heir to ease his succession concerns was to be disappointed, for the marriage was a disaster.

The mismatched couple simply could not get over their personal differences, and Henry's refusal to confirm the official status of his new son-in-law did nothing to help matters – Geoffrey did not know whether he would in time be king of England in right of his wife (in the same way as his father would be king of Jerusalem, following his marriage to the heiress there), or whether he was to be merely a 'stipendiary commander' on his wife's behalf as she took the throne in her own name.[3] By the autumn of 1129 the couple had split, with Geoffrey remaining in Anjou and Matilda returning to Normandy, where she pointedly continued to refer to herself as 'empress' rather than 'countess of Anjou'.

Given that the death of William Clito had removed the major obstacle to Henry's plans to be succeeded on the English throne by his own child, he did not hurry to address the situation, perhaps hoping that Matilda and Geoffrey might work things out for themselves. But they did not; indeed, they seemed much happier apart, and Geoffrey took a mistress who bore him an illegitimate son, Hamelin of Anjou, in 1130.

Henry finally lost patience and made a move in the summer of 1131. He had been in Normandy for several months, and when he returned to England he took Matilda with him. At a council on 8 September he reiterated Matilda's position as his heir – obliging the barons to swear once more to uphold her rights – but the payoff was that she would have to return to her husband.[4] The question of the English succession was now becoming critical: Henry was in his sixties, and his only heir was a woman approaching thirty who had been married twice and never borne a child. The Anglo-Norman royal dynasty was hanging by a thread.

The situation could not have been more different in France, where King Louis and Queen Adelaide, in the same autumn of 1131, were the proud parents of five surviving sons and a daughter, with the queen expecting another child. Their eldest, Philip, was fifteen years old and recognised by all as the heir to the throne; he had been so designated at the age of four, and had been crowned as junior king in April 1129.[5] Since then, he had supposedly been spending his time learning about the responsibilities that would one day be his alone, but opinions differed as to how assiduously he was doing this: he is variously referred to in contemporary chronicles as 'a radiant and charming boy [who] was the hope of good men and a terrifying prospect for evildoers'; someone who 'was loved by all who knew him for the sweetness and simplicity of his character'; and a young man who 'strayed from the paths of conduct travelled by his father and, by his overweening pride and tyrannical arrogance, made himself a burden to all'.[6] Whatever his personality – and there can be no real way of knowing it from the surviving evidence – what is certain is that he was increasingly associated with and involved in government, his name included on various charters as the king and queen issued them 'with the agreement of their first-born son Philip'.[7]

On 13 October 1131 young Philip was riding through Paris with some friends. The streets were crowded and busy, for King Louis had just summoned his nobles to form a host for a campaign in the Vexin, and it is possible that Philip was not paying much attention as he bantered with his companions. Without warning, a pig suddenly ran out in front of his horse, startling it. 'Taking a very bad fall,' as Suger tells us, 'the horse threw the noble youth riding it against a stone and crushed him underfoot with all its weight.' Philip's horrified friends picked up his broken and bloodied body and carried him to the nearest house, but his injuries were too severe and he died later the same day.[8]

The sudden, tragic, accidental death of a teenaged heir to the throne had caused chaos and catastrophe in England a decade earlier. But although Philip's demise was a huge personal loss ('so great, so astounding were the grief and sorrow that struck his father, his mother, and the leading men of the kingdom that Homer himself would have lacked the skill to express it'),[9] it was not the dynastic disaster for France that it could have been. Within a fortnight Louis VI's eleven-year-old second son – also called Louis and referred to as 'Louis the Young' to differentiate him from his father – was crowned as junior king. The ceremony was performed by none other than Pope Innocent II, who was in France at that time; with such powerful church backing, nobody could possibly argue thereafter that young Louis was not the true heir to the kingdom, even though he had not been born to the position. His name was included on an official document the very next day, when King Louis the elder made a donation to the Church in memory of his late son Philip 'with the consent of his son Louis, crowned king, and of Queen Adelaide'.[10] Young Louis would, of course, now need to undergo the years of training for the throne that Philip had experienced, for his own upbringing had been quite different and had been intended to

47

prepare him for a career in the Church. But an unprepared and inexperienced son was a great deal better than no male heir at all.

* * *

By the autumn of 1132, Matilda and Geoffrey had been married for over four years. King Henry may or may not have given up hope of seeing a legitimate grandchild, but at last came the news he was waiting for: Matilda was pregnant. She gave birth on 5 March 1133 to a child who was, happily for all concerned, a healthy boy. He was named Henry after the king – being known later and throughout his life as Henry fitzEmpress – and the English royal dynasty finally had a male heir to continue its line. Indeed, Matilda followed up by providing a 'spare', Geoffrey, just fourteen months later. The king travelled to Normandy, where he stayed for some while, 'to rejoice' in his grandsons and to argue with Matilda over where she should be buried: her second labour had been very difficult, and she was widely considered to be dying.[11]

In the event, she recovered and Henry could now start to plan a different sort of future – one in which he would train his grandson in kingship in place of the son he had lost, perhaps with a view to passing the crown directly to him and avoiding the tricky questions of female succession and a husband's rights altogether. But it was not to be: in the autumn of 1135 Henry was on a hunting trip when he was taken ill, and he died at Lyons-la-Forêt in Normandy on 1 December, aged around sixty-seven.[12] Had he survived for longer, the path of the English crown over the next two decades might have been smoother, but little Henry was just two and a half years old, far too young to be considered as a candidate for the throne in his own right. The dangers of infant mortality were many, and even if he survived them there was no precedent for a minority of the length that would be required, which would inevitably cause great disruption.

According to King Henry's own wishes, and the oaths of his barons, the English crown should now have passed to his daughter Matilda, but there was no rush to acclaim her; indeed, active discussions were held on the suitability of other candidates. There was little consensus either on the identity of the next king, or even on whether England and Normandy should both be inherited by the same person. After some deliberation, the barons of Normandy offered the duchy to Theobald of Blois, the eldest of Henry's nephews, but it is not clear whether this implied that they also thought he should be king of England. As it transpired, all the discussions were for nothing, for Theobald's younger brother Stephen had already crossed the Channel from his county of Boulogne, secured the royal treasury at Winchester – where his other brother Henry happened to be the bishop – and had himself crowned at Westminster.

The fact of Stephen's coronation meant that he was irrevocably the king, and so swift had his coup been that news of it reached Theobald at the same time as the offer of the Norman barons. They then decided that it would indeed be easier for them 'to serve under one lord on account of the honours they held in both provinces', accepted Stephen's *fait accompli* and rescinded their offer to Theobald. Theobald seems to have taken umbrage at being passed over in such a fashion: 'Offended at not getting the kingdom though he was the elder, [he] hurried away to see to important affairs which demanded his attention in France.'[13] Meanwhile, the news of King Henry's death did not reach Matilda, who was hundreds of miles to the south in Anjou, until much later; Stephen may even have been crowned before she was aware that her father was dead.[14]

We do not know exactly how King Louis reacted when he heard of all this, but what did become clear was that England and Normandy would be embroiled in internal turmoil for some time: 'When King Henry died ... the peace and harmony of the kingdom were buried with him', as one contemporary succinctly notes.[15] This provided the French king with a respite, during which he could attend to French affairs. Louis was by now in very poor health and earning the soubriquet by which he would hencefor-ward be known, 'the Fat': Abbot Suger wrote of him that 'the weight of his fleshy body and the toil of endless tasks had quite beaten down the lord king'.[16] The king's son Louis the younger was still only in his mid-teens, so the situation was a delicate one, and perhaps he gave thanks for the demise of his long-time rival.

However ill he might have been in body, Louis's mind was still healthy and his political acumen was as keen as ever. So, when he was presented with an opportunity to annex an extensive, rich territory to the French crown, he was able to take full advantage of it.

* * *

Duke William X of Aquitaine (a large province in the south of France) was a widower with two daughters and no sons. He was at this point only thirty-eight and perhaps intended to marry again, in order to father a male heir who would continue his ancient line; but – if this was indeed his intention – in early 1137 it was secondary in his thoughts behind a desire to make a pilgrimage to Santiago de Compostela in the Spanish kingdom of León. Recognising that such an undertaking held potential dangers, William first made arrangements for the security of his daughters: they were installed in the castle of Bordeaux, and William made a request that King Louis should take them under his protection while he was away and act as their guardian, should anything befall him. Until such time as he might return, remarry and father a legitimate son, the heir to Aquitaine was his elder daughter Eleanor, then aged around fourteen. Given her age and the lack of a son in the family, it was perhaps surprising that Eleanor had not yet been betrothed to a suitable husband; it is not clear whether this was simple oversight on her father's part or whether everyone was keeping their options open in case he should produce a male heir.[17]

As it transpired, the duke's careful provisions were necessary, for he died on his pilgrimage before reaching the shrine. On his deathbed he reiterated his request to King Louis, evidently worried that his duchy would become subject to violent conflict and that his elder daughter – who had become, at a stroke, the richest marriage prize on the market – would be fought over by ambitious lords.[18] This was a great opportunity for Louis: firstly, as he had done in Flanders a decade previously, he could stamp his authority as royal overlord on the region; and, secondly, as Eleanor's guardian he had control of her marriage. It can have surprised nobody when his choice of husband for her was none other than his son Louis the younger.

Louis junior was immediately dispatched south with a large retinue, headed by Abbot Suger of Saint-Denis and Count Theobald of Blois, and he and Eleanor were married on 25 July 1137. Whether they had the chance to introduce themselves before the wedding, or whether their first sight of each other was at the altar, is not recorded, but they had certainly never previously met. This was not an unusual situation for royal couples, whose marriages were not matters of personal preference, but rather arrangements centred on lands and dynastic concerns – any affection that might develop between husband and wife was a bonus, not a prerequisite.

Louis VI was politically and diplomatically triumphant, but he did not live long enough to celebrate, nor to meet his new daughter-in-law: he died just a week after the wedding, on 1 August 1137.[19] Over the course of his almost-thirty-year reign he had strengthened and united France, and – with this annexation of Aquitaine as his final act – he might have felt confident, on his deathbed, that his kingdom would be in the ascendant over the squabbling English for many years to come. But if those really were his dying thoughts, they were wrong.

⋙ CHAPTER FOUR ⋘

BROTHERS AND SONS

THE QUIET, PIOUS, SEVENTEEN-YEAR-OLD newlywed Louis VII now found himself sole king of France, the news reaching him while he was still hundreds of miles away from familiar ground.

The task ahead of the young monarch was great, for the territories over which he would exercise direct rule were more or less double the size of those his father had controlled: Aquitaine covered the whole of the southwest of France from the Pyrenees as far north as Poitiers, representing about a third of the total area over which the French crown claimed overlordship. This is not to say, however, that Aquitaine now formed part of the royal domain, for it did not. Louis, as king, would have been its ultimate overlord anyway, but he ruled it *directly* as duke of Aquitaine, not as king of France; and he was only the duke by virtue of his marriage to Eleanor.[1] The future status of the duchy would depend on whether the couple had any children together; if they had none, then on their deaths the crown of France would pass to Louis's next brother and his heirs, but Aquitaine to Eleanor's sister or uncle, thus separating the two territories once more.

If Louis and Eleanor were to have a family, however, the situation might change in a number of ways. If they had only one son then he would inherit everything, which might then pave the way to a closer union between kingdom and duchy; but if they had more than one, France might go to the eldest and Aquitaine to the second. If they produced only daughters, Aquitaine would go to the eldest, just as it had passed to Eleanor, and to that daughter's future husband, who would rule in her name. However, the

question of female succession to the throne was not yet settled in France.
Since the accession of Hugh Capet in 987 no French king had died without
leaving a son; thus, the question had simply not arisen and it was unclear
whether, in such a case, the crown would pass to a king's surviving brother
rather than to a royal daughter. And, finally, if Louis and Eleanor were ever
to separate and have children with different partners, France would pass to
a son of Louis's, but Aquitaine would descend to Eleanor's children, regardless of the identity of their father.

In the summer of 1137 there was no reason to suppose that the teenaged
king and queen, with time and health on their side, would not go on to
produce a large family. Like any other king, Louis would hope to father a
son, and preferably more than one, in order to secure the succession; but in
the meantime the situation of the French crown was by no means precarious, because he had a number of younger brothers. Louis VI and Queen
Adelaide had produced a total of seven sons and one daughter. The eldest,
Philip, had been killed in the accident that passed the throne to Louis VII;
another boy had died in infancy. The precise dates of birth of the others are
not known, but at the time of the younger Louis's accession in the summer
of 1137, his surviving siblings and their approximate ages were Henry
(fifteen), Robert (twelve), Peter (eleven), Constance (nine) and Philip (five).
This Philip had been born after his eldest brother's death and given the
same name; this was not uncommon practice at the time, particularly where
royal and noble families tended to use a restricted range of first names that
they wished to pass on to future generations.[2]

In view of the relatively modest nature of the direct royal holdings under
Louis VI, this was actually too many sons to provide for adequately, so both
Henry and little Philip were earmarked for careers in the Church. This did
not, incidentally, mean that they would spend their days as simple monks
living in poverty; it was common practice for the nobility to enrol some of
their sons in holy orders, and such men would rise to be bishops, abbots
or cardinals, advisors to – and socially on a par with – their lay peers. One
problematic issue was that those to be so 'donated' were generally chosen on
the basis of birth order, rather than aptitude or inclination, which resulted
in some highly unsuitable appointments over the years. Happily, this does
not appear to have been the case for Louis VI's two sons, who seemed
content with their lot: Henry would go on to be bishop of Beauvais and

then archbishop of Reims, both posts associated with the French royal family, while Philip would reach the rank of archdeacon in Paris before dying while still in his twenties.

That left Louis VII with two remaining brothers and a sister to provide for. Constance was destined to play a pivotal role in the Capetian relationship with the English royal house, and we will hear more of her later in this chapter. Peter was provided for by marriage to an heiress; he became lord of Courtenay in right of his wife. Robert, as the second surviving non-clerical son, was entitled to an apanage – a grant of land – and through this he became count of Dreux; later he also became count of Perche by his first marriage and count of Braine by his third.[3] Until such time as Louis became a father, Robert was also heir presumptive to the French crown. An heir *presumptive*, just to clarify the terminology, is the person who is currently the heir to an estate or title, but who might legally be displaced by someone else (for example, the younger brother or daughter of a king, who might be supplanted by the later birth of a son). An heir *apparent* is the person who is currently the heir and whose position cannot be altered by subsequent births – normally the king's eldest son. Robert was therefore in an uncertain position for the time being, his future prospects potentially being anything from a county to a kingdom.

Louis, although not originally intended for the throne, had had nearly six years to get used to the idea. Eleanor, on the other hand, had been subject to dizzying changes of fortune in just a few weeks: from heiress of Aquitaine, to orphan, to queen of France, a role she can hardly have anticipated. To add to her sense of dislocation, she was immediately obliged to leave her sunny southern duchy and travel to Paris, reaching it in the late summer of 1137.

One of the first problems she encountered in the French capital was linguistic: the northern French *langue d'oïl* was different from the *langue d'oc* or Occitan dialect spoken in the south.[4] But languages could be learned, and she had brought retainers with her with whom she could converse in the meantime, so she was not completely isolated. A greater issue was culture, and particularly culture as it related to the influence of the Church and to the position of women in society. The ducal court in which she had been brought up exhibited little more than conventional piety; but in Paris the Church exerted a much greater influence on day-to-day life, amplified by the fact that many of the most influential figures around Louis were clerics, such as Abbot Suger.

Male churchmen were likely to regard women, and especially powerful women, with suspicion, and the same held true for many of the lords who had been raised in the overtly religious and military northern half of France. Eleanor had been brought up in a society where married women were allowed to control property and could wield great influence in society, so she took this outlook with her into her marriage; however, this did not go down well with male magnates who were not accustomed to women acting on their own authority. Noblewomen, incidentally, were routinely expected to be active and capable – but as supportive helpmeets to the men in their lives, not as individuals in their own right.[5] However, Eleanor was determined not to fade into the background, and she benefited from several notable advantages. Firstly, Louis – the king, the sole source of royal authority – 'loved the queen almost beyond reason', as she had 'so enmeshed and captivated the heart of the young man with the charm of her beauty'.[6] Secondly, the couple were nearly the same age, something that was relatively unusual in a noble or royal marriage, where an older and more politically experienced man might be expected to have a wife many years his junior. Eleanor, aged around fifteen, was able to exert greater influence on a youth some two years older than herself than she would have done on a man decades her senior. And finally, she also had much greater personal access to Louis than anyone else at court, especially after the retirement of the queen mother, Adelaide, to her dower estates. Without making a significant impact on official charters and documents, Eleanor became, informally, the king's chief advisor. As it transpired, this did not do either of them any particular favours, resulting as it did in inexperience supporting and encouraging inexperience.[7]

Eleanor might have been able to win over the French lords and the court if she had given birth to the all-important son and heir as soon as possible, but months and then years went by without any pregnancy (or at least any viable one that we know of; miscarriage was such a common occurrence that contemporaries hardly bothered to record it). So many rumours have swirled around over the centuries about Louis and Eleanor's relationship that it is difficult to say with any certainty whether their lack of a child can be attributed to simple fertility issues, or whether Louis in fact had some squeamishness about sex. He had been brought up from his early youth in the expectation of a celibate clerical career and he was extremely devout, even by the standards of his era; one contemporary wrote of him that 'he was so pious, so just, so catholic and benign, that if you were to see his simplicity of behaviour and dress, you would think ... that he was not a king, but a man of religion'.[8] There was a definite link between kingship and religion – kings of both England and France were anointed with holy oil as part of the coronation, which was a religious ceremony, and they were seen as God's chosen – but Louis appears to have taken this a step further, to the point where he perhaps saw kingship as a religious vocation in its own right. The quote often attributed to Eleanor, that she felt she had 'married a monk, not a king', is probably apocryphal, but equally probably contains the essence of the truth.[9]

It was not until Louis and Eleanor had been married eight years that a pregnancy was carried to term, but eventually, in 1145, Eleanor was confined – it is not clear exactly where – in anticipation of the birth.[10] All of France held its breath ... and then expelled it in disappointment when the birth of a daughter, Marie, was announced.

Not long after Marie's birth, news reached western Europe that the city of Edessa had fallen to Muslim troops. The rulers of Jerusalem, Queen Melisende and her son Baldwin III, were appealing for help, and envoys from Antioch had already arrived at the papal court. Pope Eugenius III proclaimed a crusade, in which he was ably supported by the high-profile zealot Bernard, abbot of Clairvaux and a leading figure in the western Church, who gave a thundering speech at Vézelay on 31 March 1146. Enraptured with the idea of fighting for Christ, Louis became the first reigning king of either England or France to take the cross personally, setting off for the Holy Land in June 1147, after having received the *oriflamme* from the altar of Saint-Denis.[11]

To have the king leaving his realm for an unspecified length of time in order to head into the teeth of danger might enhance France's standing on the international stage, and also Louis's personal reputation, but it was a risky internal strategy – especially given that both of Louis's non-clerical brothers, Robert and Peter, accompanied him overseas, thus stripping the kingdom of every adult male Capetian. And nor would the queen be left to act as regent, for she was also to travel, although this at least had the benefit that a son and heir might be produced. France was left in the able but ageing hands of Abbot Suger of Saint-Denis, as Louis and his family set off with high hopes.

The details of the generally disastrous Second Crusade are not within the scope of this book, other than to highlight the deterioration in the relationship between Louis and Eleanor, to the point where divorce was talked of.[12] Blame for the situation has generally been placed at Eleanor's door: rumours of her supposed conduct while on crusade – and particularly of her uncomfortably close relationship with Raymond of Antioch, who was her uncle – appeared in contemporary literature. However, we must temper this with the knowledge that she was already unpopular with French clerics, and that the easiest way to slander a woman was to call her chastity into question. On the king and queen's return from the East, the intervention of the pope, who 'strove by friendly converse to restore love between them' (and, more to the point, 'made them sleep in the same bed'), saved the marriage for the time being, and even resulted in another pregnancy.[13] By now Louis was starting to worry about the increasing power of Geoffrey, the count of Anjou (of whose rise we shall hear more later in this chapter), and he had also been in disagreement with his own brothers Henry and Robert, who rebelled against his authority in 1149–50 following his return to France. This does not appear to have gone very far – armed insurrection certainly did not result – but, nevertheless, Louis must have felt that the birth of a son to guarantee the succession would relieve some of the pressure bearing down on both his kingship and his personal life.[14]

But it was not to be: Eleanor gave birth to a second daughter, Alix, in the summer of 1150. Louis was now thirty years of age and had been married thirteen years; he had no direct male heir and his relationship with his wife was growing ever worse, a situation not helped by her unpopularity among the male nobles and churchmen who made up the royal court. He was faced with a difficult decision. Divorce and remarriage might give him the chance to father a son to continue his dynasty, but he would lose the vast territory of Aquitaine, which would stay with Eleanor. Of course, he would have custody of the current heir to the duchy (his elder daughter, Marie), but she was only heir presumptive: if Eleanor were to remarry and bear a son, then Marie would lose out. However, as overlord of Aquitaine, Louis would expect to exert some influence in the choice of a second husband for

Eleanor – or none – and, in any case, the sacred cause of the French kingship was more important.

Louis and Eleanor's marriage was annulled on 21 March 1152, officially
on the grounds of consanguinity, as they were third cousins once removed.[15]
We might choose to note, however, that if the Church's rules on affinity
were applied this strictly for everyone, a large proportion of the noble
marriages in France and in England would be rendered invalid, so it would
seem no more than a political expedient. The two daughters of the union
were declared legitimate – on the basis that the parties had entered into the
marriage in good faith – and custody of them was granted to Louis. As far
as we know, Eleanor never saw either of her daughters again.

Louis, now deprived of the woman who had been at his side for almost
half his life, also lost at around this time both of his most experienced advisors. Abbot Suger, who had remained healthy and sharp of mind well into
his seventies, died in 1151, to be followed to the grave by Theobald, count
of Blois and Champagne, early in 1152. Theobald – who was the nephew of
Henry I and elder brother of King Stephen, and who, as we saw earlier,
might have been king of England and duke of Normandy himself had the
dice fallen differently – had produced a brood of children who would play
important roles in the future relationships between the ruling houses of
France and England. At the time of Stephen's accession Theobald had given
up any ambitions across the Channel in order to concentrate on his affairs
in France, and they had prospered. He had been count of Blois (as Theobald
IV) since his early youth, and had later also inherited the prestigious county
of Champagne (as Theobald II) from an uncle, thus allowing him to provide
amply for his children. He had four sons: Henry, who succeeded him as
count of Champagne; Theobald (V), who became count of Blois; Stephen,
later count of Sancerre (a less prestigious title and not on a par with the
other two; Stephen owed homage to his brother Henry); and William,
known as William Whitehands, who was given to the Church and later
became archbishop of Sens and then of Reims. There were also six daughters in the family – always useful for a nobleman who wished to arrange
strategic marriage alliances, regardless of their own feelings on the matter
– and we shall in due course hear more of the youngest, Adela.

* * *

Given the many problems by which Louis found himself beset, he was perhaps fortunate that England was, for the early part of his reign, not one of them, plagued as the kingdom was by troubles of its own. As we saw earlier, it was Stephen of Blois, Henry I's nephew, who succeeded in having himself crowned following the king's death in December 1135, much to the surprise of many of the English and Norman nobles. Henry's daughter, Empress Matilda, found herself sidelined, with little political support or practical resources, and also immobilised by pregnancy: she gave birth to a third son, William, in July 1136 at Argentan in Normandy. She did not, however, give up on her ambitions for the English crown, and when her half-brother Robert, earl of Gloucester (the eldest of King Henry's many illegitimate children), defected to her cause in the spring of 1138, she was able to start planning a campaign to take the English throne she saw as rightfully hers. Once arrangements had been made and troops assembled, she left her husband and three young sons behind in Normandy and sailed for England in October 1139.

The political and military details of the war that followed, during the period sometimes known as the Anarchy, are complex and we will touch on them here only insofar as they relate to the relationship between the two ruling dynasties.[16] Matilda enjoyed an initial surge of success and seemed to have achieved victory early in 1141, when Stephen was captured at the Battle of Lincoln; she was declared 'Lady of the English' and prepared for a coronation at Westminster. But she was driven out of the capital by forces led jointly by Queen Matilda, Stephen's wife, and Stephen's mercenary commander William of Ypres, the illegitimate Fleming whom we last met when he attempted to claim the county of Flanders back in 1127. During a subsequent engagement at Winchester later in 1141 Empress Matilda's own military commander, Robert of Gloucester, was captured; she was forced to agree to an exchange that freed both him and Stephen, and the cycle of attritional warfare started again.

Matilda's cause in England was aided – perhaps not entirely deliberately – by her husband Geoffrey, who was making great gains on the other side of the Channel. As count of Anjou (and also controlling the adjoining territories of Maine and Touraine, thus forming a not insignificant bloc), Geoffrey had long had designs on Normandy, and his marriage to Matilda, who claimed the duchy as part of her inheritance from Henry I, gave him the perfect excuse to invade it on the grounds that he was fighting for the rights of his wife and his eldest son. Geoffrey's dogged and bloody campaign inched across Normandy over the course of several years, and although he was fighting predominantly in his own interest, his success had the knock-on effect that those Norman barons who supported Stephen were too busy defending their own estates and could not help the king in his struggles against Matilda in England.

In the spring of 1144 Geoffrey finally took Rouen, the capital of Normandy. Louis VII, who had previously acknowledged Stephen as duke of Normandy, bowed to the reality of the situation and recognised Geoffrey as duke later that same year. He did make one significant gain out of the situation: as part of the recognition arrangement, Geoffrey handed over control of the castle of Gisors, possession of which had been a thorny issue during the reigns of Henry I and Louis VI, and possibly the rest of the Norman Vexin as well. Geoffrey, having ostensibly claimed the duchy in the name of his wife and son, proclaimed that he would cede Normandy to young Henry – then eleven years old – as soon as the boy came of age.[17]

Accepting Geoffrey as duke was a more difficult and complex issue for Louis than might at first seem the case, for King Stephen's son Eustace was the French king's brother-in-law, and the boy had already paid homage to Louis for Normandy.[18] Quite early in his reign Stephen had realised that he could use an ally across the Channel, and in 1139 he had sent envoys to Louis with a generous financial offer for the betrothal of the French king's only sister, Constance (then aged around eleven or twelve), to Stephen's elder son, the nine-year-old Eustace. The couple were married in 1140, Constance being dispatched across the sea to what was then a very uncertain situation in England. Within a short space of time, the two children were subject to huge changes of fortune: they had not been married a year when Stephen was captured at the Battle of Lincoln, resulting in Eustace being disinherited, as Empress Matilda (who had three sons of her own) was proclaimed 'Lady of the English'. And there was worse in store for Constance. Before setting off for what he knew would be a violent engagement, Stephen had placed his wife and his young daughter-in-law in the Tower of London for their own safety, under the supposed 'protection' of Geoffrey de Mandeville, earl of Essex and castellan of the Tower, who was a man of dubious loyalties at the best of times. True to form, once the outcome of the battle was known he came to terms with the empress; Queen Matilda was able to leave the Tower (she went on to raise troops in conjunction with William of Ypres, as we have seen), but Geoffrey kept Constance in his custody, an 'outstanding prize' whom he probably intended to use as some kind of insurance policy.[19]

No contemporary writer dwells on the plight of the young French princess, but she must have been at least anxious, and at worst terrified for her life. The next blow was that the empress, when she reached London herself, refused a petition from Henry, bishop of Winchester (who was King Stephen's brother), that Eustace, although denied the crown, should be permitted to inherit his father's personal possessions and titles: the county of Mortain, which Stephen held in his own right, and that of Boulogne, which was his wife's.[20] Constance's status might therefore fall from future queen to countess to nothing, a situation that would surely be unacceptable to Louis VII. Happily for her, she was spared having to appeal to her royal brother by Stephen's release and restoration to the throne in the autumn of 1141, which made her once again the wife of the heir to England.

As the war in England dragged on and on, it became apparent that the next generation would have to take up the fight, and that the principal protagonists would cease to be Stephen and Matilda, and would become their eldest sons, Eustace and Henry. By 1151 Henry was very much in the ascendant, being now duke of Normandy: his father Geoffrey Plantagenet had remained true to his word and stepped back in Henry's favour. Empress Matilda, who was by now living entirely in Normandy, having relinquished control of the English campaign to her son, enlisted the help of the venerable Abbot Suger shortly before his death. He had known and admired her father, Henry I, many years previously, and one of his final acts was to petition King Louis to recognise the younger Henry as duke – possibly also with the view to switching his support for the English succession from Eustace to Henry. With Suger's encouragement, the eighteen-year-old Henry and his father both travelled to Paris to meet the king in person; Louis agreed to accept Henry's homage as duke, but with the canny proviso that, in return, Henry would cede to him the whole of the Norman Vexin.[21] While they were in Paris, Geoffrey and Henry almost certainly also encountered Queen Eleanor, a meeting that would later have significant consequences.

Stephen realised that Normandy was gone, at least for the present, and that he needed to take decisive action if England were not also to slip from his son's grasp. Perhaps influenced by his alliance with the royal house of France, he tried to ensure Eustace's succession by taking a leaf from the Capetian book and proposing something that was unprecedented in England: having his eldest son crowned king during his own lifetime. This had been the custom in France for well over a century, and it had added to the stability of the royal house there, but Stephen encountered problems in trying to institute the practice. The major stumbling block was that Theobald of Bec, the archbishop of Canterbury, would not agree to perform the ceremony unless he had explicit permission from the pope to do so. Unfortunately for Stephen, the pope, Eugenius III – he who had preached the Second Crusade and attempted to reconcile Louis and Eleanor – declined, on the grounds that his predecessor Celestine II had already written to Archbishop Theobald 'forbidding him to allow any change to be made in the position of the English crown, since the transfer of it had been justly denounced, and the matter was still under dispute'.[22] As the coronation would not be valid if carried out by anyone other than the archbishop of Canterbury, Stephen was forced to give up on his plan.

Over the next two years Fortune's wheel turned further, raising Henry and casting Stephen down. Queen Matilda died in May 1152, leaving Stephen bereft, and then his son began to cause him more grief. Eustace, as we have already noted, had spent his childhood veering between extremes of status, and he had grown up into an erratic young man who revelled in the cruel excesses of warfare. War of any kind was obviously violent, and it was accepted that violence would spill over to result in non-combatant and civilian casualties – and, indeed, that such terror was a useful strategy. However, it needed to be used properly and tactically: senseless and random brutality was a different matter, as it made the perpetrator look unpredictable – something which, in a king or future king, was dangerous for all concerned. So Eustace, by actions such as 'ordering his men to set fire immediately to the houses everywhere, to kill those who came in their way and commit indiscriminately every cruelty they could think of' was sowing uncertainty in the minds of the English barons; even those who were staunch supporters of Stephen began to feel uneasy about the prospect of his son on the throne.[23]

This had many advantages for Henry, who was now increasingly seen as a better prospect and as the 'true heir' to Henry I.[24] That he was also a young man of great power and resource who would probably win the war, either with or without the support of Stephen's adherents, probably also influenced any waverers. Stephen was beginning to notice that 'some of his leading barons were slack and very casual in their service and had already sent envoys by stealth and made a compact with the duke'.[25] And stroke after stroke of good fortune came Henry's way, further enhancing his prestige and the extent of his territories. Already duke of Normandy, he became also count of Anjou and Maine in September 1151, when Geoffrey Plantagenet died of a fever at the unexpectedly early age of just thirty-eight; and then, in 1152, he became an even more threatening rival to the kings of both England and France, thanks to a sudden marriage that astonished and wrong-footed half of western Europe.

CHAPTER FIVE

A QUEEN OF TWO REALMS

T HE FIFTEEN-YEAR MARRIAGE of Louis VII and Eleanor of Aquitaine had been annulled on 21 March 1152. Although Eleanor had lost custody of her two daughters, she took the riches of Aquitaine with her, meaning that she was once more a great marriage prize. The temptation of gaining lands and power so easily was too much for some, and as Eleanor made her way south from Paris after the annulment there were several attempts to kidnap her, most notably by Theobald V, the new count of Blois, and by Geoffrey fitzEmpress, who was the second son of Empress Matilda and the late Geoffrey of Anjou. Eleanor managed to evade them both, for she had a greater alliance in mind: as soon as she reached Poitiers she met – undoubtedly by arrangement – Henry fitzEmpress, and they were married on Whit Sunday, 18 May, just eight weeks after the annulment of her first union.[1]

We should be clear that this course of action represents Eleanor taking control of the situation, of her future, in the only way that she could. Although the phraseology of contemporary accounts of her divorce from Louis depicts him as repudiating her, there can be little doubt that she wanted out of the marriage just as much as he did. She was realist enough, however, to recognise that the best way to protect Aquitaine – and her own person – was to marry again, rather than attempting to act as *feme sole*. She could have taken her pick of French noblemen, most or all of whom would have been only too pleased to accept any overtures of marriage that involved elevation to the status of duke, but Henry was the one that she chose, evidently of her own free will. That there was a personal attraction between them is undeniable – and the vigorous nineteen-year-old was certainly a great contrast to her first husband – but Eleanor's decision was also both politic and ambitious: of all the possible candidates for her hand, Henry was best placed to help her protect and defend Aquitaine, and he was also the only one who held a realistic prospect of being able to offer her a crown to replace the one she had lost.[2]

As the news of the wedding filtered out, it was met with reactions varying from astonishment to fury – and, in the case of Louis VII, both. 'This marriage brought about great enmity and discord between the French king and the duke,' notes one contemporary, and the fallout was to dominate Plantagenet–Capetian relations for decades to come.[3] Louis was disadvantaged by the match several times over. Although direct control of vassals' marriages was not strictly a privilege of French overlordship, as king he would have expected to have some say in the choice of spouses for both the duke of Normandy and the duchess of Aquitaine. We cannot say with any certainty who his favoured candidates might have been, but we can be sure that he would not have wanted Henry and Eleanor to marry each other, thus creating the huge agglomeration of lands that meant Henry controlled more of France than he did. And, of course, Eleanor's remarriage at an age when she was still very much able to bear children (she was a decade or so older than Henry, but still the right side of thirty) meant that Louis's daughter Marie might lose her place as the heir to Aquitaine.

Louis took immediate action, both martial and political. Within months his daughters Marie and Alix were betrothed respectively to the brothers Henry I, count of Champagne, and Theobald V, count of Blois (who were, incidentally, twenty-five and twenty-two to their brides' seven and two; the girls were sent to separate convents for their education and the actual marriages would not take place for another twelve years), and Louis then formed a military coalition with both of his new sons-in-law. He also swept into the alliance others whose lands or positions were threatened by Henry's dramatic rise: Louis's younger brother Robert I, count of Dreux; Henry's younger brother Geoffrey fitzEmpress; and King Stephen's son Eustace, who was more than happy to take up arms:

> The king [Louis], highly incensed at this [Henry and Eleanor's marriage],
> because she had delivered over to the Duke of Normandy the fertile

province of Aquitaine, the lawful inheritance, in his opinion, of the daughters he had by the queen, flew to arms and began very violent attacks on the duke, and allying himself with King Stephen's son Eustace, who had married his [Louis's] sister, handed over to him some castles on the border of Normandy, with the object of his making constant raids over Normandy from them and assailing the duke as heavily and hurtfully as possible.[4]

Young Geoffrey's inclusion in this list of Henry's enemies might seem surprising, but at a time when primogeniture was fast gaining ground as the preferred form of inheritance for noble fiefs, as well as crowns, the mere fourteen-month age gap between the brothers made all the difference. Henry had gained Normandy, Anjou and Maine, while Geoffrey had been left only three castles; Geoffrey had not only failed in his attempt to gain Aquitaine by forced marriage, but had subsequently seen the prize fall into his brother's lap. It can hardly be a surprise that he was jealous, though his decision to ally himself with Eustace and Eustace's two Blois cousins shows both a want of judgement and a lack of respect for his mother and her long-time enmity to that house.

The designs of the alliance came to nothing. Louis, Eustace and their companions had planned to delay their main strike until Henry was back in England and out of the way, but he was still at Barfleur, on the point of taking ship, when they invaded his lands. Perhaps forgetting that Henry had the formidable (and by no means retired) empress on his side, they had miscalculated: Matilda was by now permanently based in Rouen, close to the French border from where the attack was launched, and she managed to get a message to Henry quickly enough to stop him sailing. He turned his troops around and returned with astonishing speed, forcing the Capetian–Blois coalition to retreat without engaging in battle.[5]

* * *

By the autumn of 1152 the threat of war had receded, and Eleanor could adjust to her new status in relative peace. She was now duchess of Normandy and countess of Anjou and Maine, in addition to the titles she held by right of birth; an enviable position, but still a far cry from the anointed queen she had once been. She spent the early months of her marriage in Normandy, in the company of Empress Matilda. Much has been made over the years of the idea that two such 'strong-willed' women (an epithet almost never applied to men) could not possibly have enjoyed such close proximity, but in fact there is no evidence to suggest that their relationship was anything other than cordial. They were, after all, working towards the same goal – that of seeing Henry on the throne of England.

In what must have been a joy to her and an additional mortification for Louis, after all her near 'barren' years with him, Eleanor found herself pregnant within months of her wedding to Henry, and – just to disconcert Louis further – she gave birth to a healthy son in August 1153. The boy was called William, a name that reflected the past glories of his mother's ducal ancestors and his father's royal ones. He was the heir to the considerable estates of both parents; as a mark of his status he was invested with one of Eleanor's minor titles, becoming count of Poitou before he was out of his cradle. But it appeared that an even more glittering future awaited the tiny figure, for the war of succession in England was finally grinding to an end.

Henry had spent most of the time of Eleanor's pregnancy in England. In February 1153 there had been a stand-off at Malmesbury, in torrential rain and gales, where the River Avon had been so swollen that neither Henry's forces nor Stephen's could risk crossing it to engage the other.[6] Stephen was the first to withdraw, at which point a number of his barons offered homage to Henry; the king then swept north and eastwards through the midlands before turning his attention to Wallingford in August. This was an outpost that had held doggedly for Matilda, and then Henry, since the very beginning of the war, and Stephen was besieging it for the third time. As Henry's army approached, it looked as though there would be great bloodshed; but the barons, sick and tired of a never-ending war that was likely to end in 'the desolation of the whole kingdom', simply refused to fight. Henry and Stephen were obliged to negotiate, and the outcome of the talks was that Stephen would remain king for the rest of his life, but that he would then be succeeded by Henry.[7]

This arrangement might have satisfied the barons, who could now see the light at the end of a very long and bloody tunnel, but it seriously displeased Eustace, who found himself disinherited. He reacted in the only way he knew how: by engaging in a rampage through Cambridgeshire and East

Anglia. Then – in what was both a coincidence and a colossal stroke of luck for Henry, as well as being interpreted as an omen by various commentators in possession of excellent hindsight – he died unexpectedly of a seizure, on the very day that Henry and Eleanor's son William was born. He was little mourned by anyone except his father, his death being generally seen more as a relief than a tragedy. Indeed, it was explicitly linked to the promise of peace, 'for as long as he lived, harmony could not have interposed, and the factions could not possibly have been reconciled and united, because of both his youthful aggression and a remarkable confidence arising from his kinship with the king of France'.[8] Countess Constance, the latest in a long line of young widows, had no children; this simplified the situation in England and meant that she was still of use to her brother Louis VII on the marriage market. He summoned her back to France, and within a year she was married to Raymond V, count of Toulouse, of whom we shall hear more later.

Stephen, having already settled the question of the succession, had no heart to reopen it or to continue any kind of struggle on behalf of his younger son, William of Blois; indeed, he had no heart to continue living in the midst of so much failure and loss, and he reigned quietly before dying just a year later, in October 1154.

For the first time since the Conquest, the death of an English king did not result in a scramble for the crown, for there was no doubt who would succeed to it. Indeed, so confident was Henry in his position that he waited several weeks for better weather before he crossed the Channel; he and Eleanor were crowned at Westminster Abbey on 19 December 1154. Eleanor of Aquitaine, pregnant once more and the very picture of royal fecundity, now found herself the only woman (either before or since) to have been crowned queen of both France and England.[9]

Henry was only twenty-one, but he was taking no chances with the arrangements for the succession; in the spring of 1155 he had the barons swear allegiance to little William and also to his infant second son Henry, who had been born in February.[10] The precaution was sadly necessary, as William died in 1156, at the age of three, leaving Young Henry (as he was generally known, in order to differentiate him from his father) as heir to the throne. He was not to be alone in the royal nursery, however, as three siblings appeared in rapid succession: Matilda in June 1156, Richard in September 1157 and Geoffrey in September 1158. Henry and Eleanor would later go on to add three more children to the family: Eleanor (born in October 1162), Joanna (October 1165) and John (December 1166, at which point Eleanor was in her mid-forties).

What was the ideal family size for a reigning king? The question had always been a thorny one. The golden rule, of course, was that there should be a son; in an age of infant mortality and indifferent medical care, a second son was also valuable as an insurance policy, as was a daughter or two to use strategically in marriage. But after that, there was a fine and ever-moving line between having enough children to ensure the succession in case of disease or disaster, and having so many that they could not be adequately provided for. Louis VI had solved the issue of his large family by determining that his superfluous sons would enter the Church, and there is a small possibility that Henry and Eleanor might have intended this for their youngest, John (who was educated at Fontevraud Abbey), though there is no clear evidence either way.[11] Given that their joint holdings were so extensive, it looked as though there would be ample provision for the three older boys, split along traditional lines: the patrimony (England, Normandy, Anjou, Maine) for the eldest, the mother's inheritance (Aquitaine) for the second and a rich heiress for the third (Geoffrey was betrothed to Constance, heiress to the duke of Brittany, before he was ten). Things, as we shall see, did not quite work out as planned, partly because of the usual hazards of medieval life, and partly because Henry and Eleanor seem to have overlooked the possibility that a brood of active sons who were close in age might have a tendency to fight among themselves.

* * *

The situation of the previous generation was now reversed: the king of England had a healthy number of sons, while the king of France had none. Louis waited a little longer than Eleanor to remarry, casting about him for a bride of suitable rank and potential fertility, before settling on Constance, one of the nine children of the fecund Alfonso VII of León and Castile. The wedding took place in 1154, at which point Constance was somewhere between fourteen and eighteen years old, but Louis was to be disappointed in his hopes: his new queen gave birth to a daughter, Margaret, in 1157 and then died in childbed at the birth of another daughter, Alice, in 1160. Although a contemporary account tells us that Louis waited until 'he had put his sadness a little behind him' following Constance's agonising death, it was in fact only five weeks before the desperate, forty-year-old king married for the third time.[12] His choice of bride was Adela of Blois, teenage daughter of the late Theobald IV, count of Blois, and sister to counts Henry I of Champagne and Theobald V of Blois, who now became Louis's brothers-in-law as well as his sons-in-law.[13]

To complicate genealogical matters further, another royal marriage – and an even more unusual one – took place in 1160. We shall examine this in greater detail below, but in short: Henry, the five-year-old son of Henry II and Eleanor of Aquitaine, married Margaret, the three-year-old daughter of Louis VII and Constance of Castile, despite their tender ages and the not-inconsequential fact that the groom's mother had once been the wife of the bride's father.

Louis, meanwhile, returned to his waiting game, and five long years passed during which he must have thought he was doomed never to produce a male heir. But then, in August 1165, to the king's huge joy and relief, Adela gave birth to a healthy son: Philip, known at the time as *Dieu-donné* (God-given) but better known now by his later epithet, Augustus. The chronicler Gerald of Wales – at this time a student in Paris – would later recall being woken by the noise of the celebrations in the street.[14] It seemed nothing short of a miracle that this should happen after five years of Louis's current marriage and after a quarter of a century of him trying to father a son – and this impression was only reinforced when it took Adela another six years to carry a pregnancy to term again. She presented the king with a fifth daughter, Agnes, sometime around 1170 or 1171, by which time Louis was in his fifties and presumably realising that Philip was the only son he would ever father.[15] He did now have a grandson – his eldest daughter Marie having given birth to a son, Henry, future count of Champagne – but succession through the female line was still uncharted waters in France, and leaving the crown to a son and undisputed heir would be vastly preferable.

The answer to the question of the perfect number of sons for a reigning king remained elusive. Louis no doubt felt that one was not enough, leaving him in ever-present fear of illness or accident as Philip navigated his way through infancy and childhood; but Henry II and Eleanor of Aquitaine would come to realise that four, at least in their case, was too many.

⮞ CHAPTER SIX ⮜

'MAGNA DISCORDIA'

WITH A LARGE FAMILY TO provide for and ever-increasing ambitions of their own, Europe's newest power couple were soon on a quest for more.

Like other regions of the country that were distant from Paris, the county of Toulouse in south-east France owed allegiance to the king, but his overlordship was nominal. The distance from the capital was further emphasised by the fact that Toulouse was a different and discrete geographical entity: it was separated from the northern part of France by the Massif Central, but had a Mediterranean coast that gave it access to – and perhaps more in common with – the Spanish and Italian realms bordering that sea. The county was at this time the subject of dispute; it had been contended for some time by the dukes of Aquitaine that Toulouse was a part of their duchy and that the duke of Aquitaine should also hold the title count of Toulouse. This was enough for Henry, at Eleanor's urging, to plan an expedition. It was to be large in scale, and the forces that assembled in Poitiers in the summer of 1159 hailed from all over his domains: 'England, Normandy, Aquitaine, Anjou, Brittany and Scotland poured forth all their knightly chivalry and warlike prowess in support of the king of England.'[1]

The situation was serious for the count of Toulouse, for the nature of Eleanor's claim meant that, if she were to be successful, he would be completely dispossessed of his county, rather than merely owing allegiance to her for it. The count in question was Raymond V, who shared with Eleanor a mutual ancestor, Pons, an eleventh-century count of Toulouse. Raymond was, of course, keen to hold on to his title and lands and to pass them on to his own children (he had at this time two young sons).[2] But he could not hope to match the level of resources that the king of England could bring to bear in support of his wife's claim, and, had he been left to defend himself, he might have succumbed to the combined might of Henry's forces. However, he had one immensely valuable asset: his wife, Constance, who was the widow of Eustace of Blois and the sister of Louis VII. Raymond immediately sent an appeal for aid to his brother-in-law, and Louis responded by marching south with an army of his own.

Louis could not, in all conscience, declare that Henry's claim to Toulouse was inadmissible, for he himself had attempted to press it when he was married to Eleanor, and before Constance was married to Raymond. But equally, he could not now allow it for fear of dispossessing his sister and nephews while simultaneously increasing Henry and Eleanor's already large sphere of influence.[3] He did, fortunately, have another political card to play: as Henry was duke of Normandy and Aquitaine, Louis was, technically at least, his overlord as well as Raymond's. So when he entered the city of Toulouse and proclaimed that he was putting himself in charge of its defences, he was daring Henry to make a direct attack on his overlord.

Thomas Becket, Henry's chancellor, showed his willingness to rebel by urging the king to attack. However, Henry ('from foolish scruples and respect for the king of France', according to the rather dismissive account of Becket's contemporary biographer) was not inclined to take this serious step.[4] Quite apart from the immediate ramifications, there was the added complication that he would be setting the example of rebellion against one's lord; his own followers might then use that as a precedent against him if they were ever dissatisfied. There was no justifiable way the campaign could proceed, and he knew it. He remained in the south-east until the autumn, but by then sickness was laying his army low and he withdrew.[5] In a further blow, he then discovered the advantage of brothers who worked in harmony with each other: while he had been in the south of France, he had ordered diversionary raids in the north, but these had been effectively negated by incursions into Normandy by Louis's brothers Henry, bishop of Beauvais, and Robert, count of Dreux.[6] And, says a contemporary, 'the anger engendered between the king of France and [Henry] at the time of that expedition at last came to full term . . . and as it burst forth it disturbed with troubled commotions the peace of the regions subject to them'.[7]

In the autumn of the following year, 1160, relations between the kings soured further, ironically enough as the result of two marriages. Two years previously, they had agreed to the betrothal of Henry's son Henry to Louis's daughter (by Constance of Castile) Margaret, as part of a wider arrangement over the Norman Vexin; this area, as we saw earlier, had been ceded to France by Henry's father, Geoffrey of Anjou, and Henry not unnaturally wanted it back. Louis agreed that it would form his daughter's dowry, but that he would retain control of it until the actual wedding took place. As the prospective bride and bridegroom were at this point aged six months and three years respectively, and as the Church frowned on pre-pubescent marriages, Louis could look forward to a decade or more of uncontested rule over the whole Vexin. At least one chronicler saw it the same way, noting that 'the children, who because of their youth could not yet wed, should be joined in marriage when the time came'.[8] Louis was happy to relinquish the person of his daughter as a sign of good faith, so custody of the infant Margaret would pass to Henry; Louis's only stipulation was that she should not be placed in the direct household of his ex-wife Eleanor, so she was instead confided to the care of Robert de Neubourg, the seneschal of Normandy.[9] The opinion of Queen Constance on the fate of her tiny daughter is not recorded.

At the time, 1158, the delay was not too much of a problem for Henry, for he was looking to the long-term future of his house; and there was the additional factor that Louis, despite two marriages, had no son, so the prospect of even greater gain might have been at the back of the English king's mind. But all this changed in 1160 when Queen Constance died and Louis almost immediately announced his intention to marry the teenaged Adela of Blois, thus both providing himself with a new opportunity to father a son and allying himself with the house of Henry's rivals: Adela and her brothers were the niece and nephews of King Stephen.[10] Henry, who had both children in hand, retaliated by having Henry and Margaret's wedding carried out immediately – two weeks before that of Louis and Adela, in fact. This was a move that shocked the Church: one contemporary chronicler wrote that Henry pressed ahead with it 'although they were as yet but little children, crying in the cradle'.[11] Young Henry was five years old and Margaret three; they can barely have been aware of what they were doing as they walked down the aisle, never mind consenting to a lifelong union. But King Henry's point was made, and under the terms of the treaty the castles of the Vexin were surrendered to him. He quickly refortified and regarrisoned the great stronghold of Gisors, but his triumph came at a price: 'It is known', wrote one chronicler of the episode, 'that the two kings mentioned were never at peace with each other for long, and the peoples on each side became inured to suffering whatever madness the kings perpetrated in their arrogance.'[12]

Louis was put out by this development, but he regained his place in the dynastic competition in 1165, when Queen Adela gave birth to the all-important son, Philip; he could now plan more clearly for the future.[13] It is worth noting here that Louis has often been seen, at least in Anglophone writing, only through the prism of his failed marriage to Eleanor of Aquitaine, and he has thus sometimes been dismissed as being overly pious and weak. But this is to do him a disservice. It is undeniable that he was devout – far beyond what was required for his role as king – and he might sometimes have presented an air of unworldliness, but he certainly did not lack either intelligence or political acumen, as he would go on to demonstrate. He was also, crucially, popular with his fellow countrymen, who offered him their full support.[14] As the ruling family across the Channel grew up, Louis was well able to see the cracks appearing in their relationships and to take advantage of them for his own benefit and that of France.

One way in which Louis could discomfit Henry was by supporting Thomas Becket in the latter's conflict with the English king. As we saw above, Becket had been Henry's chancellor, a secular position. However, the king had forced through his appointment as archbishop of Canterbury in 1162 – an unexpected move, given that Becket was not even a priest. The idea had been that Henry would benefit from having a 'tame' primate who would support his own ambitions, but the plan had not been a success from anyone's point of view and the relationship deteriorated rapidly. We will not explore the details in any depth here, except insofar as they afforded Louis an opportunity to further the discord. Declaring that Henry had dealt 'harshly and cruelly' with Becket, Louis 'took counsel with his vassals' and then 'promised peace and security to the archbishop within his realm . . . He added, moreover, that it was an ancient prerogative of the crown of France that exiles, especially ecclesiastics, should enjoy peace and security within his kingdom and receive protection from the injuries of their persecutors.'[15] When Becket fled from England in October 1164, therefore, Louis offered him asylum, and it was from France – specifically from Sens, where the archbishop was William Whitehands, Queen Adela's brother – that the archbishop fired off letters and sentences of excommunication. Louis, of course, benefited twice over from his positioning as Becket's ally: not only did he antagonise Henry, but, as a deeply pious and Christian king, he could also claim that he was acting in the best interests of the holy Church.

By 1167 the relationship between the two kings had reached such a nadir that they were engaged in a petty squabble over whose envoys should be entrusted with the remittance of money that they had raised to be sent to Jerusalem. By this point there was, as a contemporary succinctly notes, 'great disagreement' (*magna discordia*) between them, with mutual raids occurring over the Norman–French border.[16]

King Henry was, in the 1160s, engaged in diplomatic activity with Emperor Frederick Barbarossa, and in early 1168 he took a leaf from his grandfather's book and married his daughter Matilda into Germany. The eleven-year-old was packed off to wed Henry the Lion, duke of Saxony, the emperor's first cousin, who happened to be a divorcee older than her father. In 1170 Matilda's younger sister Eleanor was also sent abroad, to be the consort of Alfonso VIII, the king of Castile. She at least had the slightly better fortune of a husband nearer her own age: she was eight and he was fifteen, having acceded to his throne at the age of two. Constance of Castile, the second queen of Louis VII, had been his aunt.

Louis may well have felt threatened by these alliances that surrounded him geographically, and his *magna discordia* with King Henry only escalated when the astonishing news reached him, in January 1171, that Archbishop Thomas Becket had been murdered in his own cathedral of Canterbury on 29 December, by men claiming to be acting on Henry's instructions. Whether or not the assassination was carried out on the direct or inadvertent orders of the English king, Louis was able to make political capital out of it, writing to Pope Alexander III that 'the man who commits violence against his mother [i.e. the Church] revolts against human laws ... Let an unheard-of kind of retribution be invented. Let the sword of Saint Peter be unsheathed to avenge the martyr of Canterbury.'[17] Becket was, as Louis's words imply, immediately viewed as a martyr, and soon, when accounts of miracles were attributed to him, a saint; he would be canonised in February 1173, not much more than two years after his death.[18] King Henry, meanwhile, was humiliated:

> It [Becket's murder] so blackened his fame among Christian kings that he was assailed by curses from virtually everybody, and was judged a fit object for public hatred ... he too realised that his reputation was blemished, and that he was branded with a disgrace which could scarcely be expiated. His resultant anguish was such that he is said to have tasted no food for several days ... virtually the whole world blamed the king for the murder of that blessed man.[19]

A delegation of papal legates was sent to France to pronounce judgement in the affair. Henry was exonerated from having personally ordered Becket's death, but he did not deny that the assassins had taken advantage of his unguarded words. He would eventually submit himself to a humble penance at the hands of the Church.

* * *

At the time of Becket's death in December 1170 Young Henry was fifteen years old, an age at which he would have expected to take on more responsibility. He had already been introduced to the world of politics, not only through his very early marriage but also by offering homage to Louis for Normandy as far back as 1160, in one of those situations where an English king delegated his heir to fulfil the obligation rather than performing the ritual personally. Then, in 1169, a chain of such ceremonies had taken place that cemented Young Henry's position both in his own family hierarchy and with regard to France. He paid homage to Louis VII for Anjou, Maine and Brittany, and additionally knelt before Louis's son (and his own brother-in-law), Philip, who was then four years old, in recognition of his status as the future king of France. Henry's younger brother Richard, then twelve, also did homage to Louis for Aquitaine, which was to be his inheritance from his mother and was to be held directly from the French king; he was betrothed at the same time to Louis's second daughter by Constance, the eight-year-old Alice, who was taken into Henry II's custody. And finally, Geoffrey, eleven, did homage to Young Henry for Brittany, which was to be his via his marriage to Constance, the heiress of the duchy, because he was to hold it from his brother (in the latter's position as the future duke of Normandy), rather than directly from the French king.[20]

For a short time, then, everyone knew where they stood. And there was no question that Henry II wanted his eldest son to succeed him on the throne; after the wars that he and his mother had fought for many years in order to secure their rights, he had a very firm idea of his family's hereditary right to the English crown. He had obliged the barons of England to swear allegiance to Young Henry when the boy was still an infant, as we have seen, but (as the king had no doubt heard many times from his mother, the late Empress Matilda, as part of the family lore) oaths could be put aside when barons felt they might be better served by reneging on them.[21] Thus it was that Henry sought to put the matter beyond doubt by having his son crowned king during his own lifetime. As we know, King Stephen had attempted to do this for his son Eustace, but had been thwarted because his own claim to England was under dispute. Henry suffered from no such disadvantage, his right to the throne being uncontested, and he succeeded where Stephen had failed: Young Henry was crowned in June 1170. For the first time, England had two kings.[22]

However, the situation was not quite as simple or as smooth as it might seem, for Henry II had managed to offend several important parties due to the absence from the ceremony of two key figures. One was Thomas Becket, archbishop of Canterbury, who was then in exile across the Channel; and the other was Margaret of France, Young Henry's wife and queen. The former of these absences led to doubts as to whether the rite was properly valid – coronations were, by long-standing tradition, carried out by archbishops of Canterbury, whereas the crown had been placed on Young Henry's head by the archbishop of York.[23] And the second enraged the king of France. Margaret had been in Normandy, awaiting her summons to England to take her place in the coronation ceremony, but it had gone ahead without her, an omission that Louis could only interpret as deliberate and meaning that she had been 'repudiated ... to the disgrace and contempt of her father'.[24] His immediate response was to mount an attack on the Norman border, and Henry was forced to negotiate and to agree that a second coronation would be held, and that this time Margaret would be crowned alongside her husband.[25] Louis was temporarily mollified, although, as it transpired, the ceremony would not take place until August 1172, and even then it was at Winchester, not Westminster, and the crown was placed on the young queen's head by the archbishop of Rouen, not the archbishop of Canterbury. This last, of course, was unavoidable, as Becket was dead and the see still vacant.

With his crown secure and enjoying the same official status as his father, Young Henry might have felt that his future was assured and that more responsibility would come his way. But it did not, and he was forced to see his next two brothers establish themselves with lands and authority before he could do the same. Richard, as we saw above, had already paid homage to King Louis for Aquitaine, and in 1170 Eleanor chose to cede her rights to him; Richard was invested as duke of Aquitaine and count of Poitou at the age of thirteen. This does not, incidentally, imply that Eleanor was giving up power; indeed, almost the opposite, as it can be assumed that she would have more influence over her son than she did over her husband.[26] Geoffrey's future was also assured. Henry II had forced Conan IV, the duke of Brittany, to abdicate and cede his duchy to his daughter as long ago as 1166, at which point the betrothal of the five-year-old Constance and the eight-year-old Geoffrey took place; Conan's death in 1171 sealed the matter, and Brittany came under Geoffrey's nominal and Henry II's actual control.[27] Brittany was a province of some strategic importance, sharing borders with Normandy, Maine, Anjou and Poitou, and with easy shipping access to England, so it was unsurprising that Henry wished to keep a close personal eye on it for the time being.

Meanwhile, Young Henry had all the prestige of being a king and none of the power – or the money – that came with it. It became increasingly clear to all concerned that Henry II would not share his authority while he lived; and, despite being now sometimes referred to as 'the old king' for disambiguation purposes, he was still not yet forty. So Young Henry was forced to idle away his days – a dangerous situation, for, as a contemporary observed, 'a king without a realm is at a loss for something to do'.[28]

However, if Young Henry was growing dissatisfied with his own father, he had a sympathetic father-in-law in Paris, who would help make the most of his troubles, and Louis wasted no time in his efforts to exploit the divisions further. The young couple travelled to Paris in November 1172, ostensibly as the king wished to see his daughter. However, given that his paternal affection had to date reached only as far as sending all of his daughters away as children and infants, we may infer that there was also a second motive. Louis received both Margaret and Henry 'most joyfully, as he would his children', and it does seem that he was intent on welcoming Henry to his own family so that he could extend his influence further over the Young King.[29] It was probably Louis himself who put into Henry's head the idea of asking Henry II outright for control of either England or Normandy; if he did not succeed, he and his wife should return to France and make their home there, and the French king would support them.[30] Henry II, unsurprisingly, declined the request.

In January 1173 Henry II continued in his quest to surround Louis with marriage alliances favourable to himself when he negotiated the union of his youngest son John, then six, to the daughter and heiress of Count Humbert III of Savoy. The marriage settlement needed to specify in detail what lands and castles would be included as part of the deal, and Henry announced that John should have the traditional apanage of a younger son of the count of Anjou: the castles of Chinon, Loudon and Mirebeau. However, either he had forgotten or he saw as inconsequential the fact that these castles were part of the inheritance already allocated to Young Henry – he, not unnaturally, did not want them shaved off his own portion, and declared that his father had no right to dispose of them without his permission. As it happened, nothing came of the marriage plan, because Humbert's little daughter died soon afterwards, but the damage to the Plantagenet family equilibrium had already been done. The argument that ensued indicated that this was part of Young Henry's wider discontent with his position: he was eighteen (two years older than Henry II had been when his own father ceded Normandy to him) and a crowned king, and yet he had no territories to govern and no revenues with which to maintain himself, his wife and his household; he was dependent on an allowance from his father, like a child.

If Henry II initially saw this merely as his son having an adolescent fit of the sulks, alarm bells should have started to sound when the young man dropped into the conversation the name of his father-in-law, King Louis; and they certainly rang loudly when Henry II was apprised of a plot to depose him that featured the involvement of the French king.[31] He was in Aquitaine at the time, and gave orders for his castles there to be made secure before riding for Normandy, taking Young Henry with him.

The decisive break between father and son came during this journey, when both Henrys were at Chinon castle in Touraine, just south of the Norman border, in March 1173. Young Henry left it in haste one night and rode for Paris, an act that was nothing less than a declaration of rebellion against Henry II, and one that Louis was more than happy to exploit. An added bonus was that they were shortly met by both Richard and Geoffrey, sent to join their brother at the instigation of Queen Eleanor. Eleanor's motives at this point are complex, given that the situation involved both her husband and her ex-husband, but perhaps she felt that her marriage had reached the stage where she and her sons would be better served by aligning herself with the latter over the former.[32] The coalition expanded further when the French king and the Plantagenet boys were joined by five other notable lords: Louis's brother Robert I, count of Dreux; the men who were both Louis's brothers-in-law and his sons-in-law, Henry I, count of Champagne, and Theobald V, count of Blois; Philip, count of Flanders (the son of Thierry of Alsace and Sybil of Anjou); and Philip's brother Matthew, count of Boulogne, who had been married – in rather unorthodox circumstances – to Mary of Blois, King Stephen's daughter.[33]

Henry II sent envoys to Paris to speak with his son, but they were refused access to him; when Louis asked whom they were representing, and they replied 'the king of England', he was able to retort – possibly with a smirk – that they must be mistaken, for the king of England was already with him. He added that, as Henry II had crowned his son, he had therefore relinquished the throne to him. To emphasise his point, Louis had a new royal seal made for Young Henry.[34] This was all a little disingenuous – nobody was more aware than Louis that the coronation of a 'junior' king did not mean that the senior was supplanted – but it served his political purposes.

Louis, by now in his fifties and having occupied the French throne for three and a half decades with very little peace, must have felt confident that his old rival would soon be toppled. Kings of France and England had been in various degrees of conflict for three quarters of a century – that was nothing new – but now, uniquely, Louis could congratulate himself and look on while two kings of England went to war against each other.

PART II

THE DEVIL'S BROOD

CHAPTER SEVEN

A KING WITHOUT A KINGDOM

O F COURSE, LOUIS DID NOT just sit back to watch the action as the two English kings went to war with each other; he was an active participant, if not the prime instigator of the conflict. That he acted with the collusion of his ex-wife might strike us as unusual, and this perhaps requires some exploration and explanation. Traditionally, commentators have interpreted the motives of each along gendered lines and, to generalise slightly, have tended to label his as political (he was threatened by the dominance of Henry II) and hers as personal (she was dissatisfied with Henry because she felt neglected, or because he had been engaging in affairs with other women).[1] However, it is possible to see that the reverse might also be true in both cases. In his youth Louis was very much attached to Eleanor, and even after their divorce he may well have harboured some residual goodwill towards her, especially once he was secure in the knowledge that he had fathered a son to ensure the continuity of his line. And Eleanor may have felt that, in taking the governance of Aquitaine upon himself, Henry was circumscribing her political influence there. The truth is probably a mixture of all of the above, with the personal and the political being entwined on all sides.

Contemporaries had their own views on the conflict, and certainly looked much more harshly on Eleanor's rebellion against Henry than on that of her sons or on Louis's participation in the family quarrel. While not necessarily condoning such behaviour, some could more or less understand the revolt of an ambitious son against a father who limited his authority;

one, addressing his remarks as if to the elder king directly, wrote: 'After this crowning and after this transfer of power you took away from your son some of his authority, you thwarted his wishes so that he could not exercise power. Therein lay the seeds of a pitiless war.'[2] Others thought that nothing could excuse such filial disobedience ('Thus did the king's son lose both his feelings and his senses: he repulsed the innocent, persecuted a father, usurped authority, seized upon a kingdom; he alone was the guilty one'),[3] and they certainly could not excuse such conduct in a wife against her husband. This was against what they saw as the natural order, and the Church was particularly harsh in its condemnation. A letter from Rotrou, archbishop of Rouen, to Eleanor illustrates this, reminding her of the sanctity of marriage as set out in the Gospel of Matthew, and condemning her in strong language:

> You provoke the displeasure of the lord king towards female hand and puerile counsel, a king to whom even the strongest kings bend their necks. Before the situation gets worse, return with your sons to your husband, whom you are bound to obey and live with ... Either you will return to your husband or we will be constrained by canon law and bound to exercise ecclesiastical censure against you.[4]

Eleanor does not seem to have been put off by such censure; although she remained in Poitou for the time being, there is no doubt that she was acting on behalf of the sons she had sent to Paris, and she made no moves to reconcile with King Henry. Meanwhile, the rest of the coalition gathered in the French capital in May 1173 and, in the presence of an assembly of nobles and bishops, Louis swore that he would support the cause of the three Plantagenet brothers – one his son-in-law and the others his vassals – and that he would make no peace with Henry II without their consent and that of their mother, Eleanor.[5] That Eleanor's name was publicly included in this declaration (at a time when female participation in events was routinely overlooked) indicates her involvement in, and importance to, the rebellion.

Young Henry then took centre stage, acting in his capacity as king of England to receive homage and distribute money and fiefs. Unfortunately for him, the details of the arrangements reveal just how out of his depth the teenager was in the company of the wily political figures who surrounded him. As the sudden power rushed to his head, he perhaps did not realise that the primary purpose of many of his allies was to fight not *for him*, but rather *against his father*, and that he was therefore simply a pawn, a means to an end. Equally, he seems to have been either unaware of or unconcerned about the fact that he was now forming close ties with those who were hereditary enemies, representatives of a family against whom his father and grandmother had fought a bitter war. Counts Henry of Champagne and Theobald of Blois were King Stephen's nephews, while Count Matthew was at this time ruling Boulogne in right of his daughters, Stephen's only legitimate grandchildren.

These men had very definite ambitions of their own. Count Philip of Flanders, for example, already controlled the key Channel ports of Gravelines and Wissant, and now, in return for his homage to Young Henry, he was endowed with the county of Kent, along with the major castles of Dover and Rochester – which would give him not only a large income but also a secure foothold in England from which it would be difficult to evict him. Others saw through the members of the coalition more clearly than the Young King appears to have done: 'Their pretext was zealous support for the son against the father . . . but in reality they were seeking the opportunity for the business of private hatred, as in the case of the king of France, or that of gain, as in the case of the count of Flanders.'[6]

As we cite the chronicle sources for the forthcoming war, we should sound a note of caution about the writers' own perspectives. Those who were close contemporaries, writing as the conflict was unfolding or very shortly afterwards, were working on the assumption that Young Henry, whatever happened now, was going to be the *next* king of England, in which case it was not a particularly astute career move to criticise him too harshly. This led to some creative narrative contortions, and a writer composing his text in the late 1170s somehow managed to exonerate not only Henry II (the current king) and Young Henry (the future king), but also King William the Lion of Scots (Henry II's cousin, of whom we shall hear more in a moment), which left him no choice but to lay all the blame at the feet of Louis and particularly the count of Flanders, whose 'insolence knows no bounds' and who has 'led him [Young Henry] astray'.[7] On the other hand, the writer we quoted above who claimed that Young Henry 'alone was the guilty one' could allow himself to be more critical, as he had revised his text in the light of later events. The biographer of William Marshal (of whom we shall also hear more in due course), whose only aim was to present his protagonist in the best light, more or less glosses over the whole affair by saying only that 'the war between father and son was so bitter, so savage, so deadly, harmful, and damaging to everyone' – although he does safely manage to fit in a dig at King Louis, saying that 'this deed of yours is neither just nor exemplary, to set father against son'.[8]

The situation became more perilous for Henry II when his antagonists in France were joined in their cause by others from across the Channel, notably Hugh de Kevelioc, earl of Chester (who was a great-grandson of Henry I and thus a kinsman of both kings of England); Robert de Beaumont, earl of Leicester; Hugh Bigod, earl of Norfolk; and King William the Lion of Scots. William, who was also related to both Henrys – his grandfather David I had been uncle to, and a great supporter of, Empress Matilda – had succeeded to the Scots throne in 1165, following the death of his childless elder brother, Malcolm IV. Prior to this he had been the earl of Northumberland, a family title that he had lost when Malcolm surrendered his English counties to Henry II in 1157; this was a deprivation that William could not forget, and it was at the forefront of his mind when he joined Young Henry, who promised him the restitution of the earldom of Northumberland for himself and that of Huntingdon (another previously held family title) for his younger brother David, in return for their support.

Geographically, then, Henry II's enemies were all around him. It was evident that Normandy was going to be the key battleground, as it lay at the centre of his holdings; he had to pass through it in order to travel from England to Anjou, Maine and Aquitaine. If the coalition could make inroads there, they could cut his territories into smaller pieces, and they wasted no time in mounting a multi-pronged assault. In June 1173 a force led by Young Henry, Philip of Flanders and Matthew of Boulogne marched across the French–Norman border to attack the fortress of Aumale, north of the Vexin, which they took with no trouble when the holders of it surrendered so quickly that they were suspected of collusion.[9] At the same time Louis, with an army supposedly some 7,000 strong, besieged Verneuil (about 70 miles further south, on the border of Normandy and the French county of Perche), while further agitation took place over in Brittany at the instigation of the earl of Chester. The rebels there took Dol, which lay some 12 miles west of the Norman border.

A contemporary may be exaggerating a little, but he gives a flavour of what Henry II found himself up against:

> The whole of the kingdom of France and the king, the son of the king of England, Richard his brother, earl of Poitou, and Geoffrey, earl of Bretagne, and nearly all the earls and barons of England, Normandy, Aquitaine, Anjou and Brittany, arose against the king of England the father, and laid waste his lands on every side with fire, sword, and rapine: they also laid siege to his castles, and took them by storm, and there was no one to relieve them.[10]

The coalition seemed well placed for a quick victory, but they were neither the first nor the last people to underestimate either the vigour of Henry II or the importance of luck in a military campaign. The king's response was immediate and energetic:

> Then you would have seen Henry racing through the border country, dashing from one area to another and doing three days' journey or more in a single day; his men thought he must be flying. I cannot count the number of knights he took prisoner; he put them in chains and fetters, but, being such a noble man, he did not want to hang them or tear them limb from limb ... the king had their vineyards and their woods destroyed, their houses burnt and their castles laid waste.[11]

And Fortune did not favour the rebels for long. Having taken Aumale, Young Henry and the Fleming contingent moved 15 miles deeper into Normandy to attack the strategically significant fortress of Drincourt, which lay on the River Béthune, but here they met with much stiffer resistance, resulting in hand-to-hand combat. It was during this action that Count Matthew was struck just below the knee by a crossbow bolt and – presumably afflicted by blood poisoning – died of the wound a few days later. This was a personal disaster for Count Philip, as well as a setback for the rebellion, for Matthew was not only his brother but also his heir; Philip was obliged to cease hostilities while he arranged for his one remaining brother, Peter, to leave holy orders, which meant that all momentum was lost in that quarter.[12] Young Henry, still itching for action and glory, rode south to join Louis at the siege of Verneuil.

However, while these events had been occurring, Henry II was advancing to relieve the siege of Verneuil in person, and he reached it on 8 August 1173, along with a large force of Brabançon mercenaries – probably not the 10,000 claimed by some of the more excitable contemporaries, but a significant host nonetheless.[13] This created a major dilemma for all three principal protagonists: who, exactly, was prepared to fight directly in the field against whom? Henry II had previously declined to face Louis in Toulouse back in 1159, as Louis was his overlord; but now the situation was different, as he was defending his own lands from attack, so he could have no such qualms. He might, however, have been more hesitant about taking the field against his own son. And did Young Henry really want to engage his father in a risky combat which might result in the death of either or both?

Louis, meanwhile, had additional concerns. He had spent a month and a considerable amount of money besieging Verneuil, and if he withdrew now then this would be wasted. But, on the other hand, a pitched battle was always a hazardous affair, and both evidence and precedent were against him: Henry had a much greater martial reputation than he did, and the last time the kings of France and England had faced off against each other directly (with the French king similarly supporting the claims of a young protégé against his rival) had been back in 1119 at Brémule, which had not ended well. If he, Louis, were to be captured, then the consequences for France, and for his precious nine-year-old son, would be dire. All things considered, he decided that the stakes were just too high and retreated. However, as he did so, he made an unexpected and unchivalrous move: despite agreeing a truce as Henry approached, he sacked and burned the town of Verneuil before he withdrew.[14] With Louis out of the way, Henry turned his attention to Brittany, where he succeeded in short order in retaking Dol and capturing the earl of Chester.

An attempt at negotiation was made in September 1173 when Henry met Louis, Young Henry, Richard and Geoffrey at Gisors. The English king offered to share the revenues of his domains with his sons, but they – probably with Louis's encouragement, and certainly unwisely – refused;

despite their setbacks, they still believed that they could prevail, and thus had their eye on greater prizes. Contemporaries thought they knew whom to blame for this, one writing that 'it did not suit the purpose of the king of France that the king's sons should at present make peace with their father'.[15] Henry II, it should be noted, was still not offering any substantive authority or rule, only a return to the previous status quo, so Louis undoubtedly had little trouble in persuading the boys that they should decline the offer. He reiterated his support for his protégés, and no agreement was reached. This was a miscalculation on Louis's part, for Henry senior soon carried off a series of victories in Anjou, Touraine and Poitou, while his lieutenants in England – led by his elderly uncle Reginald, earl of Cornwall, the last surviving illegitimate son of Henry I – overcame the forces of the earl of Leicester.[16]

It was in Poitou that Henry was finally able to corner the other major figure in the revolt: his queen, Eleanor. As we saw earlier, she had remained in the county while her sons rode north, encouraging (with mixed success) the Poitevin barons to support them. But, seeing Henry's forces come closer, and realising the likely consequences, she decided to flee. Dressed in men's clothing for disguise, she attempted to slip past Henry's army to seek asylum with Louis, but she was apprehended and placed in Henry's captivity at Chinon castle.[17]

* * *

There was intense diplomatic activity during the winter of 1173–74, while active campaigning was suspended. This was usual for the time of year, as travelling was difficult in the cold weather and it was almost impossible to find sufficient provisions for men and horses, so the 'campaigning season' tended to run from spring to autumn. Pope Alexander III attempted to intervene in the dispute; worried about the increasingly threatening situation evolving in the crusader states in the East, he felt that the conflict between the kings of France and England was both unnecessary and damaging. He made overtures to both sides, and also took some action that showed his displeasure at the idea of a son rebelling against his father, pointedly confirming the appointment of Richard, erstwhile prior of Dover, to the archiepiscopal see of Canterbury – this was something Henry II had approved, but Young Henry had sought to annul. Pope Alexander also wrote several times to Archbishop Henry of Reims to ask him to encourage his brother King Louis to make peace. The only war that mattered, he implied, was that against the enemies of God, who were threatening the Holy Land.[18] Once more the normally pious Louis reacted uncharacteristically, ignoring the pope's entreaties. His reasons for doing so are not entirely clear, but we may perhaps infer that he was at this point in his life more concerned about the secular future of his realm and the forthcoming rule of his son Philip. Given that Louis had been obliged to wait for so long to produce a male heir, the chances were that Philip was going to inherit the throne at a relatively young age, so it would not be surprising if Louis wanted to do all he could to hand over a kingdom that was both intact and free from crisis. And having the affable and naive Young Henry on the English throne, rather than the confident and powerful Henry II, might help.

Over the winter Louis explored another possible alliance, making tentative enquiries about marrying young Philip to a daughter of Frederick Barbarossa, the German emperor, although this eventually came to nothing. Henry II, meanwhile, held a solitary Christmas court at Caen, in the absence of his wife, who was his prisoner, and his three elder sons, who were all still at Louis's court.

Hostilities resumed in spring 1174 and Henry II wasted no time. He achieved further victories in Maine and Poitou, devastated parts of Brittany, and then decided that the situation there was stable enough for him to return to England, where King William of Scots was still causing trouble.[19] Henry sailed from Barfleur on 7 July, bringing with him several family members: the young Queen Margaret, now effectively her father-in-law's hostage; the girls who were betrothed to Richard and Geoffrey, Alice of France and Constance of Brittany; the captive Eleanor; and the couple's two youngest children, Joanna and John (then aged eight and seven), who had been living at Fontevraud Abbey for their education.[20]

Upon their arrival in England, Eleanor was sent to Salisbury castle, where she would remain for the foreseeable future. Her rebellion against her husband merited, in the eyes of contemporaries, her repudiation as a disloyal wife, but Henry could make no move to divorce her, for in doing so he would lose his rights to Aquitaine. Indeed, there might even be more serious consequences: any 'divorce' was in fact an annulment – that is, a decree that the marriage had never been valid in the first place – and this carried with it the possibility that hostile parties might call into question the legitimacy of Henry's children. Thus it was that he took the obvious course of action and simply locked Eleanor up: many husbands and wives lived separately, so this action did not invite any particular criticism.

King William had invaded the north of England, and over the course of the spring and early summer he had besieged Wark and Carlisle before turning back to Alnwick, which is where he was when Henry landed at Southampton.[21] However, the English king's first move was not to ride north, but rather east: Henry had decided to make a pilgrimage to the shrine of the recently canonised St Thomas Becket at Canterbury. He was ostentatiously humble about it, arriving barefoot and fasting, dressed only in a woollen shirt, to confess that he had (albeit unknowingly, as he still claimed) been responsible for Becket's death. He then submitted to scourging at the hands of the monks.

In what was an incredible stroke of good fortune, but naturally interpreted as a sign of favour from the saint, it was on the very same day (13 July 1174) that King William was captured as the Scots were defeated at Alnwick, as Henry discovered four days later when the news reached him in London.[22] The one remaining rebel English earl, Hugh Bigod of Norfolk, submitted, and the war in England was over. King William was taken across to Normandy to be imprisoned at Caen, and then later at Falaise; and Henry was able to travel back to France much more quickly than anyone had expected him to.

While Henry II had been thus engaged, King Louis, Philip of Flanders, Young Henry and their allies had taken advantage of his absence from Normandy to besiege Rouen.[23] And it was there, in early August, that they heard with astonishment the news that the English king – whom they had thought still safely on the other side of the Channel – was approaching their position. He had landed at Barfleur on 8 August and made 150 miles in three days, to arrive there on the 11th. It was no wonder, as we noted earlier, that 'men thought he must be flying'.[24]

The situation was not dissimilar to that at Verneuil the previous year, but this time Henry II, having defeated his enemies in England, was even more in the ascendant; there was no realistic choice for his foes but to retreat. Louis ordered his siege engines to be burned – partly as a symbolic gesture and partly to stop them falling into Henry's hands – and Count Theobald of Blois and his brother William Whitehands, archbishop of Sens, were sent to negotiate with their kinsman. It was arranged that face-to-face talks between the three kings would take place the following day, but (perhaps as Henry II had expected and allowed for) Louis and Young Henry made their exit overnight and rode back over the border into France.[25]

The single member of the coalition still left fighting was Richard, who was in his county of Poitou, but, with Henry II now free to give this part of the rebellion his full attention, Richard (still only just seventeen, let us not forget) was outnumbered, outflanked and unwillingly forced to back down. He was reportedly 'greatly indignant' over his elder brother's capitulation, and this either began a new family antagonism or fanned the flames of one that was already in existence.[26] Young Henry, Richard and Geoffrey could now do nothing but submit to their father and ask his pardon; the only question was how harsh his terms were going to be.

The king met his three sons at Montlouis (on the River Loire, just to the east of the city of Tours) on 29 September 1174, having evidently given the question of terms some thought. On the one hand, he needed to demonstrate his authority now that he had achieved victory. But on the other, he did not wish to treat the defeated young men too punitively, as of course they were his sons and his wish was for them to rule his territories after him (though not, as he had amply demonstrated, until after he was gone – preferably in old age and of natural causes). His answer to this problem was to throw money at it. Young Henry was offered two castles and an annual allowance of 15,000 Angevin pounds; this equated to some £3,750 sterling, many times the average income for an earl, and would allow him to live lavishly. Richard – whom Henry, after reviewing the evidence of the recent war, presumably now saw as the greater military threat, despite his tender age – was to have two unfortified residences and half the revenue of Poitou; Geoffrey would receive half the revenues of Brittany, with the whole to come to him once his marriage to Constance had taken place.[27]

There was an additional sting in the arrangement for Young Henry, in that he was obliged to agree to provide for his youngest brother, John, who would receive the three castles in Anjou and Maine that were one of the original causes of the dispute. John would also be given an income from Normandy and the county and revenues of Nottingham in England; this was an extraordinarily generous endowment for a fourth son, especially one who was only eight years old, and was perhaps used by Henry II as a warning to the others that he could change his intentions as to their future inheritances if he so wished. As additional provision for John, Henry arranged for the boy's marriage with Isabelle, one of the three daughters and co-heiresses of William, earl of Gloucester. This proposed marriage was well within the prohibited bounds of consanguinity, for William was the son of Robert of Gloucester, Empress Matilda's half-brother, making the youthful bride and groom second cousins. Henry pressed ahead with it regardless, including a stipulation that William would make John his sole heir, and that if he were to go on to father a son, John would still get half of the rich Gloucester inheritance. Later Henry II would decide that even this was not enough, and in 1177 he named John lord of Ireland.[28]

Queen Eleanor was excluded from all these arrangements, her name not even mentioned. Her fate was to remain captive at Henry's pleasure, which, as far as anyone could see at the time, meant indefinitely. She was not, of course, to be held in a dank dungeon; her confinement was more like a house arrest, where she had apartments of some comfort but was not allowed to leave.[29] Given that her sons had chosen to remain loyal to her in their rebellion against their father, she was to some extent a hostage for their continued good behaviour.

Henry was not quite so lenient with those defeated parties who were not his sons: he would keep the king of Scots and the earls of Chester, Leicester and Norfolk in captivity for the time being. The earls would not be released until 1177, and even then Henry ordered a number of their castles to be razed. King William was able to return to Scotland at the beginning of 1175, but his release was on punitive terms: he had to hand over castles and hostages, and also to become Henry's vassal for all his lands, including Scotland itself as well as the estates he held in England.[30]

Young Henry, then, had been defeated and humbled, forced to agree to terms that he had once considered unacceptable; and as he approached his twentieth birthday – married, a knight and a crowned king – he still had no definitive authority in any of his lands. After the peace had been concluded he initially travelled to England with his father, but after a year he was chafing and requested permission to leave. Ostensibly this was to undertake a pilgrimage to the shrine of St James at Compostela, but it is likely that the real reasons were boredom and a desire to escape from his father's direct supervision: 'Such a stay was not to the liking of the young King, indeed he disliked it ... [He] did not find it in the slightest bit amusing to be so long confined in England.'[31] With his generous allowance safely in hand and no ruling responsibilities to weigh him down, he headed across the Channel in the company of William Marshal, then a knight of burgeoning reputation aged around thirty, in April 1176. Henry first visited King Louis and then Count Philip of Flanders, who set him up with an entourage to enter a tournament – something that would take up a great deal of his time in the next few years as he waited impatiently for the family dynamic to swing in his favour.[32]

There is an argument to be made that Henry II was too lenient with the Flemings – who had, after all, had nothing in mind other than their own gain in fighting against him. Count Philip was required only to renounce any claim to Young Henry's rash promises of Kent and Dover, and even then he received a cash annuity in lieu. He did, however, voluntarily opt for a change in circumstances. As we noted earlier, Pope Alexander was at this time trying to drum up enthusiasm for a crusade, and Count Philip pledged to go to the Holy Land, whereupon Henry II – perhaps keen to see the back of him for a while – offered him a sum of money to retain knights to take with him, in memory of his late brother Matthew, count of Boulogne.[33] Philip set off in 1177. His earlier efforts to free his brother Peter from his ecclesiastical career had not had the desired outcome, for Peter had died childless in 1176; so, before leaving, Philip designated his sister Margaret and her husband Baldwin V, count of Hainaut, as his heirs to Flanders if he should die while he was away. But he would be back, as we shall see.

* * *

King Louis needed to regroup. In the immediate aftermath of the war he was feeling the financial strain of his unsuccessful campaigns; he concentrated for a while on internal matters, as any attempt to continue the conflict would be not only pointless but ruinously expensive.

Among his activities was the approval in 1175 of two church appointments that would be of import in the years to come. The first resulted from the death of his brother Henry, archbishop of Reims; this was the highest ecclesiastical appointment in France and one that was generally held by a member of the extended royal family. However, it now went to William Whitehands, archbishop of Sens, who was not a Capetian but the brother of Louis's wife, Queen Adela, and also the brother of the increasingly powerful counts Henry I of Champagne, Theobald V of Blois and Stephen of Sancerre.[34]

The second church appointment did involve a member of Louis's own family: Philip of Dreux, the third son of Louis's brother Robert, was appointed bishop of Beauvais, having been assigned to a clerical life at an early age (indeed, he was still not yet twenty). As we noted earlier, it was not unusual for younger sons of the house of Capet to be put in holy orders, but in this case it was unfortunate for Philip, as he was one of those chosen simply on order of birth and not on aptitude: all the evidence points to him being a bellicose bull of a man who was unsuited to clerical life. We will hear more of him in due course.

Louis was not to be left to his own devices for long. After a couple of years spent reimposing himself in England, in the spring of 1177 Henry decided to reopen hostilities with the French king, albeit politically, rather than militarily. In June of that year his envoys reached Louis and made two demands that were so unreasonable as to be provocative: that Louis should cede the whole of the Vexin (and not just the Norman part, as originally agreed) as part of the marriage settlement between Young Henry and Margaret; and that he should additionally hand over Bourges and other territories (something that had never been agreed at all) for the marriage of his daughter Alice to Henry's son Richard. Alice, as we may remember, had been placed in Henry's keeping back in 1169; she had remained there ever since and was now seventeen, more than old enough by contemporary standards for the wedding to have taken place.

Louis, not unnaturally, refused to make these concessions; indeed, he retaliated with a counter-demand of his own – that Alice's marriage to Richard should take place, as promised, now, without any dowry. It was insulting to him that his daughter should be left in a kind of limbo, betrothed (and thus unavailable to anyone else) but not actually married and therefore not having the legal status of duchess of Aquitaine or countess of Poitou. In this, Louis was supported by Pope Alexander, who threatened Henry with interdict if he did not comply and arrange the wedding forthwith.[35]

The French king also had another card up his sleeve, for his daughter Margaret was pregnant. Henry II's earlier hope that his son might one day succeed to the French throne had been thwarted when Louis fathered a son of his own, but now the situation was almost reversed: Louis could look forward to his grandson inheriting the English crown. And in the meantime, he was on very good terms with his son-in-law, the next king. Capetian influence on England looked to be growing, and when the pregnant Margaret fled the Angevin lands for Paris as soon as renewed conflict between her husband and her father-in-law became an imminent prospect, Louis's control looked complete. A furious Henry II, unwilling to have an heir in the direct line of succession to the English throne born in a location where he had no authority, added another demand to his list – that Margaret should be returned to him forthwith – but it was ignored.[36]

Unfortunately for all concerned, tragedy was to strike. The good news was that, just as everyone had hoped, Margaret's child – born in Paris – was a boy, who was named William. But his arrival on 19 June 1177 was premature, always a worrying occurrence at the time, and he died just three days later.

A somewhat unsatisfactory pact was agreed between the kings in November of that year, in which nothing was really resolved except mutual non-aggression, a non-date-specific undertaking to go on crusade together, and vague promises of support:

We will that all should know that we now are and henceforth wish to be friends, and that each of us will, to the best of his power, defend life and limb for the other, and his worldly honours against all men ... I Henry, to the best of my power, will aid Louis, king of France, my liege lord, against all men; and I Louis will, to the best of my power, aid Henry, king of England, as my vassal and liege-man, against all men.

Louis would follow this up in 1178 with letters patent – that is, letters meant for public proclamation, rather than messages sent to a private individual – that referred to Henry as 'our most dearly beloved brother'.[37]

By this time, differences in health and demeanour were becoming noticeable in the two kings. Henry celebrated his forty-fifth birthday in the spring of 1178, and was still fit and hale; Louis, meanwhile, was in his late fifties and not nearly as vigorous. He thus needed to plan seriously for the future, and he began to organise the coronation of his son, Philip, as junior king, with the intention that the ceremony would take place on the feast of the Assumption in August 1179, shortly before Philip's fourteenth birthday.

Before this could come to pass, however, disaster struck. In the summer of 1179 Philip was a member of a hunting party at the royal residence of Compiègne, but he became separated from the group and lost in the dense forest. Despite an increasingly frantic search for the boy, he was not found until two days and two nights had passed, by which time he was terrified and starving. He fell into a fever, and it soon became evident that his life was in danger.[38] All Louis's careful planning, his lifelong hopes for his heir, were about to come crashing down, just as those of Henry I in England had in 1120.

Louis's desperation was such that he took an unprecedented step: he resolved to travel to the shrine of St Thomas Becket to beg for the saint's intercession. He would be the first member of the house of Capet to set foot on English shores since the future Louis VI back in 1100, and the first reigning French king ever to do so. So precipitous was Louis's decision to cross the Channel that Henry II was almost caught out; he arrived in time to meet his fellow monarch off the ship only after a breathless overnight ride from London. However, after that all was cordial, and they travelled together in state to Canterbury, where Louis spent two days praying.[39]

His petitions to Becket were successful, and young Philip recovered. He was crowned and anointed at Reims on the feast of All Saints, 1 November 1179, surrounded by those who would soon seek to take advantage of him: Young Henry and his brothers Richard and Geoffrey were all in attendance, as was Count Philip of Flanders, now returned from the Holy Land, along with his brother-in-law Baldwin V, count of Hainaut. The young Plantagenet sibling group and the up-and-coming Flanders–Hainaut faction were now seen as serious rivals to the more long-standing Blois–Champagne party, which was represented at the coronation by Philip's maternal uncle William Whitehands, archbishop of Reims. It was he who placed the crown on the new king's head, but he was the only member of the family present: his siblings, counts Theobald, Henry and Stephen and Queen Adela, were all absent.[40]

Also unable to attend – sadly for him, as he had awaited this moment of triumph long enough – was King Louis. The shock of his son's illness, followed by the journey overseas, had exacerbated his health problems, and he had suffered a stroke on his return journey from Canterbury.[41] Although he survived it, he never regained his health and took no further part in government, all of which meant that Philip faced something of a crash course in ruling while surrounded by the circling sharks. It was Count Philip of Flanders – who now saw more potential for his own advancement in the young, soon-to-be-reigning king of France than in the non-ruling junior king of England, and acted accordingly – who won the first part of the race to influence Philip. He forced through a royal marriage with his niece (Baldwin's daughter), the ten-year-old Isabelle of Hainaut, in April 1180.

Louis VII lingered for some months, paralysed and bedridden, before dying on 18 September 1180 at the age of sixty. He left France – with all its friends, enemies and unresolved issues – in the hands of a boy who had just turned fifteen.

$\geqslant$ CHAPTER EIGHT $\leqslant$

'THE GOD-GIVEN'

ONE SUBSTANTIAL FACTOR IN Philip's favour was that there was no possible rival claimant to the throne. He was the only son of the previous king, crowned and anointed, recognised by all, so he did not have to begin his reign by fighting off a challenger, as had so often been the case in England. There were, however, rivals vying for the position of chief advisor to – and therefore influencer of – the king, a status all the more important given the new monarch's tender age and inexperience.

The initial success of Count Philip of Flanders in this regard was twofold, for the marriage of King Philip with Isabelle of Hainaut not only placed him and his family nearer the throne than the Blois–Champagne faction, but also offended them further in that little Isabelle had previously been intended as the bride of Count Henry's elder son and heir, also called Henry (later Henry II of Champagne).[1] Nor did the situation please the queen mother, Adela of Blois, who might have expected to exert a great deal of influence on her teenage son – as dowager queens in France had done before, most notably during the minority of Philip I, whose mother had acted as his regent when he came to the throne at the age of eight. A formal regency was not necessary now, in 1180, as the crown did not follow the custom of the nobility, which saw heirs come into their full inheritance only at the age of twenty-one; Louis VII had assumed full control of the realm at seventeen, and there seems to have been a tacit acceptance by all parties that Philip, at fifteen, could do the same. Thus the Blois faction had no official governmental responsibility, although it did still have the upper hand in the Church: Queen Adela's brother William Whitehands was now not only archbishop of Reims but also a cardinal and papal legate, a direct representative of Pope Alexander. Meanwhile the third, Plantagenet, faction observed events and bided its time, while – perhaps surprisingly – the remaining members of the Capetian family itself remained very much in the background. King Philip's paternal uncle Peter of Courtenay was at this time in the Holy Land (he would die there sometime in the early 1180s without returning to France), while the other surviving brother of Louis VII, Robert I of Dreux, was now nearing sixty and taking little part in public affairs. He had a family of twelve children from his various marriages, including his sons Robert (later Robert II of Dreux) and Philip, the bishop of Beauvais; the latter was away on the crusade, along with his uncle Peter and Henry I, count of Champagne.

It was recognised that King Philip, although 'a boy in age', was nonetheless 'mature in mind and deliberation', and he demonstrated this from the earliest days of his reign.[2] He had agreed to the Flanders–Hainaut marriage with his eyes open, for the risks, in terms of discontent in his immediate family, paled into insignificance when compared to the gains. Firstly, Isabelle was reputedly descended from Charlemagne, so any children she bore Philip (himself a descendant of Hugh Capet) would unite the bloodlines of the two legendary French kings. Secondly, the prosperous county of Artois came with Isabelle as her dowry; and thirdly, there existed also the possibility of a claim to the county of Vermandois, the possession of Count Philip's wife, as they had no children of their own. The countess of Flanders was Elisabeth, the elder daughter of Count Ralph I of Vermandois and his wife Petronilla of Aquitaine (who was the younger sister of Eleanor of Aquitaine). Ralph and Petronilla had two sons, but they both died childless, making Elisabeth countess of Vermandois in her own right in 1167. Initially she ruled jointly with her husband, Philip, but in 1175 he accused her of adultery. The charge may or may not have been true, but her alleged partner was nonetheless beaten to death on Philip's orders and Philip used this as an excuse to pressure the waning Louis VII into allowing him to disinherit Elisabeth and take complete personal control of Vermandois. Flemish authority and influence were thus pushed further south into France, and King Philip would have been keen to exploit any possibility of annexing Vermandois to the crown.[3]

Even at this early stage of his reign, it would seem that Philip was seeking not only to consolidate his royal holdings, but also to expand. Indeed, he had shown signs of wanting to take personal control of his destiny even earlier: he had removed the royal seal from the incapacitated Louis VII while the old king still lived, in order to prevent his maternal uncles from getting hold of it.[4] He also refused to let even the closest of family relationships interfere with his plans, as exemplified by his decision to confiscate his mother's lands when she, alarmed at the sidelining of Blois–Champagne influence in favour of Flanders and Hainaut, pre-emptively began to fortify them. She fled to her brother Theobald for protection, and the lines seemed to be drawn up.

But now the third faction entered the fray. Henry II of England and Young Henry had observed events, and now, for once in agreement, decided that their greatest threat with regard to influence over King Philip was Count Philip. They therefore needed to offer support to Blois–Champagne – a situation that surely would have seemed impossible a few years previously – in order to drive a wedge between the king and the count of Flanders, and then to exert more influence on Philip themselves. It helped that Young Henry was on good personal terms with his brother-in-law; and Henry II could now position himself as the older, wiser head, the benevolent advisor to and protector of the new king. Peace was at this point in his own interests, so as not to destabilise his own, currently conflict-free, empire; it is also possible that he felt that his animosity towards Louis VII had been personal and should not now be directed at his late adversary's son. Whatever his motives, he mediated a reconciliation between Philip and his mother and her brothers, agreeing a treaty at Gisors in June 1180 that mirrored the peace established with Louis VII three years earlier.[5]

As part of the reconciliation Philip's uncle William Whitehands, as befitted the archbishop of Reims and premier churchman in France, became one of his foremost advisors. The wider Church suffered a brief period of instability when Pope Alexander III died in 1181 after a long reign of twenty-two years; his successor, Lucius III, was presumably envisaged only as a short-term replacement, as he was already in his eighties at the time of his election.

Another significant fatality in 1181 was Count Henry I of Champagne, head of the Blois–Champagne faction. He had been captured and then ransomed while in Asia Minor (having been the sole survivor of a massacre) and had set off home after his release, but he had only been on French soil a matter of weeks before illness overtook him and he died. This left Champagne in the hands of his elder son, who became Count Henry II. As he was only fourteen, the county would come under the regency of his mother; she was Marie of Champagne, the elder daughter of Eleanor of Aquitaine and Louis VII, who was intelligent, well educated and a renowned patron of literature.[6] Marie had numerous younger half-siblings from her parents' various marriages. They included King Philip of France; the seven Plantagenet children of Henry II; and – somewhat confusingly – Margaret of France, who was married to Young Henry, and Alice of France, the fiancée of Richard. That Marie was able to remain on reasonably amicable terms with all of them throughout her life is testament to her political and diplomatic abilities.

In 1183 the French king, now in his late teens and wanting to exert his authority and independence, obtained the excuse he needed to break free of Philip of Flanders. This was occasioned by the death of Countess Elisabeth, which initiated a chain of events. As she had been countess of Vermandois in her own right as well as countess of Flanders by marriage, that title and the associated lands should have passed to her one remaining sister, Eleanor of Vermandois; however, as we noted earlier, Count Philip had previously persuaded Louis VII to agree that he should have sole control over them, and he now claimed Vermandois in his own name. The king came down on the side of Eleanor (telling Count Philip, with some irony, that his own earlier confirmation of Louis's grant was no longer valid as he had made it as a child) and conflict ensued. Henry II of England stepped in once more to mediate a peace, but Count Philip now harboured antagonism towards the French king.

Irked by this, and encouraged by the Blois–Champagne faction, King Philip announced in 1184 that he intended to renounce and divorce his wife, Count Philip's niece Isabelle of Hainaut. Given that the marriage had been sanctified by the Church, he could not make a case for this merely on political grounds, so he announced instead that it was because they were too closely related, and moreover that Isabelle was infertile and had not borne him a child. Given that the queen was still only fourteen at this point, the second accusation can hardly have been justified, but it was unclear whether

Count Philip could do anything about it. Any action of his, however, was pre-empted by Isabelle herself.

Queen Isabelle had started her public career as a ten-year-old pawn in the hands of her uncle and father. She had, as was usual for girls of her rank, been given no choice in her husband, and the king's reasons for agreeing to the marriage (as explained above) were more to do with the political gains that could be made than any personal preference for her. Isabelle behaved quietly and properly as her future was mapped out for her, all the while applying herself to her studies; she was both bright and literate. She was crowned and anointed in the spring of 1180, and took her new status seriously. But now she was in danger of losing it, and – rather than relying on father or uncle – she took matters into her own hands, by such means as were available to her.

Interposing herself into the male-dominated political discussions at court was not an option, so she took advantage of the two factors a queen could generally rely on: personal access to the king and public popularity. Even as a council at Senlis in March 1184 was approving her repudiation, she walked through the streets of Paris barefoot, dressed only in her shift, praying and distributing alms and publicly begging for forgiveness. The sight of a pretty and very young queen in such distress turned public opinion very much in her favour; there were demonstrations in support of her, swaying the king's opinion. He made an attempt at placating Isabelle by offering her marriage to any of his nobles that she cared to name, but she retorted to him that she wanted no other and, in a clever aside that both referenced his divinely ordained status and made public the fact that the marriage had been consummated, declared that 'It does not please God that a mortal should enter the bed in which you slept.'[7]

King Philip had no choice but to back down, and Isabelle was restored to her rightful position. She then immediately demonstrated her worth to him by interceding with her father, Baldwin V of Hainaut: in a personal interview she broke down in tears, saying that she was upset that conflict should exist between him and her husband. This was probably a major factor in Baldwin switching his allegiance from the count to the king when sides needed to be taken, which occurred in 1185 when Count Philip invaded French lands. With the support of Baldwin and other nobles, the king easily defeated the count and forced him to accept a settlement which saw his power bloc divided and a potential addition to the royal lands: while the count might retain a life interest, Vermandois would go to the late countess's sister, Eleanor, and would revert to the crown if she died without issue. As she was by this time on her fourth childless marriage, the chances of this were high; indeed, Vermandois would eventually fall into the king's hands in 1213. Philip of Flanders decided to make a second pilgrimage to the Holy Land, and we will meet him again there in due course.[8]

By the time of his twentieth birthday in the summer of 1185, then, King Philip had reunited with his wife, who at the age of fifteen had the makings of a formidable queen; he had subdued his rebellious vassals and 'the whole kingdom of France [had been] brought under the will of the king of France'. The chronicler and monk of Saint-Denis, Rigord, had also bestowed on him the epithet by which he would be known to posterity: Augustus.[9]

* * *

On top of all this domestic strife, Philip Augustus had also found the time to become involved in the internal conflict of the Plantagenets. That he had the confidence – one might even say the audacity – to do this so early in his reign and at such a young age speaks to his confidence and ambition, but it also speaks to necessity. Philip no doubt suspected that, if they ever truly banded together, the Plantagenet family would be more than capable of overwhelming both him and France. 'O good gods!' exclaimed one commentator, addressing this subject:

> If such brothers had observed fraternal agreement among themselves and filial affection as sons to their father, and had been bound together by the double bond of good will and nature, how great and beyond estimation, how illustrious and unsurpassed in the ages would have been the father's glory and the sons' victory![10]

As we saw above, Henry II and his eldest son had briefly put aside their differences in order to influence the relationship between Philip Augustus and Count Philip of Flanders after the former's accession, but by 1182 Young Henry was chafing at the bit once more. He was by now twenty-seven and, although enjoying a generous allowance, he was still no nearer any real power or authority than he had been a decade earlier. And just to rub salt into the wound, his younger brothers had come into their inheritances fully: Richard was duke of Aquitaine and count of Poitou, while Geoffrey was duke of Brittany and count of Richmond. There was little possibility of Henry achieving the same while his father, who was still on the right side of fifty, continued to enjoy robust health.

In the autumn of that year Young Henry, 'in conformity with the advice of Philip, king of France', asked Henry II once again for the outright grant of Normandy – not necessarily because he was keen to take on the responsibility for governing it, but rather 'from which he might pay his knights and servants for their services'. The elder Henry declined, and the younger removed himself to Philip's court. Henry II, meanwhile, was also busy dealing with the rebellious intentions of his third son Geoffrey in Brittany; and Geoffrey was known to be on excellent terms with Philip.[11]

One opportunity for Young Henry soon presented itself, in that his brother Richard was increasingly unpopular with the barons of Aquitaine:

> The nobles of Aquitaine hated their lord, Count Richard, on account of his great cruelty. They planned to drive him by force from the duchy of Aquitaine and the county of Poitou, and greatly desired to transfer the principality to the good and benign Young King ... for he was amiable to everyone, of handsome countenance, and especially famous for his military glory, to such an extent that he appeared second to none. He was self-effacing, responsive and affable, so that he was loved with very great affection by those both near and far.[12]

This was a chance for some real action outside the tournament field, and also possibly for advancement: if Richard could not keep control of Aquitaine, perhaps it might fall to Young Henry to govern it until he came into his full inheritance? Richard, almost obligingly, seized in late 1182 the castle of Clairvaux as part of his crackdown on rebellious barons, and began significant construction and refortification. Clairvaux was on the border between Richard's domain of Poitou and Henry's of Anjou, so the Young King was able to make a case that it came under his jurisdiction, thus enabling him to proclaim his open support for the Poitevin rebels. 'And therewith', says one commentator, 'that strife began which was not resolved until everyone all round had the worst of it.'[13]

As Aquitaine was held as a fief from the king of France – and Richard had paid homage for it – Philip would have had an excuse to intervene in what was technically an internal matter (much as Louis VI had done in Flanders half a century earlier), but he held off for now.[14] Henry II thus found himself obliged to step in to arbitrate; he called a peace conference in Angers early in 1183, at which he made his three eldest sons swear a compact of perpetual peace with each other; but within a month Young Henry, with Geoffrey his willing accomplice, had shown enough support for the Poitevin barons to goad Richard into taking up arms. This meant that Richard had disobeyed Henry II, who authorised Young Henry – as Richard's senior and the future king – to go to war with him. Having taken the precaution of sending his wife, Margaret, to her brother King Philip in Paris for safety, Young Henry collected Geoffrey and they invaded Aquitaine.

This turned out to be a huge mistake. Young Henry's martial experience had been gained on the tournament circuit, whereas Richard had spent the last decade engaged in real war, against tough opponents, and the gulf in their military standing soon became evident.[15] Henry and Geoffrey, and the rebellious Poitevin barons, began to plunder Richard's lands, but Richard responded quickly and effectively: he crushed resistance, captured a number of rebels and then decided to make an example of them. In a pointed gesture, he brought a group of prisoners to the river outside Limoges, where Young Henry and Geoffrey were staying at the time, and had some executed by drowning or the sword, and others blinded. He also threatened that any men belonging to the households of his brothers would be beheaded if he captured them.[16]

Alarmed at such ruthlessness and the potential danger for his sons (and his succession plans), Henry II rode south from Normandy. He arrived at Limoges in the spring of 1183, but Young Henry apparently suspected that his father would side with Richard; he would meet the king only while wearing his hauberk, a marked sign of distrust. Now Young Henry was in rebellion against his father, so both Henry II and Richard moved to assail Limoges – but as soon as news of this reached Paris, Philip Augustus sent a supply of mercenaries to his brother-in-law, in order to even the odds and maximise the potential of the conflict. This marked a new departure for the

French king: previously he had involved himself in the internal Plantagenet disputes via diplomatic means only – talking and persuading – but the dispatching of mercenaries was his first step into armed conflict in the matter, and it was only the beginning of what would turn out to be a lifelong campaign. The action also denoted a change of direction, for it was Richard's homage, not Young Henry's, that had been accepted by Philip for Aquitaine.

This ostensibly generous gesture by Philip had its disadvantages for Young Henry: now that he had mercenaries at his disposal, he had to pay them. Given that he was short of cash (Henry II having, not unnaturally under the circumstances, cut off his allowance), he decided that the best way to raise funds was to embark on a series of plundering expeditions in the lands around Limoges; this made him unpopular among the very people he had supposedly come to protect against tyranny, and when he returned to Limoges he found the gates locked against him. Events were spiralling out of control, and Young Henry's response was to rid himself of all of it by announcing that he had taken the cross.[17]

Philip's reaction to this news is unknown; but, in the event, it did not matter, for in May Young Henry fell ill. He was probably suffering from dysentery, a common disease among soldiers on campaign: 'He was attacked first by a fever, then by a flux of the bowels, which reduced him to the point of death.'[18] It was not long before it became apparent that his end was near, and he sent a message to his father to ask for a meeting. However, Henry II was suspicious of his son's motives, and in answer to his son's increasingly desperate pleas for forgiveness and for him to come in person, he merely sent a ring, together with the promise that the two of them could be reconciled in due course. By the time the severity of the situation had been made clear to him, it was too late: Young Henry died on 11 June 1183, at the age of twenty-eight.[19]

Despite all their differences, Henry II was distraught at the loss of his eldest son; his carefully laid plans of the last two decades now lay in tatters, and he almost began to look like a spent force. Philip Augustus, on the other hand, was just warming up.

⇒ CHAPTER NINE ⇐

SHAME ON A CONQUERED KING

When Henry II, as a boy, had been brought to the court of Louis, king of France, and Bernard, abbot of Clairvaux, of good memory, happened to be there at that time, the king asked the abbot what he thought of the boy, who was expecting to inherit such a great breadth of lands and kingdoms. The holy man looked at the boy, who happened to have glanced around and was fixing the gaze of his eyes on the ground at that point, and answered as if by a prophetic sprit: 'From the devil he came and to the devil he will go.'[1]

YOUNG HENRY'S DEATH WAS AN unexpected tragedy, and one that affected Henry II deeply, even though he had been at war with his son. 'My son has cost me much,' he is quoted as saying, but 'would that he were still costing me!'[2] But the king could not dwell on his personal feelings for long, as the loss of his heir also had great political ramifications: an immediate reorganisation of his plans for the inheritance of his estates was necessary. Richard, now his eldest surviving son, was promoted to the position of heir to the throne, and would in due course have England, Normandy and Anjou, the previous patrimonial inheritance of Young Henry. Geoffrey, the second son (and thus Richard's heir until he had children of his own) would retain Brittany; he held it in right of his wife, so it could not be reallocated. This meant that Henry II was able to move John, now sixteen, up to Richard's former position: he would have Aquitaine, as well as holding on to his previously granted English estates. In September

1183 Henry summoned them both to his side in Normandy to confirm the arrangement.[3]

However, Henry's neat theoretical plans had failed to take into account the character and easily predictable reactions of his sons, particularly Richard. Although no doubt happy to step into his elder brother's shoes as the principal heir, he had been brought up in the expectation that Aquitaine would be his; indeed, he had been ruling it and putting down rebellions there for many years, shedding blood and honing his military talents in demanding circumstances. To be now expected to hand his duchy over without a murmur to an untried youth was inconceivable. Richard attended the court, but asked his father for a few days in which to consider the proposition; when this was granted, he slipped away one night, rode back to Poitou and sent a message saying that he would never, while he lived, surrender Aquitaine.[4]

Meanwhile, a reorganisation of priorities was also taking place in Paris. Philip Augustus had successfully exploited divisions within the Plantagenet family by supporting Young Henry in his quarrels with Henry II, but of course that avenue was now closed. Philip therefore took another of the numerous options available to him and courted Geoffrey. Geoffrey had always been known as something of a troublemaker and had a reputation for being duplicitous: one chronicler calls him a 'son of iniquity', while another says that he was 'pouring out words smoother than oil ... able to unknit whatever has been joined together and with a tongue powerful enough to ruin two kingdoms ... an unreliable hypocrite and dissembler in all things'.[5] He had not continued the fight in Aquitaine after Young Henry's death, but his relations with Richard remained hostile. In June 1184 he (along with John, now of an age to join personally in the endless family conflicts) mounted an attack on Richard's lands, to which Richard responded immediately by invading Brittany. Once more, Henry II was forced to step in, and a temporary peace ensued; but the following year Geoffrey, with King Philip's encouragement, decided to contest the rule of Anjou with Richard.[6]

Geoffrey's seemingly unlimited capacity for fast talking meant that he had soon ingratiated himself even more deeply at the French court:

Count Geoffrey had by now so won over the minds of King Philip and of all the great men of France that, by their unanimous wish, he was created seneschal of France. Since he had obtained such great power and such friendship with the king, he had stirred up the king of the French and the whole of France against his father and brother with persuasive words, for he was very eloquent and agreeable, to such an extent that he would, without a doubt, have prepared for them trouble such as they had never seen before.[7]

As another part of his multi-pronged attack on Henry II, Philip began agitating for the return of control of the Vexin, which had been the dowry of his half-sister Margaret, Young Henry's widow. She, childless, was to be returned to France so she could be used again on the marriage market, and this gave Philip an excuse to say that the Vexin should come with her. At a conference between the two kings in March 1186, Philip agreed to transfer the dowry to another of his half-sisters, Alice, on condition that her long-awaited marriage to Richard should take place immediately.[8] This unfortunate woman was now in her mid-twenties and had been in English custody for seventeen years; her continuing non-marriage could not be seen as anything other than a gross insult. King Henry swore that it would be done, and the kings parted; but the wedding still did not take place. Meanwhile, Margaret was disposed of swiftly, as a good offer for her had arrived; she married Béla III, king of Hungary, in the summer of that same year.[9]

It was not long before the situation of the two dynasties changed once more, and due to another unexpected death. While taking part in a tournament in France – a dangerous activity – Geoffrey was trampled by a horse, and he died of his injuries a few days later, on 19 August 1186, aged just twenty-seven. Rather than having his body sent back to any of Henry II's lands, Philip had him buried in the cathedral of Notre Dame in Paris, where he may have overacted the part of grieving friend: one commentator claims that he was so distraught that he was ready to throw himself into the grave, and had to be held back by his companions.[10] Geoffrey's widow, Constance, was left with a three-year-old daughter, Eleanor, and was pregnant.[11] She was duchess of Brittany in her own right, so a speedy remarriage would no doubt be on the cards; the future rule of the duchy would depend to a great extent on whether the posthumous child she would bear Geoffrey was a son or a daughter. In the event, she gave birth to a boy on Easter Sunday 1187; this was Henry II's first grandson in the male line and he pressured

Constance to name the baby after him. But she – perhaps as a sign of Breton independence and as a protest against the Plantagenet control of her life – chose a name from her homeland, and the boy was called Arthur. Predictably, he immediately became the subject of competing claims for his guardianship, a subject to which we will return later.[12]

Arthur was not the only heir born in that year. Queen Isabelle of France had successfully fought off her attempted repudiation three years earlier, and she had been carrying out her queenly role in peace and with good sense ever since; she was one of Philip's greatest assets. In September 1187, at the age of seventeen, she fulfilled the most important duty of all when she gave birth to a son, who was named Louis.[13] King Philip was overjoyed, sending out messengers immediately to all parts of his realm to share the good news – and, given that he was only in his early twenties himself, he no doubt looked forward to Louis's birth being only the first in a long line that would secure the French succession for years to come.

Henry II's male line was, in September 1187, looking a little thinner than he probably would have liked: he had two surviving sons aged thirty and twenty, both unmarried and childless, plus his infant grandson Arthur of Brittany. His three daughters had given him multiple grandchildren, but (although he himself claimed the English throne through a female line) he does not appear to have considered them as candidates for the crown. His eldest daughter, Matilda, was married to the elderly Henry the Lion, duke of Saxony; they had a daughter and four sons. The second, Eleanor, was queen of Castile via her marriage to Alfonso VIII; she had so far borne him six children, of whom only two daughters survived. She would go on to have more, her eventual family consisting of six daughters and two sons who would live long enough to reach their teens, although she would sadly outlive a number of these, too. And finally, Henry II's youngest daughter, Joanna, was the queen of Sicily as the wife of William II. She had at present no children (although it is possible that she had given birth to one stillborn or short-lived son); after William's childless death she would be married again, to Count Raymond VI of Toulouse, with whom she would have two surviving children, a son and a daughter. We will hear more of all three of these women's families in due course.

* * *

The 1180s threatened catastrophe for the Latin kingdom of Jerusalem. We will explore this more fully in the next chapter, but one result was that Eraclius, the patriarch of Jerusalem, travelled to England early in 1185 to offer the crown of Jerusalem to Henry II; this was partly in deference to his power and his capabilities, and partly because his paternal grandfather, Fulk V of Anjou, had once held the position so there was some semblance of hereditary right. After some deliberation with his barons and churchmen, Henry declined the honour, on the basis that he had sworn an oath to protect and govern his existing lands. He and Philip Augustus then briefly put aside their differences to communicate about the possibility of launching a crusade; they decided at this point to send men and money, but not to go themselves.

However, the situation in the Holy Land – or Outremer, as it was more generally known at the time – continued to deteriorate, culminating in a disastrous defeat of the forces of the kingdom of Jerusalem at the Battle of Hattin in July 1187, at the hands of the man known in the west as Saladin. The loss was almost total: the surviving Templars and Hospitallers were executed, the bellicose military leader Renaud de Châtillon was apparently killed by Saladin personally in his tent, King Guy and the True Cross were both captured, and shortly afterwards Jerusalem itself surrendered.[14] The shocking news reached Europe, galvanising those who wished to defend the Holy Land; Richard, duke of Aquitaine, took the cross straight away, in November 1187. Kings Philip and Henry took more time to deliberate, but eventually did the same in January 1188.

Despite this seeming collegiality, by this time relations between the ruling dynasties of England and France were at a low point. Arguments were still ongoing about who should have custody of the young heirs of Brittany, and Henry thwarted Philip's ambitions in this quarter by imposing a new marriage on Duchess Constance: she was wed – very much against her will, as we shall see – to Ranulf de Blundeville, the earl of Chester, who now became Eleanor and Arthur's stepfather and, in name at least, duke of Brittany in right of his wife.

On top of this, Henry had still not arranged the wedding of Richard and Alice, irritating the French king further; and Richard himself caused more discord by pursuing again the question of Aquitainian overlordship of Toulouse, which led to Count Raymond V appealing to Philip; Philip told Henry that he had better order his son to desist, and threatened to invade

Normandy if he did not.[15] None of this was particularly conducive to the idea of the two kings embarking on a crusade as brothers-in-arms.

Why was Philip so implacably opposed to Henry and the Plantagenets? At the very beginning of his reign there must have been an element of fear: despite his public confidence and bravado, he was a fifteen-year-old boy who had inherited a kingdom overshadowed by a man who was not only an experienced rival king, but also a major vassal and landholder in France as well. Henry's initial bonhomie and 'affable elder statesman' act could very easily lead to him eliminating those rivals who sought to influence the youthful king, only to end up in that position himself, a situation from which Philip might find it difficult to escape. Thus Philip evidently decided, very early on, that trying to tread water and simply consolidate would be ineffective in the face of such an opponent – the best way to defend was to attack.

This proved successful, but the reasons behind the tactic seem to have altered over time. To begin with, it was seemingly just political: Philip wanted to exert control over his own kingdom while reducing the influence of Henry II. It would only be later – following the events of the Third Crusade and afterwards that we will examine below – that he developed an extreme personal antipathy to the surviving members of the Plantagenet family. It might all have ended differently, had Young Henry, who was Philip's brother-in-law and with whom he was on good terms, survived to succeed Henry II – or even if Geoffrey had lived longer. But this was not to be. Philip was left with Henry II, Richard and John; and he developed such an implacable animosity towards them that he sought to wipe them off not just the French map, but later the English one as well.[16]

Most of this, of course, still lay in the future. For now, Philip employed his tried-and-tested technique of dividing and conquering, encouraging Richard to rebel against Henry – although this became more complicated by the fact that they (and many of their subordinate lords) were all technically fellow crusaders. Whatever else might be said against Philip, he seems to have been a remarkably persuasive man, and Richard fell for his overtures of friendship despite the abundant evidence of what had happened to other members of his family who had done so before. He was in Paris by the autumn of 1187, and after he had taken the cross he lobbied his father for a public declaration of his succession plans before he set off for the East. That this was at Philip's instigation, or at least with his encouragement, seems clear, and he did it by suggesting to Richard that King Henry was going to disinherit him in favour of John – a plausible idea, given Henry's well-known preference for his youngest son.[17]

Richard and Henry agreed to meet in the autumn of 1188, but Richard antagonised his father before they had even started by turning up in the company of Philip. After a bad-tempered discussion, Richard again demanded that Henry confirm him as his heir in public, to which Henry remained silent; then, in a gesture that could hardly have been more provocative, Richard turned and knelt before Philip, offering him homage for Aquitaine and Normandy.[18]

* * *

Philip and Richard launched raids on Henry's lands early in 1189. Henry, however, was by now in a state of some ill health – he was only fifty-six, but had spent forty of those years almost constantly on horseback and in a state of agitation or conflict – and he was not able to retaliate. Instead he sought talks, but his opponents thought his illness a subterfuge and continued with their campaign throughout the spring. Discussions eventually took place at Whitsun, but no agreement was reached on the main sticking point: Henry would still not name Richard publicly as his heir.

This, of course, raises the question of *why* he would not do so, when Richard was surely the obvious candidate. One major factor in the argument against such a course of action was that Henry did not want to make almost the same mistake he had made with Young Henry – he certainly would not have Richard crowned as a fellow king within his own lifetime, but perhaps he thought that even giving him the title and status of designated heir would be enough for Richard to attempt to exert too much authority. The question of whether Henry was genuinely considering overlooking Richard for John is an interesting one; but the balance of probability is that, although he might favour the *idea* of disinheriting the son he liked less in favour of the son he liked more, he was not willing to depart so far from the accepted right of inheritance via the senior line – something he himself had spent his own youth fighting for. Thus it is more likely that he felt he was best served by attempting to keep Richard on a tight rein via uncertainty over his future. This might have been a good idea in principle, but in practice it was one that left Richard open to exploitation by Philip, who, although some eight years younger than Richard, seems to have been able to run rings around him politically and intellectually.

The armed conflict continued. Henry returned to Le Mans, only to be assailed there almost immediately by Richard and Philip. Their troops succeeded in gaining entry to the suburbs, and Henry's men, as they withdrew, set fire to the buildings there in order to impede enemy progress. However, the wind changed direction, and in the warm month of June sparks blew easily; soon the whole town was ablaze. Henry had to make a quick retreat, pausing on his way to watch his birthplace, and the site of his father's burial, burn.[19] The obvious thing to do would be to flee north to Normandy, to consolidate, to summon more troops, to fortify his castles there and prepare for a long campaign. But Henry was much sicker than Richard and Philip had been prepared to admit, and, for perhaps the first time in his life, he had no stomach for a fight. So instead of riding for Normandy, he headed south to his ancestral lands of Anjou, reaching Chinon so exhausted that he was bedridden for a fortnight.[20]

The real wind had changed at Le Mans, and the metaphorical wind was against Henry now. It was clear that he could not last much longer, so the Angevin barons surrendered one after another to Richard, throwing in their lot with the rising sun, rather than the waning one. Henry was summoned – there is no other word for it – from his sickbed to meet Philip and Richard, although his son still thought the illness was a ruse ('Count Richard had no pity whatever for him, indeed he told the King of France that he was feigning'). Henry arrived, evidently in great pain and distress, but remaining stubbornly on his horse even though the French king, shocked by his appearance, offered him his own cloak so that he could sit on the ground.[21] The English king was forced to listen to a set of humiliating demands – he was to do homage to Philip for all his continental lands; Richard was to be named as his sole heir; Richard was to marry Alice; Philip was to be paid a large indemnity; castles were to be handed over – and had no choice but to agree. There was, however, a spark of the old Henry left, shown as he leaned in to give Richard the traditional kiss of peace to seal the agreement:

When this had been said or done, but more falsely than in fact, and the kiss given, the count heard his father say this as he departed, but uttered

115

in a low voice, 'May the Lord never allow me to die until I have taken fitting revenge on you!'[22]

Henry was carried back to Chinon by those few men who remained loyal to him, including his illegitimate son Geoffrey and the knight William Marshal, who had returned to his service after the death of Young Henry. In one last burst of obstinacy, anger and energy, Henry demanded to see the list of those who had betrayed him by siding with Richard. Unfortunately for him, the first name on it was that of his youngest son, John, and this caused him such a shock that his condition deteriorated fatally. An eyewitness account of Henry's last agonising days, from William Marshal, details his suffering after he heard the terrible news:

> His body was burning hot, his blood so boiled within him that his complexion became clouded, dark, blue and livid. Because of his pain, which was so intense, he completely lost his mental faculties, hearing and seeing nothing. He was beset by this pain and suffered until the third day. He spoke, but nobody could understand a word of what he said. He suffered a blood clot in the heart, and there was nothing for him but to come to that point where Death simply burst his heart with her own hands.[23]

Delirious, lapsing in and out of consciousness and apparently uttering the immortal phrase 'Shame, shame on a conquered king!', Henry II died on 6 July 1189; he had, in the words attributed to Bernard of Clairvaux, returned to the devil.[24]

William Marshal sent word to Richard and arranged for the body to be transported to the abbey of Fontevraud, where the new king met him. For there was no question who was going to inherit the throne: for the first time in over 150 years, the English crown passed uncontested from father to eldest surviving son. Several contemporaries recount how, when Richard looked down at the corpse, it began to bleed from the nose, and this was commonly taken to mean that Richard was responsible for his father's death, although in hindsight we might blame Philip as much as Richard.[25]

William Marshal, incidentally, might have expected a cool reception from Richard, and this is an illustrative case study of how all patronage lapsed on the death of a king, and that those who were not in hereditary positions of power had to jockey for status in a new reign. In this case, and fortunately for Marshal, Richard pragmatically recognised the value of loyalty to one's king in difficult circumstances and took him into his own service. Perhaps pushing his luck, Marshal immediately reminded Richard that the old king, before his death, had promised him the hand in marriage and the lands of a very wealthy heiress, Isabel de Clare, who was countess of Pembroke and Striguil in her own right. Richard considered this and said that, although his father's grant was null and void, *he* would give the girl to Marshal. The new earl-elect wasted no time in rushing to England to have the ceremony performed, so that his new status would be guaranteed.[26]

* * *

To begin with, the outward friendship between Philip and Richard continued. On 20 July Richard was recognised as duke of Normandy and paid homage to Philip, who at the same time renewed the agreement made at the beginning of July with Henry II, with the obvious exception of those clauses relating to the late king's recognition of Richard as his heir.[27] Richard then travelled to England, a realm he had visited only sporadically since being named duke of Aquitaine nearly twenty years previously, and was crowned at Westminster on 3 September 1189.

Philip Augustus, however, was already recalculating. The amicable relationship which had been maintained while Richard was heir to the throne, and a useful foil in the French king's long-term campaign against Henry II, could not be sustained now that Richard was his principal dynastic opponent. Richard had inherited not only Henry II's entire sprawling empire, but also the almost impossible task of trying to keep it all together, and this was something that could be exploited.

However, before Philip could make any headway on future plans in this regard, events intervened. As we noted above, news of the fall of Jerusalem to Saladin had sent shockwaves around Europe, and both kings had taken the cross. Now that Richard had the resources of the English crown at his disposal, it was time to make firm plans, and Philip would have to keep up if he were to maintain his reputation as *rex christianissimus*, the 'most-Christian king' of France.[28]

Both kings would leave their realms to go on crusade.

≫ CHAPTER TEN ≪

CRUSADE

THE LATIN KINGDOM OF JERUSALEM had been established after the success of the First Crusade, at the end of the eleventh century. However, its monarchy had never quite managed to put down deep roots or establish a solid system of male primogeniture, due to a succession of kings either dying young or not fathering male heirs (or both).[1] Baldwin II, who reigned during the first third of the twelfth century, produced four daughters but no son, so his eldest daughter, Melisende, was his designated heir. The precarious situation in Outremer meant that, although royal governance could be carried out by a female ruler (and contemporaries did see and depict women as both able and powerful), she would need a husband or other male relative who was a capable soldier and military commander, and who could lead armies on her behalf. Baldwin thus embarked on a careful search for a husband for his daughter. His choice, as we saw in Chapter 3, fell on Fulk V, count of Anjou and grandfather of Henry II of England, who left his ancestral lands to travel to the East; he married Melisende and was proclaimed king of Jerusalem and co-ruler on Baldwin's death in 1131.

The stormy relationship between Fulk and Melisende, during which he tried to overrule her rights, and she fought back, does not form part of our tale here. Of relevance is that they had two sons: Baldwin III, who died childless in 1163 when only in his early thirties, and Amalric I, who also perished without reaching forty, although he left three children. These were two daughters, Sybil and Isabella, and a son, who succeeded as Baldwin IV in 1174 when he was just thirteen. Tragically for the boy, he contracted leprosy; he ruled as best he could through the pain of his deteriorating condition before dying bedridden, blind and childless at the age of twenty-four in 1185.

Knowing that his life would be short, Baldwin IV had, in 1183, crowned as co-king the only other male remaining in the royal line: another Baldwin, the frail five-year-old son of his elder sister Sybil. The child then became sole king as Baldwin V, but reigned for only a year, dying in 1186 at the age of just nine. This left the throne in the hands of his mother, Sybil, though her inheritance of it was conditional on her divorcing her unpopular husband (who was her second husband, and thus Baldwin V's stepfather, rather than his father), Guy de Lusignan. Sybil protested against this at first, but then conceded on the condition that she would be given a free choice of whom to marry next. This was agreed and she was duly crowned, at which point she was asked to give the king's crown to any man present who could govern the kingdom. What happened next shocked all the witnesses:

> She took the crown and called her husband who was before her and said to him: 'Sire, come up and receive this crown, for I do not know where better I can bestow it.' He knelt before her, and she placed the crown on his head ... Thus was he king and she queen.

This was, said another contemporary, 'a wonderful piece of cunning', but 'on account of the oath which they had made, nobody dared oppose her'. Sybil had outwitted the whole court and Guy was crowned king of Jerusalem in right of his wife, the personal influencing the political once more.[2]

The couple's first priority was to check the advance of Saladin, but, as we have seen, they were unsuccessful. Guy was captured at the Battle of Hattin; Sybil personally superintended the defence of Jerusalem when Saladin assailed it, and she managed to escape to Tripoli with her two young daughters when the city surrendered to the Muslim forces in October 1187.

Saladin, who was aware of the many tensions in the Jerusalemite court, released Guy in 1188: either out of mercy, or because he (somewhat naively) believed that Guy would hold true to the oath he had sworn never to take up arms against Saladin again, or because he realised that it would actually cause more conflict among the crusaders than keeping him in captivity. Guy and Sybil were reunited, and they travelled to Tyre, a city still holding out for the crusaders. Unfortunately for them, it was in the hands of Conrad of Montferrat, the brother of Sybil's first husband (and therefore uncle to the late boy king Baldwin V), who believed that his own claim to the throne was better than Guy's; he refused them entry and they were forced to remain outside the city walls. Saladin, by now, had conquered the greater part of the kingdom, so after a short stay in Antioch Guy and Sybil moved south to the great port city of Acre, which was held by the Muslims, to begin a siege.

* * *

This, then, was the situation as it stood in the winter of 1189–90, as Richard and Philip were planning their departure for the East. However, before they could set off, they each had some important matters to attend to in their own kingdoms.

Almost Richard's first act on being proclaimed king – before his coronation ceremony, and indeed before he had even reached English shores – was to release his mother from captivity.

Eleanor had been her husband's prisoner for sixteen years; she had endured what might at least be considered a 'comfortable' confinement, but it was only as comfortable as Henry allowed – she did not, for example, enjoy the revenues from her own lands, as Henry confiscated them for his own use, and she had to make do with the much smaller allowance he allocated for her upkeep. She was initially, in the mid-1170s, kept under relatively close supervision in Salisbury castle, but as the years went by she was permitted to visit other residences, and when her eldest daughter Matilda and her son-in-law Henry the Lion arrived in England in 1184 (following a dispute with Emperor Frederick Barbarossa that resulted in their exile from Germany) she was allowed to see them, and her grandchildren, spending almost a year in her daughter's company.[3] She appeared in public several times, which was useful to Henry II as it helped to prevent any rumours that he might have done away with her more permanently. At the time of his death in the summer of 1189 Eleanor was in Winchester; she was released from confinement as soon as news of his demise had reached England, and she had not yet left that city when William Marshal – on his way to claim his rich bride – reached her with letters from her son, the new king.[4]

Eleanor was now a widow of some sixty-five years of age who had been inactive on the political stage for many years, and there may have been some thought among the nobles (of England, if not of Aquitaine) that she would retreat into a dignified and feminine retirement. Far from it: she strode into a new phase of her life with energy and enthusiasm. Richard needed someone he could trust, and who better than his mother? The result was not merely a release from captivity, but immediate authority:

> Queen Eleanor, who for many years had been under close guard, was entrusted with the power of acting as regent by her son. Indeed, he issued instructions to the princes of the realm, almost in the style of a general edict, that the queen's word should be law in all matters.[5]

Richard was the first English king to be unmarried at the time of his accession since Henry I in 1100, and this provided another opportunity for him to demonstrate the esteem in which he held his mother. Eleanor played a prominent role at his coronation on 3 September 1189, and Richard later confirmed that not only should she, as queen mother, have the dower lands granted to her by Henry II, but also that she should have all that Henry I and Stephen had granted to their wives.[6]

Following his coronation, the new king immediately moved to award grants and patronage, and to make the arrangements for governance that would be necessary due to what would be a long absence. He also raised a great deal of money to finance his campaign, by various means including seizing the moveable wealth of those who died intestate and selling off offices, titles and lands. Or, as one contemporary put it:

> The king most obligingly unburdened all those whose money was a burden to them ... joking one day with his companions who were standing by, he made this jest: 'If I could have found a buyer I would have sold London itself.'[7]

The remaining members of the reduced royal family were dealt with in different ways. John, now in his early twenties, was the greatest beneficiary:

he was to have six counties in England and the county of Mortain in Normandy, as well as confirmation of his existing title of lord of Ireland. This made him by a long way the wealthiest baron in England – dangerously so, in fact – and these generous grants led many to believe that Richard intended John to be his heir. However, Richard (perhaps taking a leaf from his father's book, now he was the one wearing the crown) did not make any explicit announcement to that effect, and John's hopes were dampened rather than encouraged when Richard obliged him to marry his fiancée of long standing, Isabelle of Gloucester, on 20 August 1189; this prevented John from trying to form an advantageous – and therefore potentially threatening – royal match abroad.

As we noted earlier, the male Plantagenet line was by now looking rather thin, but there were two other candidates who might rival John's position: the toddler Arthur of Brittany, and Henry II's eldest illegitimate son, Geoffrey, now in his mid- to late thirties and with the general respect that came from having stayed loyal to his father to the bitter end. Richard tackled any potential ambitions of Geoffrey's by forcing the canons of York to elect him archbishop of York, and thus obliging him to be ordained as a priest.[8] We may assume, however, that Richard thought any question of naming an heir either temporary or unnecessary; he no doubt intended to survive the forthcoming crusade and to father a son. He certainly intended to get married, as we shall see below.

Richard did not stay in England long after his coronation, crossing the Channel to meet Philip Augustus at Nonancourt, on the Norman–French border, at the end of December 1189, where each swore to act in good faith towards the other and to defend the other's lands as he would his own.[9] As part of the agreement, Richard promised that he would marry the long-suffering Alice; now that his father was dead, there was nothing to stop him. But, tellingly, he did not specify a date.

King Philip was also busy making plans for the governance of France while he was away, and looking forward to an addition to his line of succession. He already had an all-important son, Louis (now two years old), and was in the fortunate position of having a very capable queen, who was pregnant once more and young enough to produce a large family as time went on. Philip may well have compared his situation complacently with Richard's unmarried state when the two met again in March 1190 to discuss the schedule for their departure on crusade, which was set for 24 June; but even as the conference was actually taking place, a messenger arrived to see the French king. He carried shattering news: Queen Isabelle had died in child-birth. Philip was speechless, 'so completely devastated that he was on the verge of deciding to abandon his plans for the pilgrimage'. In a further blow to Philip's dynastic plans, Isabelle had given birth to twin sons, who had both also died.[10]

However distressed Philip was on a personal level – and the instructions he gave for Isabelle's funeral and the care of her immortal soul indicate that he did feel affection for her – he could not cancel his crusade plans. However, the situation in France had now changed drastically, and he drew up a very detailed testament. His son Louis, of course, was to be his heir, guarded and guided in the event of Philip's death 'until he reaches the age when he can, with God's counsel, govern his realm'.[11] In an age of high infant mortality, Philip also addressed the question of what should happen if he and Louis should both die; but, interestingly, relating only to the distribution of his goods and treasures, without mentioning the all-important question of who should be the next king of France. Did he think that his more distant relatives – the remaining Capetian descendants of Louis VI, or perhaps the husbands and sons of his elder sisters – would form an orderly and amicable queue for the crown? This seems unlikely, although we cannot discount the possibility (especially as he was shocked and grieving) that he saw the future only in terms of himself and his son, and would leave France to take its chances if they were both gone. It may be that he was reluctant to name a secondary heir in case that man attempted to supplant the toddler Louis if Philip should die. Or perhaps Philip simply could not bring himself to believe that he would die abroad; his father, after all, had returned safely from his crusade, as had many other French lords. Whatever the case, he would leave his kingdom in the hands of his mother, Adela, and her brother William Whitehands, archbishop of Reims, while he was away; his testament gave very detailed instructions on the nature and extent of the authority that would be theirs in his absence.[12]

Much of this, of course, would have been unnecessary if Isabelle and her twins had survived; leaving the anointed queen and mother of three male heirs in charge of France would have made Philip's life more straightfor-ward at this point. Many of the travails of his later reign would also have been avoided if Isabelle had lived to fulfil her potential; as it was, she was buried in a magnificent tomb in the cathedral of Notre Dame in Paris before she reached her twentieth birthday.

Practical preparations for the crusade proceeded apace, with cash, food and weapons being stockpiled and men and horses assembled. On 24 June 1190, the feast of St John the Baptist, Philip received his pilgrim purse and staff and the *oriflamme* from Saint-Denis.[13] He then travelled to Vézelay (where Bernard of Clairvaux had so eloquently preached the Second Crusade back in 1146) to meet Richard, and they set off in early July. Their way lay together as far as Lyon, and they were keen, perhaps ostentatiously so, to demonstrate their amicable relationship in public: 'They frequently paid their respects to each other with great munificence, showing each other mutual honour and esteem . . . They completed their daily stages with eagerness and joy.'[14] Once the army reached Lyon it divided, not because of any disagreement, but rather for practical purposes: the countryside could not support such a large joint force so it was better to take different routes. Equally, they could not all embark together, so Philip rode for Genoa, where he had hired a fleet, and Richard for Marseille, where his own ships were waiting; the arrangement was that they would rendezvous at Messina in Sicily.

It is not clear exactly when the news reached them, given the distances involved, but both kings were at some point in the summer informed of a tragedy that would have a profound negative effect on the crusade. They were not the only monarchs who had taken the cross; the elderly but still vigorous Emperor Frederick Barbarossa, a veteran of the Second Crusade of forty years before, had also pledged himself to the enterprise. Indeed, given his exalted status, he was seen as the real leader of the crusade, rather than either of the kings. He and his forces had set out much earlier, as long ago as May 1189, taking the time-consuming overland route through Europe and Asia Minor. However, on 10 June 1190 he had drowned while crossing a river in Cilicia. He had left his eldest son and heir, Henry, in charge of the Empire, so the German army was continuing on its way under the command of his inexperienced second son, Frederick, duke of Swabia.[15]

Philip was the first of the two kings to land in Messina. Richard arrived a week later and – as would become a pattern – with a great deal more pomp: 'People of all ages, a crowd beyond number, came to meet the king [Richard], marvelling and declaring how much more gloriously and impressively this king landed than did the king of France.'[16] Sicily was at this time in a state of some instability: King William II (the husband of Richard's sister Joanna) had died in November 1189, and because he had no children, there was a tussle for the crown. The claimants were William's official heir, his paternal aunt Constance – who was married to Henry of Hohenstaufen, Frederick Barbarossa's eldest son and heir (and now Henry VI, king of Germany and emperor-elect, following his father's death) – and Tancred of Lecce, an illegitimate cousin of the late William. The widowed Joanna was caught in the middle, and at the time of the kings' arrival she was being held captive by Tancred, a situation Richard could not ignore. As soon as he set foot in Sicily he became embroiled in armed conflict – a conflict in which Philip declined to become involved, thus introducing (or increasing) the bad blood between them. Tancred was no match for Richard, and he soon came to terms.[17]

One of the clauses of the negotiated agreement was that one of Tancred's infant daughters would marry the three-year-old Arthur, 'the excellent duke of Brittany, our nephew, and, if we shall chance to die without issue, *our heir*'.[18] These two words were of huge import: what Richard was apparently promising Tancred was that, in return for Joanna's freedom and dower estates, and his support for the crusade, Tancred would one day see his grandson on the throne of England. As it happened the match never took place, but Richard was in any case playing a double or even triple game. He had succeeded in his immediate aim on Sicily, but he may have named Arthur as his heir only as a ploy to keep his brother John in check (we will hear more of John's activities during Richard's absence in the next chapter); and it was now certain that he intended to marry and father legitimate heirs of his own.

It was at this point, finally, that Richard had to break the news to Philip that he had no intention of marrying Alice. The ostensible reason, and one that he spoke about unabashedly, was that during the many years of her residence in the household of Henry II, the old king had seduced her, and had even fathered a short-lived bastard son. However, this is probably a convenient fiction put about in order to give Richard a solid reason for refusing the marriage that did not make him look like a faithless oath-breaker.[19] Philip could not force Richard to marry Alice, so instead of arguing fruitlessly he accepted the fact and set himself to getting the best advantage out of the deal. There was, of course, a discussion about the future of the

Vexin, and the agreement drawn up between the two kings at Messina in early 1191 was that it would belong to Richard and his male descendants, but that if he died without a legitimate son, it would revert to Philip. If Philip, in turn, died without a legitimate son, then the Vexin would be considered part of Normandy.[20] Alice's personal fate also had to be considered, and she would be returned to France as soon as the arrangements could be made (which was, as it turned out, not for several years and after a great deal of wrangling). She was by now thirty, having been betrothed to Richard since she was nine, and – given the male-centric nature of the records and chronicles of the time – there is unfortunately no record at all of what she, personally, thought of all this. We can have no idea of whether she still, after all these years, harboured thoughts of marrying Richard and becoming queen, or whether she was simply relieved and pleased that her long years of uncertainty were over, that her life was no longer on hold. Her story did later take something of a more positive turn: as the sister of a king, her value on the marriage market had not quite expired, and in 1195, at the age of thirty-five, she would be married to the teenage William Talvas, count of Ponthieu, going on to bear him two children and to live peacefully for another twenty years.

This was all in the future, but what now became clear to Philip was that Richard had been planning to break off his betrothal to Alice for much longer than he claimed, for he had been in negotiation for some time with Sancho VI of Navarre on the subject of an alliance via a marriage with Sancho's daughter Berengaria. The Spanish kingdom of Navarre might seem an unlikely ally for a king of England, but Richard had inherited all of his father's titles, and was thus still also duke of Aquitaine – in association with his mother – following his refusal to cede that title to John. It was therefore of the utmost importance that his southern borders should be protected, and an alliance with Sancho VI 'the Wise' (and his son, the future Sancho VII 'the Strong', who would shortly succeed him) would be the best way to achieve this.[21] That these negotiations had been under way for quite some time was evidenced by the fact that Berengaria was actually already on her way to Messina, accompanied by none other than Eleanor of Aquitaine.

Richard and Philip both spent the winter of 1190–91 at Messina, sharing a Christmas feast at which we might imagine that the conversation was not terribly amicable. The demands of the crusade notwithstanding, Richard remained in Sicily with his increasingly bored troops until such time as his bride should appear. Eleanor and Berengaria arrived in March 1191, to be welcomed by Richard, but not by Philip; the French king had already left, ostensibly to get on with the crusade, but also in some humiliation and not wanting to face either his rival's bride or his father's first wife, triumphant along with her son.[22]

* * *

Philip Augustus arrived at Acre on 20 April 1191.[23] The sight that met him as he disembarked would have been one of a sizeable and busy encampment around the city walls – an encampment that was packed with troops and non-combatants, lacking in adequate provisions and sanitation, and susceptible to disease. Food was scarce: 'The best meat that the people of the host could eat was horse meat or the meat of mules and donkeys ... when the poor people could find a dead animal they ate it as a great dainty.'[24] Two epidemics had already swept through the siege camp in October 1190 and January 1191, meaning that more crusaders may have died of disease than in combat. The camp had become semi-permanent, for the Latin forces had been investing Acre since August 1189, under the initial ineffectual command of King Guy and then the more competent leadership of Henry II of Champagne, to whom Guy seems to have ceded control of military operations after Henry's arrival in 1190. The progress of the siege had been slow, hampered as it was by a lack of men, by illness, by the excellent defence mounted by the Acre garrison and also by the ever-present threat of a Muslim relief army camped in the surrounding hills that made periodic attacks on the crusaders, even as they launched their own assaults on the city and its garrison. The result was a hellish, violent stalemate that was desperately in need of fresh impetus.

Among those ready to greet Philip on his arrival was a sizeable contingent of French lords who had travelled separately from their king and made better time. They included some of Philip's kinsmen: his nephew Henry II of Champagne, as we have just noted; his maternal uncle Stephen of Sancerre; and his paternal cousins, the brothers Count Robert II of Dreux (who had inherited the title following the death of his father, Robert I, in 1188) and Philip, bishop of Beauvais ('a man more devoted to battles than books').[25] The presence of so many high-ranking noblemen had both advantages and disadvantages for Philip and for France. On the one hand, it meant that many estates back home were in the hands of inexperienced heirs or regents; but on the other, there could be no credible threat to Philip's rule, or the potential rule of his young son, from those left behind, for the contenders were all in Outremer, where he could keep an eye on them. Robert of Dreux, as the eldest son of Louis VII's second brother, could class himself as the next heir in the male Capetian line, while Henry of Champagne, as the eldest son of King Philip's eldest sister, was also a plausible candidate.

Also present at Acre was Count Philip of Flanders, by now an experienced crusader who had once defeated Saladin himself at Montgisard, and a man who was related to the royal house of Jerusalem, as his mother, Sybil of Anjou, had been the half-sister of kings Baldwin III and Amalric I. One notable missing face was that of the man who was both Philip's uncle and his brother-in-law, Theobald V of Blois; he had arrived at Acre the previous summer, but had died there in January 1191, meaning that his only surviving son, who was with him in Outremer, became Louis I, count of Blois.[26]

The crusading groups from other countries were by now also patchy. The remnants of the German army (some 700 men out of an initial force of 18,000) had arrived the previous autumn after their overland trek, but they were not in the best state: already demoralised by the death of Frederick Barbarossa, they had suffered many more losses in the January outbreak of disease, including Frederick, duke of Swabia, Barbarossa's son. What was left of their army was now commanded by Leopold V, duke of Austria, who would go on to play a major part in Philip's later antagonistic relationship with King Richard. Richard himself would not arrive until 7 June, some seven weeks after Philip, having delayed in Messina and then been diverted by pressing concerns in Cyprus.[27]

Philip's first task upon his arrival was to get to grips with the political situation in the Latin kingdom of Jerusalem. Queen Sybil and both her young daughters were by this time dead, having been carried off by the epidemic of sickness in October 1190.[28] Her widower, King Guy, had only held the throne in her right, so legally Sybil's heir was her sister Isabella, the last remaining child of Amalric I. One faction proclaimed Isabella queen, and she was forced to divorce her husband (who was not considered suitable kingly material) and marry the battle-hardened Conrad of Montferrat, whom we last saw defending the walls of Tyre and claiming that he had a right of his own to the crown as the uncle of little Baldwin V. However, Guy de Lusignan refused to relinquish the throne.

As a reigning king and *rex christianissimus*, Philip Augustus was recognised as a senior figure in the host, even its natural leader, and his opinion on the matter would carry a great deal of weight. His inclination was towards Conrad, who was both a better military commander than Guy and a distant relative of his own, and their burgeoning friendship had a positive effect on the siege. Guy, as we have noted, had been at Acre for some time, but without being able to compel the city to surrender; once Philip and Conrad jointly brought their forces to bear and provided fresh momentum, hope began to spread through the camp at last that there might be a successful conclusion to the seemingly never-ending engagement.

If this was to be the case, immediate action was necessary. Philip began his preparations; he rode around the city to assess its strengths and weaknesses, and had siege machinery built. This was a complex task in the late twelfth century, requiring specialist engineers who were as much an integral part of an army as knights or footsoldiers. Such machinery could take the form of battering implements (rams, picks and so on), structures that enabled combatants to engage in hand-to-hand fighting (ladders or siege towers, sometimes several storeys high and protected against attack) and projectile weapons. These last are sometimes difficult to define precisely, as medieval chroniclers – who tended to be clerics, rather than soldiers, and thus not experts – were often confused about terminology and used words such as ballista, petrary, mangonel and trebuchet indiscriminately. What seems clear from the context of the surviving descriptions of the siege of Acre is that Philip's machines were stone-throwing devices; but whether they worked by traction, torsion or counterweight is uncertain.[29]

In addition to the construction of machinery, Philip's men also began to fill in the moat around the city and to dig under it, in order to offer more potential avenues for assault. However, he had promised Richard that he would await his arrival before he made a direct attack, and at this point he had no idea when the English king was going to arrive. Impatient at Richard's increasing delay and irritated by the way in which he was seemingly prioritising his own affairs in Cyprus over those of Christendom, Philip sent his cousin the bishop of Beauvais to hurry him along, accusing Richard of 'arrogantly persecuting innocent Christians when close by there were still so many thousands of Saracens whom he should be attacking'. This abrasive approach was unsuccessful, Richard's reply being apparently unprintable: 'Such things were said as should not be written down', says the chronicler who was in his host, primly.[30] Richard was also, while on Cyprus, in personal negotiations with Guy de Lusignan, who had travelled there to seek his support in the dispute over the crown of Jerusalem – support Richard was inclined to give, partly as the Lusignans were a family from Richard's county of Poitou, and partly no doubt because he knew that Philip favoured Conrad.[31]

Richard's belated arrival at Acre only served to provoke Philip further. The fault for the total breakdown in their relationship that would ensue lies probably with both, but it would seem that very few contemporary chroniclers could take a balanced view: their depictions of the events at Acre became ever more entrenched as either pro-Richard and anti-Philip or vice versa, meaning that they could portray the same incidents in markedly different ways. One English commentator, for example, put the split down to Philip's jealousy at being overshadowed by Richard:

The king of the French had arrived at Acre before Richard and was much thought of by the natives, but when Richard came the king of the French was extinguished and made nameless, even as the moon loses its light at sunrise.

French writers, meanwhile, were convinced that Philip almost took the city before Richard even arrived, and that Richard played him false: 'The king of France could easily have taken the city had he wished. But he was awaiting the arrival of King Richard of England because they had travelled together and had made an agreement.'[32]

Richard did not help matters when he immediately offered men more money to serve him than Philip could afford. The French king was paying three gold bezants a month – considered generous – but Richard, his coffers full from the spoils of Sicily and Cyprus, offered four and managed to poach a number of individuals, as well as virtually all the Pisans.[33] However, he seemed still in no hurry to attack, instead sending envoys to Saladin suggesting that they should meet; he then fell ill, and Philip finally decided that the time had come to go ahead without him. The French host launched a concerted attack on 3 July, coming close to taking the city without Richard's help at all (which would have changed the course of future crusading narratives quite considerably). But each minor success against the walls of Acre was met with an attack from the encircling relief army, thus distracting the crusaders long enough for the city garrison to repair the damage.

Relations between the kings deteriorated further, each seemingly as keen to antagonise the other as he was to take the city. At one point, a French source tells us, Richard launched an attack at a time when Philip had offered safe conduct to a number of Muslim envoys, thus embarrassing and discrediting the French king and eliciting an extreme reaction:

> The king [Philip] was so angry that he even ordered his men to arm themselves to go and attack the king of England. He had already put on his own leg armour when the wise men in the host intervened and calmed him down.[34]

Then Philip fell ill himself. He contracted a disease known to contemporaries as *arnoldia*, which involved some very unpleasant symptoms: he suffered from a high fever, his hair and his nails fell out, and his skin peeled off in strips.[35] To compound his misery, it was while Philip was on his sickbed that he received the news that his only son and heir, Louis, was suffering with dysentery and was near death in Paris. And it was at this point that Richard may or may not have played a particularly nasty trick:

> King Richard conceived a great crime whereby he would kill the king of France without touching him ... While the king of France was lying ill, King Richard went to call on him. As soon as he arrived he enquired after his illness and how he was. The king replied that he was at God's mercy and felt himself severely afflicted by his illness. Then King Richard said to him, 'As for Louis your son, how are you to be comforted?' The king of France asked him, 'What about Louis my son that I should be comforted?' 'It is for this', said the king of England, 'that I have come to comfort you, for he is dead.'[36]

The intent was presumably to cause Philip, in his weakened state, to die from the shock; and while it is far from certain that either this anecdote or the one quoted above about Philip sending his men to attack Richard are true records of events, they do show the sort of behaviour of which commentators thought the kings capable.

While he lay on his sickbed, Philip was still able to plan. In later years, as we shall see, he would be a noted proponent of siege warfare and breaker of castles, and it would appear that he used his time at Acre to hone these skills. He 'concentrated on constructing siege machines and placing stone-throwers in suitable places', arranging for them to loose their missiles 'continually, day and night'; he 'constructed with great determination an implement which would climb up the wall . . . called a "cat" because it clung like a cat to the wall as it crept up to seize it'.[37]

The impetus provided by the English and French armies, and their associated great influx of fresh troops, outnumbering the exhausted and permanently on-duty garrison, had a positive effect on the progress of the siege. After the French attack the city offered to surrender on terms; but Richard, scenting a more complete victory, initially refused – as did Saladin, to whom the besieged had appealed for help. However, when the French engines brought down more of the city wall and shook the 'Accursed Tower', and further mining caused it to collapse, the inhabitants surrendered on 12 July, even though they did not have Saladin's permission to do so. As was the accepted procedure for a city that had surrendered (rather than being taken by storm), they were promised their lives on the payment of a large ransom, plus the return of the fragment of the True Cross that had been captured at Hattin and the release of prisoners.[38]

The crusaders entered the city and flew their banners from the walls: those of the English, French and German contingents hung alongside that of the Latin kingdom of Jerusalem as a sign of victory. But the German banner was not the emperor's; it was that of Leopold of Austria, who had inherited command of the army following the deaths of Frederick Barbarossa and his son. Richard was unable to countenance the banner of a mere duke flying beside his own, though his exact reasoning is unclear: perhaps it was due to status, or because Leopold had only recently arrived and not put as much effort into the siege as he had, or perhaps he was merely annoyed that Leopold had managed to find better accommodation in Acre than he had. In any case, Richard ordered the banner taken down, and then added an unnecessarily petty gesture: 'The duke's banner was cast into the dirt and trampled upon as an insult to him.' Leopold, 'full of wrath', left Acre and sailed home.[39]

On 28 July a settlement was reached over the division of spoils from Acre, but there was still 'an enormous disagreement' between the two kings over the question of the crown of Jerusalem, Philip and most of the other crusaders preferring Conrad, but Richard persisting in his support for Guy.[40] Richard successfully pressed for the sort of uncomfortable compromise that suited nobody, by which Guy would retain the crown for the rest of his life, but on his death it would pass to Conrad. In the meantime, Guy would hold the south of the kingdom while Conrad would have the north.

None of this did anything for the personal relationship between Richard and Philip, with the latter showing his irritation by making a claim – which might be considered both optimistic and provocative – for half of Cyprus, given that Richard had conquered it while supposedly on the crusade, and that they had previously made a pact to share their crusade conquests equally. Richard, not surprisingly, declined.

Whether or not this was the actual last straw, it was at this point that Philip decided to leave Outremer and return home. Naturally, the chroniclers from both sides interpreted the reasons for this in different ways. The pro-Richard Anglo-Norman writer Ambroise exclaims 'God's mercy! What a turnabout!', and implies that the French king was the subject of gossip: 'He was going back because of his illness, *so the king said, whatever is said about him.*' However, the French chronicler Rigord emphasises Philip's illness and says that he had 'violent suspicions' about Richard's private negotiations with Saladin.[41]

Philip left Acre on 31 July 1191, travelling via Crete and Rome and meeting Pope Celestine III and Emperor Henry VI, to both of whom he complained about Richard's behaviour. He then crossed the Alps and returned to France overland, reaching Paris on 27 December 1191 to be reunited with his four-year-old son, who had miraculously thrown off his dangerous illness – one that killed many young children – and survived.[42] Philip himself bore the traces of his own sickness, being now permanently bald and prone to a paranoia that would be lifelong. He also harboured an implacable personal antipathy towards Richard, which would manifest itself in the years to come.

Before departing Outremer, Philip had entrusted command of the French forces to Hugh III, duke of Burgundy, along with 5,000 marks in cash and his allotted share of prisoner ransom money, which would ensure that the army continued to be paid. He had not been accompanied on his return voyage by any of the great lords who were his kinsmen, whose fates were varied. Henry II of Champagne remained in the Holy Land, and – as nephew to both Philip and Richard – was eventually seen as a good compromise candidate for the kingship of Jerusalem; following the assassination of Conrad of Montferrat in April 1192, he was immediately married to the widowed (and pregnant) Queen Isabella.[43] Philip's cousins Robert II of Dreux and Philip, bishop of Beauvais, both stayed in Outremer for the present, though they would later return safely to France, as we shall see. The king's uncles Theobald V of Blois and Stephen of Sancerre were both dead, as was Count Philip of Flanders, who had succumbed to illness at Acre on 1 June 1191. This may well have been a factor in Philip Augustus choosing to return to France in order to exploit opportunities in Flanders, Vermandois and Artois, this last involving a title he could still claim as part of his queen's dowry, even though she had died; we may also add that finding a new queen, so that he could father more sons to secure the succession, would have been a priority. The deaths of so many heads of houses – the counts of Vendôme, Clermont and Perche in addition to those named above, and shortly to be joined by the duke of Burgundy himself while still in the Holy Land – would cause instability in France, which would thus benefit from having its king back.[44]

Philip and Richard's supposedly joint crusading venture had succeeded in some of its military aims; but in terms of the relationship between them, and between the ruling houses of England and France for years to come, it was a disaster. One chronicler sums up the events of the crusade quite neatly:

> In every affair in which the said kings [Richard and Philip] and their people had united, they were less successful than they would have been if they had acted separately, for the king of France and his men looked contemptuously on the king of England and his people, while he and his people did the same to the others.[45]

* * *

Richard remained in the Holy Land for another fifteen months after Philip's departure, during which time he recorded victories over Saladin at Arsuf and Jaffa, but also carried out a horrific massacre of 2,700 prisoners-of-war from Acre, offered his sister Joanna as bride for Saladin's brother, and never reached Jerusalem.[46] On hearing disturbing rumours about his brother John's actions in England he decided to return to his kingdom, sailing from Acre on 9 October 1192. We might choose to interpret his decision to leave Outremer with the crusade's aims unfulfilled, in order to attend to matters in his own realm, as being very similar to Philip's; but because Richard benefited from better PR and more obsequious chroniclers, he has not had opprobrium heaped on him in the same way, either at the time or since. We might even choose to go further, noting (perhaps controversially) that although Richard received most of the plaudits for the Third Crusade, the only major success of the expedition – the fall of Acre – happened while Philip was there.[47]

Richard's journey first took him via ship to Corfu, but then he had to consider his route carefully, due to the long list of rulers he had managed to antagonise. He could not sail for France and then ride through Aquitaine or Provence, as Philip would be informed of his arrival as soon as he got there. Germany was equally out of the question, if he did not want to run the risk of capture by Emperor Henry (who was offended by Richard's support in Sicily for Tancred, against Henry's wife Constance, William II's original designated heir). North-western Italy was dominated by the Montferrat family, now enemies of Richard after he was rumoured to have had a hand in the assassination of Conrad. When Richard did embark again from Corfu, it is possible that he was intending to go through the lands of the king of Hungary (risky, as Béla III was Philip Augustus's brother-in-law) in order to reach those of Henry the Lion, widower of Richard's sister Matilda, but he was blown off course and ended up landing between Aquileia and Venice in north-east Italy. He then rode through Carinthia with only a small retinue, uncharacteristically trying not to draw attention to himself; but when he reached Vienna, on 20 December 1192, he was recognised and arrested by men loyal to the still-enraged Leopold V of Austria. Leopold had him taken to the castle of Dürnstein and informed Emperor Henry, who (after some haggling) paid him a fee to transfer Richard to his own custody; the emperor then wrote to King Philip, confident that the news 'will afford most abundant joy to your own feelings'.[48]

It would be no surprise if Philip were to have felt 'abundant joy', and he no doubt hoped that his fellow king's imprisonment would be a long one. This would give him the chance to cause lasting harm to Richard and his dynasty, initially by allying himself with the only other surviving Plantagenet brother, John.

≈ CHAPTER ELEVEN ≈

'THE DEVIL IS LOOSE'

JOHN HAD BEEN BUSY WHILE his brother was overseas. A suspicious Richard had initially obliged him to swear an oath that he would not set foot in England for three years from the date of Richard's departure, but – with the lobbying of their mother – he had been persuaded to release John from this promise even before he left. John was thus able to take full possession of his counties and their revenues, to play a part in the governance of the realm in the absence of its king – and to concern himself with the question of who would be the *next* king, and how soon that accession might come about. Richard was childless and crusades were dangerous.

England was accustomed to having a king who was not a permanent resident; Henry II had spent much of his time in his continental domains. However, these were relatively close by – a messenger from England would be able to reach him in a matter of weeks, and he would be expected to flit back and forth across the Channel with at least some regularity. Richard's going on crusade was completely different. The distances involved and the nature of the expedition would stretch message time from weeks to months, and his expected absence from months to years. This was unprecedented, and there was a sense of unease in England: 'As the earth shudders at the absence of the sun, so the face of the realm was altered at the king's departure ... Castles were strengthened; towns were fortified; and moats were dug.'[1]

John threw himself willingly into this power vacuum. Conscious that – as had been the case several times previously in England – a vacant crown was likely to fall into the hands of the man nearest and quickest to seize it, regardless of any official designation as heir, he travelled around the country with an armed retinue, letting himself be seen as a representative of the royal family and letting his supporters refer to him openly as the heir to the throne. There was no one with sufficient authority to stop him: he was the pre-eminent baron of the realm, and the archbishop of Canterbury and the queen mother were both absent, the former on his way to the Holy Land with Richard, and the latter on her round trip to collect Berengaria and take her to Sicily. John, therefore, was free to set up what was, in effect, a rival administration, with his own justiciar and chancellor.[2]

By the end of 1191 King Philip was back in France; and by the spring of 1192 John was openly spreading rumours that Richard would never return. In the late summer or autumn of that year John's whispering campaign against his brother received a morale boost from an unlikely source: Philip, the bishop of Beauvais. Most of the remaining French contingent in the Holy Land left for home in the summer of 1192, the bishop among them, and:

> When he landed in Germany, at every stage of his journey he spread the word amongst the people that that traitor, the king of England, from the very day of his arrival in Judea, had arranged to betray his lord, the king of the French, to Saladin; that he had had the marquis's [Conrad of Montferrat's] throat cut so that he might seize Tyre; that he had made away with the duke of Burgundy by poison; that at the end he had sold the whole army of Christians who did not submit to him; that he was an extremely savage man, iron-hearted and unlovable in his ways, skilful in wiles and most skilful in dissimulation.[3]

Moreover, when he got back to France the bishop 'secretly whispered in his king's ear that the king of England was sending assassins to France to kill him'. This, of course, only added to Philip's existing paranoia, brought about by some mental aspect of his serious illness, and he set bodyguards to watch over himself night and day.[4] Philip then made further overtures to John, which were eagerly accepted. The French king had already made the perhaps overly hopeful offer that John (his own wife Isabelle of Gloucester notwithstanding) should marry the cast-off Alice and be rewarded with recognition of his rights to all of the lands Richard held from the French king; but John was not keen – and anyway, his now-returned mother pointed out to him the folly and possible repercussions of such action.[5]

And then came the news that was everything that John and Philip could have wished and prayed for: Richard had been captured, and was now in the custody of Emperor Henry VI. 'His mother was distressed when she heard this, but it did not grieve his brother,' says one commentator, with admirable understatement.[6] It was far from certain that Richard would ever be released, and Philip and John certainly hoped this would be the case. Indeed, Philip sent a delegation to the emperor headed by none other than the bishop of Beauvais, who advocated against setting Richard free (which Henry was not about to do) and asked about the possibility of selling his custody to King Philip (which Henry was not about to do either). The emperor set an enormous ransom fee of 150,000 marks – £100,000 sterling or 100,000 lbs of silver – two or three times the total annual revenue of England, moved Richard to the remote castle of Trifels in the mountainous south-west of Germany, and that seemed to be that.

John rushed across the Channel in January 1193, first to Normandy and then to Paris, where he performed a somewhat pre-emptive homage to Philip for the lands in France that he felt sure would now come to him, and declared himself willing to put aside his wife and marry Alice.[7] Frustratingly, we are once again uninformed about her feelings on the matter. Richard's imprisonment and John's reaction to it show the extent of his ambitions: it was now that his thoughts could move from the prospect of *succeeding* Richard to the idea of *replacing* him. It seems almost bewildering that John should ally himself with Philip in this way, falling for exactly the same trick that the French king had played on all his older brothers one after the other, but perhaps he was blinded by his own greed and ambition.[8] Philip, meanwhile, had dealt with the Flanders inheritance and taken control of Artois. This made him overlord of the coastal counties of Guînes and Boulogne, and thus in a position to threaten a seaborne invasion of England; he began to assemble a fleet at Wissant in the county of Boulogne. The count at this time was Renaud de Dammartin, who had kidnapped and forcibly married Ida of Boulogne, who was countess in her own right. She was the daughter of Matthew of Alsace (who had been killed at the siege of Drincourt in 1173, as we saw in Chapter 7) and Mary of Blois, daughter of King Stephen.[9]

But everyone had discounted the determination of one person: Eleanor of Aquitaine. Now in her seventies, she was still far from retiring and would certainly spare no effort where her favourite son was concerned. She organised defences against the potential invasion threat of Philip (which he was undertaking with Danish support, of which more in a moment), and such was her authority that one chronicler referred to her as 'Queen Eleanor, who at that time ruled England'.[10] She found an ally in the new archbishop of Canterbury, Hubert Walter, who arrived in England at Easter 1193 with instructions from Richard to ensure that the ransom was raised, and as quickly as possible. Eleanor immediately levied a 25 per cent tax on income and on moveable property, confiscated the entire year's wool crop from the Cistercian order of monks and 'borrowed' gold and silver plate until 'there was not a single chalice or censer left in any church in England'.[11] She harried the nobles for donations, perhaps pointing out to them that in Richard's letter he had requested to know how much each individual contributed, 'so that we may know how far we are bound to return thanks to each'. She also wrote letters to Pope Celestine III, detailing her anguish and urging him to act.[12]

Philip, meanwhile, having temporarily shelved his plans for an invasion of England, launched attacks into Normandy. Richard's status as a crusader was supposed to protect his lands in his absence, but the fact that he had been captured while on his way home – that is, with his crusade completed – meant that Philip could use the letter, if perhaps not the spirit, of the law to move against him now. His troops captured the perennial thorn in Norman–French relations, Gisors castle, and then moved to lay siege to the city of Rouen.[13] He enjoyed less success in Aquitaine, thanks to Richard's marriage alliance; Philip managed to stir up a minor rebellion, but this was quelled when Queen Berengaria's brother Sancho the Strong arrived in the region with a large force of knights.[14]

It would seem that John was now prepared to take a large gamble – a trait that will reappear later on, as we shall see – in order to cement his position. A letter patent of January 1194 proclaimed that he had made an agreement with Philip: in return for the French king's recognition of his rights, he gave to Philip 'Normandy on the French side of the river Seine to the English Channel, except the city of Rouen itself and two leagues around', as well as various other pivotal strongholds not only in Normandy, but also in

Maine, Touraine and Anjou; he was to hold his continental lands as Philip's vassal.[15] The timing of such a public declaration of John's intent was spectacularly bad, as Richard was released from captivity on 4 February. Philip received the news first and sent a message to John 'that he must take care of himself, for the devil was now let loose'.[16]

* * *

By this time Philip also had other problems. The question of the French succession had been pressing since Queen Isabelle's death in 1190, and he needed to marry again. He had been able to leave it this long as the situation was not desperate, for he already had a son and heir, the five-year-old Louis, who was thriving; but healthy young children could turn into sick and dead children with frightening rapidity, and it was too dangerous to invest the whole future of the dynasty in just the one son, especially when Philip was single and still only in his late twenties. Besides, a marriage would provide him not only with a queen, but also with a useful political alliance. In early 1193 – and thus during Richard's period of captivity – he found a lady who appeared to be the ideal candidate: Ingeborg, the sister of King Cnut VI of Denmark. Politically, Denmark had a vestigial claim to the English crown (from the line of Cnut the Great, who had been king of both realms in the eleventh century), which might be of use in Philip's ongoing conflict with the current English royal house; and it also had a fleet. Personally, Ingeborg was around eighteen and reputed to be a great beauty, as well as one of the most pious royal women in Europe.[17] She had a distant connection to French territories, as her grandfather had been the first cousin of Charles the Good, count of Flanders from 1119 until his assassination in 1127.

The arrangements were made and Ingeborg arrived, along with her Danish retinue, in August 1193. She was as beautiful as the reports had promised; Philip had not been duped. She, on beholding the prematurely aged man some decade her senior, may have been less impressed, but that was the price of becoming queen of France – and, besides, she had no choice in the matter anyway. The wedding took place on 14 August, the bride and groom having met each other for the first time earlier that same day and having no common language except some Latin. The young couple were crowned by Philip's uncle William, archbishop of Reims, and all seemed to be proceeding according to plan.

But then, in a development which has baffled commentators both at the time and since, on the morning after the wedding night Philip announced that he was repudiating Ingeborg; he sent her away to a convent, refused to see her again and declared his intention to seek an annulment.[18] Many reasons for this abrupt decision – some more plausible than others – have been put forward over the years, from Philip discovering that Ingeborg had bad breath to her being *so* pious and beautiful that he was rendered temporarily impotent. The latter should perhaps be given some credence, given that Philip would later self-incriminatingly state that the marriage had not been consummated. Whatever the precise cause, the reasons for this extraordinary event certainly seem to be personal, rather than diplomatic: the relative situations of France and Denmark had not changed overnight.

However, if Philip thought that he could rid himself of his new wife with ease, he was very much mistaken, and he had very much underestimated Ingeborg's strength of character. In the initial rush to action it seemed that he would be successful, and he began with the standard excuse: at a hearing on 5 November 1193 he claimed that he and Ingeborg were related within the prohibited degree, as Ingeborg was related within the fourth degree to Philip's first wife, Isabelle of Hainaut. The ten-man council (handily composed of eight lords and bishops who were related to the king and another two who were members of his household) declared on the basis of this that Philip and his queen could separate.

Ingeborg, meanwhile, had no representation at this council, and was more or less a prisoner: she was confined in a convent, unable to speak French and denied contact with any of her fellow countrymen. However, she could not accept a dismissal on such terms. To be sent packing, back to her brother, labelled in some obscure way as damaged goods, would be humiliating and would certainly impair her prospects of making another match. Moreover, she was now the crowned queen of France, as well as Philip's legal wife – the laws of God and man had joined them together. Her first reaction to being denied a voice in France was to go over the king's head, and she appealed directly to the pope, Celestine III, in a series of letters, as did her brother Cnut. Unfortunately for her Celestine reacted slowly, and it would be several years before he sent two papal legates to France to investigate the situation. But Ingeborg never gave up, never wavered, and we shall hear more of her as we go on.[19]

* * *

This, then, was Philip's personal situation at the time he heard of Richard's release from captivity early in 1194. Moreover, he knew that Richard was aware of his alliance with John, as the emperor had, for political purposes of his own, most obligingly kept his captive informed and showed him their letters encouraging a lengthy incarceration. Exactly how Richard would react now that he was free remained to be seen, though a great deal of ill feeling and an escalation in hostilities could probably be expected.[20]

Richard arrived back in England alongside a triumphant Eleanor (who had taken the ransom to Germany personally) on 13 March 1194. He was not, however, accompanied by Queen Berengaria – the only queen of England, before or since, never to have set foot in the kingdom during her tenure – in whom he seems to have had less and less interest. This was not the almost visceral antipathy that Philip had shown to Ingeborg, but rather a simple indifference which remains puzzling on several counts. The Navarrese alliance had served Richard well, so it would seem odd to jeopardise good relations by neglecting Berengaria. Richard was now thirty-six, and the question of a son and heir must surely have been on his mind; but there was no chance of producing one while his queen remained on the opposite side of the Channel. Perhaps he thought her barren; if so, this seems harsh, given the very small amount of time they had spent together during their marriage so far, and he made no announcement about putting her aside or seeking another wife. He simply ignored her. As far as can be ascertained, he did not see her again until April 1195, when they met at Le Mans, and she would also spend Christmas that year at his court in Poitiers. She was still only thirty at that point, so hopes of an heir can surely not have been despaired of; but there is no recorded meeting at all after this time.[21] As is often the case with medieval women, we have absolutely no information on Berengaria's own views of her situation. There has, of course, been much debate over the years on the question of Richard's sexuality, some of it based on misreadings or misunderstandings of the comments of chroniclers; but he had, in the past, gained an unsavoury reputation for attacking the wives and daughters of his Aquitainian nobles, and he was the father of at least one illegitimate son, so this can surely not be the crucial factor in his apathy towards Berengaria.[22]

Upon his arrival in England, Richard wasted no time in reimposing his authority. John (then in France) was summoned to face trial for his actions during Richard's absence, his lands to be forfeit if he did not appear; yet he failed to arrive. Others were not so daring or so foolhardy: as soon as the king's identity was verified, those castles held against him surrendered, and the castellan of St Michael's Mount allegedly died of fright when he heard who was approaching.[23] So swift was Richard's reassumption of power that he was able to take ship for Normandy by early May, confident that England would remain at peace during his new absence. Once there he met John in person and, despite the latter's non-appearance in England and the supposed penalty of forfeiture of his estates, Richard forgave him anyway, because he was his brother and merely 'a child'. John was twenty-seven.[24]

Once the touching family reunion was out of the way Richard set about regaining the lands in Normandy that had been lost to Philip during his captivity. Philip now held much of Normandy east of the River Seine, and his position in the north of France had been strengthened by his acquisition of Artois; the lands under his control now reached perilously close to Rouen.[25] In May 1194, prior to Richard's arrival, he was still seeking to press his advantage and was besieging Verneuil; but Richard now made his move, first sending a force to break through Philip's lines to reinforce the garrison, and then leading his main army up behind the French to cut off their supply lines.[26] On 29 May Philip was forced to retreat: the first step backwards for some time in his long-term campaign against the Plantagenets, and perhaps a sign of things to come. He did not go quietly, however, moving on to Évreux (held by John, who, since the reconciliation, was doing so in Richard's name rather than Philip's) and capturing a castle that was no more than 5 miles from Rouen. He proposed a three-year truce with Richard, but they could not agree terms, as Richard did not see that those who had turned against him should be left in peace.[27]

Richard then turned south to Touraine and Aquitaine, where his brother-in-law Sancho the Strong had been fighting on his behalf (thus making Richard's overt neglect of Berengaria even more inexplicable), but had subsequently been forced to return home following the news that his father was on his deathbed. Sancho VI would die on 27 June, meaning that the younger man ascended the Navarrese throne as Sancho VII and would be busy with matters there for the foreseeable future; Richard would have to fight his own battles.

Philip also marched south, thus making an armed engagement more likely, and an encounter of sorts took place at Fréteval in Touraine on 4 July 1194. It is sometimes called 'the Battle of Fréteval', but in reality it was no more than a skirmish. Philip was encamped there, in the valley of the Loire, when Richard moved in front of him to block his route. Philip declared – either as a ruse or through misplaced bravado – that he would attack the next day, and Richard replied with equal swagger: 'The king of England joyously receiving his message, sent word back to him that he would wait for him, and, if he should not come, would pay him a visit on the following morning.'[28]

Rather than advancing, however, Philip turned to retreat up the valley. Richard set off in pursuit but only managed to catch the rear of the French forces, including the slow-moving baggage train. The available sources that describe what happened next are, naturally, split along partisan lines, with the French chroniclers playing it down and the English ones maximising the engagement; but whatever the exact nature and number of the casualties, the outcome was a loss of face and money for Philip. Like all kings of this period, he carried with him when he travelled not only his household goods but also the apparatus of governance, and among his losses were treasure, his own seal (a great propaganda coup for Richard) and a list of those of Richard's subjects who had defected or been minded to defect to Philip while the English king was in captivity. Philip himself was not captured; he was towards the front of his forces and had stopped in a local church to attend Mass, meaning that the pursuit either did not find him or went straight past. Such chases, incidentally, could be risky: there was always the danger that the force being hunted might stop and regroup while the chasers were scattered. Richard, therefore, commended William Marshal for obeying orders and having the presence of mind to remain in place with a reserve force, instead of joining in a headlong pursuit which could have become chaotic and dangerous.[29]

The forces of the two kings then went their separate ways: Richard southwards and Philip northwards, where he took John by surprise at Vaudreuil, on the border of the Vexin; having ceded it to Philip earlier in the year, John was now besieging it. Philip scored a quick success, forcing John to flee and capturing his siege machinery.[30]

A truce was announced in July 1195, but it fell through when Philip discovered that Emperor Henry was encouraging Richard to invade France, with the promise that he would do the same from the other side. This was reminiscent of the pact of 1124 between Henry I of England and Emperor Henry V; and, like that plan, it never happened.[31] There were skirmishes and sporadic peace talks through the rest of 1195. Richard finally released Philip's long-suffering sister Alice, and it was now that she was married to the count of Ponthieu, thus strengthening Philip's alliances in the north-east of France; we may hope that she achieved some measure of contentment in her new life. There was some talk that Richard's eleven-year-old niece Eleanor of Brittany might marry Philip's son Louis, now eight, with the Norman Vexin as part of the arrangement, but the idea proceeded no further. A peace treaty was finally agreed in January 1196, thus giving all parties something of a breathing space.[32]

* * *

By now the marital and succession issues being experienced by both kings had intensified. Philip had still not managed to divest himself of Ingeborg, who continued to petition the pope, and Celestine had in 1195 declared that the annulment of the marriage on the grounds of consanguinity was in itself invalid.[33] Philip would need to seek another means of effecting a divorce, but in the interim he complicated the situation further: in June 1196 he took another wife, Agnes, daughter of Berthold IV, duke of Merania (part of the Empire). There was outrage both in Denmark and in France, including among the clergy, who had hitherto been loyal to Philip, with even Rigord of Saint-Denis describing those who supported the king in this as 'mute dogs who no longer knew how to bark'.[34]

Philip's new line of attack against Ingeborg was that the marriage had not been consummated because of sorcery – a serious charge. She, meanwhile, insisted that it had, and further impasse ensued. She was assisted in 1198 by the death of the elderly Celestine and the accession of a remarkably young and energetic new pope, the thirty-seven-year-old Innocent III, who took her part. She needed his support, for in 1198 Agnes bore Philip a daughter, Marie, and then in 1200 an all-important second son, Philip (known as Philip Hurepel, due to his wild hair and in order to differentiate him from his father). King Philip would do everything possible to ensure that his second son was considered legitimate, which was not the case if the marriage to Agnes was bigamous in the eyes of the Church, so he redoubled his efforts to rid himself of Ingeborg, claiming they had never been legally married in the first place. Innocent, however, flexing his new papal muscles, declared the union with Agnes invalid, and threatened serious measures if Philip did not take back his rightful queen. Philip was not prepared to do this, and Innocent would later lay France under an interdict. This was the most severe punishment the Church could inflict, meaning that Mass could not be celebrated anywhere in the kingdom and that the sacraments were forbidden – for everybody, not just for the individual who had caused the sentence to be pronounced. It was a sure way of making a king unpopular with his own subjects, who were unable to marry, or to bury their loved ones in consecrated ground.[35]

We will hear more of these developments later, but suffice it to say that at the time of his marriage to Agnes in 1196 Philip found himself losing popularity in his own kingdom, amid a swell of sympathy for Ingeborg, and he no doubt prayed that nothing would happen to his one indisputably legitimate son before the situation could be clarified.

In this respect Philip, despite his travails, was better off than Richard, who had no legitimate children at all and who would need to designate an heir in the event of this situation continuing – which was almost certain, given that he had by now given up all personal contact with Berengaria. John was the obvious candidate, as Richard's only remaining brother and the son of Henry II, but he was unstable, as well as unpopular; and moreover he also had no legitimate children, despite his six-year marriage to Isabelle of Gloucester. The only other descendants in the male line of Henry II were Arthur and Eleanor of Brittany, the children of Geoffrey, who was the younger brother of Richard and (crucially, as it would later turn out) the older brother of John. As an infant, Arthur had been designated by Richard as his heir, but this could be considered to have been superseded by Richard's later reconciliation with John. Moreover, Arthur was still only a young boy and, far from being part of the family firm, he could even be considered a kind of 'anti-Plantagenet', as he had been brought up by his independent mother, Constance of Brittany; he was a pawn in the hands of King Philip and had never visited England. We will hear more of Arthur, Eleanor and Constance in the next chapter.

Richard, of course, had other nephews. The best placed of these were the sons of Matilda and Henry the Lion of Saxony, not only because Matilda had been Richard's eldest sister, but also because the boys had spent much of their youth in England and were known to Richard (and his influential mother) personally. The eldest, Henry of Brunswick, was now Count Palatine of the Rhine and busy with his affairs in Germany, and the second, Lothar, had died; but the third, Otto, now aged around twenty, was a viable candidate. He had grown up in England and was known there as a member of the Plantagenet family; Richard had named him count of Poitou and was currently engaged in negotiations to marry him to Margaret, elder daughter and heir presumptive of King William the Lion of Scots. This was all to come to nothing, however; in 1197 Emperor Henry VI died and Otto returned to Germany to pursue a claim to that throne, as we shall see shortly.

It was also in 1196 that Richard arranged a new marriage for his youngest sister, Joanna, the widowed former queen of Sicily. Her second husband was to be Raymond VI, count of Toulouse, which would give Richard at least one border to his lands on which he was not facing trouble. Raymond VI was the son of Count Raymond V and Constance of France (who was the daughter of Louis VI and, as we might recall, once the wife of Eustace, son and heir of King Stephen); he was thus a first cousin of Philip Augustus, so it was worth Richard's while to get him on side. Finally, the match also went some way to settling the long-running dispute between the dukes of Aquitaine and the counts of Toulouse, as Richard ceded his claims there as part of the arrangement.[36]

* * *

Military matters did not stop while kings were embroiled in personal concerns, and it was also in 1196 that Richard began an ambitious project. The site of Les Andelys, a naturally defensible position on a tall outcrop of rock overlooking the River Seine, 60 miles north-west of Paris and 25 miles south-east of Rouen, on the Norman side of the French border, was of such strategic import that both kings had been explicitly forbidden from forti-fying it under the terms of the peace treaty of January that year.[37] Richard was having none of this, and nor did he care that the site was owned by the Church; he seized it from the archbishop of Rouen and began planning a castle, to be known as Château Gaillard.[38]

As with any castle, Château Gaillard was erected to perform both defen-sive and offensive duties. It was needed to block the route from Paris to Rouen, and also to fill the gap in the Norman border fortifications caused by the loss of Gisors to the French. But it was also envisaged as the launch pad for the reconquest of the parts of Normandy that had been lost, and even the invasion of France itself. It was to be Richard's personal project, and he would spend much time there during its construction. He used all the practical knowledge of castle design and siege warfare that he had gained on his travels to ensure that it would be the finest and strongest in Normandy or France. A keep was surrounded by three baileys – the inner with the middle one around it, surrounded by a deep ditch and accessible only via a bridge from the outer – each with its own high walls. The walls of the middle and outer baileys were punctuated with cylindrical towers, and each bailey had its own well, so the garrison would have water, even if they had to retreat behind the next set of defences. The whole was set on a rock 300 feet high and dominating the river.

The castle also benefited from the latest defensive innovations. It was one of the first in Europe to use machicolations, stone projections at the top of a wall that allowed objects to be dropped through them on to anyone at the bottom of the wall on the outside. The gatehouse leading from the middle to the inner bailey had towers flanking its entrance, to avoid having a blind spot in front of the gate. Most impressively of all, the walls of the inner bailey were curvilinear (that is, wavy, with semi-circular projec-tions), which meant that they were effective at withstanding attacks from siege machinery, and that arrows could be loosed at all angles to provide a complete field of fire, with no dead spots.

The most remarkable thing about Richard's new castle, however, was the speed with which it was built. Many other fortifications took decades to construct, but Château Gaillard was finished in only two years. This was principally because Richard was prepared to throw a huge amount of money and resources at it: the final cost was some £12,000 sterling, used to pay many hundreds of labourers, as well as to purchase materials; this was more than he spent in total on all the castles in England during his entire reign. Château Gaillard was reputed to be impregnable, and it was a stunning symbol of Richard's power and his intentions.[39]

While the castle was being built, hostilities continued and escalated, with Richard's cruelty in particular increasing. In the spring of 1197 he raided Ponthieu and burned the town of St Valéry, carrying off much booty and leaving the surviving inhabitants destitute. He had previously given orders that English merchants were not to trade with Flanders, with a view to forcing the new count, Baldwin IX (who had succeeded following the death of his mother, Margaret), to review his loyalties via economic sanctions. When Richard now found English ships in the harbour of St Valéry loaded with grain and food, he seized the cargoes, burned the ships and hanged the crews.[40]

Richard then moved on to raid the Beauvais area, where his forces captured his long-time antagonist Philip of Dreux, bishop of Beauvais and King Philip's cousin. This was a great coup, as the bishop 'was one of the men that he hated most in the whole world'; the king was 'full of joy'.[41] There was some limited indignation at Richard imprisoning a churchman, but, as he pointed out himself, 'It was not as a bishop that he was taken captive, but as a knight of great reputation, fully armed and with his helmet laced.'[42] Bishop Philip was, as we have noted previously, a warlike man, and he received short shrift even from the pope. When he wrote to Celestine to complain that 'I was taken prisoner and thrown into heavy chains and fetters; neither the dignity of my order, nor reverence for God, afforded me any relief or mitigation', the reply he received showed little sympathy for his plight:

> That it has turned out unfortunately for you is not to be wondered at ... Throwing aside the peaceful bishop, you have assumed the warlike knight ... You have borne the shield in place of the chasuble, the sword in place of the stole, the hauberk for the alb ... Into the pit which you have made, you have deservedly fallen.[43]

Bishop Philip would remain in captivity for the rest of Richard's life, but we will meet him again later.

Richard next returned to Normandy, taking a castle only 4 miles from the French-held Gisors. In the summer of 1197 his combination of sanctions and bribes had the desired effect when Baldwin IX, count of Flanders, defected to him and then immediately invaded Artois.[44] Philip, who had been concentrating on defending the Vexin, could not ignore this open rebellion by one of his vassals; he rode for Flanders, but became bogged down in guerrilla warfare and was forced to declare a truce. All three parties met for talks in September 1197, and we might imagine the awkwardness of young Baldwin at being stuck in between the two hostile kings. A peace was agreed that was supposed to last until January 1199, but in the event – and perhaps unsurprisingly – it did not.

Further complications arose when Emperor Henry VI died unexpectedly of a fever while in Sicily, at the age of just thirty-seven, in September 1197. His only son, Frederick, was not quite three years old and thus not a contender for the imperial crown, in a competition that boiled down to two candidates who represented rival families. Both were young, and whichever was chosen could therefore be expected to enjoy a long reign, and so the decision was a weighty one. The Hohenstaufen, supported by Philip Augustus, was the twenty-year-old Philip, duke of Swabia, a son of Frederick Barbarossa and thus the late Emperor Henry's younger brother; he was elected king of Germany (the first step to becoming emperor) in March 1198 by a party of princes mainly situated in the south of the Empire. However, there were some who were opposed to this dynasty, and they were encouraged both by King Richard and by the new pope, Innocent III. Their preferred candidate would have been Henry of Brunswick, Richard's eldest nephew, but he was away on crusade and they could not wait for him to return. Thus it was that they put forward Otto, the next surviving brother, then twenty-three; he in turn was elected by a mainly northern contingent in Cologne in June 1198, and crowned at Aachen in early July.[45]

With his nephew on the throne in Germany, Richard's threat to France was greatly enhanced, and he now moved to surround Philip further by making another alliance, this time with Renaud de Dammartin, count of Boulogne, whose lands included the major sea ports on the Channel. Other French lords, swayed by Richard's bribes (he was 'a good deal richer, both in land and money, than the king of France' and he, 'by presents, enticed all who were powerful in the French kingdom into friendship with him'),[46] were also wavering. Among these were Louis, count of Blois, and Geoffrey, count of Perche, who was married to Richard's niece Richenza, Otto's sister.

One French chronicler says that King Richard was by now so confident and puffed up with pride that he believed he could threaten Paris itself.[47]

Philip made alliances with some of Richard's discontented vassals in Aquitaine, but it was not enough, and he did not have the same level of resources with which to buy favours. Small-scale conflicts continued to pepper northern France, particularly Flanders and the Vexin, for another year, with reported atrocities escalating. At one point Philip, caught unawares by the presence of Anglo-Norman forces led by Richard himself, had to take refuge in Gisors castle in order to avoid capture, which would have been catastrophic for France.[48] He was now at the point where he had to use all his intelligence and experience to hold off a better resourced foe, but the tide was not in his favour.

But then, in the spring of 1199, 'God visited the kingdom of the French'.[49] Richard had ridden south against those Aquitainian nobles who had sided with Philip, and March 1199 found him besieging the small castle of Châlus-Chabrol, 20 miles south-west of Limoges. On the evening of 26 March he went out, unarmed except for an iron cap, to inspect the progress of the siege, and was hit by a crossbow bolt loosed from the walls, which struck his left shoulder. Thinking the wound minor, he retired to his tent and tried to pull out the bolt himself, but he only succeeded in breaking off the shaft, leaving the barbed iron head embedded in his flesh. A surgeon was summoned, but it was only 'after this butcher had carelessly mangled the king's arm in every part' that the head was removed.[50] The wound became infected, and as Richard watched the blood poisoning spread, he knew his end was near. With little or no thought of his wife, he wrote to his mother, who had for several years been enjoying a kind of semi-retirement at the abbey of Fontevraud, near Chinon and around 130 miles north of his current position. He was able to hold on long enough for Eleanor to reach him, and he died in her arms on 6 April.[51]

This pathetic and bathetic end sent waves of shock through England, France and much of western Europe. Richard was only forty-one and had seemed almost invincible. Amid the shock, though, one stark fact stood out: whatever his achievements had been as crusader and as king, Richard had failed in one primary royal duty: he had not fathered a legitimate son. And this was a situation that Philip fully intended to exploit.

≥ CHAPTER TWELVE ≤

KING ARTHUR?

A T THE TIME OF HIS uncle Richard's death, Arthur of Brittany had just turned twelve. He and his sister Eleanor had passed a childhood that might best be described as unstable, pulled this way and that between the competing priorities of Henry II, Richard and Philip while their devoted mother fought to do what was best for them.

Constance, duchess of Brittany, had been compelled into marriage as a young girl, being betrothed to Henry II's son Geoffrey when she was just five years old, shortly after her father had been forced by Henry to abdicate in her favour.[1] This left both Constance and Brittany in Henry's hands, and she grew up in his household – an experience she does not appear to have enjoyed, judging by her subsequent actions – while he ran her duchy with no reference to her, installing his own men in key positions of authority. So keen was he to keep Brittany in his own grasp, in fact, that he delayed the moment of the actual wedding as long as possible, and Constance was twenty when it finally took place in 1181, far older than many other royal or noble brides.

This put the duchy under Geoffrey's rule, with Constance reduced to the role of consort, although at least she was now living back in her homeland, and there is some evidence that her husband consulted her more than his father had done.[2] She bore Geoffrey two daughters and was expecting a third child when he was killed in an accident in 1186, after just five years of marriage. Constance was thus left in a challenging position: she was a widow of twenty-five, pregnant, either the mother of two toddler daughters or mourning the recent loss of one of them,[3] and she had the whole of Brittany to control amid the pressures applied by the kings of France and England.

However, the situation did have its advantages. As duchess in her own right, Constance could not be shunted aside to dower estates, in the same way as could a widow who had held her position only by marriage. She had been legally subject to Geoffrey while he was alive, and subordinate to Henry II before that; now she had the chance to exert her own authority. First, she needed to survive the dangers of childbirth, which she did, and her long-term plans were given a boost when the child she bore on Easter Sunday, 29 March 1187, was a boy. She immediately used the birth of a male heir as an opportunity to assert her independence. Her two daughters had – perhaps at Geoffrey's instigation – been given names from the Plantagenet family, Eleanor and Matilda. The new baby was Henry II's only grandson in the male line, and the king wanted him to be named after him; however, as we have seen, Constance pointedly ignored his wishes and called the baby Arthur, a name of Breton significance.[4] We should not underestimate the magnitude of this gesture of defiance – at a time when she was at her most vulnerable, Constance had chosen to challenge the most powerful man in western Europe.

The choice of name is also an indication that, at the time of his birth, Constance's ambitions for Arthur related primarily to his Breton inheritance. Richard, Henry's heir, was still only twenty-nine and unmarried, and there was no reason to suppose that he would not go on to have children of his own. If there had been the possibility of Arthur one day succeeding to his grandfather's dominions (which would perhaps be Constance's perfect revenge for her own powerless upbringing), it might have been more sensible to call him Henry, in order to curry favour with the king.

The most important immediate priority from Constance's point of view was that Arthur should remain in her custody. If he were to be taken away by Henry to be raised in the Plantagenet court, it was possible that she could be forced to abdicate in his favour (as her own father had been), leaving Henry free to exercise power on Arthur's behalf. However, she also needed to be wary of the motives of King Philip, who might use any uncertainty in Brittany as an excuse to further his own designs.

As the holder of a noble title and extensive estates, it was inevitable that Constance would be forced to marry again; and in 1188 Henry arranged a match that suited his political objectives, but which was personally distasteful, seemingly to both parties. Ranulf de Blundeville, earl of Chester, was just eighteen – some nine years younger than Constance – and had only recently come into possession of his estates, having inherited them as a minor when his father Hugh de Kevelioc (whom we last saw back in 1177, being released from captivity after an abortive rebellion against Henry) died in 1181. Ranulf's Norman lands bordered Brittany, and his English ones were close to the holdings of the earldom of Richmond, which was associated with the duchy. The union did not meet with Constance's approval, but she had little choice in the matter, so the wedding took place. However, this time around she fought with greater determination to keep her own rights, and the Breton barons took her part: they never recognised Ranulf as their lord. He, in turn, sporadically made use of the title 'duke of Brittany', but seemed otherwise uninterested, continuing to reside in England or Normandy, while Constance lived in Brittany.[5]

This was the situation, then, as Arthur was in his infancy. It was inevitable that he and his sister Eleanor would be used as pawns in the dynastic game, and the change of English king from Henry II to Richard in 1189 did nothing to alter this. In 1190 Richard – with no apparent reference to Constance – arranged Arthur's marriage with a daughter of Tancred of Sicily, although this did not in the end transpire. In 1193, as part of the negotiated terms of his release from captivity, Richard promised Eleanor as a bride for the son of Duke Leopold of Austria, and the ten-year-old was actually on her way there in 1194 when news of Leopold's death reached her party; the arrangement fell through and she turned back.[6] Both children were also of interest to King Philip, and he attempted to claim wardship of Arthur, while proposing the idea of Eleanor marrying his own son and heir, Louis.

In the spring of 1196 Richard summoned Constance to his court in Normandy, probably in an attempt to persuade or force her into giving up custody of Arthur, but she had hardly crossed the border when she was kidnapped by Ranulf. Richard tried to put it about that this was merely a matrimonial dispute, but it seems very unlikely that Ranulf would defy his king so far as to kidnap Constance and spirit her away when she was actually on her way to meet Richard. Richard thus at least tacitly approved of the abduction, and may even have ordered it himself.[7] Fortunately for

Constance, Arthur was at that time in the care of some of her loyal Breton advisors; they put him into hiding and then spirited him away to Philip's court in Paris, while at the same time renouncing their allegiance to Richard and appealing to the French king for help. Arthur would remain in Paris for a couple of years, joining the household of Philip's son Louis, who was the same age. This was not an unusual scenario: the heirs of kings were often surrounded by the heirs to, or young holders of, noble estates, which had the dual advantage that they could undertake knightly training together, while also forming bonds of friendship and loyalty that would be useful in the future.[8]

From Philip's point of view, this was an ideal time for Arthur and Constance to make overtures to him: earlier in 1196, John had defected from the French king's camp back to Richard's, and so – in the absence of any more Plantagenet brothers – Philip was only too pleased to have a nephew to set against them. Constance, meanwhile, remained in captivity, and it may be that this was partly voluntary: it seems a logical assumption that Richard would have released her in return for Arthur, but that she chose to remain in his custody rather than give up her son.[9] She does at least appear to have been kept in reasonable comfort, rather than close confinement, and was able to send letters to her children and her officials.

Constance was held captive for nearly two years, not being released until 1198. By this time Arthur was eleven; he had weathered the worst dangers of infancy and childhood, and his mother could more justifiably associate him with her rule in Brittany, issuing charters that included both of their names.[10] They remained for the time being under Philip's protection, but Constance was as wary of letting Brittany come under his close control as she was about it being under Richard's. The time was, in any case, ripe for her to reconsider her allegiances, as the situation had developed: Richard had by now been married for seven years and was still childless, meaning that the English crown itself might be within reach. This would mean returning to Richard's favour, so Arthur (ostensibly in his own name, but in reality guided by Constance) renounced his fealty to Philip and agreed to be guided by Richard in his dealings with the French king.[11] Constance was freed and finally succeeded in having her marriage to Ranulf annulled; she could now devote herself to her son and his ambitions. Ranulf would marry for a second time in 1200, and we will meet him again later.

In April 1199 the unexpected news burst on Constance that Richard had died suddenly, throwing all her plans into disarray. Although she may have harboured long-term ambitions for Arthur in that direction, it was too soon: he was only twelve, a long way from being able to govern or to become involved in a potentially deadly war. But she would nevertheless be forced to act, for the circumstances demanded it.

The situation was uncertain, as there were at the time no absolute rules of inheritance for the English crown. On the grounds of primogeniture, Arthur's claim was better, as his father Geoffrey had been older than John; moreover, Richard had designated him heir back in 1190. However, primogeniture – although of increasing importance – was not yet the defining factor in the succession, and there was some uncertainty about how it should be applied. Did the younger son of a reigning king take precedence over the claims of a grandson who, although descending from a senior line, was the son of a father who had never ruled? In general, the customs of Anjou, Maine and Touraine would favour the grandson (and Brittany could be persuaded to agree, at least in the present case), but England and Normandy would favour the son. These were the richer and more powerful of the territories at stake, and added to this was the idea that – his declaration of 1190 notwithstanding – Richard might have changed his mind on his deathbed to favour John, given that the two of them had been reconciled following Richard's return from captivity.[12]

One man who became involved in these events was William Marshal, who had been a loyal subject of Richard since his accession and who had been richly rewarded; he was now a senior nobleman, an earl in right of his wife, the holder of extensive lands and the father of a daughter and three or four sons. He thus had much at stake if he wanted the tide of good fortune to continue in his favour, at a time when personal royal patronage was an important factor in a noble career. There is an interesting episode in his biography that deals with this rather intense period, based on his own later reminiscences, that is worth quoting in some detail.

At the time of Richard's death William was in Rouen, where the catastrophic news reached him late on the eve of Palm Sunday, just as he was 'having his boots removed' before he went to bed. 'In a state of violent grief', he immediately went to call on Hubert Walter, the archbishop of Canterbury, who was also in Rouen, so that they could discuss the matter in private before the news was disseminated more widely.[13] The actual dialogue which is then attributed to them is obviously fictional (it is unlikely that they spoke in rhyming couplets, which is how the original text is presented), but it summarises quite neatly the dilemma in which the barons of all the late king's lands now found themselves.

At first the conversation seems to indicate that neither of the potential candidates was seen as a particularly good choice. 'The king is dead?' exclaims the archbishop:

> What solace is there for us now? None, so help me God! With him gone, I can think of nobody to choose to rescue the realm or come to our aid in anything. The realm is now on the road to destruction, grief and desti- tution. We can be sure it won't be very long before we see the French rush upon us to take everything we have.

William notes that 'we should be thinking of choosing quickly . . . a man to make king', and Hubert says that 'by right' this ought to be Arthur; but William replies that this would be a 'bad decision' because Arthur has 'treach- erous advisors', he is 'unapproachable and overbearing' and 'he does not like those in our realm'. He suggests that John is the preferred choice, because he 'is nearest in line to claim the land of his father'. The archbishop is eventually persuaded by William's argument that 'the son is indisputably closer in the line of inheritance than the nephew is, and it is right that that should be made clear', although he does give an ominous warning: 'I tell you, you will never come to regret anything you did as much as what you're doing now.'

In later years, then, William could claim that he had considered the merits of both claimants, rather than jumping to immediate support of John. Also of note is that, according to this account, it is up to the great men to 'choose' a king (the word occurs several times in the conversation). As is clear both from the uncertainty surrounding the hereditary principle and from the unorthodox way in which the English crown had been appropri- ated several times since the Norman Conquest, succession was not auto- matic on the death of the incumbent: the support of the barons was needed. However, here the actual agency seems to be vested in the barons, rather than the candidates.

The depiction of Arthur as 'unapproachable and overbearing' seems to be a product of hindsight, given that Marshal later went on to serve John, and it is probably unfair given Arthur's age and the fact that William can have had very little personal contact with him. So, too, is the accusation that he did not like those in England, although this is perhaps less a personal comment and more a recognition that Arthur had in fact never been across the Channel. The barons might therefore be justified in worrying that his accession – with his mother as a regent, or at least as a figure with great influence over him – would result in a Breton-based overturning of various English customs and practices that currently favoured them.

They were, however, entirely correct to suspect the motives of Philip Augustus.

As soon as Philip heard of Richard's death he invaded Normandy, seizing Évreux and Conches and devastating the surrounding region.[14] Having the only two remaining male Plantagenets at each other's throats was of great advantage to him: not only would they cause damage to each other and their mutual family, but the situation provided him with an opportunity for gain. His previous tactics had been to support any junior member of the family who was rebelling against someone more senior, and so it now seemed natural to favour Arthur, the underdog; Philip was aided in this decision by Constance, who appealed to him for help. As we have seen, she may originally only have wanted to secure Arthur's Breton inheritance, but now she had no choice but to push his claim to the throne. This was not simple ambition (although that clearly did play a part), but was also a defensive manoeuvre. If John became king, even without opposition, he would always see Arthur as a potential threat, so the boy would never be safe. The only way to counter this danger to her son was to move pre-emptively on to the attack; for this, she would need a powerful ally, and there was only one realistic candidate for that role.

John, meanwhile, could probably hardly believe his luck. In the normal course of events he, as a fourth son, would have had little to no prospect of ever acceding to the throne. But his hopes and expectations had been gradually rising throughout his life – firstly thanks to the obvious preference shown towards him by Henry II, and then due to the successive deaths of his elder brothers. Now the crown was within reach and – having seen off the glamorous and popular Henry, the clever and conniving Geoffrey and the intimidating and violent Richard – he was not about to be kept from it by a twelve-year-old boy and his Breton mother.

* * *

Events moved apace in the weeks after Richard's death. John, enjoying the support of William Marshal and other Norman barons, realised straight away the importance of appropriating money and resources, and he moved quickly to take control of the Angevin royal treasury at Chinon.[15] Constance, meanwhile, began raising troops; her army quickly seized Angers, the capital of Anjou, and there a group of barons declared Arthur their lord on Easter Sunday, 18 April 1199. The Normans, however, had no wish to be ruled by a Breton, so they in their turn proclaimed John as duke in Rouen on 25 April. The person of Arthur was, of course, of the greatest importance, so Philip 'at once sent him to Paris under charge of a guard'. This left no one – or at least no male figure – in charge of Arthur's domains, so Philip then 'received into his care all the cities and castles which belonged to Arthur'.[16]

The most significant objective, of course, was the crown of England itself and the recognition that came with the coronation ceremony. Here John was quickest off the mark: he crossed the Channel and had himself crowned and consecrated at Westminster on 27 May 1199. He was now, in the eyes of God and his contemporaries, the king, and this was going to make Arthur's task (or, rather, Philip's, as it effectively was at this point) all the more difficult. Philip was not deterred, however, and now he pulled off a clever political move, knighting Arthur and accepting his homage not only for Anjou, Maine, Touraine and Brittany, but also Normandy.[17] Homage, as we have noted before, had a two-way effect: Arthur recognised Philip as his overlord, but in return Philip recognised Arthur's claim to those lands. Philip's acceptance of Arthur's homage for Normandy meant that John was now technically considered a usurper there, which meant that Philip had no qualms about invading and taking control of towns and fortifications, all the while keeping Arthur safely in Paris.

Arthur had his mother on his side, but John had a formidable mother of his own. Eleanor was now in her late seventies, but still ruling Aquitaine; as duchess in her own right her position had not been altered by Richard's death, even though she had shared power with him while he lived. The resources of the duchy were considerable, and she now made a tour through Poitou, securing for John the support of the nobles and the Church as she went.[18] While engaged on this tour, she suffered a second loss hard on the heels of Richard's, which was a great personal blow. Her daughter Joanna, countess of Toulouse, had been enduring marital problems and had left her husband's court with a view to seeking protection from Richard in Normandy, even though she was pregnant and such a journey would be dangerous to her health. She had reached Poitou, and Eleanor, when she heard of Richard's death. After a visit to Richard's grave at Fontevraud she attempted to travel on, but was too ill; she returned to Fontevraud and died there in September 1199. Her baby, a son, was delivered by Caesarean section after her death, but lived only long enough to be baptised.[19]

In August 1199 the two parties in the dispute met for negotiation. Philip initially asked John to cede Poitou to Arthur on top of his other four territories (with Philip as his overlord, as per their earlier act of homage), but he was aware by this stage that the momentum was with his opponent. Both England and Normandy were holding fast for John, partly based on the fact of his coronation and partly because the barons saw his rule, rather than Arthur's, as being in their best interests. With the added support of Aquitaine, those areas still holding out for Arthur – Anjou, Maine, Touraine and Brittany – were in danger of being surrounded. John therefore felt himself to be in a strong enough position to reject the terms.[20]

A surprising development occurred sometime between August and October 1199 when Constance married again, this time apparently of her own volition. Her choice was a Poitevin nobleman named Guy of Thouars, who was the younger brother of Aimery, viscount of Thouars; Guy's date of birth is not known, but he was probably some six or seven years older than Constance. He was an unlikely selection from a purely political point of view – there would have been candidates of higher profile and greater influence if Constance's objective had been to provide impetus or resources for Arthur's campaign – so it seems likely to have been a choice based at least in part on personal preference.[21] Her new marriage actually had an adverse effect on her efforts on Arthur's behalf, as she bore Guy two daughters (Alix in 1200 and Catherine in 1201), and the periods of pregnancy and post-birth recovery must have put her out of action for lengthy periods of time.

Arthur and Constance were due to meet John for talks in November 1199, but Arthur was warned in advance (by a party unnamed in the sources) that John intended to put him in prison. Given John's reputation for treachery, this had to be taken seriously, and the warning seems to have been proved correct by another of his actions: on the very same day John obliged Aimery, viscount of Thouars – Constance's brother-in-law since her recent marriage, and thus suspect in John's eyes – to hand over Chinon castle to him. Rather than appear before him, all three made an overnight escape to Angers.[22]

Further negotiations took place between John and Philip in January 1200. One minor consequence was the release from captivity of the bishop of Beauvais (although only after he was forced to pay 2,000 marks of silver in recompense for the expense of his long imprisonment),[23] and the major outcome was the Treaty of Le Goulet, which was finalised and sealed in May. On examination of the terms of the treaty, it might appear superficially as if Philip had backed down on most of his earlier demands: he now recognised John as Richard's lawful heir, and thus accepted that Arthur would lose Anjou, Maine and Touraine (he would keep his birthright of Brittany, although he would hold it from John, not Philip; and, although not mentioned specifically in the treaty, he would continue to be seen as John's *de facto* heir until John had children of his own). But in fact Philip used the situation to wring every last concession he could.[24] John would recognise Philip as his overlord in Normandy, and Philip would keep under his direct control those parts of Normandy he had already gained.

Many such treaties included the promise of a marriage between the families to seal the bargain, and this was no exception. Philip's son Louis would be married to a niece of the childless John, although this was not to be Eleanor of Brittany but Blanche of Castile (the daughter of John's sister Eleanor and her husband Alfonso VIII of Castile), for whom John provided a lavish dowry in both cash and land.[25] Blanche would thus be queen of France in due course, and, given John's lack of legitimate issue, there was even a vague possibility of a claim to the English throne in the future. Louis and Blanche, who were both twelve, were in fact married the very day after the treaty was sealed; the indefatigable Eleanor of Aquitaine had already made the long journey over the Pyrenees to fetch her while the negotiations were ongoing, taking advantage of the opportunity to see her daughter Eleanor, her only surviving child except for John, for the first time in thirty years.[26]

As we might expect, nobody thought to record Blanche's opinion; the power that queens and noblewomen exercised was dependent on what they did *after* they were married, not on having a choice of husband in the first place. One chronicler does at least attempt a short description of her:

> Blanche [meaning 'white' in French], white in face and heart, and announcing by her name the merit with which she shone both on the outside and the inside; she came of royal stock on both her father's and her mother's side, and would rise even above them by the nobility of her soul.[27]

The age of the parties suited Philip, for he was to keep the dowry castles and territories in his own hands until such time as the marriage should be consummated, which was likely to be some while. Meanwhile, Eleanor of Aquitaine retired once more to Fontevraud, where by now the prioress was her granddaughter (Alix, the youngest daughter and namesake of Eleanor's second daughter by Louis VII). She expected her residence there to be permanent, but she would be called into action once more, as we shall see.

Philip was resigned for now that John would take Richard's place as the lord of a vast expanse of land, but he must have been aware that they were very different people. He knew John relatively well, and so would be looking for weaknesses to exploit; John would make a mistake sooner or later. And then, right on cue, he did.

John had been married to Isabelle of Gloucester for ten years, but she had borne him no children and they had been estranged since around 1196; she had pointedly not been crowned alongside him in May 1199. Now that he was king he had the political influence necessary to get rid of her, so he conjured up the familiar convenient excuse of consanguinity and their marriage was annulled in the autumn of the same year.[28] John was thirty-four, still easily young enough to father a brood of children, and he would need to look about him for a bride of suitable standing who would bring him political advantages. His catastrophic error in this was not so much his choice of new wife, but rather the way he went about acquiring her.

Isabella was the only child and heiress of Aymer, count of Angoulême, and she was also a close relative of Philip Augustus, as her mother was

Philip's first cousin (being the daughter of Peter of Courtenay, a younger son of Louis VI). She was thus of royal stock, but with no issue of consanguinity for John; moreover, the county of Angoulême was of strategic significance, as it lay between the Plantagenet strongholds of Poitiers and Bordeaux. She was eminently suitable as a bride for a man in John's position. However, Isabella was already betrothed. A neighbouring county to Angoulême was La Marche, then under the rule of Count Hugh IX de Lusignan; he wished to unite the two estates, and a marriage between a member of his house and the heiress of Angoulême would bring this about. Isabella was no more than eleven or twelve, so the obvious candidate for groom would be Hugh's son (the future Hugh X), who was seventeen; however, Hugh senior – then in his late thirties or early forties and with no wife, his marriage having been annulled – had decided to marry her himself. The arrangements had already been made when John stepped in, seizing Isabella and marrying her himself on 24 August 1200.[29] She then travelled to England with him and was crowned queen at Westminster on 8 October.

Hugh IX de Lusignan was outraged, but instead of compensating him or seeking to calm the situation, John dismissed any claims he and his family might have had, treating them with contempt and seizing their property when they complained. By autumn 1201 Hugh had married Isabella's cousin Matilda of Angoulême, renounced his allegiance to John and defected to Philip, appealing to him – as the overlord of them both – for his intervention. In April 1202 Philip took the opportunity to pronounce against John a sentence of the forfeiture of his estates in France, which would serve as a convenient pretext for launching a campaign against him.[30]

* * *

While all this was taking place, Arthur of Brittany was dividing his time between the French court in Paris, where he engaged in the knightly training that was usual for boys of his class and age, and Brittany, where he spent time with his mother, stepfather and their two young daughters. But then, in September 1201, Constance suddenly died.[31] This was a great blow to Arthur and his ambitions, as she had been the driving force behind his campaigns and indeed his very survival. However, he was by now fourteen – not much younger than Philip Augustus had been when he inherited the

French throne – and he could begin to play a more active part in the management of his own affairs. Or so he thought. Being an inexperienced teenager in a position of such prominence was difficult enough at the best of times, but being an inexperienced teenager stuck between John and Philip was never going to end well.

At Easter 1202 John summoned Arthur to do homage to him once more; but Arthur, perhaps fearing a trap, as he had done in 1199, instead went to Philip.[32] This was just the time when Philip declared John's French lands forfeit, and so Philip was presented with a dual opportunity. He proposed a marriage between his infant daughter Marie (born to Agnes of Merania, his disputed third wife) and Arthur. With the resources of the French crown behind him, Arthur – now duke of Brittany in his own right – would have a greater chance of challenging John's position in his other territories, so the prospect must have seemed attractive. There was still unrest in Poitou, led by the disaffected Lusignans, and this now turned into a full-scale revolt in Arthur's name against John. John's principal ally in the region, his father-in-law Aymer of Angoulême, had recently died, leaving the Lusignans as the major power in the region. Philip sent Arthur there, deeming him now old enough to ride at the head of his own troops, while he himself launched an invasion of Normandy.

When Arthur reached Poitou the lords there 'welcomed him with great joy and made him their commander in chief',[33] but unfortunately his youth and inexperience quickly led to disaster. Eleanor of Aquitaine, forced out of retirement once more by the situation of her son's making, was at the castle of Mirebeau, on the border of Anjou and Poitou. Arthur, sensing a high-profile scalp, moved to assail it. But although his forces took the town, the castle inside it had separate defences, and Eleanor was able to retreat there while managing to get a messenger out to John. In an unusual display of decisiveness and organisation, he was able to march his troops 80 miles in just forty-eight hours, arriving at Mirebeau before Arthur and the Poitevins could possibly have expected him.

That they were unprepared for the attack that fell on them early in the morning of 1 August 1202 was evident from the fact that John's men entered through an unsecured gate, and that the Poitevins were unarmed and still eating breakfast.[34] There was fierce fighting in the streets and Arthur had nowhere to go, trapped between the oncoming army and the walls of the castle still holding out behind him; the defeat was total and he was captured by William de Briouze, one of John's adherents, who handed him over to the king. In total John took over 200 prisoners (including Hugh IX de Lusignan and his brother Geoffrey), thus quelling the revolt completely.[35]

Arthur was taken to Falaise castle in Normandy, and initially John made it known that he would be open to negotiations over his release. This did not, in the event, transpire, and in January 1203 Arthur was taken to a much closer confinement in Rouen, from which he never emerged. His sister Eleanor, then eighteen, also found herself in John's custody shortly after the events at Mirebeau, and she was sent to England to be imprisoned. The main danger in her case was that she might one day marry, thus giving her husband and any children a claim to John's throne. With the exception of one short period that we will discuss later, she would spend the whole of the rest of her life in captivity.[36]

* * *

Arthur's exact fate remains unknown. There is little doubt that he was murdered, but exactly how, when and by whom is unclear. There seems to be a general consensus among contemporaries that he was held in harsh conditions and that he was dead within less than a year, but after that their information is sketchy and sometimes contradictory: he 'suddenly disappeared', or he was blinded and castrated, or he was not blinded and castrated but the Bretons were *told* that this was so, or he was drowned.[37] The two accounts that correspond to the greatest extent are, strangely, from very different places. One is that of William the Breton, a chaplain and chronicler based at the French royal court who, naturally, would have had an interest in Breton affairs. He claims that John had Arthur put in a boat, that he rowed him out into the Seine, stabbed him and then dumped his body overboard.[38] The second is the annals of Margam Abbey in south Wales, which sounds obscure until we take into account the fact that the annalist there would have been in a position to get his information from the same William de Briouze who had captured Arthur and who had been concerned in the arrangements of his custody. This annalist writes that:

> After King John had captured Arthur and kept him alive in prison for
> some time, at length, in the castle of Rouen, after dinner on the Thursday
> before Easter [3 April 1203], when he was drunk and possessed by the
> devil, he slew him with his own hand, and tying a heavy stone to the
> body cast it into the Seine.[39]

The correlation of John's personal involvement and the use of the Seine for
disposing of the corpse is significant, and John is known to have been in
Rouen on the date given by the Margam annals. This, of course, is not
conclusive, but what is certain is that Arthur was never seen alive again.[40]

Rumours as to his demise began to circulate very soon after the alleged
event:

> An opinion about the death of Arthur gained ground throughout the
> French kingdom and the continent in general, by which it seemed that
> John was suspected by all of having slain him with his own hand; for
> which reason many turned their affections from the king from that time
> forward.[41]

This, of course, was a situation that King Philip was bound to exploit for his
own ends. His long-time ploy of playing younger members of the Plantagenet
family off against their seniors had perforce come to an end, for there were
no more candidates to back. But this was now irrelevant, as Philip no longer
needed the tactic. He had as his antagonist a man who was little trusted,
even by his own adherents, and who was nowhere near as politically experienced or astute as himself. He was, finally, no longer on the defensive,
protecting France from a stronger foe: he could seek to act aggressively.[42]

Philip had started to line up his required pieces on the board even while
John's conflict with Arthur had been ongoing, and in the first years of the
new century he benefited from a number of upheavals in some of France's
richest provinces and the emergence of a new generation that he could
influence and control. In 1200 he made peace with Baldwin IX of Flanders,
who later departed on the Fourth Crusade, briefly became the Latin emperor
of Constantinople and died in mysterious circumstances as a prisoner of the
tsar of Bulgaria in 1205. A widower, Baldwin left two young daughters, Joan
and Margaret, as his heirs in Flanders, and they became Philip's wards.[43] In

1201 Philip also came to terms with Renaud de Dammartin, count of Boulogne. Renaud had one child, a daughter and heiress named Matilda, and Philip arranged for her to be betrothed to his second son, Philip Hurepel, while both were still in swaddling bands. He also granted to Renaud the county of Mortain, which had once been John's but was now under Philip's control, in a sign of how far the pendulum had already swung. And finally, Philip also gained from the unexpected death in 1201 of Count Theobald III of Champagne, his nephew, when still only in his early twenties. Theobald's wife, Blanche of Navarre (the younger sister of Sancho VII and of Berengaria, dowager queen of England) was heavily pregnant at the time of his death; she gave birth to a son barely a week later, who was immediately declared Theobald IV of Champagne. But a very long minority beckoned, and although Blanche acted as the regent of the county, Philip exercised a great deal of influence and some direct control there. Little Theobald was taken from his mother and placed in the household of Philip's son Louis and his wife to be brought up; we will hear more of him later.

John, at this point, was also basking in his recent successes. He had eliminated his potential rivals for the throne and considered that the crown was now secure on his head. But, as he was to discover, there was a great difference between obtaining a kingdom and a duchy and keeping them.

CHAPTER THIRTEEN

THE FALL OF NORMANDY

A KING'S RIGHT TO ACCEDE to his throne was based on a combination of factors – hereditary principle, conquest and acclamation among them – and his succession was sealed by the coronation ceremony and its attendant divine approval. He alone was the monarch, but once he began to reign he needed others: no king could rule without the consent and support of his barons, whose loyalty was essential. As amply demonstrated by the other members of John's family, loyalty might be inspired or coerced in a huge variety of ways, including popularity, martial prowess, inspirational leadership, effective governance, trustworthiness or plain fear. John's problem was that he proved to be spectacularly bad at all of them.

As we have seen, following John's second marriage and his subsequent sour relations with the Lusignans, they turned to King Philip, as did other barons, including the viscount of Thouars. John's cruel treatment of the Poitevins captured at Mirebeau did him no favours, and the plausible rumours of Arthur's murder in the spring of 1203 led to further defections by various magnates in Anjou and Poitou, not to mention unrest and rebellion in Brittany.[1] John found the borders of his continental territories increasingly unsafe, and he began to muster men and resources in Argentan, the great fortress situated centrally in southern Normandy.

To add to his troubles, he was short of the cash necessary to amass men and provisions. 'The worldly wealth which accrues to kings ... gives power', wrote one well-placed contemporary financial administrator, baldly but accurately. 'Their power indeed rises and falls as their portable wealth flows or ebbs. Those who lack it are a prey to their enemies, and those who have it prey upon them.'[2] This was certainly the case for John now. To some extent, it was an inherited problem: Henry II had amassed a great deal of wealth during his long reign, but Richard's constant military spending (and especially his habit of keeping a standing army, whose knights and men were paid by the day whether they were fighting or not) had depleted the royal coffers – as, of course, had his crusade and his subsequent enormous ransom payment. He had also spent a great deal of money in Normandy, which was particularly expensive as it had a long border with France that needed to be defended.[3] However John did not help himself by compounding these problems: the more he alienated his barons, the more they initiated local rebellions, which caused further expense as he was forced to attempt to quell the troubles he had created, while at the same time he lost the income from their taxes and fees.

John's situation was not improved by the fact that Philip was at the same time getting richer. This was in part thanks to his territorial gains over the last few years (by the Treaty of Le Goulet he had added half of the county of Évreux to the French royal domain, and had formalised his hold on other areas, such as the valleys of the rivers Epte, Eure and Avre); but it was also due to an overhaul of the French royal administrative systems and the appointment of efficient men in key positions.[4]

Financially and militarily, then, Philip was in a good position, and his spiritual and political situation had also improved within the last couple of years. Pope Innocent III had, in January 1200, laid France under an interdict, following Philip's refusal to reinstate Ingeborg and his continuance of the relationship with Agnes of Merania, which was variously criticised as either bigamous or adulterous (as well as vaguely consanguineous, as his maternal grandmother was descended from the same branch of Bavarian nobility as Agnes). Eventually, the pressure from the pope and from his own clergy began to tell, and Philip pledged a reconciliation with Ingeborg, which led to the interdict being revoked in September 1200. However, this all seems to have been nothing more than an empty promise on Philip's part: Agnes was not removed from court and Ingeborg was not released. Indeed, she was moved to a captivity that seemed even more punitive: she later wrote to Innocent to 'describe my miseries', pointing out that:

My lord husband persecutes me . . . I have no comfort and I suffer innumerable and unbearable harms; for no one dares to visit me . . . No person or messenger from my native land is permitted to come or to speak with me, with or without letters. My food is given sometimes very scantily; I daily have the bread of tribulation and the drink of anguish, nothing medicinal for the needs of human frailty . . . There is no supply of clothes, not such as would be suitable to a queen . . . I am closed in such a house and cannot leave it.[5]

But, yet again, she was to be disappointed in any hopes of freedom or aid. Agnes's death in 1201, while upsetting Philip, conveniently freed him from any accusations of bigamy or adultery, so the fact that he was separated from his queen became of secondary importance in the eyes of the papacy. Innocent's attention was by now elsewhere and he wrote to both John and Philip, urging the former 'devoutly to consider the things which pertain unto peace' and the latter 'to make an enduring peace with King John'; the alternative was that 'however great our love in the Lord for both of you' he would be forced to impose dire sanctions.[6] His main concern by now was the Fourth Crusade, but if he believed that ceasing to harass Philip about his treatment of Ingeborg would free up the French king's attention for the campaign, he was mistaken: Philip's thoughts were much closer to home.

* * *

Philip had, of course, already made some moves on Normandy as part of his support for Arthur. He had taken Lyons-la-Forêt (the site of Henry I's death) in July 1202, before moving on to Gournay and capturing it with an ingenious manoeuvre: seeing that it was well defended by deep moats engineered from the flow of the River Epte, he did not assault it directly but instead broke a dam that lay higher up the river, creating a huge flood that broke down and swept away the walls, forcing those inside to surrender.[7] Arthur's capture at Mirebeau in August 1202 was a setback for Philip, but it did not stop him – his campaign against John and Normandy had always been about more than Arthur's rights. In January 1203 troops under the command of the French marshal, Henry Clément, took Alençon, on the border of Normandy and Maine – a great blow to John, especially as this was achieved bloodlessly, with the connivance of Robert, count of Alençon, who, hitherto loyal to John, 'became a cowardly renegade, transferring his allegiance to the king of France, becoming his ally and doing homage to him, and letting the French into his town'.[8] John was losing friends and allies at an alarming rate, and it was at this point that he moved Arthur, his prize captive, from Falaise to Rouen.

Later in the spring of 1203, shortly after the assumed date of Arthur's murder, Philip moved along the Loire into Anjou.[9] The castles and towns here were not his primary objective, but with this strike into Plantagenet heartlands he did enough to destabilise the area and distract John's attention; Philip then left matters there in the hands of others and returned to his main goal, Normandy.

The Norman–French border was protected by a chain of castles, their areas of influence overlapping to form a formidable barrier. This meant that a relatively small number of men, when garrisoned in these fortresses, could impede the progress of an invading army many times its size, so long as they based their strategy around the castles and did not attempt to engage in pitched battle on open ground. Philip's task, then, was to break the stranglehold of these castles by taking them one by one, preferably leaving them intact rather than being forced to destroy them; that way, he could garrison them himself and turn them to French advantage.

A standard tactic – if we may use such a term, when the design and terrain of fortifications varied so widely – was for an attacking army to isolate an individual castle by burning and plundering the surrounding land (in order to gain resources for themselves, while simultaneously depriving the garrison), and then to set up a siege camp that threatened violence and prevented those inside from making any contact with allies. Negotiations would then take place with the castellan; he might sometimes agree to surrender straight away, or an arrangement might be made whereby he would be allowed to send a message to his lord asking for help, and then surrender if no help were sent within a specified time. In these cases it was common practice for the garrison and the civilian population of the castle to be allowed to leave unmolested, though whether they were also permitted to take any belongings with them would depend on the goodwill of the besieger; the castellan himself might be kept (also unharmed) for ransom. If no such arrangement were reached, then the besieger would attack the castle via any means at his disposal. This was a risk for both sides: those outside might well run out of food before those inside, and they were vulnerable not just to attacks from any approaching relieving force, but also to the weather and the ravages of disease caused by the inevitable unsanitary conditions; meanwhile, the defenders might also starve and were liable to be massacred if the castle were taken by storm.

A decade earlier, Philip had gained a reputation in the Holy Land as a breaker of castles, and he lived up to it now. He was well prepared, with a host comprising not only mounted knights and footsoldiers but also engineers, miners and other siege experts. He had the finances to enable him to retain, feed and pay them (hungry and dissatisfied men did not make an effective army), and his siege machinery was mobile, capable of being dismantled in order to be transported from one engagement to the next in a slow, but nevertheless reliable, baggage train. This was the opportunity he had been building towards for the whole of his reign, and he was taking no chances.

Conches fell to him early in the summer, and then he moved on to Vaudreuil. This was held for John by two barons, kinsmen named Robert Fitzwalter and Saer de Quincy, and it had recently been strengthened and reprovisioned against the expected attack. A lengthy siege might therefore have been anticipated; but unexpectedly (and for reasons that remain unclear to this day), Fitzwalter and de Quincy surrendered without a blow being struck. They were both taken into Philip's custody until such time as they could pay their ransoms – which they had to raise themselves, as John declined to contribute (as he had previously done for others, provided they had surrendered with his permission). The two barons were unhappy with John's refusal to help them out, and their disaffection grew; we will hear more of them later.[10]

The capture of Vaudreuil was a huge coup for Philip, not only for its own sake – a valuable fortress in a key position, obtained with very little trouble or expense – but also because it was a preliminary line of defence for Château Gaillard, which was in itself the key protector of Normandy's capital, Rouen, and thus by extension the whole of the duchy. The way to Château Gaillard, the prize jewel, now lay open, and it is no exaggeration to say that Normandy would stand or fall depending on Philip's success or failure there. We might perhaps also speculate that Philip would have felt a private sense of satisfaction at the prospect of taking the castle that had been the personal pet project of Richard, his long-time antagonist.

Château Gaillard was reputed to be unconquerable – Richard had once said that he could hold the castle if it were made of butter[11] – so any assault on it would need the full range of Philip's ingenuity and resources. His clerk William the Breton, who was an eyewitness to the events of the siege, gives some idea of what he was up against:

The site was already fortified by nature, but Richard made it even more impregnable. He enclosed it in a double wall and built high towers all round, equally spaced ... He fortified the summit of the rock and built a citadel. The position, beauty and fortifications of the place had made the name of Château Gaillard renowned throughout the world.[12]

Philip and his army arrived in late August 1203, and he was able to survey the ground and consider his options. An immediate frontal assault on the main fortification would be both ineffective and costly in lives; there was plenty of preliminary work to do before such an action could be attempted, and in the meantime the garrison could be softened up via starvation. In order to cut off their supplies he needed to isolate the castle completely, so he set his men to this – they began by taking a smaller fortification on an island in the middle of the river, and then built a pontoon bridge, which would enable them to cross and to control river traffic. Their success here left the small walled town of Petit-Andely open to attack, and the citizens (some 1,500 of them) fled up to the castle to be admitted behind its sheltering walls.

King John, who was 30 miles away at Rouen, had by now heard of the siege and knew he had to take immediate action. His plan was to send a force under William Marshal to seize the pontoon bridge, thus allowing a flotilla of small ships to reinforce and resupply the garrison. However, this expedition proved to be a disaster: the Anglo-Norman force attacked the outer reaches of the French camp and killed a number of defenceless camp followers and other civilians, but it was then chased away by a counter-attack from the French before it could make any attempt on the bridge, and no ships could land their cargoes. William Marshal was forced to flee igno-miniously, which is no doubt the reason why his normally loquacious biog-rapher fails to mention the siege of Château Gaillard at all.

The blockade of the main castle was now almost complete, and Philip finished it off by having his men dig deep trenches from river to river, as well as behind his own camp, so that they could not be taken by surprise by any further relieving force. It was clear that this was going to be a long haul over the autumn and winter, so the French replaced their tents with sturdier buildings of wood and thatch, while Philip – keen not to become so immobile that he neglected his other interests – temporarily left the scene to supervise personally another siege at the castle of Radepont, some 15 miles to the north.

The castellan of Château Gaillard was Roger de Lacy, a man who had no landed estates in Normandy and who owed his position entirely to John's goodwill. He was thus determined to hold the castle, come what may; but after the failure of the relief attempt he had to accept that he was on his own for the time being. There were enough stores inside the walls to feed the garrison for a full twelve months, but this did not take into account the large influx from Petit-Andely of additional mouths to feed. His initial decision to admit the citizens had been taken when he expected to be relieved or resupplied, but that was no longer the case. Holding the castle against Philip had to be his primary objective, so he now took the decision to pick out the 500 or so of those least able to contribute to the castle's defence and expel them.

His tactic worked: the French army parted to let these non-combatants – the old, the sick, the weak – pass unharmed. De Lacy therefore did the same again a few days later with another batch, who were similarly permitted to leave unmolested. However, word of this reached King Philip, who was being kept informed of progress, and he sent back orders that no more people were to be allowed to leave the castle: it was in his best interests to keep as many mouths as possible confined within, so they would eat through the provisions all the more quickly. And so it was that when de Lacy expelled a final cohort, probably of some 500–600 souls, they were met not with the opening of the French lines, but with a hail of missiles. They fled back to the castle, only to find the gates locked; they pleaded to be let back in but were chased off with arrows and stones. They had no choice but to remain out in the no-man's-land on the steep slopes outside the castle, where they would remain through three months of a harsh winter: starving, kept alive only by the water of the Seine, a few roots and herbs and the odd livestock escapee, and trying to scrape out what pitiful shelter they could in the hollows of the hillside.

The question of who was more to blame for the plight of these individuals is a debatable one. In *theory*, both King Philip and Roger de Lacy were following a textbook course designed to maximise their own side's chance of winning the siege: Philip by reducing the garrison to starvation as quickly as possible, and de Lacy by trying to prevent this, so that he could hold out long enough for a further relief effort to be attempted. To this we may add that, of the two, de Lacy had more of a duty to shelter the refugees, as they were the citizens of a town that was supposed to be under the castle's protection. However, he would no doubt argue that he needed to prioritise the wishes of the overlord to whom he was answerable: King John would be more concerned about the fate of the castle than the population of the town.

But theory, of course, is one thing; practice quite another. The net result was another example of innocent people, simply trying to go about their lives, being stuck in the middle of violence that did not really concern them. In the overall scheme of things their crops, their trade and their taxes would be only minimally affected by a change of regime at the castle, or even in Normandy as a whole; a Plantagenet–Capetian conflict had little relevance to them. They, however, were the ones to suffer the sharp consequences of the dynastic struggle, as they became pawns in a horrific waiting game: each side expected the other to blink first, to take pity and to let the civilians back into the castle or out through the French lines. But neither was prepared to back down, and the result was horror, as those who were trapped eventually resorted to cannibalism and other desperate practices in an attempt to stay alive.[13]

* * *

The French army made no direct assault over the winter of 1203–04, instead spending its time in engineering works – levelling the approach to the outer bailey and filling the moat, so that men and machinery would be able to approach the walls – and plundering the surrounding countryside, so that it had adequate rations while the besieged were forced to consume their dwindling supplies. John, meanwhile, more or less gave up the ghost: he had several castles between Château Gaillard and Rouen razed, so that Philip would not be able to take and make use of them, and then on 5 December he took ship for England. He seems to have done this almost clandestinely:

As he left, he told some of his men that he would go to England to seek advice and help from his barons and those in his household and then make a speedy return. But the fact of the matter is that he took the Queen with him, so there were many who feared that his stay would be a very long one. He soon made ready his departure, for he had already sent his wagon-train and all his effects ahead of him secretly.[14]

Once in England John made noises about raising money for a fresh campaign in the spring, which he would lead personally, in order to drive Philip out of Normandy; but this would never happen.

Philip arrived back at Château Gaillard in February. He had been miles away when he had issued his original order about the civilians, but now he came face to face with the full horror of the suffering he had caused. The few starving survivors begged for mercy, and he relented and let them pass, ordering them to be fed. His faithful chronicler puts this down to the king's great 'compassion' and his desire to 'save the unfortunate',[15] but we might also choose to note that such course of action was to Philip's own benefit: his reputation as a merciful Christian king was enhanced, and he moved the unfortunates much further away from his own men, thus avoiding any danger of disease, which could sweep speedily and lethally through a siege camp. Besides, the emaciated wretches before him were certainly no military threat. Their sufferings were unfortunately not over: many of those who had somehow managed to survive the privations of the winter died from the effects of overeating on an empty stomach when they gorged themselves on the food offered by the French troops.

Philip's attention was not held long by the refugees: after a winter of preparation it was now time for the big push against the castle defences. He brought his siege machinery to bear on the outer bailey, and a tall belfry was dragged up to the walls, enabling the French crossbowmen and archers to shoot down at the garrison inside. Meanwhile, his miners began digging at the foundations of the outer bailey's towers, which eventually came crashing down. This created a breach through which the French could enter, and they poured through; the rubble further filled the moat, allowing easier passage across it for more troops. At de Lacy's command, the outnumbered garrison gave the outer bailey up as lost, torching the buildings in it as they retreated.

The middle bailey had a ditch and walls of its own, but Philip's men found one weak spot. Richard's original design had been flawless, but John had impaired the defences by the addition of an extra building, which housed a chapel on its upper floor and a latrine on its lower – both of which provided potential entry points. A small group of the French were able to scramble down into the moat and then up the other side until they reached it, and then, either by climbing up the latrine chute or in through the chapel window, to get inside. They ran through the building out into the middle bailey, setting fire to a door and making as much noise as possible. This confused the garrison, who, thinking they were under mass attack, retreated long enough to enable the group to open the gate and lower the drawbridge, so that the waiting French knights and footsoldiers could enter. The middle bailey was taken and the garrison retreated to the inner bailey and keep.

Once again the French were faced with a ditch and a high, thick wall – this one with the added defence of D-shaped towers that formed waves and allowed the defenders to shoot from all angles. Philip's men would have to regroup and re-engineer. They attempted another mine (sheltered under the cover of the bridge between the middle and inner baileys, which was ill-advisedly a permanent one of stone, rather than a wooden drawbridge), but this time de Lacy was wise to the tactic and had a counter-mine dug; his men forced the French to retreat before they could complete their work. But Philip had other resources at his disposal, and by early March a large petrary was brought up. The rubble from previous encounters provided plenty of ammunition, and the machine bombarded the wall with large blocks of stone; the wall, weakened by both the attackers' mine and the defenders' counter-mine, could not withstand the barrage and eventually collapsed. The breach was stormed and hand-to-hand combat ensued. The defenders, astonishingly, fought on, but there was nowhere else to go and they were soon overwhelmed by force of numbers.

As we noted earlier, when a castle was taken by storm the vanquished defenders were liable to be executed. However, whether in recognition of their bravery, or out of relief at finally achieving victory, or perhaps with one eye on his finances, Philip had the castellan, his 36 surviving knights (only 4 had died during the siege) and 120 men-at-arms held for ransom. However, he could not resist one triumphant symbolic gesture. When called upon to surrender at multiple points during the last few months, Roger de Lacy had repeatedly declared that he would never give up the castle, even if dragged out by his feet – and he was indeed removed from Château Gaillard in this humiliating manner.[16] John, at least, recognised the lengths that de Lacy had gone to on his behalf: he contributed £1,000 towards the ransom and, on his release, made him sheriff of Yorkshire and Cumberland.

Philip had conquered the jewel in his old enemy's crown and he had done it in style, taking the supposedly impregnable fortress by storm rather than by starvation, treachery or surrender. However pleased he was with himself, though, Philip did not get carried away by his victory at Château Gaillard; he remained in tight control of his overall strategy. It would have been tempting to head straight to Rouen, but Rouen was heavily fortified and difficult to cut off from resupply; the result would be another long siege, which might give any of John's remaining adherents elsewhere in Normandy the time to regroup. Philip thus embarked instead on a circular sweep south and then west, visiting each of the major towns and fortifications, threatening them with a siege and persuading or intimidating their holders to hand them over. Towns were guaranteed to keep their rights and privileges if they submitted, and any Norman baron who was prepared to recognise Philip as his overlord, rather than John, would be allowed to keep his lands, a tempting offer in a time of war, especially given John's abrupt retreat to England and the slim prospect of him returning to take back control. Philip could also offer a comforting moral high ground: under the terms of the Treaty of Le Goulet, John had recognised the French king as his overlord for Normandy, and by his condemnation of John in 1202 Philip had, quasi-legally, deprived him of the duchy. Thus, any baron who submitted to Philip and renounced John could claim he was acting within the law.[17]

Philip seized the castle of Argentan, one of the great Norman hubs of trade, travel and arms manufacture, with little effort; Falaise, the birthplace of William the Conqueror, fell to him in just seven days. He moved into western Normandy, where Domfront, Caen, Bayeux and Lisieux were all taken with very little or no resistance.[18] His allies in Brittany, by now convinced that John had murdered their young duke, overcame Mont-Saint-Michel and Avranches. They were led by Guy of Thouars, acting as regent on behalf of his three-year-old daughter Alix, now *de facto* the duchess; he then moved to meet Philip at Caen.[19] Rouen was by now isolated, the only city in Normandy still holding out, so it was finally time for Philip to advance on the ducal capital.

The citizens of Rouen were well aware of the way the wind was blowing, and Philip did not even need to have his siege engines unpacked and assembled. The military commander of the city requested a truce on 1 June to enable him to send a message to John, on the understanding that he would surrender if no help were forthcoming within thirty days. John, in England, recognised the futility of the situation and did nothing, sending back a laconic reply that they could do as they saw fit; the citizens therefore saw sense and opened their gates to Philip on 24 June, before the truce had even expired.[20] The French king now had the whole of the duchy of Normandy under his control.

* * *

The power of the Plantagenet dynasty was waning, and during the spring of that year it had lost one of its greatest members. On 1 April 1204, while Normandy was in the process of collapsing in the face of the French king's onslaught, Eleanor of Aquitaine died at Fontevraud. She was eighty-two and had been queen of France and queen of England; she had ruled, rebelled, been imprisoned and then released to rule again. Widowed, and at an age when many or most women might have retired gracefully, she had taken up with energy the cause of her favourite child, Richard, helping and advising him, and later taking charge of the campaign to secure his release from captivity; it is doubtful if his enormous ransom would have been raised so quickly if it were not for her efforts. Then, on Richard's unexpected death, she had done it all again for John, possibly regretting that she had lived long enough to see him lose the respect of his barons, lose his brother's supposedly unassailable castle, and about to lose the whole of Normandy. Her husband's empire was no more.[21]

In Aquitaine, where Eleanor had been duchess for sixty-seven years, it was truly the end of an era. Many of the Poitevin barons who had been faithful to John only out of personal loyalty to Eleanor – and who recognised the significance of the change of regime in Normandy – now defected to Philip. His conquest of the duchy represented an even more momentous break with the past: Normandy had been a domain of the English king since 1066, and had not been under direct French royal control since Charles the Simple had ceded it to the Viking leader Rollo in 911.

Having inherited a small kingdom overshadowed and threatened by a powerful antagonist, Henry II, Philip had spent a quarter of a century doggedly and shrewdly fighting back against Henry and all his family, using every conceivable resource at his disposal and at last gaining the upper hand on French soil. The border between the lands controlled by the king of England and the king of France was no longer the Vexin, but the English Channel. This put the victorious and resurgent Philip in such a favourable position that he could now expand his dynasty's ambitions to an extent previously unthinkable: the conquest of England itself.

1. In the last decade of the eleventh century King Philip I of France abandoned his wife and queen, Bertha of Holland (here seen in the tower), to elope with Bertrade de Montfort. She would bear him two illegitimate sons and would scheme to put one of them on the throne.

2. In November 1120 Henry I of England lost his son and heir in the *White Ship* disaster, throwing England and Normandy into a succession crisis.

3. Louis VI also lost his heir in a tragic accident. His eldest son Philip, then aged fifteen, was thrown from his horse when it was frightened by a pig in the streets of Paris, and he died of the injuries he sustained.

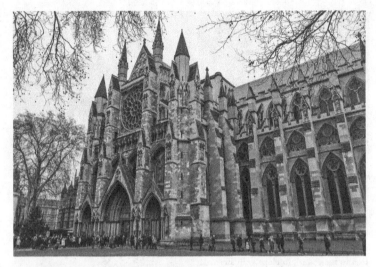

4 & 5. Westminster Abbey and Reims Cathedral, the traditional coronation sites of the kings of England and France.

6. Geoffrey of Anjou, also known as Geoffrey Plantagenet, married Empress Matilda, the daughter and heiress of Henry I. Their son Henry II was the first 'Plantagenet' king of England.

7. Louis VII was desperate to father a son and heir. Here he prays for divine assistance and is rewarded when his third wife, Adela of Blois, gives birth to Philip Augustus.

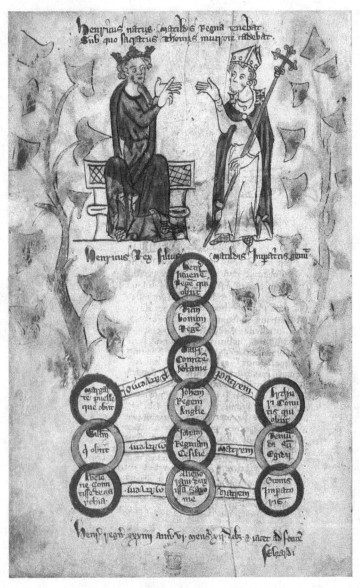

8. Henry II of England suffered from no such fertility issues, fathering four sons who would live to adulthood and three daughters who would make prestigious international matches.

9. Fontevraud Abbey, situated on the borders where Poitou, Anjou and Touraine met, was a foundation favoured by both the English and the French royal houses.

10. Philip Augustus of France and Richard the Lionheart of England agreed to go on crusade together. Philip (right) landed at Acre first; here he greets Richard and the latter's sister Joanna, the recently widowed queen of Sicily, upon their arrival.

11. Château Gaillard. After ordering its construction, Richard the Lionheart boasted that he could hold it even if the walls were made of butter. When Philip Augustus took it from King John in 1204 it was a catalyst for the fall of Normandy.

12. The effigy of Eleanor of Aquitaine at Fontevraud Abbey. Her death in 1204 tore a huge hole in the Plantagenet family and deprived her son King John of valuable support.

13. The Battle of Bouvines in 1214 was a pivotal event in the history of the two rival dynasties. Philip Augustus defeated the allies of King John and was then able to reign untroubled in France for the rest of his life.

Appliat Lod.Wians.

14. By 1216 the Capetians were in such a position of ascendancy that Philip's heir, the future Louis VIII, was invited to England and was proclaimed its king. Here Louis is depicted landing on the Isle of Thanet with a company of knights, clergymen and civilian administrators.

15 & 16. There was some resistance to Louis in the name of the new boy king, Henry III, and Louis's forces were defeated in battle at Lincoln in May 1217. The castle held out against the combined French and rebel army and the French commander, Thomas, count of Perche, was killed in an engagement outside the cathedral.

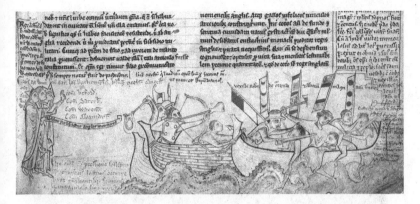

17. Prince Louis's wife, Blanche of Castile, mustered reinforcements and sent them across the Channel, but they were defeated in the naval Battle of Sandwich in August 1217.

18. When Louis VIII died in 1226, at an unexpectedly early age, he left a large family of young children. He was succeeded on the French throne by his twelve-year-old eldest son, Louis IX, with the widowed Blanche of Castile acting as regent.

19. Louis IX was pious in the extreme. In 1239 he welcomed the Crown of Thorns to Paris, constructing the magnificent Sainte-Chapelle to house the relic.

20. In England the royal succession was hanging by a thread. In 1236 the twenty-eight-year-old Henry III had married the twelve-year-old Eleanor of Provence (he is seen here putting the wedding ring on her finger) but it would be several years before she bore a child. Eleanor's sister Margaret was already queen of France by virtue of her marriage to Louis IX.

21. Henry III and Louis IX, as brothers-in-law, became firm friends. It was during Henry's sojourn in Paris at Christmas 1259 that Louis IX's eldest son and heir, the sixteen-year-old Louis, died, and Henry acted as one of the pallbearers at his funeral. The carved end panel of the young man's tomb commemorates the occasion: Henry is the slightly worn but recognisably crowned figure second left.

22. When Louis IX and Henry III died, in 1270 and 1272 respectively, it was the end of an era in both realms. The new kings, Philip III and Edward I, were first cousins thanks to their mothers' sibling relationship. Here Edward pays homage to Philip for his remaining French lands.

23. Edward I's marriage to Eleanor of Castile was happy and of long duration. It was also productive: Eleanor gave birth to at least fourteen children and possibly more, although only one of the couple's sons, the future Edward II, survived his father.

24. The French royal family in the early years of the fourteenth century. The enthroned Philip IV is flanked by his four surviving children: from the left, his third son, Charles, later Charles IV; his second son, Philip, later Philip V; his daughter Isabella, queen consort of England by virtue of her marriage to Edward II; and his eldest son Louis, later Louis X and already king of Navarre via his mother's line. Also depicted (far right) is Philip IV's younger brother Charles of Valois, whose line would inherit the French throne after all three of Philip's sons died without male heirs.

Part III

THE CAPETIAN KING
OF ENGLAND

CHAPTER FOURTEEN

FIRST STEPS

A very bad man was King John, crueller than any other; he ... brought shame to many of the great men of the land, which made him much hated.[1]

S O WRITES A CONTEMPORARY OBSERVER in the part of his narrative that deals with John's return to England after the loss of Normandy; the earliest criticism of this type and a foreshadowing of the opprobrium that would be heaped on the king by many others in later years. In the immediate term, it was these same 'great men' of England who would have to deal with John most closely, as he would perforce have to reside in the kingdom from now on.

We should be clear that, at this time and in the context of the Anglo-Norman realm, it was a sign of failure for a king of England to have to spend most of his time in England; since the Conquest, Stephen was the only monarch to have done so.[2] John's loss also brought about a new development in the idea of what it meant to be 'English' or 'Norman'. In the years following the Conquest, up until around the 1120s, chroniclers based in England such as Henry of Huntingdon and William of Malmesbury had seen the population as two distinct groups – Norman rulers and English subjects; but a couple of decades later these lines were becoming more blurred, and in his account of the Battle of the Standard of 1138 Henry of Huntingdon depicts the mixed English and Norman host as standing together against the Scots and being urged before the engagement to 'consider well who you are and against whom you are fighting this battle'. By the 1170s the distinction had almost completely disappeared, and a contemporary was able to note that 'nowadays, when English and Normans live close together and marry and give in marriage to each other, the nations are so mixed that it can scarcely be decided ... who is of English birth and who of Norman'.[3] But now that had all gone backwards, with England and Normandy separate once more.

John, with no choice but to focus on England, began in a surge of energy, spending the second half of 1204 and the first half of 1205 on the road, from Devon to Yorkshire, hauling the entire royal household with him as he offered royal audiences and judged legal cases in person.[4] But his almost frenzied activity may have been covering a deeper anxiety about Philip Augustus's motives, and a fear of possible imminent invasion: John summoned a great council, the members of which agreed on a statute for the defence of the kingdom and announced that every man in England should swear a personal oath of loyalty to the king.[5]

John, still retaining the title 'duke of Normandy' in his style, however hollow it sounded, made preparations for a campaign there in 1205 that never happened; Philip was in full control of the duchy and consolidating his hold by the day. Those who held lands on both sides of the Channel were forced to make a choice: if they swore allegiance to Philip for their Norman estates, John would confiscate those they held in England, and vice versa. This affected a large number of lords and barons, who dealt with the situation in different ways. Some families – perhaps thinking or hoping that the situation was temporary – split their holdings between brothers or sons, with one taking the English part and the other the Norman; others threw in their entire lot with one king or the other. There followed a redistribution of lands on a scale not seen for over a century, as Philip and John each awarded their own loyal adherents with estates confiscated from those who had chosen to support the other.[6]

One man who managed to keep hold of his estates in both jurisdictions was the canny William Marshal, ever dedicated to his own career. Sent by John on a diplomatic mission to Philip, he paid a fee to the French king and promised to do homage to him for his Norman lands if John failed to take back the duchy within a year and a day – but with no mention of renouncing his English lands or his allegiance to John. That this was unusual and, by the mores of the day, unethical is indicated by the fact that William's biographer spends hundreds of lines justifying his hero's action: the 'worthy Marshal' had no intention of being a traitor, even though he did, after the time was up, pay homage to Philip 'unreservedly'. Indeed, it is the man who informs King John that Marshal has done this who has spoken 'treacherous words' and who is a 'base flatterer'. William himself goes on to claim to John that he had acted with his permission. The result of all this was that he 'was on bad terms with the king for a long time' apparently 'without justification and through no fault of his'.[7] He did keep both sets of lands, though, meaning that he might be storing up trouble for himself if John were to invade Normandy in an attempt to retake it: in such a case, with his divided loyalties, which side would William be on?

William Marshal and a few others aside, the sundering of England and Normandy was almost complete, with lords and families generally settling for one or the other now that the major ties between them were cut.[8] For a brief time, then, it seemed as if the two ruling dynasties would go their separate ways – although 'dynasties' is almost the wrong word by this point, as direct members of both families were very thin on the ground. A time of renewal was just around the corner, however, as a new generation would soon emerge.

In 1205 John stood almost alone, the future of his house precarious: he had no legitimate children (although he had acknowledged some half a dozen bastards with various women), and he also had no legitimate brothers and no nephews in the male line. The only living descendant of any of his brothers was Geoffrey's daughter Eleanor of Brittany, whom John had safely locked up so that she could not challenge his own position. He did have a number of nieces and nephews from his sisters, chief among them Ferdinand, the current heir to the Castilian throne; Ferdinand's sister Blanche, the future queen of France; Raymond, the future count of Toulouse; and Otto of Brunswick, who had been pursuing his claims in the Empire. John's decision in 1200 to marry a girl who was no more than twelve had obviously postponed any plans for a direct heir, but by the middle of the decade Isabella was in her mid- to late teens and therefore entering her childbearing years. John must have felt a combination of pride, pleasure and relief when she bore him a son, Henry, in October 1207; the succession was further stabilised by the arrival of a second son, Richard, in January 1209, and three daughters (Joan, Isabelle and Eleanor) would follow.

Over in France, King Philip was still keeping Ingeborg in captivity, their twelve years of marriage having been spent entirely separately. He had taken no further wife since Agnes's death, so no more legitimate children were to be expected, although he acknowledged a bastard son, Peter Charlot, who was born to an unnamed mother sometime between 1205 and 1209 and who was destined for a career in the Church. Philip's two children by Agnes, Marie and Philip Hurepel, had survived the perils of early infancy and had been legitimised by the pope, so they could in theory take their place in his succession plans (they had both already had marriages arranged for them), although questions could and would always be raised about their legitimacy, given the doubts over the validity of their parents' marriage at the time of their births.

Philip's main hope for the future of his dynasty was thus his eldest son, Louis, born to his first and undisputed queen, Isabelle of Hainaut. In 1205 Louis turned eighteen and his wife, John's niece Blanche of Castile, gave birth to their first child, a daughter. Tragically for the couple – although not unusually, given contemporary rates of infant mortality – the baby survived only a few days. Louis and Blanche would go on to have a son and heir, Philip, in 1209, at which point Philip Augustus became the first king in the history of the Capetian royal dynasty to have a son and a grandson, two generations of direct heirs, alive simultaneously during his own lifetime. Louis and Blanche would, in time, see off very thoroughly the fertility problems that had plagued the kings of France for the last couple of generations, although they suffered a disproportionate number of losses, even by the standards of the day: in total they had a family of two daughters and ten sons, of whom only five (the younger girl and four of the boys) lived to adulthood.[9]

* * *

John's problems were not confined to England and Normandy; by 1206 Aquitaine was in danger from both north and south. Back in 1170, when John was three years old, his sister Eleanor had married Alfonso VIII of Castile. Alfonso was now claiming that Gascony (the southern part of Aquitaine) had been his wife's dowry, to be handed over to him when her mother died. If this ever was part of the arrangement – there is no documented evidence to say so, and Henry II surely would not have agreed to such a large part of the lands under his control being ceded – then only Alfonso remembered it three and a half decades later. However, claim it he did, and he was sure enough to launch an invasion in 1205.[10] Meanwhile, Philip Augustus was menacing Poitou, the northern part of Aquitaine, following his triumphs in Normandy, Maine and Anjou.

John had to act if he were not to lose what remained of his continental lands. In the spring of 1206 he commandeered and mustered a fleet of ships, taking into his service a pirate based in the Channel Islands, known as Eustace the Monk, of whom we shall hear more later. The fleet sailed in June for the port of La Rochelle, where John was met by those Poitevin barons who remained loyal to him. With the relatively meagre resources at his disposal there was no realistic way he could wrest back control of those areas that had submitted to Philip, but he was at least able to support those places still holding out for him; these included Niort, being stoutly defended on his behalf by a baron named Savari de Mauléon.

Next, John shifted his attention southwards, moving into Gascony and laying siege to Montauban (about 130 miles south-east of Bordeaux and 30 miles north of Toulouse), where Castilian forces – although not Alfonso himself – were entrenched following their incursion. Here John scored a notable success:

And when, after fifteen days, they had destroyed a great part of the castle by the incessant assaults of their petrariae, and the missiles from their ballistas and slings, the English soldiers, who were greatly renowned in that kind of warfare, scaled the walls and exchanged mortal blows with their enemies . . . The well-fortified castle of Montauban was taken.[11]

John went back to Niort and then made some raids into northern Poitou, reaching even as far into Anjou as Angers; however, Philip reacted with a show of force, by mobilising an army and marching to the Poitevin border, where he made his headquarters at the erstwhile Plantagenet stronghold of Chinon. However, although fully prepared to defend what he already held, he made no attempt at further conquest, too pragmatic to risk overreaching himself; he merely oversaw the deployment of troops and commanders at various strategic sites and then returned to Paris. Normandy, and the consolidation of his hold there, would remain his principal concern for some time to come.

In the face of the French threat John did not push his luck and sued for peace; a truce was agreed on 26 October 1206 that would last for two years. Under its terms, each king would retain the lands and loyalties in Poitou that he then held, and any further dispute in the area would be put to arbitration by a committee whose members included Savari de Mauléon acting for John and Hugh IX de Lusignan for Philip.[12] Meanwhile, Alfonso had made little headway with his territorial claims – the barons of Gascony being much less willing to submit to a Spanish monarch than the barons of Poitou were to a French king – and he was recalled to Castile by a threat of Muslim incursion on his own southern border. His interest in Gascony eventually petered out.[13]

John could thus return to England in a certain degree of triumph, having achieved some limited objectives and gained a much better idea of what he would have to do if he were to tackle the larger goal of regaining his ancestral lands. It was clear that Philip would undertake at all costs to defend his newly acquired territories, which meant that any campaign in Normandy would be a substantial undertaking. If he were to attempt it, John would need two things: money and a powerful ally. He set about the first by imposing taxes, fees and reliefs (a system whereby the heir to an estate had to pay a substantial sum in order to come into his or her inheritance) in England in a manner that amounted almost to extortion and that made him increasingly unpopular with his barons. For the second he would look to Germany, as his father and great-grandfather had done before him.

However, John had forgotten about – or was perhaps ignoring the influence of – the major third party in any interaction between European kings and realms: the Church. No monarch could properly concentrate on a dispute with a peer if he were also embroiled in a quarrel with the papacy (as Philip Augustus had come to realise over the years), and John was by this stage taking along a perilous path.

Hubert Walter, the archbishop of Canterbury, had died in July 1205, so a successor needed to be elected. This task fell, as was customary, on the monks of Canterbury; clerical appointments were church business. However, it would be disingenuous to say that a king could not bring influence to bear in such a situation, either by delaying the election or by pressuring the electors to choose his own preferred candidate. John had previously been accused by Pope Innocent of just such interference: when the see of Lincoln fell vacant in November 1200, John had ensured that the election was delayed for over two years, causing Innocent to write to him in February 1203 to 'rebuke' and 'upbraid' him for many offences against the Church:

> You are claiming for yourself power beyond your rights, you are applying the revenues of the churches to your own uses, you are attempting to prevent elections, and in the end by your unlawful persecution you are forcing the rightful electors to choose in accordance with your arbitrary decision – as you are known to have done in the church of Lincoln, where you refuse to allow an election to be held, so that you may keep its large revenues still longer in your own hands.[14]

Innocent concluded his letter by noting, a little ominously, that he had 'delayed exercising our duty perhaps longer than we should', but that if John '[did] not personally undertake to correct the wrongs herein stated and to abstain from similar wrongs', he would 'by no means hesitate to carry out such duty as is fitting, after such prolonged waiting and such fatherly warning'.[15]

The election for the new archbishop of Canterbury was not unnecessarily delayed, taking place in the autumn of 1205, but John became mired in further dispute. He had put forward a preferred candidate (John de Gray, the bishop of Norwich) and some of the monks bowed to the king's will by choosing him; however, another faction asserted their independence by instead electing their own sub-prior, Reginald. Both sides appealed to Innocent to recognise their choice, but he – pulling rank as only a pope could – set aside both claims and instead appointed Stephen Langton, an Englishman based in Rome who was already a cardinal. From a disinterested point of view, Langton was a good choice for the archbishopric of Canterbury: he was one of the foremost biblical and theological scholars of his time, and had studied and travelled widely. But the point was that he was not the choice of either electoral party, so his appointment was controversial.[16]

John refused to acknowledge Langton as archbishop, despite Innocent's now even less veiled threat that the king might 'involve yourself in a difficulty from which you could not easily be freed' but that 'if you will humbly agree with us, we will take care to provide adequately for you and your successors'.[17] John did not agree, humbly or otherwise, and the course of his relations with the papacy for the foreseeable future was set. He could not stop Langton's consecration, which took place in Rome, but he did prevent the new archbishop from entering England and then seized the revenues of the see of Canterbury and declared Langton's supporters to be public enemies.[18] In May 1208 England was placed under interdict, but John merely used this as an excuse to appropriate more money and property from the Church; in November 1209 Innocent declared him excommunicate.[19]

* * *

While John was busy dealing with his barons, his bishops and the pope, Philip was free to deal with internal matters in France. He had his own ongoing travails with the papacy, of course, although these had by now lessened a little. Ingeborg was still in captivity, but Innocent, far from lobbying for her freedom, wrote to her in 1210 to urge her to 'accept humbly that your patience [is being] tested' and tell her that she 'should bear everything with equanimity' because it was God's will that she should be tested. He did, however, finish by noting that he would 'never withdraw the support of apostolic favour from you', indicating that Philip still needed to watch his step.[20]

Philip's main concern for the last few years had been overhauling the governance of Normandy. Major changes had taken place since his conquest of it – around a third of the lands had changed hands following the redistribution of loyalties and homages – and he also intended to run it differently. No longer would it be a duchy under a duke who would be subject to him as king and overlord; instead, it would be incorporated into the royal domain and he would rule it directly. For the first time in centuries there would be no duke of Normandy, and he did not take the title himself. This meant a wholesale change to the administrative systems: Philip removed a number of men from office – in some cases abolishing the positions altogether – and replaced them with officials who were French, not Norman, and loyal to him. He shut down the separate Norman exchequer and integrated it into the main French treasury, almost doubling his income from royal lands.[21] While he was concentrating on all this, his ambitions towards an invasion of England were put on hold, but he had not forgotten them: he was merely laying the groundwork. Normandy had to be a firm base on which to stand before he could risk another step forward. In the meantime he could start to formulate further plans, and they would involve his eldest son.

One of the items high on Philip's agenda in the early 1210s was to find something for the now-adult and warlike Louis to occupy himself with. There was no recent precedent for an adult heir to the throne, the last having been Philip's grandfather, the future Louis VI, over a century earlier.[22] Given Philip's previous involvement with the family of Henry II, we might assume that he would wish to avoid making the same mistakes as his old nemesis – that is, giving an adult son and heir no authority or autonomy, and ending up with a filial rebellion on his hands. If this was the case then he started off in a less-than-ideal manner, with a series of actions that might have been considered provocative. The sons of kings were often knighted at very young ages; Louis was almost twenty-two by the time his father authorised the ceremony for him. Every previous king of the Capetian dynasty had crowned his heir as junior king during his own lifetime, in order to ensure the continuity of the succession; Philip did not do the same for Louis.[23] Louis was by right count of Artois (the inheritance of his late mother); Philip did not officially name him so.

On top of all this, Louis resembled his great-grandfather in being rest-less and extremely fond of martial pursuits, wanting an outlet for his aggression and energy in preference to kicking his heels at the Parisian court and talking to clergymen about politics. As a teenager in 1206 he had taken part in a short campaign in Brittany, which had given him some early and valu-able military experience, but nothing had presented itself since. By 1212 he was champing at the bit and decided to take the initiative himself, launching a targeted and lightning campaign into Flanders.

The heiress of Flanders, as we saw in Chapter 12, was Joan, the elder orphaned daughter of Baldwin IX, who had departed on crusade and never returned. Before he left for the East Baldwin had seized two towns, St Omer and Aire, that were part of the county of Artois, which technically at least belonged to Louis, as part of his mother's inheritance. The question of the towns lay dormant while both Louis and Joan were underage; but in January 1212 Joan had been married to Ferrand, an ambitious younger son of the king of Portugal, who became count of Flanders in right of his wife and who refused to cede the two towns. Louis therefore gathered up some friends and a host – not entirely with King Philip's permission, it must be said – rode for Flanders and captured both places swiftly and with very little trouble, making no attempt to attack anywhere else.[24]

Ferrand was forced to agree to a treaty by which he ceded St Omer and Aire in return for Louis making no claim on the rest of Flanders, but he was henceforward antagonistic to both Louis and Philip. The obvious place to turn in such circumstances was to John, and Ferrand began to make overtures to him; this interested John greatly, for Flanders, with its sea coast and command of Channel shipping lanes, would be a valuable ally in any attempt to launch a campaign on the continent. Moreover, John had already come to an agreement with another renegade French lord who controlled important ports: Renaud de Dammartin, count of Mortain and Boulogne. Renaud had agreed to the marriage of his daughter and heiress, Matilda, to King Philip's son Philip Hurepel as long ago as 1201, and the wedding had taken place in 1210, even though both bride and groom were still underage at nine and ten, respectively. But Renaud had been covertly in contact with King John for some months, arousing Philip's suspicions, and their mutual distrust grew. A spat over border castles between Renaud and the Dreux family, cousins to the French king, in 1211 was the catalyst for a complete breakdown of relations, and in 1212 Renaud also defected and paid homage to John.[25]

The dissatisfaction of two French counts, however influential they were, was not enough on its own to cause conflict between the Plantagenet and Capetian kings; but events of greater international significance were afoot, and these were to envelop all the participants as they led inexorably down the path to open war.

* * *

The Empire had been the scene of much turmoil over the preceding decade. As we saw in Chapter 11, Henry VI – the son of Frederick Barbarossa and the one-time captor of Richard the Lionheart – had died in 1197, leaving a son who was not quite three years old. The boy was overlooked in the subsequent tussle over the throne, while different parties of electors supported the Hohenstaufen Philip, duke of Swabia (Henry VI's younger brother, and the candidate favoured by Philip Augustus) or Otto of Brunswick (John's nephew and, naturally, his choice for the imperial throne). Both were crowned king, but Otto's coronation had been carried out by the archbishop of Cologne, the traditional celebrant, and thus carried more weight. The struggle had continued for a decade, with both men gaining and then losing the upper hand, until the matter was settled with great finality by Philip of Swabia's murder in 1208. Otto was then acknowledged as the German king and was crowned emperor by Pope Innocent in October 1209. To cement his position in Germany he married Beatrice, the eldest of the late Philip's four daughters, though he was widowed less than three weeks after the wedding.[26]

This left Philip Augustus short of a valuable ally, but while the dispute over the imperial throne had been dragging on Henry VI's young son, Frederick, had been growing up. He had been king of Sicily (an inheritance from his mother, and therefore one that could not be claimed by either Otto or Philip of Swabia) since the age of four, and had been living there safely away from the disputes in Germany. By the spring of 1212 he was seventeen and ambitious; backed by Pope Innocent, who had initially favoured Otto, but later turned against him and excommunicated him, Frederick had himself declared king of Germany.

By the autumn of that year Frederick's position was secure enough for Philip Augustus to risk supporting him publicly. He sent his heir, Louis, to represent him at a face-to-face meeting, the outcome of which was a treaty, sealed on 19 November, recording that Frederick and Philip each promised to support each other and that neither of them would make peace with John, Otto or any of their allies.[27] Frederick was crowned king in December in Mainz, though he was recognised only in the southern part of Germany; Otto still held sway in the north.

Frederick's attention would naturally be on internal matters in the Empire for the foreseeable future, so although he was favourably disposed toward France, he could not be relied on as an active ally at this stage. France was expanded and powerful, but it stood alone. Philip did what he could to strengthen ties with the Empire by marrying off his daughter Marie (who was at this point a fourteen-year-old widow) to Henry I, duke of Brabant (a widower of nearly fifty, with six children, most of them older than his new wife) in early 1213. However, this paled into insignificance compared to

John's useful web of relationships that surrounded the French royal domain. England, with its abundant resources, was allied to Flanders and Boulogne, with their strategically important Channel coasts; and also to Otto, who had powerful supporters and wealth at his disposal that could be used to threaten France from the other side, especially if this helped him with his own designs in Germany.

However, if Philip Augustus had demonstrated one thing during the three decades of his reign, it was that he believed attack to be the best form of defence. His ambitions were undiminished, and he still wanted to finish his life's work by wiping the last Plantagenet off the map. A major conflict was looming, and the pieces on the board were almost in place.

* * *

One crucial player, though, was still missing: Philip could make no further move against a fellow monarch without the support of the Church, or at least an absence of active papal hostility. To this end, it was in the spring of 1213 that he finally yielded to Ingeborg's tenacity, conceding that their marriage had been genuine and reinstating her as queen, some twenty years after their wedding. This is not to say that they were reconciled personally as husband and wife, for they were not, and they did not live together as a couple; however, she was released from custody, she returned to court and her rights and dignity were restored. This removed the last obstacle to Philip's harmonious relationship with Pope Innocent, as well as smoothing his relations with Denmark under its king, Ingeborg's second brother Valdemar II, who had succeeded the childless Cnut VI in 1202.[28]

Philip might now be basking in papal approval, but the same could not be said of John. England was still under interdict and he was still excommunicate, the combination of which had led to England being almost emptied of bishops, as many of the prelates fled across the Channel to avoid the conflict of interests. Perhaps piqued at John's nonchalant acceptance of his excommunicate status, or worried that what was meant to be his ultimate sanction would lose its potency, Innocent now took further steps. In March 1213 he wrote to Archbishop Stephen Langton and other bishops to instruct that 'because sometimes the perversity of the wicked passes down by succession of blood from father to son', if John did not make his peace with the Church, then 'neither you nor any others should presume to anoint or crown any of his heirs to be king'.[29] That Innocent should threaten the future of a five-year-old boy in this way is indicative both of the seriousness of John's position and the pope's confidence in his own authority over the monarchies of Europe.

If this did not shake John, then rumours that Innocent had announced his actual deposition and his replacement by Philip Augustus certainly did. Some chroniclers reported these tales as fact: 'Stephen archbishop of Canterbury,' wrote one, 'informed the pope of the divers rebellions and enormities perpetrated by the king of England from the time of the interdict up to the present time, by unceasingly laying the hands of rage and cruelty on the holy church in opposition to the Lord.' The pope, he continued, was 'deeply grieved', and

> definitively decreed that John king of England should be deposed from the throne of that kingdom, and that another, more worthy than he, to be chosen by the pope, should succeed him. In pursuance of this decree, our lord the pope wrote to the most potent Philip, king of the French, ordering him, in remission of all his faults, to undertake this business, and declaring that, after he had expelled the English king from the throne of that kingdom, he and his successors should hold possession of the kingdom of England forever.[30]

If we examine the language of this piece of narrative carefully, the story seems less likely. Whatever his spiritual authority, did any pope have the right to depose a king, or to 'order' another to do anything? And a king as politically experienced as Philip Augustus is unlikely to have submitted to such a command – even though it instructed him to do exactly what he wanted to do anyway – because of the precedent that it would set about the relationship between the pope and the king of France. Other contemporaries gave much less credence to Innocent's supposed decree, believing that Philip's plan to invade England was his own: 'It happened that King Philip of France was asleep in his bed one night when he jumped up as if in astonishment and said, "God, what am I waiting for, why don't I go and conquer England?"'[31]

Whatever the precise nature of the pope's intentions, Philip was not about to miss out on such an outstanding opportunity. In April 1213 he summoned a council of his nobles at Soissons – for the French kings had a tradition of working in consultation with their barons – at which the question of an English invasion was discussed. With the sole and notable exception of Count Ferrand of Flanders (who said he would not assent to anything unless the towns of St Omer and Aire were returned to him by Louis), the council agreed to support his project.[32] Philip announced that, if successful, he would not take the English throne himself, but would bestow it on his eldest son. This would be something of a win–win situation for him, ticking off two of his goals at once: John would be gone and the Plantagenets defeated, and Louis would have a kingdom of his own and an outlet for his martial aggression, without Philip having to cede one inch of France from his grasp.

* * *

Armed conflict between the kings of France and England was nothing new, but this phase would see a fresh development in the theatre of war, in that the Channel would be of pivotal importance. Since 1066, the kings of the Anglo-Norman realm had needed ships to transport them and their households across the sea relatively frequently, and they may have kept a small number of their own for this purpose, but now the Channel was no longer a kind of internal waterway within their own lands; it was the border with France. Ships were therefore needed in greater number and in a variety of types, for fighting as well as transport.

King Richard, when he had required ships for his crusading travels, had simply commandeered them, and to some extent John could do the same: in early 1213 he 'ordered a list to be made of all the ships in each of the ports of England . . . found capable of carrying six horses or more' and commanded them to muster at Portsmouth 'well-equipped with stores, tried seamen, and good soldiers, to enter into our service'.[33] He could also rely on the use of vessels from the Cinque Ports, whose citizens owed service to the crown; however, as this amounted in a normal year to fifty-seven ships for fifteen days of service, this was not going to be enough either to defend against a potential French attack or to launch one of his own. John therefore needed to construct ships for his own use. He had been aware of this since his loss of Normandy, and so (fortunately, given the situation he now found himself in) the groundwork had been laid in terms of sourcing labour and materials. He then accelerated the pace of building: between 1209 and 1212 twenty new galleys and thirty-four other ships were constructed.[34] By the spring of 1213 John's navy, as we may now call it, was in control of Channel shipping under the command of his half-brother William Longsword, the earl of Salisbury. William was around ten years younger than John, and probably the youngest of Henry II's illegitimate children; he was among John's firmest baronial supporters.

King Philip also found himself in need of a navy, now that he had control of the Norman coastline and could call on the services of a number of ports in northern France. Following the almost unanimous agreement of his nobles at the Council of Soissons, he began preparations in earnest for an invasion of England, mustering a large fleet at Damme that comprised a combination of commandeered and newly built vessels. Of course, ships needed men who were able to sail and command them, and Philip's cause had recently received a boost when one of John's most experienced captains, Eustace the Monk, defected to him. Eustace, as his epithet implies, had once been in holy orders, but he had left his monastery and entered the service of Renaud de Dammartin, count of Boulogne. However, he later fell out with Renaud, and the two men became antagonists as Eustace embarked on a career of piracy from a base in the Channel Islands. As we have seen, he had been in John's service for several years, but in 1212 he left it, switching his allegiance to Philip when he discovered that Renaud had made the opposite move. Eustace had 'performed many evil acts', and his combination of experience and unscrupulousness made him a valuable addition to the French king's naval forces.[35]

John's situation was perilous: unpopular in England, excommunicate and in dispute with the Church – including, as we have seen, a threat against his heir as well as himself – and now directly menaced by invasion from France. It was time for a huge gamble, and in May 1213 he wrote to the pope to capitulate, not only agreeing that he would accept Stephen Langton as archbishop of Canterbury, but also, astonishingly, ceding the whole of England to Innocent and offering to hold it from him as a papal fief. This evidently caught many in England by surprise, but in hindsight it was a masterstroke, as one chronicler explains:

The king provided wisely for himself and his people by this deed, although to many it seemed ignominious and a monstrous yoke of servitude. For matters were in such extremity . . . there was perhaps no other way of evading the impending danger. For from the moment he put himself under apostolic protection and made his kingdom part of St Peter's patrimony, there was no prince . . . who would dare attack him or invade his lands.[36]

The effects were predictable. 'The pope was delighted to hear this message', wrote one contemporary, noting that 'the king was absolved and gained his peace'; Innocent addressed John in his next letter as 'the illustrious king of England', a marked change from his recent missives. He then sent a legate to Philip in France and 'forbade him to cross to England to do wrong, for the whole realm of England was the pope's fief; and if he did make the crossing he should know that the pope would do justice upon him and upon his land'. The U-turn was complete.[37]

Philip was understandably furious:

The French king was much enraged when he heard this, and said that he had already spent sixty thousand pounds in the equipment of his ships, and in providing food and arms, and that he had undertaken the said duty by command of our lord pope.[38]

However, he was also newly reconciled to the papacy after two decades of conflict, and statesman enough to admit when he had been outmanoeuvred; he submitted to the pope's will and cancelled his invasion. But worse was to come.

In his frustration, Philip turned on Ferrand of Flanders (who, as we might recall, was the one French noble not to declare his support at the Council of Soissons), attacking his lands and authorising his equally angry son Louis, now deprived of his potential English kingdom, to do the same. Ferrand, who had been wavering in his allegiances for some time, sent a direct appeal to John for help, and John responded by sending his own ships across the Channel. On 30 May his fleet, commanded by William Longsword, found the French fleet at anchor at Damme, sparsely guarded as Philip's troops were engaged inland in Flanders. They attacked and defeated the few men left guarding it, took the supplies for themselves and then set fire to the vessels, the ships burning and 'belching forth smoke as if the very sea were on fire'.[39]

Philip's plans for an invasion of England had turned to ashes; John was triumphant, at least temporarily. But, as ever, he was erratic and now he decided to overreach himself. With his ploy of ceding England as a papal fief he had gambled and won, defending his ground; now he decided to raise the stakes and attack.

❧ CHAPTER FIFTEEN ❧

BOUVINES

JOHN'S PLAN WAS TO REGAIN everything that he had lost in France a decade previously in one sweeping campaign. He would land in Poitou and attack from there north and west into Anjou and Brittany, while his allies – Otto, Renaud and Ferrand – would combine with a further English contingent, led by William Longsword, to invade France from the north and north-east. Philip Augustus would be caught between the armies, unable to fight on all fronts at once, and would be crushed.

It was very early in the campaigning season when John embarked; he crossed the Channel safely and landed at La Rochelle on 16 February 1214, while at the same time William Longsword sailed for Flanders. The army John had with him was not of sufficient size for the task at hand, as he had encountered difficulties in recruitment. The barons and knights of England owed military service to the king, but this was generally for a limited period of forty days in any one year, and there does not seem to have been a consensus on whether this was due if the service in question was abroad (either for a war of conquest or the defence of existing possessions), so many nobles now used this as an excuse. By the early thirteenth century military service could be 'bought out' by a payment called scutage, thus enabling the king to hire paid soldiers, which is what John intended to do in Poitou; but in this particular case it does not appear that many of the English barons paid that, either.[1] One lord notable by his absence was William Marshal; he had sent his knights to John but refused to take part in the campaign personally, as he could not (or would not) take up arms against Philip, his overlord in Normandy. 'The Marshal was left behind', notes his biographer in an attempt to gloss over the inconvenient situation, 'to protect his towns, castles and domains.'[2]

Despite these difficulties John got off to a good start: from La Rochelle he advanced without much trouble, taking various smaller castles in the course of March and accepting the homage of a number of the notoriously fickle Poitevin barons. One of his great antagonists in the region had, for some time, been Hugh IX de Lusignan, the original fiancé of John's queen, Isabella. But Hugh had always been fluid in his loyalties and he was now open to negotiations; when John proposed a marriage alliance between the two families – his four-year-old daughter Joan to be betrothed to Hugh's son and heir, the twenty-something Hugh junior – this was accepted with alacrity.[3] A letter that John sent back to England showed his confidence in the campaign so far: 'Now, by the grace of God, an opportunity is afforded us of attacking our mortal enemy the king of France. And we inform you thereof that you may rejoice in our successes.' His position south of the Loire secure, he then marched into Anjou before turning westwards to Brittany.[4]

Following the death of Duke Arthur and the imprisonment of his sister Eleanor, their younger half-sister Alix had been declared duchess in her own right as the inheritance of her late mother, Constance, with her father Guy of Thouars acting as regent while she was underage. Alix was still only thirteen or fourteen, but was by now married, so her husband held Brittany in her right; he was Peter of Dreux, the second son of Philip Augustus's cousin Robert II, count of Dreux. He was in Nantes as John approached it, along with his elder brother, another Robert.

John had, rather unexpectedly, brought the captive Eleanor of Brittany with him across the Channel, perhaps in the hope that the Bretons would desert Peter and Alix in her favour, as being the eldest of Duchess Constance's daughters; but if this was his plan, there is no evidence that it worked. Nantes held firm and Eleanor would be sent back to England and to an incarceration lasting until her death in 1241, thirty-eight years after her initial capture.

Nantes was fortified, and the sensible thing would have been to remain behind the walls. However, Robert of Dreux rather unwisely made a sortie out of the city with a small party of knights, intending to try to hold a bridge against John's forces; they were soon overwhelmed and captured. John then attempted to use Robert as leverage to force Peter to surrender Nantes, which was more of a threat than might normally be the case: noble hostages were generally treated with respect, but John had previously killed or maimed men (and children) in his custody in similar situations. But Peter refused to capitulate. Nantes posed too great a challenge at this stage, so John decided against a full-scale siege and left it behind, taking Robert with him.[5]

John headed back along the Loire, taking Ancenis on 11 June and Angers (where the walls were still in a state of disrepair after previous campaigns) six days later before moving on to La-Roche-aux-Moines. This was a recently built castle that had been erected in order to defend the main route from Brittany through Anjou, and thus could not be left behind in French hands if John wished to advance further in safety. John arrived outside its walls on 19 June and set up a siege, bombarding the castle for two weeks and attempting psychological warfare by erecting a gallows outside and threatening to hang the entire garrison. However, they held firm because they knew that their situation was not extreme: help would soon be on its way.

* * *

As had been amply demonstrated by his career up until this point, Philip Augustus was a master of strategy, to the extent that it has often been said that he much preferred politics to war. But he was certainly not averse to getting in the saddle himself when the need arose, nor of engaging in seemingly difficult military enterprises; he had, after all, taken Acre in 1191 and Château Gaillard in 1204.[6] On hearing in February that John had landed at La Rochelle, he had swiftly mustered an army and ridden south, together with his son Louis. They were already in Poitou when the news reached them of the second invasion occurring behind them in the north.

This was the point at which Philip felt the full advantage of having an heir who was both a grown man and a keen soldier and commander; he was able to turn back himself to face Otto and the others while leaving Louis to deal with John. Louis was aware that the English king was at La-Roche-aux-Moines, static for the time being, and needed to make a decision: would he ride there and attempt to lift the siege by engaging the English and Poitevin forces in what would be open battle, or would he await developments at La-Roche-aux-Moines and then seek to block John's progress elsewhere in a less risky manner? Louis, as he had shown in Flanders two years previously, was capable of impetuous action; but in this case his decision to engage John seems to have been supported by the older and wiser head of Henry Clément, the French marshal whom Philip had left with his son's forces.[7] The order was given, and the French troops advanced towards John's position.

John, engaged in siege operations, heard that Louis's force was approaching, and publicly he welcomed the idea of battle, as he had a much bigger army at his disposal. However, his confidence began to waver when it became clear that the Poitevins, both lords and mercenaries, were unwilling to take the field against the actual heir to the French throne. To use an anachronistic term, they could get away with plausible deniability so long as they limited themselves to besieging castles held by their peers, while fighting under the command of the man who was the duke of Aquitaine; but engaging in a pitched battle against their future king was a very different state of affairs.

With the loyalty of his army in doubt, and wary of being trapped between the oncoming forces and a potential sortie from the castle garrison (a likely event when Louis was seen approaching), John took the decision on 2 July to flee. The English chroniclers try to paint this as an orderly and strategic retreat, but it was in fact something of a rout. John ran away so quickly that he left behind his baggage, his all-important siege machinery and most of his army; he made the 70 miles back to La Rochelle in two days. His men followed him, but on the way they needed to cross the River Loire, which caused a bottleneck, and many of them were still on the wrong side when Louis arrived. The exact number of casualties is not recorded, but a significant proportion of John's force was killed, drowned or captured, and Louis was able to seize much useful booty: armour, weapons, provisions and valuables.[8]

Satisfied with his gains, and wary of becoming involved in a disorganised chase after the departed and now resourceless John, Louis elected not to pursue him in person. Instead, he regrouped and took back a number of the strongholds that had previously surrendered or succumbed, including the damaged city of Angers. He also mourned the loss of Henry Clément, one of the few French casualties of the engagement, who died of his wounds some days later, and sent a messenger north to inform Philip that the southern threat had been eliminated.

* * *

'Emperor Otto, Count Ferrand, Count Renaud and Earl William Longsword ... divided France up between them. Ferrand wanted Paris; Renaud wanted Normandy; the emperor wanted Orléans and Chartres and Estampes.'[9] So self-assured were the allies, according to one commentator, that they were discussing the division of the spoils before they even had them in hand. Indeed, confidence in the spring of 1214 in their forthcoming victory was so contagious that Duke Henry of Brabant, who had become King Philip's son-in-law only the previous year, pushed through the marriage of his eldest daughter to Otto, deserting Philip to join Otto's coalition – and thus making young Marie one of many women and girls in the Middle Ages whose futures were sacrificed to the cause of a failed peace negotiation, and who were forced to see their husbands and their fathers fight each other. And a fight there would be, because the French king was certainly not about to let go of his kingdom without one.

Philip had made good time back from Poitou with his troops, an effective army of different types of combatant: he had 'collected an army of earls, barons, knights, and soldiers, horse and foot, together with the commoners of the cities and towns, and advanced in great force to meet his enemies'.[10] The lords had answered his call in great numbers: the almost existential threat to France, similar to the one faced by his grandfather Louis VI ninety years previously, had resulted in a similar response, and the supporters riding and marching under Philip's fleur-de-lys and *oriflamme* banners hailed from all the northern half of France. With the king were, among others, his cousins Robert II of Dreux and Robert's brother Philip, the bishop of Beauvais (still preferring martial pursuits to clerical ones after all these years); his brother-in-law William, count of Ponthieu (the husband of Philip's long-suffering sister Alice); Odo III, duke of Burgundy; and Walter II de Châtillon, count of St-Pol. The count of Blois, Theobald VI, was afflicted by leprosy and thus absent, and the count of Champagne was Theobald IV, who was only thir-teen; he did not attend in person, but there were contingents of knights and militias from Champagne present, under their seneschal. A slightly older teenager, Thomas, count of Perche, was in the host himself, prepared to fight for the king to whom he owed allegiance, even though he was Otto's nephew.[11]

The Church militant was represented in Philip's host not merely by the bishop of Beauvais, but also by a fascinating (and inexplicably little-known) character known as Brother Guérin. Guérin was not, as his name might imply, a cloistered monk; he was a former Hospitaller knight of great experience who had fought in the Holy Land in the 1180s, surviving the bloody Battle of Hattin, and who had later risen to the prestigious position of keeper of the seal and Philip's chief advisor. He would shortly be consecrated as the bishop of Senlis and later appointed chancellor of France, but for now his military under-standing and skill were invaluable. There were also various non-combatant clergy present, including Philip's chaplain and clerk, William the Breton, who provided a detailed eyewitness account of what was to follow.[12]

In total, Philip had a force of around 1,300 cavalry (mainly knights, but a few lightly armoured mounted sergeants) and between 4,000 and 6,000 infantry; once the allies were assembled, he could expect to face a larger army of around 1,500 cavalry and 7,500 infantry.[13] However, numbers alone were not everything, and much would come down to the structure of each host and its hierarchy. Philip's army had the advantage here, with a clear line of command: each separate contingent reported to its own count or duke, who would be with them in the field, but they in turn understood that they took their orders from Philip alone. By contrast, the allies were attempting a kind of leadership by committee, which was never ideal. Otto was the highest ranking among them, but Renaud and Ferrand were contributing large contingents of men and were on home ground, while King John was financing most of the costs of the campaign, meaning that William Longsword carried a great deal of authority. Some differences of opinion were evident: they could not agree whether they wanted to fight Philip directly in the field, and if so, whether they were prepared to fight on a Sunday, and if so, where. Eventually Renaud's belli-cosity came out on top ('For even on this very Sunday ... I will stand up in battle, even to the death')[14] and they tried to manoeuvre Philip into a pitched battle. This type of engagement, as we have noted before, was generally avoided, if possible, because of the risks, but sometimes it proved either the best or the only option. What the allies needed was a swift victory, preferably one that resulted in Philip's death or capture. If they were to become bogged down in a long series of sieges, it would tip the advantage towards the French king.

The encounter they wanted came about on 27 July 1214 (a Sunday) at a place called Bouvines, which was on the road from Lille to Tournai. It was the site of a bridge across the River Marcq, and the ground in the immediate vicinity of the river was marshy; a large party wanting to cross had thus to funnel along a narrow, raised road and over the bridge a few at a time, which would take some while. If half an army was on one side and half on the other, it would be the ideal place for an ambush.

Philip was not necessarily looking for a pitched battle himself; it would seem that he was, at least initially, trying to outmanoeuvre his opponents rather than seek direct confrontation. His army was halfway over the bridge in the direction of Lille when he heard that the allied host was behind him and advancing from Tournai, the worst of all positions and potentially disastrous. However, the bickering of the allies and the late arrival of some of Otto's troops meant that Philip had enough time to stop his army, order it to turn round and cross back, and then form up on a plain away from the marshy ground. There was now no chance of avoiding battle: he had his enemies in front of him and only the bridge behind – which he destroyed to avoid any temptation for him or his men to flee.

Each side formed up in three wings. Philip placed himself in the centre of his line, together with around 200 mounted knights and 2,000 infantry, under the *oriflamme*. To his right were the knights of Champagne and Burgundy, commanded by the duke of Burgundy, the count of St-Pol and Brother Guérin (who 'rode rapidly among the men, encouraging them to fight vigorously for the honour of their king and kingdom ... and telling them to guard at all costs against a more numerous enemy outflanking and surrounding them');[15] they were supported by a small force of mounted sergeants and a number of the militia groups. To Philip's left were the Bretons and the men of Dreux, Perche and Ponthieu, commanded by Count Robert II of Dreux and William of Ponthieu. Finally, Philip left a rearguard of some 150 sergeants behind him near the remains of the bridge.

Facing them was the allied army. Otto was in the centre, along with a small elite bodyguard of knights and supported by infantry from the Empire, all under the imperial banner of a dragon and an eagle. To Otto's right, facing Philip's left wing, were Renaud and William Longsword, with English knights and Brabant infantry and, on the extreme right flank, a small group of English archers. The allied left wing was under the command of Ferrand, with knights and infantry from Flanders and Hainaut. The plain was almost flat, so neither side had the advantage of high ground, but Philip's forces were facing south-east with the bright summer afternoon sun behind them; the allied army had the sun in their eyes.

The allied forces took longer to form up, and were still not quite in position when Guérin launched a charge against the Flemings, who were then also engaged against the knights of Champagne; the count of St-Pol's forces broke right through Ferrand's line, enabling them to turn and attack again from the rear. Fierce close-range fighting occupied the French right and the allied left for some time. In the meantime, Otto's centre division moved forward to meet Philip's, targeting the king in person; the French knights launched a counter-charge. And over on Philip's left the Dreux brothers were engaged by the advancing English forces under William Longsword.

Looking at the battle in overview like this, it almost seems like a game of chess. But a medieval battle was more than just wings of cavalry or blocks of infantry: it was individuals, getting close enough to kill and maim and hack at each other face to face, surrounded by noise, sweat and blood. This is vividly depicted in several places in William the Breton's narrative:

> Lances are shattering, swords and daggers hit each other, combatants split each other's heads with their axes, and their lowered swords plunge into the bowels of horses ... The combatants are engaging each other over the whole plain in such a close melee that those who are striking and those who are being struck are so close to each other that they barely have room to raise their arm to strike another blow ... Loose horses are running here and there across the field, some giving out their last breaths, some with entrails spilling out of their stomachs, some kneeling and falling to the ground ... There is hardly one place where you cannot see dead men and dying horses.[16]

And, as it happened, it was a number of individual encounters that changed the course of the battle.

King Philip was the undoubted target, and logically so: if he were to be killed then the French forces would soon collapse, and the whole realm would be thrown into instability, especially with Louis several hundred miles away. While the French and imperial knights were engaged in the battle's centre, German footsoldiers were able to force their way through the melee; one of them managed to hook his polearm into Philip's mail armour and drag him from his horse. Falling heavily, Philip was able to get to his feet, but was surrounded by men carrying long billhooks and pikes whom he could not reach with his sword as they stabbed at him. He was saved by a heroic act of self-sacrifice: one of his household knights, Peter Tristan, dismounted, offered his horse to Philip and then threw himself bodily between the king and his attackers. He was killed, but his actions gave Philip time to mount and get away from the immediate danger. He rallied and continued to fight on horseback in the central battle.

The tide in the centre began to turn, and now Otto was in danger as French knights hacked their way through to him. One grabbed his bridle and attempted to drag him out of the melee to capture him; another aimed a stab at his chest, but succeeded only in thrusting his dagger into the eye of Otto's horse, which had reared up at that exact moment. The horse managed to stagger away a little before collapsing and dying, giving one of Otto's bodyguard knights the time to offer him his own mount (an escapade which he survived, unlike Peter Tristan); Otto mounted and began to retreat. His elite knights bought him time to get away, but the imperial standard was captured.

Meanwhile, over to the allied left, Count Ferrand and the Flemings had been fighting a desperate action, surrounded as they had been since the early stages of the battle; after several hours in the searing heat the exhausted and wounded Ferrand was captured, triggering a collapse. The remaining Flemings were killed or captured, or chose to flee the field.

Over on the allied right flank, the earl of Salisbury was fighting in the melee when he came face to face with Philip of Dreux. William Longsword was tall and well built, like his half-brother Richard the Lionheart, but he was no match for Richard's old nemesis. The pugnacious bishop of Beauvais, now in his sixties, clubbed the younger man on the head with a mace 'that he just happened to have in his hand', crushing his helm and knocking him off his horse so that he fell heavily, 'his body making a dent in the ground'. Bishop Philip then battered the earl into submission and had him taken prisoner.[17]

That just left Renaud, in the same part of the field. He must have been aware to some extent of what was happening to the other parts of his army, but of all the allies he had the most to lose – a renegade lord taking the field against his king, and without the insurance policy of being related to a royal family, as Ferrand was – so he refused to give up. He formed his remaining infantry into a circle of two ranks, bristling with pikes and axes, while he and his knights remained mounted in the middle. From here they launched sortie after sortie against the French, retreating each time back inside to rest and regroup before attacking once more. Even William the Breton was forced to admire Renaud's 'indomitable courage' as he cut a distinctive figure, taller than those around him and wearing a garishly decorated helm.[18] The tactic proved effective for so long that soon they were the only part of the allied army still left fighting, and King Philip was able to order men forward in great numbers to overwhelm them. Renaud was knocked from his horse and trapped underneath it, unable to move, whereupon he was almost killed in a scramble; he was rescued only by the timely arrival of Brother Guérin, to whom he surrendered.

King Philip had won a huge victory, so significant that the ramifications probably did not sink in straight away. His immediate response was twofold: to give thanks to God in a nearby chapel, and to regroup, rather than to over-reach himself by attempting to chase the escapees. There was no need: the battle was over.[19] It could have been different, of course. If Philip had been killed at that pivotal moment when he was unhorsed, then life would have been very difficult for Louis, who would have had to fight his way up to Paris to try and gain his throne – all of which serves to remind us again why pitched battles were routinely avoided, if other options were available. As it happened, Philip had not only survived but had lost none of his major supporters.

The same could not be said for the enemy forces, the remnants of an alliance that was now in tatters. Otto had escaped (as, incidentally, had Henry of Brabant, although the content of any conversations he might have had with his wife on the subject of the battle remains unrecorded). But the former emperor was a spent force: he made it back to Germany, but he was no longer any threat to Frederick of Hohenstaufen and he died in internal exile in Brunswick in 1218, 'poor and miserable'.[20] King Philip sent Otto's broken standard to Frederick as a gift, both as a gesture of their friendship and as a none-too-subtle reminder of whom he had to thank for the unop-posed route to the imperial crown he would now enjoy.

Renaud and Ferrand, as counts of France who had committed treason by rebelling against their king, were liable to the most severe penalties, and nobody would have censured Philip if he had chosen to have them summarily beheaded. He did not, however, opting instead to incarcerate them in separate prisons, where Renaud was additionally loaded with chains. Ferrand's wife, Joan (who was countess of Flanders in her own right), was allowed to continue her rule there under closer royal supervision. Renaud was stripped of his lands and titles in favour of his daughter and heiress, Matilda; as she was married to Philip's son Philip Hurepel and they were both underage, direct control of Mortain and Boulogne fell to the king.

As time went by, both the renegade counts might have ended up wishing that they had been granted the mercy of a swift death. Ferrand was not released until 1227, thirteen years into his imprisonment and several years after King Philip's own death. This clemency was not extended to Renaud (who remained chained to a heavy log and unable to walk more than a pace in any direction), either because it was felt that he still had not paid his debts, or because he was considered a threat to what was by then Philip Hurepel's personal rule in his counties. It was in 1227, after Ferrand's release, that Renaud gave up hope and took his own life.

William Longsword, earl of Salisbury, owed no fealty to Philip and therefore needed to be treated differently. Realising his debt to the Dreux family, Philip awarded custody of William to Count Robert, with the intention that he could be exchanged for Robert junior, who was still in John's hands following his capture at Nantes. This did eventually come about, but it took so long, and John stalled so much, that William might have been forgiven for thinking that his half-brother did not want him back at all.[21]

* * *

Philip was triumphant and, in another sign of divine favour, his daughter-in-law Blanche had given birth to a second surviving son, Louis, during the momentous spring of 1214. The French king had two sons, two grandsons, most of his enemies under lock and key and his kingdom at peace. There was just one more thing to tick off his list, and the circumstances were as favourable as they had ever been. John's great gamble had failed, and he had been utterly defeated. He returned to England physically unscathed, but he had set in motion a train of events that he would not be able to stop.

CHAPTER SIXTEEN

INVITATION AND INVASION

J OHN WAS NOT, BY THIS point, a popular king. As we noted earlier, since his loss of Normandy in 1204 he had been making unreasonable financial demands on his barons, and this had caused great discontent. In theory, there were only three occasions on which a king of England could call on the financial resources of his barons: for the ransoming of his person (as Richard had done back in 1194), for the knighting of his eldest son and for the first marriage of his eldest daughter. However, there were also fines for various infractions and a system of reliefs, whereby, as we noted earlier, the heir to an estate, on the death of the previous incumbent, paid a sum to the crown in order to come into the inheritance. The problem for the barons was that, according to the exchequer, 'there is no fixed amount which the heir must pay to the king; he must make his own terms'[1] – and John's terms were that he needed money and he would go to almost any lengths to get it.

There are many examples of John's unreasonable financial demands from the decade between 1204 and 1214, but two stand out that would have repercussions later down the line. Geoffrey de Mandeville, the earl of Essex (the great-great-nephew of his namesake whom we met earlier, acting nefariously during the reign of King Stephen), had been forced to offer the huge sum of 20,000 marks (£13,333) for marrying John's ex-wife, Isabelle of Gloucester. This was at least twenty times the annual income he might expect from her earldom; and, as she was at least twenty years older than him, the deal was presumably not even expected to include the provision of heirs. Geoffrey ended up heavily in the crown's debt, unable to meet the strict schedule of payments stipulated by John, and saw some of his new estates confiscated. But there were worse fates, as illustrated by the almost complete destruction of the family de Briouze. As we saw in Chapter 12, William de Briouze had been the man who captured Arthur of Brittany back in 1202 and handed him over to John; he was at that time high in royal favour, but had subsequently fallen foul of some of John's exactions. When John demanded that he hand over his sons as hostages as security for his debts, William's wife, Matilda, made the mistake of saying out loud that she would never hand over her children to the man who had murdered his own nephew. Once that statement was in the public domain there was no way back, and she was hit with a demand for the almost unimaginable sum of 50,000 marks (£33,333) for 'the king's grace'. When she could not pay, she and her eldest son were imprisoned and starved to death; William fled to France, but died there a couple of years later.[2]

These examples serve to illustrate not only John's insatiable appetite for money, but also the way in which he sought to rule by fear and insecurity. He trusted nobody who was not in his power, either because they owed him money or because he held their family members in his custody as hostages. The extortionate reliefs, fees and fines were one way in which he achieved this: being in John's debt meant a constant sword hanging over the head of the unlucky debtor, aware that the king could decide to call in the full amount at any time and that this would cause destitution. This state of affairs was already worsening before the disastrous 1214 campaign in France, which is why many of John's barons did not wish to support him in the venture. They now knew – if they had not been aware before – the depths of his unpredictability and his viciousness. He then stirred the situation further by leaving the unpopular Peter des Roches, bishop of Winchester, as justiciar and regent during his absence. Peter continued John's demands for money and for service, and was disliked as he was a 'foreigner' – the definition of 'Englishness' having by now reached the point where a man who hailed from either Poitou or Touraine was considered foreign by English barons whose own family origins lay in Normandy or Anjou.[3]

When he returned from France in the autumn of 1214, John could see the threat on the horizon, and he immediately began strengthening the garrisons of royal castles with troops of mercenaries – mostly Poitevins, thus compounding the barons' distrust of the way the king relied on 'aliens'

– under the command of one Falkes de Bréauté. Falkes was the illegitimate son of a Norman knight, and had carved out a career for himself as a mercenary captain and ruthless enforcer.[4] In January 1215 John met the disaffected barons in London, a conference at which great emphasis was placed on the coronation charter of Henry I, from more than a century previously, which contained clauses on upholding ancient laws and liberties and the rights of the nobles.[5] John procrastinated about coming to an agreement, and both sides appealed to Rome. Given that John supposedly held England as a papal fief, there was little doubt as to whose side in the dispute Innocent would take, as two letters, both dated 19 March 1215, attest. One was addressed to the barons of England:

> It is a grievous trouble to us that, as we have heard, a difference between some of you and our well-beloved son in Christ, John, illustrious king of the English, has arisen . . . We utterly condemn it, if (as alleged by many) you have dared to form leagues or conspiracies against him and presumed arrogantly and disloyally by force of arms to make claims which, if necessary, you ought to have made in humility and loyal devotion.[6]

The other was sent to Archbishop Stephen Langton, 'to express surprise and annoyance' that he had

> until now ignored the differences between [John] and certain magnates, barons, and associates of theirs, wilfully shutting your eyes and not troubling to mediate for a settlement . . . Some indeed suspect and state that, in the issues recently raised with the king, you are giving help and favour to his opponents.[7]

In order to curry further favour with the pope, on Ash Wednesday in March 1215 John took the cross. It seems likely that this was nothing more than a cynical ploy; he evidently had little intention of actually going on crusade, but rather wanted the protected status that came with being a crusader. Following this development, the disaffected barons held another meeting in April. Prominent among the ringleaders were Geoffrey de Mandeville, now earl of both Essex and Gloucester but greatly in John's debt; and Robert Fitzwalter and Saer de Quincy, who, as we saw in Chapter 13, had been in a dispute with John about the payment of ransoms following their uncontested surrender of Vaudreuil eleven years earlier. These men were also linked by a web of relationships: de Mandeville's first wife had been Fitzwalter's daughter, and Fitzwalter was de Quincy's kinsman as well as his old comrade-in-arms. The whole group gave John an ultimatum that he should abide by the Articles of the Barons, as the demands were now known, but he refused.[8]

Rebellion then turned to outright war, as the barons formally renounced their homage to John and 'defied' him on 3 May, moving to attack his castles of Northampton and Bedford.[9] A key moment in the conflict came on 17 May, when London opened its gates to the rebels; from there they wrote to those lords still siding with John:

> [The rebels] advised [the royalist lords] with threats, as they regarded the safety of all their property and possessions, to abandon a king who was perjured and who warred against his barons, and together with them to stand firm and fight against the king for their rights and for peace; and that, if they refused to do this, they, the barons, would make war against them all, as against open enemies.[10]

John still had the support of a few of the highest men in the land: his half-brother William Longsword, earl of Salisbury; his cousin William de Warenne, earl of Surrey; William Marshal, earl of Pembroke; Ranulf de Blundeville, earl of Chester; and William d'Aubigny, earl of Arundel.[11] Thanks to his status as the holder of a papal fief, John also retained most of the representatives of the Church – with the possible exception of Stephen Langton, archbishop of Canterbury, who was suspiciously neutral, and the definite exception of Giles de Briouze, bishop of Hereford, who was firmly with the rebels and predictably so, given what had happened to his father, mother and elder brother at John's hands. But many other earls and barons sided with the rebels, and the momentum of the waverers was flowing that way; with his capital now in the hands of his opponents, John realised he had little choice but to submit to the baronial demands. He set his seal to the document that would later become known as Magna Carta on 15 June 1215.[12]

However, John was by no means reconciled to losing his kingly authority in this demeaning fashion. Almost immediately after sealing the charter he wrote once again to Pope Innocent, and once again he received the full backing of the papacy. In a letter dated 24 August 1215, Innocent wrote:

> We utterly reject and condemn this settlement, and under threat of excommunication we order that the king should not dare to observe it and that the barons and their associates should not require it to be observed: the charter, with all undertakings and guarantees whether confirming it or resulting from it, we declare to be null, and void of all validity for ever.[13]

Galvanised by this support, John rescinded his agreement to the charter in September.

The barons were now forced to come to the conclusion that they would not be able to control John, so they came up with a next step that was logical, albeit radical: they would have to overthrow him. This, of course, meant that they were faced with the obvious question of who should succeed him on the throne – they were not republicans, seeking to topple the monarchy as a whole, but rather subjects who wanted a better king than John. There does not seem to have been any idea of replacing John with one of his sons (who were aged seven and six), as an adult man who could impose himself on the situation was greatly to be preferred. As we noted in Chapter 14, however, male members of the Plantagenet family were by this stage almost non-existent, so the barons would have to look elsewhere. They did not want to elevate one of themselves, probably out of a combination of respect for the institution of monarchy and a realisation of the jealousy and chaos this would cause. So they needed someone who was already of royal blood, and their gaze turned across the Channel.

That the barons of England should contemplate inviting a Capetian to sit on the throne of England might, in hindsight, seem odd, but in the contemporary context their choice was based on sound reasoning on several counts. The French monarchs had a tradition of involving their foremost lords in decision-making processes, via a council of nobles, which was naturally a precedent that appealed to the English barons exasperated with John's autocratic demands. Having a representative of the French royal house on the throne of England would also mean that the barons could go back to having just one overlord, possibly with the hope of the restitution of their ancestral lands in Normandy. It was only eleven years since John had lost the duchy, so most of the current cohort of earls and barons had grown up with the idea of a cross-Channel monarchy; indeed, it was John's permanent residence in England that seemed the oddity, not the other way round. Perhaps at the back of their minds was also the idea that their chosen king would elect to reside mostly in France, thus leaving them with a greater freedom to pursue their own agenda in England. Finally, they were aware that many of John's mercenaries were Poitevins, who might show some reluctance to fight against a member of the royal house of France, thus depriving John of their services.

A Capetian therefore seemed to be the logical choice; the only further question was which one. Again, there does not seem to have been a great deal of discussion on this point, with Louis being preferred from the outset to Philip. It was he, after all, who had been touted a few years earlier as a potential English king, and it was he, rather than his father, who possessed at least the shadow of a blood claim, as his wife Blanche was John's niece and a granddaughter of Henry II and Eleanor of Aquitaine via their only surviving daughter, Eleanor. Louis was also younger and more vigorous (twenty-seven to Philip's forty-nine), an important consideration if military action were to be necessary. He had proved his worth on campaigns before, and he would – or at least the English barons assumed he would – benefit from abundant resources, as his father would throw the whole might of the French monarchy behind the mission. The decision was made, and Robert Fitzwalter and Saer de Quincy sailed to France in September 1215 to make the offer personally.[14]

John, still convinced that he could fight his corner, was waiting for another contingent of Poitevin mercenaries to arrive; he rode to the south coast to receive them, but there was a storm in the Channel and all that arrived were bodies washed up on the shore, while the coin and treasure to pay them sank to the bottom of the sea.[15] The barons took advantage of this unexpected bonus by seizing Rochester castle and thus both barring John's way back to London and securing the mouth of the Medway where it flowed into the Channel. An experienced knight named William d'Albini (a cousin of Robert Fitzwalter, not to be confused with William d'Aubigny, the earl of Arundel mentioned above) was installed as the garrison commander. John had little choice but to assail it, but he approached the task with energy and an unusual efficiency, destroying the bridge over the Medway to prevent reinforcements arriving from rebel-held London and organising a full-scale siege.

John remained at Rochester for all seven weeks of the siege – the longest he spent in any one place during his entire reign – supervising a twenty-four-hour bombardment with his machinery, the operators working in shifts through day and night. He had sappers dig a mine under the curtain wall, causing the south-eastern corner to collapse and allowing his men to storm in for hand-to-hand combat; the defenders retreated to the keep, but another mine caused its south-east corner tower to collapse. The keep was of an unusual design, with a reinforcing wall that effectively divided it internally into two separate halves, so the defenders were still able to hold out in one half; in order to make their supplies last as long as possible, they ejected those least able to fight. In a horrifying echo of the atrocity at Château Gaillard in 1203, one chronicler claims that John refused to let them pass peaceably through his lines, instead having their hands and feet cut off.[16] The expulsion of these unfortunates did not actually buy the defenders much more time – after a further week had gone by and with 'not a morsel of provisions remaining amongst them' they were starved into surrendering on 30 November. John's first instinct was to hang the whole garrison, but he was persuaded against it on the grounds that similar treatment might later be meted out to royal garrisons by the rebels; in the end only one man was executed, a crossbowman who had previously been in John's own service.[17]

While all this was going on, Robert Fitzwalter and Saer de Quincy had arrived in Paris, at which point they made a proposal unique in the history of the two houses and the two kingdoms: they offered the crown of England to the son of the king of France.

* * *

Since his success at La-Roche-aux-Moines and his father's at Bouvines, Louis had not been idle. The south-eastern area of France had for some years been riven by a conflict that would later become known as the Albigensian Crusade: to summarise briefly, a sect had grown up around a belief known as Catharism, which was Christian but so far removed from the orthodox doctrine that it had been declared heresy, and various means had been sought to stamp it out, with violence escalating since the papal legate to the region had been murdered in 1208. Pope Innocent had demanded action of Philip, who had not been averse (this providing him with an opportunity to send Louis on a military campaign to keep him occupied), but his attention had been distracted by the proposed invasion of England in 1212. Louis was eventually dispatched south early in 1215, along with some of his companions and the elderly, but indefatigable, bishop of Beauvais, to take his place in a host led by the experienced campaigner Simon de Montfort.[18] He returned in the autumn at the end of the campaigning season, having been part of a successful attempt to capture the city of Toulouse, and was in Paris to meet Fitzwalter and de Quincy in person and to receive their offer and their homage.

Louis was keen to take up the opportunity, but he and the two barons were taken aback by Philip's apparently lukewarm reaction. This might have been natural caution; the French king liked to examine a situation from all angles before taking action. It might have been because the pope was against it, and Philip had not long been reconciled with the Holy See after two decades of conflict caused by his marital situation. There also exists the vague possibility that he was offended – that, although he himself had planned to install Louis on the English throne several years before, he might now have preferred the crown to be offered to him in the first instance, so he could graciously nominate his son in his stead. But there is another, and perhaps more likely, explanation: that he was playing a double game. He would not overtly support a plan that was opposed by the pope, but in fact he would not contest it or forbid his son from taking action, and in private he would actually support it by clandestine means. When Louis immediately announced his acceptance of the crown and his support of the baronial cause, therefore, Philip did not gainsay him; and when Louis raised an initial force of 120 knights and sent them across the Channel in December 1215, Philip did nothing to stop him. (As it happened, the first, unintended, consequence of this action was the loss of one of the leading rebel barons: during a tournament that was held as part of a joint military training exercise, Geoffrey de Mandeville, earl of Essex and Gloucester, was accidentally killed by a French knight.)[19] Another fleet of twenty ships followed in January 1216.

As was customary in France, such a momentous proposal needed to be put before a council of nobles, and – notwithstanding the actions Louis had already taken – the campaign could not be considered a settled plan until it was agreed upon. The council, later known as the Assembly of Melun, took place in late April 1216, with Philip presiding but remaining neutral, allowing Louis to put his case to the nobles and them to respond. Louis had arranged for his team of advisors – chief among whom was Simon Langton, the younger brother of the archbishop of Canterbury – to prepare a legal argument for his right to the English crown, but it was thin, to say the least. It rested on three points of varying degrees of spuriousness: that John had lost his right to the English throne, that Louis was the legitimate heir to that vacant throne, and that the papacy had no right to intervene in the matter.[20]

The instability of the legal ground on which Louis stood was not an issue for the eager council of nobles. The two principal outcomes of the assembly were resounding support for Louis's claim and forthcoming campaign, and the start of a long-term enmity between him and the papal legate Guala Bicchieri, who had argued vociferously against the plan while Louis looked upon him 'with a scowling brow'.[21] Guala left the French court to travel to England, muttering imprecations about Louis and Philip and threatening them with excommunication, but Pope Innocent made no personal comment on the situation at all, leading us to the intriguing possibility that he might also have been playing something of a double game.

King Philip ostensibly remained neutral, and contemporary chroniclers took a range of views on his motives. William the Breton, ever keen to present Philip in the best light, states conclusively that Louis acted 'against the will of his father' and that the king refused to support his son, so as not to offend the pope. The gossipy Minstrel of Reims, meanwhile, depicts a stand-up row between father and son, during which Philip shouts, 'Do whatever you like, but you will never succeed, because the English are traitors and felons.' The Anonymous of Béthune, one of our best-informed sources at this point, is perhaps nearest the mark when he says that Philip 'publicly made it appear as though he did not want to be involved because of the truce he had gained [reconciliation with the pope]; but privately, it was believed that he had advised him [Louis]'.[22] The bottom line is that the king could have prevented Louis from launching his campaign, but he did not. As an aside, the fact that he could let Louis take so many of France's nobles and fighting men abroad showed that he was in no danger at home;

his alliance with the Empire was secure and his lifelong war against the Plantagenets had moved from the defensive to the offensive.

Louis began raising troops, but he had a problem: without Philip's official and public backing, he could not call upon the resources of the French crown. He thus had to recruit privately, and although he was not short of volunteers from among those who fancied some overseas adventure and the chance for gain, the force he ended up with was nothing like the size it could have been – or that the English barons might have been counting on. This would become a recurring theme and perhaps the defining characteristic of the invasion, as we shall see. As it was, a fleet began to assemble at the Channel ports of Wissant, Gravelines and Boulogne, to be commanded at sea by Eustace the Monk; it would carry a force of some 1,200 knights and their horses, and probably two or three times as many non-knightly combatants.[23]

* * *

John knew what was coming, but he was powerless to stop it. He was not helped by the fact that more than half his knights were from either Poitou or the Low Countries, and might refuse to fight against Louis, or even defect to him.[24] He did what he could by dividing his army in half. He deployed one part, under William Longsword and Falkes de Bréauté, to remain in the south-east and keep an eye on London – not to attempt to retake it, but rather to try to keep the barons pinned down there and stop supplies entering. William and Falkes took their instructions about reimposing royal authority seriously, and carried out brutal raids in Essex, Hertfordshire and Cambridgeshire, including sacking Ely, where a contemporary noted that 'they made great slaughter, as they did everywhere they went, sparing neither age, nor sex, nor condition, nor the clergy'.[25] The smoke from burning buildings could be seen from London, and was no doubt intended as an incentive for the inhabitants to rethink their loyalties; but they did not.

John himself went north, to launch devastating raids of fire and pillage in the lands of his opponents, moving swiftly from St Albans through Northamptonshire and Nottinghamshire. His methods were as brutal and direct as ever: when he advanced on Belvoir castle, held by Nicholas d'Albini – son of the William who had commanded, and been captured at, Rochester and was now being held in close confinement at Corfe castle –

John ordered Nicholas to surrender, otherwise his father 'should never eat again but should die a disgraceful death'. Given John's previous record, this was no empty threat and, coupled with the knowledge that no help would be forthcoming to relieve a siege, Nicholas surrendered.[26]

By early 1216 John was in Yorkshire, pillaging and burning his way north to encounter the forces of the teenaged King Alexander II of Scots (the son and successor of William the Lion, whom we last met in Chapter 7), who had taken advantage of the chaos in England to launch an invasion of his own, burning Newcastle. John's advance caused Alexander to retreat, and soon John reached Berwick, which he sacked. He initially looked to move even further north, but Alexander was able to defend his own borders and John, on receiving news from London that a further party of French reinforcements had arrived, turned around. He was back in Bedford by the end of February 1216, after a swift campaign that had caused much damage, but was not really sustainable – the rebel commanders and their allies in the north knew that John would not be able to remain there for long, so they sprang back up once his back was turned, and indeed Alexander had already recrossed the border to attack Carlisle before John reached Bedford. John's campaign could even be considered counter-productive, in that he had been attacking his own subjects, causing untold suffering and misery to those who would thus have no cause to appreciate or respect him in the future. That he used foreign mercenaries to do this only added insult and ill-will, as the chronicler Roger of Wendover describes:

> The whole surface of the earth was covered with these limbs of the devil like locusts, who assembled from remote regions to blot out everything from the face of the earth, from man down to his cattle; for, running about with drawn swords and open knives, they ransacked towns, houses, cemeteries and churches, robbing everyone, and sparing neither women nor children; the king's enemies wherever they were found were imprisoned in chains and compelled to pay a heavy ransom. Even the priests whilst standing at the very altars, with the Cross of the Lord in their hands, clad in their sacred robes, were seized, tortured, robbed and ill-treated.[27]

John had succeeded in depriving his opponents of resources, while also extorting enough money to pay the mercenaries who were acting for him;

but he had also succeeded in alienating his subjects, who began to turn away not just from him but from the whole idea of his dynasty, under which they had known little peace. John's five children were, at this time, being brought up entirely separately from each other, although almost all in the orbit of Peter des Roches, which did not make them any more popular. His heir, the eight-year-old Henry, was under the bishop's personal guardianship, initially in Winchester, but later (as the threat of invasion on the south coast increased), being taken further west to Marlborough and then Devizes. Second son Richard, aged seven, was based at Corfe castle, in the hands of one of Peter's loyal men; two-year-old Isabelle was in the household of another crony; and baby Eleanor was at Taunton, another of Peter's castles.[28] The only exception was John's eldest daughter, the five-year-old Joan, who was in France, being brought up in the household of her intended husband, Hugh de Lusignan junior. If John wanted to secure his children's future, he would need to face up to the invasion that was now imminent.

* * *

Louis sailed from France on the evening of 20 May 1216, the auspicious feast of Pentecost, after bidding a temporary farewell to his pregnant wife. In his flagship, commanded by Eustace the Monk, were, among others, his chief advisor, Simon Langton, and his kinsmen Robert of Dreux the younger and Robert de Courtenay. His campaign did not get off to the best start when a storm blew up in the Channel, scattering his fleet and meaning that when he arrived on the Isle of Thanet the following day, he was accompanied by only six other ships. They anchored at Stonor while they waited for the rest to assemble – fortunately for him, they had been blown off course, rather than sunk – but Louis was impatient and he waded ashore. He was met by a small but not belligerent crowd of locals, among whom was a priest carrying a crucifix. As a symbolic gesture, Louis sought him out and kissed the crucifix. This was not to be an invasion in the true sense of the word; as far as he was concerned, he was the rightful king, invited to take the crown, so he was merely on his way to claim his rights in peace, rather than to kill his new subjects and burn their lands. If he met no resistance, he would cause no unnecessary violence.[29]

More French ships arrived and they mustered at Sandwich, taking control of the town and port on 23 May. Louis opted not to begin a siege of Dover castle straight away: it was large, well provisioned, well fortified and well garrisoned with Flemish knights under the command of John's justiciar Hubert de Burgh (who had replaced Peter des Roches in that post in the aftermath of Magna Carta the previous year), so any attempt on it would be time-consuming. It would need to be addressed eventually, of course, but first Louis should meet the barons who had invited him, so he bypassed Dover and rode directly for London. Canterbury surrendered to him on the way; the papal legate Guala was there, but he left hurriedly to meet John in Winchester, declaring Louis excommunicate as he went.[30]

The barons left the capital to meet Louis along the way at Rochester. Among them were Robert Fitzwalter and Saer de Quincy, along with William de Mandeville (brother of the late Geoffrey), the new earl of Essex, and others including William Marshal junior, eldest son of the earl of Pembroke. Whether the latter had genuinely decided to fight against his father, or whether they were playing a similar sort of ruse to that of Philip Augustus – making sure that one member of the family would be on the winning side, no matter what the outcome – is unclear. These barons paid homage to Louis and, while they were there, retook Rochester castle from the small force that John had left after his triumph of the previous year, the damaged walls doing little to prevent them.

Louis entered London on 2 June 1216. Not only was there no resistance, but he was openly welcomed: he was cheered through the streets by the assembled population and welcomed at St Paul's by the canons. Once there, he swore on the gospels that he would restore to his new vassals all their rightful inheritances and previous good laws. Louis was not, at this stage, crowned – a point to which we will return later. He therefore continued to style himself 'eldest son of the king of France', rather than 'king of England', but in other ways he behaved as a new monarch would. He took up residence at the royal palace of Westminster, named Simon Langton his chancellor, wrote to King Alexander of Scots and then also to all the barons who had not yet done homage to him, ordering them to do so or to leave the realm.[31] There was something of a rush to acclaim him; his arrival, after so many years of talk, and the unopposed welcome he had received so far, convinced many who had previously wavered that the tide had turned. As far as they were concerned, John's reign was over and they should submit to the new king before it was too late. Among the big names who came over to Louis at this point were three of the four notable Williams who had previously remained loyal to John: the earls of Salisbury, Arundel and Surrey.

And what of John himself? With the defection even of his cousin and his half-brother, all seemed to be over. He had, in fact, made his way to the coast when he heard that Louis had been sighted; but for reasons best known to himself he decided not to attack, even when only seven ships of seasick men arrived. As might be expected, different chroniclers put different interpretations on this, with the English point of view being that John 'did not venture to attack Louis on his landing, lest in battle they [John's men] might all leave him and go over to the side of Louis; he therefore chose to retreat for a time, rather than to give battle on an uncertainty', while the French opinion was that 'forgetting his promise and his royal pride, [John] preferred to flee rather than fight'.[32] In either case he made good speed westwards, away from Louis's army, first to Dover, and then on to Guildford and Winchester. He was on the run, and it would seem that his once-mighty dynasty had fallen.

≈ CHAPTER SEVENTEEN ≈

'HELL IS MADE FOULER'

The obvious thing for louis to do at this point was to have himself crowned. During the twelfth and early thirteenth centuries in England it was the fact of coronation and anointing, and the approval of God and the Church that was thereby implied, that made a king, regardless of any apparently superior hereditary claim. This convention had been exploited by Henry I, who had a surviving older brother at the time of his accession in 1100, and by Stephen, who in 1135 had two living older brothers as well as a cousin who was the child and designated successor of the previous king, all of whom would have been higher up the nominal queue. The situation now, in 1216, was different, in that the previous king was very much alive; but, given that Louis's argument at the Assembly of Melun had been that the English throne was vacant, a formal coronation would be an immeasurable boost to his own claim.[1]

Unfortunately for Louis, there were several hurdles in the way. Chief among them was the decree of excommunication that had been made against him by the papal legate Guala as he fled from Canterbury; as an excommunicate, Louis was officially barred from church services, and this would certainly include a coronation ceremony. He made light of it at this stage, having Simon Langton put out a statement that the sentence had been pronounced only by the legate – who had publicly argued with Louis at Melun and who might have a personal grudge – and not by the pope himself. Therefore, the reasoning went, the excommunication should not be considered final, as Innocent would surely rescind it once he heard the facts.

There was also, perhaps, a thought that excommunication might be losing its terror due to recent overuse: John and Philip Augustus had both been under the sentence for years, but had been happily welcomed back into the fold by Innocent as soon as they acquiesced to his demands, and neither of them had suffered any lasting spiritual or reputational damage.

Of greater immediate import were the questions of place and celebrant. Most of the churches in London ignored Guala's decree and welcomed Louis – including St Paul's, where he had taken his oath to restore good laws; but one of those that did heed the legate and close its doors to him was Westminster Abbey, the traditional coronation site. Moreover, the sole right to crown and anoint kings of England was invested in the archbishop of Canterbury, but Stephen Langton was in Rome, suspended from his post by Pope Innocent, thanks to his sympathy for and involvement with the rebel barons.[2] Louis therefore had two options: press ahead with a ceremony that could later easily be called invalid by his opponents, or defer it until the correct procedure could be followed. If he had been as politically astute as his father he might have chosen the former, on the basis that any coronation was better than none; but in fact he opted for the latter, preferring instead to concentrate on subduing those parts of the realm that remained antagonistic to him in a military campaign.[3]

This was a clearer path, with two easily identifiable goals: to bring to heel and accept homage from those barons who had not yet recognised Louis as king; and to eradicate John, who would continue to be a danger for as long as he was still at large and continued to enjoy the support of the powerful earls of Pembroke and Chester as well as the justiciar, Hubert de Burgh. It was also a path that could not be followed by remaining in London, so Louis would need to saddle up and get out into what he considered to be his new realm. He could not be everywhere at once, of course, so he divided his forces into three: one part would remain in London as a garrison to keep the capital secure; one part, under Robert Fitzwalter, would move into the eastern counties; and Louis himself would take the rest westwards to pursue the fleeing John.

From London Louis moved first towards Winchester, where John was known to be, via Reigate (where William de Warenne, earl of Surrey, had the castle gates left open for him), Guildford and Farnham. The combined French and baronial force reached Winchester on 14 June to find it ablaze:

John had heard that they were on the way, fled further west to Corfe and ordered the city suburbs fired as he went. The two castles of Winchester (a larger, royal one and the smaller Wolvesey, belonging to the bishop of Winchester, currently in the hands of one of John's illegitimate sons) were still standing and garrisoned, so Louis set up simultaneous sieges; both soon surrendered.[4] Winchester was thus secured, so Louis could leave his own garrisons there and set off again in pursuit of John.

Corfe was a very well-defended castle – hence it being used to hold high-profile prisoners – but John did not feel safe even there, and preferred further flight to the danger of being pinned down by a siege. He made his way deeper into the West Country, while ordering Falkes de Bréauté to ensure the garrisoning and provisioning of Wallingford, Wareham, Bristol and Devizes as well as Corfe. This was probably John's best tactic under the circumstances, as the constant need to stop and set up sieges would slow Louis's momentum. The major castles Louis had left behind him in the areas he otherwise controlled – Dover and Windsor – were already causing him problems, and he could not afford to keep advancing while leaving enemy-held strongholds behind him. He would have to take them or break them one at a time, allowing John to stay one step ahead.

The pursuit now took Louis to Portchester and then the small castle of Odiham, whose tiny garrison of three knights and ten soldiers managed to stand out for a whole week before surrendering – as a mark of respect for their bravery, Louis not only allowed them to leave unharmed, but also to take their horses and armour with them. At this point an unexpected bonus came his way when a message arrived from the castellan of Marlborough, announcing a pre-emptive surrender. Marlborough was not, of course, the only town to yield to Louis; but this particular episode is significant, because it illustrates a problem that was going to dog him during the whole of his English campaign: how was he going to balance the needs and wants of the English barons who had invited him over with those of the French lords who had followed him in the expectation of reward? In this instance Louis accepted the submission and gave the town and the castle of Marlborough to his kinsman Robert of Dreux the younger, but this was immediately contested by William Marshal junior, who felt that his family connections in the area entitled him to the award, and who had already complained about being overlooked for the position of marshal of Louis's army. The dispute threatened to escalate, but Louis was fortunate in being able to compromise: the surrender of Worcester followed swiftly on the heels of Marlborough's, and he was able to allocate this to Marshal junior. But he would need to be aware that there would effectively be two claimants for every town and stronghold he took, and the political acumen needed to keep the two very disparate halves of his support happy might have taxed even Philip Augustus. The young Marshal would soon be back asking for more; his hold on Worcester did not last long, and the town was quickly retaken by forces loyal to John under the command of Ranulf, earl of Chester, and Falkes de Bréauté.[5]

Louis had only taken one third of his troops with him on this southern campaign, and now they were stretched out thinly all along the south coast and into the West Country, making him potentially vulnerable. He thus decided to pause his pursuit of John in order to pull back and consolidate, heading back to London to receive dispatches on how the other parts of his support were faring. The news was good: Robert Fitzwalter had enjoyed success in Essex, Norfolk and Suffolk, while another baronial adherent, Gilbert de Gant, had advanced northwards to Lincoln, where he had a hereditary claim to the earldom that had been in abeyance for half a century. He had there taken the town, although the castle within it was still holding out under its castellan, a widow in her sixties named Nicola de la Haye, who had purchased a truce. Perhaps scenting an opportunity to redress the balance of French and baronial rewards, Louis welcomed the cash that Gilbert brought as a result of the truce and named him earl of Lincoln. He also heard that inroads had been made into Yorkshire on his behalf, and that King Alexander of Scots was besieging Carlisle. In short, Louis now had the support of around two thirds of the barons, and around half of England's geographical area was under his control.[6]

This was all very pleasing, and Louis could now give some thought to how he could govern his new realm once he was master of all of it. He had already named a chancellor, instituted some rudimentary systems of justice and made grants of land and titles (some of which were tenuous, given that there were existing holders who were loyal to John), but his further attempts at governance met with little success, as England was just in too much chaos for the normal systems to function properly. He could not impose widespread taxation, only *ad hoc* financial exactions – and, even then, only from lands under his control; and he was not in a position to mint his own coins, a significant marker of kingship.[7] He was also still awaiting news from Rome following his appeal against Guala's sentence of excommunication, the result of which would have a great influence on the course of his campaign. But when a messenger did eventually arrive, it was with the surprising news that Innocent III, who was only in his mid-fifties, had died suddenly in mid-June. This would mean a time of great uncertainty not just in England, but all over western Europe; a successor would be elected in due course, but there was no knowing whether he would follow Innocent's policies or set out on a completely different path. And, in the meantime, there was a power vacuum at the highest level of the Church.

There was nothing Louis could do about the papal situation, but he could continue military action. He decided against another pursuit of John, opting instead to turn his attention to the places where there were still pockets of resistance in lands otherwise under his control, in the form of castles holding out against him. He sent Robert of Dreux (junior) and another leading compatriot, Hervé, count of Nevers (whose daughter and sole heiress was betrothed to Louis's elder son, Philip), to Windsor, while he himself headed for the mighty fortress of Dover. He arrived there on 25 July 1216 and settled in for a long siege.

* * *

John had succeeded in eluding Louis so far, but he was by now little more than a fugitive in his own kingdom. Louis's static position at Dover gave John the opportunity to emerge from his bolthole, and he regained some support over the late summer by exploiting the divisions between the French and baronial elements of Louis's party. To summarise a complex situation briefly, the more the English barons defected to Louis, the less the French liked it (as this would decrease their own opportunity for gain) and the more the tensions between the two disparate parties became obvious; a few well-placed offers and bribes might thus lure some of the barons back to John's camp. This did not produce anything like a tidal wave of U-turns, but it did tempt some, among them the disgruntled William Marshal junior.

In early September John went on the offensive, leaving the West Country to move swiftly across the south midlands; he was at Oxford by the middle of the month before skirting Windsor (not engaging in battle with the besiegers there, but ravaging the countryside and burning enough of the harvest-season crops to draw some of them off to protect their food supplies) and heading for Cambridge and into Suffolk. Next he turned north to try to give some relief to Lincoln, reaching the city by the end of September to liaise with Nicola de la Haye, although not engaging in any military action there either.[8] Then he headed to Lynn in Norfolk, where he was feasted by the townspeople, but later began to feel ill; he may or may not have known straight away that he had contracted dysentery, but this must have become clear to him as his condition worsened rapidly. Nevertheless, he left Lynn on 11 October in the direction of Swineshead Abbey, 30 miles north-west. In order to get there, his large party had to cross the marshy ground of the Wash, and it was during this journey that some kind of mishap occurred that resulted in the loss of some or all of his baggage train. The contemporary accounts are confused as to how serious this incident was and what losses (of both life and goods) were sustained, but it was in any case a setback that the now seriously ill John did not need.[9] He stayed at Sleaford on 14 and 15 October, from where he wrote a letter to the new pope, Honorius III, to say that he believed his life was in danger and to beg Honorius to take the kingdom of England and his young heir under papal protection.[10] From Sleaford the party travelled to Newark, John by now in a litter as he was too ill to ride. The abbot of Croxton, a nearby Premonstratensian foundation, was summoned to hear his confession, and John made a will. Normally a royal testament would be detailed, with specific bequests spelled out, but this one was brief because John was 'overcome by a grievous sickness, and thus incapable of making a detailed disposition of [his] goods'. In line with England's status as a papal fief, the list of executors was headed by the papal legate Guala, followed by Peter des Roches, bishop of Winchester; it then included among others William Marshal, Ranulf de Blundeville and Falkes de Bréauté. Once this was achieved, John had nothing to do except to contemplate his mortality and to pray for himself and his son amid the increasing pain he was experiencing. He died at Newark during the night of 18–19 October.[11]

Although in his younger days John had met Philip Augustus more than once, he had never come face to face with Louis – neither in Poitou or at La-Roche-aux-Moines in 1214, nor in England in 1216; and now he never would, leaving to others the task of fending off the Capetian invader. There is no denying that John was unpopular with contemporaries, and despite sporadic attempts over the years and centuries to rehabilitate him, he is still generally considered one of the worst kings ever to sit on the English throne. Gerald of Wales, ever a critic of the Plantagenets, was robust in his assessment:

> John ... since he was not able to equal his outstanding brothers or his parents in good, being one who, just as he was younger in age, so too was far worse in bitter emotions and wicked deeds, strove not only to surpass them in evil but to surpass all vicious people in the enormity of his vices, and especially, with all his effort, to outdo all the tyrants whom the present age or the long memory of antiquity can recall, with the detestable deeds of his wicked tyranny.[12]

The most commonly quoted of the thirteenth-century epitaphs of John is Matthew Paris's *'Anglia sicut adhuc sordet foetore Johannis, / Sordida foedatur foedante Johanne gehenna'*, a translation of which is 'With John's foul deeds England's whole realm is stinking, / As does hell, too, wherein he is now sinking', but which is often rendered more simply and pithily as 'Foul as it is, hell is made fouler by the presence of John.'[13]

John's body could not be taken to Westminster for burial, as London and its outlying suburbs were under Louis's control; instead, and as he had specified, he was interred at Worcester Cathedral. He had been the last adult male of the Plantagenet family, and his dynasty was now hanging by a very slender thread. His heir, Henry, who had celebrated his ninth birthday only a fortnight previously and who was lodged safely at Devizes castle, was now brought to Gloucester, being met on the way by William Marshal and others in a touching scene that Marshal's biographer covers in some detail:

> The Marshal came forward to meet him and greeted him, and the well-brought-up child said to him: 'Welcome. I wish to tell you truly, that I give myself to God and to yourself, so that in God's name you may take charge of me. And may our true God, the protector of all that is good, grant that you so manage our affairs that you may take good care of them.' The Marshal replied: 'Fair lord, I can tell you sincerely, and may

God protect my soul, that I will be yours in good faith and will not neglect you as long as I have the power to do so.' The King wept, and those standing round him wept tears of compassion, and the Marshal likewise wept pitifully.[14]

The Plantagenet future looked bleak, but it lay not only in the hands of a tearful and overwhelmed nine-year-old child: it was also in those of the older and wiser men around him. And it was these men who recognised something Louis had missed: the pivotal importance of having a coronation – any kind of coronation, no matter how unorthodox – to confer legitimacy. 'The sooner the better,' Marshal's biographer has one of them say, 'for, upon my faith, there is no question of waiting; if we wait too long, we might end up with nothing.' They would therefore press ahead, on the basis that Henry III was John's hereditary heir.[15]

As a prelude to the coronation Henry was knighted, despite his tender age, and then the ceremony took place on 28 October 1216, the day after Henry's arrival in Gloucester and a Friday – the lords did not want to wait even another two days, in case Louis took advantage of the delay to have himself crowned in London first. So Henry's coronation was, like the one Louis might have organised for himself in June, if he had been so minded, not at Westminster Abbey and not celebrated by the archbishop of Canterbury: the legate Guala sang the Mass and Peter des Roches placed the crown on his head. Or, in fact, not a crown: they did not have one available, and so the item placed on the boy's head was a circlet donated by his mother. He was dressed in 'child-sized robes of state', and afterwards 'those inside the cathedral carried him out in their arms'.[16]

It is perhaps ironic that Henry was at this point considered the 'English' king in opposition to the 'French' invader, as he was, of course, almost entirely French himself. His mother was Isabella of Angoulême, a woman of Poitevin and French ancestry (and indeed a great-granddaughter of Louis VI), and his father was John, himself the son of an Aquitainian mother and a father who was half-Angevin. Only one of Henry III's eight great-grandparents, Empress Matilda, could in any way claim to be 'English'. But in a time of an emerging proto-national feeling, that was how it was framed; and, as we will see, Henry would later prove to be the first of what we might call the Anglo-centric kings of England.[17]

Of immediate concern was the fact that there would be a long minority, a situation that had not arisen since the Conquest. Sensibly under the circumstances, full vice-regal power and control of the king were not vested in one man alone: William Marshal (now aged around seventy) would be the regent, but Peter des Roches would have personal guardianship of Henry, and both would be subject to the oversight of the pope in the person of the legate Guala. Someone who would play no part at all in the new regime was the queen mother, Isabella of Angoulême, although it is not entirely clear whether this was her own choice or simply because the coterie surrounding the new king did not consider her for any kind of formal role, such as those that other dowager queens had previously played in both England and France. The traditional narrative, perhaps emphasised or exaggerated by male chroniclers in possession of hindsight, has been that she abandoned her children; however, it is equally likely that she was excluded from power by male nobles and politicians who distrusted the influence she might wield over her young son, and she was not mentioned in John's deathbed testament.[18] Isabella would leave England less than a year after her son's coronation, never to return, though we will meet her again in France in due course.

* * *

Louis, as we saw earlier in this chapter, had settled down in front of Dover castle in July. Dover was one of the largest and best-fortified castles in England, having been much enlarged and improved by Henry II; it was set on a hill and boasted a solid keep with walls up to 20 feet thick, and surrounding curtain walls broken only by a twin-towered gatehouse that was itself further protected by a wooden barbican. It was in the hands of the justiciar, Hubert de Burgh, who had a large garrison and ample supplies. Louis was, therefore, in no doubt that taking it would require a great deal of resources, time and patience – all things he did not exactly have in abundance. He did, however, have plenty of military experience and a tactical mindset, so he did everything he could with the means available to him. One part of his force remained in the town of Dover, on one side of the castle, while the other moved to a hill in front of the gatehouse, which gave him the advantage of higher ground. His siege engines were erected there and the bombardment began; at the same time, his ships blockaded the harbour, so that the castle could not be resupplied by land or by sea. When the bombardment made little progress against the walls he tried other standard tactics, building a siege tower and setting men to undermine the walls.

Hubert, meanwhile, did not sit idle and wait for Louis's troops to breach the defences. He sent out waves of men on frequent sorties who were able to charge on horseback, inflict damage and casualties on the siege camp, and then retire back behind the walls. This state of affairs lasted for several weeks, at which point it became apparent that Louis's besieging force was starting to haemorrhage men. Some of his noble French companions had signed up for adventure and gain, not to sit still and be shot at by crossbow-wielding snipers on the walls of Dover, and they began to make excuses to slip away; some knights felt that their obligatory period of military service was up, as they had served their forty days; some of his mercenaries felt they were not being paid enough, and deserted.

Louis's depleted force did make a breakthrough in the middle of August, thanks to a direct and bloody attack on the barbican which ended in its capture; but they could make no progress against the stone gatehouse behind it. King Alexander of Scots arrived (having made his way, remarkably, the entire length of England without incident or attack) to offer him homage for his English lands, and so did a party of reinforcements from France led by the younger of the two Dreux brothers, Peter, duke of Brittany, and by Thomas, count of Perche, whom we last saw at the Battle of Bouvines.

In early September the painstaking work of the miners finally paid off when one of the gatehouse towers collapsed, allowing the French to pour in for long-awaited hand-to-hand combat, but the defenders threw themselves into the gap, holding off the attackers and filling in the breach with timbers taken from buildings inside the castle walls. The French could penetrate no further into the castle, despite their efforts and some casualties, so the siege reverted to its prior situation. The stalemate served nobody, so Louis and Hubert agreed a truce and Louis withdrew temporarily from the siege on 14 October, little realising that momentous news would soon come his way.[19] He was back in London when the information reached him, probably on or around 22 October, that John was dead.

From one perspective, the death of Louis's antagonist might seem like a wonderful opportunity for him to cement his domination over England,

and indeed almost his first move was to send word to Hubert de Burgh at Dover that he should now surrender the castle, on the grounds that the king for whom he was holding it was no more; if he did so, then he would be welcomed into Louis's fold with a high position. Hubert, however, declined, stating that if John were truly dead then he now served John's children.[20] It was a good start for Henry at the beginning of his reign, and even better was to come, thanks to a move from the regency council that was both ingenious and astonishing: they met at Bristol on 12 November and reissued Magna Carta.

The significance of this manoeuvre should not be underestimated – in short, they were voluntarily agreeing to something that John had gone to war and involved the papacy to prevent. The reissue had the immediate effect of pulling the rug out from under the feet of any baron who was justifying his support of Louis on the grounds that John had reneged on the charter.[21] Moreover, it asserted Henry's willingness to work with, rather than against, his barons, while at the same time emphasising his innocence in any previous dispute. The flow of barons from the royal party of John and Henry to that of Louis was thereby stemmed, and it might even be possible, with the right combination of carrot and stick, to reverse it. William Marshal 'immediately sent letters to all the sheriffs and castellans of England, enjoining them each and all to obey the newly crowned king, and promising them possessions and many presents besides'.[22]

Those barons who sided with Louis, and any who were wavering, were faced with a dilemma. Their primary, and much-publicised, complaint was against John; but John was dead, and in his place was a blameless nine-year-old boy who could hardly be cast as a tyrant, thus changing the political face of the conflict at a stroke. Indeed, we might even go so far as to say that John's dying was actually the most useful thing he could have done for the cause of his dynasty in England.[23] However, there also needed to be taken into account the very practical consideration that Louis might well win the war, in which case the barons wanted to be on his side. There was something of a hiatus while everyone waited to see what everyone else would do, and seemingly no one could make up his mind:

> There was a great deal of wavering amongst the barons of England, to which ruler they should entrust themselves, whether to the young Henry

or to Louis ... [Louis] had retained in his own possession the lands, possessions, and castles of the said barons, which he had subdued with their help, and had placed foreign knights and people in charge of them. On the other hand, it seemed a disgrace for them to return their allegiance to a king whom they had renounced ... [The barons were] thus in difficulty every way.[24]

The deadlock continued over the winter of 1216–17, except that the regent's blandishments won over the long-suffering William d'Albini, who had been in prison (and threatened with execution by starvation, as we have seen) since his heroic but unsuccessful defence of Rochester in 1215. Perhaps realising that he might never be freed, he agreed to come to terms, raised a ransom and was released to join Henry's party – although, as security, his wife and one of his sons had to remain as hostages in his place. Some of John's previous techniques were evidently still useful.[25]

Louis gained no more new followers, and still did not have sufficient troops or resources to push for a final victory. He left Dover to its own devices for now (the garrison there, incidentally, had broken the truce as soon as his back was turned, emerging to burn the siege camp, ravage the countryside and replenish their stores) and settled instead for besieging and taking a series of smaller castles, such as Hertford and Berkhamsted.[26] Campaigning in the winter was difficult, and the feast of Christmas was often a time when hostilities were suspended – especially when both parties declared themselves faithful sons of the Church (in Louis's case despite his excommunication, which had been upheld by Pope Honorius) – so a general truce was agreed over Christmas, to expire on 13 January 1217. Louis observed the dates punctiliously but started campaigning again as soon as the peace expired, taking the castle at Cambridge, at which point the regent proposed a further truce, involving a complete cessation of hostilities by both parties until the end of April. Louis, perhaps running out of ideas and glad of the breathing space himself, consented (on the proviso that a number of other castles be surrendered to him, which was agreed), and everyone in England had a short respite while they considered their options. Louis decided that what he needed to do was consult with his father and find more troops, so he temporarily left England in February 1217 to sail for France.

* * *

In the nine months that his son and heir had been away, Philip had enjoyed peace and stability in France, nobody daring to contest the authority of the victor of Bouvines. His court and the lordships owing allegiance to him had been little disturbed by Louis's campaign, as participation in it was largely split along generational lines; the heirs and younger sons had gone to England, while the counts themselves and the older heads had stayed put. There is no knowing exactly how much Philip worried about his son's safety while he was away; but if he was anxious, then it was likely to be on a personal, rather than a dynastic, level. Philip was still only fifty-one and intending to rule for many years yet; and even if something happened to him *and* to Louis, the crown of France would pass safely to another Capetian, for Louis and Blanche now had three sons – Robert had been born in September 1216, joining Philip, seven, and Louis, two, in the royal nursery – and Philip Hurepel was by now in his late teens.

Louis's arrival back in Paris in late February, seeking reinforcements, shattered the tranquillity of the royal court. In keeping with his public declaration that he did not support the campaign, Philip ostentatiously refused to meet his excommunicate son in person; however, equally in keeping with the double game he was probably playing, he did not make any attempt to stop Louis raising more troops, and a letter from Pope Honorius urging him to forbid Louis from returning to England mysteriously failed to reach Philip's hands until after Louis had already departed.[27]

Another major player now came to the fore: Blanche. By the spring of 1217 she had recovered from her latest confinement and now became a more active force in support of her husband. She was clever, well educated, very fond of Louis and had as firm a knowledge of what he would need to succeed as any non-combatant could hope to have. She was also, presumably, quite keen to be queen of England, given that she would probably not become queen of France for some time; and she had multiple sons to provide for, so it was in her own best interests and those of her children to help Louis in his quest. Although John had been her uncle, and little Henry was her cousin, there appears to have been no question of divided loyalties: she had been married to a Capetian for more than half her life and her allegiance lay squarely with the French royal house. She waved Louis off as he sailed again for England (with some extra men, but not as many as he had hoped for or needed) on 22 April 1217, and then set to work on his behalf.

The situation, then, as Louis set foot on English soil once more, was that the realm was split more or less down the middle by a line running north–south, with Henry's party controlling the western half and Louis's the eastern, including London but excepting the isolated strongholds of Dover, Windsor and Lincoln. Louis also had Alexander of Scots and Llewelyn of Wales harassing the northern and western borders of England; perhaps not exactly on his behalf, but at least in his favour. The problem for everyone was that neither of the two major parties had a standing army of sufficient size to overwhelm the other, so a long war of attrition beckoned, which would not be to anyone's benefit. There needed to be a final push one way or the other, and – as had been the case in France three years earlier – the outcome would be settled in battle.

⋟ CHAPTER EIGHTEEN ⋞

A TALE OF TWO BATTLES

A S SOON AS LOUIS WAS known to have sailed for France, the regent broke the agreed truce and organised forces to attack Ely, Rochester, Chichester, Portchester, Farnham and Odiham in his absence. William Marshal has over the centuries developed a great reputation as a chivalrous hero, an uncomplicatedly loyal man of his word who served his royal masters without question, but this is almost entirely due to the uncritical praise of his contemporary biographer, who was being paid by Marshal's son and who therefore made sure that he portrayed his protagonist in the best light. In fact Marshal was a much more complex character, imbued in the 'chivalry' of the day – basically that might was right, so long as you were of a certain social status – who did not hesitate to do whatever was necessary in order to bring about a desired outcome.[1] In this particular case, even his biographer recognised that some explanation was necessary, and tried to justify his actions on the rather thin pretext that Louis's return to France meant that he 'had no intention of keeping the truce', so Marshal's action was a kind of pre-emptive retaliation.[2] Morally dubious the regent's breaking of the truce might have been, but it was also effective, and that was the point: several high-profile defections followed, including those of the notable waverers the earls of Salisbury, Surrey and Arundel.

Louis docked at Sandwich on 23 April 1217 to find that, in addition to the places mentioned above, Winchester, Southampton and Marlborough had by now all fallen, and Mountsorrel (in Leicestershire) was also under attack by Ranulf de Blundeville, the earl of Chester. On top of all this, the papal legate Guala had somehow managed to proclaim Henry's cause a holy crusade. Louis would be facing an uphill task if he were to continue with his campaign for the crown of England, but he decided to persevere. In his appraisal of Louis's character and prediction of his actions the regent had erred, for it seems that he had expected the temporary withdrawal to turn into something more permanent, and was taken aback when he heard that the Capetian had landed once more in England: 'The Marshal heard about Louis's return, and was not one bit pleased when he did.'[3]

Marshal was right to be wary, for an irritated Louis swept across the south of England with greater fury and violence than the previous year. He burned Sandwich as he left it, and then stormed with his cavalry via Canterbury, Malling and Guildford to reach Farnham only four days after landing. There he attempted to set up a siege, but he had outpaced his baggage train and so did not have his heavy machinery. Before it could catch up, he received word that Henry and William Marshal were both at Winchester; this was an opportunity not to be missed, so he raced off again. The capture of Henry would put an end to the war, and the detention or death of the regent would be almost as effective. William Marshal had intended to defend Winchester, one of the places he had retaken while Louis was away, but he changed his mind when he heard that the Capetian was on his way in person, beating a retreat, with Henry in tow, to Marlborough. As he left Winchester he burned the luckless city once again, probably leaving the citizens to reflect that they would not mind who was on the throne if it would only guarantee peace. Louis arrived, but, seeing that his quarry had eluded him again, stayed only long enough at Winchester to regarrison the castles and order repairs before he rode back to London. He had completed his reconquest of the south of England in only two weeks.[4]

While Louis had been thus engaged, a combined French and baronial force under Saer de Quincy, Robert Fitzwalter and Thomas, count of Perche, had headed north to relieve Mountsorrel and then move on to Lincoln, where the truce bought by Nicola de la Haye the previous autumn had now expired. At Mountsorrel, the earl of Chester was mistakenly informed that Louis himself was in the approaching army, which was enough to make him destroy his siege machinery and retreat to Nottingham. Mountsorrel was relieved without further action (and claimed by Saer de Quincy, in whose possession it had been before the war) and the party moved on to Lincoln.

A baronial force under the same Gilbert de Gant whom Louis had named earl of Lincoln was in control of the town, but the castle within it, protected by its own defences, was holding out, still under the command of the redoubtable Nicola. Gilbert was confident that, with the extra impetus provided by the new force, the castle would soon fall.[5]

When John had visited Lincoln in the autumn of 1216, he had confirmed Nicola in her position as castellan, and had additionally appointed her sheriff of Lincolnshire, despite her protests that she was too old – interestingly, nobody seems to have raised any concern that she was female, indicating that she was a well-known and well-respected local figure.[6] This was one of John's last acts, and it proved to be one of his best: Nicola had continued to defend the castle in the name of the royalist cause no matter what Gilbert de Gant and his compatriots had thrown at it. It had been subject to a ceaseless bombardment throughout March and April; it was now mid-May and the garrison was still resisting.

Word reached William Marshal of the situation at Lincoln, and he realised what a blow, possibly a fatal one, it would be to Henry's cause if the castle were to capitulate; Lincoln was England's second-largest city, and control of the stronghold there would give Louis a sphere of uninterrupted influence in the eastern half of the kingdom and allow him to stretch further north. John's campaign had managed to avoid direct combat whenever possible, opting instead for a guerrilla-style war, but now there seemed to be little choice. Lincoln must be relieved, and the only way to do that was to advance upon it with an army prepared to fight. Marshal sent out letters summoning everyone who was loyal to Henry (except Hubert de Burgh, who was still defending Dover) to muster at Newark. He made his own way there as soon as the letters were sent, bringing Henry in person to aid morale, along with Peter des Roches and Guala. Among those who answered the call were a number of England's other bishops, the earls of Chester, Salisbury, Aumale and Derby (but not, interestingly, Surrey and Arundel, who appeared to be still hedging their bets), the recently reconciled William d'Albini, Falkes de Bréauté and a nephew of the regent named John Marshal.

Once they were assembled, William Marshal gave them all a stirring speech and Guala reminded them that they were engaged in a holy crusade.[7] He re-excommunicated those besieging the castle (which, incidentally, implies that they were ignoring the sentence first time round, in the same way that Louis was seemingly oblivious to his), and he now also included in the decree the citizens of Lincoln, who, he believed, had succumbed to the enemy forces too easily. This last was a deeply unfair accusation, as the merchants and shopkeepers of the city were hardly experienced in war or trained to repel the army of professional soldiers that had fallen upon it. After that there was nothing to wait for: on 19 May Henry and Guala retired to Nottingham, while the rest of the army started to march the 20 miles north-eastwards towards Lincoln.[8]

The city was built on a hill, with the castle at the top, to the north-west, and the river at the bottom to the south. The castle, unusually, had two keeps, each on a separate mound, with the whole inside a large bailey encircled by walls. It was in a prime position: to the south, the defenders could command the steep descent towards the river, and to the west they could look out over the valley of the Trent and the highway. The outer castle wall was surrounded by a deep ditch and had two principal gateways: one in the east wall leading into the city, and a smaller postern to the west, giving access to open country. The city of Lincoln surrounding the castle was itself walled, with gates to the north, south, east and west. The French and baronial forces were spread throughout the city, with the largest concentration being around the castle as they besieged it, and most of the citizens were still resident, no doubt keeping to their homes as much as possible as the danger of battle came nearer.

The army under William Marshal was marching from Newark, which under normal circumstances would take them via the main road to Lincoln; but this would bring them to the city's south gate, meaning that they would need to cross the river, enter the city and fight their way up the steep streets before they could get anywhere near the castle to relieve it. This was hardly an ideal tactic, so instead they took a less direct route via Torksey, arriving on the open ground to the west of the city early on the morning of Saturday 20 May. The regent then divided his army into four parts: three divisions, each comprising a mixture of mounted knights and foot sergeants, to be commanded by himself, Ranulf de Blundeville and Peter des Roches; and a group of some 300 crossbowmen led by Falkes de Bréauté. There is some confusion in the sources over whether any communication took place between the army and the castle garrison, but if it did then it can only have been minimal, with the French and baronial forces placed in between them.[9]

Meanwhile, a reconnaissance party left the city to assess the oncoming army, but confusion reigned. Saer de Quincy and Robert Fitzwalter went out first, returning with the news that the enemy were approaching 'in good order, but we are much more numerous than they', and giving their opinion that they should leave the city to engage in battle on open ground.[10] However, on hearing this, the senior-ranking but young and comparatively inexperienced Thomas, count of Perche (who was still only around twenty-one), rode out to see for himself and thought differently, apparently after miscounting the enemy: each knight had two banners, one with him and one in the baggage train; but with all of them flying at once Thomas thought that the host was twice as big as it actually was. He therefore overruled the others and ordered the French and baronial force to remain within the city. He set one part to defend the walls and gates, and the other to continue the attack on the castle; if they could seize it now, at the last minute, and get inside, they would be in a much better defensive position. As it transpired, they could not, and the fight would take place in the streets, while they were trapped between the oncoming army and the castle garrison behind them.

The regent's army now split into the preordained divisions: Chester's attacked the north city gate, drawing the French that way, while the crossbowmen under Falkes slipped into the castle via the postern that opened outside the city walls and the Marshal himself attacked the city's west gate. There was some fierce fighting in the narrow streets, with men on horseback too close together to mount a proper charge. The crossbowmen who had infiltrated the castle stationed themselves on the ramparts, raining their bolts down on the men operating the siege machinery and shooting the horses of the French and baronial forces, which clogged the streets up further. Falkes and his men then took advantage of the chaos and made a sortie into the city to join the hand-to-hand fighting on foot.

The biography of William Marshal, unsurprisingly, gives a detailed account of the battle, including Marshal's own contribution and a flavour of the turmoil of the general combat:

Had you been there, you would have seen great blows dealt, heard helmets clanging and resounding, seen lances fly in splinters in the air, saddles vacated by riders, knights taken prisoner. You would have heard, from place to place, great blows delivered by swords and maces on helmets and on arms, and seen knives and daggers drawn for the purpose of stabbing horses.[11]

Under the combined assault, the French and baronial army was gradually forced east and south, down the hill. Thomas of Perche, who 'performed many great feats of arms that day', attempted to rally his men in front of the cathedral – one of the only flat open spaces in the city – but he was killed when a thrust from a lance or sword entered the eye-slit of his helmet.[12] The loss of their ranking nobleman caused his men to hasten their retreat, and they were pushed southwards, defending themselves as they went. The regent's army now had the significant advantage of fighting downhill in the steep streets, and their opponents were forced back and out of the city via the south gate. This gate was very narrow and the congestion caused a last stand; an opportunity not for slaughter, but for the victorious lords to capture the rebel noblemen for ransom. Saer de Quincy, Robert Fitzwalter and Gilbert de Gant were all among those taken prisoner.

The battle was over – or at least it was for the defeated combatants. The citizens of Lincoln, however, now suffered from Guala's decision to excommunicate them, as they were considered fair game. The army that had ostensibly come to 'rescue' them from the French now turned on them with a vengeance, and lives, as well as goods, were lost:

Baggage, silver vessel and various kinds of furniture and utensils all fell into their possession without opposition. Having then plundered the whole city to the last farthing, they next pillaged the churches throughout the city, and broke open the chests and store-rooms with axes and hammers, seizing on the gold and silver in them, clothes of all colours, women's ornaments, gold rings, goblets and jewels. Nor did the cathedral church escape this destruction, but underwent the same punishment as the rest . . . Many of the women of the city were drowned in the river, for, to avoid insult [i.e. rape by the soldiers of Marshal's army], they took to small boats with their children, their female servants, and household property . . . The boats were overloaded, and the women not knowing how to manage the boats, all perished.[13]

William Marshal rode in person to Nottingham to tell Henry and Guala of the victory, and then set about dividing up the spoils. Prisoners and their ransoms were distributed to his lieutenants, the captives ordered to be kept in close custody until they could pay up. Thanks to a distant family tie with Thomas of Perche (William's mother and one of Thomas's great-grandmothers had been sisters), Marshal appropriated for himself the English lands of the late count; and he appointed William Longsword, earl of Salisbury, as sheriff of Lincoln and castellan of the castle. In so doing he disinherited, in an almost inexplicable act of ingratitude, the courageous Nicola de la Haye; she would dispute her claim to Lincoln with William Longsword for many years to come.[14]

News of the defeat at Lincoln reached Louis at Dover five days later; he was, predictably, 'full of anger and rage' at the dent in his ambitions.[15] However, although the outcome of the battle was certainly a blow, it was not catastrophic: other than the count of Perche, his barons were imprisoned rather than dead, and could rejoin him once their ransoms were paid; he still held nearly half of England, including its capital; and he was aware that more troops might soon be available from France. He did not, therefore, rush off in a panic – he remained at Dover for a few days more, in order to send messages across to France. Then he burned the ships that still remained to him (to avoid them falling into the hands of Hubert de Burgh, who was sure to emerge from Dover castle as soon as Louis was gone) and rode for London, where he arrived at the beginning of June. There he met up with some 200 knights who had managed to flee Lincoln without being captured, and awaited the arrival from across the Channel of reinforcements sent by his wife.

* * *

As soon as Louis had left France in April 1217, after his temporary sojourn, Blanche had set to work on his behalf. She did this in the most practical manner possible, riding through Artois and those lands where she and Louis had most personal sway, in order to harangue the lords there in person, rather than merely writing them letters. By midsummer she had drummed up enough men and money to equip a small fleet; but it was still not going to be enough, so she took the intimidating step of approaching the king himself.

As we have seen, Philip Augustus had so far publicly denied support to his son for the English campaign, refusing even to see him when he returned to Paris to ask for help. He could hardly, however, decline to see his irreproachable daughter-in-law, the mother of his royal heirs, so he agreed to receive her. He must by this stage have been aware of the force of Blanche's personality, some seventeen years after she had first joined his family; but, even so, he seems to have been taken aback by the whirlwind that confronted him and persuaded him to do what nobody else had been able to do: open the royal treasury and hand over some of his gold.

One entertaining interpretation of the interview is offered by the Minstrel of Reims. The scene he presents is almost certainly fictional, but it does give a flavour of the way in which Blanche was popularly perceived and depicted at this time:

[Louis] asked his father, in the name of God, to send him some money. And the king replied that, by the lance of St James, he would not.

When my lady Blanche knew this, she went to the king, saying 'Are you going to let my lord your son die in a foreign country? Sire, in God's name, he ought to reign after you; send him what he needs, at least from the revenues of his own lands.'

'Certainly, Blanche, I will do no such thing,' replied the king.

'No, sire?'

'No,' said the king.

'In the name of God,' said my lady Blanche, 'then I know what I will do.'

'And what will you do?' asked the king.

'By the grace of the mother of God, I have fine sons by my lord; I will pawn them all and see what I can get for them.'

Then she parted furiously from the king, and when he saw her go he knew that she meant what she said. He called her back and said, 'Blanche, I will give you my treasure, as much as you want, and you can do with it whatever you wish, but I will not send any to him.'

And a great deal of treasure was delivered to my lady Blanche, and she sent it to her lord.[16]

Imaginary as the detail of this scene is, it contains at least a grain of the truth: in acting as he did, Philip could just about claim that he was not going against the pope's wishes, as he was giving money to Blanche, not to Louis. It was therefore up to her what she did with it – he would not support an excommunicate, but she might if she chose.

By late summer the fleet, of ten large ships carrying men and horses and some sixty small supply vessels, was ready to embark; Blanche saw it off personally from Calais on 20 August 1217. It was commanded at sea by Eustace the Monk, and the senior-ranking nobleman in charge of the troops was Robert de Courtenay, a Capetian kinsman of Louis's via his descent from Louis VI. They were both on board the command vessel, known as 'the great ship of Bayonne', which was so loaded down with men, horses, baggage, treasure and the pieces of a trebuchet that it was barely out of the water.[17]

If the French reinforcements could reach London and join up with Louis's existing army, he would probably have sufficient resources to carry the day. It was therefore imperative from the regent's point of view that they be intercepted before they could land, so that the two parts could not unite. Hurried preparations began as soon as the French fleet was known to be on its way, and the Channel weather was in William Marshal's favour: the French ships had almost reached Dover when a storm blew them back across the Channel. They turned again as soon as they could, but it was the night of 23–24 August by the time they neared England again, and the three-day delay had given the regent's forces precious extra time, so they were in a state of greater readiness.

Marshal had summoned all loyal nobles to muster at Sandwich, which is now several miles from the coast but which was at the time a sea port, where he had manned and equipped a fleet of eighteen large and twenty smaller vessels. As we noted earlier, the concept of Henry as an 'English' king might have been somewhat nebulous in terms of his personal bloodline, but the regent was at this point able to call more definitively on a sense of national identity, as there were no English barons on board the enemy ships at all – they were to a man French invaders. 'God gave you the first victory over the French on land. Now they return to England to claim the land as theirs, against God's will,' Marshal's biographer has him saying during his pre-battle oration; and, just in case patriotic feeling was not a sufficiently strong motivation, to incentivise his troops further he promised them any plunder they could take from captured French vessels once the battle was over.[18]

The composition of his army was to be very different from the one that had taken to the streets of Lincoln; earls and barons, brought up to fight on horseback, would be markedly less adept at combat on a heaving deck out at sea, so many of them contributed ships, knights and men without boarding personally. Henry and Guala, as non-combatants in any case, would remain on shore, and with them stayed a group of bishops, William Marshal and several other earls including William Longsword of Salisbury and William de Warenne of Surrey. The fleet would be commanded at sea by Hubert de Burgh (who had left Dover once Louis's siege ceased), and by Philip d'Albini, a long-time admiral of John's who had been patrolling Channel waters since 1207.[19]

The French ships initially sailed towards Dover as they crossed the Channel, but once in sight of the coast they turned; on the morning of 24 August 1217 they could be seen sailing northwards, parallel with the shore, with the idea of rounding the Isle of Thanet and sailing up the Thames to London.[20] The English fleet left Sandwich as the French ships were passing, Hubert de Burgh's vessel at the front. To start with they headed out to sea, into the wind (which was blowing from the south-east), and passed behind and to the south of the French; it looked as though the French had made it past the danger, with a clear sea between them and the mouth of the Thames. However, they had not taken into account the skill of the English sailors: by dint of excellent seamanship, their ships came swiftly about (all except Hubert's, which had got too far ahead and therefore overshot the turn, thus putting him at the rear) and then approached the French at speed with both the wind and the sun behind them. Taking advantage of the wind direction, the English launched volleys of powdered lime at the French before the ships engaged, blinding and choking those on board so they were unprepared for the attack that would follow.[21]

The first English ship to reach the French was one owned by William de Warenne. It caught up with the French command vessel – which was not very manoeuvrable, as it was so heavily laden and sat low in the water – and rammed it. Warenne's ship was followed by a large cog belonging to the regent that sat higher in the water than the French vessel, thus allowing the English to rain down arrows and crossbow bolts on their already inca-pacitated opponents. Grappling hooks were thrown; the ships were lashed together; English knights and footsoldiers poured across. This situation was replicated across the fleet, the rigging of the French ships being cut so they became unmanoeuvrable and easily rammed and boarded.

The main encounter took place on the 'great ship of Bayonne', soon surrounded by four English ships, where the regent's forces carried the day in hand-to-hand fighting, hacking their way across a deck so crowded that there was barely room to swing a sword:

> Eustace and his men defended themselves by hurling and throwing missiles and firing arrows. They slaughtered a great many Englishmen and defended themselves courageously. Eustace knocked down a good number of them with an oar which he was holding. Some had their arms broken, others their heads smashed. This one was killed and that one laid out; one was knocked down and another wounded, while a third had his collar-bone shattered.[22]

As the encounter reached its inevitable conclusion, the outnumbered French common soldiers and sailors were massacred: 'They [the English] lost no time at all in killing those they found on board and throwing them into the sea as food for the fish.'[23] A group of men from the regent's fleet, drunk on violence, did attempt to kill the knights and nobles as well, but they were saved by the English knights for ransom – they had not forgotten Marshal's promise of monetary gain. Robert de Courtenay was among those captured; he was imprisoned at Dover castle. Among the notable gainers was Hubert de Burgh, whose ship arrived belatedly, albeit in time for him to seize two French vessels and some valuable prisoners.

Eustace the Monk, 'a most disgraceful man and a wicked pirate', had survived the encounter and was dragged out from where he was hiding in the depths of the ship's hold; he did make a huge ransom offer, but must have known his life would be forfeit. He was apparently offered the choice of being beheaded on the trebuchet or beheaded on the ship's rail; none of our sources record his answer, but the sentence was carried out and his severed head was later paraded on a spear around the towns of the south coast that he had terrorised for years.[24]

As at Lincoln, there were great gains to be had for the common English soldiery, as well as the nobles – though at least this time they were taken from enemy combatants rather than innocent townsfolk. The French fleet had been carrying supplies and money for Louis to pay his troops, as well as the horses, armour and personal possessions of those on board; so much booty was taken that 'the sailors were able to share out the coins in bowlfuls', and there was even enough left over to found a hospital in honour of St Bartholomew, whose feast day it was.[25] Accounts differ as to the precise extent of the French losses – whether all their ships were sunk or captured, or whether some made it back to Calais; but, in either case, none landed successfully in England and Louis received no reinforcements.[26] The game was up.

Louis had been in London for several weeks, launching a few raids into surrounding areas but not moving far while he waited for news of reinforcements. Once the fate of his fleet was known to him he realised that no further resources would be available, so he agreed to negotiate. The regent, meanwhile, was aware that Louis did still have sufficient support to cause more trouble if he were so minded, so the talks were very much discussions of a truce and a peace treaty rather than a surrender. The amicable atmosphere was also no doubt enhanced by two other points: firstly, that Marshal, as one of the only men still holding lands in England and in Normandy (thanks to his prior arrangement with King Philip), would know that Louis would one day be his overlord for his French estates, so he would not want to antagonise him; and secondly, that if his son and heir were to be in any real danger, or if the reputation of France were to be under threat, King Philip might finally move to muster the considerable resources of the French monarchy to intervene.

An initial meeting took place on 5 September 1217 between William Marshal and Hubert de Burgh on one side, and Louis and Robert de Courtenay (who could be thankful that the swift negotiations meant his imprisonment was a short one) on the other. The resulting Treaty of Lambeth was finalised a week later. Under its terms, Louis agreed to relinquish his claim to the English throne, but was in return to receive a payment of 10,000 marks (£6,667) of silver, around a quarter of the crown's annual income. Other clauses were that all lands and rights were to be restored to their pre-war holders, all prisoners taken during the war were to be released (the English rebels among them only on swearing an oath of obedience to Henry), and further ransoms were not to be collected, although those already paid could be kept.[27] Louis, absolved from excommunication, sailed back across the Channel on 28 September 1217.

* * *

The Capetian project in England was over. Some contemporaries were baffled as to how it had not succeeded, and could only put it down to divine intervention:

> It was truly a miracle that the heir of the king of France, having advanced so far into the heart of the country with a great army and having succeeded in occupying so much of it, helped by the barons, and had taken it so quickly, was forced to abandon this kingdom without hope of recovering it. It is because the hand of God was not with him.[28]

The Plantagenets had survived – just. But the struggle between the two dynasties was far from over: the theatre of conflict had merely shifted location once more from England to France. And the situation for the Plantagenets was still precarious, for while France had two grown men at the helm, one a shrewd king with decades of political experience behind him, and the other a restless heir keen on military adventure, England had a small boy, an old man and a pack of squabbling advisors who would soon come to blows.

➤ CHAPTER NINETEEN ➤

LOUIS REX

T HE WAR IN ENGLAND WAS over; now the task was to ensure peace and to restore and maintain systems of governance, law and administration. This was complicated by the fact that the realm would be subject to the first royal minority since the Conquest, a minority that would be of some length, given the new king's tender age, so new and different ways of working would need to be found.

To start with, new ways were not terribly apparent; it seemed almost as if John's reign were continuing, for the men in charge were those who had served him for years. But things soon took a different turn once the prominent nobles – both those on the council and others – realised that for the foreseeable future they would be able to function without the direct and overbearing oversight of a powerful but unstable adult king. Self-interest became the order of the day.[1] England was ruled by an uneasy coalition of William Marshal as regent, Peter des Roches as the king's guardian and the legate Guala as the pope's representative. Hubert de Burgh remained the justiciar, but his role had effectively been downgraded: normally the justiciar was the king's right-hand man and his representative while he was away; but as the present king was already represented by a regent, Hubert's exact position was unclear.

It was not long before changes took place both in the council and in the wider realm. A group of nobles, many of whom had been on opposing sides during the recent war, put aside their differences and departed in 1218 on the campaign that would later be known as the Fifth Crusade. Among them were Ranulf de Blundeville, earl of Chester; William d'Aubigny, earl of Arundel; Saer de Quincy, earl of Winchester; and Robert Fitzwalter. They joined up with contingents from France, Hungary and the Holy Roman Empire in a force led by Andrew II of Hungary and Leopold VI, duke of Austria (the son of Leopold V, who had been Richard the Lionheart's antagonist and captor two decades previously). Together with the king of Jerusalem, John of Brienne – a French nobleman who had married Queen Maria of Montferrat, the Jerusalemite royal house having continued its long tradition of producing female heirs – they besieged and took the port city of Damietta in Egypt. However, they were later defeated as they marched south along the Nile, and were forced to restore Damietta as part of the negotiated settlement.[2] Robert and Ranulf would eventually return from the expedition; Saer died at Damietta and William on his way home.

Meanwhile, in England, the original ruling triumvirate had dissolved. Guala retired as papal legate to England in the autumn of 1218, to be replaced by Pandulf Verraccio, who had previously spent time in England (he was involved in the Magna Carta negotiations) but who had been in Rome during the intervening three years.[3] It was also in the autumn of 1218 that the aged William Marshal began to suffer from poor health; he died in May 1219. He was succeeded as earl of Pembroke – but not as regent – by William II Marshal, the eldest of his five sons. During Marshal senior's final illness, Peter des Roches had played a more prominent role in the government, and he sought to have himself named as replacement regent by Marshal when the latter was on his deathbed. This was denied, however, and with good reason: as the bishop was already the personal guardian of the king, this would invest too much power in one man. He retained his guardianship, but the new great seal that had been struck in November 1218 would be in Pandulf's keeping. The two of them formed a new triumvirate with Hubert de Burgh.[4]

However, there were tensions between Peter and Hubert. Peter, as we noted earlier, was not a particularly popular man in England, associated as he was with the most detested aspects and draconian policies of John's reign, which he had enforced during the period he was regent. Hubert, on the other hand, was more generally accepted simply by virtue of being more of an unknown quantity. He had served John during the defence of Normandy, but had been captured in 1204 and did not return to England for nearly a decade, thus managing to stay distanced from the conflict that built up towards Magna Carta and civil war. His tenacious defence of Dover castle during the war had both enhanced his reputation and, again, kept him away personally from most of the other nobles. Peter did not get on particularly well with Pandulf, either, though they did have one thing in common: a dislike of Stephen Langton, the archbishop of Canterbury.[5] However, they would need Langton for the important and symbolic event that was now thought necessary.

As we noted above, Henry III had been 'crowned' in October 1216, the ceremony taking place in Gloucester and without the authorised celebrant. Now that the dust had settled a little in England, the council felt that it was time to ensure that a proper, traditional, legal coronation should take place, in order to allay any fears that a further challenge from France might involve a declaration that Henry's kingship was not valid because his coronation had been irregular. Thus it was that the twelve-year-old Henry was crowned in May 1220 in Westminster Abbey by Archbishop Langton; this time there was a real crown, along with a golden sceptre and a silver staff.[6] He remained for now under the tutelage of Peter des Roches, and his education continued. We do not have any exact details of Henry's programme of instruction, though it certainly included a thorough grounding in politics as well as the usual accomplishments in literacy and religion. Presumably Henry was also trained in martial matters, although – unlike many other members of his dynasty – he displayed little interest in or aptitude for military pursuits in later life.[7]

By the summer of 1220, following the second coronation, more cracks were becoming evident in the relationship of the ruling trio. Hubert had by now more or less replaced Peter as the head of the administration; Pandulf resigned as legate in 1221 and Peter his position as Henry's guardian shortly after, meaning that for a short while Hubert was effectively in sole charge, with a council to consult about major decisions.[8]

A key question that was now looming on the horizon was when the young king would officially gain his majority and begin his personal rule. This was an even more thorny issue than might otherwise have been the case, due to his complete reliance up until this point on his advisors. Having been deprived of both of his parents before he was ten, and with no surviving legitimate uncles or aunts, Henry had no family network to rely on and, other than one younger brother, no provision to make for members of his extended family. A huge amount of patronage was therefore up for grabs, and the declaration of the king's majority was the point at which it would become available. Up until now, all grants of land and titles made during Henry's reign had been temporary and subject to ratification once he came of age; thus, whichever of his advisors held the upper hand when the momentous day finally came would expect rich pickings, so it is no surprise that opinions on the best date varied.

Although there was no Anglo-Norman or Plantagenet precedent for a royal minority in England, there had been others in recent memory in Europe. Frederick II, the current Holy Roman Emperor, had been declared of age as king of Sicily when he was fourteen, before he went on to make his ultimately successful claim to the imperial throne. Fourteen was an age invested with significance, marking the end of one of the 'seven ages' as a boy became an adolescent.[9] Henry would turn fourteen in October 1221, perhaps rather sooner than some of the great lords would like. There was also the king's personal development to take into account; Henry does not seem to have had the overwhelming drive that his father, uncle or paternal grandfather had at a similar age, and there seems to have been no serious attempt to declare him of age in 1221, although the landmark of his fourteenth birthday may have hastened the departure of Peter des Roches from his post, on the grounds that the now adolescent king did not need a guardian. Other possible dates for the formal declaration of Henry's majority would be 1223 (when he would turn sixteen) or 1225 (eighteen), but the widely accepted definition of adulthood was twenty-one – which is when earls or counts who were minors could legally come into their estates – and this would not happen until October 1228.

While these questions were being debated in the early 1220s, England did at least benefit from peace with France. The truce agreed following the Battle of Bouvines in 1214 was due to expire at Easter 1220, but (much to the relief of those governing England) King Philip 'most kindly' agreed to extend it until spring 1224.[10] This meant that the ruling council was free to focus on its own internal discord, and by the autumn of 1223 relations had broken down completely. Peter des Roches was forced out by an alliance led by Hubert de Burgh and supported by Archbishop Stephen Langton, William II Marshal, earl of Pembroke, and William Longsword, earl of

Salisbury and the king's uncle. They used the familiar 'anti-foreigner' rhetoric against Peter, who, as we noted earlier, hailed originally from either Poitou or Touraine, although he had been in England for at least twenty years. The same ill feeling was directed at his vocal supporter Falkes de Bréauté, who, as we might remember, was John's mercenary leader and his often violent enforcer during the war. The squabbling looked set to go on.

But then news arrived from France that would change everything.

* * *

Philip Augustus had welcomed his son back to France in the autumn of 1217 with very little ceremony – as might be expected, given that he had not returned with a crown on his head and Philip had not officially backed him in his quest for one anyway. Neither of them had come out of the situation badly, as it happens; Louis's military reputation was still intact (he had been forced to withdraw due to lack of resources, not because he had been personally defeated in the field) and he still had the French throne to look forward to, while Philip retained his superior status (he was a king and his son was not) and could also rest assured that England was going to be in no position to mount a challenge to France in the foreseeable future. However, the downside was that the king was now once again faced with the question of what to do with a restless adult heir, and he was fortunate that two opportunities of very different types soon presented themselves.

The first was a rather unexpected offer that arrived from Castile, offering the crown to Louis and Blanche, or to one of their sons if they would care to choose one and dispatch him south. The background to this is complex; in brief, the elder of Blanche's two brothers and the heir to the Castilian throne, Ferdinand, had died in 1211 at the age of twenty-two, while returning from a campaign against the Muslims in the south of Spain, meaning that when Alfonso VIII died in 1214, he was succeeded by his youngest child, Henry, then a boy of ten. Henry had reigned for three years before being killed in an accident while he was out playing; this meant that the crown passed to the eldest of his surviving sisters, Berengaria. She had been married to Alfonso IX of León and had four children by him, but – very much against their wishes – Pope Innocent III had dissolved their marriage on the grounds of consanguinity, so they were now separated and she had been living in Castile and acting as regent for her younger brother.

Berengaria was declared queen of Castile in her own right in 1217, only to resign the crown immediately in favour of her eldest son, Ferdinand, who became Ferdinand III of Castile, as well as the heir to León. However, this caused issues with Pope Honorius (who considered Ferdinand illegitimate, due to the consanguinity issue) and with the Castilian nobility, who feared interference in their affairs from León. They therefore managed to unearth what they claimed was a proviso left by Alfonso VIII saying that if his son Henry should die childless, the Castilian throne should pass to his daughter Blanche and her heirs. They dispatched a messenger north, though it was not clear how or whether they would have felt the involvement of France in their affairs to be any better than that of León. As it transpired, the question did not arise, as Louis and Blanche declined the offer for themselves and for their sons – thus depriving Castile of a monarch who would have been descended from both the Plantagenets and the Capetians, as well as its own royal house. Ferdinand III retained the throne (eventually uniting it with that of León) and reigned for over thirty years.[11]

There is, alas, no evidence to show what Philip Augustus might have felt about the Castilian opportunity; but after it was declined he was able to find Louis something else with which to occupy himself, in the form of the still ongoing Albigensian Crusade. Simon de Montfort had been engaged for some time now against Raymond VI, count of Toulouse, and his son the future Raymond VII, and had been besieging the city of Toulouse through the autumn and winter of 1217 and the spring of 1218. In June 1218 he was killed by a stone launched from a petrary on the walls, and without its charismatic leader the crusade lost ground. At the behest of Pope Honorius, and with Louis's enthusiastic approbation, Philip agreed that his son could take the cross in November; Louis spent the winter making preparations and set off in the spring of 1219. On the way to Toulouse he allowed his men to engage in a horrific massacre of civilians at Marmande; but he had little success against the mighty walls of Toulouse and by the autumn of 1219 he was on his way back north.[12]

The next three years were peaceful ones in France, giving Philip the opportunity to rule without trouble or challenge, increasing his income as he did so and taking an ever firmer grip on Flanders. Count Ferrand was still in prison and would not be released in Philip's lifetime, but the many other Flemish lords who had been captured at Bouvines were gradually paying off their ransoms, which swelled Philip's coffers even more.[13] Louis and Blanche, meanwhile, were able to spend more time together, and the result was three more sons in quick succession, although their joy was tempered by the loss of their eldest son and heir, Philip, shortly before his ninth birthday. The next eldest, Louis, was immediately recognised as the new heir, and King Philip was at leisure to take an interest and spend some time with him, something the younger Louis would remember fondly in later life.[14]

In the autumn of 1222, Philip fell ill. The bouts of fever he suffered may or may not have been linked to his long-ago serious illness in the Holy Land, but they were certainly debilitating, and the situation prompted him to draw up his testament. He used the opportunity to salve his conscience to some extent, leaving vast sums to the Church, to widows, orphans and lepers, and to his long-suffering queen, Ingeborg.[15] The fever was described as quartan – meaning that it struck every fourth day – so in between the attacks Philip was still able to continue with his duties and govern personally; he had held France grasped in his hands for more than forty years, and he was not about to let go until those hands were well and truly cold. His decline continued throughout the spring of 1223, as he steadfastly refused to take his doctors' advice to go on a diet and abstain from wine, and by July he was on his deathbed. His son and grandson were both summoned, and were with him when he died on 14 July 1223. 'Death, which spares nobody, neither great nor small, came for him,' records the Minstrel of Reims, simply, while William the Breton, who had known the king personally for many years, expends many lines extolling the late king's virtues.[16] A lesser-known chronicler offers a more balanced analysis:

[Philip had] an agreeable appearance, well-formed body, cheerful face, a bald pate, ruddy complexion. [He was] given to drink and food, prone to sexual desire, generous to his friends, miserly to his foes, skilled in stratagems, orthodox in belief, solicitous of counsel, holding to his word, a scrupulous and expeditious judge, fortunate in victory, fearful of this life, easily moved, easily assuaged, putting down the wicked of the realm by sowing discord among them, killing no-one in prison, availing himself of counsel of lesser men, bearing grudges only momentarily, subduing the proud, defending the Church, and providing for the poor.[17]

Philip, insisting to the last on keeping up with his royal itinerary, had died at Mantes; his body was transported the 35 miles to his capital, and he was interred at Saint-Denis.

During his reign, Philip had expanded France and brought more of it under direct royal control. Formerly troublesome areas that nominally owed allegiance to the crown, but in reality went their own way, had been brought closer to the fold (and in some cases under his complete control), meaning that his successor could expect little trouble from Champagne, Blois, Flanders, Brittany or Normandy. He had instituted the sort of administrative reforms that rarely make headlines, but which contributed to the smooth running of his realm and his government.[18] He had also raised France's international profile, not merely by his crusading activities but also via his relationship with the Holy Roman Empire and his unceasing efforts to weaken the power of England and the Plantagenets. But although the scourge of Henry II, Henry the Young King, Richard and John was no more, his death did not signal the end of the conflict between his house and that of his rivals; indeed, it was the signal for a renewal of hostilities.

* * *

The news that Philip was dead reached England in late July 1223, and Hubert de Burgh, as might be expected, immediately took steps to try to turn the situation to Plantagenet advantage. Despite the defeats of 1204 and 1214, and the reality of the present situation, Henry III still styled himself 'duke of Normandy' and 'count of Anjou'; Hubert wrote to the lords of Normandy inviting them to return to Henry's allegiance. Pushing his luck slightly, he also decided to send Archbishop Stephen Langton to France in an effort to persuade Louis to delay his coronation. This was on the rather spurious grounds that Louis had, Hubert claimed, promised as part of the Treaty of Lambeth in 1217 to return Normandy and the Angevin lands to Henry once he acceded to the French throne. Unsurprisingly, there is no mention whatsoever of any such undertaking in the written text of the treaty; it remains open to conjecture whether Louis had made some kind of vague verbal assurance in the heat of the moment, one that was never recorded, or whether the canny politician Hubert was in fact stretching the truth. In either case, the archbishop of Reims brooked no delay and Louis dismissed the claim outright, replying that 'he held possession of Normandy and other lands as his right, as he would be prepared to prove', and that the oath of the English king as part of the Treaty of Lambeth had been violated, because 'not only were the bad laws brought into force again in their old state, but others had been made even worse than they throughout England'. This sounds suspiciously like a threat, and on hearing it the archbishop and his companions, 'being unable to obtain any other [reply], returned home and told the king'.[19] Such was the position of authority in which Louis now found himself.

Rarely can medieval Europe have witnessed a smoother transition of power than the one that took place in France in 1223. Louis was thirty-five and an experienced leader; he was popular among the nobility, particularly with those of his own generation; and he had been one of his father's right-hand men for more than a decade. Although he was the first of the Capetian dynasty not to have been crowned 'junior king' during his father's lifetime, he had been recognised as the heir to the throne since his birth, and no voice was raised – or could possibly be raised – to deny his right. Moreover, he offered stability both present and future: in contrast to his father and grand-father, he had been happily married for over two decades to the same woman, and he had five sons, Louis (nine), Robert (seven), John (four), Alphonse (three) and Philip-Dagobert (one). A long-awaited daughter, Isabelle, would follow in 1224, and a sixth son, Stephen, in 1225.

A new king might seek to impose his authority by sweeping away all his predecessor's systems, and Louis did add a few new advisors to the royal household, among them Simon Langton, the brother of the archbishop of Canterbury, who had been with him in England. However, he also recog-nised the worth of the officials Philip had appointed and promoted over the years, and retained most of them, including Brother Guérin, now in his late sixties, whom he named chancellor. This ensured a smooth administrative transition to the new regime, adding to Louis's advantages as he inherited a stable, well-run kingdom with plenty of money in the treasury. Louis and Blanche were crowned and anointed at Reims on 6 August 1223, as planned, at which point the man who had narrowly failed to become king of England and declined to become king of Castile could finally style himself Louis *rex*.[20]

Apart from Louis's wife and young children, the immediate Capetian family was by this time a little sparse. The new king's half-sister, Marie, duchess of Brabant, would die less than a year after his coronation. His half-brother Philip Hurepel was now in his mid-twenties and count of Clermont, an apanage given to him by his father some five years previously; he also ruled the county of Boulogne in right of his wife, Matilda de Dammartin (daughter of Count Renaud, still in prison following his defeat at Bouvines), and they had a daughter, Joan. Philip Hurepel occupied a slightly ambiguous position in the royal family, due to the irregular marital circumstances of his parents at the time of his birth; but as Louis had so many sons Philip was unlikely ever to inherit the crown, so the question of his legitimacy could be conveniently shelved.

With no other siblings, Louis's next nearest companions were his second cousins of the Dreux family. Chief among these were the two eldest brothers, Robert (now Robert III, count of Dreux, following his father's death in 1218) and Peter, duke of Brittany. Another distant kinsman who was also a close companion of Louis was Guy de Châtillon, count of St-Pol. These four men were all of a similar age and had been raised together since their early youth; they formed a close-knit group. A younger companion who had been brought up in Louis's entourage and who would assume great significance later in the reign was Theobald IV, count of Champagne (who had been born posthumously to Theobald III and who had finally come of age in 1222, after a minority that had lasted his whole life). As well as being the lord of one of France's richest counties, Theobald was in line for the throne of Navarre via his mother, Blanche, who was the younger sister of the childless Sancho VII the Strong and of the dowager Queen Berengaria of England.[21]

There were high expectations of Louis at the time of his accession. William the Breton took up his pen once more to write an addendum to his *Philippide*, addressed to Louis:

[Poets] will sing of the brilliant start to your reign, and will tell of the transports of joy and the applause with which France welcomed her new king ... You will be a subject worthy of their songs ... You will suffer no longer to reign in peace this new king who dares to bear the English sceptre which, taken from his father by just sentence, belongs only to you, is reserved only for you through the rights of your wife, and which was conferred on you by the unanimous election of the clergy, the people and the nobles of England. This enterprise calls you, and you will prepare for it after Easter following the expiration of the truce which John begged from your father. Therefore, joyfully taking up arms under favourable omens ... start to re-establish the rights of your kingdom, and add a kingdom to a kingdom, giving the signal for combat ... Take no rest until the child of England, vanquished by your armies, has resigned into your hands the sceptre to which he has no right, so that you may at last reign over both realms.[22]

Philip might have been content, during the final years of his reign, to be at peace with England; but at the beginning of his, Louis certainly was not, and he wasted no time picking up on his unfinished business with the Plantagenets. He might not have succeeded against them in England itself, but he could now continue his father's work of trying to eradicate their presence on French soil. The truce extension agreed by Philip was due to expire in May 1224; Louis announced that he would not be renewing it.[23]

* * *

Poitou was still in the hands of the English king by virtue of his position as duke of Aquitaine, another style Henry retained although he had never crossed the Channel. He did, however, have one very close relative in the region: his mother. Isabella of Angoulême had left England in July 1217, some nine months after her young son's accession, and had returned to her native Poitou. There she was reunited with her daughter Joan, who was being brought up in the Lusignan household. Count Hugh IX, who had been betrothed to Isabella before her marriage to John, died in 1219 and was succeeded by his son Hugh X, Joan's fiancé, who was in his mid-thirties. Joan was still only nine, and it was not long before the arrangement was dropped in favour of a different one: Hugh junior married Isabella herself on 10 May 1220, a marital arrangement that 'caused much talk', as one contemporary succinctly noted.[24] Isabella was by this stage around thirty-two years of age and already a mother of five, but she would go on to have a second family of five sons and four daughters with her new husband, of whom we shall hear more later.[25] A widowed queen might generally be expected to offer gifts or monetary donations in return for prayers or Masses for the soul of her late husband, or to establish a foundation in his name, but following Isabella's return to France not one of her extant letters or charters mentions John; she concentrated all her attention on her new life and her new family.

Isabella and Hugh – now count of Angoulême as well as La Marche – were the major powers in the region. Hugh was in an unusual situation, being (nominally at least) the stepfather of the king of England, while owing allegiance to the king of France as his overlord. His main loyalty, however, was to himself, and he exploited the events of the 1220s to his advantage, responding to the overtures of the new King Louis VIII. Louis's political intelligence might not have been quite of the calibre of his father's, but he was nonetheless astute enough to recognise that the one thing Hugh had missed out on following his marriage to Isabella was the Isle of Oleron. This was an inhabited island of fertile land lying just off the west coast, which Hugh and his family had long coveted; it was to have formed part of Joan's dowry, but was not included in the terms of his marriage settlement with Isabella. Louis thus made Hugh a tempting offer: if he could use Hugh's lands as a base for his campaign against the remaining territory in the region held by Henry, he would cede control of the Isle of Oleron to Hugh as soon as they captured it. Hugh agreed.[26]

This news must have distressed Henry when it reached him; but at that time, in 1224, he had little attention to spare for Poitou as he was embroiled in internal problems in England. As we have seen, Hubert de Burgh's rise to prominence had been smoothed by his relative anonymity; but as the years went by and his confidence increased, he began to overreach himself in a way that the great noblemen of the country found unpalatable. After being twice widowed, Hubert married as his third wife Margaret of Scotland, the sister of King Alexander, thus attaining royal connections; he was later named earl of Kent, which put him on a par with some of the older, more established noble families – a subject to which we will return in the next chapter.[27]

What started as 'loud murmurings' against Hubert turned into open revolts, the most serious of which was orchestrated by Falkes de Bréauté.[28]

Falkes was outlawed in June 1224 by a group of justices who found against him on charges of seizure of property in Bedfordshire. Falkes's brother, William, who held Bedford castle in his name, then kidnapped one of the royal justices, an affront to the king's authority that required immediate action.[29] The teenaged Henry arrived in person, accompanied by Hubert de Burgh, Archbishop Langton and an army of soldiers and engineers, to besiege the castle. Huge resources were brought to bear, siege engines were constructed and quarrying began to find stone for ammunition. Eventually the castle was taken, though not until mid-August. The royal justice was freed and the women who had been inside the castle (including Falkes's wife, who incidentally sought an immediate divorce) were allowed to depart; but the serious challenge to royal authority had to be punished appropriately, so William de Bréauté and the eighty-man garrison were hanged.[30] On hearing the news, Falkes voluntarily surrendered all his English possessions and went into exile; he would die in Rome two years later. The siege of Bedford was a success for the king in terms of reimposing royal authority on rebellious barons, but Henry and his major supporters had been occupied there for two months, meaning that they had taken their eye off what was happening in France.

Louis VIII was not a king who was inclined to hang around, especially when a military campaign was on offer. One of his major problems in England had been a lack of resources, but this was no longer an issue now that he had the considerable riches of the French crown at his disposal. He summoned all royal vassals, mustering an army that included combatants from Brittany, Normandy, Flanders and Champagne, as well as the royal domain, at Tours in June 1224.[31] With him were, among others, Brother Guérin; Philip Hurepel; Robert III, count of Dreux; Guy II, count of St-Pol; and Theobald IV, count of Champagne. The second Dreux brother, Peter, duke of Brittany, was tasked with remaining at Lusignan castle, Louis not entirely trusting the word of Count Hugh that he would continue to be loyal.

The French royal army marched first on Montreuil-Bellay, where a truce was agreed with the viscount of Thouars; this was the same Aimery VII, now in his seventies, who had tussled with King John many years previously. Then it turned south-west to work its way through to the main goal, La Rochelle; this was the major port on this part of the coast, and it was where kings of England landed when they came to visit their territories in France. The town of Niort, commanded by the English seneschal of Poitou, Savari de Mauléon (whom we last saw on John's campaign of 1206 in Chapter 14), surrendered after a short siege in the first week of July. Savari and his men – as was the custom following a surrender – were allowed to depart, and they retreated to La Rochelle. Next in the army's path was St Jean d'Angély, where 'those in the town heard of the approach of the king' and 'gave themselves up' with no resistance.[32] The way to La Rochelle lay open.

The town was defended by an English garrison, and the sympathies of its inhabitants could be expected to lie across the Channel, as they depended for much of their prosperity on trade with England. There was no pre-emptive surrender, so Louis set up a siege, which began in mid-July. An eyewitness gives a flavour of the preparations:

> Here a knight polishes his helmet to remove traces of rust. Shields are made ready; swords are sharpened so that their steel points can inundate the earth with blood and turn the green grass red ... Footsoldiers make ready their catapults, and a mass of lead is converted into balls; machines are constructed which are destined to break down the walls and to cast blocks of stone to destroy towers and houses, to kill enemies ... Hands are full of darts and javelins, quivers are filled with arrows ... They are not short of bows, heavy blades, cruel axes or falchions; each also arms himself with a sharp steel sword.[33]

The bombardment began. The town was well fortified, and the garrison, having had due warning of the French army's approach, had stockpiled supplies. They were confident that they could withstand the assault until they received relief and reinforcements from England, but of course these were never to arrive. By the beginning of August this reality had become apparent, and the citizens were rethinking their priorities: if they surrendered, they stood more chance of surviving with their lives and businesses intact than they would if La Rochelle were taken by storm. After some discussion they opened their gates, and Louis made a triumphal entry. The citizens, as they had hoped, were left unmolested on the condition that they swore fealty to the French king, which they did. The English garrison were allowed to sail away unharmed, and thus 'the English, who had long been lurking in this part of Aquitaine, left either voluntarily or under duress the kingdom of France'.[34]

Henry had kept Bedford but lost Poitou. However, although the exchange was hardly comparable in terms of wealth and revenue, in hindsight it is difficult to see what else he could have done. If he had invested his time, money and troops in trying to defend La Rochelle and the other towns, only to lose his grip on the kingdom of England, the implications would have been much worse. The rebellion against his father was still a recent memory in England, so the imposition of royal authority there was of the utmost importance.

This did not prevent blame being assigned for the losses in Poitou. When Savari de Mauléon reached England he was badly received, accused of surrendering too easily and threatened with a charge of treason. He took umbrage at this and sailed back to France to submit to Louis, offering his allegiance in December 1224.[35] Given his valuable local knowledge, he was a useful man for Louis to have on the ground in Poitou, and he was given the command of La Rochelle. In the meantime, the Isle of Oleron had submitted to Louis without a fight; he kept his promise to hand it over to Hugh de Lusignan, who had – for now, at least – been equally true to his word and held his lands for Louis behind the royal army's advance.

Henry would belatedly send a force across the Channel in August 1225, a whole year later. This was commanded by his brother, Richard, who was now sixteen and earl of Cornwall; in anticipation of regaining his territories Henry had also rather optimistically named him count of Poitou, one of the subsidiary titles of the duke of Aquitaine. Richard was under the guidance of two very experienced heads, his uncle William Longsword, earl of Salisbury, and the naval commander Philip d'Albini; they had some success holding on to Gascony (the southern part of Aquitaine), but were ineffective in Poitou.[36] Louis had by now stationed his own garrisons in the towns there; the county was to be integrated into the royal domain in much the same way that Normandy had been, and would later form an apanage for his son Alphonse. Gascony may well have been next on Louis's hit list in his quest to sweep the English out of France, but events elsewhere intervened; Fortune's wheel was about to turn in the most dramatic way imaginable.

* * *

While all the conflict had been occurring in Poitou, the Albigensian Crusade was still going on. The seemingly never-ending war had engulfed a new generation, with the crusaders now being led by Amaury VI de Montfort, son of the Simon who had been killed at Toulouse in 1218, and the southerners by Raymond VII of Toulouse, son of the late Raymond VI. The younger Raymond was Henry III's first cousin, his mother having been King John's sister Joanna; he had been gaining ground because Amaury, although dedicated to the cause, could not quite live up to the standards of his father as a military commander.[37]

Louis, fresh from his triumphs and always keen to ride and fight rather than sit and talk, decided to address the matter once and for all. It would take some time to plan and assemble the force and the supplies he would need, but he set matters in motion. He also started to put some administrative affairs in order, and this included drawing up his testament in June 1225. Like his great-grandfather Louis VI, he had almost too many sons to provide for, but thanks to his own gains and the considerable acquisitions of Philip Augustus he could do something for nearly all of them. Louis junior, then aged eleven, was to have the crown of France and the royal domain; Robert, nine, was to be count of Artois, Louis VIII's maternal inheritance; John, six, would be count of Anjou and Maine, recovered by Philip from the English; and Alphonse, five, would be count of Poitou (the claims of Richard of Cornwall notwithstanding) following Louis's conquest there. After that the available lands ran out, so Philip-Dagobert, three, would enter the Church, as would any further sons born after the testament was drawn up. Louis's only daughter, Isabelle, would have a dowry in cash rather than estates, but the enormous sum of £20,000 (Parisian) that was allocated to her would certainly be a temptation for any king or prince.[38]

Louis set off for the south in June 1226. There was by now a further incentive to end the crusade: Amaury de Montfort, realising that he could not win the war, had ceded all his rights in Languedoc to Louis as his overlord, so there were vast territorial gains on offer as well as the blessing of the Church. Raymond of Toulouse appealed to his cousin King Henry for aid, but it was in England's interests for Louis to be engaged in Languedoc as long as possible, and besides, Henry had a growing reputation for piety, so he was not inclined to help a man who was excommunicate and fighting against the forces of the established Church.

Louis's army was held up at the great city of Avignon by a siege which lasted from June to September. The king's close companion Guy, count of St-Pol, was killed in an assault. Others began to grumble that their forty-day period of service was up, and even to desert; among these were, notably, Peter, duke of Brittany, and Count Theobald IV of Champagne. In the burning sun of the Provençal summer the unsanitary siege camp became a place of sickness and death, ravaged by famine and by 'large black flies, which made their way inside the tents, pavilions and awnings, and affected the provisions and liquor; [the French] being unable to drive them away from their cups and plates, they caused sudden death among them'.[39]

Avignon surrendered in September, but by that time Louis was already ill. At first he tried to ignore it, leading his depleted and sickness-ravaged army towards Toulouse; but by the time they got there it was mid-October and his forces were in no state to begin a siege that would last all winter. Reluctantly, he decided to head back to Paris, intending to return to the south the following spring. But he would never make it home: his dysentery grew worse and he died on the journey, at the small castle of Montpensier, on 8 November 1226.[40]

This was a huge shock for France. Louis was thirty-nine and had been on the throne for just three years and three months – a marked contrast to two centuries of long, stable periods of sovereignty, his six immediate predecessors having enjoyed reigns of between twenty-nine and forty-nine years each. Those who were with Louis scrambled to take the necessary decisions and to organise the transportation of his body to Paris for burial.

There was, at least, a clear and undisputed heir. The principle of father–son succession was long established in France and on his deathbed Louis VIII had reiterated that the crown was to pass to his eldest son, Louis. And thus it was that on 29 November 1226, three weeks after his father's death, a twelve-year-old boy became the second Louis *rex* to be crowned at Reims within less than four years. A long minority following a sudden death now beckoned in France, just as it had in England a decade earlier. The pendulum between the two dynasties had been swinging in favour of the Capetians for many years, thanks to the ascendancy of Philip and Louis over John and Henry. Was it now about to make a swift change of direction?

Part IV

SAINTS AND SINNERS

≈ CHAPTER TWENTY ≈

WOE UNTO THE LAND . . .

Woe unto you, O land, when your king is a child.

                                                        Ecclesiastes 10:16

ENGLAND HAD CERTAINLY SUFFERED its share of ups and downs since the accession of a minor in 1216; the question now was whether the same would happen in France a decade later. The two young kings were first cousins once removed, Henry's father having been the brother of Louis's maternal grandmother, and superficially there were a number of similarities between the two situations: in each realm the unexpected early death of a king from dysentery, while embroiled in an internal conflict, had resulted in a young boy succeeding to the throne rather earlier than he or anyone else had anticipated. But there, as we will see, the similarities ended: France would take a very different path from the one trodden by its neighbour over the preceding ten years.

One of the major factors in this divergence was the character and actions of the two widowed dowager queens. Isabella of Angoulême, as we have seen, had left England less than a year after her son's accession and then concentrated her attention on her growing second family. Little Henry had been left to the mercy of his advisors, with no parent to guide or care for him, and Isabella appears to have had scarcely any contact with her first family – except to take her daughter Joan's intended husband for herself and then return the little girl to England in the autumn of 1220. Henry was thus effectively an orphan, and one who needed to act as the head of his family from a very young age. His only other adult relative, his trusted uncle William Longsword, earl of Salisbury, had died in 1226, following his return from the expedition to Aquitaine that we mentioned in the previous chapter.

Henry and his advisors had, by 1226, already arranged alliances for two of his three sisters: the now sixteen-year-old Joan was the queen of Scotland, having been married to Alexander II in 1221, soon after her return from France; and eleven-year-old Eleanor was the countess of Pembroke, following her marriage to William II Marshal, twenty-five years her senior, in 1224. Isabelle, twelve, was not yet betrothed, as Henry was holding her back for a prestigious international alliance as and when the opportunity should arise. Henry's brother Richard, his heir presumptive until such time as he should have a son of his own, also needed to be provided for with titles and lands appropriate to his rank; he was now seventeen, earl of Cornwall in fact and 'count of Poitou' in name.

Louis IX's mother could hardly have been more different from Henry III's. At the time of her son's accession Blanche was a widow (a grieving one, unlike Isabella), the mother of seven children all aged under thirteen, and pregnant with an eighth. But this did not stop her taking immediate action on behalf of her eldest son, who would become the almost exclusive focus of her life from that point onwards. As we have seen, Louis VII and Philip Augustus had assumed full regal power at their accessions, even though they were aged only seventeen and fifteen respectively; but Louis IX was just twelve, and those few years made all the difference: he would need an adult to act for him. Louis VIII, on his deathbed, had named Blanche as the regent for their son during his minority, a choice that might seem unusual when there was at least one adult male relative available, but in fact it was both reasonable and uncontroversial.[1] Previous kings of France had left their mothers in charge during a period of absence – one example that we have already seen being Philip Augustus's trust in the abilities of Adela of Blois while he was away on crusade – and the rule of a mother during a minority was a well-established custom among the nobility of France. Blanche of Navarre had controlled the county of Champagne during the recent long minority of her son Theobald IV, and the incumbent duke of Burgundy, in 1226, was the teenage Hugh IV under the tutelage and rule of his mother. There were, of course, obvious worries about entrusting the care of a boy king to a paternal male relative who might himself have a claim to the throne. But a mother, it was thought, could be relied upon to do her utmost in the cause of a son.

In Blanche's particular case, the fact that she was 'foreign' worked to her advantage: as a member of the Castilian royal family she was above internal French rivalries, was not allied to any of the great French houses and would therefore not be suspected of trying to favour one at the expense of the others. She was further assisted by the fact that her long residence in France, where she had lived since she was twelve, had given her a close acquaintance with those same internal rivalries so she was well aware of what she and her son were stepping into. She accepted the position and put aside her grief so that she could work in the best interests of France and its new king, Louis IX.

After Louis VIII's funeral Louis and Blanche set out from Paris to make their way to Reims. They broke their journey at Soissons, where Louis, despite his youth, was knighted. The coronation itself was calm, and it took place in the usual venue and followed the usual format; there were no irregularities that might call it into question, such as those that had occurred at Gloucester in 1216. The only difference from the established order of events was that the celebrant was the bishop of Soissons: the honour of crowning and anointing a new king of France normally belonged to the archbishop of Reims, but the see was vacant, Archbishop William de Joinville having accompanied Louis VIII on his campaign and having also died on the way back, just a few days before the king. In a further sign of stability in the kingdom and a signal that established precedent still held, the next archbishop of Reims – a post often associated with the Capetian royal family – would be Henry of Dreux, third son of the late Count Robert II and brother to both Robert III, count of Dreux, and Peter, duke of Brittany. The bishop of Soissons was assisted at the ceremony by the aged Brother Guérin, chancellor and bishop of Senlis, now serving his third French king and providing another link to the past.[2] The Church and the nobility of France were represented by as many as could reach Reims in time, given the tight timescale, and they swore oaths of allegiance to Blanche as well as to Louis. However, there were three notable absentees, of whom we will hear more presently: Theobald IV, count of Champagne; Hugh X de Lusignan, count of La Marche and Angoulême; and Peter de Dreux, duke of Brittany.[3]

Blanche of Castile had spent a large proportion of the preceding seventeen years either pregnant or recovering from her frequent confinements, which was of course a primary duty, but one that perhaps gave her less time to interest herself in political life than she would like. In early 1227 she gave birth to her final child, Charles, in the sad knowledge that he would never know his father, but also with the recognition – and perhaps the relief – that her childbearing duties were now firmly and finally over. The boy survived, although the family suffered the loss of the next youngest, the toddler Stephen, later that same year. Blanche would continue to supervise the education of all her remaining seven children, but her principal focus was unambiguously on Louis and the establishment of his reign. There has been a prevailing view for many years that Blanche was overbearing, that she dominated Louis for the remaining years of her life, but – as we will see – this view needs to be nuanced. In the very early stage of his reign, while he was pre-pubescent, of course she took the lead and must have been the driving force behind most of the decisions made; but, even then, she never forgot that she was acting merely in his name, and later on they would become a very effective partnership.[4]

The immediate road in front of Blanche, as she started out on the long minority, was not an easy one; as one sympathetic thirteenth-century writer points out, 'her children were small and she was a lone woman in a foreign country, and she had to outwit a number of great lords'.[5] The lords whom she had to outwit in the short term were led by the trio mentioned above who had been absent from Louis's coronation, and there were additional difficulties in the shape of Philip Hurepel.

Philip Hurepel was now in his mid-twenties and the holder of extensive lands, thanks to Philip Augustus and Louis VIII. He was the young king's nearest paternal adult relative, and might have considered himself unlucky that he was not named regent. From the available evidence, it would appear that he was not overtly ambitious – perhaps he realised that the shadow of the circumstances of his birth would forever be an issue – and he made no direct move. Indeed, he was one of those present at Louis VIII's deathbed who ensured that the late king's wishes were carried out. However, he was an adult son of Philip Augustus, the great king who had only been dead three and a half years and who was still fresh in popular memory (and whom he resembled physically), which meant that he would inevitably be the focal point for anyone who *did* wish to incite rebellion against young Louis, as he was the only possible rival candidate. And this is what happened almost immediately, although Philip Hurepel prudently does not seem to have played an active part himself. 'They said they would make him king,' relates the Minstrel of Reims, 'but he would not be wise at all if he believed them.'[6] 'They', in this case, were the other three.

Peter de Dreux, duke of Brittany, was a member of a cadet branch of the Capetian family and had been one of Louis VIII's closest companions since boyhood. As the second son of Count Robert II of Dreux he had inherited no family lands, but had gained a duchy by marriage, though he was now only its regent: his wife, Alix (who was duchess in her own right), had died in 1221, leaving Peter with a four-year-old son, John, in whose name he now ruled, and a three-year-old daughter, Yolande. The duchy of Brittany had previously been held by members of the Plantagenet family, as we have seen, and it had long been associated with the earldom of Richmond in England; Peter entered into negotiations with Henry III about the possibility of gaining those lands by paying homage to him, which would effectively return Brittany to English overlordship. The discussions were positive, and a marriage alliance was proposed between Peter's daughter, Yolande, and Henry. This was perhaps not the most prestigious international match that Henry could hope for, but it would bring Brittany into his orbit, thus going some way towards his goal of rebuilding the cross-Channel empire held by Henry II; and, given that Peter had only one son and that children's lives were precarious, there was also the possibility that Yolande might end up as the heiress of Brittany, thus bringing the duchy into Henry's direct possession. Peter was satisfied with the way things were going, and he shared his plans with his two co-conspirators.[7]

Theobald IV, count of Champagne, had besmirched his reputation in France by deserting Louis VIII at the siege of Avignon and returning home – indeed, there were even rumours floating about that he had poisoned Louis, although these are almost certainly fictional. Theobald had been gone over a month by the time Louis fell ill, and the king had spent the intervening time in cramped and unsanitary military camps surrounded by sick men, so dysentery seems the likeliest cause. However, given Louis's subsequent death, the blame attached to Theobald in the popular imagination was great, and Blanche had forbidden him from attending Louis IX's coronation. Hugh X de Lusignan, meanwhile, had inherited his father's propensity for fluid loyalties, and now he saw more potential for gain in joining Peter and Theobald than in remaining loyal to Louis and Blanche, though he would continue his family's tradition of changing sides whenever it was convenient.

These three lords began to advance their own ambitions by stirring up discontent with Blanche's regency, and then went so far as to challenge Louis's kingship in the name of Philip Hurepel, on the grounds that Louis was too young to rule and that his regent was a woman and a foreigner. This was a dangerous moment, as it would not be the first time that the claims of an adult uncle had been set against those of a boy nephew (as events in England and the Empire had demonstrated within living memory), but they were hampered by Philip Hurepel's lack of enthusiasm for the venture, and by the fact that they had very much underestimated the queen.

As we saw in Chapter 18, Blanche had taken bold and practical action to assist Louis VIII during his English campaign, and she wasted no time in doing the same for Louis IX now. At the first hint of insurrection in early 1227, she sprang into action – something all the more impressive when we recall that she must have been either heavily pregnant or recovering from a recent confinement at the time, given that her son Charles was born at around the same date. Her first move was a diplomatic one, as she managed to separate Theobald from the other two and talk him round. Contemporaries were so baffled by her skill in achieving this that they could only explain it by promulgating the idea that the two of them were having an affair, but this seems extremely unlikely.[8] There was no doubt some kind of personal element to the talks – they were related, Theobald's mother Blanche of Navarre being Blanche's cousin, and they had known each other a long time, Theobald having been placed as a child in the shared household of Blanche and the future Louis VIII – but the rapprochement now was almost certainly due to political necessity on both sides. The queen's anger over Theobald leaving the Albigensian Crusade early might have cooled a little, especially as she realised that he could not really be blamed for Louis VIII's death, and she would appreciate that her position as regent meant she had to make compromises and allies where she could. And Theobald might have had his future, as well as his present, situation in mind: if he acted now as a rebellious vassal, it would set a bad example to those who would be his own vassals once he was king of Navarre; and when that day arrived, he would need Louis as an ally.

Whatever the precise nature of the talks, Theobald agreed to remain loyal to the crown. Safe from any danger left behind them in Champagne, Blanche and Louis were therefore able to ride with the royal army – which included Robert III, count of Dreux, Peter's elder brother, who had remained faithful to his sovereign – to Chinon, the best place strategically to keep an eye on Brittany and La Marche as well as being prepared for any English-backed advance out of Gascony.[9]

Backed up by this threat of military action, Blanche brought Peter and Hugh to the negotiating table. The woman who had once faced down the great Philip Augustus evidently had little difficulty with these two barons, and she was able to talk them out of their hostile position and persuade them to pay homage to Louis. She also managed to break up the planned English–Breton marriage alliance; as part of the deal, Peter would have to cancel his daughter's betrothal to King Henry and instead affiance her to John, the third of Blanche's sons and the one due to inherit Brittany's neighbours Anjou and Maine. As a concession, Peter would hold Angers in John's name until the wedding took place. Similar arrangements were made to tie Hugh X de Lusignan to the French royal house, his position as Henry III's stepfather notwithstanding: he agreed to marry his son and heir – a six-year-old somewhat inevitably called Hugh – to the three-year-old Isabelle, Blanche's only daughter. Philip Hurepel was not party to these discussions, but his compliance was bought or assured with the promise of a large cash allowance; he would also have the wardship of Yolande of Brittany until her marriage could take place. This was not likely to be for some while as, at time of the treaty, she was eight and John seven.[10]

While all this was happening in the northern half of France, the Albigensian situation was still ongoing. As we saw in Chapter 19, Amaury VI de Montfort had ceded all his rights in Languedoc to the crown, so the campaign had come under royal leadership. Manoeuvres had continued after Louis VIII's death, but with a different strategy: the royal forces had adopted a policy of economic devastation, ravaging the fields and harvests, and driving the people – whether heretics or not – to the edge of starvation. By the spring of 1229 they could take no more and Raymond VII submitted uncon-ditionally to Blanche, his first cousin (their mothers, Joanna and Eleanor Plantagenet, having been sisters) and to the Church. The Treaty of Paris officially ended the conflict, and yet another marriage alliance was arranged:

Joan of Toulouse, Raymond VII's only child and heir, would marry Blanche's fourth son, Alphonse (this despite their close family relationship – a dispensation was sought from and agreed by Pope Gregory IX). The eight-year-old prospective bride was taken to Paris to be brought up in the royal household along with her nine-year-old fiancé, the long-disputed county of Toulouse would henceforward be tied more closely to the crown, and the value to a ruling dynasty of having 'spares' as well as heirs was demonstrated. With his daughter at the royal court, Raymond VII would be obliged to remain loyal, and after his death either the county would be in the hands of the king's brother and his descendants, or – if Alphonse and Joan had no children – it would be subsumed into the royal domain.[11]

Blanche and Raymond's other cousin, Henry III, cannot have been pleased when he heard of the treaty. Toulouse bordered Gascony, his remaining possession in France, and having that county in the hands of a member of the French ruling house would jeopardise his interests. There was little he could do about the betrothal, but the other continuing murmurs of unrest in France provided him with an opportunity he did not want to miss.

* * *

In January 1227 King Henry (then aged nineteen and three months) had declared that henceforward he would issue charters under his own seal, thus effectively ending his minority at an in-between date that caught some of his advisors off-guard.[12] Hubert de Burgh was the major beneficiary, being named earl of Kent and given lands in that county and in south Wales, but this made him more unpopular with the established nobility, many of whom also continued to resent his ambitious marriage to Margaret of Scotland.

Henry's major goal at this early point of his personal rule was the restitution of his family's lands in France, and, as we have seen, he entered into negotiations with Peter, duke of Brittany. Peter's submission to Blanche in 1227 and the breaking of the proposed marriage alliance between his daughter Yolande and Henry had put a stumbling block in the way of Henry's ambitions, but Peter was not yet finished. Still dissatisfied with his position in France, and keen to gain the Richmond lands in England, he met Henry in the autumn of 1229 and did what he had threatened to do before: he paid homage to the English king. He also actively encouraged an attack on Louis. 'The king of France is a young boy, a child,' he is reported as telling Henry, 'not of an age to wear the crown ... You could recover everything that your father lost.' This enticement was evidently music to Henry's ears.[13]

Blanche summoned Peter to appear before her and Louis, in order to explain himself; but, in what amounted to a statement of defiance and revolt, he refused to attend. In January 1230 they raised a force to besiege and occupy castles and towns along the Loire, taking back Angers from his control as they went. But the situation was escalating: thanks to Peter's homage and the literal safe harbour this provided, Henry arrived in person with a fleet of some thirty ships at St-Malo in May. Blanche's marriage, all those years ago, had been a symbol of peace between the Plantagenets and the Capetians, but that time seemed long gone as she now found herself fighting against her cousin on behalf of her son. The French forces were able to contain Henry and Peter to the area around Nantes, while Henry, demonstrating that he did not have the martial fervour of many previous members of his dynasty, seemed almost paralysed and made no move to launch a major attack, or even to lead ravaging expeditions; he simply sat still. 'The king of England all this time was lying with his army at the city of Nantes,' said one English commentator, 'doing nothing except spending his money.' Meanwhile 'the earls and barons ... devoted themselves to eating and drinking by turns, as though they were keeping Christmas'.[14]

The Capetian monarchy now demonstrated once again that it worked in concert with its nobles. At a council convened in June, Blanche and Louis were supported unanimously by a group that included, among others, Theobald IV of Champagne, reconciled with them, at least for now; Amaury VI de Montfort, relieved to be free of his lifelong war of attrition in Languedoc and now constable of France, in return for having ceded his rights in the south; and Ferrand of Flanders, who had been released in 1227 from his thirteen-year post-Bouvines captivity and was keen to demonstrate his loyalty. The council condemned Peter and were prepared to support their king and his regent with all the resources at their disposal; this was too much for Henry and Peter, and they sued for peace.[15]

A truce was agreed in August 1230. However, it did not seem to have any definitive effect in ending the conflict, or the appetite for conflict, one way or the other. Henry sailed back to England in October, having achieved very little. But three of his major magnates – William II Marshal and his brother Richard Marshal (who held, separately and respectively, the English and the Norman estates that had once belonged to their father, who had managed to retain both after the fall of Normandy in 1204), and Ranulf, earl of Chester – remained in Brittany. Along with the undeterred Peter, they began launching raids into Normandy. This forced Blanche and the now sixteen-year-old Louis to saddle up once again in order to invade Brittany itself via Normandy, which was now part of their royal domain. Peter was forced to back down and agree to a settlement that confined him to Brittany; the chief negotiators for Blanche and Louis were Peter's brother Henry of Dreux, the archbishop of Reims, and Philip Hurepel, who had by now come to the realisation – if he ever doubted it – that his best interests lay in being the loyal supporter of his nephew, who was consolidating and strengthening his position on the throne as every day went by.[16]

The failure of the expedition was not well received in England. Henry had taken his army across the sea, wrote one commentator, 'where he lost many of his men, expended a great deal of money, and recovered little or nothing of his lands'.[17] Hubert de Burgh bore the brunt of the blame, and his enemies – including Peter des Roches, who had recently returned from crusade – succeeded in bringing him down in 1232. He survived the experience, but was put in prison.[18]

By this time a new face had appeared on the English political scene: a young man named Simon de Montfort. He was the younger brother of Amaury, constable of France, and the son of Simon de Montfort the elder, the Albigensian Crusade leader who had died at Toulouse in 1218.[19] The family had a historical claim to the earldom of Leicester in England via Simon senior, who had been the son of Amice, sister of the childless Robert de Beaumont, who had died in 1204, bringing to an end the male Beaumont line that had held the earldom since the time of Henry I. This Robert had had two sisters: Amice and another named Margaret, who had married Saer de Quincy, the earl of Winchester, who had fought on the baronial side during the war against King John. Robert's estates should have been divided between the heirs of both his sisters, but with the de Montforts settled in France as vassals of the French king, it had become difficult for them to make any claim; and with Simon the elder and Amaury fully engaged in the

Albigensian Crusade for much of their lives, the question had lapsed. The lands (but not the title of earl of Leicester) were currently in the hands of Ranulf de Blundeville, the earl of Chester, himself childless.

Simon junior was an ambitious young man, in his early twenties at this point, who wanted more than a younger brother's portion. With Amaury, the elder, secure in his position in France and unwilling to jeopardise it, Simon persuaded him to sign over any rights he might have to lands and estates in England, and set sail. He was received in a friendly manner by Henry, who was not averse to him having the Leicester lands, if Ranulf could be persuaded to resign them, and a discussion would ensue about this.[20] Had the king known the trouble that would come his way in later years from this new friend, he might have put Simon straight back on a ship and pushed it out to sea himself.

* * *

Tragedy struck the French royal family in 1232 when two of King Louis's younger brothers, John and Philip-Dagobert, died aged thirteen and ten. Amid the sorrow at such bereavement on top of earlier losses – Louis now had just one sister and three surviving brothers of the large family that had once existed – there were repercussions for the future of the kingdom, in the form of the apanages that Louis VIII had stipulated in his testament. There was no change for second son Robert, who celebrated his sixteenth birthday in 1232 and who would retain Artois, the county originally allocated to him, or for Alphonse (who would turn twelve at the end of the year), who was count of Poitou and would also later be count of Toulouse, thanks to his marriage; but Charles (aged five) would benefit. He had not been born when Louis VIII's original testament had been drawn up, and was thus one of the 'any further sons' destined to enter the Church; but he now stepped into the shoes of the late John to become count of Anjou and Maine. This, coupled with the deaths of Stephen and Philip-Dagobert, also originally intended for clerical careers, meant that all the family remained in the secular world. The brothers were generally known by the names of their estates, not their places of birth: Robert of Artois, Alphonse of Poitiers and Charles of Anjou.[21] Their sister Isabelle, aged eight in 1232, was betrothed to young Hugh (later Hugh XI) de Lusignan, but even at this early age she was beginning to demonstrate an extreme piety and a desire never to marry, and she would later extricate herself from the arrangement.

The death of young John put an end to the royal family's projected marriage alliance with Brittany, and set in motion a complicated chain of further arrangements. Yolande of Brittany, John's intended bride who had previously been destined for Henry III, was now betrothed to Theobald IV of Champagne, who was some twenty years her senior; but, like her other engagements, this would not result in marriage. She would eventually make it to the altar at the fourth attempt, in 1234, when she married Hugh, the very same son and heir of Hugh X de Lusignan and Isabella of Angoulême who had been spurned by Princess Isabelle.

The year 1234 proved to be a momentous one in both realms. In England, Henry finally found himself free of both Hubert de Burgh and Peter des Roches. The former had been in prison for two years, and now Henry allowed the office of justiciar itself to lapse, naming no replacement. In part, this was a sign that he wanted to exert his independence to a greater extent; but also, an office whose primary purpose was to represent the king in England when he was abroad was not really necessary when the king spent all his time in England, having failed to regain his lands across the Channel. Peter des Roches had by now also fallen: since his return three years previously, he had made himself unpopular through financial exactions on Henry's behalf and the appointment of cronies, thus reminding the English barons of why they disliked him and his influence in the first place:

> All this time Peter bishop of Winchester and his colleagues had so perverted the king's heart with hatred and contempt for his English subjects, that he endeavoured by all the means in his power to exterminate them, and invited such legions of people from Poitou that they entirely filled England, and wherever the king went he was surrounded by crowds of these foreigners; and nothing was done in England except what the bishop of Winchester and this host of foreigners determined on.[22]

Peter would die in 1238 and Hubert in 1243, both as spent old men who never recovered their previous influence. However, Henry's newfound independence was also a worrying sign of a possible return to the bad old days of his father's arbitrary rule, and he was reminded by his nobles that he had reissued Magna Carta and promised to abide by its terms. A council held in Gloucester in 1234 insisted on the basis of this that Henry must govern in concert with councils – later to be called 'parliaments'.[23]

In France, Philip Hurepel died, only in his mid-thirties and apparently of wounds sustained during a tournament, leaving a widow, Matilda de Dammartin, who was countess of Boulogne in her own right, and a daughter, Joan, who was the sole heiress not only of Boulogne but also of all her father's other lands. Louis and Blanche accepted Matilda's homage but kept a very close eye on her and her daughter, who could only be married with their express permission. Joan would later marry Walter IV de Châtillon, son of the loyal count of St-Pol who had died fighting for Louis VIII at Avignon; but they had no children, and so Philip Hurepel's line died out.

It was also in 1234 that Theobald IV of Champagne inherited the crown of Navarre, becoming King Theobald I, following the death of his uncle Sancho VII the Strong (Theobald's mother, Blanche, and his childless aunt, Berengaria, having predeceased their brother). He retained his lands and titles in France, but moved to take up residence in Navarre and would be safely occupied there for some time. In the same year the truce confining Peter de Dreux to Brittany expired and he decided to leave the realm, as well as the duchy, departing on crusade. This ended any lingering ideas of a Breton alliance with England, meaning that Henry III now had no foothold in France further north than Gascony, so any attempt at invasion was unlikely. Louis IX was safe and secure: during the years of his minority, woe had not been visited upon his land.

In the spring of 1234 Louis celebrated his twentieth birthday. He had three younger brothers, but the Capetians had a long tradition of the throne passing from father to son, so thoughts were naturally turning to the question of his marriage – and a similar situation was occurring in England, where the twenty-six-year-old Henry was still worryingly single. In a curious twist to our story, one family was about to bring about a profound change in the nature of the relationship between the Capetians and the Plantagenets.

⇒ CHAPTER TWENTY-ONE ⇐

FOUR SISTERS

O NCE UPON A TIME, A count and countess had four beautiful daughters who all grew up to be queens. It sounds exactly like the start
of a fairy tale, but in the case of the family of Raymond-Berengar
IV, count of Provence, and his wife Beatrice of Savoy, it is in fact a true story.

Provence was a county on the Mediterranean coast, east of and bordering
Toulouse; it covered an area stretching from the Rhône valley in the west to
the Alps in the east. Although today it lies in France, in the early thirteenth
century it was part of the Empire, so Count Raymond-Berengar owed allegiance to Frederick II. Savoy, the county from which his wife hailed, bordered
Provence immediately to the north. Beatrice was not the heiress of Savoy,
having six brothers, but her marriage sometime around 1219 to Raymond-
Berengar brought the two provinces closer together. They had produced six
children, but the two boys – who were probably twins – had died in infancy,
leaving them with four daughters, Margaret, Eleanor, Sanchia and Beatrice,
born around 1221, 1223, 1228 and 1231 respectively.[1]

In the spring of 1234 the rulers of France and Provence realised that an
alliance between them could be mutually advantageous. Raymond-Berengar,
a Catholic of impeccably orthodox beliefs, had long been a rival of Raymond
VII of Toulouse, and was now threatened by the fact that Emperor Frederick
(who was at this point in dispute with Pope Gregory IX and had already been
excommunicated twice) seemed to be favouring the equally religiously suspect
Raymond. An alliance with France, a strong neighbour to the west, would
therefore help bolster Raymond-Berengar's position. France, meanwhile, had

only recently gained a strong foothold in Languedoc and was moving towards direct control of Toulouse. Everything seemed to favour an alliance with Provence: it was a stable and well-governed county on the other side of Toulouse; Louis needed a wife and an heir, and Beatrice of Savoy and her daughters were renowned for their beauty; and, as Raymond-Berengar had no sons, a match with his eldest daughter held out the promise of direct control over Provence one day.

Queen Blanche opened negotiations by offering to arbitrate in the dispute between Counts Raymond and Raymond-Berengar, on the condition that the latter agreed to the marriage of his eldest daughter with Louis whatever the outcome. He consented, the arbitration predictably found in his favour, and the wedding of Louis and Margaret took place at Sens in May 1234, the barely teenage Margaret being crowned queen the following day. According to various accounts, the virtuous Louis took some obscure words of scripture literally and delayed the consummation of the marriage for three days, so that the couple could dedicate their first three nights together to prayer.[2]

One of the other driving forces in the agreement had been the ambitious brothers of Beatrice of Savoy, who now found themselves uncles to the queen of France; indeed, it was one of these uncles, William of Savoy, bishop-elect of Valence, who brought Margaret to her wedding and gave her away, rather than her father. We will hear more of William later in this chapter.

Becoming a married man effectively ended Louis's minority, and in any case he reached the age of twenty-one a few months later. He assumed full autonomous power in April 1235, although there was never an official declaration that the regency was at an end – none was needed, for the transfer of power had been so gradual and so smooth that it was not marked by an obvious break.[3] By any standards, Blanche's regency had been an unqualified success. None of the problems normally associated with such a situation had occurred: she had not sought to sideline or remove Louis from power while she had the upper hand, but rather had led by example while teaching him and involving him in government from the very start. There had been no falling out between them, and when he took over there was no antagonism, or any attempt from him to push her away. In fact, even though he was now the sole king, Louis continued to rely on Blanche to a great extent – this is not an indication of him being dominated, but rather a recognition that he was extremely fortunate to have a political advisor of her calibre available who was guaranteed to remain absolutely loyal to him. It would make no sense to attempt to replace her, for who could do the job better?

Blanche's powerful and positive influence on the king and the kingdom was recognised by those closest to Louis, including the man who was his confessor, who later wrote:

> With what force, hard work, justice, and power his mother guided, protected, and defended the rights of the realm . . . Thanks to the merits of his innocence and the wise foresight of his mother, who always proved a manly woman, combining her feminine spirit and sex with the heart of a man, those who would upset the kingdom went down in confusion while the justice of the king triumphed.[4]

Blanche had been at France's helm for so long that old habits died hard, and for some while she continued to be known simply as 'the queen', while Margaret was referred to as 'the young queen' to avoid confusion. Indeed, between 1234 (when Louis married) and 1236 (when Ingeborg died) there were actually three queens in France, the widowed and respected Ingeborg being known as 'the queen of Orléans' after her place of residence.[5]

* * *

Now that he was married, Louis would no doubt expect to be the father of heirs before too long; and with three brothers all heading for marriageable age, the Capetian succession seemed secure. The situation in England, however, was very different.

By early 1236 King Henry was twenty-eight and still unmarried; a precarious position for the succession, and one that was exacerbated by the fortunes of the rest of the family. He had recently scored a significant diplomatic coup when he arranged for his one remaining available sister, Isabelle, to marry Frederick II, the twice-widowed Holy Roman Emperor. The wedding took place in 1235, at which point she was twenty-one (an unusually mature age for a royal bride) and Frederick forty.[6] Henry had been holding Isabelle back for just such a prestigious alliance, but unfortunately it did not work out very well for her on a personal level. She was empress in name, but Frederick kept her in virtual captivity in Noventa Padovana (in northern Italy, just east of Padua), where he visited her solely for the purposes of procreation; she never appeared at his court or at his side, and had no political influence. Even the mild-mannered Henry III would later be moved to complain about her treatment.[7] At this point, the beginning of 1236, Isabelle had borne no children, and neither had Henry's other sisters, Joan, queen of Scots and Eleanor, countess of Pembroke.

The sole member of the Plantagenet family who had managed to become a parent was Richard of Cornwall, but this only came at the expense of conflict with his brother. The circumstances are complex, but in brief: in 1231 Gilbert de Clare, earl of Hertford and Gloucester, had died, leaving a widow who was Isabel Marshal, the second daughter of the renowned William I Marshal. She was a rich prize in her own right, and given that not one of her five brothers had managed to produce any children, there was also the chance of a share in the great Marshal inheritance in the future. Gilbert de Clare had only been dead five months when Richard, almost a decade Isabel's junior, married her in a hurried ceremony without first consulting Henry, who was furious.[8] However, the king's ire later cooled and Richard and Isabel's union was not challenged. She had already proved her fertility, having borne six children to her first husband, and now she began another family. A first son and a daughter both died as toddlers, but in November 1235 Isabel gave birth to another son, Henry (later to be known as Henry of Almain, to distinguish him from the many others who shared the same name at this time), who would survive.[9] The Plantagenet family had thus, after a long hiatus, entered a new generation – and in the male line, too. But King Henry needed sons of his own, and he also needed an alliance that would help him achieve his ambitions.

Henry III's primary goal, as we have seen, was to regain his family's ancestral lands in Normandy, Anjou, Maine and Poitou, plus their erstwhile hold on Brittany, but his attempts to do so had so far met with little success. A proposed marriage alliance with Brittany and one with the county of Ponthieu (which was not large or overly wealthy, but was strategically well placed for any incursions into Normandy) had both fallen through due to Capetian opposition. Henry did, however, retain his hold on Gascony, the southern part of Aquitaine that bordered on Toulouse as well as Poitou, and his recent marriage strategy had centred on this. The union of Isabelle and Emperor Frederick, whose powerful sphere of influence lay on the other side of France, had been a great boost, and it now seemed expedient to reinforce this alliance by Henry marrying into the Empire himself, with the family of Provence being the most ideally placed. Such a relationship would also, to some extent, counterbalance the advantage that Louis had gained by marrying into the same family.

During the summer of 1235 Henry's envoys travelled to Provence to negotiate with Raymond-Berengar, and also with his influential coterie of brothers-in-law, including William of Savoy. Before they left, Henry had considered all the possibilities and had given them six different sets of letters, all dated 11 October 1235 and each demanding a different amount (from 20,000 marks down to 3,000) for Raymond-Berengar to bestow upon his daughter as a dowry. The idea was that the envoys would negotiate the best deal that they could and then produce whichever was the relevant letter, thus demonstrating that the amount agreed upon was the one they had been aiming for all along, while also avoiding the necessity of long journeys back and forth to gain Henry's approval of each step.[10] However, after their departure Henry found himself so keen on the marriage that he sent a further letter after them, saying that if all else failed, they were to agree to the match without any payment at all – which, in the event, is exactly what happened.

The deal was reached; the envoys inspected Eleanor in person and approved of her appearance (nobody bothered to record what she might have thought of them, or of this rather humiliating experience), so all was set. The union was made binding when Eleanor made her promises by proxy, one of the envoys standing in for Henry, and then she set out on the long winter journey – accompanied, as her sister had been, not by her father but by her uncle William of Savoy. She was, of course, guaranteed safe passage through France by her brother-in-law King Louis.

Eleanor reached England safely, disembarking at Dover and then moving swiftly to Canterbury, where she and Henry were married on 14 January 1236.[11] They had never met, so the occasion must have been a bewildering and rather overwhelming one for a girl of twelve in a chilly foreign land. However, fortune favoured her. Henry was some sixteen years her senior, which might have been intimidating, but the evidence we have both of Henry's personality prior to this point and of his behaviour towards Eleanor afterwards indicates that he was kind to her on a personal level, as well as welcoming her for political reasons.

After the wedding the royal party moved to Westminster, where, in a lavish spectacle, Eleanor was crowned and anointed on 20 January.[12] There would be much for her to learn, not least new languages: the Anglo-Norman dialect of French spoken in England was different from the Occitan that was probably her mother tongue, and English – of which she would have had no knowledge at all – was increasing in popularity at the highest levels, after having been suppressed in the decades since the Conquest. Given her youth, there would be some relief from immediate pressure to bear a child; but twelve was the canonically accepted age of marriage for girls, so it is probable that the union was consummated straight away, and with England's need for an heir weighing so heavily she would not expect sympathy for long if she did not fall pregnant.

Henry's marriage to Eleanor of Provence had a separate consequence, one that was both familiar from the past and ominous for the future. The history of the relationship between the nobility and Peter des Roches and his associates must have given Henry some inkling that he needed to be careful when favouring 'foreigners', but it was not long after his marriage that he appointed Eleanor's uncle William of Savoy as one of his chief advisors. He then attempted, contrary to the now established practice of free clerical elections, to have him appointed bishop of the rich see of Winchester. William was not in fact an ordained priest – hence his status as 'bishop-elect' of Valence, which gave him the status without the troublesome business of taking holy orders – so this would have been a double insult to the Church.[13] The usual complaints began to surface: William had 'cunningly managed' matters such that Henry 'suffered this bishop to pull his kingdom to pieces' and 'allowed foreigners – Poitevins, Germans, Provençals and Romans – to fatten themselves on the good things of the country, to the injury of his kingdom'.[14]

These were internal English concerns, at least for now. The major international consequence of Henry's marriage was that the ruling houses on either side of the Channel were more closely linked than ever before; the kings of England and France were now brothers-in-law, and their children would be first cousins.

* * *

With both dynasties now represented by sets of siblings in their teens and twenties, it is no surprise that the 1230s were a season for weddings. In 1237 King Louis's next two brothers were married, Robert to Matilda of Brabant and Alphonse to his long-time fiancée, Joan of Toulouse.[15] The fourth brother, Charles, was still only ten, so it made sense for Louis to hold him back for now until an advantageous deal could be made. Louis's only sister, Isabelle, would steadfastly refuse to marry at all, despite being later pressured by no less a personage than Pope Innocent IV to accept the hand of Conrad of Hohenstaufen, a son of Emperor Frederick.

In England, Henry's youngest sister, Eleanor, had been widowed in April 1231 at the age of sixteen when her much older husband William II Marshal died. She was easily young enough to have a second alliance arranged for her, but with Henry's permission she took a vow of perpetual chastity in the presence of the archbishop of Canterbury. This did not make her a nun – she would not take holy orders or reside in a convent – but the vow was binding and meant to be lifelong. She kept to it for several years before being smitten with the personable and ambitious Simon de Montfort; she married him in January 1238, and their first child (a boy, somewhat predictably named Henry) was born at the end of the same year.[16]

Richard of Cornwall, meanwhile, was widowed when Isabel Marshal died in childbirth in 1240; the child was also lost, leaving Richard with a single son, Henry of Almain, then aged four. By this time neither Richard nor his son was in the direct line of succession, as a momentous event had occurred: Queen Eleanor, then aged fifteen or sixteen, had given birth to a male heir in June 1239. The boy was named Edward, after Henry's favourite saint – the first time an Anglo-Saxon name had been given to any member of the Anglo-Norman-Plantagenet family since the Conquest and an indication that the monarchy was now more Anglo-centric in nature.[17]

Richard must have known that he would eventually be supplanted in the succession, but he had been the heir to the throne since he was seven years old, so possibly he did feel disconcerted. Moreover, the new official arrangements made in case of the king's death, as well as naturally naming Edward as the heir, also nudged Richard further out in favour of Eleanor and her Savoyard uncles (several more of whom were by now in England), which did not go down well. It was possibly as a consolation, then, that following Isabel Marshal's death Henry suggested a match between Richard and

Sanchia of Provence, the third of Raymond-Berengar's daughters and the sister of the queens of both England and France. It was a prestigious alliance for a second son who was no longer in the line of succession, and Richard accepted with alacrity. Queen Eleanor arranged the match, and the wedding took place in 1243; Sanchia would give Richard a second son, Edmund of Cornwall, in 1249.

Both Richard of Cornwall and Simon de Montfort, the king's brother and brother-in-law, were ambitious and in possession of strong personalities, stronger indeed than the king's; their voices became dominant around the court. Richard and Eleanor were by now Henry's only two surviving siblings, Joan having died in 1238 and Isabelle in 1241.

* * *

The queens of the two realms being sisters did not, at first, stop age-old disputes and grievances from resurfacing, and it was not long before the situation deteriorated alarmingly.

Louis IX's brothers, as we saw earlier, had been apportioned various apanages, with full control of their estates being granted when each reached his majority and was knighted. In the case of Alphonse, this happened in 1241, when he turned twenty-one; he was invested as count of Poitou and received the homage of its lords. However, the perennially self-interested Hugh X de Lusignan and his wife Isabella of Angoulême were unhappy with the situation. In the long absence of a count who actually resided in the region (there had not been one since Richard the Lionheart, prior to his accession to the English throne) Hugh, as the major landholder in Poitou, had enjoyed a great deal of autonomy, something that was now threatened: with the title in the hands of the king's brother, closer oversight from the French crown was inevitable. Moreover, despite her lack of contact with him for most of his life, Isabella was displeased at her son Richard being deprived of the title. She was also irritated at what she felt was the lack of deference shown to her by the Capetian family; during a recent meeting with Louis she had been treated as a countess, rather than, as she expected, with the respect due to her as dowager queen of England.[18] Hugh and Isabella were the leading figures in a confederacy that was hostile to Alphonse, and in December 1241 Hugh went to Alphonse's Christmas court and publicly renounced his homage, an insult that could not be ignored.[19] They were joined in their rebellion by some, though by no means all, of the other Poitevin lords.

In the spring of 1242 Louis IX came to the aid of his brother in person, in order to reimpose royal authority in the region. He assembled a large force – of around 4,000 knights and another 20,000 who were a mixture of sergeants, footsoldiers and crossbowmen – at Chinon, and then spent May and the first half of June taking a number of rebel-held castles. He acted punctiliously, on the one hand garrisoning or destroying castles that had been held against him and ravaging the lands of those in rebellion against their king, but on the other refusing to act indiscriminately or to punish those who were merely following the orders of their superiors. His carrot-and-stick approach resulted in the defection of a number of the Poitevin rebels, leaving Hugh and Isabella isolated.[20]

Hugh and Isabella, recognising the weakness of their position, sent envoys to England to beg for Henry's help. Henry and Richard – who was still claiming to be count of Poitou himself – mustered a force of their own and sailed from Portsmouth, landing at Royan, on the northern bank of the mouth of the River Gironde, about 60 miles north of Bordeaux, in mid-May.[21] On their arrival, they saw their mother in person for the first time since she had left England in the summer of 1217, when Henry had been nine and Richard eight; unfortunately we do not have any details of the encounter except the knowledge that it took place. The English troops, when added to those of the Poitevin rebels, formed an army that was probably slightly larger than Louis's in total, but with fewer knights. Henry sent envoys to Louis to complain that the French king's activities in besieging and razing castles had broken the truce between them, to which Louis, 'with a calm look', not unreasonably replied that if he chose to take action against those of his own barons who were rebelling against him, this was an internal French matter and nothing to do with the king of England.[22]

Henry now formally declared war on Louis, on 8 June (the news not reaching Louis until eight days later), which enabled him to take military action of his own with a clear conscience. The English king was, of course, hardly a renowned warrior, and he had been strikingly unsuccessful in his previous campaign in Poitou in 1230; but now, with the support of Hugh and other Poitevin barons, he thought he had enough troops and resources to succeed and was more confident. What a triumph it would be to regain some of the lands lost by his father. However, he immediately lost his momentum by moving to Saintes and sitting still for a fortnight, instead of attempting an advance across the River Charente and into Poitou while Louis was engaged in a siege at Hugh de Lusignan's stronghold of Frontenay. This gave Louis the time to press the siege, accept a surrender and then move in good order, under his *oriflamme* banner, to Taillebourg, where the two armies came face to face on either side of the Charente on 21 July 1242.

Taillebourg, a town guarded by its own castle, was a strategically important location due to its stone bridge over the Charente. Either army would need to cross it in order to make an incursion into the lands held by the other, the river being too deep for any attempt at fording and there being no other substantial bridge nearby. The exact sequence of events, as the armies faced each other, is unclear: either the English and the Poitevins made the first move, attempting to charge across the bridge, only to be met with a counter-charge from the French knights that drove them back; or the English tried to retreat without crossing, and the French, unwilling to let them get away, charged across to engage them and they turned to defend themselves. In either case, there was combat on the bridge, in reality not much more than a skirmish, although Joinville calls it 'a fierce and furious fight', possibly for the purposes of glorifying Louis, who 'rushed headlong into danger with the others ... The moment the English saw the king cross over, they lost heart and fled.'[23]

The English and the Poitevins escaped southwards towards the town of Saintes, about 7 miles distant, leaving the French in control of the bridge, so they could cross in good order; they camped overnight on the spot where the English had been the night before. An advance guard followed the English army, probably harassing them en route, Louis's superior numbers of knights now coming into play as mounted and heavily armed men were much more effective in a pursuit situation than footsoldiers.

The knights were also to play their part the next day, when a second engagement took place, this time out in the open, albeit 'in the narrow roads between the vineyards' near Saintes.[24] Again the details are sketchy, though one French chronicler makes the most of his side's victory:

There was a marvellous and mighty battle and a great slaughter of people and the bitter and hard-fought battle lasted a long time, but in the end, the English could not sustain the French attacks and fled. When King Henry saw what was happening, he was shocked and retreated as quickly as he could ... Seeing that they were retreating, the French pursued them in great haste and killed many and took a great many prisoners.[25]

The French were victorious and the English retreated again, many being captured as they fled. Rather than engage in a further long pursuit, leaving Saintes as a threat behind them, Louis and Alphonse consolidated their foothold by turning their attention to the fortified town; after either a very short siege, or merely the threat of one, the citizens surrendered and handed over the keys.[26]

Henry, meanwhile, made it all the way to Bordeaux, with his military reputation further diminished in the eyes of his barons. Simon de Montfort was openly critical of him, apparently telling the king to his face that it would be better if he were locked away, as had happened to a king named Charles the Simple in the tenth century. It was an ominous threat.[27] Hugh and Isabella surrendered to Louis on 24 July and – under the circumstances – were treated with some leniency, being forced to give up many gains but keeping their joint ancestral lands of Lusignan, Angoulême and La Marche.

With the English king's relationship with his barons in disarray and his army afraid to come out of Bordeaux, Louis was now in a position to sweep into Gascony and attempt to complete the work of his father and grandfather by forcing the English out of France altogether. It is intriguing to speculate on what might have happened, but an outbreak of dysentery in Louis's army compelled him to pause. Worse still, he contracted the disease himself, throwing into a panic those who remembered his father's death sixteen years previously from the same condition while on campaign.[28] Louis survived, but was not in a fit state to continue the campaign; he headed back to Tours, and thence to Paris, which he reached at the end of August.

By this time many of the English lords, including Richard of Cornwall, had sailed for England; Henry remained in Bordeaux for almost another year, but achieved nothing of significance.[29] In March 1243 he asked Louis for a truce of five years, which was granted, the agreement being sealed at Pons on 1 August; it was to run until 1248 and left Louis in possession of all he had gained during the war, including Poitou and the Saintonge area, thus taking another bite out of Henry's remaining French lands.[30]

Henry returned to England in the autumn of 1243 and immediately ran into more discord with his barons, who were dissatisfied with the rapacity and swift rise to prominence of the queen's Savoyard uncles. William of Savoy was by now dead, but three of his brothers had embedded themselves in Henry's confidence and his purse. Thomas was count of Flanders by virtue of his marriage to Joan, countess in her own right and a widow since the death of Ferrand almost a decade previously; he was now in receipt of a large cash pension from Henry. Peter had been created earl of Richmond (the lands that had previously been coveted by Peter de Dreux), and was thus among the realm's more significant barons. And Boniface had, through 'the strenuous exertions of the king' and 'to the astonishment of many' managed to get himself elected archbishop of Canterbury.[31] The three brothers now formed a not-insignificant power bloc, becoming even more unpopular when a fourth, Philip of Savoy, accompanied Sanchia of Provence on the journey to her wedding with Richard of Cornwall and was richly rewarded for his 'expenses' in doing so. Indeed, the only one of Queen Eleanor's Savoyard uncles who was not now a member of the English court was the eldest, Amadeus, who had inherited Savoy and was occupied there. Henry either did not see the discontent of his English lords or thought he could ignore it, but he was storing up trouble for the future.[32]

* * *

The 1240s were a time of royal family renewal on both sides of the Channel. Queen Eleanor, as we saw earlier in this chapter, gave birth to a son and heir, Edward, in 1239; she then bore Margaret in 1240, Beatrice in 1242 (at Bordeaux, where Eleanor was accompanying Henry) and Edmund – named, like his brother, after an Anglo-Saxon saint – in 1245, all of whom would survive childhood. There was also a little-reported but significant royal death in England: that in 1241 of Eleanor of Brittany, the daughter of Duchess Constance and the sister of the long-dead Arthur, whom we last saw back in Chapter 15. She had been imprisoned for thirty-eight years for no crime other than having royal blood and an arguably better right to the throne than John.[33] As the years and decades had passed – and particularly when she became too old to bear children – her claims had gradually faded from public consciousness, but she remained a symbol of how women's lives could be blighted by the dynastic concerns and ambitions of their male relatives. Henry paid for a chaplain to celebrate Mass daily for Eleanor's soul, though his generosity had apparently never run to the idea of releasing her from captivity. Her death marked a final break with the past and a sign that the Plantagenet dynasty could concentrate on its future.[34]

Meanwhile, in France, Queen Margaret gave birth to a daughter, Blanche, in 1240. The disappointment of her bearing a girl was tempered by joy at the royal couple producing any child at all, something that was becoming a concern after six years of marriage. The lack of offspring naturally prompted concerns over Margaret's fertility, it being implied that responsibility lay with her, despite the fact that the saintly Louis abstained from sleeping with his wife 'through all of Advent and all of Lent, and also on certain days of the week and similarly during vigils and major feast days', as well as 'on solemn days when he was to take communion . . . and for many days before and after', which would have drastically reduced the chances of conception.[35] A second daughter, Isabelle, arrived in 1241, and then – after another worrying gap and to the kingdom's great joy – Margaret bore three sons in quick succession: Louis in 1244, Philip in 1245 and John in either 1246 or 1247. The Capetian family continued to suffer from the heartbreak of infant mortality, losing both Blanche and John before they were four, but leaving the succession safe with two sons, and future marriage alliances possible with a daughter.

In August 1245 Raymond-Berengar of Provence died. Under the terms of his will, drawn up in 1238, he had left the county of Provence to his fourth and youngest daughter Beatrice (presumably thinking that the others were already amply provided for), so she was a rich, single heiress. Nobody had seen fit to take this bait while Raymond-Berengar was still alive, but following his death, when the will was no longer in danger of being changed in favour of one of the other daughters, there was an almighty scramble. Henry III could have no stake in this; he had no other brothers, and his son Edward could not be a contender for Beatrice's hand as she was his aunt. But Louis IX had one unmarried brother remaining – the eighteen-year-old Charles of Anjou, who would be an eminently suitable match for the fourteen-year-old Beatrice, at least in Louis's eyes.

There was, as might be expected, stiff competition. Raymond VII of Toulouse put in a bid, but was thwarted by having to seek a papal dispensation, as he and Beatrice were related in a prohibited degree. Emperor Frederick dispatched a fleet in an attempt to kidnap young Beatrice to secure her for his son Conrad of Hohenstaufen, and James I of Aragon sent an army into the Rhône valley, presumably also on behalf of a son, given that he himself was already married. The widowed Countess Beatrice, sensible of the dangers, locked her daughter away in the fortress of Aix and appealed to Pope Innocent IV for help. He in turn sought support from the Capetians, and a deal was reached whereby he would back Charles of Anjou as the preferred candidate for young Beatrice's hand in return for Louis promising to support him militarily against any future move by Emperor Frederick, who was still the subject of papal disapproval. This arrangement was also favoured by Boniface of Savoy, the archbishop of Canterbury, whose word carried weight both in the Church and in the family. Beatrice and Charles were married in Aix in January 1246.[36] The four sisters were now the wives of two sets of brothers, kings and princes of England and France, binding them all in a tight network of relationships that would later be tested almost to destruction.

⋑ CHAPTER TWENTY-TWO ⋐

CAPTIVE KINGS

THROUGHOUT THE 1240S LOUIS IX's religious fervour became ever more apparent. He had always been devout, but the arrival in France in 1239 of what was claimed to be the original crown of thorns from the Crucifixion marked the start of a new phase in his spiritual life. On first seeing it he experienced an epiphany, standing 'dumbstruck' and 'transfixed with such fervour' that he thought he saw 'the Lord in person carrying the Crown of Thorns at that very moment'. On Louis's orders, he and his brother Robert carried the crown in its reliquary through the streets of Paris barefoot, dressed only in their shirts; he would later build the magnificent Sainte-Chapelle to house the relic.[1]

Religion, of course, had always been of importance to the Capetian royal house; Louis VII had been noted for his piety, as had Louis VIII and Blanche of Castile. However, theirs was what we might call a kind of 'secular religion' that was compatible with royal and governmental duties, while both Louis IX and his sister Isabelle tended towards a much more ascetic spirituality, which they sometimes took to extremes. Louis, for example, undertook physical chastisement:

> After he had made his confession he would always receive discipline from his confessor with five identical slender iron chains ... When the disciplines were finished, these little switches would be folded up and stored away. He would carry this case secretly in a purse that hung from his belt ... If his confessor was sometimes lenient with his blows, and

the king thought he was sparing him in this way, he would nod to him as a sign to strike harder.[2]

Indeed, Louis even expressed a desire to retire from the world, planning 'from heartfelt devotion that when his eldest son should come of age he would give up his kingdom, obtain his wife's consent, and enter a religious order'. However, the queen had 'absolutely no desire to accede to his request', and pointed out to him that it was God's will that he should be king.[3] No such stricture applied to Isabelle, of course, and – despite the fact that she was his only sister and would therefore be of great value in forming a marriage alliance – Louis would allow her in 1243 to turn down the offer of the hand in marriage of Conrad, son of Emperor Frederick, and retire from the world. She did not actually become a nun, but took a vow of perpetual virginity and lived in a convent, later refusing to become its abbess so she could live out her days humbly in prayer.[4]

Louis was of a delicate constitution, as noted by two chroniclers who knew him intimately: the king rested on his bed every day after dinner, wrote one, while the other observed that Louis's desire to wear a hair shirt as a permanent penance had to be abandoned because 'it was extremely painful to his delicate skin', making repeated reference in his text to various illnesses and the king's 'bodily weakness'.[5] In late 1244 Louis fell seriously ill, and by January 1245 his life was despaired of. Indeed, it was thought at one point that he was actually dead:

> [The king] came at last so near to dying that one of the two ladies who were tending him wanted to draw the sheet over his face, maintaining that he was dead. But another lady, who was on the opposite side of his bed, would not allow it, and said she was sure his soul was still in his body.[6]

On hearing this conversation, Louis regained consciousness, and was so overcome by his miraculous revival that he swore he would go on a crusade if he recovered fully. Blanche, on hearing this news, 'mourned as much as if she had seen him lying dead' – as well she might, given the way she had lost her husband. She attempted to persuade Louis that a vow made in the throes of a serious illness was not binding, but he was not to be moved and repeated his promise when his health improved.[7]

Crusading was in Louis's Capetian blood. His father had led one, albeit within the boundaries of his own kingdom; his grandfather had fought in the Holy Land in the 1190s and his great-grandfather in the 1140s. Now Louis would do the same, bringing together his duty as a Christian king and his religious fervour as a pilgrim in the greatest cause of all. He began to plan, but such was the enormity of the undertaking that it was 1248 before all was ready for his departure. As well as the logistical matters of troops, transport, provisioning and so on to organise, he also had to make arrangements to ensure that France would be safe in his absence, and this naturally included negotiations with Henry III. The truce agreed back in 1243 would expire in 1248, so talks began on the subject of extending it, and even on the possibility of a permanent peace. This latter could not be achieved at this time as, although both kings were predisposed to want peace, the demands each made of the other were irreconcilable: in short, Louis would agree to enduring peace if Henry would resign all claims to his former lands in France, while Henry would only agree to it if those lands were restored. However, despite the absence of any settlement for the longer term, an extension to the temporary truce was arranged – something which Henry would have had little choice about in any case, as Louis's status as a crusader meant that all his lands would be under papal protection while he was away, and Henry was not the sort of man to challenge the pope's spiritual authority.[8]

Louis would, of course, leave his mother as his regent; but, alarmingly for Blanche and for the French succession, he intended to take all three of his brothers with him, leaving only his young children (Isabelle, then aged seven; Louis, four; and Philip, three) in France. They were a slender thread on which to hang the entire Capetian dynasty if things should go awry in the Holy Land, and they would be deprived of both their parents for an indefinite period, as Margaret would accompany Louis to the East – a necessity for a queen of childbearing age whose husband envisaged an absence of several years. The same was true of the wives of the royal brothers, so Margaret would have their female companionship during the adventure, though Matilda, countess of Artois, would have to join them later, unable to travel with the main party as she was pregnant with her first child and close to her confinement.

Louis's brothers seemed just as keen as he was to join the adventure, albeit possibly for different reasons. They had all received the same upbringing from their devout mother, but Alphonse and Charles took after their father in displaying a more conventional type of royal piety, being by no means as ascetic as Louis IX but, rather, happy to live with the trappings of privilege. Charles, in particular, exhibited a very worldly ambition for lands and territories, as we shall see later. Robert, the brother closest to Louis in age and beloved by him, despite the disparity in their characters, was of a different stamp altogether: a much more bellicose specimen who was happiest when fighting, impulsive, and not above the odd robust practical joke.[9]

The French king was the undisputed leader of the expedition that later became known as the Seventh Crusade, with no other European monarch taking part; the army was predominantly French, with a small English contingent led by William II Longsword, who was King Henry's cousin. The legendary animosity of the Third Crusade was evidently still being talked of, and William 'most earnestly entreated his followers not to allow the usual French pride and envy to excite disagreements between them and the English, as he heard had happened in the time of the English king Richard'.[10] After collecting the *oriflamme* and a pilgrim staff from Saint-Denis in mid-June 1248 Louis rode south towards Aigues-Mortes, a port that he had built expressly for the purpose on the Mediterranean coast now that the French royal domain stretched all the way to the sea in that direction. There he embarked on 25 August 1248 with an army consisting of around 15,000 men, of whom 3,000 were knights and 5,000 were crossbowmen; some 7–8,000 horses also needed to be transported.[11] The army overwintered on Cyprus before setting sail again – not for the Holy Land, but for Egypt, on the basis that subduing it would give them a firm base for future attempts to recapture Jerusalem, and that Egypt was the capital of the Ayyubid empire and thus the financial crux for Muslim control of the Holy Land.

Louis and his army reached Damietta in June 1249, and to great jubilation they took it with little resistance ('miraculously' by God's intervention, according to one commentator). But they either failed to capitalise on their momentum or did not take local conditions properly into account: once they were there, the Nile flooded and they were stranded for six months.[12] It was the end of the year before they were able to march again. There was some discussion about whether they should head for Alexandria or Cairo; most of Louis's advisors favoured the former, but his brother Robert of

Artois argued for Cairo, because 'it was the chief city in the kingdom of Egypt, and if you wished to kill the serpent, you must first of all crush its head'. The result was that 'the king rejected the barons' advice in favour of his brother's', and to Cairo they were to go.[13]

On the way, the crusading army had to pass the town of Mansurah in the Nile Delta. As it was fortified and garrisoned, with further Egyptian troops encamped near it, they could not simply bypass it and leave it behind them, so combat was inevitable. In early February 1250 the crusaders were victorious in an attack on the camp outside the walls, and opinion was then split on whether they should mount an immediate assault on the town itself. Many of Louis's nobles advised caution, but the impetuous Robert of Artois would not be prevented, thinking to press an advantage. Unaware that a trap had been laid, Robert led a party that included, among others, William II Longsword and some 300 Templar knights and charged through the open gates, thinking that the town lay undefended before them. Once they were inside, the gates were shut and the crusaders were attacked from all sides. The result was a massacre: Robert was killed, along with William and all but five of the Templars.

Louis was devastated to hear of his brother's death (Joinville, who was present when the news reached him, depicts the king in tears), but he had no time to grieve.[14] The loss of so many knights and the victory of the Egyptians meant that he would have little chance of making it through to Cairo, so instead he began a retreat towards Damietta, during which the crusaders were harassed, starved and prey to disease. On 6 April the weakened army was attacked at Fariskur and annihilated; all Louis's troops were either killed or captured, and among those taken prisoner were the king himself and both of his surviving brothers, Alphonse and Charles.[15]

This was the greatest disaster to befall the Capetian dynasty for many generations, if not ever. The king, the *rex christianissimus*, was not only a captive, but the prisoner of Muslims; and the other adult male members of the royal family were either likewise captive or dead. Louis, moreover, was suffering from an attack of dysentery so serious that he fainted from the pain several times, and his diarrhoea was so bad that his attendants were forced to cut away the lower half of his braies. His survival was by no means certain.[16]

Leadership of the French now fell, nominally at least, to Queen Margaret, who was then in Damietta. The stress she was under must have been almost unbearable: not only did she have to cope with the dangers of the military situation but she was heavily pregnant, only days away from her confinement. Joinville depicts her having continuous nightmares about the possibility of attack by 'Saracens' and the safety of her unborn child, keeping an elderly knight in her room night and day and making him swear that he would kill her, rather than allow her to be taken prisoner, if the city should fall.[17] Three days after she heard the news of Louis's capture she gave birth to a son whom she named John-Tristan (from the French *tristesse*, meaning 'sadness'). We have no idea which of Margaret's female companions were with her at the time, for no chronicler recorded such a detail, but her sister Beatrice, countess of Provence and Anjou, and Matilda, the recently widowed countess of Artois, were both in the crusading party at this time, so it is likely that they were all together. Matilda was also pregnant: having delivered a daughter, Blanche, in 1248 before she left France, she would bear Robert a posthumous son and heir, Robert II of Artois (of whom we shall hear more later) in September 1250. Beatrice had already given birth once during the crusade, while they were in Cyprus over the winter of 1248–49, to a son who had died, and she would bear a surviving daughter (inevitably named Blanche) at some point in 1250 – the month is not known, so she may have been either pregnant or the mother of a very young baby at this time.

Most of the accounts we have of the crusades – both contemporary and modern – focus almost exclusively on the male protagonists and the military action.[18] But we should not overlook the contributions and the bravery of the many women who travelled thousands of miles and who lived alongside these men in extreme conditions, enduring the same hardships often while pregnant or with infants and small children to care for. And while women did not generally take an active part in the pitched battles that took place, they were often caught up in sieges and ambushes; depending on their rank, they might expect ill-treatment, rape, slavery or death if captured, and the fear of such consequences must have been ever-present.

News of Louis's capture eventually made it back to Europe, reaching Henry in England in August 1250. This could have been a huge opportunity for him; he was, of course, under oath not to attack Louis's lands while he was away, but a less scrupulous (or more effective) king might have found a way to get round this somehow, with France in the hands of an elderly woman – even if she was the renowned Blanche of Castile – and its future now seemingly dependent only on two small boys. But Henry made no move to press an advantage. Indeed, in March 1250 – long before he heard of Louis's imprisonment, and more likely to have been in response to news of Louis's earlier swift victory at Damietta – he had actually taken the cross himself, hoping to stir his subjects into joining him as he began preparations for a crusade. He was probably sincere in his desire, but his expertise in military matters did not match his enthusiasm, and nor were his barons particularly fired up by the idea; so, although Henry did succeed in raising a great deal of money for his putative crusade, in the end he never left English shores.[19]

* * *

It was very soon after John-Tristan's birth that Queen Margaret, from her bed in Damietta, took the lead in the ransom negotiations to secure Louis's release. Louis had made a tentative offer to his captors, who had asked him why he could not be definitive, to which he had replied 'that he did not know whether or not the queen would consent, since, as his consort, she was mistress of her actions'.[20] An enormous sum, equivalent to around a third of the French crown's annual income, was eventually settled on, together with the surrender of Damietta and Louis's promise to leave Egypt and not return.

Louis, his brothers and the survivors of the army were set free in May 1250, on payment of the first instalment by Margaret. Louis, a man of his word, arranged to leave Egypt, but instead of sailing for home after his two-year absence, he decided to head for the Holy Land itself. He sent Alphonse and Charles back to France with a letter addressed to the public, announcing his intention to stay in the East until he had achieved something of note, lest his crusading vow go unfulfilled. In this he demonstrated a strikingly self-aware humility, in contrast to the sometimes bombastic reports issued by other kings and crusade leaders.[21] In France the two brothers were reunited with their mother, now in her sixties and beginning to suffer from poor health; Alphonse remained in Paris to help her with the regency even though he had, while he was away, become count of Toulouse (Raymond VII having died in 1249) and had much to attend to in that county. Charles, meanwhile, preferred to pursue his own interests – specifically the opportunities that had arisen following the death of Emperor Frederick in December 1250 – and this caused some friction between the brothers.

Louis and Margaret sailed for Acre, the scene of his grandfather's triumph half a century previously and now the capital of the Latin kingdom after the latest fall of Jerusalem; but despite remaining in the Holy Land for several years, he achieved little more than consolidation. Heedless of the pleas of some of his nobles that he should return to France, he showed no signs of budging, declaring that his duty was to protect the Holy Land and that it might fall for want of defenders if he left.[22] So obsessed was he by now that he paid little attention even to letters from his mother urging his return, and he ignored his own wife and children almost completely (since John-Tristan's birth in 1250, Margaret had borne Peter in 1252 and Blanche in early 1253, all in difficult circumstances and apparently with little interest from her husband). Louis's lack of concern shocked even the faithful Joinville:

> The queen, who had but lately recovered from her confinement on giving birth to the Lady Blanche at Jaffa, now arrived at Saida [where Louis was then staying], having come there by sea. As soon as I heard that she was there, I got up from where I was sitting beside the king and went to meet her, and escorted her back to the castle. When I returned to the king, whom I found in his chapel, he asked me whether his wife and children were well. On my telling him they were he remarked: 'When you got up and left me I knew very well that you were going to meet the queen, so I have asked them to postpone the sermon until your return.' I am telling you this because during all the five years I had been with the king he had never once spoken to me of his wife and children, nor, so far as I know, to anyone else. In my opinion it does not seem right and proper for a man to be so detached from his own family.[23]

That Louis was more concerned for Joinville not missing the sermon than he was for his wife, and that he preferred to stay in the chapel rather than going out to meet his family on their arrival, speaks volumes about his growing religious fanaticism – though we must take into account that this particular writer was later one of the witnesses for Louis's canonisation and may have been seeking to emphasise the king's piety.

However, there was one piece of family news that had the power to shock Louis and cause him to take action. In the spring of 1253 he received a message from France: his mother had died the previous November. 'He was so prostrated with grief', wrote Joinville, 'that for two whole days no one could speak to him'; to which Louis's confessor adds details of his 'sobs and tears'.[24] Since Blanche's death all government in France was being carried out in the name of the heir to the throne, the nine-year-old Louis, who was acting as regent with the help of his uncles Alphonse and Charles. This was hardly an ideal situation, and it at last brought home to Louis the responsibilities he held as a king of France, rather than as a crusading Christian monarch. 'Great danger was looming for his kingdom, as much from England as from Germany,' as one commentator noted.[25] He would go home.

The return journey was eventful, involving hardship, shipwreck and various near-death experiences; but eventually the royal party reached Paris in September 1254, by which time Louis and Margaret had been absent for six years. There was great jubilation in the capital, with celebratory processions, but Louis, 'this true lover of humility', seems to have been something of a killjoy, unimpressed with 'the follies of dances and sumptuous splendors and vanities of this sort'; he 'declined all these things [and] was displeased by the many honors of immense and superfluous expense which he saw'.[26] The children whom the king and queen had left in France had been apart from them for more than half of their short lives and must hardly have recognised their parents, and they now met their three younger siblings for the first time. At the time of her arrival in Paris Margaret was pregnant again, which must have made the long and dangerous journey even less pleasant; she would give Louis another daughter, a namesake Margaret, early in 1255. At almost the same time she would see her eldest, with whom she had only just been reunited, depart for marriage: in April 1255 the now fourteen-year-old Isabelle was married to Theobald II, king of Navarre (son and successor of Theobald I, whose many exploits we recounted in earlier chapters, who had died in 1253). The alliance between France and Navarre would prove to be of great import in later years, as we shall see, and it would also have a bearing on France's relationship with England.[27]

* * *

During the six years of Louis's absence, Henry III had been experiencing an increasing number of problems with his barons. Partly this was due to his continuing reliance on, and open favouritism towards, those 'foreigners' disliked by the English magnates. The queen's Savoyard uncles had been unpopular for some time, but they had now been in England so long that the other barons were beginning to accept them, and Henry could have taken advantage of this. However, from the late 1240s onwards the old grievances were raked up again when members of another family began to arrive: the king's own half-siblings from Poitou.

Isabella of Angoulême had nine children with her second husband, Hugh X de Lusignan: five sons and four daughters, who all survived to adulthood. Isabella died in 1246, at which point the eldest son of her second marriage, Hugh XI de Lusignan, succeeded her as count of Angoulême, the title she had held in her own right. Both Hughs enlisted for Louis IX's crusade; the father died at Damietta in June 1249, so the son then became count of La Marche and lord of Lusignan as well, but he did not live long enough to return to his ancestral estates, being killed at the Battle of Fariskur in April 1250, the engagement at which King Louis was captured. This left all the accumulated lands and titles in the hands of his eldest son, Hugh XII, who was probably no more than twelve and thus subject to the regency of his mother, so the French royal family would expect less trouble from that quarter for a few years.

Some of the late Hugh XI's brothers and sisters were by this point already settled in France, but five of them decided to try their luck in England: Guy, Geoffrey, William, Aymer and Alice de Lusignan all arrived in 1247. Within months King Henry had arranged two very favourable marriages, that of William to Joan de Munchensi, a granddaughter and co-heiress of William I Marshal, and that of Alice to John de Warenne, the young earl of Surrey, who was a royal ward. In 1250 Aymer, who was only in his early twenties at the time, was elected bishop of Winchester thanks to the pressure brought to bear by the king.[28] None of this pleased the more established noble families, who had marital and ecclesiastical ambitions of their own but were forced to stand by and see the prizes falling to the newcomers. To add to the discord the Savoyards, once themselves resented by the barons, now in turn resented the even more lately arrived Lusignans.

Henry seemed oblivious to all of this, no matter how many times Simon de Montfort and others pointed it out. The Lusignans took advantage of their royal connections, acting contrary to England's laws and pursuing personal vendettas against the Savoyards and the English barons almost with impunity, as Henry declined to restrain them – and indeed protected them on several occasions – while continuing to shower them with gifts. The frustration of the nobles is evident in the work of the chronicler Matthew Paris, whose text for the years of the late 1240s and the early 1250s is peppered with frequent references to various outrages and complaints. Ominously, there are also direct references to Henry 'openly following the example of his father', not only in respect of his foreign favourites, but also due to his continuing financial exactions and increasingly arbitrary style of rule.[29]

During these years the influence of Simon de Montfort, now fully invested as earl of Leicester, continued to increase. By 1252 he was one of Henry's closest advisors and the father of five sons by the king's sister Eleanor (Henry, Simon, Amaury, Guy and Richard; they would later also have a daughter, named Eleanor after her mother). King and earl had experienced some notable fallings-out over the years, but in 1248 Henry appointed Simon as his lieutenant in Gascony, to rule there for a projected term of seven years.[30] However, Gascony was a difficult province to govern, and a combination of belligerent landholders and Simon's ruthless methods when attempting to control them led to an uprising in 1252 – one which was supported by Alfonso X of Castile, who resurrected the old claims to Gascony of his great-grandfather Alfonso VIII that we mentioned in Chapter 14.

So serious was the situation that Henry relieved Simon of his position and sailed for Gascony in person in the summer of 1253, leaving Queen Eleanor as his regent in England – a responsibility that had not fallen on a queen there since the days of Eleanor of Aquitaine. She would rule the realm in her husband's name, capably, for ten months, before travelling to Gascony to join him at the end of May 1254.

Henry's trip was successful, if not spectacular: Matthew Paris sums it up rather underwhelmingly as 'after much toil and useless expenditure of money, the king of England gained possession of his own castles in Gascony'.[31] A truce was agreed with Alfonso X, under the terms of which Alfonso would resign any residual claims to Gascony based on his descent from Henry II, but that Henry III would cede Gascony to his son Edward, who would marry

Alfonso's half-sister Eleanor of Castile. Alfonso, interestingly, would not finally approve the arrangement until he had seen Edward in person – perhaps he was curious about the extent to which Edward resembled his father in character or in appearance, the answer in both cases being 'not at all'. When he did meet the young man, Alfonso was happy and the wedding took place in Burgos in 1254.[32]

Following the ceremony the young couple spent some time in their province of Gascony. Edward was fifteen and Eleanor thirteen, so their ages were a little more compatible than many other royal couples. Despite their youth, they were both of the accepted canonical age, and the birth of a short-lived daughter in 1255 while they were in Gascony indicates that Edward chose to consummate the union almost straight away – a decision that would have health consequences for Eleanor, as giving birth at such a young age was not optimal. She was not rendered sterile by it, but she would lose at least another two children to infant death or stillbirth while in her teens, and it would be over a decade after her marriage before she would bear a surviving child.[33]

After some correspondence between Louis and Henry, and encouraged by their wives Margaret and Eleanor, the English king and queen travelled back from Gascony via France. In December 1254 they were in Paris, where they were joined by the queens' other sisters, Sanchia and Beatrice, as well as by their mother Beatrice of Savoy. The occasion was celebratory in nature, rather than an opportunity for serious political discussion, but it laid the foundations for the future relationship between the two kings, who, crucially, took an immediate liking to each other. They had almost met once before, across the bridge at Taillebourg twelve years earlier, but that conflict was now forgotten, or at least pushed aside, as Louis showed Henry around his capital's most impressive buildings and churches; Henry, in return, was generous in his gifts and charitable donations.[34]

All four sisters, meanwhile, had a chance to meet and to catch up on family news as well as on international diplomacy, the two subjects being in their cases very much intertwined. The two youngest had by now started families: Sanchia had one son, Edmund of Cornwall, while Beatrice had so far borne Charles of Anjou two daughters and a son, and would go on to have another daughter and two more sons.

Despite having children old enough to be married, the two elder sisters would also continue to add to their nurseries. After a long interval, during which Henry and Eleanor might have thought that their family was complete (their four children ranging in age at that time from fourteen to almost nine), they had rejoiced in the safe arrival of a daughter, Katherine, in November 1253. Sadly, all was not well: she may have suffered from a developmental or degenerative disorder, and would live only until May 1257. Both her parents were devastated by her death, falling ill themselves for some weeks. During Katherine's illness Henry had made offerings to various shrines; after her death he arranged for a sumptuous tomb with a silver effigy to be erected at Westminster, and he rewarded the nurses who had cared for her.[35] The rates of infant mortality in the twelfth and thirteenth centuries were so horrific, early death so common, that there can be very few historians who have not found themselves writing phrases such as 'the eldest surviving child of' or 'of their surviving children', often without too much thought. However, each loss was a tragedy in its own right, and contemporary parents were by no means untouched by grief, despite it being such a frequent occurrence.

Louis and Margaret would later go on to have two more children, Robert in 1256 and Agnes in 1260; but by the time the latter arrived they, too, were deep in parental mourning, a circumstance of which we will hear more in the next chapter.

* * *

To return to our main narrative, Henry had in 1254 ceded Gascony to Edward, who was, of course, also expected to inherit the English throne; and it was in that same year that Henry became involved in a plan to obtain another crown for his second son, Edmund.

Frederick II had died in 1250. As well as holding the title of Holy Roman Emperor he had been the king of Sicily, a separate inheritance from his mother. The kingdom encompassed not only the island of Sicily, but also southern mainland Italy up as far as Naples and Capua, meaning that it and the Empire sandwiched Rome and the papal states in between them. Since Frederick's death both his realms had been in the hands of his son Conrad IV, who had been elected king of the Romans (a subsidiary title in the Empire, and one, despite its name, that effectively meant king of Germany) as far back as 1237. Conrad was proving to be just as much of a headache for the papacy as his father, and Pope Innocent IV had determined to try to replace him on the Sicilian throne with a candidate of his own choosing. Such a candidate would need to be of royal blood and would preferably be an adult man, but Innocent's overtures to Richard of Cornwall had been declined and those to Charles of Anjou had been vetoed by King Louis – who, although revering the Church, also had a strong sense of royal authority; he could not countenance the overthrow of a fellow monarch. Innocent was therefore obliged to rearrange his plans, and he had offered the Sicilian throne to Edmund, an offer accepted by Henry in February 1254 on behalf of his then nine-year-old son.

Henry had a great enthusiasm for the idea, and even went so far as to have Edmund crowned king of Sicily (at Westminster) in April 1255. However, any actual, physical attempt to claim the kingdom would require a great deal of effort and resources – and the English barons did not see why they should support an idea that they considered a vanity project, or why they should pay for it. The fact that the plan had the eager backing of the queen's Savoyard uncles (one of whom had already, and rather prematurely, been granted a province in Edmund's new kingdom) made the prospect even less appealing.[36]

To add to Henry's dynastic ambitions, Edmund was not the only member of the English royal family to be crowned king of a realm to which he had no hereditary right. Conrad IV died, leaving Sicily nominally to his two-year-old son Conradin, but in practice under the powerful regency of his illegitimate half-brother Manfred. Manfred was fully engaged in Sicilian affairs – he would usurp his nephew there in 1258 – and thus did not make any attempt on the Empire, where his illegitimacy would have debarred him from the throne in any case. The Hohenstaufen dynasty was more or less exhausted (Frederick II's only other legitimate son, Henry, whose mother was Isabelle, Henry III's sister, had died in 1253), leaving the German princes no choice but to look elsewhere, and in December 1256 Richard of Cornwall was elected king of the Romans, with the full support of his brother Henry III.[37] Richard and Sanchia made their way to Aachen, where they were crowned on 17 May 1257, thus making Richard the second king among his siblings and Sanchia the third queen among hers.

Richard's accession did not go down particularly well in France, where Louis was naturally anxious about having a Plantagenet in charge of the Empire; and neither was it particularly welcomed in England, where the relationship between the king and his barons had been going from bad to worse. Henry's seemingly boundless – and expensive – ambitions for his family, his own lavish lifestyle, his obvious favouritism for foreigners and his autocratic rule had caused increasing discontent. As ever, though, 'foreign-ness' was in the eye of the beholder: the Lusignans were unpopular because of their origins, but Simon de Montfort was not considered foreign, even though he had been brought up in France and was the son of a famous French commander and the brother of the former constable of France.[38]

By 1258 there was open and mutual animosity between the Lusignans and the Savoyards. The queen had a preference for the Savoyards, while the king supported his Lusignan half-siblings, something which led to an increasing divide between Henry and Eleanor. The barons, meanwhile, disliked the new interlopers even more than the old ones, and Simon de Montfort was one of the leading voices calling for reform.[39] In the absence of his brother, whose forceful personality had often backed him up – and whose seemingly boundless reserves of cash had bailed him out more than once – Henry could not control the warring parties, and his grasp began to slip. The situation was not helped by the poor harvests of 1256 and 1257 (a result of adverse weather), which meant that food was expensive and hunger rife across England, with thousands of deaths from starvation, including many in London, where bodies were piled up in the streets.[40]

In April 1258 Henry summoned a parliament at Westminster, the principal purpose of which was to seek yet more financial aid, and relations broke down irrevocably. The tipping point came when a member of the queen's household who had been attacked by Aymer de Lusignan demanded justice; Henry declined to take any action against his half-brother, thus 'denying justice' in direct contravention of the relevant clause in Magna Carta. A group of barons, including Simon de Montfort, swore to support each other against the Lusignans and to address the question of justice in the realm; they then stormed into Henry's presence, armed.[41] Henry had no choice but to agree to accept the formation of a committee of twenty-four barons that would oversee reform in England.

Henry was entitled to nominate half the members of the committee, but when it became apparent that all his choices were Lusignans and their adherents, the barons realised that further steps were necessary. When parliament reconvened in Oxford in June they determined to remove the

Lusignans altogether by blaming them for Henry's misrule. A list of griev-ances was drawn up, a further oath of solidarity was sworn, and they moved against the helpless king, demanding that he

> should faithfully keep and observe the conditions of the charter of the
> liberties of England, which his father, King John, had made and granted
> to his English subjects . . . which said charter he, the present King Henry,
> had many times granted and sworn to observe.[42]

By the end of June Henry had been forced to hand over a number of royal castles to baronial castellans, and under 'the Provisions of Oxford', as they were known, a ruling council of fifteen magnates was formed, to which he transferred power. His son Edward also – albeit unwillingly – swore to uphold the provisions, and the Lusignans left England. It was over: Henry was still the king in name, but he was no longer the ruler of his kingdom, holding no more personal power than he had done as a boy of nine, forty-two years previously.[43]

The bemused Henry did not know where to turn. But the example of the peaceful realm across the Channel, ruled by a king who was revered by his vassals, must have been an object of admiration and envy. Fortune's wheel had turned again, and it would not be long before the unthinkable would happen: the king of England would ask the king of France for help in a war against his own subjects.

CHAPTER TWENTY-THREE

BROTHERS-IN-LAW, BROTHERS-IN-ARMS

EACE WITH FRANCE HAD also been on the agenda of the 1258 parliament, and the question was picked up again in 1259 once the dust
had settled a little in England. Louis was keen to reach an arrangement, for reasons that were both family-related and overtly religious:

> The most pious king of France was now diligently studying the means
> of establishing a lasting peace between the two kingdoms of France and
> England; for, said he, 'the greatest efforts should be made to establish
> a firm and durable peace between my sons and those of the king of
> England, who are cousins, and who will, under God's favour, become
> kings, that the two kingdoms may no longer gnaw each other at the
> instigation of the enemy of the human race [i.e. Satan], nor the inhabit-
> ants reciprocally pillage and slay each other, and thus be thrust into
> hell'.[1]

As we may recall, a permanent peace between the two realms had been
impossible to agree, due to the incompatible aims of the two parties with
regard to the lands in France formerly held by the Plantagenets. Henry no
doubt still harboured a personal desire for the reconquest of those lands; but
by now he was in no position to bargain, especially as his council urged him
to settle the matter. 'As the king had not the courage to regain his lost territory by force of arms,' writes one commentator, bluntly, 'nor money enough
to collect an army, and above all, as he saw that his subjects were on the

point of rising against him, he accepted [Louis's] conditions of peace, being in some measure compelled to do so.'[2]

Louis's conditions were draconian. Henry would relinquish all claims to Normandy, Anjou, Maine, Touraine and Poitou, meaning that the cross-Channel empire of his forebears and any dreams of recovering it were absolutely at an end. He would retain Gascony, and, as a concession, Louis agreed the transfer of some lands on the Gascon borders, with more promised if Alphonse of Poitiers and his wife, Joan of Toulouse, should die without heirs, resulting in their estates being subsumed into the royal domain. This was a reasonable offer, given that the couple were by now both nearing forty and had been married for twenty-two years without producing a child, and Henry was glad to accept.

Louis was so much in control of the negotiations that his magnates even complained about the concessions, saying he had been too generous:

> In making peace with the king of England, King Louis acted against the advice of his council, who had said to him: 'It seems to us that Your Majesty is needlessly throwing away the land you are giving to the king of England; for he has no right to it, since it was justly taken from his father.' To this the king replied that he was well aware that the king of England had no right to the land, but there was a reason why he felt bound to give it to him. 'You see,' said he, 'our wives are sisters and consequently our children are first cousins. That is why it is most important for us to be at peace with each other.'[3]

Agreement was reached and Henry crossed to France in November 1259, ratifying the Treaty of Paris in person on 4 December.[4]

Henry's continuing usage of the styles 'duke of Normandy' and 'count of Anjou' had long been fanciful at best, but now he would give them up officially. There was no protest from the English barons about this; it was more than half a century since Normandy had fallen, so any residual hopes of them regaining ancestral lands there had long faded. Henry might retain the style 'duke of Aquitaine', but there was a catch: despite his claims that it was his own sovereign territory, Louis insisted that it was a fief of the French crown, meaning that Henry would have to pay homage to him for it as his vassal. As we saw earlier, when previous English kings had owed homage for

Normandy or other French lands, they had circumvented the question by having their sons perform the ceremony in their stead.[5] Here Henry had a ready-made excuse, in that Gascony was supposed to be Edward's; but he did not avail himself of it, performing the homage himself and thus providing the spectacle of the king of England kneeling to the king of France. This allowed Louis to conclude the justification to his magnates, quoted above, with an indisputable line of reasoning: 'Besides, I gain increased honour for myself through the peace I have made with the king of England, for he is now my vassal, which he has never been before.'[6]

With the holder of Gascony now publicly his vassal, Louis's own sovereignty stretched all the way to France's far southern border, a useful circumstance given his interest in, and alliances with, no fewer than three of the Spanish kingdoms. As we saw earlier, his eldest daughter, Isabelle, was the queen of Navarre; Louis's second son, Philip, would later marry Isabella of Aragon, daughter of James I. The links with the royal house of Castile – to which Louis no doubt felt an affinity, as it was his mother's family – were strengthened twice over: the French heir, Louis, was at this time betrothed to Berengaria, Alfonso X's eldest daughter, and King Louis's second daughter, Blanche, would later marry Alfonso's heir, Ferdinand. When taken in the context of Louis's own marriage into the house of Provence, those of his brothers in Provence and Toulouse, and the rule of his brother and latterly his nephew in Artois, this meant that his influence ran from the Low Countries and the Channel to the Pyrenees and the Mediterranean.

Marriages were also on the mind of the English king and queen, specifically the one they had arranged for their second daughter, Beatrice, with John de Dreux, heir to the duchy of Brittany (son of John I and grandson of the Peter de Dreux whose exploits we recounted earlier). The wedding was due to take place in January 1260, so, following the ratification of the Treaty of Paris, Henry and Eleanor remained in the capital as guests of the French king and queen over Christmas. However, the ceremony was postponed due to tragic circumstances. Louis, the eldest son of Louis and Margaret and the designated heir to the throne, fell ill over Christmas, possibly of appendicitis, and he died in January, at around the time of his sixteenth birthday.

Louis's pain was profound: 'He fell into such grief that no one could calm him ... The king went on mourning for his son whom he loved so much, and he was so full of sorrow that nobody could elicit a single word from him.'[7] Perhaps inspired by the memory of his own education at his mother's knee, Louis had – since his return from the Holy Land – taken much more interest in the education and personal development of his children than was generally the case with a reigning king. 'Before he went to bed the king used to send for his children,' noted Joinville,

> and tell them of the deeds of good kings and emperors, at the same time pointing out that they should take such men as an example. He would also tell them of the deeds of wicked princes, who by their dissolute lives, their rapacity, and their avarice had brought ruin on their kingdoms.[8]

Louis would also oblige his children to learn and repeat to him the religious Hours, intertwining the faith that meant so much to him with their more secular education in literacy and politics. As the heir to the throne, young Louis had been educated with particular care with regard to his responsibilities – he had already acted as regent once, as we saw earlier – and his loss was devastating, particularly as he had survived the many perils of childhood and, now 'marvellously wise and gracious', was on the verge of taking his place in the adult world.[9]

The funeral took place on the day originally scheduled for the wedding and, remarkably, one of the pall-bearers was none other than Henry III – an event of such significance that it was depicted on the young man's tomb chest, which is still extant.[10] Louis had not been crowned as junior king: following the deliberate omission of this ceremony for the future Louis VIII and the accidental one for Louis IX, it had lapsed; Philip Augustus remains the last Capetian monarch to have been crowned in the lifetime of his father.

Louis and Margaret had now suffered the loss of three of their children, but life and responsibilities had to go on, however sorrowing they were. Thankfully for the succession, they were still left with four sons and four daughters; their next son, Philip, aged fourteen, became the heir to the French crown. He was only a year younger than his deceased brother and they had been brought up in close proximity, but (as would become evident in later years) Philip had not benefited from the exacting education given to the heir to the throne, and it is probable that he did not match up to his lost brother in terms of intellect.[11]

The delayed wedding of Beatrice of England and John of Brittany took place a week after the funeral, and the French king and queen exerted themselves enough to attend. The union was one of lands as well as individuals: Beatrice brought the long-disputed earldom of Richmond to the marriage, so her husband would hold estates on both sides of the Channel. She and John were well suited in terms of age (at the time of the wedding, he was twenty and she seventeen) and they would go on to enjoy a successful partnership; they gave their eldest son the traditional Breton name of Arthur.

* * *

Henry travelled back to England in April 1260. His sojourn in France had given him the opportunity to witness at first hand the respect and reverence in which Louis was held in his kingdom, in marked contrast to his own situation. But emulation was impossible: despite some superficial similarities in terms of their piety, the two kings were very different. Louis's religious character, as we know, tended towards the ascetic, and following his return from crusade in 1254 this had become even more marked: he banned gambling and punished blasphemers by having them branded on the lips; he wore simple clothing, ate plain food, fasted regularly and washed the feet of lepers.[12] Henry, meanwhile, made lavish gestures, such as feeding hundreds of the poor while wearing expensive garments, and spending a great deal of money on an extravagant lifestyle. Louis had embarked on a wholesale review of the systems of justice and administration in France and had overhauled them for the benefit of all his subjects; Henry had denied justice while allowing his personal favourites to flout the law with impunity.[13] He simply did not have the personal or moral authority over his people that Louis enjoyed.

The next king of England bid fair to have plenty of authority, but it looked as though he would exercise it very differently from his father. In 1260 Edward turned twenty-one, an adult ready to play his part in the governance of the realm, but there were already some concerns about his behaviour. Physically and in character he seems to have inherited a different set of family traits to his father, resembling his great-uncle Richard the Lionheart in being tall, strong and violent. And, also like Richard, he had developed a reputation for cruelty in his youth. He surrounded himself with bully-boys who harassed and stole from traders, townsfolk and monasteries:

disturb[ing] the peace of the inhabitants of the country through which they passed, by plundering their possessions as well as abusing their persons, and that by his permission, to such a degree that the injuries perpetrated by the king his father were considered trivial when compared to those committed by him.

Such rough-housing might be excused as the youthful folly of the privileged, but there was also a more serious and crueller streak to Edward's character:

As he was passing through a peaceful part of the country at a time of peace, a young man met him, and Edward, without any pretext for killing or maiming the young man being given him, ordered one of his ears to be cut off, and one of his eyes to be pulled out, which was done, though contrary to every rule of justice. Many ... began to despair of him, remarking, 'If this occurs when the tree is green, what is to be hoped for when it is old and dry?'[14]

Edward had not liked the terms of the Treaty of Paris. Technically, Gascony was meant to be his, but his father's personal homage to Louis for it implied that he, Edward, was only a lieutenant; and whichever of them held it did so only as a vassal of Louis anyway. All other Plantagenet ancestral lands had been surrendered, thus denying Edward – a keen warrior – any future opportunity to fight to regain them. And it was not only his father's submission in France that displeased him: he had also agreed only very unwillingly to the terms of the Provisions of Oxford, and would take any opportunity to overturn them. Evidently he did not intend his rule, when it came into being, to be constrained in the same way that Henry's was.

As it happened, Edward was helped in this endeavour by the discord that arose within the ranks of the barons who had promulgated the provisions. By 1260 their relations had begun to break down, with a particular rift between Simon de Montfort and Richard de Clare, the earl of Gloucester, who was the second-richest magnate of the realm, after the king's brother, Richard of Cornwall.[15] A further boost to the royalist cause came in 1261, when a papal bull released Henry from his obligation to support the provisions; he immediately dismissed all the officials who had been imposed on him. Rebellion threatened, but in an attempt to avoid outright war both sides agreed to submit their case for arbitration, and agreed on an authority who was acceptable to them both: not the pope, but Louis IX of France.

That this astonishing step could have been taken speaks volumes about both the toxic situation in England and the growing reputation of Louis throughout Europe: he was trusted to be neutral, and indeed had already been called upon to arbitrate in other international disputes.[16] On a slightly more cynical note, it is possible that both sides believed that Louis would favour them due to personal connections: Henry because Louis was his brother-in-law and friend, and Simon because his own family's stock had been so high in recent French history and because he was aware of Louis's commitment to reform in his own realm.

The cases were submitted to Louis in December 1263 – Henry's by him in person and Simon's by proxy, as he had recently been thrown from a horse and had broken his leg – and the French king considered everything carefully before coming to a decision. As well as the specifics of the case, he also had to take into consideration the wider picture, and this is evident in the judgement he gave on 23 January 1264, known as the Mise of Amiens, in which he did not mince his words. He had, as we have noted previously, a great respect for the concept of royal authority – something which outweighed even his dynastic concerns (one cannot help thinking that previous French kings, including Louis's revered grandfather Philip Augustus, might have taken advantage of such an open goal for Plantagenet destruction) – with the result that he came down firmly on Henry's side, as some representative quotes show:

> By our present decision or ordinance we quash and annul all the aforesaid provisions, ordinances, statutes and obligations, however called, and whatever has followed from them or by occasion of them ... ordaining that as well the said king as all the barons and others who have consented to the present arbitration, and who in any way have bound themselves to observe the aforesaid [provisions], shall be utterly quit and absolved of the same ...

> We also decree and ordain that the aforesaid king at his own volition may freely appoint, dismiss, and remove the chief justice, chancellor, treasurer, counsellors, lesser justices, sheriffs, and any other officials and ministers of his kingdom and his household, as he was used and able to do before the time of the provisions ...

We repeal and quash the statute made to the effect that the kingdom of England should henceforth be governed by natives and that all aliens should leave the kingdom ...

We declare and ordain that the said king shall have full power and unrestricted rule within his kingdom and its appurtenances, and shall in all things and in every way enjoy such status and full power as he enjoyed before the time of the aforesaid [provisions].[17]

Just to top it all off, Louis also noted that the pope had already proclaimed the provisions 'quashed and annulled', thus adding even more weight to his own rulings. It was a devastating blow for the barons (and the bishops associated with the cause), whose claims had been utterly dismissed. Despite having agreed beforehand to abide by Louis's decision, they found this unambiguously one-sided decision intolerable, and the war that had been threatening for years finally broke out, preceded by an increasingly bad-tempered exchange of letters. The barons wrote to Henry to claim that

some people who are about your person have heaped lies upon lies concerning us ... It is our wish to preserve the health and safety of your person ... It is our purpose to punish, as far as it lies in our power, not only our own enemies, but yours.

Henry replied:

It is clearly evident ... that you do not observe towards us the fealty due to us, and that you do not care at all for the security of our person ... We do not care either for your fidelity or your love.

This was not worded strongly enough for Edward and Richard of Cornwall, who (perhaps sensing that they were the ones being set up to take the fall, as the king's so-called evil counsellors) sent a letter of their own to the barons to say that 'we defy each and all of you as public enemies, and inform you that henceforth we will use all our endeavours to do you injury, both in person and in property, wherever we can find the means to do so'. They concluded by calling the barons 'perfidious traitors'.[18]

Armed conflict was now inevitable, and the two sides met in open battle at Lewes on 14 May 1264. Initially the royalists looked to be having the best of it, as Edward's division routed the barons' contingent of poorly trained Londoners, but he then committed the cardinal error of engaging in a long pursuit, chasing them for around 4 miles and thus removing his own cavalry from the field. By the time he regrouped and got back, it was all over: Richard of Cornwall's central division had been defeated, with Richard himself taking ignominious shelter in a windmill, and Henry's reserve had been forced to withdraw to a nearby priory. Edward attempted a counter-attack, but it was too late, and he also retreated to the safe confines of the priory. Victory belonged to Simon de Montfort and the barons: King Henry, Edward, Richard and Richard's son Henry of Almain were all taken prisoner.[19] A new agreement, the Mise of Lewes, was drawn up; under its terms, Henry was a captive, agreeing to uphold the Provisions of Oxford, to rule via his council and to remove all 'traitors' from his household. Even then, he was not to be trusted: both Edward and Henry of Almain would remain as hostages to ensure the king's compliance.[20]

The sole remaining royals at large, Queen Eleanor and her teenaged second son, Edmund, were at this point in France – which, ironically, was a safer place for the queen of England than her own realm. Here Eleanor agitated on her husband's behalf, writing letters to Alphonse of Poitiers (in whose domain the port of La Rochelle lay), appealing to him to muster ships on her behalf and to seize any English vessels in the port.[21] By 1 June she was in Paris, seeking her brother-in-law King Louis's approval for her to take control of Gascony (so that Simon would not be able to do so in Henry's name), and also trying to persuade him into rather more radical action: an invasion of England.

Louis was 'upset and angry' to hear that Henry was in captivity, and sent envoys to Simon to demand that he release the king.[22] He was also horrified at the terms imposed on Henry, saying he would rather break clods behind a plough than submit his own kingship to such an indignity. In England, the belief that Louis was about to launch an invasion was so strong that the barons put out a public statement (in the king's name), saying that 'since it is known for sure that a great horde of foreigners is readying ... to invade the kingdom by force of arms', all knights and tenants should 'prepare yourselves with horses and arms manfully and powerfully ... to march thence with us against the foreigners'. An army was mustered in London and marched into Kent, prepared to defend the coast.[23]

Meanwhile, Queen Eleanor took steps of her own, mustering a fleet at Damme along with her uncle Peter of Savoy. However, they delayed, sitting in the port all through September, October and into November, by which time the troops' agreed period of service was over and the money to pay them was running out. This delay was probably due to concern for the safety of Edward and Henry of Almain: Henry III had already written to Eleanor and Louis to express his fears for his son and nephew if any invasion should be attempted.[24] The execution of the heir to the throne would, under normal circumstances, be unthinkable; however, it was technically permissible via the accepted code by which hostages' lives were forfeit if the terms of an agreed pact were violated. And the situation in England had deteriorated to such an extent in recent years that Simon de Montfort might just go through with it. Eleanor was not willing to risk her son's life.

It was Edward himself who eventually resolved the situation: in May 1265 he escaped from captivity, and he immediately began to rally royalist forces.[25] On 4 August the two sides met in battle again, at Evesham, and the result was a complete reverse of the earlier engagement: Simon de Montfort and his eldest son, Henry, were killed and their army annihilated. In a savage departure from the norms of war up until that point, Simon's body was subsequently mutilated. The only moment of danger for the royalists came when Henry III, who had been dressed in plain armour and brought into the fray by his enemies, was almost killed by his own supporters before he managed to cry out to them and confirm his identity.[26]

The remaining rebels held out for as long as they could, retreating to Kenilworth and holding out there through the summer and autumn of 1266. But they were eventually forced to surrender, and the war was brought to an end in October by the Dictum of Kenilworth, which unambiguously restored royal authority.[27] Simon's surviving sons fled the country; his widow, Eleanor, was the king's sister and therefore not in danger of her life; but she, too, left England and would never return. As he celebrated the fiftieth anniversary of his accession – an occurrence unprecedented in English history – Henry was back on his throne.

* * *

King Louis had not invaded England, but he was at this time, 1266, also embroiled in other international concerns, particularly those of Sicily. As we saw earlier, he had been reluctant to help dethrone Conrad, in view of the fact that Conrad was a legitimate monarch; but the situation had changed since then. Edmund of England, whom Henry had proclaimed as king, had no hereditary right at all, and since that time Henry had, due to his domestic concerns, been completely unable to forward his son's claim or support it in any practical way. The realm of Sicily had therefore been ruled since 1258 by Manfred, who was both a usurper and a bastard and thus also had no claim, in Louis's eyes, to be a legitimate king.

In 1263 Pope Urban IV, tired of waiting for Henry to take action, had ceased supporting Edmund's claim to Sicily and switched his backing to his predecessor's choice, Charles of Anjou. Urban died the following year, but his successor Clement IV continued the same policy – which may or may not have been linked to the fact that both popes were French – and appealed to Louis IX to support his brother. This time Louis agreed, and he put resources at Charles's disposal. Charles travelled to Rome, where he and Beatrice were crowned on 5 January 1266, thus making her the fourth and final queen among her sisters (although she did not enjoy the status long, dying the following year), before making his move on the kingdom of Sicily itself. As his cause had been declared a crusade he had little trouble raising troops, and he led an army of some 6,000 knights and mounted sergeants and 20,000 footsoldiers, mainly French and Provençal. It was in the event something of a lightning campaign: he initially marched towards Naples, but on hearing that Manfred was mustering forces at Capua he turned and crossed the Apennines, and the two armies met near Benevento on 26 February. Manfred was killed in the battle, and resistance across the kingdom immediately collapsed – there was no point holding out for a king who was dead – allowing Charles to take possession of both halves of the kingdom, southern mainland Italy and the island of Sicily itself. All of this had occurred within two months of his coronation.[28]

He might have found conquering the kingdom straightforward so far, but there was a nasty addendum, one which demonstrated both that Charles was very different in character from Louis, and that the conventions of war had changed for the worse in recent years. As we noted in Chapter 22, the last legitimate Hohenstaufen king of Sicily, Conrad, had left a young son,

Conradin, who had been usurped by Manfred. Those opposed to Charles now persuaded Conradin to stake his own claim, which he did, moving from Bavaria, where he had been living, through Italy at the head of a multi-cultural and somewhat rag-tag army. His campaign, unfortunately for him, was abortive: he was defeated at the Battle of Tagliacozzo in August 1268, and then captured in October the same year. Charles had Conradin executed by beheading, despite the fact that he was just sixteen years old.[29]

We do not know what Louis's reaction was upon hearing of his brother's callous action, but by now it was too late to stop the momentum of the powerful Charles. He was undisputed king of Sicily and a senator of Rome, and he would later make a play for the kingdoms of Albania and Jerusalem, as well as retaining his interests in France; he may even have had designs on the Empire itself following the death of Richard of Cornwall in 1272. The youngest, posthumous son of Louis VIII was now the social equal of, and more than a match for, his eldest brother.[30]

Louis IX declined to become involved any further in the affairs of Sicily, and left his brother to it. By the time of Conradin's death he was deeply involved in a new project, one which would bring together the royal houses of France and England: another crusade.

❧ CHAPTER TWENTY-FOUR ❧

THE END OF TWO ERAS

L OUIS IX HAD ALWAYS considered his crusading as unfinished business. So when Sultan Baibars, the leader of the Mamluks, made sweeping gains during the 1250s and 1260s, this led Louis to take the cross once more in 1267. Not everyone was as keen as he was on the idea: even the faithful Joinville was later moved to write that

> I considered that all who had advised the king to go on this expedition committed mortal sin. For at that time the state of the country was such that there was perfect peace throughout the kingdom, and between France and her neighbours, while ever since King Louis went away the state of the kingdom has done nothing but go from bad to worse.[1]

In a repeat of the events of two decades earlier, Louis spent several years raising money and troops, making careful plans and sorting out the logistics of the enterprise, finally collecting the *oriflamme* in March 1270 before riding south and embarking from Aigues-Mortes on 1 July. In another, somewhat foolhardy, echo of previous events, he emptied France of every adult male member of the ruling house, taking with him his brother Alphonse, his three eldest sons, Philip, John-Tristan and Peter, and his nephew Robert II of Artois, recently knighted; he arranged for his other brother, Charles of Anjou, to join them once they were overseas. The only Capetians left in France were children: Louis's youngest son, Robert, then only thirteen or fourteen, and the king's grandchildren.[2] These grandchildren were in direct line for the throne: Louis's heir, Philip, had been married to Isabella of Aragon eight years earlier, and she had already fulfilled her progenitorial duty in abundant fashion. Three sons, Louis, Philip and Robert, were already in the royal nursery, and as the crusade departed she was recovering from her confinement with a fourth, Charles.[3]

Someone else who was keen to join Louis's crusade was Edward of England. Politically this was not a particularly wise decision: the dust from the civil war was still settling, and removing the heir to (and, by now, power behind) the throne from the kingdom had the potential to destabilise matters. Crusading was also very expensive, and an attempt to raise finances for the campaign would not be popular. We must, therefore, conclude that Edward's participation stemmed from a personal desire to join what was seen as the greatest military adventure of the times, perhaps added to a desire to enhance the prestige of the English crown on the world stage. Edward was a warrior at heart and perhaps welcomed the opportunity to escape from domestic politics into purely military pursuits, where he had a clear-cut view of right and wrong, and where violence was not only acceptable but expected. On crusade, therefore, he would go, to join and collaborate with the king of France.[4]

England would not be left quite so bereft of royal males as France. King Henry, of course, was still on his throne, though his health was starting to fail, and his younger son Edmund (now earl of Lancaster) would remain with him for now. Richard of Cornwall – who was still titular king of Germany, but who had enjoyed little success in pushing his claims to the imperial throne – was also in England, and he had two adult sons of his own. The elder, Henry of Almain, would accompany Edward, while the younger, Edmund of Cornwall, would remain in England. And Henry also had grandchildren in the direct line of succession: Edward and Eleanor of Castile had two sons, four-year-old John and two-year-old Henry, as well as a baby daughter, Eleanor. As Edward intended to take his wife with him on the crusade, they would leave their children in the care of Richard of Cornwall.

Edward experienced some difficulties with finance and recruitment, and his party did not embark from Dover until the second half of August 1270. The overland journey through France then took some time, and it was not until mid-September that he reached Aigues-Mortes, by which time Louis and his host had long departed.

As had been the case back in 1248, Louis did not travel directly to the Holy Land, but rather to north Africa, in this case Tunis, which he reached on 18 July 1270. The precise reasons for this choice are unclear, but may have been political rather than military.[5] The French set up camp near Carthage and waited for Charles and his Sicilian contingent to join them; but the press of people and animals packed together in the blistering summer heat meant that an outbreak of disease was almost inevitable. Dysentery duly swept through the camp, with Louis and his two elder sons all being stricken. In the first week of August John-Tristan, the French prince who had been born in sorrow at Damietta during Louis's captivity on his earlier crusade, died at the age of twenty. By that time Louis was so ill that the dreadful news can barely have registered with him; he, too, succumbed, dying on 25 August 1270.

The loss in such circumstances of a king so revered was a great shock to contemporaries. Their descriptions and epitaphs are fulsome:

When the king was near to death he called on the saints to help and protect him ... then he called to his aid Saint Denis, patron saint of France ... The saintly king asked to be laid on a bed covered with ashes, where he crossed his hands on his breast, and looking towards heaven, rendered up his spirit to our Creator ... It is a pious duty, and a fitting one, to weep for the death of this saintly prince, who ruled his kingdom and kept guard over it so righteously and loyally, who was so generous ... As the scribe who, when producing a manuscript, illuminates it with gold and azure, so did our king illuminate his realm.[6]

When clear signs showed that he was approaching the end, he worried about nothing except those things that properly concerned God alone and the exaltation of the Christian faith ... As the strength of his body and speech ebbed away little by little, striving as best he could to speak, he did not stop asking for the prayerful support of the saints dear to him, and especially of the blessed Denis ... The servant of Christ, approaching his last hour, and lying down on a bed of ashes spread out in the shape of a cross, rendered his joyful spirit to its creator, at the very hour at which the Son of God expired, dying on the cross for the life of the world.[7]

Charles of Anjou arrived on 27 August only to find his brother dead. With the new King Philip too unwell to command his army, and Louis's remaining son, Peter of Alençon, only nineteen, Charles assumed temporary command. The French forces were in no state to mount any sort of serious campaign, so he prudently brokered a peace deal with the sultan of Tunis, ratified in November 1270.

The first act of the new king, Philip III, from his sickbed, was to declare his brother Peter regent on behalf of his young son Louis in the event of his own death, a possibility that could not be ruled out for some while. His second was to become involved in an unseemly spat with his uncle over the fate of Louis IX's body: he thought it should be returned to France, while Charles – no doubt with one eye on the distinct possibility of Louis's canonisation and the prestige it would bring to his own realm to have the relics there – argued for Sicily. Philip eventually recovered from his illness and immediately made plans to abort the crusade and return to France; but, despite his wishes, he found it would be impossible to convey his father's decomposing remains that far. A compromise was then reached: in a process known as *mos Teutonicus*, 'the Germanic custom', Louis's corpse was boiled to separate the flesh from the bones, with the latter to be returned to France and the former, with the king's viscera, to be interred in Sicily.[8]

Philip set off home, but his accession and his journey were to be afflicted by a series of appalling losses that fell like hammer blows one after the other. He had already lost his father and the brother closest to him in age. During a stopover on land in between the legs of the sea voyage his wife, Isabella of Aragon, then six months pregnant with her fifth child, was thrown from a horse; she went into a premature labour, gave birth to a stillborn baby and died in agony shortly afterwards from a combination of her injuries and childbirth complications. Philip's brother-in-law and ally Theobald II of Navarre, who was a member of the French crusading party, died in Sicily in December; he was followed to the grave by his widow, Philip's sister Isabelle, a few months later. Philip's uncle and aunt, Alphonse of Poitiers and Joan of Toulouse, died within days of each other in Italy during their own return journeys. And, to cap it all, when the new king reached Paris in May 1271 it was to the news that one of the many faces of infant mortality had carried off his son Robert.

The funeral of Louis IX took place the day after Philip's return, his bones interred at Saint-Denis; reports of miracles occurring at his tomb began to circulate soon afterwards.[9] The widowed Philip, who had buried his wife and his brother John-Tristan along with his father, was crowned at Reims on 15 August 1271 with no queen at his side. He would later go on to marry again – to Marie of Brabant (the niece of Matilda of Brabant, widow of Philip's uncle Robert I of Artois) – and start a second family, but this would cause him further heartache. Intelligent, cultivated and dazzling, Marie was also ambitious and, perhaps not unnaturally, preferred her own children to those of the late Isabella; there were reports in France that she wanted to put them ahead of their half-siblings in the succession, much as Louis VI's stepmother had attempted many years before, as we saw back in Chapter 1. These allegations reached a peak when Philip's eldest son and heir, Louis, died in 1276 at the age of eleven, just as Marie was about to give birth to her own first child. It was rumoured that she had had the boy poisoned, and speculation did not abate when she gave birth just days later to a son who was given the name Louis; the accusations were serious enough that Philip ordered an inquest. However, this eventually came to nothing, and as the king had two other surviving sons from his first marriage, and Marie could hardly have expected to get rid of both of them as well without arousing suspicion, the circumstances are more likely to have been the result of unfortunate coincidence.[10] In any case, it was Philip's second son by Isabella, another Philip, who became the heir to the throne.

* * *

Edward arrived in Tunis just as the French contingent was leaving. As a peace treaty had already been agreed there was little point in him beginning a campaign there, so he returned to Sicily with the others to spend the winter there and make alternative plans. In February 1271 he received word from England that his father was seriously ill and that he should come home, but he merely sent his cousin Henry of Almain back to monitor the situation. Henry never made it: he was murdered at the altar of a church in Viterbo in March 1271 by his other cousins Guy de Montfort and Simon de Montfort the younger. They proclaimed that this was in revenge for the deaths of their father and eldest brother at Evesham, although Henry of

Almain had not been at the battle in person, as he was at that time still in captivity.[11]

The terrible news did not take long to reach Edward, but so keen was he to continue with his crusade (rather than to return ignominiously to England having done nothing, to the detriment of his reputation) that even this did not turn him from his purpose. In April 1271 he and his English troops sailed for Acre. Once in the Holy Land he recaptured Nazareth, but his army was too small to make any significant challenge to Baibars's forces. His brother, Edmund of Lancaster, arrived in August with reinforcements, which emboldened Edward; but he was still short of the massive army that would be necessary to make any real gains, and he was only able to under-take raids, rather than mount a sustained campaign.

Eleanor of Castile gave birth to a daughter, known throughout her life as Joan of Acre, in April 1272. A truce with Baibars was agreed in May, at which point Edmund departed again.[12] The royal situation in England had by now deteriorated: King Henry continued in poor health, while Richard of Cornwall, who had been acting as protector of the realm, had suffered some kind of seizure (probably a stroke) in December 1271 and died in the spring of 1272. As his son Henry of Almain was already dead and both of King Henry's sons were away from England, that left the ailing king with only his younger nephew, Edmund of Cornwall, and his little grandsons.

This was still not enough to persuade Edward to leave the Holy Land; but he changed his mind after a serious incident in June 1272, when an assassin was sent to kill him. He was attacked while alone by a man wielding a poisoned knife and, although he was able to fight the assailant off and kill him, he had been struck by the blade and fell ill. He survived, but his recovery was slow. Unable to fight or to lead his army, he convalesced until September before deciding that enough was enough and leaving the Holy Land for Sicily.[13] It was while he was there that two pieces of family news reached him: tidings of the death of his elder son and heir, John, and then of his father. Charles of Anjou, his host, was surprised to find that Edward seemed to care little about the loss of his son, although he was extremely upset about King Henry. 'To have more sons is easy,' explained Edward, 'but the loss of a father is irredeemable as he cannot be replaced.'[14]

Edward was the king of England – and, in a departure from previous practice, he was considered so from the moment of Henry's death, even though he had not yet been crowned. For centuries, the death of almost every king of England had been followed by a scramble for the crown, with the victor not certain until he had it placed on his head in the proper ceremony. Two things were different this time. Firstly, Henry's reign had been so long that Edward had been the designated heir for all of his thirty-three years, so the idea of a rival candidate seemed almost impossible; and secondly, he was on crusade – and therefore doing God's work – and could not feasibly be expected back in England for many months, no matter how quickly the news reached him or how swiftly he then set off home. Henry's death meant the end of government in his name, which only left three choices: elect a new king straight away from the available candidates in England, thus bypassing Edward (which was unthinkable); accept Edward as the heir, but endure a long interregnum until he could be crowned; or declare him king straight away and govern in his name. The nobility of England, probably by pre-arrangement, opted for the third choice, and swore allegiance to him at Henry's funeral, as soon as the old king was buried.[15]

The epitaphs of Henry III were more subdued than those of his contemporary Louis IX. Where possible they concentrated on his piety, which was undoubted, while damning him with faint praise for the more secular aspects of his life. 'In proportion as the king was considered to be deficient in prudence in worldly actions, so he was more distinguished for his devotion to the Lord,' wrote one commentator, while another called him 'a religious and pious man' and added that 'he was simple in affairs of state, but his largesse to the poor was to be admired'.[16]

Henry was in his grave at Westminster Abbey, and Louis (or at least his bones) in his at Saint-Denis. After long reigns in both realms, France and England stood on the verge of new eras – but the problem with eras ending, especially in dynastic monarchies, was that *someone* had to keep going. In this case, it was Henry's and Louis's sons, both very different from their fathers. And this meant that the relationship between the two dynasties was about to change again.

* * *

Edward I and Philip III were related to each other multiple times over. As Louis IX had earlier emphasised to his nobles, they were first cousins, as their mothers were sisters; additionally, on their fathers' sides they were second cousins once removed, Edward's grandfather John and Philip's great-grandmother Eleanor having been brother and sister. And further back still, via various lines of descent, it so happened that both kings were descended from Henry I of England *and* Louis VI of France.

Both new kings had their work cut out to impose themselves, due to the length of their fathers' reigns: Louis had been on his throne for forty-four years and Henry on his for fifty-six, so there were not many people around in either realm who had any meaningful memory of any other monarch. Philip was perhaps in the more challenging situation of the two, for how could he possibly hope to live up to the memory of the revered Louis IX? He responded, as we will see, by throwing himself into many a foolhardy enterprise. His epithet, *le Hardi*, is rendered in English as 'the Bold', but the connotations of the term are not entirely positive.[17]

Edward was in a stronger position, having been for some years a more dominant force in English politics – and certainly in English warfare – than his father. As we noted above, the nobility of England had already sworn allegiance to him, and his confidence in his authority is evidenced by the fact that he still seemed to be in no hurry to return to his kingdom. He left Sicily in January 1273, reaching Rome in February and making a fairly leisurely journey, with many stops, through Savoy and France. In France the royal couple left their infant daughter Joan of Acre to be brought up in the care of her maternal grandmother, Joan of Ponthieu, and Edward did homage to Philip III 'for all the lands I ought to hold from you', a suitably vague statement that would allow for much reinterpretation later on.[18]

England's king finally reached his kingdom on 2 August 1274. That his confidence was not misplaced is indicated by the fact that nobody had made any kind of rival claim in the intervening time, and there appears to have been very little in the way of nobles using the absence of a king to stir up private rivalries for their own benefit. Edward and Eleanor were crowned at Westminster on 19 August, a year and nine months after the death of his predecessor, but this did not mark the start of his reign: due to the unusual and novel circumstances, he was the first English king to date his reign from the day of his accession, rather than of his coronation.[19]

We have already heard of the many losses that the French royal family had endured in recent generations, due to infant and youth mortality. Up until now the English house had suffered less in this regard, but Edward and Eleanor reversed the trend very sadly. By the time of the coronation in August 1274 Eleanor had borne at least nine children, of whom only four (Henry, aged six; Eleanor, five; Joan, two; and baby Alfonso) were still living, and Henry would die just two months later. This left the royal couple with only Alfonso as a male heir, a dangerous situation for the succession, and one that was exacerbated when their next five children in a row were girls.[20]

Royal fathers were not expected to be hands-on parents: Henry III and Louis IX (when he was not distracted by the exigencies of a crusade) had been the exceptions, rather than the rule. Indeed, there is an argument to be made that Henry's extreme devotion to family, in its wider sense, may have been one of the defining problems of his reign. But even by the standards of the day Edward appears to have been particularly offhand, having little interest in any of his children other than the fact of fathering them. Charles of Anjou had been surprised by his callous attitude to John's death; Edward had left Joan in France without a second thought; and he did not bother to travel the short distance from London to Guildford to see his heir, little Henry, during his final illness in the autumn of 1274. Of course, royal children were often brought up in separate households to their parents, so we should not read too much into that; but the old belief that medieval parents did not care for their children because they were so likely to lose them has long been questioned, and there are many examples of parents exhibiting profound grief at their losses. Edward's only recorded statement on the subject, however, is the one we noted above: that more children were easy to come by.[21] Easy for him, maybe; Eleanor, whose body was doing the actual work of repeated pregnancies and labours, might have felt differently.[22]

Edward was concerned with issues more important to him than whether his many children lived or died – he had international matters of state to attend to and conquests to plan. His crusade had been an objective failure, and he was thwarted by the Treaty of Paris from taking further action in France for the present; he now turned his attention nearer to home, launching campaigns into Wales in 1276 and 1282.[23] He was not to be able to concentrate fully on his Anglo-Welsh wars, however, as he also experienced rebellion against his rule in Gascony. As he held the duchy there as a vassal of the French king, the agitators had been able to appeal to Philip III as their ultimate overlord, and in 1279 – in between his two Welsh campaigns – Edward had found the time to cross the Channel to discuss the matter in person. It was his first meeting with the French king in six years, and the cousins managed, at this stage at least, to continue the cordial relationship that their fathers had established; each made concessions to the other, and agreement on the immediate future of French–Gascon relations was celebrated with feasts and jousts.[24]

This was a rare and temporary moment of peace for Philip. While Edward had been engaged in his Welsh wars, Philip had been busy botching his relationships with France's other neighbours, leading the royal cousins into a series of tit-for-tat rival alliances with the various Spanish kingdoms that would have far-reaching and sometimes unexpected results.

Both parts of France's earlier double alliance with Castile had fallen through. Louis, King Philip's older brother (he whose coffin Henry III had helped to carry), had not lived long enough to fulfil his proposed union with Alfonso X's daughter Berengaria. And although Philip's sister Blanche had married Alfonso's son and heir, Ferdinand, the young man had died within his father's lifetime, so she would never be queen of Castile. The circumstances surrounding Ferdinand's death had caused a dispute: Blanche had borne him two sons, but King Alfonso overlooked them in his succession plans and named his own second son, Sancho, as his heir. Blanche, unsurprisingly, appealed to her brother for help, and Philip responded by attempting to launch an ill-advised and ill-prepared military campaign that never even made it across the Pyrenees. Blanche's sons were sent to Aragon for their safety, and were never reinstated to the Castilian succession; relations between France and Castile remained strained.[25] This suited Edward of England, whose relationship with Alfonso X was strong, given that his queen, Eleanor, was Alfonso's half-sister.

In Navarre the situation was reversed, and here Philip was able to steal a political march on his English rival. Theobald II of Navarre and his queen, Isabelle of France (Philip's sister), had died during and just after Louis IX's last crusade, as we saw earlier. They had been childless, so the throne had passed to Theobald's younger brother, who became Henry I of Navarre. Henry was to suffer a tragedy: his only son, another Theobald, died at the age of three when he eluded his nurse one day and then fell from the great height of a castle battlement. Henry himself died within a year, in July 1274, leaving Navarre to his only surviving child, his one-year-old daughter Joan, under the regency of her mother.

Naturally, little Joan became a great marriage prize, and King Edward was among those seeking her as a bride for one of his sons, of whom he had two living at the time. Unfortunately for him, however, Joan's mother and regent was another member of the French royal house: Blanche of Artois, King Philip's first cousin (the daughter of Louis IX's brother Robert, who had been killed at the Battle of Mansurah). Blanche fled to Paris and placed Navarre under French protection, and Philip III quickly betrothed Joan to his then second son, Philip.[26]

Edward was not best pleased by this outcome, but as it turned out the situation resulted in a different and unexpected marriage tie between the houses of France and England, for the widowed Blanche of Artois went on to marry Edward's brother, Edmund of Lancaster, in February 1276. There were various political advantages to the match; but as widow and widower, they had a little more say in their marriage choice than many others, and it would appear that these two representatives of the rival dynasties married out of mutual attraction – one of a surprising number of such unions in this book, when we come to count them, and all of them second or subsequent marriages for the woman concerned.[27] Blanche and Edmund's relationship was approved by both dowager queens, the sisters Eleanor and Margaret of Provence, though the news was less well received by the bride's brother, the belligerent Robert II of Artois, who was 'most displeased and angry' at the link between the two families, because 'he well knew that the king of England had no love for the king of France'.[28] And Edmund himself was still uncomfortably close to the prospect of becoming king of England, for at the time of his marriage Edward and Eleanor had only one living son, Alfonso.

* * *

Edward's brother marrying Philip's cousin might have made it seem as though relations were cordial, but it was not long before a third Spanish realm, Aragon, would cause friction between the English and French kings.

In news that might at the time have seemed tangential to the Anglo-French relationship, there had been trouble in the kingdom of Sicily. Charles of Anjou, who had been king there since 1266, faced a rebellion in 1282 instigated by locals and supported by Peter III of Aragon – whose wife, Constance, was the daughter of Manfred, Sicily's previous king who had been killed in battle, and in whose name he therefore had a claim to the crown. The rebellion became known as the Sicilian Vespers, as it broke out into violence on the evening of the Easter vigil.

By September Peter of Aragon had been crowned on the island of Sicily as its king. Philip of France, seemingly aware neither of Peter's determination to secure and defend another crown nor of the resources he could put behind his effort, rallied to his uncle's support. A French army led by the king's younger brother Peter of Alençon – he who had been named as putative regent if Philip had died while ill in Tunis at the time of his accession – and his cousin Robert II of Artois, by now a noted military commander, arrived in December 1282. Peter of Alençon was killed just a month later by Aragonese troops, and the eventual result of the war was that the kingdom was split into two halves: Peter of Aragon would keep the title and the island of Sicily, while Charles of Anjou would retain the mainland part, henceforward to be styled the kingdom of Naples.[29]

There was, as might be expected, bad blood thereafter between France and Aragon, something Edward of England was prepared to exploit to the full. In 1282 he had betrothed his eldest daughter, Eleanor, to Alfonso, eldest son and heir of Peter III, in order to cement a link between England and Aragon.[30] Philip of France countered with a rival Spanish alliance of his own: the long-awaited wedding of his son Philip and Joan of Navarre took place in August 1284, when she was eleven. Philip junior was by now the heir to the French throne, following the earlier and possibly suspicious death of his elder brother Louis, and he now also became absentee king of Navarre in right of his wife. Despite young Louis's demise, the French royal succession was at this point looking strong. Philip III had three surviving sons – Philip and Charles from his first marriage and the other Louis from his second – and also several nephews in the male line; his heir's Navarrese marriage meant that he would, in due course, also expect grandsons in the direct line of succession.

The male future of the English house, meanwhile, was once more hanging by a thread. After what was at least her fourteenth – and might even have been her fifteenth or sixteenth – pregnancy, Queen Eleanor had finally given birth to another boy, Edward, in 1284. Tragically for her, the baby was only four months old when his brother Alfonso, the only other son in the family, died. He was ten years old and so had probably made it past the most dangerous period of childhood, and Eleanor's political hopes must have been invested in him, as well as her personal feelings; that she felt his loss deeply is evidenced by the fact that, alone of all her children, she had Alfonso's heart kept, so that it could be buried with her own.[31]

King Edward, meanwhile, being now the father of five surviving daughters but only one baby son, and with a wife who was well into her forties, would soon have to consider the possibility of female succession, a point to which we will return in the next chapter.

* * *

King Philip could not let the situation with Aragon lie, and he prepared to take military action against Peter III. In this he was supported by the pope (now Martin IV, another Frenchman), who had excommunicated Peter over his actions in Sicily, and even went so far as to declare him deposed in Aragon itself. This gave Philip the excuse he needed to invade, nominally on behalf of his teenaged second son, Charles of Valois, whom he intended to have crowned king of Aragon. Two of the Spanish kingdoms would then be under Capetian rule, which would expand his area of influence.

Both sides in this Franco-Aragonese conflict appealed to King Edward for help, Philip summoning him as a vassal to join his host and Peter requesting his aid on the basis of the proposed marital alliance between their children (which had been put on hold, due to the excommunication and the refusal of Pope Martin to grant the required dispensation, as the two parties were related). Edward's reply to Peter was that he could not go against his homage to Philip, so he could not help; but he did not join Philip either.[32]

It was Philip's rashness that saved Edward from having to make a firm decision one way or the other. Despite the deaths of both Charles of Anjou, the king of Naples, in January 1285 and Pope Martin IV a few weeks later (which might have indicated to anyone else the desirability of delay and the possibility of negotiations), Philip launched his campaign against Aragon at Easter. His preparations had been flimsy and he was without sufficient supplies, naval support or planning; his forces were defeated at sea and unable to engage with the Aragonese on land – they simply evaded the French until the French, short of food and ravaged by an epidemic illness, were forced to retreat.[33] Philip (whom one chronicler describes rather optimistically as 'sad and angry, because he thought he should have been able to take all of Aragon and the whole of Spain') was one of those who fell ill and, like his father and grandfather before him, he succumbed to dysentery while away on a campaign; his army had barely made it back over the Pyrenees and on to French soil when he died, in October 1285, aged only forty.[34] Peter III of Aragon died only weeks later, meaning that all four of the main protagonists in the ill-fated war involving Sicily, Aragon, France and the papacy had died within the same year, and Edward could step back from the situation with some relief.

Epitaphs of Philip tend towards the conventional, rather than the enthusiastic; or else they damn him with faint praise, such as the writer who tells us that 'day by day the courage and the will to subdue his enemies grew in him', conveniently glossing over the fact that although the will might have been there, the actual success was not.[35]

The new king of France, despite any ambitions that the dowager queen Marie of Brabant might have had, was Philip's eldest surviving son from his first marriage, Philip, who was already the king of Navarre and the count of Champagne in right of his wife. His accession to the French throne was uncontested, and he was proclaimed Philip IV and crowned on 6 January 1286. He was a bellicose youth, just seventeen years old, and he would provide Edward with a new and different type of opponent, both in politics and in war.

CHAPTER TWENTY-FIVE

THE IRON KINGS

IN THE ROLL OF FRENCH kings, Philip IV is generally known as *Philippe le Bel*, 'Philip the Fair', but he also has the lesser-known nickname of *le Roi de Fer*, 'the Iron King'. In a manner reminiscent of his ancestor Philip Augustus, who had inherited the throne at a similar age, he was determined from the first to strengthen the French monarchy and to resolve some of the issues caused by his predecessor's rash decisions; one immediate consequence of this was that he distanced himself from some of Philip III's foreign policy.[1] The younger Philip had not approved of his father's invasion of Aragon, so a cessation of hostilities occurred directly. He and Aragon's new king, Alfonso III, were first cousins (Philip's mother, who had died so tragically on her way back from a crusade when he was only a small child, had been Isabella of Aragon, Peter III's sister) and they agreed upon a peace.[2] Alfonso was at this time betrothed to Eleanor, the eldest daughter of Edward I of England, an alliance that might eventually have complicated his relationship with France, but the arrangement was mired in controversy and he would die in 1291 before the wedding could take place.

Edward, in his position as duke of Gascony, was required to travel to France at the accession of the new king in order to pay him homage for the lands he held there. He sailed from England in May 1286 and made his way without undue haste to Paris, where he did homage and also raised the question of the Gascon lords bypassing his authority and making appeals directly to the French king. Philip accepted the homage, which was again worded vaguely, and made some concessions in Edward's favour with regard to Gascony; the new royal relationship appeared to have got off to a good start.[3]

Like Philip, Edward is also known to posterity by two different soubriquets, one related to his appearance and one to his character and actions: 'Longshanks' and 'the Hammer of the Scots'. He received the latter following another campaign on his borders that would distract his attention from France for some while.

By the late 1280s Edward had become embroiled in Scottish affairs, an episode that we will summarise only briefly here. King Alexander III of Scots (the son of Alexander II, whom we last met fighting against King John in Chapter 16) had at one time been Edward's brother-in-law, as he was married to Edward's sister Margaret until her death in 1275. Alexander III's three children all predeceased him, so when he was killed in an accident in 1286, he was succeeded on the Scots throne by his only grandchild: this was Margaret, generally known as 'the Maid of Norway', his daughter's daughter by King Eric II of Norway. She was three years old at the time and, in an echo of Philip III's reaction to the earlier situation in Navarre, she was immediately betrothed to King Edward's baby son Edward, despite the fact that he was her first cousin once removed. This meant that – if all went according to plan – Edward I's grandchildren would in due course inherit the Scots throne; in the shorter term, young Edward would become king there in right of his wife, as Philip IV of France was in Navarre. A more immediate benefit for King Edward was that, due to the extreme youth of the parties concerned, he would have effective control of Scotland in the name of his son and daughter-in-law as soon as they were married.

Tragically, however, little Margaret died at the age of seven, leaving Scotland with no monarch at all, no clear successor, and over a dozen distantly related claimants who put forward their cases for the crown.[4] King Edward was asked to arbitrate, in much the same way as Louis IX of France had once been called upon to make a judgement on affairs in England. However, the results were very different: Edward decided in favour of one of the claimants, John Balliol, but then attempted to claim sovereignty over the whole of Scotland himself. Scottish kings had previously owed allegiance to their English counterparts, but, other than a brief interlude under William the Lion, only for lands they held in England (much as the king of England did for lands he held in France).[5] Edward's claim was a whole new situation, and one that would result in conflict between England and Scotland for decades to come.[6]

Outside of Scotland there were two other significant consequences of Edward's actions. The first was that Edward recognised the danger to a kingdom of being left without either a male heir or a clear designation of whom the crown should pass to in such a situation. He did not, of course, actually intend to die without leaving a son to succeed him, but at this point he was left with just one, his youngest child, Edward; and having already lost his three older sons, he must have been well aware of the dangers of child mortality. The basic choice that faced Edward was: if he died with no living son to succeed him, should the crown pass to (or through) his daughters, or should it remain in the male line and go to his brother, Edmund of Lancaster, and then his male heirs? Edmund, as we will recall, was married to Blanche of Artois; they had by now three sons, so if Edward's own line failed, the succession would be secure there.

Edward's preference, however, was for the children of his body rather than his brother, even if this meant the crown passing to or through the female line. He was prompted to make his decision official in April 1290 on the occasion of the wedding of his second daughter, the then eleven-year-old Joan of Acre, to Gilbert de Clare, the powerful earl of Gloucester (who was, incidentally, in his mid-forties and the father of two daughters who were older than his new wife). In what was perhaps an attempt to stop Gilbert becoming overly ambitious, Edward decreed that if he should die without a male heir, the throne should pass to his daughters and their heirs in order of seniority – that is, that his eldest daughter Eleanor was next in line after young Edward. Eleanor was still, at this time, betrothed to Alfonso III of Aragon, and after his death in 1291 her position in the English succession might have made her a great international marriage prize; bizarrely, she was married off to the relative nobody Henry, count of Bar, in 1293.[7]

The question of female succession – the possible claims of the unfortunate captive Eleanor of Brittany notwithstanding – had not been officially addressed in England for more than 150 years. The last occasion had been in the 1120s, when Henry I declared his daughter Empress Matilda his heir; Edward must have been aware of the consequences of that, but he pressed ahead anyway. As it happened the point was not tested, for young Edward survived his father, but the vexed question of succession to the crown via the female line would raise its head bloodily in France in the fourteenth century and in England in the fifteenth.

The second international consequence of Edward's intervention in Scottish affairs was that in 1295 Scotland and France would agree an alliance to support each other against England; under the terms of the treaty, if England attacked either realm then the other would invade English territory. The 'Auld Alliance', as it later became known, was one of the longest-lasting international agreements, renewed by subsequent French and Scots kings until the sixteenth century.[8]

* * *

Philip IV no doubt also recognised the seriousness of a king dying without a male heir, and the duty incumbent on him to continue the line that had now worn the French crown in direct father–son succession for three centuries. But he and the rest of the immediate Capetian royal family were young. At the time of his accession, Philip had one surviving full brother, the fifteen-year-old Charles of Valois; he also had a half-brother, nine-year-old Louis (the baby who had been born to Marie of Brabant in the same month that Philip III's eldest son had died), as well as two younger half-sisters, Margaret and Blanche, who were little more than toddlers. He had no children of his own and his wife, Joan of Navarre, was twelve years old. This was not only a hurdle to the succession, but also a symbol of the wider lack of female authority at the French court during the early years of Philip's reign. Such a young queen would not, of course, be expected to exercise a great deal of influence, although Joan would grow into the role in due course.[9] There was, further, no queen mother to assist the young king: the dowager queen, Marie of Brabant, was Philip's stepmother and they were not on particularly good terms. He did have a dowager queen grandmother, Margaret of Provence, but she was now feeling the effects of age. Although she had been active in political life while her son was on the throne, she was not able to continue during the reign of her grandson; she retired to a convent sometime in the early 1290s and died at the end of December 1295, in her mid-seventies.

At the time of her death, Margaret was the last of the four sister queens; over in England, the queen mother Eleanor of Provence had died in June 1291, having also retired to a convent. This was a further blow to Edward, who had lost his wife, Eleanor of Castile, only months before in November 1290. His queen's death appeared to affect him much more deeply than the loss of any of his children; as her body was conveyed from Lincoln to Westminster, he ordered a stone cross to be erected at each of the twelve places where her cortege stopped overnight en route – an imitation of an earlier Capetian innovation, the series of crosses erected to mark the stages of the journey of Louis IX's body when it was brought back to France.[10] Eleanor's heart was interred at Blackfriars, London, alongside that of her son Alfonso; her body was buried at Westminster on 17 December 1290, and for the rest of the decade there was no senior adult royal female figure in either realm.[11]

Edward had contemplated no serious move against France early in his reign, possibly because he was already occupied in Wales and then in Scotland. With both of those now apparently subdued, at least temporarily, he had leisure to turn his attention across the Channel, and particularly to exploit the vague wording of his homage to Philips III and IV. The situation of the king of England holding lands as the liege man of the king of France was always likely to lead to trouble, and with the belligerence of the Iron King on one throne and the Hammer on the other, probability became certainty. Edward and Philip were about to overturn decades of peaceful relationships between the two dynasties, and head down the road to open war.

* * *

It started with various scuffles between the sailors of rival territories: mariners from the Cinque Ports in England were hostile to those of Flanders and Bayonne, while a feud between English and Norman sailors in 1292 spilled over into violence. Various raids on rival ships both in port and at sea continued into the following year, and in May 1293 there was an encounter that could fairly be described as a battle between an English convoy and a Norman fleet off Cap Saint-Mathieu, the most westerly point of Brittany.[12] Although much booty was gained by the English and brought home, King Edward would not accept any of it himself, in an attempt to stay out of what he considered at this stage to be a private war. He was, in any case, making preparations to embark on another crusade to the Holy Land, which was taking up much of his time and attention.

Various embassies went back and forth between the two kings in an attempt to calm the situation, but this only served to escalate it from a local, private conflict to a national one. In the eyes of some French chroniclers, this was due to Edward's duplicity:

> Edward, king of England, putting into action the iniquitous projects he had – it was said – been planning for a long time, made great preparations on the pretext that he would soon depart for the Holy Land. Having equipped his ships at Bayonne and many other ports, and made immense preparations for war, he then wickedly attacked the people of King Philip, in Normandy and elsewhere, by land and by sea. He killed and captured an infinite number, destroyed most of their vessels and took the rest to England filled with goods and merchandise.[13]

According to this same writer, Edward's men also attacked La Rochelle, leading Philip to order him to hand over the ringleaders to face justice. When he did not, and Philip's messenger was ill-treated, the French king had his constable seize all of Gascony, an action that was (in the eyes of the writer) entirely justified by the circumstances, as an overlord confiscating the lands of a rebellious vassal.

English observers, of course, took a different view. One accuses the French king of 'a great act of treachery by design', and says that he and his advisors wished to use the unrest in Normandy as an excuse to summon Edward before a court of French peers, at which 'by premeditated deceit they have [already] given judgement', thus allowing Philip to deprive Edward of Gascony.[14] In this telling, it is the unfairly treated Edward who is advised to seek redress for his loss; he is urged by his counsellors to make alliances with foreign partners, in order to take on Philip by force of arms.[15]

Edward responded eagerly to his advisors' suggestions, seeking (like his grandfather John before him) to surround the king of France with enemies, by making overtures to Adolf of Nassau, the king of Germany; Guy of Dampierre, the count of Flanders; and Otto IV, the count of Burgundy. We should note at this point that the *county* of Burgundy was distinct from its neighbour, the *duchy* of Burgundy; the latter was part of France, while the former owed allegiance to the Empire. It was the count of the territory in the Empire with whom Edward sought to make an alliance, not the French duke. He also went back to his English barons and people, telling them 'how Aquitaine was lost by treachery' and that he needed to tax them heavily in order to claim it back.[16] This was not popular.

Edward's recruitment drive for the campaign, as exemplified by an order sent to the sheriffs of England, ordered 'all men possessing land and rent to the value of £20 per year [or more]' to 'at once provide themselves with horses and arms and hold themselves fit and ready to join us and to go with our own person for the safeguarding and defence of themselves and of our whole kingdom'. Of interest is the fact that he positions this service as being in defence of the whole realm: it is only later in the writ that he indicates that the service will take place abroad, as 'we have now decided to set our crossing to the lands beyond the sea'. He ends with a slightly ominous exhortation to 'devote yourself to the execution of this our mandate with all speed, lest – which God forbid! – our crossing be delayed through your default and we be obliged to chastise you severely'.[17]

Philip IV was not the first young king of France to face off against a more experienced English counterpart early in his reign, and, unfortunately for Edward, he went about it with a combination of determination and political and military talent that matched those of his ancestor Philip Augustus. Firstly, he took advantage of the time Edward needed in order to make his alliances and preparations. The final embassy between the two kings had failed in 1294, but Edward, in conflict with so many of his neighbours at once, was delayed by a rebellion in Wales in 1294–95, and then by his decision to march against the Scots in person in 1296, during which campaign he forced John Balliol to abdicate and declared he would rule Scotland directly.[18] Setting up an administration there was time-consuming, and although Edward was able to send contingents of men to Gascony from late 1294 onwards, it was not until 1297 that he was ready to depart himself.

In the meantime, Philip had launched a counter-attack; an army led by his brother Charles of Valois and his cousin, the vastly experienced military leader Robert II of Artois, invaded Gascony at Easter 1295. By midsummer the French had taken most of Gascony, with the remaining English garrisons holed up in Bourg and Blaye in the north of the duchy and Bayonne in the south. To press his advantage further, Philip next ordered raids on seaports on England's south-east coast; attacks were made on Dover, Winchelsea and

Hythe, with casualties on English soil arising from an Anglo-French conflict for the first time since the invasion of the future Louis VIII in 1216–17.

The French war on land continued simultaneously, and the English stronghold of Bayonne was besieged in 1296. The garrison there was commanded by Edward's brother, Edmund of Lancaster – who, as well as being a member of the English royal house, was both the brother-in-law of Robert of Artois and the stepfather of the French queen. Edmund fell ill and died in June, while the siege was at its height; the rest of the defenders, short on morale and money, trickled away.[19] Philip was moving ever closer to his goal of imposing direct royal authority on all parts of his kingdom, though the financial strain was beginning to show. The problem for everybody was that the ongoing conflict was expensive: for Philip, who had to leave standing garrisons in each place he took, and for Edward, who had to send men and supplies across the sea.

Time was passing. The age difference between the two kings, which had previously favoured Edward's experience over Philip's youth, now reversed its influence: in the summer of 1296 Edward turned fifty-seven and, having been active all his life, was on the verge of seeming elderly next to the vigorous twenty-eight-year-old Philip in his prime. The same might be said of the dynasties: Philip by now had sons as well as brothers, while the English succession rested solely on the shoulders of Edward's only son, Edward, now in his teens. If he were to die, then the situation would be murky indeed: Edward's eldest daughter, Eleanor, had by now borne the count of Bar a son; but, as a foreign subject, if he were ever to attempt to claim the English throne he could expect to face stiff competition from the de Clare family (the children of Edward's second daughter, Joan) or even the sons of the late Edmund of Lancaster – Thomas, the 2nd earl, Henry and John.

By the autumn of 1297, when Edward was at last in a position to make a move in person, there was little point in heading to Gascony. Instead he sailed for Flanders, at which point everything began to go wrong. Before he even arrived, his ally Count Guy had been defeated at the Battle of Furnes on 20 August by the indefatigable Robert II of Artois (whose only son, Philip, would later die of wounds sustained in the engagement), and King Philip announced that Flanders was to be absorbed into the royal domain. The Iron King was in no mood to offer concessions to a county rebelling against his authority: during the campaign, a number of Flemish villages were razed and harvests burned.

Philip also took action against the count's family. A potential marriage between Prince Edward of England and Guy of Dampierre's daughter Philippa had previously been touted; this was not the most prestigious of matches for Edward, as Philippa was not by any means Guy's heir (Guy had eight sons, as well as a number of older daughters), but it would have cemented the Anglo-Flemish alliance and put Guy in a stronger position against his French overlord. The union was forcibly prevented by King Philip, who took the unfortunate girl into his own custody and held her in Paris.[20] It was a comfortable captivity, during which Philippa was maintained and educated; but it was captivity nonetheless, and it lasted until her death in 1304 – another female life wasted due to the political concerns of male relatives.

Philip was in the ascendant, and he now received an enormous spiritual and political boost: after a long campaign, his grandfather Louis IX had been canonised by Pope Boniface VIII on 4 August 1297. The Capetian house could now number a genuine saint among its recent members.[21]

By the time Edward arrived in Flanders, at the end of August, Lille had fallen to the French and he could find no support in Bruges, which would shortly also surrender to Philip. Edward thus took up residence in Ghent. His Burgundian allies and his son-in-law Henry, count of Bar, launched some raids into French territory in his support, but with little effect; Adolf of Nassau prevaricated and then did nothing. In October Edward received the devastating news from home that his forces in Scotland had been heavily defeated at the Battle of Stirling Bridge the previous month.[22] Being at war on both fronts simultaneously was not working out well, so he was amenable to Pope Boniface VIII's offer to mediate between him and Philip. Philip's motives for agreeing to the arbitration are less clear, given that he had very much the upper hand (one factor may have been that he owed a great deal to the pope's recent canonisation of St Louis; another that waging war continued to be expensive), but agree he did, and this led to a temporary truce. Edward returned to England in March 1298.

As ever, it took time for the full terms of peace to be negotiated, particularly as matters were complicated by Edward having the Flemings as allies and Philip the Scots.[23] But when matters were settled, one of the proposals was the age-old idea of intermarriage between the two dynasties – two marriages, in this case. Under the terms of the Treaty of Montreuil of June 1299, King Edward agreed to the union of his son and heir, Edward (then fifteen), with Philip's four-year-old daughter Isabelle, the wedding to take place at a later date; King Edward himself would marry Philip's young half-sister Margaret (the daughter of Philip III by his second marriage to Marie of Brabant) straight away. They were, of course, related in a prohibited degree, as Edward's mother and Margaret's paternal grandmother had been sisters, but – as usual when kings set their minds to something and the pope agreed – this difficulty was overcome.

This was another match that exhibited a massive disparity in age: Edward was sixty and Margaret in her late teens, certainly younger than most of his children. But dynastic politics overrode any such considerations, so the wedding went ahead at Canterbury on 10 September 1299. As we might expect, contemporary chroniclers focus on the political implications of the match, without paying much attention to Margaret or her personal feelings; but she was undoubtedly placed in an awkward position – not only because her new husband was old enough to be her grandfather, but also because she arrived in England as the foreign sister of the king with whom the realm had recently been at war. She appears to have dealt with the situation extremely well, pleasing Edward, making herself popular with the English lords by undertaking a queen's traditional intercessory role, and forming good relations with her stepchildren.[24] The union also served its purpose in dynastic terms: in 1300, sixteen years after his next youngest child had been born and more than forty years since he first became a father, Edward was delighted when Margaret gave birth to a son, Thomas of Brotherton. She would present him with another, Edmund of Woodstock, the following year, and he could finally feel more secure about the succession as he entered his declining years.

The French succession was by now also secure, or so Philip must have felt. His queen, Joan of Navarre, had borne him seven children, of whom four would survive to adulthood: three sons, Louis, Philip and Charles, and a daughter, Isabelle.

The conflict between the two realms reared its head again in 1302, not by any personal action of Edward's or Philip's, but due rather to the Flemings, who rebelled against their French overlord. Philip sent an army to quell the insurrection, but he suffered a huge and unexpected reverse when his cavalry host was defeated by a well-organised force of urban infantry at the Battle of Courtrai on 11 July. Philip's top military commander, his cousin Robert II of Artois – who had fought in every French campaign at home and abroad since Louis IX's crusade back in 1270 – was killed in the engagement, pulled from his horse and battered by the *goedendags* (a type of long, spiked mace) of the Flemish footsoldiers.[25]

Edward had not been involved personally in the battle, but he was still allied to the Flemings, and there was great delight in England when news of the French defeat crossed the Channel. He did not seek to press an advantage by making any further move against the French king himself; he was bound by the terms of the Treaty of Montreuil, and of course he was now Philip's brother-in-law, his two young sons Philip's nephews. Any hint of ongoing conflict was brought to a definitive end by the Treaty of Paris of May 1303, under the terms of which Philip restored Gascony to Edward, Edward agreed to cut all his ties with Flanders, and the formal betrothal of the younger Edward and Isabelle took place, following the 1299 contract for their marriage.[26]

Philip IV reasserted his supremacy over Flanders by personally leading his troops in a definitive victory at Mons-en-Pévèle in August 1304; Edward turned his attention back to Scotland and to internal matters in England. The Plantagenet and Capetian kings were once again closely related, but for now they had gone their separate ways, and the terms of their latest treaty seemed to ensure that the two rival houses had, at last, sheathed their swords.

HAPPILY EVER AFTER . . .

ON 25 JANUARY 1308, A lavish wedding took place in Boulogne.
The groom was the king of England: the tall, handsome,
twenty-two-year-old Edward II. He had succeeded his father
some six months previously and had resolved to fulfil the terms of the treaties with France. His bride was Isabelle, the only surviving daughter of
Philip IV, now twelve years old and of an age, canonically at least, to be
married.

It was a glittering occasion. King Philip was present, as were two of his
sons: his heir, Louis, king of Navarre since his mother's death, and third
son Charles, together with their wives Margaret of Burgundy and Blanche
of Burgundy.[1] Also in attendance were the dowager queens of France and
England, Marie of Brabant and Margaret of France; King Philip's brother
Charles of Valois; Charles II, king of Naples, the son of Charles of Anjou; and
Albert of Habsburg, king of the Romans. A plethora of dukes, counts and earls
from England, France and the Empire were also in attendance, and sumptuous
wedding gifts of jewels, plate and furs had been offered to the young couple.
The guests exemplified the way in which the two dynasties of France and
England were already woven together: Earl Thomas of Lancaster, for example,
was both the groom's cousin and the bride's uncle, while Philip IV was the
bride's father and the groom's second cousin. The hope was that the intertwining would continue. At some point in the future, it was assumed, there
would once more be kings of France and England who were first cousins. The
future looked bright.[2]

The marriage, planned a decade previously, was meant to symbolise peace, but it would not be long before all went disastrously awry. Little Isabelle did not, as the ring was placed on her finger, know that her husband would snub her for his male favourites, and that he and they would become her political enemies. Edward was equally unaware that his young wife would later take her revenge for this by overthrowing him and ruling England together with her lover. None of the guests was aware that in the years to come, various among them would be accused, betrayed, deposed, imprisoned or executed. And nobody could possibly have predicted that within two decades the centuries-old edifice of the Capetian royal house, safe and secure in its direct father–son succession since before the turn of the millennium, would come crashing down. The consequences of this wedding would be far-reaching, leading to renewed conflict between the two dynasties in the form of a war that would last for over a hundred years.

NOTES

Full references to all works cited may be found in the bibliography. Quotations from primary sources originally written in Latin, Old French or Anglo-Norman have been taken from published English translations where possible. Where works are only available in their original language, translations into English are my own (except where otherwise stated), as are all those from secondary literature written in French or German. For information on my specific approach to referencing, see the 'Reading this book' section of the introduction.

Introduction

1. There is a vast literature on William, the Conquest and its effect both domestically in England and in international terms. For an introduction, see Bates, *William the Conqueror*; Morris, *The Norman Conquest*; Chibnall, *Anglo-Norman England*; Bates, *The Normans and Empire*; and the early chapters of Bartlett, *England under the Norman and Angevin Kings*. The chapter 'Reshaping Western Europe' in Wickham, *Medieval Europe*, gives an excellent overview of developments in England and France, as well as in other European countries.
2. For an introduction to French history prior to 1100, see Dunbabin, *France in the Making*; Beaune, *Naissance de la nation France*; and the early chapters of Bradbury, *Capetians* and Menant et al., *Les Capétiens*.
3. For a wide-ranging discussion on this point, see Bartlett, *Blood Royal*, pp. 114–23.
4. For more on Fortune's wheel in the Middle Ages, see Bothwell, *Falling from Grace*; Radding, 'Fortune and Her Wheel'.
5. As a start, see Duggan (ed.), *Queens and Queenship in Medieval Europe*; Parsons (ed.), *Medieval Queenship*; Erler and Kowaleski (eds), *Women and Power in the Middle Ages*; Bennett, *Medieval Women in Modern Perspective*; Castor, *She-Wolves*. Recent biographies of individual medieval women include Turner, *Eleanor of Aquitaine*; Grant, *Blanche of Castile*; and Hanley, *Matilda*; there are many others listed in the bibliography.
6. There is perhaps an argument to be made that some English queens of the fourteenth and fifteenth centuries were also designated 'queens of France' because their husbands claimed the French throne, but in practice none of them reigned over both realms in the way that Eleanor of Aquitaine did.
7. Many of the full-length biographies of individuals that will be cited in the notes as we go along contain initial chapters that deal briefly with their subjects' early lives; more

general studies on childhood in the Middle Ages include Orme, *Medieval Children*; Orme, *From Childhood to Chivalry*.

8. The restricted range of first names used by comital houses may have been, in itself, a symbol of dynastic power: see Bouchard, 'Family Structure and Family Consciousness'.

9. For discussion on the 'of the people' construction as used in the Middle Ages, see Bartlett, *Blood Royal*, p. 428. Uniquely among present-day European monarchies, the death or abdication of the king of the Belgians does not result in the immediate accession of his successor; rather, the designated heir must appear before a joint session of the two houses of parliament and take a constitutional oath. Only then will he (or, nowadays, she; absolute primogeniture replaced male-preference primogeniture following a new act of succession in 1991, meaning that the heir at the time of writing is female) accede to the throne.

10. On this subject, Bartlett notes that 'before becoming king of England William I had been duke of Normandy for thirty years and he had the instincts and priorities of a French feudal prince' (*England under the Norman and Angevin Kings*, p. 12).

11. On nationhood and national identity, see, for example, Forde et al., *Concepts of National Identity in the Middle Ages*; Davies, 'Nations and National Identities in the Medieval World'; the section on national identity in Gillingham, *The English in the Twelfth Century*; McGlynn, '"Pro patria": National Identity and War in Early Medieval England'.

12. A thorough summary of the English economy, its currency and coinage, is Bolton, *Money in the Medieval English Economy*. For a wider European perspective, see the essays in Naismith (ed.), *Money and Coinage in the Middle Ages*. On coinage specifically, see Grierson, *Coins of Medieval Europe*.

Part I

Chapter 1

1. For more on porphyrogeniture, see Hollister, *Henry I*, p. 105; Dagron, 'Nés dans le pourpre'.

2. For an overview of all these events and the sources for them, see Hollister, *Henry I*, pp. 99–130. On William Rufus's death, see OV, vol. 5, pp. 289–95; WM, *Chronicle*, pp. 344–46; Benoît, pp. 165–70; *ASC*, pp. 235–36. On Henry's accession and marriage, see OV, vol. 5, pp. 295–301; WM, *Chronicle*, pp. 427–28; *ASC*, pp. 236–37. For a physical description of Henry, see WM, *Chronicle*, pp. 446–47.

3. See Lewis, 'Anticipatory Association of the Heir'; Bradbury, *Capetians*, p. 74. As it happened, the crown of France passed directly from father to eldest surviving son for over 300 years, including the entire two centuries that will be the focus of our attention here – a marked contrast to the chaos that ensued following the deaths of a number of English kings.

4. OV, vol. 6, p. 51. Louis's appetite for food and drink was renowned, and he would in later life become known as 'Louis the Fat', the epithet by which he is still distinguished today from all the other kings of France named Louis. King Philip's poor health also seems related to obesity, as we are told that he 'gave himself over to gratifying his desires', 'indulged himself too much' and did not take care of his health (Suger, p. 61); Orderic calls him 'indolent, fat and unfit for war' (OV, vol. 5, p. 215).

5. On Louis's presence at the Christmas court, see SD, p. 582; RH, vol. 1, p. 192. On the letter from France, see OV, vol. 6, pp. 51–55 (quote p. 53). All further references to the work of Orderic Vitalis are from vol. 6, so the volume number will be omitted from citations from now on. See also Bournazel, *Louis VI*, pp. 43–46 and 49.

6. OV, p. 53.

7. On Louis's activities as king-designate in the years 1101–08, see Suger, pp. 29–43 and 55–60; Bournazel, *Louis VI*, pp. 53–77. Orderic Vitalis tells of Bertrade's apparent further attempts to get rid of Louis via sorcery and poisoning, but they sound increasingly implausible.

8. This is necessarily a very brief overview. For further details on Rufus and Curthose and their relationship, see, for example, Gillingham, *William II*; Aird, *Robert Curthose*.

9. On Curthose's exploits on crusade, see HH, pp. 39–42; Wace, pp. 200–01; Benoît, pp. 161–62; *GT*, p. 46; Aird, *Robert Curthose*, pp. 153–90.

10. Williams Clito and Adelin were not really known by their soubriquets until later in life, but we will use the names throughout in order to avoid any ambiguity. It should also be noted that Matilda was Henry I's first *legitimate* child; he already had a large family of illegitimate children, of whom we will hear more below.

11. OV, p. 87.

12. For more on the Battle of Tinchebrai, see OV, pp. 87–93; Benoît, pp. 176–77; Robert Helmerichs, 'Tinchebrai, Battle of', *OEMW*, vol. 3, p. 357; Bradbury, 'Battles in England and Normandy', pp. 182–93; Morillo, *Warfare under the Anglo-Norman Kings*, pp. 169–70.

13. OV, p. 93.

14. Bertrade sensibly decided to exit the political scene following Philip's death; she became a nun at Fontevraud (WM, *Chronicle*, p. 438). From the available evidence, it would seem that Louis left her in peace there until her death from natural causes in 1117. Although she never succeeded in putting one of her sons by Philip I on the French throne, she would become the foremother of two other royal dynasties: descendants of her son from her first marriage, Fulk V of Anjou, would in due course rule over both England and Jerusalem.

15. Quote from OV, p. 177. On Henry's personality, see WM, *Chronicle*, pp. 447–48; Green, *Henry I*, pp. 312–16; Hollister, *Henry I*, pp. 496–98. On Louis's preference for action and enjoyment of military exploits, see Menant et al., *Les Capétiens*, pp. 201–02; Suger, pp. 24–28.

16. On the subject of homage and the significance of the homage ceremony, see Hyams, 'Warranty and Good Lordship in Twelfth-Century England'. For a discussion of Normandy's feudal relationship with France at this time, see Hollister, *Henry I*, pp. 239–40.

17. Bournazel, *Louis VI*, pp. 103–04; Hollister, *Henry I*, pp. 239–40.

18. Suger, p. 71. The Epte had formed the border between the French Vexin and the Norman Vexin since the tenth century; Gisors was located on the Norman side, in a small loop of the river, about 40 miles north-west of Paris (see Suger, p. 71, note e). For more on this episode, see Hollister, *Henry I*, pp. 222–23; Bournazel, *Louis VI*, pp. 103–05.

19. Suger, pp. 73–74; Bournazel, *Louis VI*, pp. 104–05. On bridges and their significance as meeting places, see Schneider, 'Mittlelalterliche Verträge auf Brücken und Flüssen'; and for a general overview, Cooper, *Bridges, Law and Power in Medieval England*.

20. Suger, pp. 76–80; Hollister, *Henry I*, p. 224.

21. For details of these events, see Suger, pp. 111–18.

22. Henry I's only legitimate daughter was called Matilda (known to posterity as Empress Matilda, as we shall see later). Rather confusingly, three of his illegitimate daughters also shared the same name; the Matilda who became duchess of Brittany should therefore not be confused with the empress, the countess of Perche or the abbess of Montvilliers, all of whom are referred to in various contemporary sources as 'Matilda, daughter of Henry, king of the English'.

23. OV, p. 181. For more on William Adelin, his childhood and youth, see Andrews, *Lost Heirs*, pp. 19–23.

24. Lucienne's exact age is not known, but Suger notes with certainty that 'she was not yet of an age to wed' and that the relationship was never consummated (Suger, p. 41).

25. On the arrangements and the wedding, see Bournazel, *Louis VI*, pp. 130–32; on Adelaide's official acts and influence on Louis, see ibid., pp. 184–87. Commenting on Adelaide's role and reputation as queen, Huneycutt notes that she was 'among France's most powerful and visible queens consort, exercising the privileges of sovereignty to a degree unprecedented in Capetian history' ('The Creation of a Crone', p. 28).

26. For more on Flanders, and the complex family relationships of its counts, see Oksanen, *Flanders and the Anglo-Norman World*.
27. 'King Louis was assisting the exiled William to recover his heritage, and most of the Normans were whole-heartedly on his side' (OV, p. 185).
28. The scant information available on this engagement is summarised by Hollister, *Henry I*, p. 252, where he notes that the sources are 'confusing and unsatisfactory'.
29. Suger, p. 114. Suger goes on to say that the would-be assassin was 'mercifully condemned to losing his eyes and genitals' instead of being put to death (ibid.). See also WM, *Chronicle*, p. 416.
30. Cnut IV had been overthrown and murdered when Charles was a young boy; Adela had fled back to her native Flanders, taking her son with her and leaving the Danish crown in the hands of Cnut's brother Olaf I. Charles had grown up at the Flemish court and remained there when his mother left to travel to Italy for a second marriage.
31. For more on the strategic importance of castles, see DeVries and Smith, *Medieval Military Technology*, pp. 223–33; Hanley, *War and Combat*, pp. 15–17; Jones, 'Fortifications and Sieges', pp. 163–64; and, more generally, the articles by Oliver Creighton and Michael W. Thompson in *OEMW*, vol. 1, pp. 336–46. On the visual domination of castles and castles as symbols of power, see also Coulson, 'Structural Symbolism'; Wheatley, *The Idea of the Castle*; Steane, *Archaeology of Power*.
32. OV, pp. 217–19; Bournazel notes that this appears to be the first recorded use of the French battle cry 'Montjoie!' (*Louis VI*, p. 143 and p. 420, note 56). See also Hibbard-Loomis, 'L'oriflamme et le cri "Munjoie"'.
33. Quote from OV, p. 231; the burning of the town was apparently done with the permission of the bishop of Évreux, on the promise of rebuilding the cathedral on a grander scale than before. On the attack on Évreux, see OV, pp. 229–31; Hollister, *Henry I*, pp. 262–63. On the conduct of war, and ravaging as a tactic, see Contamine, *War in the Middle Ages*, pp. 260–302; Hanley, *War and Combat*, pp. 42–45; Bachrach and Bachrach, *Warfare in Medieval Europe*, pp. 365–68; McGlynn, *By Sword and Fire, passim*; Allmand, 'War and the Non-Combatant'.
34. For more on the Battle of Brémule, see *ASC*, p. 248; Suger, pp. 117–18; OV, pp. 235–43; RT, pp. 31–32; HH, pp. 54–55; Robert Helmerichs, 'Brémule, Battle of', *OEMW*, vol. 1, pp. 171–72; Hollister, *Henry I*, pp. 263–66; Menant et al., *Les Capétiens*, p. 234; Bournazel, *Louis VI*, pp. 145–48; Morillo, *Warfare under the Anglo-Norman Kings*, pp. 171–73; Aird, *Robert Curthose*, pp. 262–63. The most detailed study is Strickland, 'Henry I and the Battle of the Two Kings: Brémule, 1119'.
35. For the details of Louis's discussions with the pope, see OV, pp. 257–59; Bournazel, *Louis VI*, p. 149; Aird, *Robert Curthose*, pp. 264–67.
36. SD, p. 601. For further discussion of the terms of the peace, see Hollister, *Henry I*, pp. 274–76 (who calls it a 'dazzling diplomatic triumph' for Henry); and Bournazel, *Louis VI*, pp. 150–51, who points out that Louis also gained, because Henry's offer of his son's homage confirmed his recognition of Louis's position as the overlord of Normandy.

Chapter 2

1. OV, p. 297.
2. OV, p. 301. For more on the *White Ship* disaster, see *ASC*, p. 249; OV, pp. 295–307; SD, pp. 601–02; Wace, pp. 206–07; Benoît, pp. 172–74; WM, *Chronicle*, pp. 455–57; HH, pp. 55–56; Hollister, *Henry I*, pp. 276–79; Hanley, *Matilda*, pp. 43–46; Andrews, *Lost Heirs*, pp. 21–23; Aird, *Robert Curthose*, pp. 268–70.
3. Wace, p. 206.
4. Louis's eldest son, Philip, was formally acclaimed as his heir to the throne in 1120, when he was just four years old; Bournazel, *Louis VI*, p. 155. He would be crowned and anointed as associate king in 1129.

5. There was some wrangling over the return of little Matilda's dowry; Fulk was entitled to a 'refund', as the marriage had never been consummated, but Henry did not see this as a priority. See *ASC*, pp. 250–53; SD, p. 607; Hanley, *Matilda*, p. 46; Hollister, *Henry I*, p. 290. Matilda would not marry again and later became a nun at Fontevraud, apparently at her own request.

6. See Power, *Norman Frontier*, p. 379 and n. 70.

7. 'All this hostility was because of the son of Earl Robert of Normandy, called William [. . .] *the king of France and all the earls and all the powerful men held with him*, and said that the king held his brother Robert in captivity wrongfully, and [that he had] put to flight his son William out of Normandy unjustly'; *ASC*, p. 254. 'So it was that *many men*, seeing that King Henry's legitimate heir had perished, and that the king was growing old without legitimate descendants, *passionately embraced the cause of his nephew William, and devoted all their energies to raising him to power*'; OV, p. 329 (my emphasis in both cases).

8. OV, p. 201.

9. For details of the minor engagements, see SD, pp. 610–11; OV, pp. 331–37 and 341–47; Hollister, *Henry I*, pp. 294–96.

10. Quote from OV, p. 351. For more on the Battle of Bourgthéroulde, see *ASC*, pp. 253–54; OV, pp. 349–53; Robert Helmerichs, 'Bourgthéroulde, Battle of', *OEMW*, vol. 1, pp. 162–63; Hollister, *Henry I*, pp. 298–301; Bournazel, *Louis VI*, pp. 166–67; Morillo, *Warfare under the Anglo-Norman Kings*, pp. 173–74. On the mutilation of the ringleaders, see OV, pp. 353–55. On the effectiveness of fighting on foot, see Bennett, 'The Myth of the Military Supremacy of Knightly Cavalry'.

11. OV, p. 359.

12. One of the many people who drowned in the *White Ship* disaster of 1120 was an envoy of the emperor who was at that time attached to Henry I's court: see OV, p. 305; Hanley, *Matilda*, pp. 31–32. For more on the relationship between England and the Empire at this time, see Leyser, *Medieval Germany and Its Neighbours*, pp. 191–214.

13. This was also recognised in the name of the realm: before Louis VI's reign, the term 'Francia' denoted only the land between the Meuse and the Loire, but it was afterwards applied to the whole kingdom of what we now recognise as France. For a more detailed examination of the extent of royal domains, see Power, *Norman Frontier*, pp. 85–88.

14. All the direct quotes in the account that follows are from Suger, pp. 127–31. See also Bournazel, *Louis VI*, pp. 168–71.

15. For further discussion on the symbolism of this act and on the patronage of St Denis, see Bournazel, *Louis VI*, pp. 384–88. See also Bradbury, *Capetians*, p. 144 (who notes that the *oriflamme* later became fictitiously linked with Charlemagne); Dunbabin, *France in the Making*, p. 258; Hibbard-Loomis, 'L'oriflamme et le cri "Munjoie"'.

16. Menant et al. note that the reign of Louis VI 'is traditionally presented as the first great step in the affirmation of the French monarchy and the territorial unification of France' (*Les Capétiens*, p. 242).

17. Quote from OV, pp. 165–67. On the annulment, see also Hollister, *Henry I*, pp. 304–05; Andrews, *Lost Heirs*, p. 14; Aird, *Robert Curthose*, p. 270.

18. Emperor Henry was only thirty-eight, but he had been ill for some months with what modern historians believe to be cancer. See Chibnall, *Empress Matilda*, pp. 39–41; Fuhrmann, *Germany in the High Middle Ages*, pp. 94–95.

19. On the elective nature of the imperial succession, see Wilson, *Holy Roman Empire*, pp. 301–11; Fuhrmann, *Germany in the High Middle Ages*, pp. 96–97. At the time of his appointment in 1125, Lothar was in his fifties with only a single daughter, which indicates that the electors were seeking an emperor, and not necessarily a dynasty.

20. For more on Robert of Gloucester, see Given-Wilson and Curteis, *Royal Bastards of Medieval England*, pp. 74–93. For a discussion of the issues with Robert's potential claim to the throne, see McDougall, *Royal Bastards*, pp. 123–28; on his character and the idea that he was no more than a safe pair of hands, rather than a leader, see Hanley, *Matilda*, pp. 198–99 and 240.

21. On Henry's deliberations, see WM, *Historia*, pp. 3–4; Hollister, *Henry I*, pp. 308–17; Andrews, *Lost Heirs*, pp. 23–6; Chibnall, *Empress Matilda*, pp. 50–1; Hanley, *Matilda*, pp. 46–9 and 54–5. On the oath-taking ceremony, see WM, *Historia*, pp. 4–5; Benoît, pp. 182–83; Hollister, *Henry I*, pp. 317–18; Chibnall, *Empress Matilda*, pp. 51–53; Hanley, *Matilda*, pp. 55–58. On the question of female succession, see Beem, *The Lioness Roared*, pp. 30–34 and 49–52; Castor, *She-Wolves*, pp. 64–66; Hanley, *Matilda*, pp. 58–59 and 143–47.
22. Quote from OV, p. 371. On these events, see ibid., pp. 369–71; Bournazel, *Louis VI*, pp. 177–79.
23. Suger notes that Charles 'governed the well-populated land of Flanders with valour and care', and that 'besides being a splendid defender of God's church, he was prominent for generous almsgiving and a noteworthy guardian of justice' (Suger, p. 138).
24. Galbert, p. 119; see also Suger, p. 139; OV, p. 371; SD, p. 616.
25. Galbert, p. 164.
26. Quote from Suger, p. 138. Details of the punishments – for those who really want to know – may be found in Galbert, pp. 208–13 and Suger, p. 141. Hollister adds that large numbers of men were subject to 'grisly tortures and agonizing executions, the vengeance extending beyond the murderers and their fellow conspirators to their followers, many of whom were presumably innocent' (*Henry I*, p. 319 n. 149).
27. According to Galbert, King Louis pointed out in public that William was not only illegitimate, but of very low status on his maternal side: he had 'an ignoble mother who continued to card wool as long as she lived' (Galbert, p. 187).
28. Galbert, pp. 194 and 196; Suger, p. 140 (my emphasis in all cases). On Clito's succession, see also Nangis, p. 12.
29. Galbert, pp. 201–08. On the way in which the towns of Flanders took advantage of the political disturbance caused by the Flemish succession crisis, see Dunbabin, *France in the Making*, pp. 270–71.
30. For details, see Galbert, pp. 260–71.
31. This translation of Clito's letter appears in King, *King Stephen*, p. 34.
32. HH, p. 59.
33. Suger, p. 135.
34. Galbert, p. 278.
35. Galbert, p. 291.
36. Galbert, p. 298.
37. For more on the Battle of Axspoele, see Galbert, pp. 297–99; Bournazel, *Louis VI*, p. 189.
38. Galbert, p. 307; see also OV, p. 377; SD, p. 616.
39. OV, p. 377.
40. OV, p. 381.
41. Galbert, p. 312. Of the last four counts, Robert II had been trampled to death in battle in 1111; Baldwin VII had died of wounds in 1119; Charles the Good had been murdered in 1127; and William Clito died of wound infection in 1128. For more on the conflict in Flanders in 1127–28 and on William Clito's claims and acts there, see SD, p. 616; Hollister, *Henry I*, pp. 318–26; Bournazel, *Louis VI*, pp. 179–90; Aird, *Robert Curthose*, pp. 271–73; Oksanen, *Flanders and the Anglo-Norman World*, pp. 20–29; Duby, *France in the Middle Ages*, pp. 141–51; Hicks, 'The Impact of William Clito'.

Chapter 3

1. For more on Matilda's time in the Empire, see Hanley, *Matilda*, pp. 17–34; Chibnall, *Empress Matilda*, pp. 18–44; Castor, *She-Wolves*, pp. 52–64.
2. Baldwin II of Jerusalem had four daughters and no sons. His eldest daughter, Melisende, was recognised as his heir, but due to the unique military situation of the kingdom, it was imperative that a male warrior should be at its head. Baldwin had been seeking a

suitable husband for Melisende for some time when his choice fell on Fulk, who was an experienced warrior, a widower and a nobleman who had visited Jerusalem before. See Riley-Smith, *Crusades*, pp. 74–75; Hanley, *Matilda*, pp. 64–65; and below, Chapter 10.

3. Quote from OV, p. 483. On the early stages of Matilda and Geoffrey's marriage, see Hanley, *Matilda*, pp. 68–72; Chibnall, *Empress Matilda*, pp. 55–59; Castor, *She-Wolves*, pp. 67–69.

4. On the council, see HH, p. 63; Hollister, *Henry I*, pp. 463–64; Chibnall, *Empress Matilda*, p. 59; Hanley, *Matilda*, p. 71.

5. Nangis, p. 13.

6. Suger, p. 149; OV, p. 421; and Map, p. 285, respectively. We should note that different chroniclers might have had very different purposes and points of view as they wrote their narratives.

7. Bournazel, *Louis VI*, p. 191.

8. Suger, pp. 149–50. For more on this incident, see OV, pp. 421–23; RT, p. 41; HH, p. 62; WM, *Historia*, p. 10; Nangis, p. 15; Bournazel, *Louis VI*, pp. 194–95; Sassier, *Louis VII*, pp. 15–16. Philip's short life is the subject of a fairly recent biography: Pastoureau, *Le roi tué par un cochon*.

9. Suger, p. 150.

10. Bournazel, *Louis VI*, pp. 195–96; Sassier, *Louis VII*, pp. 19–23.

11. Quote from HH, p. 63. See also RT, p. 44; Hanley, *Matilda*, pp. 73–74; Chibnall, *Empress Matilda*, p. 61.

12. OV, pp. 449–51. See also Hollister, *Henry I*, pp. 467–69 and 473–75.

13. OV, p. 455, describing Theobald doing the twelfth-century equivalent of taking his ball home.

14. On the specific chronology of these events, see Hanley, *Matilda*, pp. 80–83; on Stephen's seizure of the crown more generally, see Benoît, pp. 188–89; HH, pp. 66–67; WM, *Historia*, pp. 14–16; OV, p. 455; King, *King Stephen*, pp. 41–48.

15. GS, p. 15.

16. Suger, p. 151.

17. On Eleanor's early life up to this point, see Turner, *Eleanor of Aquitaine*, pp. 10–37.

18. Suger, p. 156; OV, pp. 481–83; Bournazel, *Louis VI*, pp. 202–03; Turner, *Eleanor of Aquitaine*, pp. 37–38.

19. Suger gives us a long and possibly embroidered account of the piety of Louis's last days and his deathbed: pp. 152–59. It does appear, though, that he was with the king in person: 'When he saw that I was weeping ... he said, "Dearest friend, do not weep for me, but rather celebrate with great joy"' (Suger, p. 155). For a slightly more abridged account, see Bournazel, *Louis VI*, pp. 204–05. Summing up Louis's reign as a whole, Dunbabin notes that it was 'a decisive turning point in the history of the French monarchy' (*France in the Making*, p. 265).

Chapter 4

1. Louis and Eleanor were 'crowned' with ducal coronets in a ceremony in Poitiers on 8 August 1137, a rite that emphasised that this title was distinct from the French crown (see Sassier, *Louis VII*, pp. 60–61; Turner, *Eleanor of Aquitaine*, p. 49). The chronicler Orderic Vitalis confuses this event with a royal coronation (OV, p. 491), but as it took place only seven days after the death of Louis VI, it is unlikely that the news would have travelled so far so quickly, and even more unlikely that there would have been time to organise such a ceremony or to transport the necessary regalia.

2. The French royal family of the Middle Ages was particularly keen to pass on the names Philip and Louis; they are frequently given to two or more sons in the same family, with the result that every king of France from 1060 to 1316 was either a Louis or a Philip.

3. An apanage was a system used in various parts of Europe, but most commonly in France, whereby a lordship or grant of land was made to a younger royal son, sourced either from his mother's inheritance or by carving a small lordship off the main patrimony. It provided a middle ground between equal inheritance of all sons (which would eventually weaken a kingdom by splitting it into smaller and smaller parts) and sole primogeniture (which handed everything to the eldest, but then created the danger that younger sons would rebel because they had everything to gain and nothing to lose). An apanage would revert to the royal domain if the line became extinct. In this particular case, the county of Dreux remained in the hands of Robert's descendants until 1355.

4. The names reflect the words used for 'yes' in each language. For a detailed history of the two dialects, see Abalain, *Le français et les langues historiques de la France*.

5. On Aquitanian customs with regard to women and property, see Turner, *Eleanor of Aquitaine*, pp. 37–38. On the expectation that women in the twelfth century would be capable and active, see the discussion and examples from primary sources in Hanley, *Matilda*, pp. 240–41. For a discussion of the issues of female rule over a wider chronological period, see Beem, *The Lioness Roared*, esp. pp. 1–12.

6. Quotes from JS, p. 53 and WN, vol. 1, p. 129, respectively. John of Salisbury also later adds the detail that Louis 'loved the queen passionately, *in an almost childish way*' (JS, p. 61; my emphasis). Abbot Bernard of Clairvaux, of whom we shall hear more later in this chapter, rebuked Eleanor for the extent of her 'harmful influence' over the king; Sassier, *Louis VII*, p. 129.

7. For more on Eleanor's influence on Louis during these early years of their marriage, see Turner, *Eleanor of Aquitaine*, pp. 53–57.

8. Hallam and Everard, *Capetian France*, p. 89, citing Stephen of Paris's *Fragmentum Historicum de Ludovico VII*.

9. On this quote, see Turner, *Eleanor of Aquitaine*, p. 47.

10. In the twelfth century, to be 'confined' meant just that, at least for those of a certain rank: an expectant mother was shut into her apartments with her female attendants. On the specifics of childbirth in the Middle Ages, see Leyser, *Medieval Women*, pp. 126–30. For an in-depth survey of childbirth traditions and cultures, see Burnett et al. (eds), *Pregnancy and Childbirth in the Premodern World*.

11. On the fall of Edessa and the call to crusade, see Phillips, *Holy Warriors*, pp. 75–83. On Bernard's speech at Vézelay, see Sassier, *Louis VII*, pp. 146–48. On the significance of Louis receiving the *oriflamme*, see Naus, *Constructing Kingship*, p. 86, where he notes that 'in the long term, this was an important moment in the history of France and its monarchy [...] Louis had become not merely another crusader; he had become a crusader king – the first to come from France and the first to lead a major expedition to the East.' We should note that Louis was not the first member of either the French or the English royal houses to go on crusade (Robert Curthose and Hugh of Vermandois had both served with distinction during the First Crusade), but the significance of a crowned, reigning king participating was substantial.

12. As the Second Crusade was an undertaking of Louis's that did not have a significant impact on the Capetian relationship with the English ruling house, we have passed over it very briefly here. A contemporary account written in Old French is *GC6*, pp. 7–64; see also Nangis, pp. 31–34. For more on the Second Crusade, see Phillips, *The Second Crusade*; Phillips, *Holy Warriors*, pp. 89–102; Asbridge, *Crusades*, pp. 201–21; Riley-Smith, *Crusades*, pp. 93–104; Menant et al., *Les Capétiens*, pp. 390–93.

13. Quotes from JS, p. 61. On the rumours surrounding Eleanor's conduct, see ibid., pp. 52–53; Sassier, *Louis VII*, pp. 186–89; Turner, *Eleanor of Aquitaine*, pp. 87–91. On Eleanor's part in the crusade, see Pangonis, *Queens of Jerusalem*, pp. 130–55.

14. Robert's discontent seems to stem from him blaming Louis for the failure of the Second Crusade (Sassier, *Louis VII*, p. 197), and Henry's from an ecclesiastical dispute: JS, pp. 69–70; Sassier, *Louis VII*, pp. 216–17.

15. *GC6*, pp. 67–68; Nangis, pp. 35–36. For more discussion on the divorce, see Sassier, *Louis VII*, pp. 231–37; Turner, *Eleanor of Aquitaine*, pp. 104–07.
16. For more on this civil war, see for example Crouch, *The Reign of King Stephen*; Bradbury, *Stephen and Matilda*; King, *King Stephen*; Chibnall, *Empress Matilda*; Hanley, *Matilda*. The principal primary sources are *GS*; WM, *Historia*; HH.
17. On the fall of Rouen, see RT, p. 58 ('Geoffrey, who had until this time been count of Anjou [. . .] became duke of Normandy'). See also Hanley, *Matilda*, p. 192. On the arrangements relating to Louis's recognition of Geoffrey as duke of Normandy, see Sassier, *Louis VII*, pp. 133–34; on the extent of Louis's gains in the Vexin at this point, see Power, *Norman Frontier*, p. 392 and n. 23.
18. As we noted earlier, English kings sometimes got round the issue of needing to kneel to the king of France by having their young sons perform homage for Normandy, in return for recognition of their status as heirs. In this case, Eustace was probably around seven when he performed homage in 1137; see Andrews, *Lost Heirs*, pp. 36–37.
19. On this episode, see WN, vol. 1, p. 69; Hanley, *Matilda*, p. 159; King, *King Stephen*, pp. 193–94.
20. WM, *Historia*, pp. 57–58. This might sound cruel, but was actually the only possible response from Empress Matilda at this point – why would she grant the son of her defeated opponent the titles, lands and resources with which he could mount a retaliatory campaign against her? On this point, see Hanley, *Matilda*, p. 153; Andrews, *Lost Heirs*, pp. 37–38.
21. Hanley, *Matilda*, pp. 206–07. On the question of whether Louis received the whole of the Vexin at this point, or whether Geoffrey had already ceded it to him in 1144 when he handed over the castle of Gisors, see Power, *Norman Frontier*, p. 392 and n. 23.
22. JS, pp. 85–86. This interpretation of events is confirmed by Henry of Huntingdon: 'The pope in a letter had forbidden the archbishop to elevate the king's son as king. It was understood that this was because Stephen has seized the kingdom contrary to the oath' (HH, p. 88).
23. *GS*, p. 223.
24. As an indication of how prevalent this attitude was by this point, even the noticeably pro-Stephen *Gesta Stephani* begins to refer to Henry as 'the lawful heir' to the English throne (*GS*, pp. 205, 215 and further subsequent instances).
25. *GS*, p. 235.

Chapter 5

1. On these events, see RT, p. 66; Gervase, vol. 1, p. 149; *GC6*, p. 68; WN, vol. 1, pp. 129–30; Warren, *Henry II*, pp. 44–45; Turner, *Eleanor of Aquitaine*, pp. 107–09; Sassier, *Louis VII*, pp. 237–38. Having been divorced by Louis on the ostensible grounds of consanguinity, Eleanor now found herself married to a man to whom she was almost as closely related: she, Louis and Henry were all direct descendants of Robert II the Pious, king of France from 996 to 1031.
2. For a more thorough discussion of Eleanor's decisions at this point, see Turner, *Eleanor of Aquitaine*, pp. 100–03. Barber also emphasises that Eleanor's decision was motivated by political, rather than personal, reasons (*Henry Plantagenet*, p. 46).
3. HH, p. 88. Although Henry II did not use the surname Plantagenet himself – it being his father's personal soubriquet – it has become so well known an appellation for his family and descendants that, as noted in the introduction, I will use it as shorthand for 'the ruling house of England' from now on.
4. *GS*, p. 227.
5. On this episode, RT, pp. 66–67; Gervase, vol. 1, pp. 149–50; Hanley, *Matilda*, pp. 208–10; King, *King Stephen*, pp. 267–69; Warren, *Henry II*, pp. 45–48; Sassier, *Louis VII*, pp. 239–41; Andrews, *Lost Heirs*, p. 40.

6. HH, pp. 90–91.
7. Quote from *GS*, p. 239. For more details on these negotiations, see RT, p. 73; HH, pp. 92–93; WN, vol. 1, p. 127; Hanley, *Matilda*, pp. 216–19; King, *King Stephen*, pp. 276–81; Warren, *Henry II*, pp. 48–53.
8. WN, vol. 1, p. 125.
9. On the coronation, see *GS*, p. 241; HH, pp. 95–96; Gervase, vol. 1, p. 159.
10. On the oaths, see RT, p. 77.
11. On this point, see Turner, *Eleanor of Aquitaine*, p. 195.
12. Quote from *GC6*, p. 71.
13. Although this marriage strengthened Louis's alliance with the house of Blois, and therefore his hand against Henry II, it did mean that his third wife was just as closely related to him as his first, whom he had divorced on the grounds of consanguinity; Adela and Louis shared the same mutual ancestor as Eleanor, Robert II the Pious of France. As it happens, Adela could also claim a link to the English royal line, as she was the great-granddaughter of William the Conqueror, so any children born of her marriage to Louis would therefore be descended from both houses.
14. *GC6*, pp. 89–91; Sivéry, *Philippe Auguste*, pp. 25–26. Gerald of Wales also claims – with some hindsight – that a woman told him that 'We now have a king given to us by God and a powerful heir to the kingdom by God's gift, through whom shame and loss, punishment and deep disgrace, full of confusion and disaster, will accrue to your king' (GW, p. 675). For detailed analysis of contemporary reactions to Philip's birth, see Lewis, *Royal Succession in Capetian France*, pp. 64–73.
15. Agnes's story is another one of young royal girls having their futures and their happiness sacrificed for political gain. In 1178, at the age of around eight, she was shipped to Constantinople to be brought up alongside her future husband, Alexios II Komnenos, who was about two years older. They were married in 1180. Three years later Alexios was murdered by his cousin, who became Andronikos I Komnenos; in order to bolster his position, the approximately sixty-five-year old Andronikos married the twelve-year-old widow. A Byzantine observer said that 'she shrank from the union [...] she loathed his roughness [...] she alone knew what she suffered' (as translated in Bartlett, *Blood Royal*, pp. 36–37). Andronikos was later deposed and murdered; Agnes survived him and married for a third time, but her fate thereafter is unknown.

Chapter 6

1. *Becket*, p. 47. For a more detailed explanation on the background to this dispute, see Warren, *Henry II*, pp. 82–85. On the campaign being at Eleanor's instigation, see Turner, *Eleanor of Aquitaine*, pp. 134–35. On the campaign itself, ibid., pp. 136–38; Barber, *Henry Plantagenet*, pp. 95–97; Favier, *Les Plantagenêts*, pp. 237–38.
2. Raymond V's struggles with Henry II and his sons over the years are summarised in Déjean, *Les comtes de Toulouse*, pp. 211–19. For additional detail and a family tree illustrating the conflicting claims, see Bowie, *Daughters of Henry II*, pp. 71–73.
3. William of Newburgh emphasises that Louis was prompted to act out of family loyalty and to fight 'on behalf of his nephews'; WN, vol. 2, p. 47.
4. *Becket*, p. 48.
5. One of the casualties of this sickness was William of Blois, count of Boulogne and Mortain, the only surviving son of King Stephen, who had thrown in his lot with Henry; he fell ill and decided to return to England, but had only reached as far as Poitiers when he died, at the age of just twenty-four.
6. RT, pp. 89–90; Warren, *Henry II*, pp. 87–88; Favier, *Les Plantagenêts*, pp. 238–39.
7. WN, vol. 2, p. 55.
8. WN, vol. 2, p. 99.
9. Sassier, *Louis VII*, p. 279.

10. In hindsight, we can see that Henry II was secure on this throne and that the house of Blois did not make any further claim on England, but this was far from certain at the time; Adela's brothers Henry and Theobald were ambitious young men, and their other uncle Henry of Blois, the canny and experienced bishop of Winchester, still exercised considerable influence there.

11. RH, vol. 1, p. 258. For more on the unusual nature of this marriage, see Strickland, *Henry the Young King*, pp. 30–33.

12. WN, vol. 2, p. 101.

13. On the celebrations attending Philip's birth, see Sassier, *Louis VII*, pp. 371–72; Bradbury, *Philip Augustus*, pp. 1–2.

14. The chronicler Walter Map tells us of an occasion when Louis took a nap in a forest, outside any wall or fortification, and with only two guards for company. When one of his lords reproached him for risking his life in this way, Louis replied that he could sleep alone and safe because no one wanted to do him harm (Map, p. 282).

15. *Becket*, p. 94. For a contemporary account (somewhat biased in Becket's favour) of the archbishop's elevation and change in behaviour, see ibid., pp. 50–58; and on the dispute itself, see ibid., pp. 59–91. For a detailed modern analysis of the dispute, see Warren, *Henry II*, pp. 447–517. On Louis's involvement in the affair, see Sassier, *Louis VII*, pp. 373–98. For more on Becket generally, see Barlow, *Thomas Becket*; Guy, *Thomas Becket*.

16. RT, p. 103; Latin in *CRSHR*, vol. 4, p. 230. One modern historian calls it a 'smouldering rivalry' (Power, *Norman Frontier*, p. 398); an apt description, given that the situation could have erupted in flames at any moment.

17. RH, vol. 1, p. 339. For an account of the murder itself, see ibid., pp. 335–37; *Becket*, pp. 148–59; WN, vol. 2, pp. 103–07.

18. This rapidity was remarkable, even by the standards of the age. As a comparison, another great churchman of the era, Abbot Bernard of Clairvaux, died in 1153 but (despite both his fame and his piety) he was not canonised until 1174.

19. WN, vol. 2, p. 107.

20. On the sequence of homage ceremonies, see RT, p. 109. Alice was to go to her marriage with no dowry (Gillingham, *Richard I*, p. 39), a point to which we will return later.

21. Empress Matilda, whom we last saw aiding Henry against the Capetian–Blois alliance of 1152, had remained in Normandy since that time, ruling it very effectively as his regent while he was engaged in other parts of his far-flung territories, and negotiating with both Louis VII of France and the Emperor Frederick Barbarossa. She died in 1167, having lived long enough to see her son succeed to everything she had fought for and produce a brood of children to continue her line. Henry's two younger brothers were also both dead by this time (Geoffrey in 1158 and William in 1163), neither of them leaving any children.

22. For more on the ceremony and a list of those present, see RT, p. 111–12; Strickland, *Henry the Young King*, pp. 84–91. Pope Alexander may not have been as supportive as Henry hoped or implied; Henry's biographer notes that 'the ports had to be closely watched to prevent letters of prohibition reaching the English bishops' (Warren, *Henry II*, p. 111).

23. Nangis, p. 45. Subsequent to this incident, the tradition was formalised: Pope Alexander issued a papal bull, *Quanto majorem*, in 1171, in which he decreed that the sole right to conduct coronations in England was henceforward to be invested only in archbishops of Canterbury.

24. *GRH*, vol. 1, p. 6.

25. For more on Louis's reaction, see RH, vol. 1, p. 326. The same chronicler gives us an example of the potential confusion caused by having two kings of the same name in the same realm, and the disambiguation that became necessary: 'the king of England, the

father, leaving the king his son behind in England, crossed over into Normandy' (p. 326); and later, 'Henry, king of England, the son of King Henry' (p. 333).

26. Henry II actually continued to use the title 'duke of Aquitaine' himself; during his father's lifetime, Richard was generally referred to as the count of Poitou. On this point, see Turner, *Eleanor of Aquitaine*, p. 189.

27. On the Breton succession crisis, see Dunbabin, *France in the Making*, pp. 331–32.

28. JF, p. 5.

29. RT, p. 117. With regard to Louis's track record as a father, his two daughters by Eleanor of Aquitaine, Marie and Alix, were betrothed at the respective ages of seven and two, and sent away to convents for their education, deprived even of each other. Margaret, as we have seen, was placed in Henry's custody before her first birthday. Louis's second daughter by Constance of Castile, Alice, was betrothed to Henry II's son Richard at the same time as he gave homage to Louis for Aquitaine in 1169, when she was eight; she was then also placed into Henry's custody – a move that was to have unfortunate consequences for her, as we shall see. Louis's one remaining daughter, Agnes, was at this point only two or three years of age, but she would also be sent away as a prepubescent: see above, note 15 to Chapter 5.

30. William of Newburgh writes only of 'certain persons' who 'whispered in his ear' (WN, vol. 2, p. 117), but Roger of Howden attributes the idea to Louis: RH, vol. 1, pp. 362 and 367. On the additional suggestion that the couple should return to France, see *GRH*, vol. 1, p. 34.

31. *GRH*, vol. 1, p. 41; see also Warren, *Henry II*, pp. 117–18 and Strickland, *Henry the Young King*, p. 131.

32. For a more detailed discussion of Eleanor's actions and motives at this point, see Turner, *Eleanor of Aquitaine*, pp. 216–21.

33. Philip had succeeded his father, Thierry of Alsace, in Flanders in 1168. As was the custom, his younger brother had received no part of the paternal inheritance, so he had bettered his position by other means: in 1160 Matthew had abducted Mary, the sole surviving child of King Stephen and a professed nun, from her cloister. He married her in order to claim the county of Boulogne – which had become hers in name after the death of her brother William of Blois the previous year – but during their ten-year union she never ceased to petition the pope for an annulment, a wish that was eventually granted in 1170, at which point she returned to her convent. She had borne Matthew two daughters, and he now ruled Boulogne in right of the elder. For more on Mary of Blois and this episode, see Andrews, *Lost Heirs*, p. 46. Philip and Matthew were also first cousins of Henry II: their mother, Sybil of Anjou, was the sister of his father, Geoffrey of Anjou.

34. On the conversation, see WN, vol. 2, pp. 117–19; see also Warren, *Henry II*, p. 118. On the seal, Favier, *Les Plantagenêts*, p. 398.

Part II

Chapter 7

1. For analysis of Eleanor's motives in particular, see Turner, *Eleanor of Aquitaine*, pp. 224–27; Warren, *Henry II*, pp. 118–21; Strickland, *Henry the Young King*, pp. 134–37.

2. JF, p. 3.

3. RH, vol. 1, p. 367.

4. Letter of Archbishop Rotrou of Rouen to Eleanor of Aquitaine; the full Latin text of the letter, plus an English translation, may be found on the Epistolae site at https://epistolae.ctl.columbia.edu/letter/143.html

5. On this event, see Sassier, *Louis VII*, p. 451.

6. WN, vol. 2, p. 121. See also Barber, *Henry Plantagenet*, p. 170.

7. JF, p. 9. Theobald of Blois is also criticised for his 'great arrogance' (ibid.) For a discussion on Jordan Fantosme's approach to all these participants, see Hanley, *War and Combat*, pp. 91–92.

8. *HWM*, vol. 2, pp. 113 and 117.

9. WN, vol. 2, p. 121. For more on this point, see Strickland, *Henry the Young King*, p. 158.

10. RH, vol. 1, p. 368.

11. Wace, p. 4.

12. On Matthew's injury and death, see RT, p. 119; WN, vol. 2, p. 123; GM, p. 65. Count Philip and his wife Elisabeth of Vermandois had no children. He had therefore named Matthew as heir to the rich county of Flanders, but Matthew's death, leaving only two young daughters, meant that Philip had to find another option. His first choice was his one remaining brother, Peter, but Peter was the bishop of Cambrai; it took some time to arrange for him to leave the Church and marry, in order that the family line could be continued. As it transpired, he produced no children either before his death in 1176, so Philip then named as his heir his sister Margaret, whose husband Baldwin, already count of Hainaut, would become count of Flanders in right of his wife.

13. For the figure of 10,000 men, see JF, p. 7; *GRH*, vol. 1, p. 51. Roger of Howden goes even further, claiming the force was 20,000 strong (RH, vol. 1, p. 368).

14. RH, vol. 1, p. 371. For a discussion of this uncharacteristic move, see Sassier, *Louis VII*, pp. 453–54; Strickland, *War and Chivalry*, pp. 126–27.

15. RH, vol. 1, p. 374; another contemporary notes that Young Henry 'bowed to Louis's advice in all matters' (WN, vol. 2, p. 117). See also Favier, *Les Plantagenêts*, p. 401.

16. RH, vol. 1, p. 375.

17. Gervase, vol. 1, pp. 142–43; see also Turner, *Eleanor of Aquitaine*, p. 227.

18. Alexander's letters are in *PL*, vol. 200, year 1174; discussion of these missives to Archbishop Henry may be found in Sassier, *Louis VII*, p. 455. See also the chapter on Alexander III and France in Clarke and Duggan (eds), *Pope Alexander III*.

19. An alternative interpretation is possible: Henry II's biographer believes that Louis deliberately held back at this stage, waiting for Henry to cross the Channel so he could attack Normandy in his absence, and that he encouraged King William to provide the distraction that would induce Henry to go (Warren, *Henry II*, p. 132).

20. For the embarkation date and the ship's passenger list, see Eyton, *Court, Household, and Itinerary*, p. 179.

21. For details on the sieges of Wark and Carlisle, see JF, pp. 41–57; Strickland, *Henry the Young King*, pp. 183–88.

22. On Henry's pilgrimage to Canterbury, see RT, p. 122; RH, vol. 1, p. 381. On King William's defeat at Alnwick and his capture, see JF, pp. 129–37; WN, vol. 2, pp. 135–39; Strickland, *Henry the Young King*, pp. 195–97.

23. For details of this siege, see WN, vol. 2, pp. 145–51.

24. Wace, p. 4.

25. RH, vol. 1, pp. 384–85; Young Henry's biographer believes that Henry II suspected that this would happen and that he was 'wise enough to let his son and King Louis escape comparatively unscathed' (Strickland, *Henry the Young King*, pp. 202–03).

26. RH, vol. 1, p. 385.

27. RH, vol. 1, pp. 385–88. As Strickland notes, these terms reflected 'the over-whelming strength of [Henry II's] position and pointedly granted considerably less than he had first offered young Henry and his brothers in the talks in September 1173 but they had rejected' (*Henry the Young King*, p. 212).

28. For more on John as lord of Ireland, see Warren, *King John*, pp. 33–37; Church, *King John: England*, pp. 19–27; Morris, *King John*, pp. 31–33.

29. A chapter dedicated to Eleanor's imprisonment may be found in Turner, *Eleanor of Aquitaine*, pp. 231–55. On the imprisonment of women more generally, see Seabourne, *Imprisoning Medieval Women*.

30. WN, vol. 2, p. 157; RH, vol. 1, pp. 398–401. For further details on the release arrangements, see W.W. Scott, 'William I (known as William the Lion), c. 1142–1214', *ODNB*.
31. *HWM*, vol. 1, p. 123.
32. On Count Philip providing the Young King with resources for the tournament, *HWM*, vol. 1, p. 127; the text adds that he then 'journeyed for at least a year and a half' taking part in such events (ibid., p. 131). On Henry's tourneying period, see Strickland, *Henry the Young King*, pp. 239–58.
33. *GRH*, vol. 1, p. 133.
34. GM, p. 68; Nangis, p. 48.
35. RH, vol. 1, pp. 463–64. On Henry's demands and Louis's reaction, see also Gillingham, *Richard I*, p. 57.
36. *GRH*, vol. 1, p. 169.
37. RH, vol. 1, quotes from pp. 464 and 470, respectively.
38. RT, p. 132; *GC6*, pp. 92–94; Rigord, pp. 11–13. For further discussion of the episode and its effects on Philip, see Sivéry, *Philippe Auguste*, pp. 19–23.
39. RT, pp. 132–33; RH, vol. 1, pp. 516–17; GW, p. 447.
40. Henry of Champagne was at this time in the Holy Land, but his brothers appear to have absented themselves in protest at the prominent role played by Philip of Flanders, who had the honour of carrying the new king's sword. For a discussion of the looming conflict between the houses of Flanders–Hainaut and Blois–Champagne over their influence on the new king, see Favier, *Les Plantagenêts*, pp. 517–20.
41. This is necessarily a modern diagnosis; see Sassier, *Louis VII*, p. 470, who discusses the symptoms and comes to what seems an obvious conclusion about the nature of Louis's illness. A contemporary notes that Louis 'had an attack of paralysis and lost the use of the right side of his body' (RH, vol. 1, p. 518).

Chapter 8

1. On Isabelle's previous betrothal, see GM, pp. 60 and 74.
2. GW, p. 571.
3. On the alleged adultery and subsequent murder, see *GRH*, vol. 1, pp. 99–101; RH, vol. 1, p. 402; GM, p. 34, n. 138. On the subject of Philip Augustus's (and Louis VII's) ambitions to annex more lands to the crown, and their increasing use of the term *corona regni* ('the crown of the kingdom') to denote royal rights, see Dunbabin, *France in the Making*, pp. 267–68.
4. This does not represent a conflict with Louis VII, but rather a recognition that he was no longer capable of exerting personal rule, and that – according to his own wishes – he would rather see his son ruling France than anyone else. Bradbury notes that in his early acts and documents Philip refers to his late father with fondness (*Philip Augustus*, p. 43). From November 1179 to April 1180 documents were issued in the names of both kings; after April 1180 the majority are in Philip's name alone, mainly confirming Louis's prior gifts and decisions. See Sivéry, *Philippe Auguste*, p. 48.
5. RH, vol. 1, pp. 520–23. On Henry's mediation and seemingly genuine wish for peace, see Baldwin, *Government of Philip Augustus*, pp. 16–17; Strickland, *Henry the Young King*, pp. 265–66.
6. Marie of Champagne (sometimes known as Marie of France, but not to be confused with her almost-contemporary, the writer and poet Marie de France) presided over a noted literary court and was the patron of, among others, Chrétien de Troyes. She ruled Champagne as regent for many years, both during her son's minority and during the absences of her husband and later her son on crusade. For more on Marie, see Evergates, *Marie of France*.
7. On the council and those present, and Isabelle's actions, see GM, p. 85. The admittedly partisan Gilbert says that 'evil plans' were formed against her by 'a council of ill-

intentioned men', but that the prayers and supplications of the poor to 'deliver her from their evil power' were successful. The dialogue between Philip and Isabelle appears in a manuscript belonging to the Bibliothèque nationale de France, BN ms. fr. 17264 (see Sivéry, *Philippe Auguste*, pp. 68–69 and 394, n. 44). For discussion of the proposed divorce and Philip's change of heart, see Sivéry, *Philippe Auguste*, pp. 68–73. For more on the little-studied Isabelle of Hainaut, see Hornaday, 'A Capetian Queen as Street Demonstrator'.

8. On the conflict over Vermandois, see *GC6*, pp. 122–26; Rigord, pp. 35–38; WB, *Vie*, pp. 196–97; Sivéry, *Philippe Auguste*, pp. 66–67; Bradbury, *Philip Augustus*, pp. 56–57; Power, *Norman Frontier*, pp. 406–11.

9. Rigord, pp. 6–7.

10. GW, p. 483.

11. Quotes from RH, vol. 2, p. 14; see also *GRH*, vol. 2, pp. 286–89.

12. Gervase, vol. 1, pp. 303–04; translation in Strickland, *Henry the Young King*, p. 272. On the reasons for the barons' offer being less than complimentary to Young Henry, see Andrews, *Lost Heirs*, pp. 57–58.

13. *HWM*, vol. 1, p. 323. On the subject of Young Henry's ambitions to rule over Aquitaine himself, see Gillingham, *Richard I*, pp. 66–67.

14. For a discussion of this point, see Favier, *Les Plantagenêts*, pp. 528–29.

15. 'What is striking is the extent to which the Young King could create a considerable chivalric reputation for himself by means of the tournament circuit, despite his conspicuously inglorious failures in war itself' (Strickland, *War and Chivalry*, p. 108).

16. *GRH*, vol. 1, p. 293; on these events and threats, see also Strickland, *Henry the Young King*, pp. 289–90; and Strickland, *War and Chivalry*, pp. 52–53, where he notes that Richard's actions had 'few parallels within the context of warfare between members of the Anglo-Norman or Frankish aristocracy' and was a 'violation of customary behaviour'.

17. RH, vol. 2, p. 24. This may have been genuine, or it may have been a ruse to trick Henry II: for a discussion on this point, see Strickland, *Henry the Young King*, pp. 297–98.

18. RH, vol. 2, p. 26.

19. On Young Henry's death, see *HWM*, vol. 1, pp. 351–55; RH, vol. 2, pp. 26–27; RT, pp. 146–47; Strickland, *Henry the Young King*, pp. 306–09. For a summary of his character, see GW, pp. 475–77.

Chapter 9

1. GW, p. 701–03.

2. *HWM*, vol. 1, p. 365.

3. On these succession plans, see Barber, *Henry Plantagenet*, pp. 212–14.

4. *GRH*, vol. 1, p. 308. See also Warren, *Henry II*, pp. 596–97; Favier, *Les Plantagenêts*, pp. 531–32.

5. RH, vol. 2, p. 25 and GW, p. 481, respectively.

6. Michael Jones, 'Geoffrey, duke of Brittany (1158–1186)', *ODNB*; Gillingham, *Richard I*, pp. 78–79.

7. GW, p. 479. Gillingham points out that seneschal of France was a post traditionally claimed by the counts of Anjou, so Geoffrey may have been publicising his ambitions in that quarter (*Richard I*, p. 80).

8. For more on this conference, see Warren, *Henry II*, p. 598.

9. *GC6*, pp. 149–50; Rigord, pp. 58–59; Nangis, p. 58.

10. On Philip's supposed overreaction (and one cannot help feeling that the companions who needed to 'hold him back' might have been strategically placed for the purpose), see GW, p. 479. Everard believes that Geoffrey may have died of illness and that the story of the tournament might therefore have been a convenient fiction to deflect attention

NOTES to pp. 110–117

from any perceived culpability. She adds that 'it would have been extremely embarrassing that an Angevin prince had fallen ill and died while a guest of the king of France' and that therefore 'a lavish show of mourning and respect was the least the Parisians and the royal court could do' (*Brittany and the Angevins*, pp. 144–45).

11. On Geoffrey's surviving family: Eleanor of Brittany had been born in 1184; there was also a second daughter, Matilda, whose date of birth is uncertain and who died in infancy (it is not clear from the surviving evidence whether this occurred before or after Geoffrey's death). Judging by the eventual date of birth, Constance must have been only in the early stages of her third pregnancy when she lost her husband.

12. RH, vol. 2, p. 61; see also Barber, *Henry Plantagenet*, p. 220; Favier, *Les Plantagenêts*, pp. 535–36.

13. GM, p. 109; *GC6*, p. 166, which notes that the whole city of Paris was filled with joy on the occasion and that the celebrations at the birth of a male heir went on for seven days and nights. No doubt some of this was due to relief – many of the older citizens would have remembered Louis VII's agonisingly long wait for a son to secure the succession.

14. On the patriarch's visit, see GW, pp. 523–27. On Henry and Philip's deliberations, see Warren, *Henry II*, pp. 604–05; Sivéry, *Philippe Auguste*, pp. 91–92. On the situation in the Holy Land, see Rigord, p. 70; Asbridge, *Crusades*, pp. 343–64; Phillips, *Holy Warriors*, pp. 126–35; Tyerman, *God's War*, pp. 354–74. On Saladin's personal execution of Renaud de Châtillon, see *Eracles*, p. 48. Saladin had been ruling Egypt since 1169 and Syria since 1176, but his name did not become well known in Europe until the events of 1187; he quickly became a popular bogeyman, and the tax that Richard and Philip would later impose to raise money for their crusade would be known as the 'Saladin tithe' (on which, see Bennett, *Elite Participation*, pp. 41–44). A recent biography of this great leader is Phillips, *Life and Legend of the Sultan Saladin*. A summary of the Battle of Hattin is Alan V. Murray, 'Hattin, Battle of', *OEMW*, vol. 2, pp. 245–46.

15. Rigord, pp. 78–79. This episode is explored in more detail in Warren, *Henry II*, pp. 610–16; Sivéry, *Philippe Auguste*, pp. 92–93.

16. Carpenter states plainly that Philip was 'unwaveringly clear' from the very start of his reign that his objective was 'to increase his power and diminish that of Henry II and his successors' (*Struggle for Mastery*, p. 243).

17. Gervase, vol. 1, p. 435; Gillingham, *Richard I*, pp. 94–95.

18. Gervase, vol. 1, pp. 435–36; *GRH*, vol. 2, p. 50; GW, pp. 609–13; *HWM*, vol. 1, pp. 413–17. See also Bradbury, *Philip Augustus*, p. 66; Warren, *Henry II*, p. 621.

19. GW, pp. 659–61; *HWM*, vol. 1, pp. 445–47. We should spare a thought at this point – as none of the principal combatants seems to have done – for the citizens of Le Mans, many of whom would have lost their homes and livelihoods through no fault of their own.

20. Henry's biographer interprets this move, rather poetically, as a sign that the king 'was weary unto death, and was going home to die' (Warren, *Henry II*, p. 625).

21. *HWM*, vol. 1, pp. 457 (quote) and 459. See also GW, pp. 665–67.

22. GW, p. 681. For details of the full terms, see RH, vol. 2, pp. 109–10.

23. *HWM*, vol. 1, pp. 461–63. On Henry II's discovery of John's perfidy, see also GW, p. 679.

24. Quote from GW, p. 683.

25. *GRH*, vol. 2, p. 71; GW, p. 695; RH, vol. 2, p. 111; RW, vol. 2, p. 76.

26. *HWM*, vol. 1, pp. 475–77. Isabel de Clare was at this point around seventeen and William Marshal in his early forties; the marriage made him, at a stroke, one of the wealthiest men in England. Nobody asked Isabel what she thought of the arrangement.

27. Rigord, pp. 83–84; Sivéry, *Philippe Auguste*, p. 96.

28. France had been the first state recognised by the Church, and the title of 'most-Christian king' was often applied to its monarchs. For more on the term and its history, see Krynen, '*Rex Christianissimus*'.

Chapter 10

1. Gerald of Wales pulls no punches in his description of the Jerusalemite royal line: 'Added to these problems was the fact that the royal stock had been almost completely exhausted and depleted by the weakness and sickness of the heirs and also by the feebleness of the female sex' (GW, p. 519).

2. Quotes from *Eracles*, p. 26 and RH, vol. 2, p. 62, respectively. For more on the history of the kings and queens of Jerusalem mentioned in this section, see Hamilton, *The Leper King and His Heirs*; for more on the specific subject of women and their role in the crusader states, see Hodgson, *Women, Crusading and the Holy Land*; Hamilton, 'Women in the Crusader States'; Pangonis, *Queens of Jerusalem*.

3. Turner, *Eleanor of Aquitaine*, pp. 246–47.

4. *HWM*, vol. 1, p. 483.

5. Diceto, vol. 2, p. 67 (translation in Turner, *Eleanor of Aquitaine*, p. 258); see also RW, vol. 2, pp. 77–78.

6. For a detailed description of the coronation ceremony itself, see *GRH*, vol. 2, pp. 80–83; RH, vol. 2, pp. 117–20. On Richard's grants to Eleanor, RH, vol. 2, p. 132.

7. RD, p. 9. For more on Richard's fundraising activities, see Gillingham, *Richard I*, pp. 114–15. On Eleanor of Aquitaine's somewhat overlooked influence on the Third Crusade, see Bennett, *Elite Participation*, pp. 112–14.

8. On Geoffrey's reluctance for this appointment, and the possibility that he may have had other ambitions, see Gillingham, *Richard I*, pp. 109–10; Warren, *King John*, p. 39.

9. *GRH*, vol. 2, pp. 104–05; RW, vol. 2, p. 88.

10. On the news of the queen's death reaching Philip while he was in conference with Richard, see Ambroise, p. 33; *IP*, p. 148 (including the quote). Childbirth was dangerous in the twelfth century, as evidenced by the many fatalities of both mothers and babies, and delivering twins was especially risky given the added complications and the fact that the births were often premature and/or the babies small. Twins occur relatively frequently in the French royal family tree, although none survived their first year until the fifteenth century, and none reached adulthood until the eighteenth; see Volkmann, *Généalogies complètes des rois de France*, which (unusually) lists all known children born to the kings and queens of France, even those who died in infancy.

11. *GC6*, p. 193.

12. For more on the details of Philip's testament, see *GC6*, pp. 187–94; Rigord, pp. 86–91; Sivéry, *Philippe Auguste*, pp. 105–09.

13. *GC6*, pp. 185–86; Rigord, pp. 84–85. Naus notes that Philip's departure ceremony and his receiving of the *oriflamme* were deliberately patterned on those of his father Louis VII in 1146 and his grandfather Louis VI in 1124 (*Constructing Kingship*, pp. 123–24).

14. *IP*, p. 151.

15. On the emperor's death, see *Eracles*, pp. 87–88; GW, pp. 653–55; GM, p. 129. For more on his long and eventful life, see Freed, *Frederick Barbarossa*.

16. RD, p. 16. For more on the contrast in style between the two kings' arrivals, see *IP*, pp. 156–57; Bradbury, *Philip Augustus*, p. 82. Baldwin notes that this continued throughout the crusade: 'At every stage he [Philip] arrived first, unobtrusively took command, and laid careful plans, only to be upstaged by the later appearance of Richard, whose greater wealth and flamboyant manner generated disturbances and raised rival objectives' (*Government of Philip Augustus*, p. 77).

17. For more details on Richard's time in Sicily, see Ambroise, pp. 37–44; *IP*, pp. 154–72.

18. RH, vol. 2, p. 165 (my emphasis); see also RW, vol. 2, p. 95; Gillingham, *Richard I*, p. 136.

19. *GRH*, vol. 2, p. 160. For discussion on this subject, see Barber, *Henry Plantagenet*, pp. 65–66 and 227. Turner gives more credence to the rumours; see his *Eleanor of Aquitaine*, pp. 235–36.

20. Gillingham, *Richard I*, p. 142. The chronicler Richard of Devizes claims that Richard enlisted the help of his cousin Philip, count of Flanders, to mediate with Philip Augustus,

noting that the count 'was a most eloquent man, with a tongue on which he set a high price' (RD, p. 26).

21. Sancho VI the Wise had been king of Navarre for forty years, attempting to bring peace to a disputed region, and he was no doubt thrilled to arrange such a prestigious match for his eldest daughter. His son, Sancho VII the Strong, who succeeded him in 1194, was a renowned warrior, so shared interests might have encouraged the two younger men to be friends on a personal level, as well as political allies. The younger Sancho's nickname and military prowess may have had something to do with the fact that he stood an astonishing 7ft 3in tall – something which sounds like it ought to be an exaggeration, but was confirmed by examination of his bones following their exhumation in the 1950s (see Del Campo, 'La estatura de Sancho el Fuerte'). Sancho VI's second daughter, Blanche, would marry Theobald III, count of Champagne (the younger brother and eventual successor of Henry II of Champagne); we will hear more of them later. For a detailed examination of the negotiations over the marriage, see Gillingham, 'Richard I and Berengaria of Navarre'.

22. For an analysis of Philip's position and probable feelings at this point, see Bradbury, *Philip Augustus*, pp. 85–86. The French chronicler Rigord puts a more positive spin on Philip's decision, claiming that he was keen to leave because he was 'burning with desire to achieve his goal' (Rigord, p. 97).

23. In line with the theme of this book, the examination of the siege of Acre that follows in this chapter will focus principally on the relationship between Philip and Richard. The siege has been analysed in depth in many publications: for the fullest treatment, see Hosler, *Siege of Acre*; see also Sean McGlynn, 'Acre, Siege of', *OEMW*, vol. 1, pp. 2–4; Tyerman, *God's War*, pp. 402–47; Asbridge, *Crusades*, pp. 398–420; Phillips, *Holy Warriors*, pp. 144–54; Favier, *Les Plantagenêts*, pp. 577–80.

24. *Eracles*, p. 94.

25. *IP*, p. 76.

26. For a fuller list of those present at the siege of Acre, see *IP*, pp. 76 and 97–98.

27. On Richard's time in Cyprus, see Ambroise, pp. 48–62; *IP*, pp. 182–95; RD, pp. 35–38; Gillingham, *Richard I*, pp. 144–54.

28. *IP*, p. 101; RH, vol. 2, p. 172. For more on Sybil's death, see Pangonis, *Queens of Jerusalem*, pp. 228–30.

29. For more on siege machinery of this period, see Fulton, *Artillery in the Age of the Crusades*; DeVries and Smith, *Medieval Military Technology*, pp. 117–36 and 165–81; Bradbury, *Medieval Siege*, pp. 241–95; Hanley, *War and Combat*, pp. 18–20. On Philip's machines at Acre, see Hosler, *Siege of Acre*, p. 110. On the role of engineers, see Purton, *The Medieval Military Engineer*.

30. *IP*, p. 192 and Ambroise, p. 58, respectively. The word 'Saracen' is now considered a racial slur and I do not use it in my own text; however, I retain it here and in other direct quotes from contemporary material, in order to show that it was in use at the time.

31. For discussion on the conflict between Guy and Conrad for the crown of Jerusalem, see Gillingham, *Richard I*, pp. 147–49.

32. Quotes from RD, p. 42 (English) and *Eracles*, p. 99 (French). Another French chronicler goes so far as to make a pun on the name *Richarz* by calling the English king '*li rois Tricharz*' (meaning 'cheat'; *GC6*, p. 199).

33. On this point, see Bradbury, *Philip Augustus*, p. 90; Hosler, *Siege of Acre*, pp. 117–18.

34. *Eracles*, p. 105.

35. WB, *Vie*, p. 207. For a possible modern diagnosis, see Bradbury, *Philip Augustus*, pp. 92–93; Sivéry, *Philippe Auguste*, pp. 116–17. An in-depth analysis may be found in Wagner and Mitchell, 'The Illnesses of King Richard and King Philippe'.

36. *Eracles*, p. 109. On Philip receiving news from Paris about Louis, see also RD, p. 48.

37. *IP*, pp. 208 (stone-throwing machines) and 210 (cat).

38. *IP*, pp. 218–21; RH, vol. 2, p. 214; Hosler, *Siege of Acre*, pp. 134–35. Hosler points out that 12 July 1191 was the 653rd day of the siege – one of the longest ever recorded (ibid., p. 133).

39. RD, pp. 46–47.

40. Quote from *IP*, p. 222.

41. Ambroise, pp. 104–05 (my emphasis); *IP* adds that Philip's decision was 'shameful' and 'outrageous' (p. 223). Quote from Rigord, p. 105; William the Breton's conclusions are similar (WB, *Vie*, p. 207).

42. *GC6*, p. 204; Rigord, pp. 100–01. For discussion of Louis's illness and recovery, see Hanley, *Louis*, pp. 17–18.

43. On the assassination and Isabella's subsequent marriage, see *Eracles*, pp. 114–16. Henry II of Champagne remained in Outremer for the rest of his life, which was not long: he was killed in an accident in 1197, when a balcony or trellis gave way beneath him and he fell from a first-floor window of the palace in Acre (Nangis, p. 81). Queen Isabella, who married again and lived until 1205, followed in the tradition of the Jerusalemite royal family by giving birth to five or six daughters, but no surviving son; she was succeeded on the throne by Maria, her daughter by Conrad of Montferrat. Henry was succeeded in Champagne by his younger brother Theobald (see note 21 in this chapter).

44. For a list of the considerable number of noble fatalities among the crusader army during the siege of Acre, which encompassed many clerics (including both the patriarch of Jerusalem and the archbishop of Canterbury), as well as numerous lords and some ladies, see RH, vol. 2, pp. 187–88. Of the French losses, Baldwin notes that Philip 'had left the major barons of his father's generation buried in the Syrian sands' (*Government of Philip Augustus*, p. 80).

45. RH, vol. 2, p. 211.

46. For more on Richard's crusade after Philip's departure, see Ambroise, pp. 106–91; *IP*, pp. 227–380; Gillingham, *Richard I*, pp. 166–221. For an in-depth discussion of the horrific massacre of prisoners at Acre, see McGlynn, *By Sword and Fire*, pp. 107–12; Hosler, *Siege of Acre*, pp. 150–57; Asbridge, *Crusades*, pp. 450–55.

47. For opposing views on Philip's crusading effectiveness from modern biographers of the two kings, see Gillingham, *Richard I*, pp. 164–66 and Bradbury, *Philip Augustus*, p. 95. Philip's pivotal role in the siege of Acre is slowly being reappraised: see the discussion in Naus, *Constructing Kingship*, pp. 124–26 and Hosler, *Siege of Acre*, pp. 162–71.

48. RH, vol. 2, p. 279. One particularly gossipy chronicler, known only as the Minstrel of Reims, gives (in his amusing but highly dramatised and fictionalised text, written in the 1260s) a story about how a minstrel named Blondel travelled from castle to castle singing a song known to him and to Richard, until one day he heard the king's voice joining in the song from inside a window (MR, pp. 41–44). In reality, the fact that Richard was being kept at Dürnstein was well known.

Chapter 11

1. RD, p. 30.

2. For more on John's activities during this period, see RD, pp. 29–35; Warren, *King John*, pp. 40–44.

3. RD, p. 80.

4. Quote from RD, p. 80. See also *GC6*, pp. 215–16; Rigord, pp. 108–09.

5. RD, pp. 60–61; *GRH*, vol. 2, pp. 236–37. See also Church, *King John: England*, p. 51; Gillingham, *Richard I*, p. 229; Turner, *Eleanor of Aquitaine*, p. 268.

6. *HWM*, vol. 1, p. 499.

7. RH, vol. 2, p. 287.

8. The thirteenth-century biographer of William Marshal notes that King Philip 'thought him [John] a fool, and completely pulled the wool over his eyes' (*HWM*, vol. 2, p. 9).

9. Mary had herself been abducted from her convent and married against her will when the county fell to her in 1159; see above, note 33 to Chapter 6.

10. Gervase, vol. 1, p. 515.

11. *Eracles*, p. 123.

12. The full text of Richard's letter appears in RH, vol. 2, pp. 290–92. See also *HWM*, vol. 1, pp. 507–09; Turner, *Eleanor of Aquitaine*, pp. 272–73; Gillingham, *Richard I*, p. 239. The full text of Eleanor's letters to the pope, both in the original Latin and in English translation, may be found on the Epistolae site at https://epistolae.ctl.columbia.edu/woman/24.html. It is in one of these missives that Eleanor famously styled herself 'by the wrath of God, Queen of the English'.

13. Gervase, vol. 1, pp. 514–15; Gillingham, *Richard I*, pp. 241–42.

14. RD, p. 59; for more on this, see Gillingham, *Richard I*, p. 230.

15. A translation of sections of the letter appears in Church, *King John: England*, pp. 55–56, citing *Layettes du Trésor des Chartes*, ed. A. Teulet, 4 vols (Paris, 1863–1902), vol. 1, no. 412. See also Rigord, pp. 114–17; Sivéry, *Philippe Auguste*, pp. 123–24; Favier, *Les Plantagenêts*, pp. 609–10.

16. RH, vol. 2, p. 297.

17. Rigord, p. 112.

18. On Ingeborg's arrival, the wedding and the immediate aftermath, see *GC6*, pp. 220–21; Rigord, pp. 112–13; RH, vol. 2, p. 304.

19. The fullest examination of Ingeborg's experiences as Philip's wife, and her struggle to retain her position, may be found in Conklin, 'Ingeborg of Denmark'. See also Sivéry (who gives more credence to possible political reasons behind Philip's decision to repudiate her), *Philippe Auguste*, pp. 193–208; Baldwin, *Government of Philip Augustus*, pp. 82–87; Bradbury, *Philip Augustus*, pp. 177–85.

20. This was to prove true: as Strickland notes, 'contemporaries were of the opinion that the wars of 1194–9 between Richard and Philip were waged with an intense animosity hitherto unseen' (*War and Chivalry*, p. 164).

21. For further discussion on this point, including possible political motives on Richard's part, see Gillingham, 'Richard I and Berengaria of Navarre'; for the dates of the couple's meetings, see Elizabeth Hallam, 'Berengaria [Berengaria of Navarre] (c. 1165–1230)', *ODNB*.

22. The sexuality debate is summarised, with references, in Gillingham, *Richard I*, pp. 263–66. In short, there was a view in the mid-twentieth century that Richard might have been homosexual, but this has been treated with less and less credence ever since. The primary misunderstanding arises from a comment by Roger of Howden that, after declaring a political alliance against Henry II in 1187, Richard and Philip Augustus shared a bed (RH, vol. 2, p. 64). However, it was common at the time for people of the same sex to share a bed, and this is meant to imply political unity, not a sexual relationship. (For an opposing view, see Trindade, *Berengaria*, pp. 59–60 and 70–76, who argues that Richard probably was either bi- or homosexual.) Richard's illegitimate son was Philip of Cognac, born sometime in the early 1180s to an unknown mother. He was alive in 1201, as a pipe roll entry of John's reign lists a payment to him in that year, but little is known of him otherwise (his portrayal in Shakespeare's play *King John* is almost entirely fictional). He was acknowledged by Richard as his son, but not raised to prominence in the same way as Henry I or Henry II's illegitimate offspring.

23. RH, vol. 2, p. 314.

24. 'John, have no fear. You are a child, and you had bad men looking after you' (*HWM*, vol. 2, p. 21). This patronising comment gives us a damning verdict on how Richard saw John, his talents (or lack thereof) and his ambitions. One of John's biographers points out that 'throughout his life so far he had been overshadowed by brothers who had made a name for themselves in the world [...] In his efforts to emulate them he had shown only caricatures of their qualities: where young Henry had been gay, he was frivolous, where Geoffrey had been cunning he was sly, where Richard was bold he was merely bombastic [...] His assumption of authority in England during Richard's absence had been a hollow mockery. He stood in 1194 as a traitor and a fool' (Warren, *King John*, p. 46).

25. Philip's gains had been substantial: 'By July 1193 the king of France had gained Arques, Drincourt, Aumale, Gournay and the whole Norman Vexin, with its fortresses of Gisors, Neaufles and Chateau-sur-Epte. By the spring of 1194 he had taken Pacy and Ivry, and Nonancourt had fallen to the count of Dreux' (Power, *Norman Frontier*, p. 414).

26. *HWM*, vol. 2, pp. 23–25; RW, vol. 2, pp. 135–36.

27. On the proposed truce and Richard's refusal to agree to it, see RH, vol. 2, p. 327. For more details of the campaigns in Normandy in 1194–96, see Gillingham, *Richard I*, pp. 283–300; Bradbury, *Philip Augustus*, pp. 114–22.

28. RH, vol. 2, p. 327.

29. *HWM*, vol. 2, pp. 31–35; RH, vol. 2, pp. 327–28. For more on this engagement, see Steven Isaac, 'Fréteval, Battle of', *OEMW*, vol. 2, pp. 138–39; Powicke, *Loss of Normandy*, pp. 152–54; Gillingham, *Richard I*, pp. 288–89; Bradbury, *Philip Augustus*, pp. 117–18. Favier notes that the loss of some of Philip's governmental documents and records at Fréteval was a factor in him deciding to make Paris the permanent home of French archives, initially based at the fortress of the Louvre (*Les Plantagenêts*, p. 616).

30. Rigord, pp. 120–21.

31. On Emperor Henry's offer, see RH, vol. 2, p. 369.

32. On the proposed Eleanor/Louis marriage, see RH, vol. 2, p. 370. For the text of the peace treaty, see Rigord, pp. 124–30.

33. The text of some of Ingeborg's letters to Celestine may be found on the Epistolae site at https://epistolae.ctl.columbia.edu/woman/68.html

34. Rigord, p. 113.

35. For more on the accession and papal rule of Innocent III, see Sayers, *Innocent III*. The new pope would prove to be much more interventionist than his predecessors in the internal politics of both England and France; Baldwin notes that Innocent 'set as his highest goal the extension of papal influence through assertion of supreme authority to judge all matters within the church's competence [. . .] These included the whole realm of matrimony, to which Philip's divorce and remarriage were an affront' (*Government of Philip Augustus*, p. 84).

36. On the details of the marriage settlement, see Gillingham, *Richard I*, p. 307.

37. Rigord, p. 129.

38. Richard's appropriation of the land led to the archbishop travelling to Rome to protest, which led in turn to an interdict being laid on Normandy, during which time 'the bodies of the dead were lying unburied throughout the lanes and streets of the cities of Normandy' (RH, vol. 2, p. 397). A financial settlement was later agreed and the interdict was lifted in April 1197.

39. For more on the construction of the castle, see Kelly DeVries, 'Château-Gaillard', *OEMW*, vol. 1, pp. 368–69; Salch (ed.), *Dictionnaire des châteaux*, pp. 32–36; Gillingham, *Richard I*, pp. 301–05.

40. RH, vol. 2, pp. 398–99; RW, vol. 2, p. 167. Baldwin IX was the brother of the late Queen Isabelle of France, and the son of Margaret, countess of Flanders in her own right, who had died in 1194.

41. On the bishop's capture, see Gervase, vol. 1, p. 544; RH, vol. 2, p. 396. Quotes from *HWM*, vol. 2, p. 65.

42. *HWM*, vol. 2, p. 81. On the significance of the phrase 'with his helmet laced' in contemporary writings, see Hanley, *War and Combat*, pp. 61–62.

43. The full text of both letters may be found in RH, vol. 2, pp. 400–03. On the bishop's capture and appeal, see also Strickland, *War and Chivalry*, pp. 47–48; Jones, *Bloodied Banners*, pp. 115–16.

44. Rigord, p. 134; WB, *Vie*, p. 214; Bradbury, *Philip Augustus*, p. 123.

45. Henry VI's death, just as he had initiated new policies and reformed the imperial administration, has been described as 'a catastrophe for Germany' (Fuhrmann, *Germany in the High Middle Ages*, p. 186). For more on the elections of 1198, see Baldwin, *Government*

of Philip Augustus, pp. 204–05; on elections in the Empire more generally, see Wilson, *Holy Roman Empire*, pp. 301–05.

46. AB, *Rois*, p. 758 and RW, vol. 2, p. 167, respectively.
47. WB, *Vie*, p. 217.
48. *GC6*, pp. 246–47; Rigord, p. 141.
49. WB, *Vie*, p. 219.
50. RH, vol. 2, p. 453.
51. On Richard's final siege and the circumstances of his death, see RH, vol. 2, pp. 452–55; Gillingham, *Richard I*, pp. 323–28.

Chapter 12

1. On Conan's rule in Brittany and his forced abdication, see Borgnis Desbordes, *Constance de Bretagne*, pp. 71–99.
2. Geoffrey's first known ducal charter records that he issued it with Constance's consent, and Constance also exercised some authority in her own name and with her own seal: see Everard, *Brittany and the Angevins*, pp. 99–100.
3. As we noted earlier (see note 11 to Chapter 9), Constance's second daughter died in infancy, but it is not clear whether this happened shortly before or shortly after Geoffrey's death.
4. On the significance of the name, see Borgnis Desbordes, *Constance de Bretagne*, pp. 260–63; Favier, *Les Plantagenêts*, p. 536; Warren, *King John*, pp. 81–82.
5. On Constance and Ranulf's married life and the lack of evidence of any cohabitation, see Everard, *Brittany and the Angevins*, pp. 157–58.
6. On Eleanor's journey and Leopold's death, see RH, vol. 2, pp. 345–47. Leopold's end was a gruesome one. While out riding he suffered a fall, and the horse rolled over his foot, crushing it so badly that broken and splintered bones projected through the skin. The wounds became infected and he knew that the foot would need to be amputated if his life were to be saved, but he could not find anyone willing to perform the operation. In the end he held an axe against his leg himself, while instructing a servant to hit it with a hammer. The foot was severed, but it was too late: the blood poisoning had already spread, and he died the following day. The same writer attributes Leopold's painful demise to God's punishment for imprisoning a crusader (ibid., p. 347).
7. On this incident, see Borgnis Desbordes, *Constance de Bretagne*, pp. 325–27; Gillingham, *Richard I*, pp. 297–98; Bradbury, *Philip Augustus*, pp. 119–20.
8. On Louis's household at this time, see Hanley, *Louis*, pp. 22–23 and 30–33.
9. Both Constance's and Arthur's biographers support this view: see Borgnis Desbordes, *Constance de Bretagne*, pp. 335–37; Michael Jones, 'Arthur, duke of Brittany (1187–1203)', *ODNB*.
10. See, for example, the formulation *cum assensu et bona voluntate Arturi filii mei* (Constance, p. 67); and also similar wording in other charters in ibid., pp. 64, 66, 72 and 73.
11. Jones, 'Arthur, duke of Brittany', *ODNB*; see also Andrews, *Lost Heirs*, p. 65.
12. One chronicler noted that 'when the king was now in despair of surviving, he devised to his brother John the kingdom of England and all his other territories' (RH, vol. 2, p. 453), though others do not mention it. The legal situation of the claimants is discussed in depth in Holt, 'King John and Arthur of Brittany'; see also Borgnis Desbordes, *Constance de Bretagne*, pp. 381–88. The only contemporary who states explicitly that John's accession was an 'injustice' because 'Arthur should have succeeded Richard, because he was the son of John's elder brother' is William the Breton (WB, *Philippide*, p. 149). Given his place of origin, it is perhaps not surprising that he should take the part of the duke of Brittany.
13. *HWM*, vol. 2, p. 93. The rest of this conversation and the quotes from it are in ibid., pp. 93–97.

14. *GC6*, p. 251; RH, vol. 2, p. 455.
15. RH, vol. 2, p. 456.
16. RW, vol. 2, p. 180.
17. RH, vol. 2, pp. 462–63; RW, vol. 2, pp. 182–83. Church points out that Philip's knighting of Arthur was a snub to John, as Arthur was his nephew and the heir to the lands that John claimed (Church, *King John: England*, p. 72).
18. On Eleanor's activities during this period, see Turner, *Eleanor of Aquitaine*, pp. 282–86.
19. D.S.H. Abulafia, 'Joanna [Joan, Joanna of England], countess of Toulouse (1165–1199)', *ODNB*; see also Turner, *Eleanor of Aquitaine*, pp. 285–86. Caesarean sections were not unknown in the Middle Ages, but they were carried out only when the mother had died, in the hope that the child might survive, or at least survive long enough to be baptised. On this subject, see Bednarski and Courtemanche, '"Sadly, and with a Bitter Heart": What the Caesarean Section Meant in the Middle Ages'.
20. See Warren, *King John*, p. 53.
21. The circumstances of Constance's remarriage are discussed by Borgnis Desbordes, who tends towards some complex political explanations (*Constance de Bretagne*, pp. 418–22), and by Michael Jones, who says the union with Guy was 'a move probably designed to widen her political contacts, but which also brought her considerable personal happiness' ('Constance, duchess of Brittany (1161–1201)', *ODNB*).
22. RH, vol. 2, p. 464; RW, vol. 2, p. 183. See also Gillingham, *Richard I*, p. 337. On John's reputation for treachery more generally, see Favier, *Les Plantagenêts*, pp. 654–55.
23. RH, vol. 2, p. 462.
24. One of Philip's biographers goes so far as to say that the treaty 'was a recognition of Philip's strength' (Bradbury, *Philip Augustus*, p. 133).
25. The text of the treaty appears in Rigord, pp. 148–53; see also Powicke, *Loss of Normandy*, pp. 200–05. John does not appear to have consulted either Alfonso or Eleanor before arranging Blanche's marriage.
26. Eleanor outlived eight of her ten children, having lost William in 1155 (the only instance of infant mortality in either of her families), Henry in 1183, Geoffrey in 1186, Matilda in 1189, Marie and Alix in 1198, and Richard and Joanna in 1199. The younger Eleanor would survive until 1214, by which time she had endured the loss of a number of her own children.
27. WB, *Philippide*, p. 152. William was, of course, writing in hindsight, in the knowledge that Blanche would go on to play a great role for the French monarchy; but still, this is one of very few descriptions of women or girls, and one of even fewer that mention character and do not simply note conventionally that a woman was 'noble' or 'beautiful'.
28. See Church, *King John: England*, pp. 81–82; Warren, *King John*, p. 66. John retained for himself the right to dispose of Isabelle's estates and would later grant the earldom of Gloucester to her nephew Amaury, count of Évreux, who had lost out under the terms of the Treaty of Le Goulet: his lands had been among those conquered by Philip Augustus that Philip was to keep.
29. There has been much speculation over the years on the reasons for John's marriage to Isabella, including some suggestions that he fell in love (or in lust) with her at first sight, despite her age; but there seems little real doubt that his motives were political, rather than personal. For accounts set in the relevant historical context, see Vincent, 'Isabella of Angoulême'; Church, *King John: England*, pp. 82–92; Warren, *King John*, pp. 67–69. On the question of Isabella's age, contemporaries noted that she looked about twelve, but this may only have been because that was the lowest canonically accepted age for adult marriage; she might actually have been younger. It is unlikely that she was much older than twelve, given that her last child was born more than thirty years later.
30. For more on the Lusignans' appeal and the decision of Philip and his council of barons to deprive John of his lands, see Bradbury, *Philip Augustus*, pp. 135–36 and 140–43; Warren, *King John*, pp. 73–76.

31. Constance was forty, which even at the time was not considered particularly elderly. Curiously, contemporary sources disagree as to whether her death was due to childbirth or leprosy; for a discussion on this point, see Borgnis Desbordes, *Constance de Bretagne*, pp. 436–38 and n. 200.

32. The written notification of Arthur's homage to Philip in 1202 may be found in Constance, pp. 131–32.

33. AB, *Dukes*, p. 106.

34. AB, *Dukes*, p. 107.

35. For a thorough discussion of this engagement and the sources for it, see McGlynn, *Blood Cries Afar*, pp. 36–40. Some of the less important Poitevin prisoners were shipped over the Channel to imprisonment in the dungeons of Corfe castle, where they were kept in such harsh conditions that they attempted a desperate break-out. They were surrounded and their food supplies cut off until they surrendered; they refused, and twenty-two of them starved to death as a result (Margam, p. 26).

36. For more on the details of Eleanor's captivity, see Michael Jones, 'Eleanor of Brittany, 1182x4–1241', *ODNB*; Andrews, *Lost Heirs*, p. 74.

37. RW, vol. 2, p. 205 ('disappeared'); RC, pp. 139–41 (blinded) and 145 (drowned).

38. WB, *Philippide*, pp. 173–74.

39. Margam, p. 27.

40. For a detailed analysis of all the contemporary sources for Arthur's death, see Powicke, *Loss of Normandy*, pp. 453–81. See also the chapter on Arthur and Eleanor in Andrews, *Lost Heirs*, pp. 62–74; Church, *King John: England*, pp. 108–11; Warren, *King John*, pp. 81–84; Jones, 'Arthur, duke of Brittany', *ODNB*.

41. RW, vol. 2, p. 206.

42. One of Philip's biographers points out that towards the latter stages of the John/ Arthur conflict 'he began to think in terms of the destruction or diminution rather than simply the containment of the Plantagenets' (Bradbury, *Philip Augustus*, p. 137).

43. For more on Baldwin and the extraordinary events of his later life, see Wolff, 'Baldwin of Flanders and Hainaut'. The Fourth Crusade does not form part of our tale here; for details, see (among many other works) Phillips, *The Fourth Crusade*; Queller and Madden, *The Fourth Crusade*; Phillips, *Holy Warriors*, pp. 166–96; Asbridge, *Crusades*, pp. 526–32.

Chapter 13

1. On the subject of various Angevin and Poitevin barons giving homage to Philip at Easter 1203, see Church, *King John: England*, p. 112; Baldwin, *Government of Philip Augustus*, p. 192; Favier, *Les Plantagenêts*, pp. 667–68. On the unrest in Brittany, see Power, *Norman Frontier*, pp. 440–42. McGlynn notes that John's 'crass insensitivity' towards the Lusignans illustrated his 'hopeless inability to manage people or inspire them to place their confidence in him as their lord' (*Blood Cries Afar*, p. 33).

2. *Dialogus*, p. 1.

3. For a discussion of John's finances in the opening years of his reign, with regard to military expenditure, see Warren, *King John*, pp. 58–63, who notes that 'Normandy was crippled by expenditure on defence [...] In plain fact, Normandy was bankrupted by the tasks Richard imposed on it, and only credit operations and the flow of English silver averted collapse' (p. 63).

4. On the territorial gains, see Power, *Norman Frontier*, p. 423. Favier calculates that Philip had increased his revenues by 72 per cent in the two decades since his accession (*Les Plantagenêts*, p. 666). For details of the funds Philip had available to make war on John, see Carpenter, *Struggle for Mastery*, pp. 266–68. A detailed examination of Philip's finances at various points in his reign may be found in Baldwin, *Government of Philip Augustus*, pp. 45–58, 144–75, 239–48 and 351–54; see also Barratt, 'Revenues of John and Philip Augustus'.

5. The full letter is available on the Epistolae site at https://epistolae.ctl.columbia.edu/letter/24140.html. For more on Philip's sham gesture, see Bradbury, *Philip Augustus*, pp. 184–85.
6. Innocent, p. 62 (to John) and p. 59 (to Philip).
7. WB, *Philippide*, pp. 159–61. See also Powicke, *Loss of Normandy*, pp. 221–22.
8. *HWM*, vol. 2, p. 131. For a discussion on the loss of Alençon and the loyalties of the count, see Power, *Norman Frontier*, pp. 438–40.
9. For more details on this short campaign, see Powicke, *Loss of Normandy*, pp. 235–36; Warren, *King John*, p. 86.
10. On the surrender of Vaudreuil, see RW, vol. 2, p. 207; Warren, *King John*, p. 86; McGlynn, *Blood Cries Afar*, p. 40.
11. GW, p. 671.
12. WB, *Philippide*, pp. 178–79. See also the description of the fortifications above, in Chapter 11. William the Breton's account of the siege of Château Gaillard is unsurprisingly the fullest (see WB, *Philippide*, pp. 176–210; WB, *Vie*, pp. 222–23 and 226–34), and what follows here is largely compiled from those passages – we will not reference each individual event separately. The siege also features in passing in the writings of Rigord (p. 164), Roger of Wendover (RW, vol. 2, pp. 207–08 and 213–14), the Anonymous of Béthune (AB, *Dukes*, pp. 109–11), and (in a highly dramatised account) the Minstrel of Reims (MR, pp. 136–40). Late-nineteenth- and early-twentieth-century interpretations may be found in Oman, *Art of War*, vol. 2, pp. 33–36, and Powicke, *Loss of Normandy*, pp. 374–77. The most detailed modern account and analysis is McGlynn, *Blood Cries Afar*, pp. 42–59; see also Laurence Marvin, 'Château-Gaillard, Siege of', *OEMW*, vol. 1, pp. 370–71; Warner, *Sieges of the Middle Ages*, pp. 124–34; Bradbury, *Philip Augustus*, pp. 146–50; Favier, *Les Plantagenêts*, pp. 674–76. A useful pictorial representation, showing the successive phases of combat, is Bennett et al., *Fighting Techniques*, pp. 194–95.
13. For more on the appalling plight of these poor souls (the details are not for the faint-hearted), see WB, *Philippide*, pp. 197–201; WB, *Vie*, pp. 231–32; McGlynn, *Blood Cries Afar*, pp. 49–55; McGlynn, *By Sword and Fire*, pp. 164–70.
14. *HWM*, vol. 2, p. 141.
15. WB, *Philippide*, p. 201.
16. AB, *Dukes*, p. 114; MR, pp. 138 and 140. Another chronicler notes de Lacy's 'prowess and incomparable fidelity' during the siege (RW, vol. 2, p. 208).
17. Church (*King John*, p. 113) notes 'the authority of a king enforcing the confiscation of the lands of a vassal who had refused to obey him [...] Philip was not making an unprovoked attack against a fellow ruler, he was punishing a vassal deserving of punishment, and asserting his rule over lands that were rightfully his.'
18. WB, *Vie*, p. 234; WB, *Philippide*, p. 213.
19. For more on Guy's activities at this point, see WB, *Vie*, pp. 235–36; Favier, *Les Plantagenêts*, pp. 671–72; McGlynn, *Blood Cries Afar*, pp. 60–61; Warren, *King John*, p. 97; Bradbury, *Philip Augustus*, p. 152.
20. RW, vol. 2, p. 214.
21. On Eleanor's death and posthumous reputation, see Turner, *Eleanor of Aquitaine*, pp. 295–98 and 299–313, respectively; see also Favier, *Les Plantagenêts*, pp. 676–78 and Martindale, 'Eleanor of Aquitaine: The Last Years'.

Part III

Chapter 14

1. AB, *Dukes*, p. 116.
2. For a discussion on this point, see Bartlett, *England under the Norman and Angevin Kings*, where he calculates that all of the kings since the Conquest had spent more than half

their time out of England, with the exception of Stephen, who, like John, was 'beaten out of his domains in northern France'. He concludes that 'the pattern is obvious. The only kings of England to spend prolonged periods in England were the military failures' (pp. 12–13).

3. Quotes from HH, p. 70 and *Dialogus*, p. 53, respectively. For further discussion on this point, see Gillingham, *The English in the Twelfth Century*, pp. 128–31 and 140–42.

4. On John's activities in the year following his retreat from Normandy, see Warren, *King John*, pp. 100–11; Church, *King John: England*, pp. 125–36.

5. Gervase, vol. 2, pp. 96–98.

6. For details on individual lords and families, see Power, 'King John and the Norman Aristocracy'.

7. *HWM*, vol. 2, pp. 145–61 *passim*.

8. We should note that the question of magnates holding lands in both realms did rumble on for several more decades: as late as 1244 Louis IX told his lords who held lands on both sides of the Channel that 'as it is impossible that any man living in my kingdom, and having possessions in England, can competently serve two masters, he must either inseparably attach himself to me or to the king of England' (MP, vol. 1, p. 481).

9. Louis and Blanche lost four of their twelve children, including a set of twins, in early infancy, and another three between the ages of nine and thirteen; for more details on their family, see Sivéry, *Louis VIII*, pp. 348–52; Hanley, *Louis*, pp. 209–12.

10. Shadis believes that Alfonso's claim was 'unlikely' and that he was probably 'taking shrewd advantage of John's disinterest in and difficulties with maintaining his continental lands' (*Berenguela of Castile*, p. 31). See also Carpenter, *Struggle for Mastery*, p. 266.

11. RW, vol. 2, p. 219.

12. For more on John's campaign of 1206, see RW, vol. 2, pp. 218–19; AB, *Dukes*, p. 118; Warren, *King John*, pp. 116–20; Church, *King John: England*, pp. 141–43; McGlynn, *Blood Cries Afar*, pp. 82–84. The text of the truce may be found in Rigord, pp. 174–77.

13. See Shadis, *Berenguela of Castile*, pp. 31–32.

14. Innocent, pp. 48 and 50–51.

15. Innocent, p. 53.

16. For more on the election following Hubert Walter's death, see Knowles, 'The Canterbury Election of 1205–6'; on clerical elections in England during John's reign more generally, see Cheney, *Pope Innocent III and England*, pp. 121–78; on John's role and his antagonism towards the appointment of Stephen Langton, see Warren, *King John*, pp. 159–63; on Langton and his life, see Christopher Holdsworth, 'Langton, Stephen (c. 1150–1228)' *ODNB*.

17. Innocent, pp. 89–90.

18. Barnwell, vol. 2, p. 199.

19. The pope wrote in a letter of May 1208 to the bishops of London, Ely and Worcester that 'because the king has refused to submit to sound counsels, granting neither liberty to the Church nor paying meet respect and due honour to the archbishop [Stephen Langton]' they were commanded to 'cause the sentence of Interdict [. . .] to be inviolably observed without appeal', 'allowing no ecclesiastical office to be celebrated [in England] except the baptism of infants and the confession of the dying' (Innocent, p. 103). In 1209, he noted that John had been 'adding transgression to transgression' by his 'repeated outrages' and that the bishops should therefore 'publicly and solemnly pronounce sentence of excommunication on John, king of the English' (ibid., pp. 115 and 123). See also RW, vol. 2, pp. 245–47 and 250–51; Warren, *King John*, pp. 168–73; Webster, *King John and Religion*, pp. 154–61.

20. Innocent's full letter to Ingeborg may be found on the Epistolae site at https:// epistolae.ctl.columbia.edu/letter/442.html

21. On Philip's governance in Normandy during the first years after he gained it, see Bradbury, *Philip Augustus*, pp. 274–78; Sivéry, *Philippe Auguste*, pp. 183–87. On the Norman exchequer, see Baldwin, *Government of Philip Augustus*, pp. 418–20.
22. Louis VI had been around twenty-seven at the time of his accession in 1108; as we have seen, Louis VII was seventeen and Philip Augustus just fifteen when they became sole king in 1137 and 1180 respectively.
23. For a discussion on the possible reasons why Philip chose not to have his heir crowned, see Hanley, *Louis*, pp. 35–36.
24. See AB, *Rois*, pp. 764–65; Sivéry, *Louis VIII*, pp. 86–88, Hanley, *Louis*, pp. 41–42.
25. WB, *Vie*, pp. 251–53; GC6, pp. 301–02. For more on the complex reasons for Renaud's break with King Philip, see Baldwin, *Government of Philip Augustus*, pp. 201–02. In Francophone scholarship, opinions vary on John's personal success or otherwise in forming a coalition hostile to Philip; for an analysis calling it a 'brilliant diplomatic coup', see Menant et al., *Les Capétiens*, pp. 303–04; for an evaluation focusing on 'John's errors', see Favier, *Les Plantagenêts*, pp. 691–98.
26. The unfortunate Beatrice is one of many women and girls who led fascinating lives and/or met tragic ends, while making only the most fleeting impression on contemporary (male) chroniclers or on official records. At the time her father was murdered she was ten years old; she lost her mother only weeks later when the pregnant widow fled, miscarried and died. At the age of eleven, Beatrice was betrothed to the thirty-four-year-old Otto; they married three years later, only for her to die of unspecified causes just nineteen days after the wedding, at the age of fourteen.
27. WB, *Vie*, p. 250; GC6, p. 299. For more on the meeting, see Baldwin, *Government of Philip Augustus*, pp. 205–06; Hanley, *Louis*, pp. 42–43. For more on the life and extraordinary career of Frederick II, see Abulafia, *Frederick II*; Kantorowicz, *Frederick the Second*.
28. On Ingeborg's restoration as queen, see Sivéry, *Philippe Auguste*, pp. 221–23; see also Conklin, 'Ingeborg of Denmark'.
29. Innocent, p. 142.
30. RW, vol. 2, p. 259
31. AB, *Dukes*, p. 126. On the question of whether Pope Innocent actually deposed John and commissioned Philip to invade England in so many words, or whether this was merely Philip's interpretation of events or indeed a fabrication, see Cheney, 'The Alleged Deposition of King John'.
32. WB, *Vie*, p. 256; AB, *Dukes*, p. 126; Favier, *Les Plantagenêts*, pp. 700–01.
33. RW, vol. 2, pp. 261–62.
34. The Cinque Ports were Hastings, Dover, Hythe, Romney and Sandwich, and their obligation dated from the time of William the Conqueror; he had required from them the naval equivalent of the military service owed by his other English vassals. On John's navy-building and his use of ships at this time, see Rose, *England's Medieval Navy*, pp. 35–36 and 44–45; Stanton, *Medieval Maritime Warfare*, pp. 227–30; Warren, *King John*, pp. 120–25.
35. For more on Eustace the Monk, see D.A. Carpenter, 'Eustace the Monk (c. 1170–1217)', *ODNB*. Eustace is also the subject of a medieval romance text – the tales in it are so embroidered that 'biography' is probably not the right word – see *Eustace*, pp. 50–78 (quote from p. 76).
36. Barnwell, vol. 2, p. 210; translation in McGlynn, *Blood Cries Afar*, p. 73. A transcription of the letters patent by which John made this agreement appears in RW, vol. 2, pp. 265–70.
37. Quotes from AB, *Dukes*, p. 129; the form of greeting in the pope's letter is in Innocent, p. 149. See also Warren, *King John*, pp. 206–10; Church, *King John: England*, pp. 198–201; Webster, *King John and Religion*, pp. 161–65.
38. RW, vol. 2, p. 271; on this episode, see also Favier, *Les Plantagenêts*, pp. 702–05.
39. *HWM*, vol. 2, p. 233; see also RW, vol. 2, pp. 272–73; Sivéry, *Philippe Auguste*, pp. 263–67; Warren, *King John*, pp. 204–05; Hanley, *Louis*, pp. 49–51.

Chapter 15

1. On military service and the composition of armies, see, among others, Contamine, *War in the Middle Ages*, pp. 77–90; France, *Western Warfare*, pp. 128–38; Housley, 'European Warfare'. On the barons of 1214 avoiding scutage payments, see Warren, *King John*, p. 225; Holt, *Northerners*, pp. 18–20 and 98–102.
2. *HWM*, vol. 2, p. 237. Carpenter notes that Marshal's 'refusal to go on the 1206 campaign shows how right John was to force a choice on everyone else' (*Struggle for Mastery*, p. 269)
3. The text of the treaty between John and Hugh may be found in WB, *Vie*, pp. 262–65.
4. On this early part of John's campaign, see RW, vol. 2, pp. 293–95 (quote pp. 294–95); Warren, *King John*, pp. 217–21; Baldwin, *Government of Philip Augustus*, pp. 213–14.
5. On Robert's capture and the events at Nantes, see WB, *Vie*, pp. 265–66; WB, *Philippide*, pp. 285–87; *GC6*, pp. 314–15; AB, *Dukes*, pp. 141–42.
6. 'Philip has in the past been given the reputation of a wily, rather tricky manipulator, timid, even cowardly', writes one of his more revisionist biographers. But 'if Philip was such a feeble, unpleasant figure, how did he keep so many men loyal to him, and how did he win the greatest battle of his age?' The answer is that Philip, while not 'a perfect human being' was 'an effective and able king, a warrior and leader as well as a diplomat and administrator' (Bradbury, *Philip Augustus*, p. 279).
7. WB, *Philippide*, pp. 293–94; AB, *Rois*, p. 767.
8. On the siege of and engagement at La-Roche-aux-Moines, from differing points of view, see WB, *Vie*, pp. 270–73; WB, *Philippide*, pp. 290–97; *GC6*, pp. 320–24; Nangis, pp. 112–13; AB, *Dukes*, p. 142; Sivéry, *Louis VIII*, pp. 121–26; Sivéry, *Philippe Auguste*, pp. 271–74; Favier, *Les Plantagenêts*, pp. 708–11; Hanley, *Louis*, pp. 55–56; McGlynn, *Blood Cries Afar*, pp. 96–100; Bradbury, *Philip Augustus*, pp. 293–95.
9. MR, p. 146.
10. RW, vol. 2, p. 299.
11. Count Theobald VI of Blois had succeeded his father Louis I in 1205, after the latter's death on the Fourth Crusade. He had campaigned against the Muslims in Castile and contracted leprosy while he was there; he returned home to a self-imposed isolation and died childless in 1218, at which point the direct male line of Blois ceased. Thomas, who was probably around eighteen, had inherited Perche at the age of seven after the death of his father Count Geoffrey III, Philip Augustus's first cousin; Thomas's mother was Richenza of Saxony, who was Otto's sister and King John's niece.
12. The literature on Guérin is unfortunately almost non-existent. One rather obscure work is Dufresne, *Mémoires pour servir à l'histoire du chancelier Guérin*; see also information at various points in Baldwin, *Government of Philip Augustus*, pp. 115–18, 215–19 (on Guérin's service at Bouvines) and 413–18. William the Breton's two narratives (*Vie*, pp. 274–92 and *Philippide*, pp. 299–349) are the major primary source for the Battle of Bouvines. What follows is largely based on his accounts, with support from RW, vol. 2, pp. 299–302; *GC6*, pp. 326–54; AB, *Rois*, pp. 767–70; MR, pp. 146–51; Nangis, pp. 113–15.
13. Contemporary medieval chroniclers are notorious for their exaggeration of troop numbers (often inflating the number of the enemy and minimising their own, in order to claim a greater victory or a more heroic loss). These figures are based on the calculations in McGlynn, *Blood Cries Afar*, p. 107 and Verbruggen, *Art of Warfare*, pp. 223–29. See also the appendix on 'Knight Service at Bouvines' in Baldwin, *Government of Philip Augustus*, pp. 450–53.
14. RW, vol. 2, p. 300.
15. WB, *Philippide*, p. 323.
16. WB, *Philippide*, pp. 325 and 327–28.
17. WB, *Philippide*, p. 342.
18. WB, *Philippide*, p. 333 (height and helm) and 344 (courage in rearguard action).
19. The Battle of Bouvines is a pivotal moment in the history of France and England, and of western Europe in the Middle Ages. The most in-depth analysis may be found in two

dedicated books: Duby, *Le dimanche de Bouvines*, and Barthélemy, *La bataille de Bouvines*; details may also be found in John France, 'Bouvines, Battle of', *OEMW*, vol. 1, pp. 163–65; Sivéry, *Philippe Auguste*, pp. 278–94; Bradbury, *Philip Augustus*, pp. 295–311; Baldwin, *Government of Philip Augustus*, pp. 215–19; McGlynn, *Blood Cries Afar*, pp. 102–17; France, *Western Warfare*, pp. 235–41; Oman, *Art of War*, vol. 1, pp. 467–90. A pictorial representation, showing the deployment of the different troops, is Bennett et al., *Fighting Techniques*, pp. 118–19. Perhaps the most succinct summary of the battle's international impact is that of Carpenter: 'In Germany it undermined Otto and set up Frederick II. In Normandy it ended the chance of Angevin recovery. In Europe it made King Philip supreme. In England it shattered John's authority and paved the way for Magna Carta' (*Struggle for Mastery*, p. 286).
20. MR, p. 151.
21. On the prisoner exchange, see AB, *Dukes*, p. 143.

Chapter 16

1. *Dialogus*, p. 96. Despite there being no fixed amount, reliefs were by established custom supposed to be 'just and legitimate'; the *Dialogus* mentions the sum of £5 per knight's fee (ibid.) and a reasonable relief for an earl – at a time when an earldom might be expected to bring an income of between £200 and £400 per annum – was around £100. John routinely demanded sums far in excess of this; see the discussion in Warren, *King John*, pp. 183–84.
2. On Geoffrey de Mandeville, see Warren, *King John*, pp. 182–83. The fate of Matilda de Briouze seems barely credible, but the death by starvation of a noblewoman was such a heinous event that it was related in detail by all the major chroniclers: see RW, vol. 2, p. 255; Warren, *King John*, pp. 185–87 and Warren's list of sources that mention Matilda's death on p. 314 (at note 3 for p. 187). An analysis of the feelings and actions of the barons throughout this period of unrest is Crouch, 'Baronial Paranoia in King John's Reign'.
3. For more on Peter's actions during the time he was left as John's regent, see Vincent, *Peter des Roches*, pp. 89–113.
4. McGlynn notes that Falkes's relationship with John was 'not built on respect but on the surer foundations of money and reward' (*Blood Cries Afar*, p. 141). For more on Falkes, see D.J. Power, 'Bréauté, Sir Falkes de (d. 1226)', *ODNB*, who notes that in his service to John, Falkes 'soon demonstrated his ruthless and dauntless character, as well as his unquestioning loyalty to the Angevin kings, earning the lasting hatred of barons and monastic chroniclers alike'.
5. On Henry I's charter and its importance to the barons, see RW, vol. 2, pp. 303–04; Warren, *King John*, pp. 226–28; Church, *King John: England*, pp. 215–16. The full text of the charter is given in RW, vol. 2, pp. 276–78 and *SECH*, pp. 46–48. A summary of the barons' grievances is given by McGlynn: 'These wrongs included being denied privileges and rights; having castles, lands and offices withheld without justification; corrupted justice and extortionate fines; excessive, punitive, royal debt collection; the favouritism towards foreigners; personal affronts to family and honour; exorbitant demands for failed military campaigns; and the sheer arbitrariness of a vindictive royal will' (*Blood Cries Afar*, p. 130).
6. Innocent, p. 194.
7. Innocent, p. 196.
8. For discussion of the Articles of the Barons, see Church, *King John: England*, pp. 22–24.
9. RW, vol. 2, pp. 306–07; McGlynn, *Blood Cries Afar*, pp. 134–35.
10. RW, vol. 2, pp. 307–08.
11. The earl of Arundel was the grandson of Queen Adeliza, widow of Henry I, who had married the 1st earl, another William d'Aubigny, after the king's death. Ranulf de

Blundeville was the earl of Chester who had once been married to Constance of Brittany (see above, Chapters 9 and 12). William de Warenne's father had been Hamelin of Anjou, the illegitimate half-brother of Henry II whose birth we noted in Chapter 3. Hamelin had been awarded the hand in marriage of the heiress Isabel de Warenne and became earl of Surrey in right of his wife; his descendants were thus known by the name Warenne, in keeping with origins of the earldom.

12. RW, vol. 2, pp. 308–24; see also AB, *Dukes*, pp. 143–48. The details of Magna Carta do not form part of our story here, but there is a wealth of information and analysis available. See, in particular, Carpenter, *Magna Carta*; see also Holt, *Magna Carta*; Holt, *Northerners*, pp. 109–28; Danziger and Gillingham, *1215: The Year of Magna Carta*; the essays in Loengard (ed.), *Magna Carta and the England of King John*; the Magna Carta project at https://magnacartaresearch.org. For a Francophone view, see Favier, *Les Plantagenêts*, pp. 723–26. The full text of the charter may be found in *SECH*, pp. 115–26.

13. Innocent, p. 216. See also AB, *Dukes*, p. 148; RW, vol. 2, pp. 325–34.

14. AB, *Rois*, p. 770.

15. AB, *Dukes*, pp. 149–50; RW, vol. 2, pp. 336–37.

16. Barnwell, vol. 2, p. 226.

17. For more on the siege of Rochester, see RW, vol. 2, pp. 335–39 (quote p. 338); AB, *Dukes*, pp. 152–55; McGlynn, *Blood Cries Afar*, pp. 143–48; Steven Isaac, 'Rochester, Siege of (1215)', *OEMW*, vol. 3, pp. 182–83; Humphrys, *Enemies at the Gate*, pp. 45–49.

18. The Albigensian Crusade will not be examined in detail here; for more on the conflict, see (among other works) Pegg, *A Most Holy War*; Oldenbourg, *Massacre at Montségur*; McGlynn, *Kill Them All*; Roquebert, *Histoire des Cathares*. Primary sources available in English translation are WP, PVC and *SCW*. On Simon de Montfort, see the early chapters of the biography of his son and namesake: Ambler, *Song of Simon de Montfort*. I refrain from giving him a number, because he is known both as Simon IV and Simon V and I have no wish to introduce additional confusion. On Louis's sporadic involvement in the ongoing war, see Hanley, *Louis*, pp. 45–46, 75, 182–90, 213–22. Philip, bishop of Beauvais, would die in 1217, in his late sixties; despite all his warring, his death appears to have been due to natural causes.

19. On the force of 120 knights, see AB, *Dukes*, p. 155. On the death of Geoffrey de Mandeville, see ibid., p. 157; AB, *Rois*, p. 770.

20. For details of the discussions at the Assembly of Melun, see RW, vol. 2, pp. 362–65; Hanley, *Louis*, pp. 77–85; Sivéry, *Louis VIII*, pp. 148–53. Interestingly, nobody at all seems to have raised the point that Louis was himself a direct descendant of William the Conqueror, via his paternal grandmother Adela of Blois.

21. RW, vol. 2, p. 362.

22. WB, *Vie*, p. 321; MR, p. 153; AB, *Rois*, p. 770.

23. On the number of men in the host, see Hanley, *Louis*, pp. 86–87. AB, *Dukes*, pp. 158–60 gives a list of names.

24. Church, 'The Earliest English Muster Roll'. See also McGlynn, *Blood Cries Afar*, p. 150, who notes that 'the conflict was never simply a matter of English against the French'.

25. RC, p. 178.

26. RW, vol. 2, pp. 350–51 (quote p. 351).

27. RW, vol. 2, p. 351. For the details of John's campaign in the north during the winter of 1215–16, see AB, *Dukes*, pp. 155–57; McGlynn, *Blood Cries Afar*, pp. 153–56; Warren, *King John*, pp. 249–51. On the atrocities, see McGlynn, *By Sword and Fire*, pp. 222–33.

28. Vincent, *Peter des Roches*, pp. 153–54.

29. On Louis's arrival in England, see Hanley, *Louis*, pp. 89–90; Sivéry, *Louis VIII*, pp. 155–56.

30. AB, *Dukes*, p. 163; Guala, pp. xli and 43–44.

31. On Louis's actions following his arrival in London, see RW, vol. 2, pp. 364–65; Hanley, *Louis*, pp. 95–100.
32. RW, vol. 2, p. 364 and WB, *Vie*, p. 324, respectively.

Chapter 17

1. On the pivotal importance of coronations at this time, see Andrews, *Lost Heirs*, p. 8; Hanley, *Louis*, pp. 243–46. The difference between being crowned or not, regardless of heredity or acclamation, is why Robert Curthose, Empress Matilda, and Arthur and Eleanor of Brittany were never considered by contemporaries to have been monarchs, while Henry the Young King was.
2. As we noted earlier (see note 23 to Chapter 6), following the dispute over the coronation of Henry the Young King in 1170, Pope Alexander III had in 1171 issued a papal bull, *Quanto majorem*, stating that the sole right to conduct coronations in England was henceforward to be invested only in archbishops of Canterbury.
3. For more on Louis's strategic error in declining coronation at this point, see Hanley, *Louis*, pp. 97–100.
4. AB, *Dukes*, pp. 165–66.
5. For more details on Louis's military campaign across the south coast of England between May and July 1216, see AB, *Dukes*, pp. 164–68; RW, vol. 2, pp. 365–66; McGlynn, *Blood Cries Afar*, pp. 170–73; Hanley, *Louis*, pp. 101–07; Sivéry, *Louis VIII*, pp. 160–62.
6. According to Carpenter's calculations, of the 133 baronies in England, the holders of 36 remained loyal to John, while 97 had gone over to Louis; of the 27 greatest lords, eight were for John and nineteen for Louis (*Minority of Henry III*, p. 19).
7. On Louis's attempts at governance in England, see Sivéry, *Louis VIII*, pp. 168–78.
8. On John's activities during this period, see RW, vol. 2, pp. 376–78; McGlynn, *Blood Cries Afar*, pp. 180–83.
9. On the extent of the loss in the Wash, and discussion of the incident, see RC, p. 184; RW, vol. 2, p. 378; Warren, *King John*, p. 254.
10. The full text of this letter (in untranslated Latin) may be found in Guala, pp. 105–06.
11. On John's death, see RW, vol. 2, pp. 377–79; HWM, vol. 2, pp. 259–63; Warren, *King John*, pp. 254–56 (text of the will on p. 255); Church, *King John: England*, pp. 246–49; Church, 'King John's Testament and the Last Days of his Reign'.
12. GW, p. 703.
13. The literal English translation appears in RW, vol. 2, p. 379; the original may be found in the 1872 Rolls Series edition, in untranslated Latin, of the works of Matthew Paris (which, for the portion dealing with events up until John's death in October 1216, is copied from Roger of Wendover), vol. 2, p. 669. Warren is more sympathetic to John than many modern observers, but even he admits that 'it was his own fault that the baronial cause fell into the hands of violent men [...] John's one answer to opposition was to crush it out of existence, instead of trying to build up the sure defences of goodwill [...] He had the mental abilities of a great king, but the inclinations of a petty tyrant' (Warren, *King John*, p. 259). Church calls him 'a catastrophic failure [...] No king can leave a legacy like John's and expect to be remembered kindly by posterity' (*King John*, p. 248).
14. HWM, vol. 2, p. 265.
15. HWM, vol. 2, p. 267. On the question of how to present Henry's accession, Carpenter notes that 'one idea was to convoke an assembly at Northampton to "elect" Henry king, but since Louis also claimed to have been elected, this would merely place Henry on a par with his rival. Instead, therefore, it was decided to plunge ahead at once with the coronation and base Henry's title on what John called "perpetual hereditary succession", Louis's claim "by succession" – that he was married to a granddaughter of Henry II – being tenuous in the extreme' (*Minority of Henry III*, p. 13).

16. *HWM*, vol. 2, p. 269. On the coronation, see also Guala, pp. 28–29. There is some confusion over whether the royal crown had been lost in John's baggage incident in the Wash, whether it had survived that episode and then subsequently been stolen in the confusion, or whether it was simply the case that the coronation regalia was out of reach at Westminster. In any event, it was not available in Gloucester.

17. On the development of national identity, and the role of this particular campaign in shaping it, see McGlynn, "*Pro patria*": National Identity and War in Early Medieval England'.

18. Wilkinson notes that 'Isabella of Angoulême was a queen consort of England whose reputation suffered greatly at the hands of near-contemporary writers, all of whom were male clerics whose accounts were coloured by their knowledge of the disastrous events of John's reign' ('Maternal Abandonment', p. 103). She later adds that 'the regency council was probably reluctant to allow Isabella to exercise any influence over her young children due to her lack of experience [...] [and] the possibility that she might be a destabilising force' (ibid., p. 111). For further discussion on Isabella's exclusion from the regency, see Woodacre, 'Between Regencies'.

19. For more on the siege of Dover during July–October 1216, see the detailed account in AB, *Dukes*, pp. 169–71; also RW, vol. 2, pp. 374–75; McGlynn, *Blood Cries Afar*, pp. 176–80; Hanley, *Louis*, pp. 109–14; Humphrys, *Enemies at the Gate*, pp. 49–55.

20. RW, vol. 2, p. 381.

21. Warren notes that 'it is the supreme irony of Magna Carta that, after being demanded by rebels and killed by the pope, it should have been brought back to life as a royalist manifesto' (Warren, *King John*, p. 256). On this reissue, see also Guala, pp. 29–31; Carpenter, *Minority of Henry III*, pp. 22–24.

22. RW, vol. 2, p. 380.

23. This is best summed up in Carpenter's vivid expression that 'Henry shrugged and the weight of John's crimes fell from his shoulders' (*Minority of Henry III*, p. 22).

24. RW, vol. 2, p. 385.

25. On William d'Albini's defection, see Hanley, *Louis*, p. 125; Nicholas Vincent, 'Aubigné, William d' [William d'Albini] (d. 1236)', *ODNB*.

26. On these smaller sieges, see RW, vol. 2, pp. 381–83; AB, *Dukes*, p. 173; McGlynn, *Blood Cries Afar*, pp. 191–92.

27. On Philip's actions, see WB, *Vie*, pp. 325–26; Bradbury, *Philip Augustus*, pp. 320–22; Baldwin, *Government of Philip Augustus*, pp. 333–36; Hanley, *Louis*, pp. 135–36.

Chapter 18

1. William Marshal is slowly being reassessed. One of King John's more recent biographers notes that Marshal's reputation for having 'an unimpeachable record of honourable service to two generations of Angevins' is 'not always deserved' (Church, *King John: England*, p. 251). For more on the new regent, see Crouch, *William Marshal*; Asbridge, *The Greatest Knight*. There is a vast literature available on the concept of chivalry and its development over the centuries; for a brief introduction, see Maurice Keen, 'Chivalry: Overview', *OEMW*, vol. 1, pp. 374–85. Full-length works include Keen, *Chivalry*; Kaeuper, *Chivalry and Violence in Medieval Europe*; Jones and Coss (eds), *A Companion to Chivalry*; Flori, *Chevaliers et chevalerie au Moyen Age*; Meuleau, *Histoire de la Chevalerie*.

2. *HWM*, vol. 2, p. 289.

3. *HWM*, vol. 2, p. 305.

4. For more on this swift campaign of April and early May, see AB, *Dukes*, pp. 177–80; *HWM*, vol. 2, pp. 305–07; Hanley, *Louis*, pp. 143–45.

5. On the relief of Mountsorrel and the move towards Lincoln, see AB, *Dukes*, pp. 180–81; *HWM*, vol. 2, pp. 307–09; RW, vol. 2, pp. 389–91; Carpenter, *Minority of Henry III*, pp. 35–36.

6. Nicola de la Haye is a fascinating character, and fortunately one who left more impression on the records of her time than many women; for more on her life and career, see Susan M. Johns, 'Haie, Nicola de la (d. 1230)', *ODNB*; Hill, *Medieval Lincoln*, pp. 199–201 and 205–06; Wilkinson, *Women in Thirteenth-Century Lincolnshire*.

7. *HWM*, vol. 2, pp. 309–15. Interestingly, given our earlier allusions to the development of national identity, Marshal's biographer says that as part of his speech he urged his compatriots 'to defend our land' against 'those who have come from France to take for themselves the lands of our men' (ibid., pp. 309 and 311, respectively).

8. The narrative of the engagement that follows, the Battle of Lincoln (sometimes called the Second Battle of Lincoln or the Battle of Lincoln Fair to distinguish it from the earlier engagement of 1141 that we mentioned in Chapter 4) is pieced together from a number of sources. The main primary works that focus on it are *HWM*, vol. 2, pp. 315–55 and RW, vol. 2, pp. 391–98; it is also mentioned in slightly less detail by AB, *Dukes*, pp. 181–82; Barnwell, vol. 2, p. 237; WB, *Vie*, pp. 326–27; MR, pp. 155–56.

9. Roger of Wendover thinks that those inside the castle managed to get someone out to apprise the regent of the situation within Lincoln and to offer some part of his army entry via the postern gate (RW, vol. 2, p. 394); the biographer of William Marshal, meanwhile, contradicts both this and himself by saying first that John Marshal met a knight of the garrison outside the castle, and then that in fact it was Peter des Roches who made contact and somehow managed to enter the city itself, disguised as a citizen, to find an old blocked gate that might allow entry for the army (*HWM*, vol. 2, pp. 323–29).

10. RW, vol. 2, p. 393.

11. *HWM*, vol. 2, p. 347.

12. *HWM*, vol. 2, p. 339.

13. RW, vol. 2, pp. 396–97. For further description and analysis of the Battle of Lincoln, see Carpenter, *Minority of Henry III*, pp. 36–40; McGlynn, *Blood Cries Afar*, pp. 208–16; Hanley, *Louis*, pp. 156–65; Sivéry, *Louis VIII*, pp. 181–84; Hill, *Medieval Lincoln*, pp. 201–05; Brooks and Oakley, 'The Campaign and Battle of Lincoln 1217'.

14. On Nicola's subsequent career, see Carpenter, *Minority of Henry III*, pp. 66–67; Johns, 'Haie, Nicola de la (d. 1230)', *ODNB*. As part of an attempt to solve the dispute, Nicola's only surviving relative and sole heir, her granddaughter Idonea, was married to Salisbury's son William II Longsword. As they were both minors, Salisbury would expect to control all the estates left by Nicola at her death, in his young daughter-in-law's name – and would expect to do this soon, given Nicola's age; she was around twenty-five years older than him. Unfortunately for Salisbury, Nicola outlived him.

15. *HWM*, vol. 2, p. 355.

16. MR, pp. 157–58. For more on Blanche's efforts at this point, see Grant, *Blanche of Castile*, pp. 56–57; Delorme, *Blanche de Castille*, pp. 85–87; Hanley, *Louis*, pp. 140–42.

17. *HWM*, vol. 2, pp. 371–73. In another manifestation of the complex family relationships on both sides of the war, as well as being Philip Augustus's first cousin Robert de Courtenay was also Henry III's great-uncle: he was the younger brother of Isabella of Angoulême's mother, Alice de Courtenay.

18. *HWM*, vol. 2, p. 369. The growing sense of nationalism was felt by the chronicler Matthew Paris, who included in his manuscript an illustration of the battle: it depicts the bishops who remained on shore saying 'I absolve those who are about to die for the liberation of England' (see plate 17).

19. Philip was a kinsman of the William d'Albini mentioned several times above, though it is not entirely clear how they were related. For more on his career, see Nicholas Vincent, 'Aubigny, Philip d' [Philip Daubeney] (d. 1236)', *ODNB*. I retain the spelling 'Albini' for their family name, in order to differentiate them from the unrelated Aubigny family who were earls of Arundel.

20. The narrative of the battle that follows is drawn from several sources. The principal primary works that deal with it are RW, vol. 2, pp. 399–401; *HWM*, vol. 2, pp. 361–81;

AB, *Dukes*, pp. 185–86; Barnwell, vol. 2, pp. 238–39; RC, p. 185; WB, *Vie*, p. 327; *Eustace*, pp. 77–78.

21. The lime is mentioned by all the major accounts of the battle: see *HWM*, vol. 2, p. 373; RW, vol. 2, pp. 399–400; AB, *Dukes*, p. 186; *Eustace*, p. 78.

22. *Eustace*, p. 78.

23. *HWM*, vol. 2, p. 377.

24. Quote from RW, vol. 2, p. 399. On the choice offered to Eustace, see *HWM*, vol. 2, p. 375.

25. *HWM*, vol. 2, p. 379.

26. For more analysis of the Battle of Sandwich, see Sean McGlynn, 'Sandwich, Battle of', *OEMW*, vol. 3, pp. 219–20; Stanton, *Medieval Maritime Warfare*, pp. 236–40; Rose, *England's Medieval Navy*, pp. 125–29; Carpenter, *Minority of Henry III*, pp. 43–44; McGlynn, *Blood Cries Afar*, pp. 226–34; Hanley, *Louis*, pp. 172–74; Cannon, 'The Battle of Sandwich and Eustace the Monk'.

27. The full text of the Treaty of Lambeth may be found in WB, *Vie*, pp. 328–31; on the treaty, see also RW, vol. 2, pp. 402–04; Guala, pp. 44–45; Carpenter, *Minority of Henry III*, pp. 44–49; McGlynn, *Blood Cries Afar*, pp. 236–38; Hanley, *Louis*, pp. 176–77; Sivéry, *Louis VIII*, pp. 188–91; Smith, 'The Treaty of Lambeth, 1217'.

28. Barnwell, vol. 2, p. 239. A partisan French chronicler blames 'the treason and disloyalty of the English [barons]', and claims that Louis 'would have won admirable victories if only he had received the loyalty that was due to him' (Nangis, pp. 119 and 120, respectively).

Chapter 19

1. Vincent notes that 'with the coming of peace, the common causes of civil war began to break down into a more natural pattern of self-interest. The king was a mere cypher. His courtiers enjoyed a taste of personal freedom unknown in John's reign' (*Peter des Roches*, p. 149).

2. Maria of Montferrat was the daughter of Isabella I of Jerusalem (whom we met in Chapter 10); she was the posthumous child Isabella bore to Conrad of Montferrat, following his assassination and her swift remarriage to Henry II of Champagne. For more on the Fifth Crusade, see RW, vol. 2, pp. 405–25 and 435–39; Nangis, pp. 121–27; Riley-Smith, *Crusades*, pp. 141–49; Tyerman, *God's War*, pp. 606–49; Asbridge, *Crusades*, pp. 551–62.

3. Guala, pp. xlii–xliii. For more on the two legates, see Brenda M. Bolton, 'Guala [Guala Bicchieri] (c. 1150–1227), papal official', *ODNB*; Nicholas Vincent, 'Pandulf [Pandulph, Pandulph Verraccio] (d. 1226), bishop of Norwich and papal legate', *ODNB*.

4. This early part of Henry's reign is covered fully in Carpenter, *Minority of Henry III*, pp. 50–127. On the new great seal of 1218, see Guala, p. lii. On Peter des Roches's attempt to be named regent, see *HWM*, vol. 2, pp. 403–07; Vincent, *Peter des Roches*, pp. 180–81.

5. On this shared dislike, see Vincent, *Peter des Roches*, p. 171.

6. On Henry's coronation, see RW, vol. 2, pp. 426–27; Carpenter, *Minority of Henry III*, pp. 187–91 (who notes that the regalia were probably brand new, John's having been either lost in the 1216 incident in the Wash or sold to raise money during the war).

7. On Henry's education, see Carpenter, *Minority of Henry III*, pp. 241–42.

8. For more details on the 1219–21 period, see Carpenter, *Minority of Henry III*, pp. 128–238.

9. On this point, see Orme, *From Childhood to Chivalry*, p. 6.

10. The text of the 1220 truce may be found in WB, *Vie*, pp. 338–41; the quote is from AB, *Dukes*, p. 190. See also the discussion in Baldwin, *Government of Philip Augustus*, p. 339.

11. On the Castilian offer, see Delorme, *Blanche de Castille*, pp. 93–94; Hanley, *Louis*, pp. 179–80; Sivéry, *Louis VIII*, pp. 197–99; Shadis, *Berenguela of Castile*, p. 104, who notes

that the supposed proviso was fictional, as Alfonso had 'commended the kingdom to Leonor's regency and made no mention of either daughter'. Queen Leonor, as she was known in Castile, was Eleanor, the second daughter of Henry II and Eleanor of Aquitaine; she would outlive her husband by just three weeks.

12. On Louis's participation in the Albigensian Crusade in 1218–19, see PVC, pp. 275–79; WP, pp. 64–65; Hanley, *Louis*, pp. 182–90; Sivéry, *Louis VIII*, pp. 206–10; Bradbury, *Philip Augustus*, pp. 328–31.

13. On Philip and Flanders during this period, see Bradbury, *Philip Augustus*, pp. 324–26, who notes that the lasting effect of Bouvines was that 'within France, the unrivalled power of the crown had to be respected' (p. 326). On Philip's financial prosperity in his last years, see Baldwin, *Government of Philip Augustus*, pp. 351–54.

14. LeGoff, *Saint Louis*, pp. 9–10 and 574–76.

15. The text of the testament may be found in WB, *Vie*, pp. 345–48. Ingeborg would outlive Philip by thirteen years; she was given full honours as a dowager queen by both Louis VIII and Louis IX.

16. MR, p. 160; WB, *Vie*, pp. 348–49.

17. The original quote is in *Tours*, p. 304; the English translation appears in Baldwin, *Paris, 1200*, pp. 70–71. For more on Philip's death, see WB, *Philippide*, pp. 370–74; GC6, pp. 369–71; Sivéry, *Philippe Auguste*, pp. 386–89. For an analysis of his character, see Baldwin, *Government of Philip Augustus*, pp. 356–59.

18. For an assessment of Philip's influence on internal French matters during his reign, and French public opinions of him, see Sivéry, *Philippe Auguste*, pp. 313–54.

19. RW, vol. 2, pp. 444–45. For discussion of this offer and the likelihood of its ever having occurred, see Carpenter, *Minority of Henry III*, pp. 309–11; Sivéry, *Louis VIII*, pp. 240–41, the latter being markedly more sceptical than the former. For references to the treaty itself, see above, note 27 to Chapter 18.

20. A detailed (and somewhat overblown) description of the coronation and the attendant festivities appears in NB, pp. 390–400. See also Hanley, *Louis*, pp. 195–98; Sivéry, *Louis VIII*, pp. 227–29; Grant, *Blanche of Castile*, pp. 61–63; Delorme, *Blanche de Castille*, pp. 101–06.

21. Sancho VII had been married twice, but had no children from either union. He suffered from ill health, including leg ulcers possibly caused by his great height, and lived in seclusion in Tudela; once her regency in Champagne was complete, Blanche moved to Navarre to act as his regent. Berengaria, also childless, had been residing in Le Mans for a number of years while engaging in a long-running dispute by correspondence with King John about payments owed to her as dowager queen and Richard's widow (see the letters on the Epistolae site at https://epistolae.ctl.columbia.edu/woman/79.html). She is generally known as 'the only queen of England never to visit England', although there is some evidence that she was present at the translation of the relics of St Thomas Becket in Canterbury in 1220 (AB, *Dukes*, pp. 191–92). The debts owing to her were finally paid during the reign of Henry III, and she continued to live quietly in Le Mans until her death in December 1230.

22. WB, *Philippide*, pp. 384–85.

23. *Tours*, p. 305; see also Carpenter, *Minority of Henry III*, p. 355.

24. AB, *Dukes*, p. 189.

25. The dates of birth and even the order of birth of Isabella's second family are unclear, but they all survived childhood, meaning that Isabella would (remarkably for the time) see all fourteen of her children live to be adults.

26. On this episode, see Hanley, *Louis*, pp. 201–03; Sivéry, *Louis VIII*, pp. 241–43.

27. On Hubert's marriage and earldom, see F.J. West, 'Burgh, Hubert de, earl of Kent (c. 1170–1243)', *ODNB*; Carpenter notes that it 'rocketed Hubert up the social scale' (*Henry III*, p. 35).

28. RW, vol. 2, p. 446.

29. On Falkes's condemnation and subsequent actions, see RW, vol. 2, p. 451; D.J. Power, 'Bréauté, Sir Falkes de (d. 1226)', *ODNB*; Carpenter, *Minority of Henry III*, pp. 351–58.
30. For more on the siege of Bedford, see RW, vol. 2, pp. 451–54; Amt, 'Besieging Bedford'; Sean McGlynn, 'Bedford, siege of', *OEMW*, vol. 1, pp. 137–38; Spencer, *The Castle at War*, pp. 111–13; Carpenter, *Minority of Henry III*, pp. 360–67.
31. On the composition of the host, see NB, pp. 410–12.
32. *Vie de Louis VIII*, p. 367. For more on this early part of the campaign, see *GC7*, pp. 10–11; Hanley, *Louis*, pp. 203–4; Sivéry, *Louis VIII*, pp. 243–8.
33. NB, p. 412.
34. *Vie de Louis VIII*, p. 368. For more on the siege of La Rochelle, see NB, pp. 414–17; *GC7*, pp. 11–12; RW, vol. 2, p. 450; Nangis, pp. 132–33; Hanley, *Louis*, pp. 204–07; Sivéry, *Louis VIII*, pp. 248–53.
35. *Vie de Louis VIII*, p. 372; *GC7*, pp. 12–15; Nangis, p. 134.
36. On Richard of Cornwall's campaign of 1225, see RW, vol. 2, pp. 456–58; *Vie de Louis VIII*, p. 373; *GC7*, pp. 15–17; Carpenter, *Minority of Henry III*, pp. 376–78.
37. On the 1219–25 period of the Albigensian Crusade, see Oldenbourg, *Massacre at Montségur*, pp. 201–07; McGlynn, *Kill Them All*, pp. 243–56.
38. The text of the testament is available in *Vie de Louis VIII*, pp. 379–83. For more on the apanages Louis VIII intended for his sons, see Lewis, *Royal Succession in Capetian France*, pp. 161–65.
39. RW, vol. 2, p. 480. For more on the siege of Avignon, see ibid., pp. 478–82; Nicholas de Bray's eyewitness account, NB, pp. 442–51 and 457–63; *Vie de Louis VIII*, pp. 377–78; *GC7*, pp. 20–23; MR, pp. 172–73; Nangis, pp. 135–36; Hanley, *Louis*, pp. 215–21; Sivéry, *Louis VIII*, pp. 378–90.
40. On Louis's death, see *Vie de Louis VIII*, pp. 378–79; *GC7*, pp. 23–24; Hanley, *Louis*, pp. 222–24; Sivéry, *Louis VIII*, pp. 400–05.

Chapter 20

1. On Louis VIII's deathbed testament, see Hanley, *Louis*, pp. 223–24; Grant, *Blanche of Castile*, p. 77; LeGoff, *Saint Louis*, pp. 44–46; Richard, *Saint Louis*, p. 34.
2. Guérin's date of birth is not known, but given that he had participated in the Third Crusade in the 1180s and was already a knight of some renown by that time, he must have been quite elderly in 1226. He would continue to serve Louis IX for the remaining months of his life, and he was still in post when he died in May 1227.
3. For more on Louis IX's coronation, see *GC7*, pp. 33–34; LeGoff, *Saint Louis*, pp. 54–57; Delorme, *Blanche de Castille*, pp. 136–39. On the nobles swearing an oath to Blanche, see MR, pp. 175–76; Delorme, *Blanche de Castille*, p. 138; Richard, *Saint Louis*, p. 39.
4. LeGoff believes that 'there was such an understanding between mother and son that a form of shared government between them almost imperceptibly succeeded the mother's tutelage, without allowing us to say that the son ruled without governing because his authority became apparent early on' (*Saint Louis*, p. 53). Bradbury comments that 'some believe that he [Louis IX] was dominated by his mother. It is rather the case that Louis was a strong character who respected his mother. He grew up under her wing but was never entirely dominated. They reigned together in amity' (*Capetians*, p. 203).
5. MR, p. 174.
6. MR, p. 176.
7. Peter was a complex man who led a life of many ups and downs; for more on his career, see Painter, *Scourge of the Clergy*.
8. Roger of Wendover alludes to a possible relationship on two different occasions, first saying that Theobald was 'in love with the queen' and later that he had 'defiled' her (RW, vol. 2, pp. 481 and 536, respectively); he also makes similar assertions about Blanche and the papal legate to France, Roman Frangipani (ibid., p. 536). These allegations are roundly dismissed by Blanche's biographers, one of whom calls them merely 'wild

rumours' (Grant, *Blanche of Castile*, p. 77), while the other points out that such accusations were the easiest way to undermine the reputation and authority of a woman in a position of authority (Delorme, *Blanche de Castille*, pp. 160–61). LeGoff also believes them to be 'pure slander' (*Saint Louis*, p. 62).

9. *GC7*, pp. 36–37.

10. For more on these events and negotiations, see *Tours*, p. 319; Richard, *Saint Louis*, pp. 40–43; Grant, *Blanche of Castile*, pp. 84–86. A useful summary of the putative baronial rebellion as a whole may be found in Menant et al., *Les Capétiens*, pp. 422–25.

11. For more on the Albigensian Crusade between 1226 and 1229, see McGlynn, *Kill Them All*, pp. 267–74; Oldenbourg, *Massacre at Montségur*, pp. 213–17. Oldenbourg notes that Louis VIII's death might have been a lucky break for the southerners, as it passed the throne to a boy and the regency to a widow, but that 'unluckily for Languedoc, this widow happened to be Blanche of Castile, a woman endowed with more energy and ambition than either her husband or her son ever possessed' (ibid., p. 213). For more on the Treaty of Paris and the associated arrangements, see Grant, *Blanche of Castile*, pp. 86–87; Delorme, *Blanche de Castille*, pp. 162–63.

12. RW, vol. 2, pp. 485–86; see also Carpenter, *Minority of Henry III*, p. 389.

13. *GC7*, p. 42.

14. RW, vol. 2, p. 538. On Henry's movements throughout this abortive campaign, see RW, vol. 2, pp. 534–38; and Carpenter, *Henry III*, pp. 86–93, who later notes of the campaign that 'neither the letters home nor the writings of the chroniclers suggest any kind of personal military effort' by Henry (ibid., p. 97). For more on the campaign from the French point of view, see Nangis, pp. 138–39; *GC7*, pp. 43–45.

15. On the council, see Grant, *Blanche of Castile*, pp. 89–90.

16. Opinions on Philip Hurepel's conduct and real motives differ. One of Blanche's biographers believes he showed an 'irreproachable devotion' to her and Louis from the moment of Louis VIII's death, and it was only later that his loyalty became 'more uncertain' (Delorme, *Blanche de Castille*, pp. 141 and 164); but another gives more credence to a longer-term alliance with Peter de Dreux, noting that it was only now, in 1230, that 'it must have been clear to Philip Hurepel [...] that his own interests were no longer served by an alliance with Peter of Brittany [...] The events of the previous year had revealed how limited was support for Peter among the French baronage [...] He would do better, as the new king reached maturity, to develop a role as a dependable uncle' (Grant, *Blanche of Castile*, p. 91).

17. Margam, p. 38.

18. RW, vol. 2, pp. 553–59. The complexities of Hubert's relationship with the adult Henry and his downfall are discussed by Carpenter, *Henry III*, pp. 58–105 and 108–22; see also Vincent, *Peter des Roches*, pp. 259–309.

19. As noted above (see note 18 to Chapter 16), I refrain from giving either of the Simons a number, because the elder was known as both Simon IV and Simon V de Montfort, while the younger can be either Simon V or Simon VI.

20. For more on Simon's initial arrival in England, see Carpenter, *Henry III*, pp. 85–86; Ambler, *Song of Simon de Montfort*, pp. 34–39; Favier, *Les Plantagenêts*, pp. 749–50.

21. More on the French apanage system from the date of Louis VIII's testament onwards may be found in Wood, *The French Apanages*.

22. RW, vol. 2, pp. 567–68. For more on Peter des Roches's fall, see RW, vol. 2, p. 586; Vincent, *Peter des Roches*, pp. 429–65.

23. Carpenter says of the episode that 'Magna Carta had withstood its first great test' (*Henry III*, p. 162).

Chapter 21

1. We do not have exact years of birth for any of the four sisters, and various dates have been posited. The ones listed here are those given in Howell, *Eleanor of Provence*, p. 2.

2. For more on the arrangements for Margaret's match and her wedding, see *GC7*, pp. 64–65; Nangis, p. 144; Gil, *Marguerite de Provence*, pp. 11–16; LeGoff, *Saint Louis*, pp. 84–89; Richard, *Saint Louis*, pp. 122–26; Jordan, *Louis IX*, pp. 4–6; Grant, *Blanche of Castile*, pp. 106–07; Delorme, *Blanche de Castille*, pp. 198–202; Howell, *Eleanor of Provence*, pp. 8–9. On Louis's postponing of the consummation, the biblical passage in question is the Old Testament Tobias 8:4, in which Tobias says to his new wife, 'Let us pray to God today, and tomorrow, and the next day: because for these three nights we are joined to God and when the third night is over, we will be in our own wedlock.' Although contemporaries assumed there was a scriptural basis for Louis's decision, one cannot help wondering whether there was a simpler and more practical reason for the delay, in that Margaret may have been menstruating – a subject the predominantly clerical and uniformly male chroniclers presumably knew little about.
3. Jordan argues that the silence of the chroniclers regarding any official announcement of the end of the minority is 'evidence that a gradual and quite natural shift from the rulership of the aging Blanche to that of her youthful son occurred almost imperceptibly' (*Louis IX*, p. 7). Grant notes that 'it is impossible to tell from official documents when Louis's minority ended, since all acts had been issued in his name from the start of his reign' (*Blanche of Castile*, p. 107).
4. GB, p. 74. Chroniclers generally had problems in finding the correct vocabulary to praise an active woman, their positive epithets for female subjects being generally limited to words like 'beautiful' and 'noble'; here Geoffrey resorts to complimenting Blanche by saying that she acted like a man.
5. See LeGoff, *Saint Louis*, pp. 54–55.
6. On the arrangements for Isabelle's marriage to Frederick and the wedding itself, see RW, vol. 2, pp. 607–10; Carpenter, *Henry III*, pp. 172–75.
7. See Kantorowicz, *Frederick the Second*, who notes that 'in contrast to his predecessors Frederick looked on his consorts simply as mothers of his legitimate heirs and successors; they had no importance as Empresses' (p. 352) and adds that Isabelle simply disappeared into a harem watched over by eunuchs (pp. 352–53). For more on Henry III's decision to marry his sister off to Frederick II, the magnificence of her dowry and trousseau, and her experiences after marriage, see Barber, *Magnificence*, pp. 102–03. Barber describes the match as 'a diplomatic coup for Henry' and notes that the extravagance was 'designed to impress' (ibid., p. 103).
8. For more on the circumstances of Richard's marriage and his attendant conflict with Henry, see Carpenter, *Henry III*, pp. 99 and 106; Nicholas Vincent, 'Richard, first earl of Cornwall and king of Germany (1209–1272)', *ODNB*. A biography of Richard is Denholm-Young, *Richard of Cornwall*.
9. 'Almain' is a corruption of *Allemagne* (the French and Anglo-Norman word for Germany) and was bestowed on Henry due to Richard's adventures in that country, of which we will hear more later.
10. On these letters, see Carpenter, *Henry III*, p. 176; Howell, *Eleanor of Provence*, p. 14.
11. On the arrangements for Eleanor's match and her wedding, see MP, vol. 1, pp. 7–10; Carpenter, *Henry III*, pp. 176–78; Howell, *Eleanor of Provence*, pp. 9–16.
12. On the coronation, see Carpenter, *Henry III*, pp. 178–80; Howell, *Eleanor of Provence*, pp. 16–18.
13. For more on the Winchester episcopal election and the 'improper means' by which Henry attempted to influence it, see MP, vol. 1, pp. 135–36. On William of Savoy and his career, see Cox, *Eagles of Savoy*, pp. 33–50; and Carpenter, *Henry III*, pp. 187–89, who notes that on his arrival at the English court 'the bishop-elect of Valence appeared not so much as a breath of fresh air as a thunderclap' (p. 188).
14. MP, vol. 1, p. 49.
15. Matilda of Brabant was the granddaughter of Henry I, duke of Brabant, whom we saw earlier vacillating in his loyalties, but her grandmother was Henry's first wife, not Marie

(the daughter of Philip Augustus), his second. Matilda and her new husband Robert were thus not related to each other in any prohibited degree.

16. On Eleanor's marriage to Simon de Montfort and the circumstances surrounding it, see MP, vol. 1, p. 117; Wilkinson, *Eleanor de Montfort*, pp. 61–72; Ambler, *Song of Simon de Montfort*, pp. 58–63; Carpenter, *Henry III*, pp. 200–02.

17. On Edward's birth, see MP, vol. 1, pp. 172–73. On the significance of his name, see Prestwich, *Edward I*, pp. 4–5; Howell, *Eleanor of Provence*, pp. 27–28. Carpenter describes Henry's decision to call his son Edward 'positive and innovative' and notes that the choice 'seemed to reposition the monarchy in the new post-imperial world, stressing its English rather than continental roots' (*Henry III*, p. 206). The name seems to have flummoxed a number of our contemporary French chroniclers, who resort to a variety of unusual or phonetic spellings.

18. On Isabella's interview with Louis, see Grant, *Blanche of Castile*, pp. 125–26; a letter to Blanche that documents in detail how Isabella reacted with fury and had to be calmed by her husband may be found on the Epistolae site at https://epistolae.ctl.columbia.edu/letter/725.html. For more on Hugh's dissatisfaction with the overlordship of Alphonse, see MP, vol. 1, pp. 394–96; Carpenter, *Henry III*, pp. 245–46.

19. MP, vol. 1, pp. 394–95; see also LeGoff, *Saint Louis*, p. 103.

20. On Louis's campaign and his capture of a number of castles, see *GC7*, pp. 92–95.

21. For the details of Henry's alliance with his mother and stepfather, see Carpenter, *Henry III*, pp. 248–50.

22. MP, vol. 1, pp. 414–15.

23. Joinville, p. 189.

24. MP, vol. 1, p. 422.

25. *GC7*, p. 97.

26. For more on the battles at Taillebourg and Saintes (sometimes treated separately and sometimes as one lengthy engagement), see Joinville, pp. 188–90; Nangis, pp. 150–51; *GC7*, pp. 96–99; MR, pp. 186–89; MP, vol. 1, pp. 419–23; Sean McGlynn, 'Taillebourg, Battle of', *OEMW*, vol. 3, p. 344; Sean McGlynn, 'Saintes, Battle of', *OEMW*, vol. 3, pp. 210–11; LeGoff, *Saint Louis*, pp. 105–06; Richard, *Saint Louis*, pp. 116–17; Hélary, *L'armée du roi de France*, p. 15; Carpenter, *Henry III*, pp. 259–63.

27. On this episode, the exact words Simon may or may not have used and the threat this might have implied, see Ambler, *Song of Simon de Montfort*, pp. 97–98; Carpenter, *Henry III*, p. 262.

28. MP, vol. 1, pp. 431–32.

29. On Henry's year in Bordeaux, see Carpenter, *Henry III*, pp. 266–70.

30. For the details of the truce, see MP, vol. 1, pp. 445–46.

31. MP, vol. 1, p. 458.

32. For more on Queen Eleanor's relationship with her Savoyard uncles, see Howell, *Eleanor of Provence*, pp. 24–31.

33. The extent to which Eleanor's claim to the English throne matched or surpassed John's is debatable. She was the daughter of John's elder brother Geoffrey, who would have taken precedence over John if he had survived, and this had given Eleanor's late brother Arthur a substantial basis for his claim, as we examined in Chapter 12. However, female succession was only really taken seriously in the absence of close male relatives, so Eleanor's right was weaker than Arthur's. We may note that if Eleanor's claim to the throne was never genuinely considered to be valid by contemporaries, this would make her long-term captivity even more cruel; John simultaneously tried to play down her rights while imprisoning her for the potential danger they caused.

34. On Eleanor's death, Matthew Paris notes simply that 'about this time died Eleanor, daughter of Geoffrey, count of Brittany, who had long been kept in close confinement', without mentioning any further detail of her life or situation (MP, vol. 1, p. 383). On Henry paying for Masses, see Carpenter, *Henry III*, p. 356.

35. GB, p. 79.
36. On the death of Raymond-Berengar, and on Charles of Anjou's marriage to Beatrice of Provence, see MP, vol. 2, pp. 113–14 and 130; *GC7*, pp. 113–15; Cox, *Eagles of Savoy*, pp. 146–49; Howell, *Eleanor of Provence*, pp. 46–47; Delorme, *Blanche de Castile*, pp. 282–83; Richard, *Saint Louis*, pp. 129–31; Dunbabin, *Charles I of Anjou*, pp. 41–43.

Chapter 22

1. The quote is from an eyewitness report that is cited in LeGoff, *Saint Louis*, pp. 97–98. For more on the crown of thorns and its arrival in France, see *GC7*, pp. 72–75; MP, vol. 1, pp. 323–25; LeGoff, *Saint Louis*, pp. 94–101; Barber, *Magnificence*, pp. 176–8.
2. GB, pp. 87–88.
3. GB, p. 80. For a close analysis of Louis IX's religion, see LeGoff, *Saint Louis*, pp. 609–39.
4. For more on Isabelle, her life and her later veneration as a saint, see Jordan, *Louis IX*, pp. 9–12; Jordan, 'Isabelle of France'; Michael Bihl, 'St Isabel of France', *CE*.
5. Joinville, p. 176 (resting in bed); GB, p. 89 (hair shirt and bodily weakness). For more on Louis's health, see the section on 'the sick king' in LeGoff, *Saint Louis*, pp. 707–09. It is worth noting that those who knew him but who wrote after his death may have exaggerated some aspects of Louis's ill health in order to paint him as suffering and overcoming adversity thanks to his strong faith.
6. Joinville, p. 191; see also MP, vol. 2, pp. 37–38.
7. Quote from Joinville, p. 191. On Blanche's attempts to change Louis's mind, see also MP, vol. 2, pp. 253–54. Louis's decision to go on crusade was not just a personal whim; there were also military catalysts, including the Khwarizmian sacking of Jerusalem and the Battle of La Forbie in 1244. See Asbridge, *Crusades*, pp. 574–76, who describes the defeat of the Franks at La Forbie as 'a calamity to match that of Hattin in 1187' (p. 576); see also Phillips, *Holy Warriors*, pp. 244–49.
8. For more discussion on the negotiations between Louis and Henry between 1244 and 1248, see Carpenter, *Henry III*, pp. 490–93; Jordan, *Louis IX*, pp. 25–27.
9. At his knighting in 1237, Robert arranged for Louis to be served his food by minstrels riding on the horns of oxen, a joke the king did not particularly appreciate; Robert also once drenched Theobald IV of Champagne in runny cheese – or possibly worse – just as he was about to start a royal interview. For more on Robert, see LeGoff, *Saint Louis*, pp. 585–88 (who calls him a 'brilliant knight', p. 588) and Grant, *Blanche of Castile*, pp. 159–60 (who calls him 'strong but impulsive' and 'heedlessly brave', p. 159).
10. MP, vol. 2, p. 311. What follows is a fairly brief summary of the campaign; copious details are available elsewhere. The Seventh Crusade is the main focus of Joinville's text (Joinville, pp. 191–330); other primary accounts are Nangis, pp. 155–61; *GC7*, pp. 117–59 and 170–78; MR, pp. 190–204. Matthew Paris covers the taking of Damietta at MP, vol. 2, pp. 360–64. Further details and analysis may be found in Jackson (ed.), *The Seventh Crusade*; Bartlett, *The Last Crusade*; Jordan, *Louis IX*; Strayer, 'Crusades of Louis IX', LeGoff, *Saint Louis*, pp. 128–50; Richard, *Saint Louis*, pp. 157–272.
11. Numbers, as ever, are difficult to estimate; in this case, see the discussion in Jordan, *Louis IX*, pp. 65–66.
12. 'How miraculously the Lord delivered Damietta to him', GB, p. 103.
13. Joinville, p. 210. On this incident, see also Phillips, *Holy Warriors*, pp. 252–55.
14. Joinville, p. 226.
15. Again, this is only a brief overview. For more on these events, including a detailed chronology, see Asbridge, *Crusades*, pp. 596–604. For more on the battles of Mansurah and Fariskur, see MR, pp. 196–201; *GC7*, pp. 148–53; MP, vol. 2, pp. 367–77; Nicholas Morton, 'Mansurah, Battle of', *OEMW*, vol. 2, pp. 566–68.
16. Joinville, p. 240.
17. Joinville, pp. 262–63. See above, note 30 to Chapter 10, on the use of the word 'Saracen'.

18. A notable exception is Hodgson, *Women, Crusading and the Holy Land*; individual case studies may also be found in Edgington and Lambert (eds), *Gendering the Crusades*. For more on Queen Margaret's experiences on crusade, see Gil, *Marguerite de Provence*, pp. 61–91.
19. On Henry's crusading fervour at this point, see Carpenter, *Henry III*, pp. 512–18. Howell notes that 'the fact that Henry never fulfilled his vow and that the revenues which he collected for the crusade were directed to other ends [...] has generated much debate as to his good faith in making his initial promise' (*Eleanor of Provence*, p. 59).
20. Joinville, p. 249.
21. On this subject, Asbridge notes that 'given the ardent self-promotion typical of other crusade leaders – from Richard the Lionheart to Frederick II of Germany – Louis also showed an extraordinary willingness to accept responsibility for the dreadful setbacks experienced in Egypt' (*Crusades*, p. 607).
22. GB, p. 103.
23. Joinville, p. 313.
24. Joinville, p. 315; GB, p. 105.
25. GB, p. 106.
26. GB, p. 108.
27. Navarre and England had already been in conflict, Theobald I going to war with Henry III in 1244 over the question of the exact position of the border between Navarre and Gascony. Although a truce had been agreed, the two realms remained on hostile terms, and Navarre's ever-closer connections to France would do little to remedy the situation.
28. For more on these marriages and the arrival of the Lusignans, see Snellgrove, *The Lusignans in England*, pp. 26–27; Carpenter, *Henry III*, pp. 467–72. John de Warenne was the son of William IV de Warenne, the earl who had swapped sides several times during the 1216–17 war in England between King John and the future Louis VIII, by his second wife Matilda Marshal, the eldest daughter of William I Marshal. Joan de Munchensi was another of William's granddaughters, by his youngest daughter Joan. As all five of Marshal's sons had died childless, his vast estates were divided up between his daughters and their children, so they were sought-after marriage prizes. On the election of Aymer to the see of Winchester, see MP, vol. 2, p. 395; Snellgrove, *The Lusignans in England*, pp. 56–65; Carpenter, *Henry III*, pp. 486–88.
29. MP, vol. 2, p. 437. For various other complaints about the foreigners and Henry's behaviour towards them, see ibid. pp. 246–47, 255–57, 395, 510–11 and 521. For an exhaustive examination of the money, lands, wardships and other benefits that Henry lavished on his half-siblings, see Snellgrove, *The Lusignans in England*, pp. 32–55 and 66–77.
30. Henry and Simon's relationship prior to 1252 had been so stormy that Ambler, the latter's biographer, dedicates an entire index section to 'Henry III–Simon relationship: breakdowns' (*Song of Simon de Montfort*, p. 418), which details the many and various instances. On Simon's appointment to Gascony and for an analysis of his rule there, see ibid., pp. 109–33; Carpenter, *Henry III*, pp. 499–511.
31. MP, vol. 3, pp. 34–35 and 40–42 (quote p. 40). For slightly more detail, see Carpenter, *Henry III*, pp. 568–83.
32. MP, vol. 3, pp. 41–42 (negotiations with Alfonso) and 83–84 (wedding). On the marriage, see also Prestwich, *Edward I*, pp. 9–11.
33. On the early consummation of the marriage, see Parsons, *Eleanor of Castile*, pp. 16–17. On the complex question of the dates of birth and death of Edward and Eleanor's children, and how many they had in total, see Parsons, 'The Year of Eleanor of Castile's Birth'; Prestwich, *Edward I*, pp. 125–26.
34. On this family reunion, see MP, vol. 3, pp. 105–10; Howell, *Eleanor of Provence*, pp. 135–38; Carpenter, *Henry III*, pp. 600–10; Gil, *Marguerite de Provence*, pp. 99–101.

35. On Katherine's possible health problems, see Howell, *Eleanor of Provence*, p. 101. On her final illness and death, and her parents' reactions to it, see MP, vol. 3, pp. 232 and 241; Howell, *Eleanor of Provence*, pp. 101–02.

36. For more on Henry's Sicilian plans, see MP, vol. 3, pp. 89–92, 137–38 and 225; Carpenter, *Henry III*, pp. 629–37; Howell, *Eleanor of Provence*, pp. 130–35.

37. MP, vol. 3, pp. 209–10 and 239; WG, p. 184. For more on the complex circumstances of Richard's election, see Vincent, 'Richard, first earl of Cornwall and king of Germany (1209–1272)', *ODNB*.

38. On this subject, see Crouch, *English Aristocracy*, who notes that 'foreignness was merely a characteristic imposed on the king's objectionable familiar favourites' (p. 91).

39. By this time, the Savoyards had become more assimilated and accepted; Peter of Savoy was actually one of those backing Simon de Montfort, and his brother Archbishop Boniface was influential with regard to the involvement of the Church and the bishops in the dispute. For more on the complaints against Henry, both financial and in respect of his support for foreigners, see Carpenter, *Henry III*, pp. 656–61 and 672–74, respectively. On Queen Eleanor's often-overlooked role in the crisis of 1258, see Howell, *Eleanor of Provence*, pp. 152–76. A useful summary of the whole is the chapter 'What Happened in 1258?' in Carpenter, *Reign of Henry III*, pp. 183–98.

40. MP, vol. 3, pp. 283–84 and 291.

41. MP, vol. 3, pp. 278–80; Langtoft, pp. 137–41. See also Carpenter, *Henry III*, pp. 691–97; Ambler, *Song of Simon de Montfort*, pp. 168–78.

42. MP, vol. 3, p. 286.

43. The full text of the Provisions of Oxford may be found in *SECH*, pp. 143–46. See also MP, vol. 3, pp. 285–88; WG, pp. 185–87; Jobson, *First English Revolution*, pp. 22–26; Ambler, *Song of Simon de Montfort*, pp. 198–203. Detailed analyses are Valente, 'Provisions of Oxford' and Clementi, 'Documentary Evidence'.

Chapter 23

1. MP, vol. 3, p. 301.

2. WR, p. 332.

3. Joinville, p. 178.

4. For the text of the treaty, see *GC7*, pp. 208–16. Other primary accounts are WR, pp. 331–32; MR, pp. 234–36; Nangis, pp. 172–73. For analysis, see Chaplais, 'The Making of the Treaty of Paris'; the chapter 'The Treaty of Paris' in Jordan, *A Tale of Two Monasteries*, pp. 49–65; Carpenter, *Henry III*, pp. 680–85; LeGoff, *Saint Louis*, pp. 192–99; Richard, *Saint Louis*, pp. 352–56; Favier, *Les Plantagenêts*, pp. 783–86; Menant et al., *Les Capétiens*, pp. 433–36.

5. See above, Chapter 1 (Henry I represented by his heir, William Adelin) and Chapter 4 (Stephen represented by his eldest son, Eustace); see also note 18 to Chapter 4.

6. Joinville, p. 178.

7. MR, p. 237.

8. Joinville, pp. 336–37.

9. MR, p. 237.

10. On young Louis's death and funeral, see MR, p. 237; Nangis, p. 173; *GC7*, pp. 216–17; LeGoff, *Saint Louis*, pp. 202–03; Sivéry, *Philippe III*, pp. 16–17 (who puts forward the appendicitis theory); Gil, *Marguerite de Provence*, p. 104. Louis was originally interred at Royaumont, the burial place for royal children at this time, but his remains were moved to Saint-Denis in the nineteenth century. His effigy there is of a later date, but the tomb chest on which it rests is original; on the foot end panel is a carved relief depicting his coffin being borne by four pall-bearers, one of whom is crowned to represent Henry III (see plate 21).

11. A contemporary later noted that Philip 'was not literate', although this might mean that he could not read or write Latin, rather than that he could not read at all (*GC8*, p. 4); Philip's biographer writes of his 'intellectual mediocrity' (Sivéry, *Philippe III*, p. 19).

12. For examples of Louis's rather extreme piety, see WC, pp. 133–35 and 144–47; GB, pp. 76–79 and 87–93. On the punishment for blasphemers, see GC7, pp. 188–89; GB, pp. 109–11; LeGoff, *Saint Louis*, p. 159.

13. The text of Louis's ordinance of reform may be found in Joinville, pp. 337–41. For further detailed analysis of Louis's reforms to administration and justice, see Jordan, *Louis IX*, pp. 135–81; Richard, *Saint Louis*, pp. 277–324; Bradbury, *Capetians*, pp. 213–18.

14. Quotes from MP, vol. 3, pp. 201 and 205, respectively. We should also note that Matthew Paris, who wrote these words, cannot be accused of slandering Edward's character in hindsight, in the light of his later actions when he became king, because he himself died in 1259, when Edward was twenty.

15. On the causes of the quarrel, see MP, vol. 3, pp. 326–27.

16. For some of Louis's activities in the field of arbitration, see Joinville, pp. 331–36. Jordan notes that 'the very desire for peace which animated all of Louis IX's actions and the feeling that began to grow in Christendom that the French king was above petty politics combined to elevate him in the European imagination to the level of supreme arbiter of "international" disputes' (*Louis IX*, p. 200).

17. *SECH*, p. 148. The word 'mise' in this context means a settlement reached by agreement (from the past tense of the French verb *mettre*, 'to put'). For more, see WR, pp. 338–39; WG, pp. 187–88; Wood, 'The Mise of Amiens'; LeGoff, *Saint Louis*, pp. 199–201; Richard, *Saint Louis*, pp. 361–66; Ambler, *Song of Simon de Montfort*, pp. 252–59; Howell, *Eleanor of Provence*, pp. 202–05.

18. The text of all of these letters may be found in WR, pp. 344–46.

19. For more on the Battle of Lewes, see WR, pp. 347–49; WG, pp. 191–96; Langtoft, pp. 141–45; Christian Teutsch, 'Lewes, Battle of', *OEMW*, vol. 2, pp. 505–06; Carpenter, *Battles of Lewes and Evesham*, pp. 22–34; Oman, *Art of War*, vol. 1, pp. 421–31 (with map on p. 439); Ambler, *Song of Simon de Montfort*, pp. 273–76 (with map on p. xvi); Prestwich, *Edward I*, pp. 44–46.

20. On the Mise of Lewes (the original text of which has not survived), see Ambler, *Song of Simon de Montfort*, pp. 275–77.

21. The text of these letters, and of Alphonse's rather lukewarm replies, may be found on the Epistolae site at https://epistolae.ctl.columbia.edu/woman/76.html

22. *GC7*, pp. 229–30.

23. For greater detail on these events, see Ambler, *Song of Simon de Montfort*, pp. 287–90.

24. On Eleanor's strenuous efforts during the spring, summer and autumn of 1264, see Howell, *Eleanor of Provence*, pp. 211–26. On the support she received throughout from her sister Margaret, see Gil, *Marguerite de Provence*, pp. 113–23.

25. For more on the *Boys' Own*-style tale of Edward's escape, involving subterfuge, racing and horse-swapping, see WR, p. 353; *GC7*, p. 230; Prestwich, *Edward I*, pp. 48–49; Morris, *A Great and Terrible King*, pp. 65–66.

26. On the Battle of Evesham, see WR, pp. 354–55; WG, pp. 198–202; Langtoft, pp. 145–47; Wykes, pp. 171–75; *GC7*, pp. 231–33; Christian Teutsch, 'Evesham, Battle of', *OEMW*, vol. 2, p. 31; Carpenter, *Battles of Lewes and Evesham*, pp. 37–66; Oman, *Art of War*, vol. 1, pp. 431–41; Ambler, *Song of Simon de Montfort*, pp. 321–28 (with map on p. xvii); Prestwich, *Edward I*, pp. 51–52.

27. For more on the siege of Kenilworth, see Wykes, pp. 195–96; Humphrys, *Enemies at the Gate*, pp. 56–63. The full text of the Dictum can be found in *SECH*, pp. 149–50; see also Prestwich, *Edward I*, pp. 57 and 64–65.

28. On Charles's Sicilian campaign, see Nangis, pp. 177–84; *GC7*, pp. 233–59; Runciman, *Sicilian Vespers*, pp. 82–96; Richard, *Saint Louis*, pp. 455–75.

29. Rishanger, p. 61. For more on this episode, see Dunbabin, *Charles I of Anjou*, pp. 55–59. One contemporary at least risks some criticism of Charles's execution of Conradin, noting in an indirect manner that 'some people were saying' that Conradin was only seeking to recover his father's inheritance, and that 'therefore he did not deserve to die',

and that those who witnessed the beheading 'felt great pity for Conradin, as he was such a handsome child' (*GC7*, p. 258).

30. For more on Charles and his career, see Dunbabin, *Charles I of Anjou*, who notes that Charles, despite being the youngest son in his family, had signalled his ambitions by making much of the name he shared with Charlemagne and of the fact that he was the only surviving son of his father to have been born 'in the purple', that is, after Louis VIII had been crowned a king (p. 10). For Charles's military career, see also Paolo Grillo, 'Charles of Anjou', *OEMW*, vol. 1, pp. 364–65.

Chapter 24

1. Joinville, p. 346.
2. Louis's youngest son, Robert, had an unfortunate future ahead of him. In 1279 he came of age and was knighted, but at the tournament to celebrate the event he was struck on the head with a mace; he survived, but the injury caused permanent brain damage and he lived the remaining thirty-eight years of his life as an invalid.
3. This fourth son would later be known as Charles of Valois, after the lands that constituted his apanage; his descendants would eventually become kings of France when the direct father–son Capetian line ended. For more on Louis's reasons and preparations for the crusade, see GB, pp. 116–19; LeGoff, *Saint Louis*, pp. 221–25; Richard, *Saint Louis*, pp. 513–41; Jordan, *Louis IX*, pp. 214–16.
4. On Edward's motivations and preparations for the crusade, see Wykes, pp. 217–18; Prestwich, *Edward I*, pp. 66–72. On Edward's correspondence with Louis while planning the crusade, see WR, pp. 372–73.
5. Asbridge believes that Louis headed for Tunis 'for reasons that have never been satisfactorily explained, but may well have been related to the machinations of his scheming brother Charles' (*Crusades*, p. 640).
6. Joinville, p. 349–50.
7. GB, pp. 120–21. For more on Louis's death, see *GC7*, pp. 280–82; Nangis, pp. 185–86; WR, pp. 376–77; LeGoff, *Saint Louis*, pp. 225–26; Richard, *Saint Louis*, pp. 568–70; Jordan, *Louis IX*, pp. 217–18; Gil, *Marguerite de Provence*, pp. 144–46; Sivéry, *Philippe III*, pp. 51–53.
8. GB, p. 123; LeGoff, *Saint Louis*, pp. 227–29. The *mos Teutonicus* procedure is examined in Westerhof, *Death and the Noble Body*, pp. 78–82.
9. Nangis, p. 189; GB, p. 125; *GC8*, pp. 35–37. On the funeral, see also Sivéry, *Philippe III*, pp. 79–83.
10. For discussion on this point, see Sivéry, *Philippe III*, pp. 153–57; Strayer, *Reign of Philip the Fair*, pp. 6–7. On the inquest, see *GC8*, pp. 61–64. For more on Marie of Brabant, see the chapter dedicated to her in the biography of her mother-in-law: Gil, *Marguerite de Provence*, pp. 157–61.
11. Rishanger, p. 67; Nangis, p. 188; *GC8*, pp. 31–32; WR, p. 377.
12. Despite Edmund's short stay in the Holy Land, he gained a lifelong nickname: his epithet 'Crouchback' refers not to any kind of physical deformity, but is, rather, derived from 'Crossback', i.e. a man who wore the cross of a crusader. See Simon Lloyd, 'Edmund [called Edmund Crouchback], first earl of Lancaster and first earl of Leicester (1245–1296)', *ODNB*, who notes that 'for the remainder of his life there existed almost continuously the very real prospect that he would go on crusade again'.
13. On Edward's time in the Holy Land, see Rishanger, pp. 67–71; *GC8*, pp. 24–27; WR, pp. 377–79; Langtoft, pp. 155–61; WG, pp. 204–10; Prestwich, *Edward I*, pp. 75–79; Asbridge, *Crusades*, pp. 643–44. Accounts of the assassination attempt all agree that it took place, but are confused about the details: see WR, pp. 378–79; WG, p. 208; Wykes, p. 249; Nangis, pp. 189–90.
14. Rishanger, p. 78.

15. On Edward's accession, see Morris, *A Great and Terrible King*, pp. 103–05; see also the more general discussion on coronations and succession in Andrews, *Lost Heirs*, pp. 8 and 75–76.

16. WR, p. 382 and WG, p. 212, respectively.

17. I am grateful to a number of native French speakers who discussed the nuances of this epithet with me.

18. For discussion on Edward's form of words, see Prestwich, *Edward I*, pp. 314–15; Morris, *A Great and Terrible King*, pp. 108–09. On the meeting of the two kings, see also Rishanger, p. 80; Sivéry, *Philippe III*, pp. 147–49.

19. For more on Edward's coronation, see WG, p. 213; Prestwich, *Edward I*, pp. 89–91.

20. Edward and Eleanor's daughters have often been overlooked, as discussion tends to be centred on the royal couple's quest for a male heir; a recent book that explores their lives is Wilson-Lee, *Daughters of Chivalry*.

21. In contrast to Edward's brusque remark about the death of his heir, John, a contemporary noted the grief of Edward's parents, King Henry and Queen Eleanor, at the loss of their grandson (Wykes, p. 246); see also Howell, *Eleanor of Provence*, p. 250; and Prestwich, *Edward I*, who notes that 'it is remarkable that the king, and even more so the queen, should have left their son Henry to be ill and die at Guildford without making the short journey from London to visit him', that 'little attention was paid by the king to the anniversaries of the deaths of his children', and that 'there is no mention [in the 1284 household accounts] of masses for the soul of Alphonso, who died that year' (p. 126). On attitudes to childhood in the Middle Ages and on the childhoods of English kings in particular, see Orme, *Medieval Children* and Orme, *From Childhood to Chivalry*, respectively.

22. Parsons notes that during the 1270s Eleanor was giving birth on average every fifteen months (*Eleanor of Castile*, p. 58), which means she was pregnant more than half of the time.

23. Edward's campaigns in Wales do not form part of our story here; for more on the Anglo-Welsh conflict of the 1270s and 1280s, see WG, pp. 215–23; *GC8*, pp. 59–60; Prestwich, *Edward I*, pp. 170–232; Morris, *A Great and Terrible King*, pp. 174–90.

24. For more on this meeting and the agreement reached, see Prestwich, *Edward I*, pp. 316–17; Morris, *A Great and Terrible King*, pp. 173–74; Sivéry, *Philippe III*, pp. 252–53.

25. For more on Alfonso X and his succession arrangements, see *GC8*, pp. 54–57; Nangis, p. 194; Gil, *Marguerite de Provence*, pp. 164–66; Bartlett, *Blood Royal*, pp. 219–20. For more on Philip III's botched response to it, see *GC8*, pp. 64–67; Nangis, p. 197; Hélary, *L'Armée du roi de France*, pp. 21–22; Sivéry, *Philippe III*, pp. 163–65, who refers to the episode as a 'humiliation' for Philip (p. 165); and Bradbury, *Capetians*, p. 238, who calls Philip's campaign 'reckless'.

26. For more on the Navarrese situation at this point, see *GC8*, pp. 50–52; Sivéry, *Philippe III*, pp. 150–51; Woodacre, *Queens Regnant of Navarre*, pp. 25–29.

27. To recap, marriages that we may infer came about (at least in part) due to mutual affection include those of Eleanor of Aquitaine and Henry II; Constance of Brittany and Guy de Thouars; Sybil of Jerusalem and Guy de Lusignan; Isabella of Angoulême and Hugh X de Lusignan; Eleanor of England and Simon de Montfort; and Blanche of Artois and Edmund of England. To these we might consider adding Philip I of France and Bertrade de Montfort, and Philip II of France and Agnes of Merania, though whether or not these two couples could genuinely claim to be 'married' is debatable. With all these relationships it is interesting to speculate on how the history of the two dynasties, and of the realms of France and England, might have been different had these individuals not felt and acted upon personal attraction to each other.

28. *GC8*, p. 59. On Margaret and Eleanor's approval, see *GC8*, p. 58; Gil, *Marguerite de Provence*, pp. 171–73; Sivéry, *Philippe III*, pp. 193–94.

29. On Philip's intervention in Sicilian affairs, see Sivéry, *Philippe III*, pp. 265–70. For more on the Sicilian Vespers in general, see *GC8*, pp. 82–89 and 91–95; Nangis, pp. 197–204; Gil, *Marguerite de Provence*, pp. 183–90; Dunbabin, *Charles I of Anjou*, pp. 99–113; Runciman, *Sicilian Vespers*.

30. In what is probably an example of female solidarity, Edward's wife and mother (who had both been married at the age of around thirteen and obliged to consummate their unions straight away) persuaded him that Eleanor was, at thirteen herself, too young for the actual wedding to take place straight away. On this point, see Parsons, *Eleanor of Castile*, p. 21; Wilson-Lee, *Daughters of Chivalry*, pp. 35–36.

31. Rishanger, p. 108.

32. For discussion on the difficult position in which Edward found himself, see Prestwich, *Edward I*, pp. 320–22.

33. On Philip's failed Aragonese campaign, see *GC8*, pp. 102–13; Nangis, pp. 205–07; Sivéry, *Philippe III*, pp. 270–88; Hélary, *L'Armée du roi de France*, pp. 25–26; Strayer, 'Crusade against Aragon'. Bradbury notes that 'the war had cost 1,229,000 *livres tournois* and gained absolutely nothing' (*Capetians*, p. 239).

34. For more on Philip's death, see *GC8*, pp. 117–20 (quote p. 118); Sivéry, *Philippe III*, pp. 278–80.

35. *GC8*, p. 119. See also Sivéry, *Philippe III*, pp. 281–86; the most positive summary he can come up with is that Philip was 'unlucky throughout his life' (p. 281).

Chapter 25

1. Strayer notes that '[Philip's] chief duty, as he saw it, was to establish his authority over all inhabitants of the kingdom of France', and that he therefore concentrated on this while refusing to become involved in matters in Germany, Italy, the Spanish kingdoms or the Holy Land (*Reign of Philip the Fair*, p. 314).

2. For more on Philip IV's relationship with Alfonso III at the start of their reigns, see Favier, *Philippe le Bel*, pp. 292–93.

3. On the meeting between the two kings in 1286, see *GC8*, pp. 127–29; Nangis, p. 208; Rishanger, p. 112; Prestwich, *Edward I*, p. 323; Morris, *A Great and Terrible King*, pp. 204–07. A note of caution is sounded by Favier, who says that 'the apparent cordiality did not fool anyone' (*Philippe le Bel*, pp. 206–07).

4. For more on Margaret and her short life, see A.A.M. Duncan, 'Margaret [Called the Maid of Norway] (1282/3–1290), Queen-Designate of Scots', *ODNB*.

5. As we saw in Chapter 7, in 1175 William the Lion of Scots had been forced to pay homage to Henry II for Scotland, as well as his English lands; this arrangement had lasted only until 1189, when the newly crowned Richard the Lionheart agreed to terminate it in return for a cash payment towards his forthcoming crusade.

6. For more on Edward I's intervention in Scottish affairs during this succession crisis, see WG, pp. 232–39; Langtoft, pp. 190–95; Barrow, *Kingship and Unity*, pp. 158–69; Prestwich, *Edward I*, pp. 356–75; Morris, *A Great and Terrible King*, pp. 229–61. On the dynastic situation in Scotland, and the competing claims of Balliol, Robert Bruce and others, see Bartlett, *Blood Royal*, pp. 72–74. Bartlett points out that submitting the case for judgement to an external ruler 'left the Scottish kingdom in a vulnerable subordinate position' (ibid., p. 77).

7. For more on Eleanor's position in the succession, see Morris, *A Great and Terrible King*, pp. 234–35; Parsons, *Eleanor of Castile*, p. 38; Bartlett, *Blood Royal*, pp. 144–45; and Wilson-Lee, *Daughters of Chivalry*, pp. 84–85, who notes on the subject of Eleanor's marriage that 'such a minor prince could hardly have anticipated that the great English king would bless Henri's marriage to his first-born child, who was second-in-line to the English throne. That this agreement was reached suggests a strong personal connection between Henri and Edward, and possibly a personal connection between Henri and his future bride' (ibid., p. 117).

8. The Auld Alliance was never officially revoked, but is considered by some to have ended with the signing of the Treaty of Edinburgh in 1560; its terms were certainly superseded by the accession of James VI of Scots to the English throne (as James I) in 1603. For more on the alliance, see Tanner, 'Franco-Scottish Alliance', and Durot, 'La crépuscule de l'*Auld Alliance*'.

9. Joan of Navarre would grow up to leave 'a legacy as a beloved queen consort of France who served as a model of medieval queenship and engaged in literary and religious patronage' (Woodacre, *Queens Regnant of Navarre*, p. 21); one of these acts of literary patronage involved commissioning Joinville to write his *Life of St Louis*, which we have quoted in previous chapters. Philip appears to have been very fond of her, choosing not to remarry after her early death in 1305 even though he was only in his thirties at the time. For more on Joan's life, see Woodacre, *Queens Regnant of Navarre*, pp. 21–49.

10. Exactly how much of an effect his wife's death had on Edward politically – rather than personally – is unclear. One of his biographers notes that 'there is no doubt that the character of Edward's reign changed markedly after Eleanor's death in 1290, but how far the change can be attributed to the loss of her influence on Edward is debatable, for there were many other factors at work' (Prestwich, *Edward I*, p. 125). On Eleanor's death, see also WG, pp. 227–28; Rishanger, pp. 120–21; Parsons, *Eleanor of Castile*, pp. 58–60 (and p. 209 for the imitation of Capetian practice); Wilson-Lee, *Daughters of Chivalry*, pp. 104–09.

11. For a discussion on the role played by other women at the English and French courts in the late thirteenth century, see Neal, 'Royal Women and Intra-familial Diplomacy'.

12. This engagement is described in WG, pp. 240–41.

13. Nangis, p. 218. Similar accusations and wording may be found in *GC8*, p. 148.

14. Langtoft, p. 201.

15. Further details and discussion on the early stages of Philip and Edward's dispute over Gascony may be found in WG, pp. 240–48; Rishanger, pp. 137–39; *GC8*, pp. 148–49; Favier, *Philippe le Bel*, pp. 209–12; Strayer, *Reign of Philip the Fair*, pp. 317–19; Hélary, *L'armée du roi de France*, pp. 26–28; Morris, *A Great and Terrible King*, pp. 264–70; and Prestwich, *Edward I*, pp. 376–81, who believes that 'the war, when it came, was of Philip's choice, not Edward's' (p. 381).

16. Langtoft, p. 213. For an analysis of Edward's quest for allies, see Favier, *Les Plantagenêts*, pp. 793–98.

17. *SECH*, p. 163. For a discussion on the decreasing number of men taking up the honour of knighthood during the thirteenth century, see Crouch, *English Aristocracy*, pp. 16–19.

18. Rishanger, pp. 158–59.

19. For more on the 1294–96 phase of the war, see WG, pp. 248–54 and 260–64; Rishanger, pp. 140–44 and 147–50; Nangis, pp. 221–28; *GC8*, pp. 152–64; Favier, *Philippe le Bel*, pp. 214–16; Strayer, *Reign of Philip the Fair*, pp. 319–21; Prestwich, *Edward I*, pp. 381–85. For details of the French forces and their deployment, see Hélary, *L'armée du roi de France*, pp. 148–52.

20. Rishanger, p. 153; *GC8*, pp. 154–55.

21. For more on the process of St Louis's canonisation, which had started not long after his death, see LeGoff, *Saint Louis*, pp. 230–34; Gaposchkin, *Making of Saint Louis*, pp. 48–66.

22. On Edward and Philip's time in Flanders and the mediation of the pope, see WG, pp. 315–22; Rishanger, pp. 177–79; Nangis, pp. 230–33; *GC8*, pp. 173–80; Prestwich, *Edward I*, pp. 392–96; Favier, *Philippe le Bel*, pp. 223–31; Hélary, *L'armée du roi de France*, pp. 28–31. For more on the Battle of Stirling Bridge, see Rishanger, pp. 179–80; A.A.M. Duncan, 'Stirling Bridge, Battle of', *OEMW*, vol. 3, pp. 311–12.

23. For a discussion on the negotiations, see Prestwich, *Edward I*, pp. 394–96.

24. For more on Margaret, see John Carmi Parsons, 'Margaret [Margaret of France] (1279?–1318), Queen of England', *ODNB*. On Edward and Margaret's personal relationship, see Prestwich, *Edward I*, pp. 129–31. A discussion on Margaret's relationship with her new stepdaughters may be found in Wilson-Lee, *Daughters of Chivalry*, pp. 202–04.

25. For more on the Battle of Courtrai, also known as 'the Battle of the Golden Spurs', see Nangis, pp. 242–44; *GC8*, pp. 203–09; Kelly DeVries, 'Courtrai, Battle and Siege of', *OEMW*, vol. 1, pp. 435–37; Favier, *Philippe le Bel*, pp. 239–41; Strayer, *Reign of Philip the Fair*, pp. 334–35; Hélary, *L'armée du roi de France*, pp. 31–33. For more on Robert II of Artois's military career, see Hélary, *L'armée du roi de France*, pp. 65–66 and 246; Hélary, 'Robert II, comte d'Artois'; Dunbabin, *Charles I of Anjou*, p. 186.

26. On the treaty, see Rishanger, pp. 213–14; Nangis, p. 247; *GC8*, p. 219; Favier, *Les Plantagenêts*, pp. 804–06.

Epilogue

1. Margaret and Blanche were not sisters. As we noted in Chapter 25, there was both a duchy of Burgundy and a county of Burgundy, the former part of France and the latter owing allegiance to the Empire. Margaret was the daughter of Duke Robert II, while Blanche's father was Count Otto IV. As it happens, Philip IV's other son, Philip (who was not at the wedding), was married to Joan of Burgundy, Blanche's sister.

2. Nangis, p. 269; *GC8*, p. 259. For more on the wedding, the guests and the gifts, see Brown, 'Political Repercussions'; Brown, 'Marriage of Edward II'; Menache, 'Isabella of France'.

BIBLIOGRAPHY

Primary sources and encyclopaedias

AB, *Dukes*	Anonymous of Béthune, *History of the Dukes of Normandy and the Kings of England*, trans. Janet Shirley, with historical notes by Paul Webster (Oxford: Routledge, 2021)
AB, *Rois*	Anonymous of Béthune, *Chronique des rois de France*, ed. L. Delisle, in *Recueil des Historiens des Gaules et de la France*, vol. 24 (Paris: Imprimerie Nationale, 1904), pp. 750–75
Ambroise	Ambroise, *The History of the Holy War: Ambroise's Estoire de la Guerre Sainte*, trans. Marianne Ailes, introduction and notes by Marianne Ailes and Malcolm Barber (Woodbridge: Boydell, 2011; orig. 2003)
ASC	*The Anglo-Saxon Chronicles*, ed. and trans. Michael Swanton (London: Phoenix, 2000)
Barnwell	Barnwell Annalist, *Memoriale Walteri de Coventria*, ed. William Stubbs, 2 vols (London: Longman, 1879–80)
Becket	*The Life and Death of Thomas Becket, Chancellor of England and Archbishop of Canterbury, Based on the Account of William FitzStephen His Clerk, with Additions from Other Contemporary Sources*, trans. George Greenaway (London: Folio Society, 1961)
Benoît	Benoît de Sainte-Maure, *Three Anglo-Norman Kings: The Lives of William the Conqueror and Sons by Benoit de Sainte-Maure*, trans. Ian Short (Toronto: Pontifical Institute of Medieval Studies, 2018)
CE	*Catholic Encyclopaedia: An International Work of Reference on the Constitution, Doctrine, Discipline, and History of the Catholic Church*, ed. Charles D. Herbermann et al., 15 vols (New York: Robert Appleton Company, 1907–12), available at: https://www.newadvent.org/cathen/
Constance	*The Charters of Duchess Constance of Brittany and Her Family, 1171–1221*, ed. Judith Everard and Michael Jones (Woodbridge: Boydell, 1999)
CRSHR	*Chronicles of the Reigns of Stephen, Henry II and Richard I*, ed. Richard Howlett, 4 vols (London: Rolls Series, 1884–89)
Dialogus	*Dialogus de Saccario: The Course of the Exchequer*, ed. and trans. Charles Johnson (London: Nelson and Sons, 1950)

Diceto	Ralph of Diceto, *Radulphi de Diceto Opera Historica: The Historical Works of Master Ralph de Diceto*, ed. William Stubbs, 2 vols (London: Rolls Series, 1876)
Eracles	The Old French Continuation of William of Tyre [Lyon *Eracles*], in *The Conquest of Jerusalem and the Third Crusade: Sources in Translation*, trans. Peter W. Edbury (Aldershot: Ashgate, 1998), pp. 11–145
Eustace	*The Romance of Eustace the Monk*, in *Two Medieval Outlaws: Eustace the Monk and Fouke Fitz Waryn*, trans. Glyn S. Burgess (Woodbridge: D.S. Brewer, 2009), pp. 3–87
Galbert	Galbert of Bruges, *The Murder of Charles the Good*, trans. James Bruce Ross (Toronto: University of Toronto Press, 1982)
GB	Geoffrey of Beaulieu, *Life and Saintly Comportment of Louis, Former King of the Franks, of Pious Memory*, in *The Sanctity of Louis IX: Early Lives of Saint Louis by Geoffrey of Beaulieu and William of Chartres*, trans. Larry F. Field, ed. M. Cecilia Gaposchkin and Sean L. Field (Ithaca and London: Cornell University Press, 2014), pp. 69–128
GC6	*Les grandes chroniques de France, tome sixième, Louis VII le Jeune et Philippe II Auguste*, ed. Jules Viard (Paris: Honoré Champion, 1930)
GC7	*Les grandes chroniques de France, tome septième, Louis VIII et Saint Louis*, ed. Jules Viard (Paris: Honoré Champion, 1932)
GC8	*Les grandes chroniques de France, tome huitième, Philippe III le Hardi, Philippe IV le Bel, Louis X Hutin, Philippe V le Long*, ed. Jules Viard (Paris: Honoré Champion, 1934)
Gervase	Gervase of Canterbury, *The Historical Works of Gervase of Canterbury*, ed. William Stubbs, 2 vols (London: Rolls Series, 1879–80)
GM	Gilbert of Mons, *Chronicle of Hainaut*, trans. Laura Napran (Woodbridge: Boydell, 2005)
GRH	*Gesta regis Henrici secundi Benedicti abbatis: The Chronicle of the Reigns of Henry II and Richard I, AD 1169–1192*, ed. William Stubbs, 2 vols (London: Rolls Series, 1867)
GS	*Gesta Stephani*, ed. and trans. K.R. Potter with notes and introduction by R.H.C. Davis (Oxford: Clarendon, 1976)
GT	*The Gesta Tancredi of Ralph of Caen. A History of the Normans on the First Crusade*, trans. Bernard S. Bachrach and David S. Bachrach (Aldershot: Ashgate, 2005)
Guala	*The Letters and Charters of Cardinal Guala Bicchieri, Papal Legate in England 1216–1218*, ed. Nicholas Vincent (Woodbridge: Canterbury and York Society, 1996)
GW	Gerald of Wales, *Instruction for a Ruler: De Principis Instructione*, ed. and trans. Robert Bartlett (Oxford: Clarendon, 2018)
HH	Henry of Huntingdon, *The History of the English People 1000–1154*, trans. Diana Greenway (Oxford: Oxford University Press, 2002)
HWM	*History of William Marshal*, ed. and trans. A.J. Holden, S. Gregory and D. Crouch, 3 vols (London: Anglo-Norman Text Society, 2002–06)
Innocent	*Selected Letters of Pope Innocent III Concerning England (1198–1216)*, ed. and trans. C.R. Cheney and W.H. Semple (London: Nelson and Sons, 1953)
IP	*The Chronicle of the Third Crusade: The Itinerarium Peregrinorum et Gesta Regis Ricardi*, trans. Helen J. Nicholson (London and New York: Routledge, 2001; orig. 1997)
JF	Jordan Fantosme, *Jordan Fantosme's Chronicle*, ed. and trans. R.C. Johnston (Oxford: Clarendon, 1981; facsimile repr. Edinburgh: Birlinn, 2018)
Joinville	Jean de Joinville, *The Life of St Louis*, in *Chronicles of the Crusades*, trans. M.R.B. Shaw (London: Penguin, 1963), pp. 161–353

JS	John of Salisbury, *The Historia Pontificalis of John of Salisbury*, ed. and trans. Marjorie Chibnall (London: Nelson and Sons, 1956)
Langtoft	Peter de Langtoft, *The Chronicle of Pierre de Langtoft*, ed. Thomas Wright, 2 vols (London: Longman, Green, Reader and Dyer, 1866–68)
Map	Walter Map, *De nugis curialium: On Courtiers' Trifles*, ed. and trans. Frederick Tupper and Marbury Bladen Ogle (London: Chatto and Windus, 1924)
Margam	*The Annals of Margam*, vol. 1 of *Annales Monastici*, ed. H.R. Luard, 5 vols (London: Rolls Series, 1864–69)
MP	Matthew Paris, *Matthew Paris's English History*, trans. J.A. Giles, 3 vols (London: Henry G. Bohn, 1852–54)
MR	Minstrel of Reims, *Récits d'un ménestrel de Reims*, ed. Natalis de Wailly (Paris: Librairie Renouard, 1876)
Nangis	William of Nangis, *Chronique de Guillaume de Nangis*, ed. F. Guizot (Paris: Brière, 1825)
NB	Nicholas de Bray, *Des faits et des gestes de Louis VIII*, ed. F. Guizot, in *Collection des Mémoires relatifs à l'histoire de France*, vol. 11 (Paris: Brière, 1825), pp. 387–463
ODNB	*Oxford Dictionary of National Biography*, online edition, available at: www.oxforddnb.com
OEMW	*Oxford Encyclopaedia of Medieval Warfare and Military Technology*, ed. Clifford J. Rogers, 3 vols (New York: Oxford University Press, 2010)
OV	Orderic Vitalis, *The Ecclesiastical History of Orderic Vitalis*, ed. and trans. Marjorie Chibnall, 6 vols (Oxford: Clarendon, 1968–80)
PL	*Patrologia Latina*, ed. Jacques-Paul Migne, 214 vols (Paris, 1841–55); online *Patrologia Latina* database, available at: http://pld.chadwyck.co.uk/
PVC	Peter of les Vaux-de-Cernay, *The History of the Albigensian Crusade*, trans. W.A. Sibly and M.D. Sibly (Woodbridge: Boydell, 1998)
RC	Ralph of Coggeshall, *Radulphi de Coggeshall Chronicon Anglicanum*, ed. J. Stevenson (London: Rolls Series, 1875)
RD	Richard of Devizes, *The Chronicle of Richard of Devizes*, ed. and trans. John T. Appleby (London: Nelson and Sons, 1963)
RH	Roger of Howden, *The Annals of Roger of Hoveden*, trans. Henry T. Riley, 2 vols (London: Henry Bohn, 1853; facsimile repr. Felinfach: Llanerch, 1997)
Rigord	Rigord, *Vie de Philippe Auguste*, ed. F. Guizot, in *Collection des Mémoires relatifs à l'histoire de France*, vol. 11 (Paris: Brière, 1825), pp. 9–180
Rishanger	William of Rishanger, *Willelmi Rishanger, Chronica et Annales*, ed. H.T. Riley (London: Rolls Series, 1865)
RT	Robert de Torigni, *The Chronicles of Robert de Monte*, trans. Joseph Stevenson (London: Seeleys, 1856; facsimile repr. Felinfach: Llanerch, 1991)
RW	Roger of Wendover, *Roger of Wendover's Flowers of History*, trans. J.A. Giles, 2 vols (London: Henry G. Bohn, 1849; facsimile repr. Felinfach: Llanerch, 1995–96)
SCW	*The Song of the Cathar Wars: A History of the Albigensian Crusade*, trans. Janet Shirley, Crusade Texts in Translation (Farnham: Ashgate, 2000)
SD	Simeon of Durham, *History of the Kings of England*, trans. Joseph Stevenson, in *The Church Historians of England, Volume III, Part II: Simeon of Durham* (London: Seeleys, 1855), pp. 423–618
SECH	*Sources of English Constitutional History: A Selection of Documents from AD 600 to the Present*, ed. and trans. Carl Stephenson and Frederick G. Marcham (London: Harrap, 1938)

BIBLIOGRAPHY

Suger   Suger, *The Deeds of Louis the Fat*, trans. Richard Cusimano and John Moorhead (Washington, DC: Catholic University of America Press, 1992)

Tours   *Ex Chronico Turonensi auctore anonyme S. Martini Turonensis canonico*, ed. Michel-Jean-Joseph Brial, in *Recueil des historiens des Gaules et de la France*, vol. 18 (Paris: 1822), pp. 290–322

Vie de Louis VIII   *Vie de Louis VIII*, ed. F. Guizot, in *Collection des Mémoires relatifs à l'histoire de France*, vol. 11 (Paris: Brière, 1825), pp. 355–86

Wace   Wace, *The History of the Norman People: Wace's Roman de Rou*, trans. Glyn S. Burgess (Woodbridge: Boydell, 2004)

WB, *Philippide*   William the Breton, *La Philippide*, ed. F. Guizot, in *Collection des Mémoires relatifs à l'histoire de France*, vol. 12 (Paris: Brière, 1825), pp. 1–390

WB, *Vie*   William the Breton, *Vie de Philippe Auguste*, ed. F. Guizot, in *Collection des Mémoires relatifs à l'histoire de France*, vol. 11 (Paris: Brière, 1825), pp. 181–354

WC   William of Chartres, *On the Life and Deeds of Louis, King of the Franks of Famous Memory, and on the Miracles That Declare His Sanctity*, in *The Sanctity of Louis IX: Early Lives of Saint Louis by Geoffrey of Beaulieu and William of Chartres*, trans. Larry F. Field, ed. M. Cecilia Gaposchkin and Sean L. Field (Ithaca and London: Cornell University Press, 2014), pp. 129–59

WG   Walter of Guisborough, *The Chronicle of Walter of Guisborough, Previously Edited as the Chronicle of Walter of Hemingford or Hemingburgh*, ed. Harry Rothwell (London: Royal Historical Society, 1957)

WM, *Chronicle*   William of Malmesbury, *Chronicle of the Kings of England*, trans. J.A. Giles (London: Henry G. Bohn, 1847)

WM, *Historia*   William of Malmesbury, *Historia Novella*, ed. and trans. K.R. Potter (London: Nelson and Sons, 1955)

WN   William of Newburgh, *The History of English Affairs*, ed. and trans. P.G. Walsh and M.J. Kennedy, 2 vols (Warminster: Aris & Phillips 1988)

WP   William of Puylaurens, *The Chronicle of William of Puylaurens: The Albigensian Crusade and Its Aftermath*, trans. W.A. Sibley and M.D. Sibley (Woodbridge: Boydell, 2003)

WR   William of Rishanger, *Continuation of Matthew Paris's Chronicle*, in vol. 3 of *Matthew Paris's English History*, trans. J.A. Giles (London: Henry G. Bohn, 1854), pp. 331–83

Wykes   Thomas Wykes, *Chronicon vulgo dictum Chronicon Thomae Wykes, 1066–1289*, vol. 4 of *Annales Monastici*, ed. H.R. Luard, 5 vols (London: Rolls Series, 1864–69)

Secondary sources

Abalain, Hervé, *Le français et les langues historiques de la France* (Paris: Éditions Jean-Paul Gisserot, 2007)

Abels, Richard, 'Cultural Representation and the Practice of War in the Middle Ages', *Journal of Medieval Military History*, 6 (2008), 1–31

Abels, Richard P. and Bernard S. Bachrach (eds), *The Normans and Their Adversaries at War: Essays in Memory of C. Warren Hollister* (Woodbridge: Boydell, 2001)

Abulafia, David, *Frederick II: A Medieval Emperor* (Oxford: Oxford University Press, 1988)

— 'Charles of Anjou Reassessed', *Journal of Medieval History*, 26 (2000), 93–114

Aird, William M., *Robert Curthose, Duke of Normandy, c. 1050–1134* (Woodbridge: Boydell, 2008)

Allmand, Christopher, 'War and the Non-Combatant in the Middle Ages', in *Medieval Warfare: A History*, ed. Maurice Keen (Oxford: Oxford University Press, 1999), pp. 253–72

— 'The Reporting of War in the Middle Ages', in *War and Society in Medieval and Early Modern Britain*, ed. Diana Dunn (Liverpool: Liverpool University Press, 2000), pp. 17–33

Ambler, Sophie Thérèse, *The Song of Simon de Montfort: England's First Revolutionary and the Death of Chivalry* (London: Picador, 2019)

Amt, Emilie, 'Besieging Bedford: Military Logistics in 1224', *Journal of Medieval Military History*, 1 (2002), 101–24

Andrews, J.F., *Lost Heirs of the Medieval Crown* (Barnsley: Pen & Sword, 2019)

Armstrong, Abigail S., 'English Royal Family Ties: Edward I and His Breton Nieces', in *Relations of Power: Women's Networks in the Middle Ages*, ed. Emma O. Bérat, Rebecca Hardie and Irina Dumitrescu (Bonn: Bonn University Press, 2021), pp. 85–104

Asbridge, Thomas, 'Talking to the Enemy: The Role and Purpose of Negotiations Between Saladin and Richard the Lionheart during the Third Crusade', *Journal of Medieval History*, 39 (2013), 275–96

— *The Greatest Knight: The Remarkable Life of William Marshal, the Power Behind Five English Thrones* (London: Simon and Schuster, 2015)

— *The Crusades: The War for the Holy Land* (London: Simon and Schuster, 2020; orig. 2010)

Audoin, Edouard, *Essai sur l'armée royale au temps de Philippe Auguste* (Paris: Champion, 1913)

Aurell, Martin, *L'Empire des Plantagenêt* (Paris: Tempus, 2017; orig. 2004)

Ayton, Andrew, *Knights and Warhorses* (Woodbridge: Boydell, 1994)

— 'Arms, Armour and Horses', in *Medieval Warfare: A History*, ed. Maurice Keen (Oxford: Oxford University Press, 1999), pp. 186–208

Bachrach, Bernard, 'Medieval Siege Warfare: A Reconnaissance', *Journal of Military History*, 58 (1994), 119–33

Bachrach, Bernard and David Bachrach, *Warfare in Medieval Europe c. 400–c. 1453* (London and New York: Routledge, 2017)

Balard, Michel, *Croisades et Orient Latin, XIe–XIVe siècle*, 3rd ed. (Paris: Armand Colin, 2017; orig. 2001)

Baldwin, John W., *The Government of Philip Augustus: Foundations of French Royal Power in the Middle Ages* (Berkeley: University of California Press, 1986)

— 'Qu'est-ce que les Capétiens ont appris les Plantagenêt?', *Cahiers de Civilisation Médiévale*, 29 (1986), 3–8

— 'Le Sens de Bouvines', *Cahiers de Civilisation Médiévale*, 30 (1987), 119–30

— *Aristocratic Life in Medieval France* (Baltimore and London: Johns Hopkins University Press, 2000)

— *Paris, 1200* (Stanford: Stanford University Press, 2010; orig. Paris: Éditions Flammarion, 2006)

Bandel, Betty, 'The English Chroniclers' Attitude Toward Women', *Journal of the History of Ideas*, 16 (1955), 113–18

Barber, Richard, *The Knight and Chivalry* (London: Longman, 1970)

— *Henry Plantagenet* (Woodbridge: Boydell, 2001; orig. 1964)

— *Henry II: A Prince among Princes* (London: Allen Lane, 2015)

— *Magnificence and Princely Splendour in the Middle Ages* (Woodbridge: Boydell, 2020)

Barber, Richard and Juliet Barker, *Tournaments* (Woodbridge: Boydell, 1989)

Barker, Juliet, *The Tournament in England 1100–1400* (Woodbridge: Boydell, 1982)

Barlow, Frank, *Thomas Becket* (Berkeley: University of California Press, 1986)

— *The Feudal Kingdom of England 1042–1216*, 5th rev. ed. (Harlow: Longman, 1999; orig. 1955)

Barratt, Nick, 'The Revenues of John and Philip Augustus Revisited', in *King John: New Interpretations*, ed. S.D. Church (Woodbridge: Boydell, 1999), pp. 75–99

Barrow, G.W.S., *Kingship and Unity: Scotland 1000–1306* (Toronto: University of Toronto Press, 1981)

Barthélemy, Dominique, *La bataille de Bouvines* (Paris: Perrin, 2018)

Bartlett, Robert, *England under the Norman and Angevin Kings, 1075–1225* (Oxford: Oxford University Press, 2000)

— *Gerald of Wales: A Voice of the Middle Ages* (Stroud: The History Press, 2006)

— *Blood Royal: Dynastic Politics in Medieval Europe* (Cambridge: Cambridge University Press, 2020)

Bartlett, W.B., *God Wills It! An Illustrated History of the Crusades* (Stroud: Sutton, 1999)

— *The Last Crusade: The Seventh Crusade and the Battle for the Holy Land* (Stroud: Tempus, 2007)

Bassett, Hayley, 'An Instrument of Diplomacy? The Curious Case of Princess Alice of France', in *Queens in Waiting: Potential and Prospective Queens*, ed. Sarah Betts and Chloe McKenzie (Basingstoke: Palgrave Macmillan, forthcoming)

Bates, David, *The Normans and Empire* (Oxford: Oxford University Press, 2013)

— *William the Conqueror* (New Haven and London: Yale University Press, 2016)

Bates, David and Anne Curry (eds), *England and Normandy in the Middle Ages* (London: Hambledon, 1994)

Bautier, Robert-Henri (ed.), *La France de Philippe Auguste: Le temps des mutations* (Paris: Éditions du CNRS, 1982)

Beaune, Colette, *Naissance de la nation France* (Paris: Gallimard, 1985)

Bednarski, Steven and Andrée Courtemanche, '"Sadly, and with a Bitter Heart": What the Caesarean Section Meant in the Middle Ages', *Florilegium*, 28 (2011), 33–69

Beeler, John, 'The Composition of Anglo-Norman Armies', *Speculum*, 40 (1965), 389–414

— *Warfare in England, 1066–1189* (Ithaca: Cornell University Press, 1966)

Beem, Charles, *The Lioness Roared: The Problem of Female Rule in English History* (New York: Palgrave Macmillan, 2006)

— (ed.), *The Royal Minorities of Medieval and Early Modern England* (New York: Palgrave Macmillan, 2008)

Benham, Jenny, *Peacemaking in the Middle Ages: Principles and Practice* (Manchester: Manchester University Press, 2007)

Bennett, Judith, *Medieval Women in Modern Perspective* (Washington, DC: American Historical Association, 2000)

Bennett, Matthew (ed.), *The Hutchinson Dictionary of Ancient and Medieval Warfare* (Oxford: Helicon, 1998)

— 'The Myth of the Military Supremacy of Knightly Cavalry', in *Medieval Warfare 1000–1300*, ed. John France (Abingdon: Ashgate, 2006), pp. 171–84

— 'Three Conquests of Normandy, c. 1099–c. 1204', in *La guerre en Normandie (XIe–XVe siècle)*, ed. Anne Curry and Véronique Gazeau (Caen: Presses Universitaires de Caen, 2018), pp. 25–35

Bennett, Matthew and Katherine Weikert (eds), *Medieval Hostageship c.700–c.1500: Hostage, Captive, Prisoner of War, Guarantee, Peacemaker* (Oxford and New York: Routledge, 2016)

Bennett, Matthew, Jim Bradbury, Kelly DeVries, Ian Dickie and Phyllis G. Jestice, *Fighting Techniques of the Medieval World, AD 500–AD 1500* (Staplehurst: Spellmount, 2005)

Bennett, Stephen, *Elite Participation in the Third Crusade* (Woodbridge: Boydell, 2021)

Berend, Nora, Przemysław Urbańczyk and Przemysław Wiszewski, *Central Europe in the High Middle Ages: Bohemia, Hungary and Poland, c. 900–c. 1300* (Cambridge: Cambridge University Press, 2013)

Berrou, Oliver, *The Contribution of Louis VIII to the Advancement of Capetian France* (Saarbrücken: Lambert Academic Publishing, 2013)

Birkett, Helen, 'News in the Middle Ages: News, Communications, and the Launch of the Third Crusade in 1187–1188', *Viator*, 49 (2018), 23–61

Bisson, T.N., *The Medieval Crown of Aragon* (Oxford: Clarendon, 1986)

408

Bliese, John, 'The Just War as Concept and Motive in the Central Middle Ages', *Medievalia et Humanistica*, 17 (1991), 1–26

Bloch, Marc, *La France sous les derniers capétiens, 1223–1328* (Paris: Armand Colin, 1958)

Blythe, James M., 'Women in the Military: Scholastic Arguments and Medieval Images of Female Warriors', *History of Political Thought*, 22 (2001), 242–69

Bolton, J.L., *Money in the Medieval English Economy: 973–1489* (Manchester: Manchester University Press, 2012)

Borgnis Desbordes, Eric, *Constance de Bretagne (1161–1201), une duchesse face à Richard Coeur de Lion et Jean sans Terre* (Fouesnant, Brittany: Yoran Embanner, 2018)

Bothwell, James, *Falling from Grace: Reversal of Fortune and the English Nobility 1075–1455* (Manchester: Manchester University Press, 2008)

Bouchard, Constance Brittain, 'Family Structure and Family Consciousness among the Aristocracy in the Ninth to Eleventh Centuries', *Francia*, 14 (1986), 639–58

— 'Eleanor's Divorce from Louis VII: The Uses of Consanguinity', in *Eleanor of Aquitaine: Lord and Lady*, ed. Bonnie Wheeler and John Carmi Parsons (London: Palgrave Macmillan, 2003), pp. 223–35

Bournazel, Eric, *Louis VI le Gros* (Paris: Fayard, 2007)

Bowie, Colette, *The Daughters of Henry II and Eleanor of Aquitaine* (Turnhout: Brepols, 2014)

Bradbury, Jim, 'Battles in England and Normandy, 1066–1154', *Anglo-Norman Studies*, 6 (1983), 1–12

— *The Medieval Siege* (Woodbridge: Boydell, 1992)

— *The Medieval Archer* (Woodbridge: Boydell, 1996)

— *Stephen and Matilda: The Civil War of 1139–53* (Stroud: Sutton, 1996)

— *Philip Augustus* (London and New York: Longman, 1998)

— 'Philip Augustus and King John: Personality and History', in *King John: New Interpretations*, ed. S.D. Church (Woodbridge: Boydell, 1999), pp. 347–61

— *The Routledge Companion to Medieval Warfare* (London: Routledge, 2004)

— *The Capetians: Kings of France 987–1328* (London: Continuum, 2007)

Brooks, F.W. and F. Oakley, 'The Campaign and Battle of Lincoln 1217', *Associated Architectural Societies' Reports and Papers*, vol. 26, part 2 (1922)

Broughton, Bradford (ed.) *Dictionary of Medieval Knighthood and Chivalry* (London: Greenwood, 1986)

Brown, Elizabeth A.R., 'The Prince is the Father of the King: The Character and Childhood of Philip the Fair of France', *Mediaeval Studies*, 49 (1987), 287–334

— '*Persona et Gesta*: The Image and Deeds of the Thirteenth-Century Capetians. 3. The Case of Philip the Fair', *Viator*, 19 (1988), 219–46

— 'The Political Repercussions of Family Ties in the Early Fourteenth Century: The Marriage of Edward II of England and Isabelle of France', *Speculum*, 63 (1988), 573–95

— 'The Marriage of Edward II of England and Isabella of France: A Postscript', *Speculum*, 64 (1989), 373–79

— 'Moral Imperatives and Conundrums of Conscience: Reflections on Philip the Fair of France', *Speculum*, 87 (2012), 1–36

— 'Philip the Fair of France, Nemesis of Edward I of England', in *Prowess, Piety, and Public Order in Medieval Society: Studies in Honor of Richard W. Kaeuper*, ed. Craig M. Nakashian and Daniel P. Franke (Leiden: Brill, 2017), pp. 237–64

— 'Réflexions sur Philippe le Bel', *Annuaire-Bulletin de la Société de l'Histoire de France* (2014; published 2018), 7–24

Buck, Andrew, *The Principality of Antioch and Its Frontiers in the Twelfth Century* (Woodbridge: Boydell, 2017)

Buck, Andrew D. and Thomas W. Smith (eds), *Remembering the Crusades in Medieval Texts and Songs*, special issue of *The Journal of Religious History, Literature and Culture*, 5 (University of Wales Press, 2019)

Burnett, Charles, Alessandra Foscati and Constanza Gislon Dopfel (eds), *Pregnancy and Childbirth in the Premodern World: European and Middle Eastern Cultures, from Late Antiquity to the Renaissance* (Turnhout: Brepols, 2019)

Cannon, Henry, 'The Battle of Sandwich and Eustace the Monk', *English Historical Review*, 27 (1912), 649–70

Carpenter, David A., 'Kings, Magnates and Society: The Personal Rule of King Henry III, 1234–1258', *Speculum*, 60 (1985), 39–70

— *The Battles of Lewes and Evesham, 1265/65* (Keele: Mercia Publications, 1987)

— *The Minority of Henry III* (London: Methuen, 1990)

— 'King Henry III's Statute against Aliens: July 1263', *English Historical Review*, 107 (1992), 925–44

— *The Reign of Henry III* (London: Hambledon, 1996)

— 'Abbot Ralph of Coggeshall's Account of the Last Years of King Richard and the First Years of King John', *English Historical Review*, 113 (1998), 1210–30

— *The Struggle for Mastery: Britain 1066–1284* (London: Penguin, 2004)

— *Magna Carta* (London: Penguin Classics, 2015)

— *Henry III: The Rise to Power and Personal Rule, 1207–1258* (New Haven and London: Yale University Press, 2020)

Carpentier, Elisabeth, 'Les Historiens royaux et le pouvoir Capétien: d'Helgaud de Fleury à Guillaume le Breton', in *L'Historiographie médiévale en Europe*, ed. Jean-Philippe Genet (Paris: Éditions du CNRS, 1991), pp. 129–39

Cassagnes-Brouquet, Sophie, *La vie des femmes au Moyen Âge* (Rennes: Ouest-France, 2012)

— *Chevaleresses: Une chevalerie au féminin* (Paris: Perrin, 2013)

Cassard, Jean-Christophe, *1180–1328: L'âge d'or capétien* (Paris: Bellin, 2011)

Castor, Helen, *She-Wolves: The Women Who Ruled England before Elizabeth* (London: Faber and Faber, 2010)

Cazel, Fred A., 'The Legates Guala and Pandulf', in *Thirteenth-Century England II: Proceedings of the Newcastle-upon-Tyne Conference 1987*, ed. P.R. Coss and S.D. Lloyd (Woodbridge: Boydell, 1988), pp. 15–21

Chamberlin, E.R., *Life in Medieval France* (London: Batsford, 1967)

Chaplais, P., 'The Making of the Treaty of Paris (1259) and the Royal Style', *English Historical Review*, 67 (1952), 235–53

Cheney, Christopher, 'The Alleged Deposition of King John', in *Studies in Medieval History Presented to Frederick Maurice Powicke*, ed. R.W. Hunt, W.A. Pantin and R.W. Southern (Oxford: Clarendon, 1948), pp. 100–16

— 'King John's Reaction to the Papal Interdict in England', *Transactions of the Royal Historical Society*, 4th series, 21 (1949), 129–50

— *Pope Innocent III and England* (Stuttgart: Hiersemann, 1976)

Chibnall, Marjorie, *The World of Orderic Vitalis* (Woodbridge: Boydell, 1984)

— *Anglo-Norman England, 1066–1166* (Oxford: Blackwell 1986)

— *The Empress Matilda: Queen Consort, Queen Mother and Lady of the English* (Oxford: Wiley-Blackwell, 1991)

Church, Stephen D., 'The Earliest English Muster Roll, 18/19 December 1215', *Historical Research*, 67 (1994), 1–17

— 'King John's Testament and the Last Days of His Reign', *English Historical Review*, 125 (2010), 505–28

— *King John: England, Magna Carta and the Making of a Tyrant* (Basingstoke: Macmillan, 2015)

— 'The Date and Place of King John's Birth Together with a Codicil on His Name', *Notes and Queries*, 67 (2020), 315–23

— (ed.), *King John: New Interpretations* (Woodbridge: Boydell, 1999)

Clanchy, M.T., *England and Its Rulers, 1066–1272* (London: Wiley-Blackwell, 1983)

— *From Memory to Written Record: England 1066–1307*, 2nd ed. (Oxford: Blackwell, 1993; orig. 1979)

Clarke, Peter D. and Anne J. Duggan (eds), *Pope Alexander III (1159–81): The Art of Survival* (London: Routledge, 2012)

Clementi, D.R., 'The Documentary Evidence for the Crisis of Government in England in 1258', *Parliament, Estates and Representation*, 1 (1981), 99–108

Conklin, George, 'Ingeborg of Denmark, Queen of France, 1193–1223', in *Queens and Queenship in Medieval Europe*, ed. Anne J. Duggan (Woodbridge: Boydell, 1997), pp. 39–52

Contamine, Philippe, 'L'armée de Philippe Auguste', in *La France de Philippe Auguste: Le temps des mutations*, ed. Robert-Henri Bautier (Paris: Éditions du CNRS, 1982), pp. 577–94

— "'Le royaume de France ne peut tomber en fille." Fondement, formulation et implication d'une théorie politique à la fin du Moyen Âge', *Perspectives médiévales*, 13 (1987), 67–81

— *La guerre au moyen âge* (Paris: Presses Universitaires de France, 1992)

— *War in the Middle Ages*, trans. Michael Jones (Oxford: Blackwell, 1992)

— *Histoire militaire de la France*, tome 1: *Des origines à 1715*, 2nd ed. (Paris: Presses Universitaires de France, 1997; orig. 1992)

Cooper, Alan, *Bridges, Law and Power in Medieval England 700–1400* (Woodbridge: Boydell, 2006)

Coss, Peter, *The Knight in Medieval England 1000–1400* (Stroud: Sutton, 1993)

— *The Lady in Medieval England 1000–1500* (Stroud: Sutton, 1998)

Coulson, Charles, 'Structural Symbolism in Medieval Castle Architecture', *Journal of the British Archaeological Association*, 132 (1979), 73–90

— *Castles in Medieval Society: Fortresses in England, France and Ireland in the Central Middle Ages* (Oxford: Oxford University Press, 2003)

Cox, Eugene L., *The Eagles of Savoy: The House of Savoy in Thirteenth-Century Europe* (Princeton: Princeton University Press, 1974)

Crouch, David, *The Beaumont Twins: The Roots and Branches of Power in the Twelfth Century* (Cambridge: Cambridge University Press, 1986)

— *William Marshal: Court, Career and Chivalry in the Angevin Empire 1147–1219* (Harlow: Longman, 1990)

— 'Baronial Paranoia in King John's Reign', in *Magna Carta and the England of King John*, ed. Janet S. Loengard (Woodbridge: Boydell, 2010), pp. 45–62

— *The English Aristocracy 1070–1272: A Social Transformation* (New Haven and London: Yale University Press, 2011)

— *The Reign of King Stephen 1135–1154*, 2nd ed. (Oxford: Routledge, 2013; orig. 2000)

Dagron, Gilbert, 'Nés dans le pourpre', *Travaux et mémoires*, 12 (1994), 105–42

Danziger, Danny and John Gillingham, *1215: The Year of Magna Carta* (London: Hodder, 2003)

David, Charles Wendell, *Robert Curthose, Duke of Normandy* (Cambridge, MA: Harvard University Press, 1920)

Davies, Rees, 'Nations and National Identities in the Medieval World: An Apologia', *Journal of Belgian History*, 34 (2004), 567–79

Déjean, Jean-Luc, *Les comtes de Toulouse, 1050–1250* (Paris: Fayard, 1988; orig. 1979)

Del Campo, Luis, 'La estatura de Sancho el Fuerte', *Príncipe de Viana*, 48–49 (1952), 481–94

Delorme, Philippe, *Aliénor d'Aquitaine*, Histoire des reines de France (Paris: Pygmalion, 2001)

— *Blanche de Castille*, Histoire des reines de France (Paris: Pygmalion, 2002)

Denholm-Young, Noel, *Richard of Cornwall* (Oxford: Basil Blackwell, 1947)

DeVries, Kelly and Robert Douglas Smith, *Medieval Military Technology*, 2nd ed. (Toronto: University of Toronto Press, 2012; orig. Peterborough, Ontario: Broadview, 1992)

DeVries, Kelly, Martin J. Dougherty, Iain Dickie, Phyllis G. Jestice and Christer Jorgensen, *Battles of the Medieval World, 1000–1500: From Hastings to Constantinople* (New York: Barnes and Noble, 2006)

Diggelmann, Lindsay, 'Marriage as a Tactical Response: Henry II and the Royal Wedding of 1160', *English Historical Review*, 119 (2004), 954–64

Duby, Georges, *The Chivalrous Society*, trans. Cynthia Postan (London: Arnold, 1977)
— *Le dimanche de Bouvines* (Paris: Gallimard, 1985; orig. 1973)
— *The Legend of Bouvines: War, Religion and Culture in the Middle Ages*, trans. Catherine Tihanyi (Cambridge: Polity Press, 1990)
— *France in the Middle Ages 987–1460*, trans. Juliet Vale (Oxford: Blackwell, 1994)
— 'Women and Power', in *Cultures of Power: Lordship, Status and Process in Twelfth-Century Europe*, ed. Thomas N. Bisson (Philadelphia: University of Pennsylvania Press, 1995), pp. 69–85
Dufresne, Eugène, *Mémoires pour servir à l'histoire du chancelier Guérin* (Paris, 1888)
Duggan, Anne (ed.), *Queens and Queenship in Medieval Europe* (Woodbridge: Boydell, 1997)
Dunbabin, Jean, *Charles I of Anjou: Power, Kingship and State-Making in Thirteenth-Century Europe* (London: Longman, 1998)
— *France in the Making, 843–1180*, 2nd ed. (Oxford: Oxford University Press, 2000; orig. 1985)
Durot, Eric, 'Le crépuscule de l'*Auld Alliance*: La légitimité du pouvoir en question entre Ecosse, France et Angleterre (1558–1561)', *Revue d'histoire moderne et contemporaine*, 1 (2007), 3–46
Dutton, Kathryn, 'Geoffrey, Count of Anjou and Duke of Normandy, 1129–51', unpublished PhD thesis, University of Glasgow, 2011
Dyer, Christopher, *Making a Living in the Middle Ages: The People of Britain 850–1520* (New Haven and London: Yale University Press, 2009; orig. 2002)
Edgington, Susan and Sarah Lambert (eds), *Gendering the Crusades* (Cardiff: University of Wales Press, 2001)
Engel, Pál, *The Realm of St Stephen: A History of Medieval Hungary, 895–1526* (London: I.B. Tauris, 2001)
Erlande-Brandenberg, Alain, 'L'Architecture militaire au temps de Philippe Auguste: une nouvelle conception de la défense', in *La France de Philippe Auguste: Le temps des mutations*, ed. Robert-Henri Bautier (Paris: Éditions du CNRS, 1982), pp. 595–603
Erler, Mary and Maryanne Kowaleski (eds), *Women and Power in the Middle Ages* (Athens, GA: University of Georgia Press, 1988)
Everard, Judith, *Brittany and the Angevins: Province and Empire, 1158–1203* (Cambridge: Cambridge University Press, 2000)
Evergates, Theodore, *The Aristocracy in the County of Champagne, 1100–1300* (Philadelphia: University of Pennsylvania Press, 2007)
— *Marie of France: Countess of Champagne, 1145–1198* (Philadelphia: University of Pennsylvania Press, 2019)
Eyton, R.W., *Court, Household, and Itinerary of King Henry II* (London: Taylor & Co., 1878), available at: https://archive.org/details/courthouseholdit00eyto/page/n5/mode/2up
Facinger, Marion, 'A Study of Medieval Queenship: Capetian France 987–1237', *Studies in Medieval and Renaissance History*, 5 (1968), 1–48
Favier, Jean, *Philippe le Bel* (Paris: Tallandier, 2013; orig. Fayard, 1978)
— *Les Plantagenêts: Origines et destin d'un empire XIe–XIVe siècles* (Paris: Fayard, 2015; orig. 2004)
Fawtier, R., *The Capetian Kings of France: Monarchy and Nation 987–1328* (Basingstoke: Macmillan, 1960)
Fleiner, Carey and Elena Woodacre (eds), *Virtuous or Villainess? The Image of the Royal Mother from the Early Medieval to the Early Modern Era* (New York: Palgrave Macmillan, 2016)
Fleischmann, Suzanne, 'On the Representation of History and Fiction in the Middle Ages', *History and Theory*, 22 (1983), 278–310
Flori, Jean, *La chevalerie en France au Moyen Age* (Paris: Presses Universitaires de France, 1995)
— *Chevaliers et chevalerie au Moyen Age* (Paris: Hachette, 1998)
— *Richard Coeur de Lion: Le roi-chevalier* (Paris: Payot, 1999)

Forde, Simon, Lesley Johnson and Alan V. Murray, *Concepts of National Identity in the Middle Ages* (Leeds: Leeds Studies in English, 1995)

France, John, *Western Warfare in the Age of the Crusades 1000–1300* (London: University College London Press, 1999)

Freed, John B., *Frederick Barbarossa: The Prince and the Myth* (New Haven and London: Yale University Press, 2016)

Fröhlich, Walter, 'The Marriage of Henry VI and Constance of Sicily: Prelude and Consequences', *Anglo-Norman Studies*, 15 (1993), 99–115

Fuhrmann, Horst, *Germany in the High Middle Ages c. 1050–1200*, trans. Timothy Reuter (Cambridge: Cambridge University Press, 1986)

Fulton, Michael, *Artillery in the Age of the Crusades* (Leiden: Brill, 2018)

Gaposchkin, M. Cecilia, *The Making of Saint Louis: Kingship, Sanctity and Crusade in the Later Middle Ages* (Ithaca: Cornell University Press, 2010)

Gavrilovitch, Michel, *Étude sur le traité de Paris de 1259 entre Louis IX, roi de France, et Henri III, roi d'Angleterre* (Paris: Bouillon, 1899)

Gazeau, Véronique and Judith Green (eds), *Tinchebray 1106–2006: Actes du colloque de Tinchebray (28–30 septembre 2006)* (Flers: Le Pays Bas-Normand, 2009)

Gil, Christiane, *Marguerite de Provence*, Histoire des reines de France (Paris: Pygmalion, 2006)

Gillingham, John, 'Richard I and Berengaria of Navarre', *Bulletin of the Institute of Historical Research*, 53 (1980), 157–73

— 'Richard I and the Science of War in the Middle Ages', in *War and Government in the Middle Ages*, ed. John Gillingham and J.C. Holt (Woodbridge: Boydell, 1984), pp. 78–91

— 'War and Chivalry in the *History of William the Marshal*', in *Thirteenth-Century England II: Proceedings of the Newcastle-upon-Tyne Conference 1987*, ed. P.R. Coss and S.D. Lloyd (Woodbridge: Boydell, 1988), pp. 1–13

— 'Love, Marriage and Politics in the Twelfth Century', *Forum for Modern Language Studies*, 25 (1989), 292–303

— *Richard I* (New Haven and London: Yale University Press, 1999)

— *The English in the Twelfth Century: Imperialism, National Identity and Political Values* (Woodbridge: Boydell, 2000)

— *The Angevin Empire*, 2nd ed. (London: Bloomsbury, 2001; orig. 1984)

— 'At the Deathbeds of the Kings of England, 1066–1216', in *Herrscher- und Fürstentestamente im Westeuropäischen Mittelalter*, ed. Brigitte Kasten (Cologne, Weimar and Vienna: Böhlau-Verlag, 2008), pp. 509–30

— 'The Anonymous of Béthune, King John and Magna Carta', in *Magna Carta and the England of King John*, ed. Janet S. Loengard (Woodbridge: Boydell, 2010), pp. 27–44

— 'The Meetings of the Kings of France and England, 1066–1204', in *Normandy and Its Neighbours, 900–1250: Essays for David Bates*, ed. David Crouch and Kathleen Thompson (Turnhout: Brepols, 2011), pp. 17–42

— *William II: The Red King* (London: Allen Lane, 2015)

Given-Wilson, Chris, *Chronicles: The Writing of History in Medieval England* (London and New York: Hambledon and London, 2004)

Given-Wilson, Chris and Alice Curteis, *The Royal Bastards of Medieval England* (London: Routledge and Kegan Paul, 1984)

Gobry, Ivan, *Louis VIII, fils de Philippe II, 1223–1226*, Histoire des rois de France (Paris: Pygmalion, 2009)

Goodall, John, 'Dover Castle and the Great Siege of 1216', *Château Gaillard*, 19 (2000), 91–102

— *The English Castle* (New Haven and London: Yale University Press, 2011)

Gransden, Antonia, *Historical Writing in England*, vol. I: *c. 550–c. 1307* (London: Routledge and Kegan Paul, 1974)

Grant, Lindy, 'Blanche of Castile and Normandy', in *Normandy and Its Neighbours, 900–1250: Essays for David Bates*, ed. David Crouch and Kathleen Thompson (Turnhout: Brepols, 2011), pp. 117–34

— *Blanche of Castile: Queen of France* (New Haven and London: Yale University Press, 2016)

Green, Judith A., *The Government of England under Henry I* (Cambridge: Cambridge University Press, 1986)

— *The Aristocracy of Norman England* (Cambridge: Cambridge University Press, 1997)

— *Henry I: King of England and Duke of Normandy* (Cambridge: Cambridge University Press, 2009; orig. 2006)

— 'Duchesses of Normandy in the Eleventh and Twelfth Centuries', in *Normandy and Its Neighbours, 900–1250: Essays for David Bates*, ed. David Crouch and Kathleen Thompson (Turnhout: Brepols, 2011), pp. 43–60

Grierson, Philip, *The Coins of Medieval Europe* (London: Seaby, 1991)

Grousset, René, *Histoire des croisades et du royaume franc de Jérusalem*, 3 vols (Paris: Perrin, 1991; orig. 1936)

Guy, John, *Thomas Becket: Warrior, Priest, Rebel, Victim* (London: Viking, 2012)

Hajdu, Robert, 'Castles, Castellans and the Structure of Politics in Poitou, 1152–1271', *Journal of Medieval History*, 4 (1978), 27–53

Hallam, E.M., 'Philip the Fair and the Cult of Saint Louis: Religion and National Identity', *Studies in Church History*, 18 (1982), 201–14

Hallam, Elizabeth M. and Judith Everard, *Capetian France 987–1328*, 2nd ed. (Harlow: Pearson, 2001; orig. London: Longman, 1980)

Hamilton, Bernard, 'Women in the Crusader States: The Queens of Jerusalem, 1100–1190', in *Medieval Women*, ed. Derek Baker (Oxford: Studies in Church History, Subsidia I, 1978), pp. 143–74

— *The Leper King and His Heirs: Baldwin IV and the Crusader Kingdom of Jerusalem* (Cambridge: Cambridge University Press, 2000)

Hanley, Catherine, *War and Combat 1150–1270: The Evidence from Old French Literature* (Woodbridge: D.S. Brewer, 2003)

— *Louis: The French Prince Who Invaded England* (New Haven and London: Yale University Press, 2016)

— *Matilda: Empress, Queen, Warrior* (New Haven and London: Yale University Press, 2019)

Hattendorf, J. and R. Unger (eds), *War at Sea in the Middle Ages and Renaissance* (Woodbridge: Boydell, 2003)

Heath, Ernest, *Archery: A Military History* (London: Osprey, 1980)

Hélary, Xavier, *L'armée du roi de France: La guerre de Saint Louis à Philippe le Bel* (Paris: Perrin, 2012)

— 'Robert II, comte d'Artois: Qu'est-ce qu'un chef de guerre à la fin du XIIIe siècle?', *Rivista di storia militare*, 1 (2012), 71–84

— 'Le service militaire dû au roi en Normandie au XIIIe siècle: autour de l'ost de 1272', in *La guerre en Normandie (XIe–XVe siècle)*, ed. Anne Curry and Véronique Gazeau (Caen: Presses Universitaires de Caen, 2018), pp. 63–71

Héliot, Pierre, 'Le Château-Gaillard et les fortresses des XIIe et XIIIe siècles', *Château Gaillard*, 1 (1962), 53–75

Hibbard-Loomis, Laura, 'L'oriflamme et le cri "Munjoie" au XIIe siècle', *Le Moyen Âge*, 65 (1959), 469–99

Hicks, Sandy Burton, 'The Impact of William Clito upon the Continental Policies of Henry I of England', *Viator*, 10 (1979), 1–21

Hill, J.W.F., *Medieval Lincoln* (Cambridge: Cambridge University Press, 1948)

Hodgson, Natasha R., *Women, Crusading and the Holy Land in Historical Narrative* (Woodbridge: Boydell, 2007)

Hollister, C. Warren, *The Military Organization of Norman England* (Oxford: Clarendon, 1965)

— *Henry I* (New Haven and London: Yale University Press, 2001)

Holt, J.C., *The Northerners: A Study in the Reign of King John* (Westport: Greenwood Press, 1981; orig. Oxford: Oxford University Press, 1961)

— *Magna Carta*, 2nd ed. (Cambridge: Cambridge University Press, 1992; orig. 1965)

— 'The *Casus Regis*: The Law and Politics of Succession in the Plantagenet Dominions, 1185–1247', in *Colonial England, 1066–1215*, essays by J.C. Holt (London: Hambledon, 1997), pp. 307–26

— 'King John and Arthur of Brittany', *Nottingham Medieval Studies*, 44 (2000), 82–103

Hornaday, Aline, 'A Capetian Queen as Street Demonstrator: Isabelle of Hainaut', in *Capetian Women*, ed. Kathleen Nolan (New York and Basingstoke: Palgrave Macmillan, 2003), pp. 77–97

Hosler, John D., *The Siege of Acre, 1189–1191: Saladin, Richard the Lionheart, and the Battle That Decided the Third Crusade* (New Haven and London: Yale University Press, 2018)

— 'Embedded Reporters? Ambroise, Richard de Templo, and Roger of Howden on the Third Crusade', in *Military Cultures and Martial Enterprises in the Middle Ages: Essays in Honour of Richard P. Abels*, ed. John D. Hosler and Steven Isaac (Woodbridge: Boydell, 2020), pp. 177–91

— 'Countermeasures: The Destruction of Siege Equipment at Acre, 1189–1191', in *The Art of Siege Warfare and Military Architecture from the Classical World to the Middle Ages*, ed. Michael Eisenberg and Rabei Khamisy (Oxford: Oxbow Books, 2021), pp. 163–71

Housley, Norman, 'European Warfare, c. 1200–1320', in *Medieval Warfare: A History*, ed. Maurice Keen (Oxford: Oxford University Press, 1999), pp. 113–35

Howard, Michael, *War in European History* (Oxford: Oxford University Press, 1977)

Howell, Margaret, *Eleanor of Provence: Queenship in Thirteenth-Century England* (Oxford: Blackwell, 2001)

Huffman, Joseph P., *The Social Politics of Medieval Diplomacy: Anglo-German Relations 1066– 1307* (Ann Arbor: University of Michigan Press, 2000)

Humphrys, Julian, *Enemies at the Gate: English Castles under Siege from the 12th Century to the Civil War* (Swindon: English Heritage, 2007)

Huneycutt, Lois, 'Female Succession and the Language of Power in the Writings of Twelfth-Century Churchmen', in *Medieval Queenship*, ed. John Carmi Parsons (Stroud: Sutton, 1998; orig. 1994), pp. 189–202

— 'The Creation of a Crone: The Historical Reputation of Adelaide of Maurienne', in *Capetian Women*, ed. Kathleen Nolan (New York and Basingstoke: Palgrave Macmillan, 2003), pp. 27–44

Hyams, Paul R., 'Warranty and Good Lordship in Twelfth-Century England', *Law and History Review*, 5 (1987), 437–503

Isaac, Stephen, 'The Problem with Mercenaries', in *The Circle of War in the Middle Ages: Essays on Medieval Military and Naval History*, ed. Donald J. Kagay and L.J. Andrew Villalon (Woodbridge: Boydell, 1999), pp. 101–10

Jackson, Peter (ed.), *The Seventh Crusade, 1244–1254: Sources and Documents* (Farnham: Ashgate, 2009)

Jasperse, Jitske, 'Matilda, Leonor and Joanna: The Plantagenet Sisters and the Display of Dynastic Connections through Material Culture', *Journal of Medieval History*, 43 (2017), 523–47

— *Medieval Women, Material Culture, and Power: Matilda Plantagenet and Her Sisters* (Amsterdam: Arc Humanities Press, 2020)

— 'With This Ring: Forming Plantagenet Family Ties', in *Relations of Power: Women's Networks in the Middle Ages*, ed. Emma O. Bérat, Rebecca Hardie and Irina Dumitrescu (Bonn: Bonn University Press, 2021), pp. 67–84

Jeep, John M., *Medieval Germany: An Encyclopedia* (New York: Garland, 2001)

Jobson, Adrian, *The First English Revolution: Simon de Montfort, Henry III and the Barons' War* (London: Bloomsbury, 2012)

— (ed.), *Baronial Reform and Revolution in England, 1258–1267* (Woodbridge: Boydell, 2016)

Johns, Susan M., *Noblewomen, Aristocracy and Power in the Twelfth-Century Anglo-Norman Realm* (Manchester: Manchester University Press, 2003)

Jones, Michael, 'The Capetians and Brittany', *Historical Research*, 63 (1990), 1–16

Jones, Richard, 'Fortifications and Sieges in Western Europe, c. 800–1450', in *Medieval Warfare: A History*, ed. Maurice Keen (Oxford: Oxford University Press, 1999), pp. 163–85

Jones, Robert W., *Bloodied Banners: Martial Display on the Medieval Battlefield* (Woodbridge: Boydell, 2010)

Jones, Robert W. and Peter Coss (eds), *A Companion to Chivalry* (Woodbridge: Boydell, 2019)

Jordan, William Chester, *Louis IX and the Challenge of the Crusade: A Study in Rulership* (Princeton: Princeton University Press, 1979)

— 'Persona et Gesta: The Image and Deeds of the Thirteenth-Century Capetians. 2. The Case of Saint Louis', *Viator*, 19 (1988), 209–18

— 'Isabelle of France and Religious Devotion at the Court of Louis IX', in *Capetian Women*, ed. Kathleen Nolan (New York and Basingstoke: Palgrave Macmillan, 2003), pp. 209–23

— *A Tale of Two Monasteries: Westminster and Saint-Denis in the Thirteenth Century* (Princeton: Princeton University Press, 2009)

Kaeuper, Richard, *Chivalry and Violence in Medieval Europe* (Oxford: Oxford University Press, 1999)

Kantorowicz, Ernst, *Frederick the Second: Wonder of the World, 1194–1250* (New York: Frederick Ungar, 1931; facsimile repr. London: Head of Zeus, 2019)

Keen, Maurice, *The Laws of War in the Late Middle Ages* (London: Routledge and Kegan Paul, 1965)

— *Nobles, Knights and Men-at-Arms in the Middle Ages* (London: Hambledon, 1996)

— *Chivalry* (New Haven and London: Yale University Press, 2005; orig. 1984)

King, Andy and Andrew M. Spencer (eds), *Edward I: New Interpretations* (Woodbridge: Boydell, 2020)

King, Edmund, *King Stephen* (New Haven and London: Yale University Press, 2012)

Knowles, David, 'The Canterbury Election of 1205–6', *English Historical Review*, 53 (1938), 211–20

Kosto, Adam J., *Hostages in the Middle Ages* (Oxford: Oxford University Press, 2012)

Krynen, Jacques, '*Rex Christianissimus*: A Medieval Theme at the Roots of French Absolutism', *History and Anthropology*, 4 (1989), 76–96

Lachaud, Frédérique, *Jean sans Terre* (Paris: Perrin, 2018)

Lalou, Élisabeth, 'La flotte normande à la fin du XIIIe siècle', in *La guerre en Normandie (XIe–XVe siècle)*, ed. Anne Curry and Véronique Gazeau (Caen: Presses Universitaires de Caen, 2018), pp. 73–82

Legge, M. Dominica, *Anglo-Norman Literature and Its Background* (Oxford: Clarendon, 1963)

LeGoff, Jacques, *Saint Louis*, trans. Gareth Evan Gollrad (Notre Dame: University of Notre Dame Press, 2009)

Leroy, Béatrice, *Le royaume de Navarre: Les hommes et le pouvoir, XIIIe–XVe siècle* (Biarritz: J et D Éditions, 1995)

Lewis, Andrew, 'The Capetian Apanages and the Nature of the French Kingdom', *Journal of Medieval History*, 11 (1976), 119–34

— 'Anticipatory Association of the Heir in Early Capetian France', *American Historical Review*, 83 (1979), 906–27

— *Royal Succession in Capetian France: Studies on Familial Order and the State* (Cambridge, MA: Harvard University Press, 1981)

— *Le sang royal: La famille capétienne et l'état, France X–XIV siècles* (Paris: Gallimard, 1986)

Leyser, Henrietta, *Medieval Women: A Social History of Women in England 450–1500* (London: Weidenfeld & Nicolson, 1995)

Leyser, Karl, *Medieval Germany and Its Neighbours, 900–1250* (London: Hambledon, 1982)

— 'The Anglo-Norman Succession, 1120–5', *Anglo-Norman Studies*, 13 (1990), 225–42

Loengard, Janet S. (ed.) *Magna Carta and the England of King John* (Woodbridge: Boydell, 2010)

LoPrete, Kimberly, 'The Gender of Lordly Women: The Case of Adela of Blois', in *Studies on Medieval and Early Modern Women*, ed. Christine Meek and Catherine Lawless (Dublin: Four Courts Press, 2003), pp. 90–110

— *Adela of Blois: Countess and Lord (c. 1067–1137)* (Dublin: Four Courts Press, 2007)

Loud, G.A., 'The Kingdom of Sicily and the Kingdom of England, 1066–1266', *History*, 88 (2003), 540–67

Luchaire, Achille, 'La Condamnation de Jean Sans-Terre par la cour de France', *Revue Historique*, 27 (1900), 285–90

Lyon, Ann, 'The Place of Women in European Royal Succession in the Middle Ages', *Liverpool Law Review*, 27 (2006), 361–93

Martindale, Jane, 'Eleanor of Aquitaine: The Last Years', in *King John: New Interpretations*, ed. S.D. Church (Woodbridge: Boydell, 1999), pp. 137–64

McDougall, Sara, *Royal Bastards: The Birth of Illegitimacy, 800–1230* (Oxford: Oxford University Press, 2017)

McGlynn, Sean, 'Roger of Wendover and the Wars of Henry III, 1216–1234', in *England and Europe in the Reign of Henry III, 1216–1272*, ed. Björn K.U. Weiler and Ifor W. Rowlands (Aldershot: Ashgate, 2002), pp. 183–206

— *By Sword and Fire: Cruelty and Atrocity in Medieval Warfare* (London: Weidenfeld & Nicolson, 2008)

— *Blood Cries Afar: The Forgotten Invasion of England 1216* (Stroud: Spellmount, 2011)

— *Kill Them All: Cathars and Carnage in the Albigensian Crusade* (Stroud: The History Press, 2015)

— '"Pro patria": National Identity and War in Early Medieval England', in *Nationalism, Patriotism, Ancient and Modern: An Interdisciplinary Approach*, ed. Alexander Peck, forthcoming

McLaughlin, Megan, 'The Woman Warrior: Gender, Warfare and Society in Medieval Europe', *Women's Studies*, 17 (1990), 193–209

Menache, Sophie, 'Isabella of France, Queen of England. A Postscript', *Revue belge de philologie et d'histoire*, 90 (2012), 493–512

Menant, François, Hervé Martin, Bernard Merdrignac and Monique Chauvin, *Les Capetiens, 987–1326* (Paris: Tempus, 2018; orig. 2008)

Meuleau, Maurice, *Histoire de la chevalerie* (Rennes: Ouest-France, 2014)

Meyer, Paul, '*L'Histoire de Guillaume le Maréchal, Comte de Striguil et de Pembroke, Régent d'Angleterre*: Poème français inconnu', *Romania*, 11 (1882), 22–74

Minois, Georges, *Richard Coeur de Lion* (Paris: Perrin, 2017)

Mitchell, Mairin, *Berengaria: Enigmatic Queen of England* (Burwash: A. Wright, 1986)

Morby, John, 'The Soubriquets of Medieval European Princes', *Canadian Journal of History*, 13 (1978), 1–16

Morillo, Stephen, *Warfare under the Anglo-Norman Kings 1066–1135* (Woodbridge: Boydell, 1994)

— 'The "Age of Cavalry" Revisited', in *The Circle of War in the Middle Ages*, ed. Donald J. Kagay and L.J. Andrew Villalon (Woodbridge: Boydell, 1999), pp. 45–58

Morris, Marc, *A Great and Terrible King: Edward I and the Forging of Britain* (London: Windmill, 2009)

— *The Norman Conquest* (London: Hutchinson, 2012)

— *King John: Treachery, Tyranny and the Road to Magna Carta* (London: Hutchinson, 2015)

Musset, L., 'Quelques problèmes posés par l'annexation de la Normandie au domaine royale français', in *La France de Philippe Auguste: Le temps des mutations*, ed. Robert-Henri Bautier (Paris: Éditions du CNRS, 1982), pp. 291–309

Naismith, Rory (ed.), *Money and Coinage in the Middle Ages* (Leiden: Brill, 2019)

Naus, James, *Constructing Kingship: The Capetian Monarchs of France and the Early Crusades* (Manchester: Manchester University Press, 2016)

BIBLIOGRAPHY

Neal, Kathleen, 'Letters and Political Discourse under Edward I', in *Edward I: New Interpretations*, ed. Andy King and Andrew M. Spencer (Woodbridge: Boydell, 2020), pp. 143–62

— 'Royal Women and Intra-familial Diplomacy in Late Thirteenth-Century Anglo-French relations', *Women's History Review*, forthcoming

Newman, Charlotte, *The Anglo-Norman Nobility in the Reign of Henry I* (Philadelphia: University of Pennsylvania Press, 1988)

Nicholson, Helen, 'Women on the Third Crusade', *Journal of Medieval History*, 23 (1997), 335–49

Nicolle, David, *French Medieval Armies 1000–1300* (London: Osprey, 1991)

— 'Warfare and Technology', *Medieval World*, 6 (1992), 49–54

— *Medieval Warfare Source Book*, 2 vols (London: Brockhampton Press, 1998)

— *Arms and Armour of the Crusading Era, 1050–1350* (London: Greenhill, 1999; orig. 1988)

— (ed.), *A Companion to Medieval Arms and Armour* (Woodbridge: Boydell, 2002)

Norton, Elizabeth, *England's Queens: The Biography* (Stroud: Amberley, 2012)

O'Callaghan, Joseph, *A History of Medieval Spain* (Ithaca: Cornell University Press, 1975)

Oksanen, Elijas, *Flanders and the Anglo-Norman World, 1066–1216* (Cambridge: Cambridge University Press, 2012)

Oldenbourg, Zoé, *Massacre at Montségur*, trans. Peter Green (London: Phoenix, 1998; orig. Weidenfeld & Nicolson, 1961)

Oman, Charles, *The Art of War in the Middle Ages*, 2 vols (London: Greenhill, 1991; repr. from Methuen, 1924; orig. 1885)

Orme, Nicholas, *From Childhood to Chivalry: The Education of the English Kings and Aristocracy 1066–1530* (London: Methuen, 1984)

— *Medieval Children* (New Haven and London: Yale University Press, 2001)

Painter, Sidney, *William Marshal: Knight Errant, Baron and Regent of England* (Baltimore: Johns Hopkins University Press, 1933)

— *The Scourge of the Clergy: Peter of Dreux, Duke of Brittany* (Baltimore: Johns Hopkins University Press, 1937)

— *French Chivalry: Chivalric Ideals and Practice in Medieval France* (Baltimore: Johns Hopkins University Press, 1940)

— *Medieval Society* (Ithaca: Cornell University Press, 1951)

— 'The Lords of Lusignan in the Eleventh and Twelfth Centuries', *Speculum*, 32 (1957), 27–47

Pangonis, Katherine, *Queens of Jerusalem: The Women Who Dared to Rule* (London: Weidenfeld & Nicolson, 2021)

Papin, Yves D., *Chronologie du moyen âge* (Paris: Editions Jean-Paul Gisserot, 2001)

Parsons, John Carmi, 'The Year of Eleanor of Castile's Birth and Her Children by Edward I', *Mediaeval Studies*, 46 (1984), 245–65

— *Eleanor of Castile: Queen and Society in Thirteenth-Century England* (New York: St Martin's Press, 1995)

— (ed.), *Medieval Queenship* (Stroud: Sutton, 1998; orig. 1994)

Partner, Nancy, *Serious Entertainments: The Writing of History in Twelfth-Century England* (Chicago and London: University of Chicago Press, 1977)

Pastoureau, Michel, *Le roi tué par un cochon* (Paris: Seuil, 2015)

Pegg, Mark Gregory, *A Most Holy War: The Albigensian Crusade and the Battle for Christendom* (Oxford: Oxford University Press, 2008)

Peirce, Ian, 'The Knight, His Arms and Armour in the Eleventh and Twelfth Centuries', in *Ideals and Practice of Medieval Knighthood: Papers from the First and Second Strawberry Hill Conferences* (Woodbridge: Boydell, 1986), pp. 152–64

Perry, Guy, *John of Brienne: King of Jerusalem, Emperor of Constantinople, c. 1175–1237* (Cambridge: Cambridge University Press, 2013)

Petit-Dutaillis, Charles, *Étude sur la vie et le règne de Louis VIII 1187–1226* (Paris: Bibliothèque de l'Ecole des Hautes Etudes, 1894)

— *The Feudal Monarchy in France and England from the Tenth to the Thirteenth Century*, trans. E.D. Hunt (London; Routledge & Kegan Paul, 1966; orig. 1936)

Phillips, Jonathan, *The Fourth Crusade and the Sack of Constantinople* (London: Pimlico, 2005)

— *The Second Crusade: Extending the Frontiers of Christendom* (New Haven and London: Yale University Press, 2007)

— *Holy Warriors: A Modern History of the Crusades* (London: Vintage Books, 2010)

— *The Life and Legend of the Sultan Saladin* (New Haven and London: Yale University Press, 2019)

Poulet, André, 'Capetian Women and the Regency: The Genesis of a Vocation', in *Medieval Queenship*, ed. John Carmi Parsons (Stroud: Sutton, 1998; orig. 1994), pp. 93–116

Power, Daniel, 'King John and the Norman Aristocracy', in *King John: New Interpretations*, ed. S.D. Church (Woodbridge: Boydell, 1999), pp. 117–36

— *The Norman Frontier in the Twelfth and Early Thirteenth Centuries* (Cambridge: Cambridge University Press, 2004)

— 'Les dernières années du régime angevin en Normandie', in *Plantagenêts et Capétiens: Confrontations et héritages*, ed. Martin Aurell and Yves Tonnerre (Turnhout: Brepols, 2006), pp. 163–92

— 'The Treaty of Paris (1259) and the Aristocracy of England and Normandy', in *Thirteenth-Century England XIII: Proceedings of the Paris Conference 2009*, ed. Janet Burton, Frédérique Lachaud and Philipp Schofield (Woodbridge: Boydell: 2011), pp. 141–58

— 'La chute de la Normandie ducale (1202–1204): Un réexamen', in *La guerre en Normandie (XIe–XVe siècle)*, ed. Anne Curry and Véronique Gazeau (Caen: Presses Universitaires de Caen, 2018), pp. 37–62

Powicke, F.M., *The Loss of Normandy (1189–1204): Studies in the History of the Angevin Empire* (Manchester: Manchester University Press, 1913)

— *The Thirteenth Century*, 2nd ed. (Oxford: Oxford University Press, 1962; orig. 1953)

Prestwich, J.O., 'The Military Household of the Norman Kings', *English Historical Review*, 96 (1981), 1–37

— 'Military Intelligence under the Norman and Angevin Kings', in *Law and Government in Medieval England and Normandy*, ed. G. Garnett and J. Hudson (Cambridge: Cambridge University Press, 1994), pp. 1–30

— *The Place of War in English History 1066–1214* (Woodbridge: Boydell, 2004)

Prestwich, Michael, *Armies and Warfare in the Middle Ages: The English Experience* (New Haven and London: Yale University Press, 1996)

— *Edward I* (New Haven and London: Yale University Press, 1997; orig. Methuen, 1988)

— 'The Garrisoning of English Medieval Castles', in *The Normans and Their Adversaries at War*, ed. Richard Abels and Bernard S. Bachrach (Woodbridge: Boydell, 2001), pp. 185–200

Pryor, John H. (ed.), *The Logistics of Warfare in the Age of the Crusades* (Aldershot: Ashgate, 2006)

Purton, Peter, *A History of the Early Medieval Siege, c. 450–1200* (Woodbridge: Boydell, 2009)

— *A History of the Late Medieval Siege, 1200–1500* (Woodbridge: Boydell, 2010)

— *The Medieval Military Engineer: From the Roman Empire to the Sixteenth Century* (Woodbridge: Boydell, 2018)

Queller, Donald E. and Thomas F. Madden, *The Fourth Crusade: The Conquest of Constantinople*, 2nd ed. (Philadelphia: University of Pennsylvania Press, 2000; orig. 1997)

Radding, Charles M., 'Fortune and Her Wheel: The Meaning of a Medieval Symbol', *Mediaevistik*, 5 (1992), 127–38

Richard, Jean, *Saint Louis* (Paris: Fayard, 1983)

Richardson, H.G., 'The Coronation in Medieval England: The Evolution of the Office and the Oath', *Traditio*, 16 (1960), 111–202

Ridgeway, Huw, 'King Henry III and the "Aliens"', in *Thirteenth-Century England II: Proceedings of the Newcastle-upon-Tyne Conference 1987*, ed. P.R. Coss and S.D. Lloyd (Woodbridge: Boydell, 1988), pp. 81–92

— 'Foreign Favourites and Henry III's Problems of Patronage, 1247–1258', *English Historical Review*, 104 (1989), 590–610

Riley-Smith, *The Crusades: A Short History* (London: Athlone Press, 1990)

Roquebert, Michel, *Histoire des Cathares* (Paris: Perrin, 2002)

Rose, Susan, *England's Medieval Navy, 1066–1509* (Barnsley: Seaforth Publishing, 2013)

Runciman, Steven, *A History of the Crusades*, 3 vols (Cambridge: Cambridge University Press, 1951–54)

— *The Sicilian Vespers: A History of the Mediterranean World in the Later Thirteenth Century* (Cambridge: Cambridge University Press, 1958)

Russell, Frederick, *The Just War in the Middle Ages* (Cambridge: Cambridge University Press, 1975)

Saint-Denis, Alain, *Le siècle de Saint Louis* (Paris: Presses universitaires de France, 1984)

Salch, Charles-Laurent (ed.), *Dictionnaire des châteaux et des fortifications du moyen âge en France* (Strasbourg: Editions Publitotal, 1987)

Sanders, Ivor John, *English Baronies: A Study of Their Origin and Descent, 1086–1327* (Oxford: Clarendon, 1960)

Sassier, Yves, *Louis VII* (Paris: Fayard, 1991)

Saul, Nigel, *A Companion to Medieval England 1066–1485*, 3rd ed. (Stroud: Tempus, 2005; orig. 1983)

Saxtorph, Niels M., 'Technical Innovations and Military Change', in *War and Peace in the Middle Ages*, ed. Brian Patrick McGuire (Copenhagen: C.A. Reitzels Forlag, 1987), pp. 216–26

Sayers, Jane E., *Papal Government and England during the Pontificate of Honorius III (1216–1227)* (Cambridge: Cambridge University Press, 1984)

— *Innocent III: Leader of Europe, 1198–1216* (London: Longman, 1994)

Schneider, Reinhard, 'Mittelalterliche Verträge auf Brücken und Flüssen', *Archiv für Diplomatik*, 23 (1977), 1–24

Seabourne, Gwen, 'Eleanor of Brittany and Her Treatment by King John and Henry III', *Nottingham Medieval Studies*, 51 (2007), 73–111

— *Imprisoning Medieval Women: The Non-Judicial Confinement and Abduction of Women in England, c. 1170–1509* (Farnham: Ashgate, 2011)

Searle, E., 'Women and the Legitimization of Succession of the Norman Conquest', *Anglo-Norman Studies*, 3 (1980), 159–70

Shadis, Miriam, *Berenguela of Castile (1180–1246) and Political Women of the High Middle Ages* (New York: Palgrave Macmillan, 2009)

Shadis, Miriam and Constance Hoffman Berman, 'A Taste of the Feast: Reconsidering Eleanor of Aquitaine's Female Descendants', in *Eleanor of Aquitaine: Lord and Lady*, ed. Bonnie Wheeler and John Carmi Parsons (London: Palgrave Macmillan, 2003), pp. 177–211

Sivéry, Gérard, *Blanche de Castille* (Paris: Fayard, 1990)

— *Louis VIII le Lion* (Paris: Fayard, 1995)

— *Philippe Auguste* (Paris: Perrin, 2003; orig. Librairie Plon, 1993)

— *Philippe III le Hardi* (Paris: Fayard, 2003)

Smith, J. Beverley, 'The Treaty of Lambeth, 1217', *English Historical Review*, 94 (1979), 562–79

Snellgrove, Harold S., *The Lusignans in England, 1247–1258* (Albuquerque: University of New Mexico Press, 1950)

Spencer, Dan, *The Castle at War in Medieval England and Wales* (Stroud: Amberley, 2018)

Spencer, Stephen J., '"Like a Raging Lion": Richard the Lionheart's Anger during the Third Crusade in Medieval and Modern Historiography', *English Historical Review*, 132 (2017), 495–532

Spiegel, Gabrielle, 'The Cult of Saint Denis and Capetian Kingship', *Journal of Medieval History*, 1 (1975), 43–69

Stanton, Charles D., *Medieval Maritime Warfare* (Barnsley: Pen & Sword, 2015)

Staunton, Michael, *The Historians of Angevin England* (Oxford: Oxford University Press, 2017)

Steane, John M., *The Archaeology of Power* (Stroud: Tempus, 2001)

Strayer, Joseph, 'The Crusade against Aragon', *Speculum*, 28 (1953), 102–13

— 'The Crusades of Louis IX', in *A History of the Crusades*, vol. 2: *The Later Crusades, 1189–1311*, ed. Robert Lee Wolff and Harry W. Hazard (Madison and London: University of Wisconsin Press, 1969), pp. 487–521

— 'The Costs and Profits of War: The Anglo-French Conflict of 1294–1303', in *The Medieval City*, ed. Harry A. Miskimin, David Herlihy and Abraham L. Udovitch (New Haven: Yale University Press, 1977), pp. 269–91

— *The Reign of Philip the Fair* (Princeton: Princeton University Press, 1980)

Strickland, Matthew, 'Against the Lord's Anointed: Aspects of Warfare and Baronial Rebellion in England and Normandy, 1075–1265', in *Law and Government in Medieval England and Normandy*, ed. George Garnett and John Hudson (Cambridge: Cambridge University Press, 1994), pp. 56–79

— *War and Chivalry* (Cambridge: Cambridge University Press, 1996)

— 'Henry I and the Battle of the Two Kings: Brémule, 1119', in *Normandy and Its Neighbours, 900–1250: Essays for David Bates*, ed. David Crouch and Kathleen Thompson (Turnhout: Brepols, 2011), pp. 77–116

— *Henry the Young King, 1155–1183* (New Haven and London: Yale University Press, 2016)

Strickland, Matthew and Robert Hardy, *The Great Warbow: From Hastings to the Mary Rose* (Stroud: Sutton, 2005)

Studd, Robin, 'Reconfiguring the Angevin Empire, 1224–1259', in *England and Europe in the Reign of Henry III, 1216–1272*, ed. Björn K.U. Weiler and Ifor W. Rowlands (Aldershot: Ashgate, 2002), pp. 31–41

Tanner, Roland, 'Franco-Scottish Alliance', in *The Oxford Companion to British History* (Oxford: Oxford University Press, 2009), pp. 390–91

Thompson, Kathleen, *Power and Border Lordship in Medieval France: The County of the Perche, 1000–1226* (Woodbridge: Boydell, 2002)

— 'Affairs of State: The Illegitimate Children of Henry I', *Journal of Medieval History*, 29 (2012), 129–51

Tilley, Arthur (ed.), *Medieval France* (Cambridge: Cambridge University Press, 1922)

Tout, T.F., *France and England: Their Relations in the Middle Ages and Now* (London: Longmans, Green & Co., 1922)

Trindade, Ann, *Berengaria: In Search of Richard the Lionheart's Queen* (Dublin: Four Courts Press, 1999)

Truax, Jean A., 'Anglo-Norman Women at War: Valiant Soldiers, Prudent Strategists or Charismatic Leaders?', in *The Circle of War in the Middle Ages: Essays on Medieval Military and Naval History*, ed. Donald J. Kagay and L.J. Andrew Villalon (Woodbridge: Boydell, 1999), pp. 111–25

Turner, Ralph V., *Eleanor of Aquitaine: Queen of France, Queen of England* (New Haven and London: Yale University Press, 2009)

— 'England in 1215: An Authoritarian Angevin Dynasty Facing Multiple Threats', in *Magna Carta and the England of King John*, ed. Janet S. Loengard (Woodbridge: Boydell, 2010), pp. 10–26

Tyerman, Christopher, *Who's Who in Early Medieval England* (London: Shepheard-Walwyn, 1996)

— *God's War: A New History of the Crusades* (London: Penguin, 2006)

Unger, Richard, *The Ship in the Medieval Economy, 600–1600* (Montreal: McGill-Queen's University Press, 1980)

Urbanski, Charity, *Writing History for the King: Henry II and the Politics of Vernacular Historiography* (Ithaca: Cornell University Press, 2013)

Vale, Malcolm, *War and Chivalry* (London: Duckworth, 1981)

BIBLIOGRAPHY

— *The Ancient Enemy: England, France and Europe from the Angevins to the Tudors* (London: Bloomsbury Academic, 2009)

Valente, Claire, 'The Provisions of Oxford: Assessing/Assigning Authority in Time of Unrest', in *The Experience of Power in Medieval Europe, 950–1350*, ed. Robert F. Berkhofer III, Alan Cooper and Adam J. Kosto (Farnham: Ashgate, 2005), pp. 25–41

Van den Broucke, Serge, 'Château-Gaillard: The Mighty Lock of Normandy's Gate', *Medieval History Magazine*, 1 (2003), 1–25

Verbruggen, J.F., *The Art of Warfare in Western Europe in the Middle Ages*, trans. Sumner Willard and S.C.M. Southern (Oxford: North-Holland, 1977)

— 'Women in Medieval Armies', *Journal of Medieval Military History*, 4 (2006), 119–36

Vincent, Nicholas, *Peter des Roches: An Alien in English Politics, 1205–1238* (Cambridge: Cambridge University Press, 1996)

— 'Isabella of Angoulême: John's Jezebel', in *King John: New Interpretations*, ed. S.D. Church (Woodbridge: Boydell, 1999), pp. 165–219

— 'A Forgotten War: England and Navarre, 1243–4', in *Thirteenth-Century England XI: Proceedings of the Gregynog Conference 2005*, ed. Björn Weiler et al. (Woodbridge: Boydell, 2007), pp. 109–46

Volkmann, Jean-Charles, *Généalogies complètes des rois de France* (Paris: Editions Jean-Paul Gisserot, 1999)

Wagner, Thomas Gregor and Piers D. Mitchell, 'The Illnesses of King Richard and King Philippe on the Third Crusade: An Understanding of *arnoldia* and *leonardie*,' *Crusades*, 10 (2011), 23–44.

Warner, Philip, *Sieges of the Middle Ages* (London: Bell and Sons, 1968)

Warren, John, *The Past and Its Presenters* (London: Hodder & Stoughton, 1998)

Warren, W.L., *The Governance of Anglo-Norman and Angevin England, 1086–1272* (Stanford: Stanford University Press, 1987)

— *King John*, 2nd ed. (New Haven and London: Yale University Press, 1997; orig. 1961)

— *Henry II*, 3rd ed. (New Haven and London: Yale University Press, 2000; orig. 1973)

Watkins, Carl, *Stephen: The Reign of Anarchy* (London: Allen Lane, 2015)

Webster, Paul, *King John and Religion* (Woodbridge: Boydell, 2015)

Weiler, Björn, 'Henry III and the Sicilian Business: A Reinterpretation', *Historical Research*, 74 (2001), 127–50

— *Henry III of England and the Staufen Empire, 1216–1272* (Woodbridge: Boydell, 2002)

— *Kingship, Rebellion and Political Culture: England and Germany, c.1215–c.1250* (London: Palgrave Macmillan, 2007)

Westerhof, Danielle, *Death and the Noble Body in Medieval England* (Woodbridge: Boydell, 2008)

Wheatley, Abigail, *The Idea of the Castle in Medieval England* (York: York Medieval Press, 2015; orig. 2004)

Wickham, Chris, *Medieval Europe* (New Haven and London: Yale University Press, 2016)

Wilkinson, Louise, *Women in Thirteenth-Century Lincolnshire* (Woodbridge: Boydell, 2007)

— 'The Imperial Marriage of Isabella of England, Henry III's Sister', in *The Rituals and Rhetoric of Queenship: Medieval to Early Modern*, ed. Liz Oakley-Brown and Louise J. Wilkinson (Dublin: Four Courts, 2009), pp. 20–36

— *Eleanor de Montfort: A Rebel Countess in Medieval England* (London: Continuum, 2012)

— 'Maternal Abandonment and Surrogate Caregivers: Isabella of Angoulême and Her Children by King John', in *Virtuous or Villainess? The Image of the Royal Mother from the Early Medieval to the Early Modern Era*, ed. Carey Fleiner and Elena Woodacre (New York: Palgrave Macmillan, 2016), pp. 101–24

Wilson, Peter H., *The Holy Roman Empire: A Thousand Years of Europe's History* (London: Allen Lane, 2016)

Wilson-Lee, Kelcey, *Daughters of Chivalry: The Forgotten Children of Edward I* (London: Picador, 2019)

Wolff, Robert Lee, 'Baldwin of Flanders and Hainaut, First Latin Emperor of Constantinople: His Life, Death, and Resurrection, 1172–1225', *Speculum*, 27 (1952), 281–322

Wood, Charles T., *The French Apanages and the Capetian Monarchy, 1224–1328* (Cambridge, MA: Harvard University Press, 1966)

— 'The Mise of Amiens and Saint Louis' Theory of Kingship', *French Historical Studies*, 6 (1970), 300–10

Woodacre, Elena, *The Queens Regnant of Navarre: Succession, Politics, and Partnership, 1274–1512* (New York: Palgrave Macmillan, 2013)

— 'Between Regencies and Lieutenancies: Catherine of Aragon (1513) and Kateryn Parr (1544)', in *Les alters ego des souverains: Vice-rois et lieutenants généraux en Europe et dans les Amériques (XVe–XVIIe siècles)*, ed. Philippe Chareyre, Álvaro Adot and Dénes Harai (Pau: Presses de l'Université de Pau et des Pays de l'Adour (PUPPA), 2021), pp. 185–206

Woodacre, Elena and Carey Fleiner (eds), *Royal Mothers and Their Ruling Children: Wielding Political Authority from Antiquity to the Early Modern Era* (New York: Palgrave Macmillan, 2015)

Online sources

Epistolae: Medieval Women's Latin Letters, at https://epistolae.ctl.columbia.edu/

Foundation for Medieval Genealogy, at http://fmg.ac/

Gallica (Bibliotheque nationale de France), at http://gallica.bnf.fr/

Internet Archive, at https://archive.org/

The Magna Carta Project, at https://magnacartaresearch.org/

Monumenta Germaniae Historica, at http://www.mgh.de/

My Armoury: A Resource for Historic Arms and Armour Collectors, at http://myarmoury.com

INDEX